third edition

All Children Read

Teaching for Literacy in Today's Diverse Classrooms

Charles Temple

Hobart and William Smith Colleges

Donna Ogle

National-Louis University

Alan Crawford

California State University, Los Angeles

Penny Freppon

University of Cincinnati

PEARSON

Boston • Columbus • Indianapolis • New York • San Francisco • Upper Saddle River
Amsterdam • Cape Town • Dubai • London • Madrid • Milan • Munich • Paris • Montreal • Toronto
Delhi • Mexico City • Sao Paulo • Sydney • Hong Kong • Seoul • Singapore • Taipei • Tokyo

Vice President, Editor-in-Chief: Aurora Martínez Ramos
Development Editor: Christina Robb
Editorial Assistant: Meagan French
Vice President, Director of Marketing: Quinn Perkson
Executive Marketing Manager: Krista Clark
Production Editor: Janet Domingo
Editorial Production Service: Kathy Smith/Publishers' Design and Production Services, Inc.
Composition Buyer: Linda Cox
Manufacturing Buyer: Megan Cochran
Electronic Composition: Publishers' Design and Production Services, Inc.
Interior Design: Denise Hoffman
Photo Researcher: Annie Pickert
Cover Administrator: Elena Sidorova

For related titles and support materials, visit our online catalog at www.pearsonhighered.com.

Chapter opener photo credits: pp. xxiv, 68, 98, 130, 190, 222, 262, 324, 364, and 438,
Ellen B. Senisi; p. 28, Gary Connon/PhotoEdit; p. 158, David Young-Wolff/PhotoEdit;
p. 294, Ellen Senisi/The Image Works; p. 402, Bob Daemmrich/The Image Works; p. 482,
Spencer Grant/PhotoEdit.

Printed in the United States of America

10 9 8 7 6 5 4 3 2 1   [WEB]   14   13   12   11   10

www.pearsonhighered.com

ISBN-10: 0-13-209226-3
ISBN-13: 978-0-13-209226-5

About the Authors

● **CHARLES TEMPLE** is a professor of education at Hobart and William Smith Colleges in Geneva, New York, where he teaches courses on literacy, children's literature, peace studies, and storytelling. He has written books on emergent literacy, invented spelling, writing instruction, language arts, diagnosis and remediation of reading disabilities, and children's literature. Along with Alan Crawford and Jean Gillet, he recently authored the *Developmental Literacy Inventory*, an assessment system for literacy, K–12. With Jim MaKinster, he co-authored *Intervening for Literacy*, a supplemental handbook for Jump Start, the early intervention project. Temple taught as a senior Fulbright Scholar in Portugal and Romania, and was a founding director of the Open Society Institute's and the International Reading Association's Reading and Writing for Critical Thinking Project, which has served more than 60,000 teachers in 40 countries in Europe, Asia, Latin America, and Africa. He co-directs Critical Thinking International, Inc., a non-profit organization that develops materials and fields mid-career professionals for teacher training projects around the world. He has published books for children, and he is currently working with teachers and authors in Liberia, West Africa, to develop indigenous literature for children.

● **DONNA OGLE** is Professor of Reading and Language at National-Louis University (NLU) in Chicago, Illinois, and is active in research and professional development projects. She is currently senior consultant to the Chicago Striving Readers Project, co-director of the Reading Leadership Institute and Co-Director of the Literacy Partners Project, collaboration among the Chicago Public Schools, NLU and the Chicago Community Trust. Donna also serves as a literacy consultant internationally, including Critical Thinking International and Grupo SM in Latin America. She is on the editorial review boards of *Lectura y Vida*, the *Reading Teacher*, and the *Journal of Adolescent and Adult Literacy*. Donna is a past-president of the International Reading Association (IRA) and an elected member of the Reading Hall of Fame. She also conducts research on visual literacy and content comprehension, having developed both the K-W-L and PRC2 (partner reading in content, too) frameworks. She is the author of many books, book chapters, professional articles, and curriculum materials.

● ALAN CRAWFORD is Emeritus Professor of Education at California State University, Los Angeles. He has served as President of the California Reading Association, a Fulbright Senior scholar in Ecuador, and a Researcher in Residence at the American Embassy in Baku, Azerbaijan. He has done extensive teaching, consulting, and writing on teaching reading in the elementary school, especially for English language learners. Alan has written curriculum for teaching reading in Spanish and serves on the Editorial Review Board of *Lectura y Vida*. He served as IRA's representative to UNESCO for many years and was a Senior Literacy Specialist at UNESCO in Paris during International Literacy Year (1989–90). He is currently a director of Critical Thinking International. He frequently presents workshops on a volunteer basis for international development projects in Latin America, Europe, Asia, and Africa.

● PENNY FREPPON is Emerita Professor of Literacy at the University of Cincinnati, Cincinnati, Ohio. In her tenure there she taught undergraduate and graduate courses in reading and writing and directed a Literacy Center that served urban children who struggled in reading and writing. This Center included graduate students in tutoring these children and supporting their parents in helping their children at home. Federal, state, and university grants supported her research in different instructional settings that was published in refereed journals. She has written book chapters, and co-authored articles and a book on "what it takes to be a teacher." The state of Ohio and some federal funds supported a workshop-based and literature-rich program, of which she was field-faculty member. This literacy specialist program included highly competent elementary, middle school, and high school teachers in research-based literacy learning and honing their coaching skills so that they were then able to teach and coach teachers in their schools. She has taught teachers in Uzbekistan and Africa and is a member of Critical Thinking International. Those who are afraid that current trends in reading instruction run the risk of dismantling much that is good in child-centered instruction will be much encouraged by Dr. Freppon's thoughtful attention to skills in the context of meaning-centered instruction.

Brief Contents

Contents

2

The Social and Cultural Contexts for Teaching All Children to Read   28

3

What Reading Teachers Need to Know About Language   68

Part Two

Aspects of Reading

4

Emergent Literacy   98

5

Phonics and Word Knowledge   130

6

Helping Readers Build Fluency and Vocabulary   158

7

Comprehension: Understanding and Responding to Narrative Texts   190

8

Comprehension: Understanding and Learning with Informational Texts   222

9

Critical Thinking and Critical Literacy   262

10

Teaching Children to Write 294

11

Assessing Literacy   324

Part Three

Organizing and Managing the Literacy Program

12

Putting Effective Literacy Instruction into Practice: Grades K to 2   364

13

Putting Effective Literacy Instruction into Practice: Grades 3 to 5   402

14

Putting Effective Literacy Instruction into Practice: Grades 6 to 8 438

15

Models and Strategies for Teaching ESL and for Teaching Reading in the Mother Tongue   482

Features

Developmental Milestones

Integrating Across the Curriculum

Standards and Literacy

Teach It!

The World of Reading

ASSESSMENT

DIFFERENTIATED INSTRUCTION

Being a Professional Reading Teacher

Preface

New to This Edition

The third edition of *All Children Read: Teaching for Literacy in Today's Diverse Classrooms* expands upon the strengths our readers have found in previous editions of our book. We have added a number of new elements to this edition that respond to significant developments in the literacy field.

The third edition includes:

- *A new chapter, Chapter 9, Critical Thinking and Critical Literacy,* that provides explanations of critical thinking and critical literacy and discusses their importance at all levels. The chapter explores ways of teaching students to conduct critical discussion of fictional and informational texts, and also the special and urgent challenges of applying critical thinking to electronic texts.

- *Increased coverage of new literacies throughout the book* that provides information about the impact of technology on the teaching of reading and writing. This content is highlighted by a margin note icon.

- *A new feature, Developmental Milestones,* that appears in Chapters 3–5. The Developmental Milestones feature provides at-a-glance summaries of typical behaviors in children's development of emergent literacy, phonological awareness, and word knowledge.

- *A new feature, Integrating Across the Curriculum,* which appears in Chapters 12–14. The Integrating Across the Curriculum feature provides concrete examples of curriculum integration at each of the three levels: K–2, 3–5, and 6–8. This feature shows how integrated curriculum addresses state learning standards while providing needed context for literacy instruction and freeing up valuable class time for instruction in other content subjects.

- Additional opportunities for our readers to apply the text concepts. Accompanying the book is an exciting new online resource, MyEducationLab, which provides readers with opportunities to apply the text concepts and build their teaching skills. We have also updated each of our existing chapters to reflect the newest developments and research findings in the literacy field.

- *Chapter 1: Approaches to Teaching Reading* chronicles recent major changes in the field, including a trend toward integrating instruction across the curriculum, that are affecting classroom practice. Response to Intervention (RTI), a new federal initiative, is also introduced in Chapter 1.

- *Chapter 2: **The Social and Cultural Contexts for Teaching All Children to Read*** includes regulations and implementation guidelines about the recent federal Response to Intervention (RTI) initiative and new insights about teaching reading and writing to children whose home language is African American Vernacular English. A new classroom vignette about Getting Parents and the Community Involved has been added, as well as a new section on creating a professional portfolio.

- *Chapter 3: **What Reading Teachers Need to Know About Language*** has been reorganized to provide updates of research on spelling and word knowledge development, including the work of Donald Bear, Robert Schlagal, and Richard Gentry.

- *Chapter 4: **Emergent Literacy*** has also been updated to reflect current research on teaching the alphabet and teaching phonological awareness.

- *Chapter 5: **Phonics and Word Knowledge*** now has a new section on Teaching the "Meaningful Word Parts" or Morphological Reader (Grades 3 and 4), which includes structural analysis and word journals.

- *Chapter 6: **Helping Readers Build Fluency and Vocabulary*** has again been updated. In addition, a new Assessment box feature, *Charting Students' Word Learning*, has been added.

- *Chapter 7: **Comprehension: Understanding and Responding to Narrative Texts*** includes new teaching strategies and a general update of major concepts.

- *Chapter 8: **Comprehension: Understanding and Learning with Informational Texts*** has added information about web and computer-based resources. One section introduces teachers to the importance of helping students learn to use the basic structure of websites and identifying the sources of the sites.

- *Chapter 10: **Teaching Children to Write*** includes a new section on Mixing Genres: RAFT, as well as a related strategy, Reciprocal RAFT.

- *Chapter 11: **Assessing Literacy*** has been generally updated. The section on the informal reading inventory has been greatly expanded to include: How to Administer and Score the Informal Reading Inventory, with subsections on *Administering the Informal Reading Inventory* and *Interpreting the Outcomes*.

- *Chapter 12: **Putting Effective Literacy Instruction into Practice: Grades K to 2*** provides updated information about research-based approaches to teaching students at grade levels K–2. The chapter includes a new feature on Integrating Across the Curriculum, introducing the use of learning centers to achieve integration across the curriculum. Chapter 12 also includes new information about the important relationship between oral language development and written language.

- *Chapter 13: **Putting Effective Literacy Instruction into Practice: Grades 3 to 5*** provides updated information about research-based approaches to teaching students at these grade levels. Curriculum integration is introduced through the use of thematic units, with an example provided on Endangered Dolphins.

- *Chapter 14: **Putting Effective Literacy Instruction into Practice: Grades 6 to 8*** provides updated information about research-based approaches to teaching students at these grade levels. Curriculum integration is introduced through the use of thematic units, with an example provided on medieval Europe. State standards in reading, literature, and social studies were provided to illustrate how the unit on the Middle Ages was grounded in important content learning. The opening vignette was also changed to reflect this theme. The chapter includes a section with current information on the status of NAEP results, the Reading Next report from the Carnegie Foundation, and an introduction to the Doing what works website sponsored by the U.S. Department of Education. A new section on web-based inquiry through ThinkQuest shows how technology is being used productively.

- *Chapter 15: Models and Strategies for Teaching ESL and for Teaching Reading in the Mother Tongue* includes new research and updated information about legal policies for English Language Learners, as well as a new section of Building Vocabulary with Read-Alouds.

- Students from California who use *All Children Read* will find that key terms from the **Reading Instruction Competence Assessment (RICA)** are fully developed in the text and also appear in the index. In addition, major concepts related to the assessment of students are also developed to support our readers in other aspects of the RICA.

- The *Teach It!* lesson plan booklet, written by Professor Codruța Temple of SUNY Cortland, with Jean Gillet, now appears as an Appendix containing a wide variety of ready-to-use, classroom-tested activities for teaching critical concepts in Literacy Education. All activities are correlated to lessons in the text itself.

Our Rationale for This Book

Teaching all children to read is a main task of our elementary and middle schools. This book shares the knowledge and skills needed to do that work well. What kind of skills? Many of them could be called "traditional." There are things good teachers of reading have done successfully for a long time—student-centered teaching; immersing children in good literature, both fiction and nonfiction; combining reading and writing; to name a few. We will pass on the best of those practices here. But not all past practices are as successful as they need to be. That is why we speak of "research-based instruction." Research on teaching effectiveness can, within certain limits, show us methods and practices that are most likely to be successful. We have sought the guidance of sound research in preparing this book.

- Traditional teaching won't take us far enough, though, because the circumstances of teaching have changed and are still changing.

- We are facing enormous pressure to educate better. Changes in society beyond the classroom are insisting that every student learn to read and think critically—every student. There are fewer and fewer places in society for the under-educated.

- All of us are educating all or nearly all of the children. Children with special needs have the right to be educated in the least restrictive environment, and all teachers are invited to team to plan and carry out instruction that helps every child learn.

- 460. That is the number of different languages children in our classrooms speak at home. 14,000,000 is the number of English language learners in our schools. North Carolina, South Carolina, and Indiana are some of the states that have recently seen 200% to 300% increases in English language learners. But 55% is the share of Spanish-speaking children who entered Los Angeles County schools last year. Most teachers at one time or another will teach a child who doesn't have strong English ability, and a large number will teach many English language learners every year.

- A few years ago, teachers could complain of working in a lonely profession: When they closed the door in the morning they were alone all day with the kids. The Response to Intervention Initiative (RTI) has the potential to lead teachers who teach reading to work in teams with fellow teachers and other educational professionals in the school, sharing data and ideas, and finding solutions to learning problems together.

- When teachers plan together, they often speak of ways to combine or integrate the teaching of many subjects. As long as students are reading for comprehension and writing to learn, it makes sense to focus reading and writing some of the time on social studies, science, and mathematics. Integrating curriculum makes good use of teaching time. Also, with the greater attention being paid to reading instruction, integrating curriculum buys more teaching time for social studies and science.

- Not long ago, teaching students to understand what they read was the pinnacle of reading instruction. Now we must go further and teach students not only to understand what they read but to make sure it is credible and to examine it for biases and manipulation. Critical literacy is taking its place alongside reading comprehension.

- Finally, the technology affecting what students read, how they read it, and how we should teach has been changing so rapidly that literacy educators now refer to the "new literacies," acknowledging that as students continue to encode and decode messages, and store and search for information, the technologies that they use to do these things will have a profound effect on the skills they need.

How This Book Is Organized

All Children Read is organized in three parts. Part One helps you develop a broad understanding of the processes by which students learn to read and write and the important factors such as culture, diversity, and the structure of language that we must understand in order to teach reading. Part Two looks in depth at the different aspects of reading and writing, from emergent literacy to critical literacy, and including comprehension, fluency and vocabulary, word knowledge, comprehension, writing, and assessment. Finally, Part Three describes, level by level, how to put all of this information together into an effective reading program that helps all children become readers and writers.

Part One: The Processes of Literacy

The three chapters in the first section of the book set the stage for teaching reading and writing. Chapter 1, "Approaches to Teaching Reading," describes aspects of literacy that must be taught and stages of reading development before discussing the main approaches to literacy instruction. Chapter 2, "The Social and Cultural Contexts for Teaching All Children to Read," carefully describes the cultural and linguistic diversity of America's students, and lays out guidelines for making literacy instruction work for all of them. Chapter 3, "What Reading Teachers Need to Know About Language," provides a background in the sounds, rules, and meanings of the English language, so the reader can successfully help learners navigate its challenges.

Part Two: Aspects of Reading

The chapters in Part Two of the book focus on the key aspects of literacy. Chapter 4, "Emergent Literacy," details the early concepts about language and print that lay the basis for learning to read and write. There are many ideas, systematically arranged, for helping children get off to a successful start in literacy. Chapter 5, "Phonics and Word Knowledge," covers phonics and word recognition. The chapter begins by exploring what children need to know in order to read words, and the phases through which that knowledge develops. It then presents a host of strategies for teaching children to read words and build sight vocabularies. Chapter 6, "Helping Readers Build Fluency and Vocabulary," summarizes our current understanding of reading fluency, the "neglected skill" in reading, and then presents best practices in teaching children to read fluently. The chapter uses the same theory and practice approach for teaching vocabulary. Chapter 7, "Comprehension: Understanding and Responding to Narrative Texts," explores the nature of reading comprehension and response to literature, and then helps the reader build a repertoire of teaching techniques that work with fictional texts. Chapter 8, "Comprehension: Understanding and Learning with Informational Texts," extends the discussion of comprehension to teaching students to understand and learn from informational texts. A new Chapter 9, "Critical Thinking and Critical Literacy," explores ways of having students think hard about what they read, examine messages for their credibility, and especially to think critically about technologically mediated texts. Chapter 10, "Teaching Children to Write," presents the components and phases of the writing process and then explains the writing workshop approach as well as other approaches to teaching writing in many genres. The methods include those that offer more support to beginning writers, and others that give the students more leeway to create in print. Chapter 11, "Assessing Literacy," explains a host of procedures that can be used in four "moments" of assessment: screening, diagnosing, monitoring, and outcomes-based assessment.

Part Three: Organizing and Managing the Literacy Program

The last section of the book weaves together the concepts and strategies that were presented earlier and shows how to organize instruction for different levels of learners. Three chapters in this section share approaches to teaching reading in different grade level spans, and the fourth shows how to work with English language learners at all levels. Chapter 12, "Putting Effective Literacy Instruction into Practice: Grades K to 2," explains how to set up and manage a literacy program for emergent and beginning readers, including suggestions for working with English language learners. Chapter 13, "Putting Effective Literacy Instruction into Practice: Grades 3 to 5," shows how to build reading and writing fluency and how to help children in the upper elementary grades read for meaning and learn from texts, again with suggestions for working effectively with English language learners. Chapter 14, "Putting Effective Literacy Instruction into Practice: Grades 6 to 8," continues with middle school students and adds a strong emphasis on reading and writing to learn. Chapter 15, "Models and Strategies for Teaching ESL and for Teaching Reading in the Mother Tongue," demonstrates how to set up instructional programs in ESL, reading, and writing for English language learners.

Special Features

Throughout the book, special features focus on issues of recurring importance to reading teachers and extend understanding of key concepts in reading instruction.

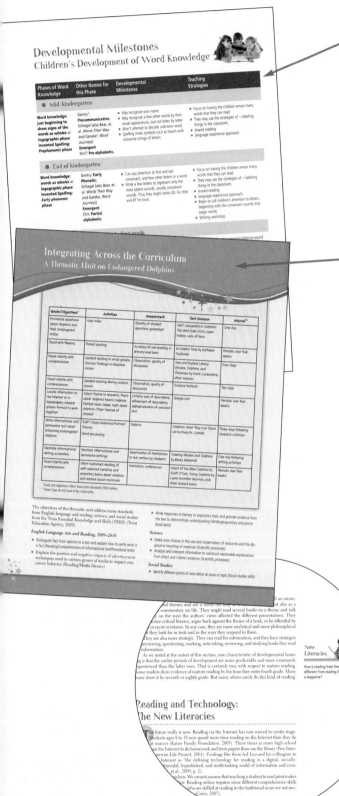

- **New! Developmental Milestones features** provide at-a-glance summaries of typical behaviors in children's development of emergent literacy, phonological awareness and word knowledge.

- **New! Integrating Across the Curriculum features** provide concrete examples of curriculum integration at each of the three levels: K–2, 3–5, and 6–8. These features show how integrated curriculum addresses state learning standards while providing needed context for literacy instruction, which frees up valuable class time for teaching other content subjects.

- Central to this text are **six overriding themes** interwoven throughout the book that are critical in reading instruction today: Language and Diversity, Family Literacy, Writing and Reading Connections, Struggling Reader, Phonics and Phonological Awareness and New Literacies. Special **marginal icons** call your attention to points in the text that specifically address these themes. Critical thinking questions attached to each icon help you extend and enhance your understanding of text concepts.

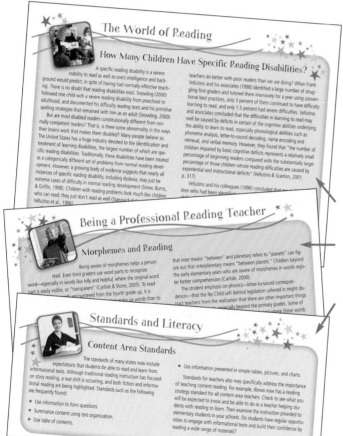

- **Graphic Organizer** and **Anticipation Guide** at the start of each chapter provide readers with an overall perspective of the chapter and the opportunity to assess their level of understanding prior to reading the chapter.

- Every chapter begins with a narrative **Classroom Story** that shares a reading teacher's experience in an active classroom. Each vignette models key concepts from the chapters and demonstrates the challenges of today's classrooms and considerations for addressing children's needs.

- **The World of Reading** boxes investigate a wide array of subjects as they pertain to the field of reading.

- **Being a Professional Reading Teacher** activities help future teachers explore their own thoughts about teaching.

- **Standards and Literacy** boxes explore standards from an objective perspective and openly discuss the pros, cons, and considerations surrounding their use in literacy education.

    In addition, the book includes an appendix, *"All Children Read and Professional Literacy Standards."* This appendix outlines the IRA *Standards for Reading Professionals—Revised 2003*, accompanied by a table correlating *All Children Read*, third edition to those standards. This special appendix also includes a table of the NCTE & IRA *Standards for the English Language Arts* and a correlation of where those standards are addressed within *All Children Read*.

Teach It!

Refer to the Teach It! appendix at the end of the book for further activities you can use to reinforce concepts discussed in this chapter.

Guided Reading and the Four Blocks

Guided reading is "a context in which the teacher supports each reader's development of effective strategies for processing novel texts at increasingly challenging levels of difficulty" (Fountas & Pinnell, 1996). The key elements of guided reading are:

- The teacher works with small groups.
- The children in each group are reading at about the same level.
- The teacher introduces stories and supports children's development of independent reading strategies.
- Each child reads the entire text.
- Independent, silent reading is the goal for each child.
- Over time, the teacher focuses on increasing the levels of text provided.
- The children are grouped and regrouped in accordance with outcomes observed and assessed by the teacher.
- Books are carefully leveled. That is, the difficulty levels of books available to the children are precisely determined so that they can progress in an orderly way.

Guided reading lessons are conducted in three essential stages. *Before the Reading* is a stage in which the teacher introduces a new and appropriate text, and children converse with the teacher about the text, asking questions and building expectations. *During the Reading* is the stage in which the teacher observes problem-solving strategies used by children. The children read the entire text, or a unified part of it, to themselves silently (or softly in the case of younger readers) and ask for help when needed. In *After the Reading*, the teacher involves the children in responding to the story through such activities as writing, discussion, paired reading, and shar-

ing personal responses. The children talk about the story, verify predictions they made before reading, and respond, usually through writing or perhaps drama (Fountas & Pinnell, 1996).

Guided reading is often combined with the structure of the Four Blocks approach (Cunningham, Hall, & Sigmon, 1999). Together, the four blocks address the five elements of Reading First and also combine many of the strengths of the basal reading program, individualized reading, and reader's workshop, while avoiding most of their limitations.

The four blocks are: guided reading, as discussed in this section; writing; self-selected reading; and working with words. Teachers can implement the multilevel aspect of the four block approach by teaching a lesson to the entire class, making the text accessible to all students with multiple settings involving read-aloud, shared reading, and paired reading in small flexible groups. They can add the writing and self-selected reading blocks of the approach as after-reading activities from the guided reading approach.

Although children in Reading First classrooms are often doing word study as a whole group, with all working on the same skills, teachers may find it more useful to teach appropriate skills in smaller groups tailored to the needs of children. For example, some children are more advanced and may not need to work with skills already mastered, and other children may lack prior knowledge needed to achieve some skills, for example, children trying to work with three-letter consonant blends such as *str* and *spl* before they have mastered two-letter consonant blends, such as *st* and *tr*.

As you can see, there are several roads to balanced literacy that also address the five major elements of Reading First: phonemic awareness; phonics; fluency; comprehension; and vocabulary. As you proceed through the chapters that follow, you will see more specific ways to apply these approaches and many others.

- **Teach It!** boxes provide readers with ready-made teaching tips for skill development, as well as for introducing new approaches to the teaching of literacy. Teach It! margin icons identify correlating activities from the *Teach It!* appendix that can be used to teach the concepts discussed.

Teach It! 9

Guided Reading and the Four Blocks Approach

DIFFERENTIATED INSTRUCTION

Reading Comprehension: Understanding and Learning with Informational Texts

SIOP Sheltered Instruction Observation Protocol

Many students who speak languages other than English in their homes do very well with conversational English, and teachers may be unaware of the need to provide specific instruction when it comes to the academic vocabulary needed for content area reading and learning. Yet this is an area deserving particular attention. Research studies have highlighted the fact that there is a great difference between conversational English and academic English competence. Teachers can do a lot to help English language learners be successful in this area of academic learning by focusing on vocabulary development.

Begin by assessing students' depth of understanding of key academic terms. For example, if the unit in social studies is about the westward movement of European pioneers across the continent, then terms like *pioneer, covered wagon, wagon train, trails, obstacles,* and *hardships* will probably be needed. These are terms that students would not encounter in normal conversational contexts. They are academic terms needed for

regular conversational English, they need to be highlighted and taught specifically.

It is often helpful to English language learners to make a list of key terms and then compare them with the same terms in their home language. Because there are many Latin-based cognates used in English, this can make the learning task much easier. For example, the science terms can be listed on one side and the Spanish terms on the other.

Opaque	opaco/a
Reflection	reflexión
Refraction	refracción
Translucent	translúcido/a
Transparent	transparente

English language learners will be much more successful if teachers focus

- **Differentiated Instruction** features highlight ways to differentiate instruction so that all students are engaged positively and productively, acknowledging the increasing diversity of today's students. Several of these features also include a **Sheltered Instruction Observation Protocol—SIOP** component, highlighting ways to differentiate reading instruction for English Language Learners.

ASSESSMENT

Involving Students in Self-Assessment

As children move into the intermediate and middle grades, they should be involved in monitoring their own growth as readers. Having students maintain Reading Logs helps them become more self-conscious about their reading habits, preferences, and strategies. Asking them to keep a record of all the books and articles they read along with their responses to the pieces is an easy starting place. Periodically, it is helpful to ask all students to record their responses to particular texts. In this way you can compare how students respond and what focus they reflect. Asking students to share their responses with each other is a good way to stimulate a discussion of the various ways readers attend to and construct meaning from texts. Reading Logs can provide an ongoing record of engagement and help teachers know if students need to be encouraged to expand their range of readings. Some students tend to stay in one genre or with very easy books.

Another way learning can be made visible to students is to have them keep samples of texts that they have marked with marginal notes

or sticky notes during the four quarters of the school year. They can return to earlier text notations and analyze changes. If students are engaged with several units and reading many informational texts over the course of the year, there should be changes in depth and range of responses they can look for. For example, students can track the number of times they make comparisons across texts, as well as the times they question authors' inferences, ask questions of a text, and visualize ideas presented. The K-W-L sheets can be a good component of this kind of activity, too. Students can evaluate the quality of their questions, the extent to which they fulfill their desires to learn new content, and the graphic organizers and summaries they create.

- **Assessment** features highlight practical aspects of assessment approaches related to chapter topics.

- **For Review** sections conclude each chapter and offer a convenient study tool in the form of a brief recap of the most important topics covered.

- **For Your Journal** sections offer ideas for using material learned in each chapter to inform development of a personal teaching journal.

- **Taking It to the World** exercises challenge readers to apply chapter material to authentic classroom situations.

- **New Literacies Connections** offer a selection of relevant websites and advice for using them to benefit professional development.

For Review

Children's literacy begins to emerge at home, well before they enter school. Once they enter kindergarten and first grade, their literacy develops through a combination of children-driven discoveries and experiences orchestrated by a teacher. A successful teacher of reading and writing in the early years must be part psychologist – a kidwatcher (see Chapter 11), a careful observer of what children have discovered and are discovering for themselves – and part bridge builder, carefully constructing experiences that will lead children from where they are to where they are going as readers and writers.

Although all children develop literacy concepts about print before they enter school, the amount of experience they have with literacy varies widely. A teacher of kindergarten and first grade must provide lavish opportunities for children to learn about print and target help for children who learn what they need to learn. The teacher can also reach out to the home, both to invite families to contribute material from their lives—family stories and traditions, for example—and to enlist the help of parents in helping children practice their literacy.

Emergent literacy refers to the period from early childhood through the first year of school in which children learn about language and print and about ways to draw meaning from and add meaning to print. In recent years, scholars have come to recognize the role of the child's own discoveries in learning to read and write, and research in literacy has identified aspects of literacy that teachers can help children develop.

For Your Journal

1. Take a moment to review your answers to the items on the Anticipation Guide that opens this chapter. Has your thinking changed? If so, write about the changes in your journal.

2. Some teachers and literacy experts expect to learn much of what they need to know about teaching from their own discoveries, from being at...

Taking It to the World

1. What are your first memories of reading and writing? Can you remember not being able to read and write? Were you curious about these activities? What things did you do to teach yourself about them?

2. Visit a preschool – a Head Start program, if possible. Ask the teachers what their approaches to supporting children's early literacy. How and when are reading and writing used during the day? How have their approaches to supporting children's early literacy changed over the last ten years?

3. To learn about efforts to involve parents in supporting children's literacy, interview an elementary school teacher or administrator. How are parents' ideas and volunteer efforts brought into the classroom? What things are sent home to help parents assist their chil-

dren? What special efforts are being made toward increasing family literacy?

4. Continuing with the interview in item 3, how are English learners being supported as they learn to read and write? How is the school working with their parents?

5. Speak with a kindergarten or first-grade teacher about how he or she assesses students' concepts about print and what types of screenings are used to assess students' reading skills.

6. Visit the Jumpstart website (www.jstart.org/about/) to determine whether there is a Jumpstart program near your community. What are some possible ways in which you might be able to volunteer some time?

New Literacies Connections

1. Visit the literacy homepage of the North Central Regional Educational Laboratory at www.ncrel.org/litweb and do a search for "emergent literacy." Examine the numerous articles and connections to useful information and materials.

2. The National Right to Read Foundation (www.nrrf.org) provides thorough information and support on phonics instruction. This website raises a number of concerns about issues such as emergent literacy and

invented spelling. Visit the "Topical Essays" page to read the critiques of these and other topics.

3. The Center for Research in Early Reading Achievement is a federally funded consortium of five universities. Its website (www.ciera.org) might be the single best site on emergent literacy, with research reports, book reviews, news of conferences, and links to other sites.

The power of classroom practice.

"Teacher educators who are developing pedagogies for the analysis of teaching and learning contend that analyzing teaching artifacts has three advantages: it enables new teachers time for reflection while still using the real materials of practice; it provides new teachers with experience thinking about and approaching the complexity of the classroom; and in some cases, it can help new teachers and teacher educators develop a shared understanding and common language about teaching. . . ."[1]

As Linda Darling-Hammond and her colleagues point out, grounding teacher education in real classrooms—among real teachers and students and among actual examples of students' and teachers' work—is an important and perhaps even an essential part of training teachers for the complexities of teaching in today's classrooms. For this reason, we have created a valuable, time-saving website—MyEducationLab—that provides the context of real classrooms and artifacts that research on teacher education tells us is so important. The authentic in-class video footage, interactive skill-building exercises and other resources available on MyEducationLab offers a uniquely valuable teacher education tool.

MyEducationLab is easy to use and integrate into assignments and courses. Whenever the MyEducationLab logo appears in the text, follow the simple instructions to access the interactive assignments, activities, and learning units on MyEducationLab. For each topic covered in the course you will find most or all of the following resources:

CONNECTION TO NATIONAL STANDARDS Now it is easier than ever to see how coursework is connected to national standards. Each topic on MyEducationLab lists intended learning outcomes connected to the appropriate national standards. And all of the Assignments and Activities and all of the Building Teaching Skills and Dispositions in MyEducationLab are mapped to the appropriate national standards and learning outcomes as well.

ASSIGNMENTS AND ACTIVITIES Designed to save instructors preparation time and enhance student understanding, these assignable exercises show concepts in action (through video, cases, and/or student and teacher artifacts). They help students synthesize and apply concepts and strategies they read about in the book.

BUILDING TEACHING SKILLS AND DISPOSITIONS These learning units help students practice and strengthen skills that are essential to quality teaching. They are presented with the core skill or concept and then given an opportunity to practice their understanding of this concept multiple times by watching video footage (or interacting with other media) and then critically analyzing the strategy or skill presented.

IRIS CENTER RESOURCES The IRIS Center at Vanderbilt University (http://iris .peabody.vanderbilt.edu—funded by the U.S. Department of Education's Office of Special Education Programs, OSEP) develops training enhancement materials for preservice and in-service teachers. The Center works with experts from across the country to create challenge-based interactive modules, case study units, and podcasts that provide research-validated information about working with students in inclusive settings. In your MyEducationLab course we have integrated this content into appropriate topics.

LITERACY PORTRAITS The Literacy Portraits section on MyEducationLab consists of video case studies showing the development of five students throughout their second grade year. Each student is shown engaging in reading and writing activities. Teacher commentary and samples of the students' work is also available.

GENERAL RESOURCES ON YOUR MYEDUCATIONLAB COURSE The Resources section on MyEducationLab is designed to help students pass their licensure exams, put together effective portfolios and lesson plans, prepare for and navigate the first year of their

---

myeducationlab

Emergent writing samples offer insight into the concepts about print and knowledge of letters and sounds held by an individual student. Complete the Building Teaching Skills and Dispositions activity "Analyzing Emergent Writing for Emergent Literacy Understandings" to develop your skills in assessing what a child knows and needs to learn. (To find this activity, go to the topic *Emergent Literacy* in MyEducationLab and click on Building Teaching Skills and Dispositions.)

teaching careers, and understand key educational standards, policies, and laws. This section includes:

- *Licensure Exams*: Contains guidelines for passing the Praxis exam. The *Practice Test Exam* includes practice multiple-choice questions, case study questions, and video case studies with sample questions.

- *Lesson Plan Builder*: Helps students create and share lesson plans.

- *Licensure and Standards*: Provides links to state licensure standards and national standards.

- *Beginning Your Career*: Offers tips, advice, and valuable information on:
  - Resume Writing and Interviewing: Expert advice on how to write impressive resumes and prepare for job interviews.
  - Your First Year of Teaching: Practical tips on setting up a classroom, managing student behavior, and planning for instruction and assessment.
  - Law and Public Policies: Includes specific directives and requirements educators need to understand from the No Child Left Behind Act and the Individuals with Disabilities Education Improvement Act of 2004.

Visit www.myeducationlab.com for a demonstration of this exciting new online teaching resource.

Supplements and Learning Aids

To get the most use of *All Children Read: Teaching for Literacy in Today's Diverse Classrooms*, third edition, a number of useful supplements are available for students and instructors.

The following resources are available for instructors to download on www.pearsonhighered.com/educators. Instructors can enter the author or title of this book, select this edition, and then click on the "Resources" tab to log in and download textbook supplements.

- **Instructor's Manual and Test Bank.** The Instructor's Manual includes a wealth of interesting ideas and activities designed to help instructors teach the course. Each chapter includes a chapter-at-a-glance grid, key concepts, student objectives, activities, discussion questions, and vocabulary and key terms. There is also a test bank for each chapter.

- **Computerized Test Bank.** The printed Test Bank is also available electronically through the computerized testing system. Instructors can use the computerized test bank to create exams in just minutes.

- **PowerPoint™ Presentation.** Ideal for lecture presentations or student handouts, the PowerPoint™ Presentation created for this text provides dozens of ready-to-use lecture aids.

Also Available for this Edition:

- **Allyn & Bacon Literacy Video Library.** This selection of videos, available for previous editions, features reading experts such as Richard Allington, Dorothy Strickland, and Evelyn English, and addresses core topics covered in the literacy classroom. Videos include *Developing Literacy in the Multiple Intelligences Classroom* (featuring Evelyn English); *Reading Strategies* (featuring Donna Ogle); *Reading and Writing: The Pathway to Meaning* (featuring Dorothy Strickland); or *Thoughtful Literacy: The Key to Student Achievement* (featuring Richard Allington). Please consult with your Allyn & Bacon representative for details and conditions on how to obtain these videos.

Acknowledgments

W e would like to thank the reviewers who took time out from busy schedules to share with us their support and expertise and provided us with the valuable feedback that helped to shape this project: Rebecca S. Anderson, University of Memphis; Diane Barone, University of Nevada-Reno; Marian S. Beckman, Edinboro University of Pennsylvania; Charlotte Black, California State University, San Bernardino; Melise Bunker, Palm Beach Atlantic College; Margaret Bell Davis, Eastern Kentucky University; Deborah Doty, Northern Kentucky University; Mary Ann Dzama, George Mason University; Callie L. Fortenberry, Texas A&M, Texarkana; David Landis, University of Northern Iowa; Darlene Michener, California State University, Los Angeles; Michael Moore, Georgia Southern University; Kathleen R. Murphy, Clarion University of Pennsylvania; John Savage, Boston College; Corlis Snow, Delta State University; Kim Truesdell, State University College at Buffalo; Marion P. Turkish, William Paterson University; Debra Whitaker-Volturo, Ocean City School District; Clairin DeMartini Wilson, Nevada State College; Valerie Wright, Saint Leo; James Zarrillo, California State University, Hayward.

Charles Temple wants to thank his colleagues and students at HWS for good cheer at all hours, the International Reading Association, the Open Society Institute, and CODE-Canada for all their support over the years, and his extended family.

Donna Ogle wants to thank her husband, niece, and colleagues for their contributions to this book. Bud has provided incredible support for this project and is a model "critical reader." Kjersten Kuhlman who directs a 21st Century Project in Massachusetts helps Donna stay current and suggested the ThinkQuest feature for this book. The teachers with whom Donna works in the Chicago area and in international contexts energized her to share their ideas. Special thanks to colleagues in CLIP and the faculty at NLU.

Alan Crawford thanks his colleagues and students in the public schools of East Los Angeles and Cal State Los Angeles for inspiration over the years; the teachers with whom he's worked—in California, Latin America, Central Asia, Central Europe, and Africa; good friends at UNESCO, the International Reading Association, and the Open Society Institute; and of course, Linda.

Penny Freppon wishes to thank her co-authors and the teachers with whom she has worked and from whom she has learned so much. She thanks Dr. Jill Dillard and Linda Headings, and Dr. Lisa Campbell for their friendship and professional guidance. She also thanks the Open Society Institute for supporting her international work. In addition, she thanks her family and extended family, and in particular, Don Gustafson, her late husband and intellectual partner, who was all she ever wanted long before she ever knew him.

Last but not least, a special thank you to everyone at Allyn and Bacon for working so hard to create this beautiful book out of our humble parts and for remaining so steadfastly cheerful and encouraging throughout: Vice President, Editor-in-chief, Aurora Martínez; Development Editor, Christina Robb; Senior Production Editor, Janet Domingo, for her project coordination; Sara Holliday for her assistance with the standards correlations, and to Kathy Smith for her good eye and detailed oversight.

---

[1]Darling-Hammond, L., & Bransford, J., Eds. (2005). *Preparing Teachers for a Changing World*. San Francisco: John Wiley & Sons.

Approaches to Teaching Reading

Anticipation Guide

The following statements will help you begin thinking about the topics covered in this chapter. Answer *true* or *false* in response to each statement. As you read and learn more about the topics mentioned in these statements, think back on your answers. See what interests you and prompts your curiosity toward more understanding.

_____ 1. Literacy makes you smarter because the vocabulary, the information, and the habit of learning from text make you better able to learn new things.

_____ 2. Among adults, there is little connection between people's level of reading ability and their income level.

_____ 3. Concerns over the media revolution are exaggerated. Students between the ages of 8 and 18 spend far less time reading online than they do reading books.

_____ 4. Most reading disabilities are caused by malfunctions of the brain, and children with reading problems need a completely different kind of teaching from what normally developing readers need.

_____ 5. Research shows that more than 86 percent of the children who get a poor start in learning to read do not catch up with their peers.

_____ 6. Differences in the amount of reading children do are not significant. What matters in teaching reading is demonstrating the skill.

_____ 7. Giving parents and caregivers ideas for helping their children at home with literacy experiences makes a considerable difference in the children's success in school.

_____ 8. Reading ability develops through stages in this order: beginning reading, emergent literacy, reading to learn and for pleasure, building fluency, and mature reading.

_____ 9. The debate between advocates of phonics instruction and advocates of whole-word instruction began in the 1980s in the United States, during the Reagan administration.

_____ 10. Formal testing is the only worthwhile means of assessing children's literacy.

Approaches to Teaching Reading

What Makes a Good Teacher of Reading and Writing?

Good teachers of reading and writing excel in many ways. They do know a great many teaching methods, but they also have a solid background in the science of language and literacy, and they manage to keep up with new developments in their field. They are keen observers of children's learning and inventive designers of lessons and techniques. They can connect with children, and children of all backgrounds and levels of ability like them, trust them, and are inspired by them. They make unusual efforts to connect with their students' families and help the families feel comfortable with the school environment and process. Good teachers of reading and writing love to read and write, and they gladly demonstrate their enthusiasm and share their knowledge with their students.

Good teachers of reading and writing are everywhere—in classrooms from Los Angeles to New York City, from the Rio Grande Valley to the fields of Saskatchewan, and all around the world. Some work in carpeted classrooms equipped with gleaming rows of computers,

but just as many make cheerful places out of storage rooms, hallways, or even tropical shelters with rattling tin roofs and open walls—always thoughtfully orchestrating the learning of an individual child or of many different children. You will find them teaching in English, Spanish, French, Kiswahili, Arabic, or more than one language at a time. You will find them in team meetings with teachers of the same grade or several grades, tracking children's progress and pondering the best ways to help all the children learn to read well; and you will find them huddled in deliberations with a caregiver and a school psychologist, trying to unlock the puzzle of a child's reading difficulty. You will see them in a school or community library, sharing just the right book with a child who is on the threshold of becoming a reader. You sometimes hear about them creating a lesson without books or paper in any one of scores of developing countries for children whose parents never knew the craft of literacy, or strategizing in a committee room at the

United Nations to help spread literacy to all of the children in the world.

The authors of this book hope that you will share with those good teachers a passion for bringing the gift of literacy to young people. We hope you will immerse yourself in understanding how reading works and how it is taught, and that you will continue to grow in your knowledge of reading and reading instruction.

Teaching every child to read and write is the most important mission of the elementary and middle school teacher. All the subjects in the curriculum contribute to the education of well-rounded children. But teaching children to read and write prepares them to learn their other school subjects and to educate themselves for the rest of their lives. The skills of literacy are centrally important for other reasons, too: Being able to read and write makes children smarter and ultimately makes their lives better. Read on!

Why Does Literacy Matter?

Teaching children to read not only reveals to them knowledge stored in print, but also makes them better able to use that knowledge. Children who read gain background knowledge about the things they read about, whether it be nature, science, history, current events, or geography (Stanovich, 1992). This knowledge helps them make sense of the new things they read (Anderson & Pearson, 1984; Recht & Leslie, 1988). Children who read gain bigger vocabularies, too, and having bigger vocabularies enables them to notice more and to make finer distinctions in their perceptions of the world (Beck, McKeown, & Kucan, 2002).

Literacy helps children to think more skillfully. Studies have shown that being readers makes a difference in people's ability to think, their awareness of words, their ability to talk about their own feelings, and even their ability to ask questions and learn about things they didn't know (Luria, 1976). Children who read and talk about books show greater self-awareness and better critical thinking skills (Almasi, 1995) and tend to engage ideas more deeply (Eeds & Wells, 1989; Goatley, Brock, & Raphael, 1995). Children who read also are better able to pick up on themes in stories, and are more likely to "get the message" (Lehr, 1988).

Among adults, being able to read leads to better health, better jobs, higher income, and better quality of life (National Institute for Literacy, 2008). These facts are important to teachers in the elementary and middle grades, too, because the experiences their students have will strongly influence whether they succeed or fail to learn to read and write (Juel, 1988; Stanovich, 1985).

Teachers of reading and writing are in a position to set children up to have better life options available for the rest of their lives. But there is a catch: Most people with limited literacy don't perceive that it is a problem. In one large study, only one in four of the poorest readers reported that they were ever troubled by not being able to read well (National Adult Literacy Survey, 1993). The task of a teacher of reading, then, will not only be to teach, but also to motivate. Even though reading ability is a ticket to a better future for all students, we cannot expect them or their parents and caregivers to know that. The teacher will have to make special efforts to encourage all children to want to be readers, and every family member to support them.

Because literacy is associated with better health and better socioeconomic standing, English as a Second Language (ESL) programs for adults are important services in all communities. (Michael Newman/PhotoEdit)

How Well Do Children in the United States Read?

For years, the media have clamored about the poor state of reading in American schools. But the critics have mostly gotten it wrong. They have missed both the considerable achievements as well as the most serious challenges in our nation's efforts to teach all children to read (Klenk & Kibby, 2000). In a nutshell, three things are true about the way children read in the United States:

- On average, American students do well at basic reading skills. In terms of basic reading (that is, reading text with essential understanding) taken as a whole, American school children do better than most other children in the world. The Office of Education and Community Development surveys students' reading achievement at fourth grade and eighth grade every four years. In 2006, fourth graders from the United States were in fifteenth place out of forty countries measured, and well above the international average—ahead of Austria, New Zealand, France, and Spain; but behind Canada, Hong Kong, Russia, and Bulgaria (PIRLS, 2009).

- Success in reading is spread unevenly among American children, however. The most successful American students do well in basic literacy tasks, but there are many students who perform poorly. The National Assessment of Educational Progress (NAEP) defines fourth graders with a **basic reading level** this way:

  Fourth-grade students performing at the Basic level should demonstrate an understanding of the overall meaning of what they read. When reading text appropriate for fourth-graders, they should be able to make relatively obvious connections between the text and their own experiences and extend the ideas in the text by making simple inferences. (NAEP, 2006, p. 20)

A third of the tested fourth graders in the United States performed below this level in 2007. Black students and Hispanic students performed better than in past years, but 60 percent of the black fourth graders tested and 56 percent of the measured Hispanic fourth graders could not read on a basic level.

A **proficient reading level** means:

[S]tudents ... should be able to demonstrate an overall understanding of the text, providing inferential as well as literal information. When reading text appropriate to fourth grade, they should be able to extend the ideas in the text by making inferences, drawing conclusions, and making connections to their own experiences. The connections between the text and what the student infers should be clear." (NAEP, 2006, p. 20)

A quarter of the fourth graders tested *could* read on a proficient level in 2007 and another 7 percent read above that, at a superior level. Many would like those figures to be higher. Noting that the literacy demands of American society are going up (as manufacturing jobs have given way to information processing jobs), a study commissioned by the Carnegie Corporation reported with concern that 70 percent of American secondary students needed remediation in reading, to get them to the proficient level.

- Differences in reading achievement are often related to economic circumstances. Schools in the United States fare worse than those in two thirds of the countries in the industrialized world when it comes to helping all children succeed regardless of their family income (Organization of Economic and Community Development, 2000; Willms, 1999). This fact is especially significant because, with 26 percent of all children in the United States living in poverty by some counts, American schools serve children with the second highest poverty rate among industrialized nations. In a typical American classroom of 30 children, eight of the children will be poor. In the same size classroom in Sweden, one of them will be poor (Bradbury & Jäntti, 1999).

Poorer children may be harder to educate:

As a result of their living in poverty, children may bring a variety of challenges to the classroom that necessitate the provision of additional services such as remediation or after school tutoring programs. These children may require basic provisions from the school, such as breakfast and/or lunch, and may lack essential supplies such as pencil and paper. (National Center for Educational Statistics, 2000, p. 14)

Struggling Reader

Why do some children have a really hard time learning to read?

Who Are the Struggling Readers?

If success in reading in the United States is spread unevenly, how many of our children have "reading disabilities"? A reading disability is said to be present when a child with normal intelligence who has had adequate instruction fails to learn to read. By this definition, experts have estimated that 10 to 20 percent of all school children have specific reading disabilities (Shaywitz, Escobar, Shaywitz, Fletcher, & Makuch, 1992). Some researchers, however, suggest that the figure might be much lower and that deficiencies can be overcome or prevented if children have enough of the right reading supports at home and proper instruction in kindergarten and first grade. (See the World of Reading box.)

Why are such early reading experiences so important? The importance of a good beginning in reading—and the damage that can be done by a poor beginning—was underscored years ago by Connie Juel (1988). Juel surveyed a group of first graders in a Texas public school, found the 20 percent who read least well, and carefully tracked the reading progress of 54 of them for three years. At the end of the study, 86 percent of those children were still in the bottom half of the class. Although reading problems had not been severe in first grade, they were serious by fourth grade. There was little reason to hope that these children would close the gap in later years. Why?

Stanovich (1986) has shown that fairly mild deficits in the early years can develop into severe reading disabilities after three or four years. We know that the more children read, the better they read. The reverse is also true. Whatever mild problem a child may have can make reading difficult, and if it's difficult, they won't practice. Proof? When Juel asked a fourth-grade subject whether he would rather do chores than read, he responded, "Lady, I'd rather scrub the mold around the bathtub than read!" (Juel, 1988). Studies of reading habits have shown us the differences in the amount of reading proficient readers and poor readers do: The most avid three or four readers in a fifth-grade classroom read in one year what the least proficient readers would read in a century (Anderson, Wilson, & Fielding, 1988). That much of a difference in practice could easily make a telling difference in reading ability. Fortunately, as we shall see in Chapter 6, there are many good ways teachers can encourage children to read more.

Family and Community Involvement

Families make a difference in children's preparation to learn to read and write. On the average, children from poor families with little education have more difficulty learning to be literate than children from middle-class homes do (Vernon-Feagans, Hammer, Miccio, & Manlove, 2001). But the exact reasons for this can be difficult to tease out. If a family is poor—and one fifth of America's children live in families that are poor—then poverty itself presents a complex set of stress factors (Ehrenreich, 2001). If you are poor, it is hard to raise a healthy and competent child. It is hard to buy and prepare nutritious food. It is hard to afford good-quality childcare. It is hard to find the time and energy between jobs to spend time with your child.

myeducationlab
The Power of Classroom Practice
www.myeducationlab.com

Learn more about the underlying causes of reading failure and the long-term repercussions of reading disabilities by completing the activity "Understanding the Matthew Effect in Reading." (To find this activity, go to the topic *Struggling Readers* in MyEducationLab and click on Assignments and Activities.)

Family Literacy

How would you persuade a skeptic that teachers should help families help their children learn to read?

The World of Reading

How Many Children Have Specific Reading Disabilities?

A specific reading disability is a severe inability to read as well as one's intelligence and background would predict, in spite of having had normally effective teaching. There is no doubt that reading disabilities exist. Snowling (2000) followed one child with a severe reading disability from preschool to adulthood, and documented his difficulty reading texts and his primitive spelling strategies that remained with him as an adult (Snowling, 2000).

But are most disabled readers constitutionally different from normally competent readers? That is, is there some abnormality in the ways their brains work that makes them disabled? Many people believe so. The United States has a huge industry devoted to the identification and treatment of learning disabilities, the largest number of which are specific reading disabilities. Traditionally, these disabilities have been treated as a categorically different set of problems from normal reading development. However, a growing body of evidence suggests that nearly all instances of specific reading disability, including dyslexia, may just be extreme cases of difficulty in normal reading development (Snow, Burns, & Griffin, 1998). Children with reading problems look much like children who can read; they just don't read as well (Stanovich & Siegel, 1994; Vellutino et al., 1996).

Going back to the definition of severe reading disabilities as not learning to read in spite of otherwise effective reading instruction, we must ask if the problem really is the instruction children receive. Can

teachers do better with poor readers than we are doing? When Frank Vellutino and his associates (1996) identified a large number of struggling first graders and tutored them intensively for a year using conventional best practices, only 3 percent of them continued to have difficulty learning to read, and only 1.5 percent had severe difficulties. Vellutino and associates concluded that the difficulties in learning to read may well be caused by deficits in certain of the cognitive abilities underlying the ability to learn to read, especially phonological abilities such as phoneme analysis, letter-to-sound decoding, name encoding and retrieval, and verbal memory. However, they found that "the number of children impaired by basic cognitive deficits represents a relatively small percentage of beginning readers compared with the substantially larger percentage of those children whose reading difficulties are caused by experiential and instructional deficits" (Vellutino & Scanlon, 2001, p. 317).

Vellutino and his colleagues (1996) concluded that most of the children who had been identified as possibly having a specific reading disability did not suffer from abnormal brain function. Rather, they suffered from confusions, delays, poor starts, and the need for finely tuned and responsive instruction that was carefully tailored to their strengths and needs.

Nonetheless, researchers have identified family literacy practices related to children's success in learning to read and write. Many of these may be influenced by the school or by the school working in concert with community partners. Here is a set of factors that the National Research Council (Snow et al., 1998, p. 123) has identified:

1. **Value placed on literacy:** By reading themselves and encouraging children to read, parents can demonstrate that they value reading.
2. **Press for achievement:** By expressing their expectations for achievement by their children, providing reading instruction, and responding to the children's reading initiations and interests, parents can create a press for achievement.
3. **Availability and instrumental use of reading materials:** By providing children's books and other reading and writing materials in the home, parents increase the likelihood that literacy experiences will occur.
4. **Reading with children:** By reading to preschoolers at bedtime and other times, listening to schoolchildren's oral reading, and providing assistance as needed, parents can promote children's literacy.

Family literacy projects that encourage families to read to children and talk with them can have success (Vernon-Feagans et al., 2001). But helping families nurture their children's literacy is not a simple matter. Communication patterns in families are hard to change—even if we agree that educators have a moral right to try to change them! Poor families offer children less verbal interaction than middle-class families do, and the shortage of interaction has a strong effect on the size of children's vocabulary and the reach of their knowledge of grammar (Hart & Risley, 1995), which in turn affects their learning how to read and write. Here is another problem: It is known that children's preschool experiences with books and print also contribute to their success in learning to read once they arrive in school (Snow et al., 1998; Teale & Sulzby, 1987). But low-income families visit the library half as often on average as middle-class families do (Baker, Serpell, & Sonnenschein, 1995). Purcell-Gates (1997) writes of an illiterate mother of an illiterate son living in Cincinnati who didn't realize there were places in the city where they would lend you books for free.

Family literacy work is not always easy, but the title of Purcell-Gates's book about the illiterate mother and the semi-literate son—*The Cycle of Low Literacy*—underscores how important it is for educators to include families in their plans for promoting literacy.

Components of Reading Ability

What goes into teaching a child to read? At its simplest, reading is the act of getting meaning from a written text. To read successfully, readers must be able to collect or construct meaning through written symbols. Readers recognize squiggles of ink on a page as letters and words. This activity is called **word recognition**. To become skilled at word recognition, readers need to be aware of the smallest sounds in language, called *phonemes*, because being **aware of phonemes** prepares readers to find matches between sounds and letters. Learning the matches between sounds and letters is knowledge of **phonics**.

Readers work with the words they recognize, and construct an understanding of what they read. This activity is called *comprehension*. Comprehension is made up of several processes and kinds of knowledge, including having some prior knowledge that can be used to understand the text, being familiar with vocabulary, knowing how text is organized, and recognizing when text is making sense and when it is not.

Readers eventually come to recognize words quickly and accurately. This activity is called *reading fluency*. It is hoped that as they have learned to read, they have made books a part of their lives and found authors they especially enjoy and have developed a **habit**

of reading. Eventually, they may learn to hone their minds by weighing an author's words, reflecting on arguments, and coming up with their own interpretations of what they have read, a skill known as *interpretation*, or **critical reading**.

Here is an illustration of these components in action. Suppose a fifth grader is asked to read this passage.

"Come quick," whispered Mother, from across the street. "The guard is looking the other way."

Rebecca clutched her doll close to her chest, crouched low, and scrambled across the empty street toward the lamppost that hid her mother. Just then a search light from atop a darkened building swept the street she had just crossed.

"Gestapo," said her mother, hugging the panting child. "They're everywhere." Rebecca squeezed the Star of David around her neck and trembled.

A number of things have to happen for this passage to be read successfully.

Phonics and Phonological Awareness

Being aware of sounds in words helps early readers get off to a good start.

Word Recognition

Of course, readers have to recognize most of the words for the meaning of the passage to be easily available to them. If they are reading the passage on their own, they should find no more than four words that they do not recognize. (That is, they should easily recognize at least 95 percent of the words in the passage.) If they are reading the passage with the support of a teacher, they would be expected to find no more than eight unknown words (a 90 percent recognition rate), according to many reading specialists (e.g., Gillet, Temple, & Crawford, 2004). As will be seen, understanding a passage is much more than the sum of understanding the words. Nonetheless, if readers have to pause and puzzle over the meanings of more than a few words in a passage, their comprehension will be impaired.

How is this word recognition done? By the time they have reached fifth grade, children will have stored thousands of words in memory that they can recognize instantly. Reading specialists call this store of instantly recognized words their **sight vocabulary**. Readers have been accumulating these words since they were in kindergarten, and as they progress through the grades, they will be learning more new words—thousands more new words—every year.

How do readers go about learning new words? In several ways. For example, if a child failed to recognize *clutched* on a first exposure, the teacher would remind the child to break the word into parts: *cl + utch + ed*. A third grader would be highly skilled at phonemic segmentation and would have no difficulty breaking the words in her speech into separate sounds, and she would be able to find matches between letters on the page and speech sounds. But also because she is a third grader, her knowledge of phonics would be a matter not just of matches between individual letters and sounds, but also of matches at the level of patterns of letters combining vowels and consonants. Therefore, she would be able to find the pattern *-utch*, which she would be able to pronounce by relating it to a word she knows: *Dutch*. She would know the *cl-* consonant blend from many words she can read, such as *clap, click, clock,* and *cloud*. She would also know the past tense ending *-ed* from her past reading and study of words. Once she worked out the pronunciation of this unfamiliar word, *clutched*, she would recognize it as a word that she has heard and used in speech but not read before. A third grader would be using phonics, but her word knowledge would include not just letter-to-sound relationships, but also knowledge of larger spelling patterns and even of grammar as a factor in word structure. The word *Gestapo*, on the other hand, would present a different problem. Here she would have to work out the pronunciation of this unfamiliar word, but once she could pronounce the word or an approximation of it, she still would not be able to associate the written word with a word she uses in speech. She would have to use other strategies—in this case, context clues—to decide what the word means. The sentence in which the word appears is

"Gestapo . . . They're everywhere."

Making and Breaking Words

She would know that Gestapo are referred to as "they," meaning that Gestapo are most likely people. From the context of the passage, she would know to equate Gestapo with the guards who were scanning the street with their searchlights. Having surmised that the girl in the passage with the Star of David was Jewish, this reader would reason that Gestapo were guards or police who hunted Jews at some time in history. Perhaps they were German soldiers or police, and perhaps the setting was the time around World War II. In this second example, the reader not only learned to pronounce a previously unfamiliar word, but also derived an approximation of its meaning. From the context of the passage, she learned a new item of vocabulary.

This example, which features a third grader who is a reasonably successful reader, illustrates how recognizing words is a complex business involving several strategies. When younger children are just beginning to recognize words, still more strategies enter the picture.

Look again at the passage on page 7. How would readers go about understanding it?

Vocabulary

"Word Conversations" for Primary Grades

Initially, readers would be helped by their knowledge of **vocabulary** (Pressley, 2000). They use their knowledge of words such as *guard*, *searchlight*, and *Star of David* to help them construct the meaning of the text; as was just seen, one reader reasoned that the word *Gestapo* provides a new name for a concept she already had: the Nazi police. Knowing vocabulary provides readers with building blocks to help them construct their understanding of the passage. But readers must also create a context in which choices among competing meanings of words can be made. Without a context to give these words meaning, a reader does not know whether a *chest* refers to a box or a rib cage, whether *scrambling* is a way of preparing eggs or of moving our bodies, whether *post* refers to a job or a pole, or whether *sweeping* is an act of cleaning or a kind of motion across a surface. So knowing the vocabulary helps a reader to construct a meaning for the text, but the meaning that is constructed for the text also helps the reader to understand the words. Thus a web of meaning is woven.

Comprehension

In addition to vocabulary, readers have background knowledge or cognitive schemes that help them to understand the passage. Words such as *whispered*, *guard*, and *searchlight* are more than vocabulary items. Together, they help young readers to construct mental frameworks for understanding that the situation described in the passage is one of danger, of stealth, of the necessity to avoid detection. It is important that readers be able to supply this framework themselves, because the situation of needing to avoid detection is not stated explicitly by the text. From the mention of *Star of David*, readers might also suppose, without being told explicitly, that the passage has to do with the flight of Jews from persecution by the Nazis during World War II—something they know about because they have read about it in other books, such as Lois Lowry's *Number the Stars* and Carol Matas's *Daniel's Story*.

Readers make inferences about what is going on in the text. Although the text never said that Rebecca was a young girl, a reader might notice the details of Rebecca's clutching her doll and depending on her mother for guidance and infer that Rebecca was young. And although the text left a gap between Rebecca's scrambling across the dangerous street and her being hugged by her mother, a reader can infer that she made it safely across the street into her waiting mother's arms.

Readers can visualize, or form mental images of, what the words in the text describe. They can picture a darkened street (even though the text never said explicitly that the street was dark), with silent, unlit buildings on each side. They might imagine a nearly silent scene. If they were asked, they could draw a picture of the street.

Visualization

If the teacher asked the young readers to say what they had read, the readers would be able to say, "A young Jewish girl snuck across the street and got away from the guards." In other words, they were able to find the main idea of the passage.

In retelling what they just read about, our young readers make it clear that they think the girl was the main character—the hero, or the protagonist—of this text and that the rest of the text might tell about her attempts to escape from the Gestapo, the Nazi police. In other words, readers assume that they are reading a story, and they use their knowledge of the structure of stories to make predictions about what will follow in the coming pages. Their knowledge and use of the structure of the text make up one more important part of their comprehension of it.

Story Maps

Reading Fluency

Another aspect of reading that is related to word recognition and comprehension is reading fluency. A child would not be considered a competent reader of this passage unless he or she could read it fairly quickly and accurately and with some inflection—some changes in the tone of voice that roughly paralleled the emotional or meaningful contours of the text. Reading fluency is both an indicator of and a contributor to successful reading. If you hear a child reading smoothly and accurately, you can infer that the child recognizes the words efficiently. If the child also reads with appropriate inflection, you can also infer that the child comprehends the text. In addition, if readers read the text fluently, their fluency will contribute to their understanding. That is because having the ability to read strings of words smoothly and accurately leaves the mind plenty of capacity to appreciate the meaning of the text (Perfetti, 1992; Pressley, 2000). To illustrate this point, imagine two bicycle riders, one to whom riding comes naturally and a novice who is still struggling to balance, pedal, and steer the bicycle all at the same time. Which one do you suppose will enjoy the scenery?

Reading experts advocate giving children instruction and practice in reading for fluency because a well-developed capacity for relatively fast and accurate reading facilitates understanding. It is also a transferable ability: Becoming a fluent reader carries over from one text to another. That is why thoughtful teachers provide children plenty of opportunities to read texts that are fairly easy for them, among other reading tasks.

Fluency Oriented Oral Reading

Critical Literacy

Critical literacy is another aspect of literacy that our third graders might or might not call into play. Critical literacy means reading with polite skepticism, examining a text's hidden assumptions and bringing to light the devices by which the text might be intended to work its effects on the reader (Luke & Freebody, 1999).

Critical reading leads us to ask questions such as the following:

- Why is the author telling us this?
- Whose voices are left unheard?
- What is this text trying to do to me?
- What questions can be asked about the message?

Critical insights that our young readers might reach could include some like these: Just as Indians used to be commonly portrayed as riding on horseback and shooting arrows at wagon trains, Jewish children are frequently and stereotypically portrayed as trying to escape persecution. Surely there are other interesting things about their lives that could be written about. Also, in American children's books, the example of ethnic persecution that is most often given has to do with Jews more than sixty years ago. Of course, the Holocaust was consummately important and should not be forgotten. But there are cases of ethnically motivated persecution going on in the world in our own time that get much less attention, particularly children's attention. Critical readers will ask why the focus on issues of justice in children's books can't be broadened to include contemporary problems that one can still do something about.

In summary, it has been shown that the act of reading has several components and that each of them has its own complexity. To read, readers must recognize words, and word recognition entails not only having words stored in memory for instant recognition, but also knowing how to pronounce a word from its sequence of letters and word parts and being able to infer the meaning of words from their context. Reading also involves comprehension, which in turn includes knowing vocabulary, having and appropriately calling to mind frameworks of prior knowledge, making inferences, visualizing, getting main ideas, and knowing and making use of the structure of the text. Furthermore, skilled reading also includes fluency: reading quickly, accurately, and with appropriate inflection. Fluency is a sign of skilled reading, and the ability to read fluently also enables meaningful reading. Finally, reading ability can include critical reading. In the chapters that follow, you will see all of these aspects of reading in more detail. But first, it must have occurred to you that the issues involved in reading might look different if one were describing youngsters just learning to read or middle school students using their reading ability to study a science text. Let's have a look at the way reading ability develops as children progress through the grades.

Phases of Reading Development

Using the word *development* to describe reading implies that the learner doesn't simply wait passively to take in reading instruction from a teacher, but rather undertakes the interaction among growth, experience, and discovery that can be called *developmental learning*. Developmental learning proceeds according to these factors:

- Cognitive growth of learners, which opens up capacities for learning
- The provision of relevant models of skilled performance and challenges in learners' own performances from their surroundings
- Active discoveries initiated by the learners themselves

To say that learning to read is developmental implies that all children go through roughly the same set of stages as they learn to read. It implies that their maturation plays a part, but that the stimulation, encouragement, and modeling of reading and writing behavior they receive are important, too. It also implies that while the teaching that learners experience can be beneficial, teaching alone will not result in meaningful learning without the learners' reorganizing and expanding their own powers through activities of discovery. Developmental learning follows predictable pathways, although a learner's development along those pathways is more predictable in the early stages than in later ones.

Emergent Literacy

The earliest period or stage of learning to read and write has come to be called *emergent literacy*. In early childhood, before children enter formal instruction, they discover useful insights about literacy; these insights become the basis on which their later learning can be built, even the learning that is orchestrated by their teachers in school. In the emergent stage, learning about literacy involves the following:

- Learning about the nature of reading
- Learning what books are, what kinds of experiences come from them, and how they are put together

- Learning about language itself, that it comes in patterns like stories and poems, and that even though you cannot see it, it is real enough to be captured in books and revisited again and again
- Learning that language comes in units of words and even smaller units and that the language one speaks while reading bears some kind of relationship to marks on a page

Teach It! 1

Reading Aloud

As awareness of emergent literacy has grown, teachers have promoted practices among families that help children's literacy to emerge. Head Start, the federally funded early childhood education program for disadvantaged children, now includes as part of its programming reading to children and other literacy activities that are embedded in children's daily play and learning activities. In some communities, parents are given a children's book when they leave the hospital with a newborn, to underscore the importance of reading to children and to make the point that it is never too early to begin reading to a child.

With their growing awareness of emergent literacy, educators have developed means of observing and assessing children's early concepts of literacy. Unlike the "readiness tests" of a previous generation, assessments of emergent literacy look at children's general familiarity with print, and also at particular indicators that have been found to predict success in learning to read. (We will look more closely at these devices in Chapter 5.) Early literacy assessments yield profiles of what children have discovered about literacy. They also raise concern when important concepts about literacy have not yet emerged in a child, because we know that those concepts will be important to the child as he or she learns to read. That point leads to the third contribution of our understanding of emergent literacy.

Learning to read in school without a fully developed foundation of emergent literacy concepts has been likened to trying to climb stairs when the first several steps are missing. Because teachers are aware of the importance of emergent literacy, they are now able to teach all children in a way that gives them another chance to develop emergent concepts about literacy. They can also provide finely tuned tutoring to children who need it so that more children can get off to the best possible start in learning to read and write.

Beginning Reading

In late kindergarten and first grade, the majority of children enter the phase of beginning reading. Most prominent in this stage is their learning to read words, but children are also learning to understand what they read. The task of learning to make words emerge from different combinations of letters on the page is so challenging that teachers often must remind children to "go back and read that line so it sounds like talk" or ask them, "Does that make sense?"

Children in the beginning phase of reading understand what reading is for and how it works. They have successfully passed through the phase of emergent reading, and are ready to learn words and expect text to make sense. As emergent readers they already understood that print, and not pictures, talks (Clay, 1985) and that a reader is not free to say just any words when paging through a text—she must come up with pronunciations of the words whose representations are printed there (Sulzby, 1985). They already have a budding sense of the patterns of stories and poems, and they know how to follow them to make meaning.

With these understandings in place, children are able to concentrate on words and develop strategies for sounding them out, as well as establish sight vocabularies (stores of words in memory that they can recognize at sight, or without having to work them out letter by letter). They are ready, though they often need reminding, to find humor, suspense, and surprise in what they read—in other words, to make meaning.

Reading for pleasure opens up a child's world and encourages imagination and inquiry. (Ellen B. Senisi)

Building Fluency

By late first grade or early second grade, children have enough experience in reading words and following messages that their reading is becoming fluent: more rapid and more accurate. For children who have often been read to, this period can be a joyful affirmation of their own competence. After a period of struggling to read texts that were far simpler and less meaningful than the stories they had long heard read to them, children are at last able to do for themselves what adults had to do for them. For children who are not so lucky, however, this period can be a hard trek through unfamiliar territory, as the fascinations of reading materialize only gradually. For the first type of child, teachers will find that their main task is to keep providing more books to a hungry reader. For the second type of child, teachers will have to celebrate gains but also gently and insistently push the child to read—and to read more challenging texts.

If the teachers are successful, then both types of children will rapidly amass sight words and steadily increase both the quantity and the speed of their reading. They will be preparing themselves for the next stage of reading, which is called *reading to learn and for pleasure*. Even so, wide differences will begin to open up here in the amount of reading children do and the size of their sight vocabularies.

Reading to Learn and for Pleasure

Teach It! 55

The Writing Workshop

By the beginning of third grade and increasingly in fourth grade, a threshold is crossed, and the emphasis shifts from learning to read to reading to learn—and, one might add, reading for pleasure. By now, children will be expected to read and follow directions and to gain information from texts. At the same time, they may be expected to read chapter books and novels and have something to say about them in their response journals, book clubs, or whatever their discussion groups are called.

A period for reading and writing instruction is still provided every day, but more and more time is given to free reading and discussion, as well as to writing workshops. These activities are useful, even essential, because children must practice literacy to develop it. Nonetheless, there is still a place for teaching the students how to comprehend, interpret, and compose. There is also still a need to make students aware of the structure of written words and the way our English vocabulary works. This is because word knowledge is not gained in the early years and then is done with. On the contrary, because the collection of words children encounter in text changes significantly at around fourth grade (from mostly words derived from Anglo-Saxon to words derived from Latin and Greek), there are new concepts to be learned about words through this period.

It is in fourth grade that problems in reading have traditionally become obvious. That is because reading shows up as a problem that is affecting students' learning in other subjects. It is also because the unsuccessful struggles to learn to read well have led children to frustration and poor motivation. Indeed, children's self-esteem might have begun to suffer because they haven't succeeded in a skill that is highly valued in school (Stanovich, 1986). Although troubled readers can and certainly should be helped to overcome their difficulties, doing so is time consuming at this stage, especially since by this grade there is much content to be learned throughout the school day. Because they now understand how earlier experiences contribute to children's reading abilities, many teachers—and whole programs such as Reading Recovery—are placing their greatest emphasis on getting children off to a good start in reading, so that the problem of the "fourth-grade slump" can be avoided wherever possible.

Mature Reading

After fifth grade and certainly by sixth grade, children who have made normal progress as readers have gradually shown other abilities that are characterized as mature reading. They read with an appreciation of the author's style, and they enjoy reading passages aloud to friends or try to imitate an author's style in their own writing. They read with an awareness of issues and themes and see a novel not only as a series of events, but also as a metaphorical commentary on life. They might read several books on a theme and talk perceptively on the ways the authors' views affected the different presentations. They might practice critical literacy, argue back against the theme of a book, or be offended by its sexist or racist overtones. In any case, they are more analytical and more philosophical in what they look for in texts and in the ways they respond to them.

They are also more strategic. They can read for information, and they have strategies for previewing, questioning, marking, note taking, reviewing, and studying books they read for information.

As we noted at the outset of this section, one characteristic of developmental learning is that the earlier periods of development are more predictable and more commonly experienced than the latter ones. That is certainly true with respect to mature reading. Some readers show evidence of mature reading by the time they enter fourth grade. Many more show it by seventh or eighth grade. But many others rarely do this kind of reading.

New Literacies

How is reading from the Internet different from reading from a book or a magazine?

Reading and Technology: The New Literacies

The future really is now. Reading via the Internet has now moved to center stage. Students ages 8 to 18 now spend more time reading on the Internet than they do with print sources (Kaiser Family Foundation, 2005). Three times as many high school students use the Internet to do homework and term papers than use the library (Pew Internet and American Life Project, 2001). Findings like these led Leu and his colleagues to describe the Internet as "the defining technology for reading in a digital, socially-networked, multimodal, hyperlinked, and multi-tasking world of information and communication" (Leu, et al., 2009, p. 2).

This matters to teachers. We cannot assume that teaching a student to read print makes her able to read well online. Reading online requires some different comprehension skills from reading print. Students who are skilled at reading in the traditional sense are not necessarily skilled at reading online (Coiro, 2007).

The differences between the new literacies and traditional literacy have been difficult to pin down, because the technology changes so rapidly. At a minimum, we can say that in reading online:

- Readers compile their own texts as they pose a question and click from site to site seeking answers. This activity is quite different from following a text that an author has scripted from start to finish. It requires that readers set out a subject and know when the information they are finding is relevant to it.

- Readers must be able to pose problems; they must decide on key words to enter into a search engine, and must detect which sources are relevant to their question once the search engine provides a listing.

- Readers must be able to locate information. They must decide what to read and what not to read when they enter a website in response to a search.

- Readers must distinguish credible information from unreliable information, because unlike most books and magazines, material is placed online with no filtering for accuracy or honesty.
    (After Leu, et al., 2009).

But the new literacies do not stop with the Internet. As Canadian educator David Booth reminds us:

What are called the new literacies are profoundly shaping the ways in which we view and use language. Just as the telephone altered communication strategies, our child will encounter a wide and perhaps unthought-of variety of information and communication technologies. Just think of video cameras, web editors, spreadsheets, list serves, blogs, Power Point, virtual worlds, and dozens more. Our traditional way of thinking about and defining literacy will be insufficient if we hope to provide youngsters with what they will need to be full participants in the world of the future. (Booth, 2006, pp. 11–12)

Thus far, this chapter has discussed reading in terms of some of its core processes: word recognition, comprehension, fluency, and critical literacy. It has also looked at reading in terms of the stages children pass through: emergent literacy, beginning reading, building fluency, reading to learn and for pleasure, and mature reading. Later sections of this book will revisit each of the aspects of reading that must be developed. Then you will see how teachers help children learn to read and write at every grade level. In the meantime, though, it may help to sketch a brief history of reading instruction. Things have been changing quickly in the literacy field, and your teaching colleagues in your school may have entered teaching with different training and different assumptions about literacy from what you are learning in your own courses.

Approaches to Teaching Reading: How We Got Where We Are

If your school is more than a few years old and the book room hasn't been cleaned out for a while, looking among the reading materials can be surprising and enlightening. You may find books based on the "look and say" method, or books that boast of their "whole language" approach, or "programmed" readers. You may even find machines that purport to train students' eye movements. It will be clear that the field of reading instruction is a restless one, with every few years bringing significant changes in materials and approaches. In the next few pages we will summarize the most significant of those changes.

Early Modern Descriptions of Reading

In 1908, Edmund Burke Huey (1908) chronicled the major approaches to teaching reading that were practiced in American schools in his time. He found an ongoing debate between teachers who preferred to emphasize words as wholes and teachers who taught students the relationships between letters and sounds. A century ago Huey noted that this distinction was already very old—perhaps 350 years old, according to one of his sources. Huey offered research—his own and that of others—that showed that the eye and brain take just as long to recognize a single letter as they do a whole word. This finding, building on a reaction to the heavy drill orientations of reading approaches in the late nineteenth century, encouraged a movement toward whole-word teaching approaches that lasted through the mid-1960s. Even then, the issue was not settled, and between Huey's time and ours, there has been an intense outpouring of research on the issue and hundreds of conferences have been attended by thousands of educators, yet the tension between different approaches to teaching beginning reading remains.

Phonics and Phonological Awareness

Arguments over the amount of emphasis to give phonics instruction have been waged for years.

Phonics versus Whole Word Reading

In the 1960s, Jeanne Chall (1967) reviewed the available research on the question of the best approaches to beginning reading. She found that in the decades leading up to the time when she was writing, most children in the United States were taught to read in basal reading programs, that is, in textbooks composed of short reading passages with graduated difficulty levels. For the most part, the basal reading programs, such as the popular Dick and Jane series, used whole-word approaches (what Chall called a "meaning emphasis") and did not teach phonics (what Chall called a "code emphasis"). According to the studies she reviewed, however, reading approaches that did use phonics showed better results than programs that did not. Following the publication of Chall's influential book, publishers began to include phonics instruction in their basal reading programs.

But that did not settle the matter. Many teachers, such as New Zealander Sylvia Ashton-Warner (1963), continued to favor whole-word approaches and argued that their use emphasized meaning, whereas the phonics approaches could lead children to focus on the small parts of reading—the letters and sounds—without an adequate appreciation of what the letters were supposed to add up to. Indeed, some of the reading materials that came into use during the 1960s focused so much on letter-to-sound regularities that they left very little meaning to be pursued. "Linguistic readers" contained text like this: "A man had a tin pin. It's a pin for a cap. It's a cap for Dan." Advocates of meaning-centered reading instruction worried that if children mostly read text as pointless as this, they could easily become confused about the true purpose of reading: to construct meaning from print.

The Cognitive Revolution

The 1970s saw a revolution in the way scholars thought of language learning. The field of psycholinguistics was developing, largely under the influence of an ingenious linguist named Noam Chomsky. The researchers whom Chomsky inspired were accumulating evidence that children learn language by exercising a built-in capacity for discovery. As long as they are in the company of people who talk to them and who model language, and as long as those around them honor children's own needs to communicate, children will learn to talk. Gradually, by stages, through an amazing exercise of finely tuned linguistic discovery processes, children learn language.

Almost immediately, theorists began to see applications of psycholinguistic theory to the process of learning to read. Frank Smith wrote an influential book called *Psycholinguistics and Reading* (1973), in which he and others argued that children could learn to read, in large part, by discovery and encouragement. One of the contributors to that book, Kenneth Goodman (1967), had offered a conception of reading as "a psycholinguistic guessing game." Goodman's work, along with that of some imaginative Australians such as Don Holdaway (1979) and Andrea Butler and Jan Turbill (1985) gave rise to what came to be known as the **whole language movement**.

The Whole Language Movement

Whole language advocates embraced many child-centered approaches to teaching. The **writing process approach** popularized by Donald Graves (1982) and Lucy Calkins (1996) was taken up by whole language advocates and became part of the movement. So did the literature-based approaches of Dorothy Strickland (1991) and Nancie Atwell (1985). Whole language classrooms were (and are) bursting with children's creativity, as children have rich experiences that stimulate talk, as they read and listen to much good literature, and as they write about and act out their own ideas.

On the psychological front, the new field of cognitive psychology yielded studies of comprehension that were relevant to reading. A U.S. government grant to the University of Illinois created the Center for the Study of Reading, where Richard Anderson and David Pearson (1984) and others elaborated a theory of comprehension called **schema theory**. As was seen in the example of children reading the passage on pages 7–10, schema theory stresses the reader's active role in making meaning. Schema theory was highly compatible with the work of both the psycholinguists inspired by Noam Chomsky and the constructivist theories of intellectual development inspired by Swiss psychologist Jean Piaget and others. The theory found ready acceptance from the late 1970s, and most

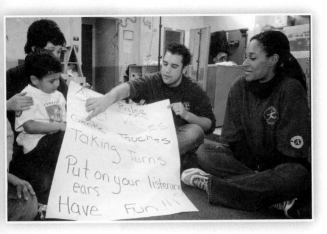

Programs such as Head Start and Jumpstart help prepare children for learning by promoting an interest in reading at a very young age. (Nancy Sheehan Photography)

reading experts still accept it today in some form or another as our guiding theory of how comprehension works. Like psycholinguistic research before it, schema theory seemed to lend support to the child-centered, discovery-oriented beliefs of the whole language movement.

The Research–Based Emphasis

Still, the disagreements between the meaning-centered advocates and the code-centered advocates continued. In the late 1980s, the U.S. Department of Education commissioned another examination of beginning reading instruction. The resulting work was *Beginning to Read* (1990), by a psychologist, Marilyn Jaeger Adams. In it, Adams concluded that exposure to print and enthusiastic encouragement might work in some cases, but that they were not sufficient to teach all children to read. Like the findings Jeanne Chall had reviewed twenty years before, the evidence Adams collected persuaded her that instruction that explicitly and systematically taught children the code that links speech sounds to patterns of letters was more successful than instruction that did not. Adams urged teachers to give primacy to teaching children to decode and recognize words, even as they immersed the children in print and encouraged them to write.

Adams also passed along another finding from late twentieth century research on reading: the importance of children's awareness of phonemes, the smallest sound units in words. In a host of studies, phonemic awareness in first grade was found to make a critical difference in whether children learned to read successfully, and Adams made a strong suggestion that teachers emphasize phonemic awareness and letter-to-sound correspondences in their early reading instruction. She said in her conclusion:

> In summary, deep and thorough knowledge of letters, spelling patterns, and words, and of the phonological translations of all three, are of inescapable importance to both skillful reading and its acquisition. By extension, instruction designed to develop children's sensitivity to spellings and their relations to pronunciations should be of paramount importance in the development of reading skills. That is, of course, precisely what is intended of good phonics instruction. (Adams, 1990, p. 416)

In 1989, then-Vice President George H. W. Bush assembled fifty state governors at the University of Virginia to work out a plan that would use U.S. schools to make American students more academically competitive in global education rankings. In an initiative called Goals 2000, led by their chairman, then-Governor Bill Clinton of Arkansas, the group agreed to specify explicit performance standards for reading and other subjects at intervals throughout the grades and to test students' abilities to meet those standards. Many states added standards for what schools of education should teach new teachers to teach. As individual states designed their standards, many drew on the work of Marilyn Jaeger Adams and like-minded writers and called for the teaching of letter-to-sound correspondences and the development of phonemic awareness. In 1996, for example, the California State Legislature passed a bill specifying that the training of all elementary teacher certification candidates include:

i. The study of organized, systematic, explicit skills including phonemic awareness, direct systematic, explicit phonics, and decoding skills.

ii. A strong literature, language, and comprehension component with a balance of oral and written language.

iii. Ongoing diagnostic techniques that inform teaching and assessment.

iv. Early intervention techniques.

v. Guided practice in a clinical setting (quoted in Snow et al., 1998, p. 302).

Also in the late 1990s, a study of early reading difficulties was undertaken by the Committee on the Prevention of Reading Difficulties in Young Children, a group of reading experts assembled under the auspices of the National Science Foundation. The resulting report, entitled *Preventing Reading Difficulties in Young Children* (Snow et al., 1998), recommended that teachers encourage students' growth in language and general knowledge, their exposure to and appreciation of literature, and their opportunities to write, while also providing instruction to boost phonemic awareness, knowledge of letter-to-sound relationships, fluency, vocabulary, and comprehension.

In 1997, Congress commissioned yet another group of experts, the National Reading Panel, to "assess the effectiveness of different approaches used to teach children to read" (National Reading Panel website, 2003). This group was organized by the National Institute of Child Health and Human Development (NICHD) at the National Institutes of Health. After reviewing what they considered to be evidence-based studies of reading over a two-year period, the National Reading Panel published their findings in *The Report of the National Reading Panel: Teaching Children to Read* (2000). In it, the panel made a number of recommendations, including a strong push for skills instruction, especially in the recognition of words and the skills that support word recognition: awareness of speech sounds and knowledge of phonics. (See the website of the National Reading Panel at www .nationalreadingpanel.org.)

With the reauthorization of the Elementary and Secondary and Education Act (U.S. Department of Education, 2001), called No Child Left Behind (signed into law on January 8, 2001), the administration of President George W. Bush mandated that every state develop learning standards in the basic subjects, including reading, and test every child annually from third grade up. (Testing was phased in over a four-year period.) The act requires that schools receiving federal funding use "evidence-based" instructional practices, and for its source of evidence, the Administration embraced the recommendations of the National Reading Panel, with special focus on five particular recommended areas of focus: phonological awareness, phonics, fluency, vocabulary, and comprehension.

Armed with the *No Child Left Behind* Legislation, for the eight years of the George W. Bush administration, the U.S. Department of Education insisted that schools receiving federal funds use methods and materials that are backed by "SBRR," or "scientifically based reading research." The results were mixed. Students from minority groups improved somewhat on tests of reading, but the results of students from other groups were largely unchanged (Lee, Grigg, & Donahue, 2007).

Being a Professional Reading Teacher

Changes in the Reading Field

If you are a new teacher just entering a school that has many experienced teachers on the faculty, the conversations about changes in the teaching of reading could be puzzling to you—even unsettling. You could easily get the impression that the focuses of educational research and teaching are as changeable as the preferred colors of kids' tee shirts or the in-brand of their sneakers. We hope the discussion you just read did not add to that impression. The truth is, things are moving forward in literacy education. The students we teach are far more diverse, and as great as the challenge of serving each of them well may be, our society as a whole is much more committed to helping every child become a success than it was a generation ago—ask your grandmother. Our knowledge base for teaching literacy has grown tremendously. Although the disagreements among theorists and practitioners have been shrill at times, we do know much more about teaching reading than we did a generation ago. Our understanding of emergent literacy; the nature of language, comprehension, the development of word knowledge; the importance of fluency and how it is learned; the way children learn to write and the way they learn literature; along with ways of serving children with special needs; ways of conducting assessment; and ways of teaching—these have all advanced tremendously. Things are moving forward. Keep your eyes open. Hold onto your hat. Be part of the change.

Balanced Reading Instruction

Today, many reading educators speak of the need for **balanced instruction** (Raphael, 1998) in teaching literacy. The term refers to an approach that, on the one hand, pays due attention to the need for giving children meaningful encounters with written language so that they will understand its purposes and forms and come to enjoy it. On the other hand, balance also means that teachers must ensure that all children learn skills that make reading possible.

There is nothing new about balanced reading instruction. The Committee on the Prevention of Reading Difficulties in Young Children (Snow et al., 1998) found that teachers need to take care to "develop children's language" and help them gain "a holistic understanding of reading." The Committee urged that renewed efforts be made to involve families in their children's literacy and called for teachers to understand and accommodate cultural and linguistic differences in literacy learning. Indeed, many teachers and specialists worry that teaching reading skills without immersing children in plentiful opportunities to speak, listen, read, and write can be unproductive. Children need skills, but they also need to understand the purposes of reading and writing and aspire to be practitioners of both.

Teach It!

Refer to the Teach It! appendix at the end of the book for further activities you can use to reinforce concepts discussed in this chapter.

Guided Reading and the Four Blocks

Guided reading is "a context in which the teacher supports each reader's development of effective strategies for processing novel texts at increasingly challenging levels of difficulty" (Fountas & Pinnell, 1996). The key elements of guided reading are:

- The teacher works with small groups.
- The children in each group are reading at about the same level.
- The teacher introduces stories and supports children's development of independent reading strategies.
- Each child reads the entire text.
- Independent, silent reading is the goal for each child.
- Over time, the teacher focuses on increasing the levels of text provided.
- The children are grouped and regrouped in accordance with outcomes observed and assessed by the teacher.
- Books are carefully leveled. That is, the difficulty levels of books available to the children are precisely determined so that they can progress in an orderly way.

Guided reading lessons are conducted in three essential stages. *Before the Reading* is a stage in which the teacher introduces a new and appropriate text, and the children converse with the teacher about the text, asking questions and building expectations. *During the Reading* is the stage in which the teacher observes problem-solving strategies used by children. The children read the entire text, or a unified part of it, to themselves silently (or softly in the case of younger readers) and ask for help when needed. In *After the Reading*, the teacher involves the children in responding to the story through such activities as writing, discussion, paired reading, and shar-

ing personal responses. The children talk about the story, verify predictions they made before reading, and respond, usually through writing or perhaps drama (Fountas & Pinnell, 1996).

Guided reading is often combined with the structure of the Four Blocks approach (Cunningham, Hall, & Sigmon, 1999). Together, the four blocks address the five elements of Reading First and also combine many of the strengths of the basal reading program, individualized reading, and reader's workshop, while avoiding most of their limitations.

The four blocks are: guided reading, as discussed in this section; writing; self-selected reading; and working with words. Teachers can implement the multilevel aspect of the four block approach by teaching a lesson to the entire class, making the text accessible to all students with multiple readings involving read-aloud, shared reading, and paired reading in small flexible groups. They can add the writing and self-selected reading blocks of the approach as after-reading activities from the guided reading approach.

Although children in Reading First classrooms are often doing word study as a whole group, with all working on the same skills, teachers may find it more useful to teach appropriate skills in smaller groups tailored to the needs of children. For example, some children are more advanced and may not need to work with skills already mastered, and other children may lack prior knowledge needed to achieve some skills, for example, children trying to work with three-letter consonant blends such as *str* and *spl* before they have mastered two-letter consonant blends, such as *st* and *tr*.

As you can see, there are several roads to balanced literacy that also address the five major elements of Reading First: phonemic awareness; phonics; fluency; comprehension, and vocabulary. As you proceed through the chapters that follow, you will see more specific ways to apply these approaches and many others.

Your Professional Portfolio

Most college and university teacher preparation programs now require that candidates prepare portfolios that reflect their professional development. In addition, many principals and school district personnel directors make new teachers' portfolios a focus of their pre-employment interviews. Your portfolio also can be a means of self-evaluation, a record of past achievement, and a plan for future professional development.

As you begin this course, you should start thinking about your own portfolio. Because reading instruction is such an important part of your new career, it should be highlighted in your portfolio. There are many formats for teacher portfolios. Most include some or all of the following:

- Sample lesson plans
- Thematic units
- Videotapes of lessons
- Descriptions of cooperative learning activities used in your lessons
- Photographs or hand-drawn plans of your classroom environment
- Student, teacher, and participant products, such as writing assignments, self-evaluations, projects, lesson plans, maps, experiments
- Plans for and evidence of continuing education or professional development, such as courses, workshops, conferences, and activities in professional organizations
- Descriptions of mentoring activities, both as mentee and mentor
- Peer observations and evaluations
- Letters of reference, commendations, and recommendations from supervisors
- An essay about your teaching philosophy (how you teach and why)
- Written reflections about planning (why artifacts are included in the portfolio); many teachers write them on stick-on notes that can be attached to items in the portfolio

Your portfolio is a dynamic, living document. It should change over time. It should reflect you as you are, which means that you should periodically remove items that no longer reflect your current status, interests, and capabilities. How large should your portfolio be? Only you can answer that. But it should be functional and useful, not a burden to you or to the person reviewing it.

Two final cautions:

- Ensure that all examples presented in your portfolio are your own original work. If you use or adapt the work of someone else, be sure to give credit.
- Proofread everything carefully; you are presenting your best face in your portfolio, including your ability to write and spell in English.

You can read more about portfolios in McLaughlin, M., & Vogt, M. (1996). *Portfolios in teacher education.* Newark, DE: International Reading Association.

Multiple Roads to Balanced Literacy

The No Child Left Behind Act of 2002 established Reading First as a "high-quality evidence-based program for students" (ED.gov, 2004). Balanced literacy is widely viewed as an outgrowth of the National Reading Panel report of 2000, combining a literature-based focus on comprehension instruction with a strong explicit phonics component. Balanced literacy consists of five major elements (National Reading Panel, 2000):

- **Phonemic awareness:** Teaching children "to focus on and manipulate phonemes in spoken syllables and words"
- **Phonics:** Teaching children "letter-sound correspondences and their use in reading and spelling"
- **Fluency:** Teaching children "to read orally with speed, accuracy, and proper expression" (expression referring to prosody, pitch, and intonation that indicates comprehension during oral reading)
- **Vocabulary:** Helping children build knowledge of word meanings so that they can make sense of print
- **Comprehension:** Teaching children the "active process that requires an intentional and thoughtful interaction between the reader and the text"

According to Strickland (2006), teachers can maintain balance in their reading programs by:

- Teaching reading skills with a focus on meaning, not as ends in themselves
- Providing daily instruction guided by the teacher and also independent work to enable students to internalize reading skills
- Helping students build knowledge as the result of a process, not by filling them up as empty receptacles
- Integrating print and electronic materials to reflect the modern multimedia world
- Interpreting standardized test scores in terms of informal assessment

There are several major approaches to reading instruction that provide these elements and that also meet Strickland's criteria for a balanced literacy program. Some of these approaches incorporate the balanced literacy elements in their basic forms, and sometimes one or more approaches are combined to address all of them. We will present a basic overview of these major approaches in this chapter in order to place them in context with the elements of Reading First and with balanced literacy. In subsequent chapters, you will find more specific and detailed treatments about how to implement these approaches in the classroom.

Basal Reading Programs

Certainly the most frequently encountered approach to reading instruction is the basal reading program, quite likely the kind of reading program that your teachers used when you were in elementary school. Most basal reading programs address all five elements of Reading First, and they are stand-alone, that is, they provide all of the materials needed for a complete reading program. Even so, most classroom teachers will supplement a basal reading program with a classroom library of outstanding children's literature on a variety of levels and topics.

The typical basal reading program consists of reading textbooks sequenced by grade level for increasing difficulty. The difficulty of vocabulary is usually carefully controlled, as is the pace of introduction of new words. Basal reading programs contain narrative stories, expository text from science, social studies, and other areas of the curriculum, poetry, plays, riddles, jokes, song lyrics, and other types of text to read. There may be four or five small reading books at the kindergarten and first-grade levels, two to four at the second-grade level, often two at the third-grade level, and one larger textbook each year from the fourth- to the eighth-grade level.

Most modern basal reading programs are anthologies of original children's literature, often in complete form and with original illustrations. Vocabulary is not controlled in these programs. Some basal readers contain excerpts of longer pieces of children's literature. Often, selections of children's literature will not have all the illustrations from the original work, or some illustrations may be partial renditions of the original. There may be simple text at the lowest levels that is designed for the teaching of reading skills. This text is usually not what we would characterize as authentic children's literature.

Lessons in basal reading programs are sometimes conducted with the entire class, although teachers that differentiate instruction according to children's needs may have two or more groups working on different levels and out of different books.

Basal reading programs also provide workbooks from which teachers typically teach such skills as phonemic awareness, phonics, comprehension, and vocabulary. They provide opportunities to practice writing as well. These may be supplemented with large charts that can be used with easels or on word walls.

Basal reading programs also incorporate assessment tools that can be used to identify each child's reading level, strengths, and needs. These assessments are frequently designed to be administered at regular intervals throughout the school year. Publishers of basal reading programs also often provide DVDs and CD-ROMs that can be used for listening centers in the classroom.

A teacher's manual always accompanies each reading textbook. This provides information about how to use the program lesson by lesson, how to use assessment measures, and other suggestions for strengthening the reading/writing program. The instructions in the manuals range from suggestions and recommendations from which teachers can choose to highly scripted programs in which every word the teacher should say to the children in teaching the lesson is provided in the manual.

Basal reading programs can vary greatly in how they are used, depending on the philosophy of reading instruction promoted. In some programs, it is assumed that children must master the sound system early, and these are characterized as *part-whole* programs. In others, children are learning more holistic skills and whole words early in the program, along with the sound system, and these are characterized as *whole-part-whole* programs.

Reader's Workshop

Reader's Workshop (Atwell, 1998) is an approach that blends independent reading with guided reading.

A typical reader's workshop time block might begin with a read-aloud in which the teacher, as an outstanding model of reading, shares different genres of children's literature for about ten minutes. There may be an interval of shared reading in which the entire class reads together with the teacher from a single text. This provides opportunities for work with fluency, word recognition skills, comprehension, and literary genres.

Guided Reading

Guided reading (see the Teach It!) is a lesson stage that may occupy thirty minutes or more. While some children have a guided reading lesson on their level, other children are completing independent work, writing, reading independently, and working in learning centers. This is often followed by a mini-lesson that addresses a need of many of the children, perhaps to decode three-letter consonant blends or to make inferences. Children may then have a guided writing activity, again accompanied with mini-lessons for some children, such as how to use the comma in a series of nouns or how to use adjectives correctly. Time for independent reading is also provided during the school day, often in the form of silent sustained reading (SSR). For a designated interval, often from ten to twenty minutes, everyone in the classroom reads a book, magazine, material from the Internet, or whatever else they might choose, including the teacher.

Students differ considerably in their reading interests. (Ellen B. Senisi)

Integrated Instruction: Literacy and Content Instruction

Another popular way to meet the varied interests and skills of students is to develop units that incorporate both literacy and content learning. A strong plus of integrated units is that students can become very motivated to read and write when they are engaged in studying some real issue or exploring a scientific phenomenon. Popular formats for developing integrated units include Concept-Oriented Reading Instruction or CORI (see http://www.cori .umd.edu), problem-based learning (see, for example, http://www.udel.edu/pbl), and Outward-bound's Expeditionary Learning (see http://www.elschools.org). Learning by Design and Civics Learning provide motivating opportunities for students to engage in real issues (see Pearson, 2008, for more elaboration on these models). Teachers also develop their own thematic units around content in their curriculum. One option many teachers follow is to have three integrated units a year: a unit combining literacy with social studies, one with science/mathematics, and one with literature. In this way teachers can develop activities, collect materials, and structure learning activities without being overwhelmed by trying to do a totally integrated approach in their classrooms.

Integrated units are popular because teachers know that they have little time to teach all the standards that are expected of them. The demands are overwhelming! So merging instruction of reading and writing with content can save valuable time. It is also more engaging for students, as the purposes for learning reading, writing, and discussion skills become more tangible and important to them. Their questions can be answered through reading. They need to use writing and note making to keep records of their observations and discuss the results of their experiments. As they read multiple sources in history, they learn from different perspectives and can then synthesize information and come to their own conclusions. In subject units, students can read and learn from multiple sources on the same topic. This helps them build their understanding of how different texts function and how they can even provide conflicting information.

Metacognitive Graphic Organizer

An important aspect of integrated curriculum is that teachers focus more attention on using informational materials and teaching students the important features and organizational structures of informational texts and the new online literacies. These resources become the major texts, rather than pieces of fictional literature. Initially students may need several teacher-directed lessons on how informational books are organized, such as how to use a table of contents, glossary, and index, and how to look for titles, main headings, and graphic features. Teachers can then model for students the ways they can locate the information needed to answer specific questions; they don't need to read texts (books, magazine articles, or websites) in their entirety, but can select portions that meet their needs.

Often, students whose reading experiences are primarily in fiction don't realize that informational material is organized very differently. In novels, for example, the chapters often don't even have titles; in informational material, in contrast, the titles and headings provide a key to the structure of the text and what the author prioritizes. Informational materials may be organized chronologically, but may also have a topical organization, or use a compare/contrast, problem-solution, or argument frame. Elementary students can and need to identify these patterns both to enhance their comprehension and to help them structure the informational reports and essays that they will write.

In integrated units teachers also have the opportunity to explore what students bring with them in their prior knowledge and preconceptions. As Bransford, Brown, and Cocking (1999) explain, there are three key components in comprehension, and the first is activating and using background knowledge. Integrated units permit exploration of what students bring to their learning because the same topic or theme is continued for several weeks. This permits teachers to more carefully match students' knowledge and interests as well as their literacy levels as part of the activities. It provides students more opportunity to engage in extended projects and deepen their learning. Teachers differentiate instruction in many ways during units and can build students' independence as they

DIFFERENTIATED INSTRUCTION

SIOP®
Sheltered
Instruction
Observation
Protocol·

What Is Differentiated Instruction?

The increasing diversity of students provides a visible reminder of how important it is that teachers provide appropriate, differentiated instruction so that all students can be engaged positively and productively each day they are in school. Students come with different background experiences and language; different interests and ways of engaging in learning activities; different levels of knowledge of print and written language skill; different levels of content knowledge and vocabulary, in addition to different home experiences and attitudes toward teachers and school. Creating classrooms where all students can learn means that both the classroom environment and the instructional program need to be designed to accommodate the range of interests and skills of students. Differentiation means taking into account all of these factors on which there are significant differences among the students and planning instruction so all students can be successful and enjoy their experiences.

It is important to start with students' strengths and help them develop the knowledge, skills, and strategies they need to become mature readers. The phrase "differentiated instruction" is used to encompass these varied ways of tailoring classroom experiences so all students can be productively learning. C. Tomlinson (2000), who has worked extensively in differentiation, defines it well:

> In the context of education we define differentiation "as a teacher's reacting responsively to a learner's needs." A teacher who is differentiating understands a student's needs to express humor, or work with a group, or have additional teaching on a particular skill, or delve more deeply into a particular topic, or have guided help with a reading passage—and the teacher responds actively and positively to that need. (p. 4)

How can new teachers become this kind of responsive teacher and still meet the needs for student growth in determined areas of study? Knowing both students and curriculum is the key. Teachers begin the year by finding out as much as they can about the students under their care. Individual interviews with the children, interviews and informal conferences with parents, and ongoing communication with the home help teachers learn more what the students are like in their out-of-school lives where they spend most of their time and energy.

Knowing the curriculum and what students need to be learning is the other starting point. Teachers need to become well-versed in the content that is to be taught. They need to know the skills that students should be developing. With this understanding, the next step is to collect information about the students' levels of knowledge and skill with that content. The teacher's task is to plan and develop appropriate instructional activities that will help students focus on what is important and that are also motivating and engaging. This means that teachers need to know students well so they can build classrooms that reflect their needs, interests, and preferences in learning activities.

Differentiation involves providing appropriate *reading materials* to students so they can be successful readers. This is one of the most important starting points in differentiating instruction. Within one classroom the range of reading levels can be substantial. Some estimates are that there is likely to be a range of 2–4 years in reading levels in the primary grades and from 4–8 years in the intermediate and upper grades. Knowing that students should read materials that are at their instructional levels for guided reading and whole class lessons, it is essential that teachers provide different texts to students, that materials are differentiated. Luckily, there are now many publishers in the United States who are producing materials on varied levels but with similar content. There is also a rich array of materials from which teachers and schools can select so students can be placed in appropriate texts as they learn to read and as they learn content in the other academic areas.

Differentiation also involves knowing students well enough to *adjust strategy and skill instruction* to particular levels of need. Knowing and adjusting to reading levels is only the starting point. Students differ in their command of the components of good reading, too, and need appropriate instruction. For example, some students will enter kindergarten knowing how to discriminate the important phonemes in English. They will benefit from some oral rhyming activities with poetry. Others will need to focus more attentively to develop discrimination of key sounds. For these students, some daily teacher-guided discrimination activities will be important. Rather than expect all students to complete the same auditory phonemic discrimination activities, differentiation is the responsive approach to these differences in students' development. With students who are non-native English speakers and those who speak dialects of English, modifications of phonemic discrimination activities and sensitivity in evaluation of students' level of mastery are needed.

engage in meaningful explorations. Reports from teachers who integrate content and literacy provide support for the effort it takes (Fogelberg, Skalinder, Satz, Hiller, Bernstein, & Vitantonio, 2009; McKee & Ogle, 2005).

Later in this book, several examples of integrated instruction are provided. In each case teachers begin by determining which standards can be combined effectively. Then they collect materials and resources, create a plan for teaching both literacy and content, and provide differentiated experiences for their students. Across the varied activities and culminating experiences, students have opportunities to monitor their own learning and see the results of their efforts. A unit approach helps motivate and engage students, honors their questions and knowledge, makes differentiation much easier with the extended time frame, and builds students' content vocabulary knowledge and disciplinary talk.

ASSESSMENT

Why We Assess

Assessment is a vital part of teaching reading and writing. Assessment allows teachers to determine how well a particular child is learning and how well an individual lesson succeeded, as well as to evaluate the effectiveness of the whole program of instruction. Assessment enables children to see for themselves how they are performing as they learn to read and write and to understand what they can do to improve. It helps school administrators to make decisions about the placement of individual children in special assistance, about the design of a curriculum, and about the inservice training needs of their faculty. Assessment also provides parents with feedback on their children's progress and identifies areas where they can provide support. It can even help parents and communities to know how their schools are performing in comparison to other schools. With the advent of the No Child Left Behind legislation of the past decade, assessment is also being used in an effort to determine which schools are performing satisfactorily in teaching children to read.

Assessment can take many forms, including testing. Although some formal and informal tests of reading and writing ability can be useful, some of the most informative kinds of assessments involve watching very carefully as children read and write under natural circumstances. The type of assessment that is used depends a great deal on what needs to be known and who needs to know it.

In this book, the topic of the assessment of literacy is covered extensively in Chapter 10. It is also integrated within each chapter. Suggestions for assessment will be provided for emergent literacy, word recognition, fluency, vocabulary, comprehension, response to literature, and writing. These suggestions for assessment will be given at every level of schooling, from lower primary to upper elementary to the middle grades.

For Review

Reading and writing are important parts of the school curriculum. They are tools that help students learn nearly everything else in the school day and continue to learn when they leave school. However, literacy is far more valuable than just a school subject. Literacy leads to habits of language and mind that take readers beyond what they would find natural to notice, think about, and communicate if they were not literate.

International comparisons show that U.S. students read fairly well—second in the world, according to one recent study. But another international comparison finds that they do not do enough deep thinking or problem solving with what they read. The benefits of literacy are not shared very equitably among students from different income groups or ethnic groups. When the National Assessment of Educational Progress has assessed reading ability, unacceptably high numbers of elementary age students have been found not to read with adequate comprehension. At the same time, studies show that few disabled readers have problems related to cognitive function. Ninety-seven percent or more, according to one study, could be remediated with appropriate instruction, although that instruction should be judiciously planned and intensively applied when necessary. These findings cast doubt on the still-continuing practice of treating so many children with "specific reading disabilities" as if there were something wrong with their brains.

The history of research on reading instruction is nearly as old as the scientific study of psychology. But debates over instructional methods in literacy—such as the whole word versus phonics debate—have lasted for many generations. Arguments between advocates of holistic approaches and skills-based approaches have been heated in the past decade, but appear to be easing with the emphasis on a balance of both. Research supports holistic instruction so that children see that literacy is meaningful; it also supports instruction in the alphabetic writing system—in phonics and the awareness of the sound system that underlies it—at least to those students who don't intuit the system.

The components of reading are interrelated, but reading can be viewed in terms of word recognition, comprehension, reading fluency, and critical literacy. Reading develops normally through stages: emergent literacy, beginning reading, building fluency, reading to learn and for pleasure, and mature reading.

To teach reading well requires that the teacher keep several things in mind. Effective reading instruction means immersing children in real literature, teaching decoding skills and coaching children in their use, giving attention to comprehension and to higher-order thinking skills, teaching learning strategies to children, making frequent assessments, involving parents in their children's learning, and respecting cultural differences.

Assessment of reading and writing ability is done for external and internal audiences. External audiences include parents, school administrators, and the general community—all of whom have a stake in knowing how well the literacy instruction program is working. External audiences usually want results from standardized tests. Assessment is also done for internal audiences, who are the children themselves and their teacher. Assessments for internal audiences typically include careful observations of children's reading and writing performance at real tasks, and are intended to shed light on what learners are doing well and what aspects of their literacy need improvement.

For Your Journal

Go back to the Anticipation Guide that opened this chapter, and consider your answers to the questions posed. Divide a page of your journal with a vertical line. On the left side, write down one of your answers that you want to think about more. On the right side, write what you think about that topic now. Repeat the exercise with at least two more questions. Take your journal to class with you, and share your comments with your classmates.

Taking It to the World

1. Interview three primary grade teachers, and ask them how they have seen the emphases in reading instruction change in the past ten years. What aspects have stayed the same? What changes have they witnessed?

2. Many adults who have poorly developed reading skills don't see their limited literacy as a problem. Call the local chapter of Literacy Volunteers of America, and ask whether this is their experience. Do many of the adults in the community who need help with literacy seek help? (A class might choose to appoint a committee to do this so as not to inundate the chapter with phone calls.)

3. The National Adult Literacy Survey noted that prisoners are more likely than the rest of the population to have reading problems. Have a member of your class interview the person in charge of education at a local or regional prison. To what extent are literacy issues related to the problems the inmates have faced?

New Literacies Connections

1. On the Internet, log on to the web pages of the International Reading Association (www.reading.org) and the National Council of Teachers of English (www.ncte.org). From what they say on these pages, can you tell what the emphases of these two organizations are?

2. The International Reading Association publishes an electronic journal called Reading On-Line. Log on and read an issue. What topics are of most interest to the readership at the moment?

Chapter

2

The Social and Cultural Contexts for Teaching All Children to Read

The following statements will help you begin thinking about the topics of this chapter. Answer *true* or *false* in response to each statement. As you read and learn more about the topics mentioned in these statements, think back on your answers. See what interests you and prompts your curiosity toward more understanding.

_____ 1. Reading and writing are both social and individual forms of communicating.

_____ 2. Differences among students in classrooms have little effect on how teachers work with children.

_____ 3. Cultural groups have distinct values regarding the importance of reading and writing.

_____ 4. Almost all English language learners are found in large urban centers.

_____ 5. African American Vernacular English is a dialect of English.

_____ 6. Children's culture is reflected in their body language, the way they manage time, and the distance they maintain between themselves and others.

_____ 7. A gifted child who is reading at grade level probably has a reading problem.

_____ 8. Boys tend to have more reading problems than girls do.

_____ 9. Some children begin school without knowing how to handle a book.

_____ 10. Children with special needs benefit from being in general education classrooms for part of the school day.

The Social and Cultural Contexts for Teaching All Children to Read

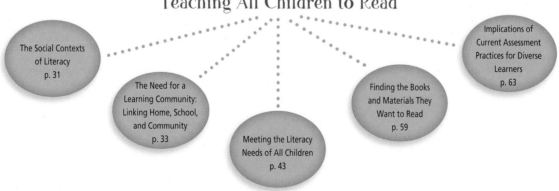

The Social Contexts of Literacy
p. 31

The Need for a Learning Community: Linking Home, School, and Community
p. 33

Meeting the Literacy Needs of All Children
p. 43

Finding the Books and Materials They Want to Read
p. 59

Implications of Current Assessment Practices for Diverse Learners
p. 63

A Classroom Story

Getting Parents and the Community Involved in the Classroom

Marguerite has been teaching seventh grade for several years. Recently, many of her students have come from newly arrived immigrant families, especially from Asia and Eastern Europe. She wants to help these students understand American society and local community life, so she uses a resource unit on community biography from the state department of education. This unit integrates language arts and history as students study their own community members. She likes this project because it helps both her new students and the rest of the class understand how local communities, schools, religious groups, businesses, and government work together. As they do their projects and learn from each other, students develop pride in being part of their town.

Marguerite also uses this project to give her students a real purpose for developing their oral and written language skills. They use language by interviewing, collecting data, and writing biographies. Each student selects a special person in the community about whom he or she will write a biography. To complete the project, students need to develop questions to use in their interviews, conduct the interviews, and write up their

findings. In addition, they conduct research on the national and international events that occurred during this person's life, create a timeline of important events that correlate with the person's life, and collect pictures and other artifacts that pertain to the report. The results of their research will be presented on a three-part bulletin board that will be shown at the *Special Persons Fair*, which is open to the public. As she organizes the time frame for this unit, she works closely with the school librarian to locate resources to help students gain more information about the local community, its history and community leadership. The librarian introduced her to the collection of local newspapers on file and suggested that the public library also had a wealth of materials that students could use.

With her careful planning and with resources well organized, Marguerite engages her students in the unit with a sense of confidence. The students benefit from her preparation and become very excited about what they learn about their own community during their research and interviews. In fact, throughout the unit students share what they are learning with each other. The enthusiasm and insights shared by students often spark

new ideas and questions from others. They make connections between their own families' experiences and those of other individuals in their community. One student who chose the school custodian as his subject developed a great history of the school through the custodian's eyes and saw how much this man had given to many generations of students. This significant contributor to the community finally received the special recognition he deserved.

The class shares their project during the *Special Persons Night*, to which they invite the subjects of their projects and other local community members to the school. The large turnout of adults interested in the recognition of local community members lets students know the value of the project. The students learn a great deal about their own community: Both students and community members are proud of the students' accomplishments.

The activity creates a positive connection between the various parts of the community—old and new, those in leadership roles and many other (less noticed, but very important) contributors, and the students and teachers in the school.

We learn from those around us. We learn to act like them, to talk like them, to dress like them, to become part of a culture. Think of how you, as an infant and young child, learned to speak by following the models of those who nurtured you or how, as a teenager, you watched and then tried to talk and look just like your friends. The power of the social context is also very strong as people develop their literacy interests and behaviors. Children who come from families in which reading is a part of the fabric of their lives—in which family members keep books by their beds to read in quiet moments, where even bathrooms have piles of magazines, and where children are read to nightly—know that reading is important. They come to school with the expectation that they will become readers like the rest of their family members. Some students enter kindergarten facile with using computers and able to read and write. Other children, however, come to school without such extensive experiences and foundations for becoming literate. Yet, they want to learn and have also probably experienced the value of family members using cell phones to text message, observed relatives reading religious materials, noted environmental print, watched adults write and read, and played with computer games. Their experiences with literacy may be different, but can provide strong motivation for learning to read and write.

In getting acquainted with our students, it is part of our job as teachers to find out about their literacy history as readers and writers. Students want to learn to read and write and to communicate well with others. We can make better connections to their expectations and experiences when we know about their lives and understand their personal purposes for literacy. The more we know about their literacy experiences, the more we can ensure that all students become part of a social network of children and adults who value literacy and who use it in many ways and for many purposes.

As teachers we also know the importance of the social nature of literacy beyond the home. Children compare themselves to those around them. Just ask students who the best readers are in their class—they know. Ask who should write the letter of thanks to the author who visited the school, and they will direct you to the best writer. Children in classrooms can easily fall into categories of participators and non-participators, achievers and non-achievers. Teachers need to know how to make the social dynamics of the classroom work positively for all students, so all can be engaged and succeed.

Twenty-first century schools have fewer and fewer classrooms composed of children from one ethnic or cultural group who all speak English as their mother tongue and who are otherwise similar to each other. In fact, about 20 percent of the children in the United States have immigrant parents, and this percentage is increasing regularly (Suárez-Orozco, Suárez-Orozco, & Todorova, 2008). One in six students in American classrooms is African American, and soon one in five will be Hispanic, but still nine out of ten teachers are white. In most American schools, teachers are working with students whose ethnic backgrounds and possibly home languages are different from their own. As cultural and linguistic diversity are increasing, educators are finding ways to make schools and classrooms inviting learning communities where families and children learn from and with each other. This chapter highlights the research and best practices that emphasize the importance of reading and writing as social activities, not just as individual skills to be acquired.

Family Literacy

How were parents and community members involved in the schools you attended?

The Social Contexts of Literacy

∙ ∙

Communities and families vary in their approaches and orientations to literacy, and many of these variations are grounded in historical and cultural circumstance. Not all Americans value the same forms of literacy in their lives. Research in mainstream American communities, as well as in varied cultural settings, has highlighted both the commonalities and the differences across families and among communities.

A classic study of variations in literacy was done by Heath (1983) and reported in her book *Ways with Words*. In this comparison of literacy in three different cultural groups in a mill town near Charlotte, North Carolina, Heath illustrates how the two working-class communities, Tracton and Roadville, provided their children with different cultural experiences related to reading and writing from those of the townspeople, whose use of literacy was more compatible with that of the schools. Roadville families' literacy was anchored

No bedtime story.

in their fundamentalist church. They saw written works as creations that they themselves were unfit to question, and they discouraged their children from asking questions or telling stories. Tracton families were more playful and collaborative when it came to reading—it was not unusual to hear a mother standing on her front stoop reading aloud a line of a letter, and have neighbors up and down the block chime in with their ideas of what it meant. At school, children from Roadville seldom ventured ideas about texts. Their teacher saw them as dull and unimaginative. The children from Tracton eagerly helped each other read aloud, even though only one child had been called upon. Their teachers saw them as unruly and even prone to cheating. Heath was able to work with the teachers to help them better connect the children's home lives and their reading tasks in school, and everyone felt more successful as a result.

Since that early work of Heath, others have explored underlying values and styles associated with literacy. Delpit (1995) has provided insights about African American cultural variations in literacy. She argues that African American children are accustomed to a more direct form of teaching and discipline and that they need that kind of clarity for success. According to Delpit, the more indirect forms of teaching and discipline preferred by many middle-class teachers leave some students out. They often don't understand the cues that teachers provide about what is important and what the students' roles should be.

Research by Kelly (2000) with a group of Mexican American mothers revealed the high level of respect they accord teachers and schools. Even when they have had few opportunities for formal schooling themselves, they want their children to succeed. Their high regard for teachers, however, has a potential negative effect. They do not want to interfere with the teachers' role by helping their children learn to read before going to school. Because of this respect for teachers and their lack of a tradition of home literacy, their children often do not enter school with the same story reading and writing experiences that other children have. These families also thought that their children could learn English in school but that Spanish would remain the language used at home. This has both advantages and disadvantages. It poses a problem in giving English language learners enough opportunities to speak and use English to become proficient. It also means that the language of intimacy and familiarity is not English, so the school associations with English need to be very positive if students are going to learn it easily. Students who speak languages other than English can be encouraged to work and talk together so that they can practice English more regularly.

Because students are coming from increasingly diverse cultural traditions with varying literacy experiences, it is valuable to try to understand something of their family and cultural values, particularly those related to literacy and schooling. It is also important to find good ways to communicate with the parents and adjust to their needs. For example, some Hispanic parents feel intimidated when asked to come to school for parent conferences. They are unfamiliar with the traditions of U.S. schools and the customary relationships between teachers and families. In an attempt to honor the different experiences of the parents, one school district in California changed its format for parent nights. Instead of having each family come alone for conferencing, the schools have small-group conferencing. After the teachers lead a discussion of students' work and curriculum expectations, they answer questions from the parents. The teachers then make themselves available to individual families who wish to talk privately. This format has worked very well. The parents feel much more secure discussing issues of school learning in a group setting rather than alone with a teacher. Instead of creating high levels of anxiety among the parents, teachers' sensitivity led to a more comfortable and relaxed way to connect with parents in small groups.

The more teachers learn about the social contexts of their community, the better able they are to respond appropriately to their students and to build new expectations and competence so that all students can attain the levels of literacy needed today. Despite the traditional values that many communities place on literacy, teachers who reach all their students successfully take time to learn about their students and expand their horizons to become versatile in their use of literacy in a wide variety of settings.

The Need for a Learning Community: Linking Home, School, and Community

Becoming aware of the relationship between community values and students' motivation and interests is a starting place for understanding the setting in which one teaches. The cultural importance of literacy activities and the ways adults and children communicate affect how teachers can help their students most effectively.

New teachers should think of themselves as working in a community, not just in a school. Before entering the school and closing out the rest of the world, take time to become acquainted with the resources around you. For example, are there libraries you can link with to help provide the variety of reading materials you will want your students to have available to them? What resources are particular to the families you will be working with, such as community clubs, religious and ethnic centers, and local leaders?

Your most powerful opportunities, however, come within the school. As a teacher, you have a very important role for the parents and families of the children in your classroom. How you meet and relate to them is critical. Understanding the families' attitudes and values will help you work with the parents as partners in developing children's literacy. You want to know them as well as possible to communicate effectively with them. Think of their needs and ways to build bridges between the school and their homes. What do they want to know? How can you support them in their efforts to help their children? Think of how you can involve them in the life of the school and the classroom. What is appropriate and beneficial for both you and them?

As a teacher, you will be part of a school community, too. The more you can participate as part of the professional team, sharing your own literacy and learning and growing with others in the building, the more successful you will be as a teacher. Do not wait until you have your classroom under control before you think about building your roles within this larger support team. Begin to envision yourself as a committed professional sharing with others.

Inside the Classroom

Along with the variation among communities in how they express the values and functions of literacy, there is also great variation within schools in how the value of literacy is expressed. A part of creating a community is designing an inviting and purposeful space in the classroom, one that maximizes the possibilities for establishing a real literacy community among students. Whether adjusting the physical environment or adapting the structure of reading and writing activities, each teacher can do a great deal to contribute to a school culture that stimulates literacy and honors students' contributions.

CREATE A LITERATE CULTURE.   One of the first statements you make to students about what is important in school is what they see in the classroom. Are desks grouped together? Are books and print materials displayed and easily accessible? Think about the classroom environment you want to create during your first year of teaching. What will the classroom look like? Remember, you will have a great deal to do in determining the kind of context you create for your students. Think of your classroom space as a visual and physical opportunity to invite your students to enjoy reading and writing. Think about some of the classrooms you have visited in recent years. How did the teachers make a clear statement that they valued reading and writing? Table 2.1 identifies things teachers can use in their classrooms to enhance the value of literacy.

One of the easiest and most important ways in which you can invite your students into literacy is by providing them with places where they can participate with others in

Table 2.1 Visual Survey of a Literate Classroom

The classroom contains:

1. A special place for reading and writing—a reading corner, a writing corner, etc.
2. A classroom library of books students can use regularly
3. A collection of books students have written either individually or in groups (these could be big books, bound books added to the classroom library, etc.)
4. A rack with magazines and newspapers appropriate for the students
5. An author's chair and/or a reader's and writer's chair from which the students read to the rest of the class
6. Books and magazines the teacher is reading, both professional and personal
7. Examples on the walls or ledges of students' responses to materials they are reading—reviews of books, story maps of key points, sketches of interesting parts of stories, shared responses, etc.
8. Charts and other visuals that serve as strategy guides for students learning to read and write—reading strategies, fix-up strategies, steps in writing, word walls to guide spelling using key patterns, etc.
9. Visual "in process" charts of students' work—I-charts, matrices of learning, K-W-L charts, responses to questions for reflection, etc.
10. Illustrations of what students are studying and learning in content areas—science process journals and social studies artifacts
11. Books, magazines, and other materials that reflect cultures represented in your class or school
12. Examples of writing in different orthographies so that students can explore the varieties of written languages

literate activities. Every classroom with a library of appropriate books, magazines, and newspapers encourages the habit of reading. As you begin to create a library, determine the range of reading levels likely among the students, identify key themes and authors that children of this age enjoy, and begin building the collection. Many schools provide sets of books for each classroom. However, you will still want to evaluate the collection and make it as appealing as possible. It should contain material on a wide range of topics of interest to your students, and some of the collection should connect to the science, social studies, and special topics that the children will study. Ensure that there are books representing the various cultures from which students in the school come. All students deserve to find and see themselves in the books and magazines in their classrooms.

Another important step is to create an attractive place for literacy activities. If space is available, create both a reading corner and a writing corner. In the reading corner, house the classroom library and additional inviting reading materials in a space where students can browse through the books and curl up on the floor or in comfortable chairs to read. Some teachers find soft chairs, pillows, or even bathtubs in which children can relax and read. You can add small bins for paper so students can make notes about special ideas they find while reading and for stick-on notes so they can mark places for sharing with each other. Some teachers involve students in creating bookmarks so they can easily access their point of reading and have extra bookmarks available in the reading center.

The writing space needs a table and comfortable chairs. The space becomes more attractive when students can enjoy a range of writing tools and a supply of writing materials. Depending on the students' age, these will vary, but a selection of colored pencils and pens, some wooden ink blocks with special designs, and a variety of kinds of paper, some with designs, make writing more fun. Computers in this area can be used for writing and editing support by parents and volunteers in early primary classes and by students as they become adept in using computers. In addition, dictionaries, thesauruses, and

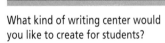

Writing and Reading Connections

What kind of writing center would you like to create for students?

other writing aids should be displayed prominently for students' use. This area can house students' writing folders so that when they are ready to write, they can enter the process easily and, when finished, can refile their works in process.

ENSURE THE SHARING OF LITERACY.   A key to helping students become lifelong readers and writers is to develop the social nature of literacy by providing regular opportunities for children to engage with each other around literacy events. Too often, as students move up in the grades, opportunities to talk with others about what they are reading and writing disappear. Yet it is through the sharing with others that students realize how central literacy can become in their own lives as part of their own enjoyment and learning. As you begin to plan for your literacy program, think carefully about including regular opportunities for students to engage with each other without the teacher dominating the discussion or exchange. Students need opportunities to work in paired reading and writing activities. They need to learn how to function as part of small cooperative literacy groups, knowing that they should be prepared with their own ideas to share and willing to listen and link to what others say. They also need to have experiences in larger groups and whole class discussions that build from their partner or small-group experiences.

For many students who are new to this country, talking in a whole-class setting is extremely difficult because they lack confidence in their command of English and of the culture of the school. Teachers can ease these students into the classroom academic life by using paired reading and talking as a first step before involving the students in larger group activities. One variation of this is called Think-Pair-Share (McTighe & Lyman, 1988). As you think about all the literacy learning activities you will structure for your students, make sure students have frequent and regular opportunities to talk and share with their peers in non-threatening settings. Don't assume that students know what it is like to discuss a book or piece of text. You might need to spend a significant amount of time getting students familiar with "talk about text." One way to develop more book discussion is to begin a Great Books program. There is full training for teachers and group leaders in this program and materials that guide students' thinking about the rich stories and texts that are included at each grade level (Plecha, 1992). Many teachers now use some form of book club (Raphael & McMahon, 1994) or literature circle (Daniels, 2002) as a way of involving students in focused talk about what they are reading. (Strategies for engaging students are discussed in Chapter 7, "Comprehension: Understanding and Responding to Narrative Texts.")

Another support for book talk is to help parents learn how to elicit reflection from their children. Some school districts have developed videotapes of the kinds of questions and follow-up comments that parents can use to help children talk about their reading. Others have prepared guides for parents to follow. One example is shown in Figure 2.1.

It is useful to help students share literacy with each other at all ages and grade levels. In this way, the shared, cultural aspects of reading and writing can become more alive for all the students in the school. A very simple way to do this is for two different grades to become partners. Students are also joined into buddy pairs for reading and writing and meet regularly (e.g., weekly, every two weeks, monthly). The children begin to share their literate activities with children older and/or younger than they are. The older readers help the younger ones as they read from books they want to share; the older students might also help write responses to the reading—what the two like about the story, characters, or information. When the younger students write their own descriptions of a trip to the nature center, the older student buddies take dictation and help to create personal accounts of the experiences.

In some schools, the students who struggle with reading also get help from older students who are trained in some basic reading strategies. In this way, both groups of students gain, and the shared understanding of literacy develops naturally. One particular program, Tall Friends, pairs middle-grade, below-level readers with second graders who are also having trouble. The reading teacher works with the older students to develop some activities that will help the second graders focus on the phonic regularities of English by doing controlled word sorts and by learning to listen to and support students as they read orally from their instructional-level materials.

myeducationlab
The Power of Classroom Practice
www.myeducationlab.com

Consider how and why a teacher has set up learning centers that allow students to practice reading and writing by completing the activity "Managing Learning Centers." (To find this activity, go to the topic Organization and Management in MyEducationLab and click on Assignments and Activities.)

Teach It! 42

Think–Pair–Share

Teach It! 35

Literature Circles

Teach It! 27

Paired Reading

Figure 2.1

Tips for Reading with
Your Child.

TIPS FOR READING WITH YOUR CHILD

1. Find a relaxed time and setting.

2. Talk about the book as you read.
   * Look over the cover, title, author, and picture and predict what you think may happen and why you like the book.
   * As you read, share connections to your life.
     "Doesnt this seem like Aunt Dorothy?"
     "This picture reminds me of our trip!"
     "Oh, I remember feeling like this!"
   * Ask questions of your child. For example:
     "Do you know anyone like this?"
     "How would you feel?"
   * After reading, share your favorite parts. For example:
     "I really liked . . ."
     ". . . was so funny!"

3. Reread favorite books.

4. Read many kinds of books—real world, poetry, folktales, humor, & fiction.

If a school does not have a vibrant, shared literacy culture, think about how to bring in some new focus to stimulate students' attention to reading and writing. There are many ways in which this can be done. One is to celebrate special days, from International Literacy Day, September 8, to Dr. Seuss's birthday, March 2. Some states have their own awards for good children's books. Illinois holds a contest each year to select students' favorite books as part of the Rebecca Caudill Awards Program. California's Young Reader Medal, sponsored by the California Reading Association, is similar. School participation in the selection of these books creates a new focus for the celebration of books. Other programs that recognize student writing can also help to add emphasis to school literacy. Inviting authors to visit the school and speak with different groups of students can make literacy and the process of writing and reading very real. Most states have some beloved and respected authors who are willing to visit schools, and bookstores will often help to bring authors to area schools.

Each of these examples highlights the importance of thinking of literacy as a community activity in the school. The more there is a climate of support for and interest in how students read and write, the more all students benefit. In addition, the more students talk with each other about their reading, the more they identify with books and reading.

START THE YEAR OUT RIGHT. Just as teachers can do much to create a warm, supportive literacy climate in the classroom, they can also help to model the importance and joy of literacy even before students start the year. Consider writing a letter to each of your new students before the year begins, introducing yourself and telling a little about your expectations for the fall. You can suggest that students bring with them an example of their own writing (if they are beyond the second grade) or a favorite book or poem. Some teachers ask students to bring pictures of themselves doing something they enjoy to put on a board for the first day. Each of these activities is an example of using literacy as a bridge to building relationships. Students love to receive mail, and some of the apprehension of starting a new year can be melted away with such simple, yet profound, gestures.

Teachers can also involve parents in events at the start of the year. By sending a letter home during the first week, introducing themselves, and describing what they will be doing in the classroom, teachers can build a bridge from school to home. Parents respond positively to a note from the teacher explaining what to expect for the fall. After an initial letter, the teacher might publish a weekly or monthly newsletter of the class events, with explanations of aspects of the reading and writing programs. Parents need to know how they can contribute. Figure 2.2 shows an example of a home-school letter that a multiage team sent to help parents understand their approach to reading development. Figure 2.3 provides an example of a letter a kindergarten teacher sent to parents and children asking them to identify favorite poems and bring them to class for all to share. This simple activity set the stage for monthly units that involved some parent participation. Knowing that they were important and were helping their children extend the resources of the class, most parents participated eagerly.

During the first week of school, literacy activities can also help the class to become better acquainted. Ask each student to bring a favorite book or magazine to share, give the students time to explain why they have selected the particular material, and listen carefully to them. This can be a good way to find out even more about the students' personal and home uses of literacy. For students for whom such selection and sharing might not be comfortable, conduct a book talk about several books and magazines in the classroom library and ask students to select the one they think they will like most. Having time to scan the materials gives each student an opportunity to share responses.

Getting to know the students quickly is important. Asking them to draw or write something about themselves is another way to elicit shared literacy activity. The bulletin board that can be created from this activity then becomes an invitation to read and learn about classmates. In one school, parents created the covers for the writing journals that the kindergarten and first-grade children were given the first week of school. Imagine the children's surprise when they realized that they would be holding a creation of their parents each time they wrote! Parents knew their children would be using their developmental spelling abilities as well as drawing to write messages each day when they spent time at the writing table.

this is brilliant

Involving Parents in the School

It is impossible to discuss social contexts of literacy without focusing on parents, for they are the children's first and most important teachers. Teachers need to know as much as possible about the parents' cultural values and styles of communicating with their children so that the adjustments to the school culture and style of each teacher can be made. Even the ability to talk about different ways of thinking, talking, reading, and writing can be useful to students, parents, and teachers. For example, you might suggest to a parent, "At school, we are trying to get the children to be independent in their reading by giving them time to figure out unfamiliar words for themselves. We ask them to look for three sources of information: visual, grammatical, and meaningful. Of course, you want them to read perfectly and fluently. Giving them the correct pronunciation of words helps this. However, right now we are trying to get the children to be more independent. If you could help reinforce our teaching strategy for the next few months, your child will feel more comfortable and, I think, reach the goal we both share." Accept that what the parents value and think is important, and then help them understand how they can assist the instructional program.

As already mentioned, relationships between parents and schools vary tremendously. In some communities, parents feel too intimidated to join the school culture. They want

Family
Literacy

What does this phrase mean:
"Parents are a child's first teachers"?

Figure 2.2   Home-School Newsletter.

"Research is an effort to do things better, it is the problem-solving mind— it is the tomorrow mind, it is a natural extension of good teaching."
(Hubbard & Power)

Welcome to the *Research to Practice* segment of our bi-monthly class news. This is the place where we hope to clarify terms, strategies, theory, research, district expectations and how it connects to what we do in our classrooms. Each newsletter will focus on a particular area of instruction, learning, and/or curriculum. It is our professional obligation to not only keep you abreast with current research, but also to align it to what we do in our classrooms. We hope that you find this portion of the newsletter informative and helpful.

- -

Rainbow Reading

Reading Levels (Jerry Johns, 2001)

Independent   The Independent reading level is the level at which the student can read fluently without teacher assistance. Materials should be read with near perfect accuracy (95–100%) and 90% comprehension.

Instructional   The instructional reading level is the level at which the student is <u>challenged</u> but not <u>frustrated</u> with teacher guidance. The student can read accurately (90–95%) with 75% comprehension.

Frustration   The frustration level is the level at which the student should not be given materials to read. Students at the frustration level (<90% accuracy and <50% comprehension) are unable to read the materials even with the support of the teacher.

Rainbow Reading

Rainbow Reading is one component of our Balanced Reading Program.* The Rainbow Reading books in our classroom are grouped into four colors: <u>Red</u> (Beginning), <u>Orange</u> (Developing), <u>Yellow</u> (Transitional), and <u>Green</u> (Fluent).

During Rainbow Reading (independent reading) students choose books from one of the four levels that are at their **independent** (95% accuracy, 90% comprehension) level. "Independent reading is essential for the development of fluency. Fluency comes from the ability to immediately and automatically identify most frequent words. This is key to the success of a life-long reader." (Cunningham, 1998)

During Reading Workshop, students are placed in materials at their **instructional** (90–95% accuracy) level. Teacher guidance provides a scaffold where students are challenged but not frustrated.

*A Balanced Reading Program provides opportunities for pleasurable, independent reading (Reading Rainbow), reading for a specific purpose (Reading Workshop, learn content, skill, strategy), and interaction through discussion, response to literature, research and inquiry. (Pinell & Fountas, 2000)

<u>**AT HOME ...**</u>
Continue to set aside a special reading time. During that time your child might be reading from the Rainbow Reading collection from school, reading a library book or other book of choice, reading to another child, or listening to you read. It is extremely important that children **hear** the language and pattern of text in the higher-level books adults read to them. Remember that reading should be pleasurable. Allow time for "easy" reading!

Happy Reading!

Figure 2.3 Home-School Letter.

March

Dear Parents,

     March is poetry month. In celebration of our featured genre of literature, please complete the following "Literature Link".

                        Thank you,
                        Debbie Gurvitz

DIRECTIONS FOR MARCH LITERATURE LINK

1. Together, choose or write a poem to be shared with our class.

2. Print the poem in the area provided.

3. Have your child illustrate his/her poem.

4. Return to school at your earliest convenience.

POEM	ILLUSTRATION

POEM

When I Was One*

When I was One,
I had just begun.
When I was Two,
I was nearly new.
When I was Three,
I was hardly Me.
When I was Four,
I was not much more.
When I was Five,
I was just alive.
But now I am six,
I'm clever as clever.
So, I think I'll be six now
forever and ever.

          A.A. Milne

ILLUSTRATION

Name_____SY

teachers to do their jobs and will support this as best they can. In other communities, parents are very involved in the schools, serving on curriculum committees, working on standards development, and visiting classrooms regularly. They might want to know a great deal about how reading is taught and might have a wealth of experience themselves guiding their own children's literacy development. When this is the case, home-school letters can be more specific with explanations of research and instructional priorities. Creating videotapes and having Parents' Nights and programs that explain how literacy develops can help to build good communication in these situations. Dealing with the variations in parent knowledge and expectations is a concern of the whole school and should be a shared decision of the faculty and administration. A key in all situations is being open to, and interested in, the parents' perspectives and concerns.

Become Part of a Professional Community

Teaching is challenging work and can be exhausting, especially for new teachers. One of the best ways you can help yourself is by seeking out opportunities to become part of the multilevel professional community of educators.

WITHIN THE SCHOOL.   At the most immediate level is the community within the school. If you are fortunate, your school will have a reading/literacy coach or specialist who is available to help you get started, who can do demonstration lessons, and who can help you manage the curriculum expectations and assessments. Most schools provide some structured times for professional development when the faculty meets regularly to discuss issues of common concern and to learn together. This may occur in grade level or departmental teams. Ask if your school has a literacy team; if it does, this group of interested teachers can help you understand the school literacy context and expectations and can also provide significant support to new teachers. These teachers will often let you visit their classrooms to watch how they conduct parts of their instructional program—from doing guided reading to initiating inquiry units. New teachers also may have the option of working with a mentor teacher in a district-based induction program. Ask if such an option exists, or if one doesn't, you might inquire about getting a personal mentor. This can be a helpful way to get to know the specific culture of the school and district and can prevent many frustrations. The school district or the larger county or service center might also have an optional set of good activities that can be used to increase effectiveness of teachers. Ask about these resources, and watch for special programs that are advertised. Many new teachers feel too busy to add another commitment, but the rewards can outweigh the time demands.

OUTSIDE OF SCHOOL.   Outside of school, teachers can seek out groups that meet regularly for discussions both of adult recreational books and of professional ones. Some teacher book clubs also read and discuss current children's books, which can help teachers become aware of new possibilities for students. With so many books published each year, it is difficult to keep up with the ones that might be appropriate for your students. You can attend book discussions hosted by bookstores and distributors with your teaching colleagues as well. They can help to identify special books and upcoming events to link into the classroom. If teachers share their search for books, magazines, and computer materials with each other, they can enjoy learning together as they find materials that are of interest to a wide variety of young people. Many school districts have Professional Development Centers where teachers in the district offer short courses and outside speakers provide seminars. If your school doesn't have a reading/literacy coach or specialist, there may be one at the district level who is available to help you get started.

As you begin your journey of professional growth, share what you are doing with your students who might not think of teachers as learners, too. Children are intrigued when they see the professional journals and books that help their teachers evaluate their own teaching and that encourage them to expand their knowledge in new directions. Keep some of your professional materials in the classroom as a visible reminder that adults are readers and learners, too. Talk about your own reflection and questions.

Join a Writing Group. If you are going to inspire children to read, you must be a reader yourself. So it shouldn't surprise you to hear us make the same point about writing. If you haven't participated in an adult writing group, you may not know how completely satisfying it can be to put your heart and soul into creating something meaningful on paper and to have other people be moved by it. The experience comes as close to genuine communication with yourself and others as anything we humans can do. Many communities offer writing classes for adults who want to be motivated to write and to have opportunities to share what they write with others. If you attend one, you will quickly see that the point is not, as many believe, to see who has "true talent" as a writer. It is rather to help you find your voice as a writer. Finding your voice takes motivation, practice, and a little inspiration. Inspiration? The ancient Greeks believed in divine creatures called *muses* who blew ideas into people's heads (that is literally what "inspire" means). We advise our own writing students to assume that the Greeks were right. Think about it: If a divine creature were to blow an idea into your head, wouldn't you be more likely to do something with it if you were writing at the time, instead of watching television or listening to your iPod? So cultivate the habit of writing. Join a group if you can. You will quickly see what a marvelous activity writing really is, and you will motivate your students with your example. And, who knows? Like Regie Routman, Nancie Atwell, Will Hobbs, Paul Janezko, Cynthia DeFelice, Jim Burke, and countless other teachers who became writers, you may connect with a large audience.

PROFESSIONAL ORGANIZATIONS. New teachers are also nurtured when they join professional organizations that hold conferences and publish journals and books designed to help teachers grow. For literacy teachers, that means becoming a member of the International Reading Association (www.reading.org) and/or the National Council of Teachers of English (www.ncte.org). These organizations have local and state groups that meet periodically to bring speakers to the area and sponsor special events; they also may offer grants to teachers wishing to attend a conference or develop some special student project. Both organizations have excellent journals that you can subscribe to either in print or online formats; *The Reading Teacher* (IRA) and *Language Arts* (NCTE) are both very useful sources of ideas and information. IRA and NCTE also jointly sponsor an important teacher support website, (**readwritethink.org**), with its large collection of lesson plans that can be downloaded and easily used. These professional organizations also provide many opportunities for teachers to develop leadership skills by speaking, being an officer, and working on advocacy when the need arises. Teachers enjoy their challenges most when they become part of the larger professional community. At a personal level, membership often results in new friends and a valuable support network. Local affiliates can be found by checking the websites of the national groups.

There are also two national professional organizations for teachers interested in the education of English language learners. Both also have state affiliates. They are Teachers of English to Speakers of Other Languages (TESOL) (www.tesol.org) and National Association for Bilingual Education (NABE) (www.nabe.org). Participation with other teachers in the school or district can help to create a strong professional learning community.

Create a Professional Portfolio

A good way you can help yourself grow and make yourself attractive to possible employers is by keeping a professional portfolio. Your university or college may already have this as part of your teacher preparation program. If not, you can easily build your portfolio on your own. Listed below are some suggestions for what to include.

- A statement of your philosophy about teaching beginning reading that provides evidence of how you view children and reading; this also provides a window on your writing abilities.
- A reflection about why you incorporated such a statement into your portfolio.
- Evidence from some experiences you have had in the levels from kindergarten to second grade (even if you intend to teach at a higher grade level) because some older children are preliterate or not literate in English. Providing evidence of your knowledge of emergent literacy and early reading can be important for any grade level.
- Lesson plans; thematic literature units; lists of high-interest, low-vocabulary children's literature and other similar artifacts.
- Examples of actual lessons you have taught, including the lesson outline and a few examples of student work; make your own reflections part of the lesson materials.
- Some photographs or DVDs of classroom environments and projects you have developed.
- A lesson plan for reading comprehension. It should include higher-order questions that lead students to activate background knowledge and use it to assimilate and then apply new knowledge from their reading. Are your only classroom experiences with kindergarten or first grade? If so, use a listening comprehension lesson in which, instead of reading themselves, the children listen to the teacher read aloud.
- Evidence of the capability to teach expository text effectively. A K-W-L chart from a lesson planned and taught during field experiences is an effective and graphic way of showing this side of your teaching.
- A list of expository text processing strategies for use in your classroom. You might divide them into three categories: anticipation strategies, knowledge-building strategies, and consolidation strategies. In this way you can explain how you can include literacy skills in content lessons. Show, for example, how you can examine the text to be read and then review your list, which will remind you of all of the possible strategies.
- Highlight your knowledge of other cultures and your ability to speak languages other than English.
  - Lesson plans in Spanish or another language, especially if the school or district interviewer is fluent in that language. (Be sure to proofread carefully.)
  - A thematic literature unit with children's literature from another language or a unit with a multicultural theme.
  - Transcripts, certificates, and/or fluency examination scores documenting proficiency in another language or culture.
  - Evidence of proficiency in teaching English as a second language.
  - Photographs of bulletin boards in another language. (Be sure to proofread carefully.)
  - Examples of volunteer work or your paraprofessional experience in bilingual classrooms, with testimonials and letters of recommendation from teachers and school administrators and/or letters and notes of appreciation from parents and students.

Two final cautions:

Be sure that all examples presented in your portfolio are your own original work. If you use or adapt the work of someone else, be sure to give credit.

Proofread everything carefully; you are presenting your best face in your portfolio, including your ability to write and spell in English.

For more about portfolios, see McLaughlin and Vogt (1996).

Meeting the Literacy Needs of All Children

An Urban Classroom

Farah Al Jabar's fourth-grade class is located in a low-income area of a major urban center. Her thirty-six students represent, in about equal numbers, four major ethnic groups: African American, Asian, Hispanic, and Anglo. Almost half entered kindergarten speaking another language or dialect of English. Although all are at least minimally proficient in English now, many have gaps in their oral language vocabularies and in the background knowledge that corresponds to that of the middle-class children for whom the school curriculum and textbooks are typically designed. According to the results of informal reading inventories that she administered in the fall, many are reading below grade level, and a few are reading markedly below grade level.

Today, one group of ten children, all reading at grade level, is beginning to read a novel by Spinelli (1990a) entitled Maniac Magee, *which was awarded the prestigious Newbery Award. It is not a particularly difficult story, but many vocabulary words are new to the children. In addition, some lack background knowledge about substantive issues that underlie the story.*

Farah ensured that she was incorporating the elements of the four-block guided reading model she applies in her classroom: guided reading, writing, working with words, and self-selected reading. Before the children read, she leads them through several brief anticipatory reading activities that prepare them to read the story with good understanding. First, she says, "Let's read the title of the book and look at the illustration on the cover," demonstrating and modeling how she makes predictions about text she will read. She asks, "What predictions can you make about this book?" One child tries to sound out the word "maniac," saying "m-m-maniac—What does it mean?" Another child quickly responds, "It's a word for a crazy person, somebody out of control." Another notices the shoes on the cover and asks, "Do those shoes belong to a boy or a girl?" Farah says, "Let's find out." She reads the two-page foreword of the book aloud to the children; it ends with a short poem:

> *Ma-niac, Ma-niac*
> *He's so cool*
> *Ma-niac, Ma-niac*
> *Don't go to school*
> *Runs all night*
> *Runs all right*
> *Ma-niac, Ma-niac*
> *Kissed a bull.**

She then explains, "The main character is Jeffrey Magee, but they call him 'Maniac Magee.' He's a boy about your age. Now what do you think the story might be about?"

Farah has already prepared the beginning of a semantic map to introduce the term *dump*, which the children will encounter early in the story. She asks, "What do you know about this word?" The children share the information they already have, and Farah records it in appropriate categories on the graphic organizer.

She then has the children close their books with their finger in place at the first page of the first chapter, and she asks them a question that will guide their silent reading of that page, beginning the guided reading part of her lesson where they will build knowledge through reading. She asks, "How does Jeffrey's life suddenly change?" They listen to the question, then open their books and begin reading silently. (Jeffrey is orphaned when his parents are killed in an automobile accident. He lives with an aunt and uncle for a short time and then runs away to live in a dump.)

---

*From *Maniac Magee* by Jerry Spinelli. Copyright © 1990 by Jerry Spinelli. By permission of Little, Brown and Company.

As they read, Farah circulates around the group, motivating them by touching shoulders, smiling, and offering encouraging comments. Some children ask for assistance with words that are unfamiliar, even after the anticipatory reading activities. She quickly provides that help so that they can maintain their comprehension. This activity also provides an opportunity for her to briefly circulate around the classroom and supervise the work of other children who are working independently as they wait for their own small-group lessons.

As the children finish reading the page and begin to raise their hands to respond to the question, Farah returns to her seat. She repeats the question and calls on a child who says, "He went to live with his aunt and uncle—they weren't too cool." Another adds, "His mom and dad were killed in a car accident." Yet another says, "He ran away." Other children add new information and share other points of view. Finally, Farah asks one student to read aloud the sentence that provides evidence for the answer that all the students finally agreed on. She then asks another comprehension-level question about the same page, following this procedure through the three pages of this first chapter of the story.

Story Maps

In a consolidation activity at the end of the lesson, Farah asks, "How did the story begin?" A child responds, "Jeffrey's parents were killed, and he went to live with his uncle and his aunt." She asks, "What happened next?" The children continue to retell the story up to that point in their own words. Farah then says, "Write a short paragraph, and predict what you think will happen in the next chapter of the story. While I teach the other group's lesson, please read from your library books." As they begin to think about that, she moves on to work with another small group of children that is reading from an anthology.

Farah has exhibited many behaviors that tell us she is an outstanding teacher, some of which relate to her strong instructional program. She uses teaching strategies that support or scaffold their comprehension and that help them build confidence. In reading aloud the preface of the book, she provided a model both of fluent reading and of thinking about what she read, as revealed in her follow-up question. She gave attention to working with words in analyzing a crucial word in the story, *dump*, whose meaning was a key to understanding the circumstances in which Maniac Magee was living. She provided guided reading in the silent reading that was directed and scaffolded by the higher-order questions she asked before they read. She provided an application and extension activity: writing a short paragraph to predict what might happen in the next chapter. And, finally, she provided time for self-selected reading.

Equally important are aspects of her approach that motivate the children, that indicate her high expectations and affection for them, and that demonstrate her deep understanding of the cultures from which they come. Choosing literature for the children's lessons is an important part of her planning. The main character of *Maniac Magee* is a boy who has very positive interactions with African American children in the story. She has also provided a large-print version of the book from LRS Large Print Publications (Spinelli, 1990b) for a partially sighted student in the group. Farah's next literature choice for this group is *By the Lake of Sleeping Children: The Secret Life of the Mexican Border* (Urrea, 1996), about life in a dump in Tijuana, Mexico, which parallels and connects with the setting of *Maniac Magee*. She takes much care to ensure that all children in her class see themselves in many different roles in the literature she provides for them. She directs the major part of her small discretionary budget each year to the purchase of sets of trade books to supplement her basal reading program.

Valuing Diversity or Coping with Differences?

We can view the diversity in Farah's classroom, and in most American classrooms, from at least two perspectives. On the one hand, teachers can consider that associating with people who are different enriches everyone. On the other hand, because diversity means that differences between children are greater than just the ordinary individual differences found among homogeneous groups of children, some teachers perceive it as a problem. Different languages can make it difficult to meet needs, group students efficiently for instruction, and provide materials that are appropriate for all children. Cultural differences arise, making teaching a complex and demanding act. These are legitimate concerns, but they should be viewed as challenges instead of problems. Teachers who take the first perspective, the positive one, view diversity as an asset to be exploited for the benefit of the children, an asset that enriches the learning of all—the students and the teacher.

Creating an inviting environment in your classroom can help promote a literacy community for all students. (Ellen B. Senisis)

CULTURAL DIVERSITY, BACKGROUND KNOWL-EDGE, AND LITERACY.   The pervasive culture in U.S. schools, according to Gollnick and Chinn (2008), is essentially "based on the knowledge and perspective of the West (Northern and Western Europe)." Many believe that this culture is apparent in textbooks and curricula and in the cadre of teachers that staff most schools. It characterizes what teachers expect students to know when they come to school, and it serves as the basis for teachers' assessment of student outcomes. It often characterizes how teachers reinforce children's behavior, both positively and negatively; how they ask children questions and accept their responses; how they correct children; how they do, or do not, make the classroom safe for children; and how they use gestures and time. Clearly, schools cannot adopt the culture of each and every child, but they can accept the culture of every child, accommodate that culture, and use its presence and teachers' knowledge of it to help teach all children. According to Fitzgerald (1995), teachers must make reading instruction congruent with the background culture that children bring to their lessons.

THE ZONE OF PROXIMAL DEVELOPMENT.   The work of Vygotsky (1978) provides another view of social constructivism that underlies children's cognitive development, with particular applications to the teaching of reading and language. The learning community includes culture, language, and important adults who guide children in their learning.

Vygotsky's concept of the **zone of proximal development** is especially important. According to his view of learning, certain tasks can be performed by a student independently; some tasks cannot be performed at all, even with help; and some fall within the "zone," which can be performed with help from others. Those *others* in the classroom are usually adults, such as teachers, paraprofessionals, and parent volunteers, but they can also be other more capable students in cooperative learning group settings.

Many implications for the classroom emerge from these concepts:

- Teachers need to design instruction that is at an appropriate level for each child—not so difficult that they fail, not so simple that there is no gain, but at a level where, with scaffolding (i.e., a support system), they can learn. A one-size-fits-all approach is not appropriate.
- Learning activities need to be done in meaningful contexts, not in isolation.
- Children need to construct their own meaning with the help of the teacher and other adults and peers in the role of facilitators.
- Children need to see relationships between what they are learning and the communities in which they live.

CULTURALLY RESPONSIVE CLASSROOM COMMUNICATION.   Children's language develops in a sociocultural context. How children use language in their homes and communities also has important effects on their use of language in classrooms, especially when they are learning to read and write. Although language arts and reading curricula often reflect a linear assumption about the development of language and literacy in all of its forms, ethnographers remind teachers that they must view how parents use language in rearing their children, the range of types of language use in the home, and the amount of exposure that children experience with respect to the diversity of languages, speakers of languages, and ways of using language outside of their homes (Heath, 1986). Culturally responsive teachers apply their knowledge of the many cultures in their classroom to the way they address children and how they respond to them, both verbally and nonverbally.

Verbal Communication. Providing feedback to students is a vital teacher activity. When feedback is provided across cultures, there is always potential for misunderstanding. Scarcella (1990) provides several categories of feedback behavior:

- Interpreting student feedback (how they indicate that they are paying attention). Most Americans nod their heads to indicate that they are listening. Asian students often nod to indicate that they are listening, but this does not necessarily indicate understanding.
- Complimenting and criticizing (how this is interpreted from both perspectives). Asian students might reject too many compliments as being insincere, whereas Hispanic students usually welcome praise.
- Teacher correction of student errors (how students view the way the teacher corrects errors). Students from some cultures want to be corrected and are concerned at a lack of correction. In other cultures, correction can be a humiliation for the student. It is important for the teacher to consider how to treat this issue with each student in the classroom.
- Student requests for clarification (how, or if, students ask for help and how teachers interpret these requests). Teachers should carefully monitor the comprehension of their students, checking for understanding and watching for nonverbal behavior that might indicate a question that has not been expressed.
- Spotlighting, or calling attention to a student's behavior in front of others. Many children do not appreciate having attention called to them, especially from across the room. Teachers might be more effective if they walk over to students and softly give instructions, especially if student misbehavior is involved or even praise for older students. The teacher can avoid turning a small problem of inattention into a major problem of defiance.
- Questioning and answering (the purpose of questions). Asking questions is an important teacher instructional behavior. American teachers tend to ask many questions for the purpose of motivating critical thinking on the part of the students. But Heath (1983) has found that African American children are often confused by the way teachers ask questions when the teachers already know the answers to them. She recommends that these children be asked questions of the type they are asked at home, such as "What's that like?" or "What's happening?" To promote higher-order thinking, teachers often ask for opinions about what a character did in a story or how an author expressed an idea. Children from some cultures are uncomfortable in offering opinions; they can gain experience and confidence in acquiring this ability in small-group work before they express themselves in front of the entire class.
- Pausing (wait-time). Teachers tend to provide insufficient wait-time for students. They need to allow students time to think about their responses before going on to another student or accepting a response from students who always seem to know the correct answer before anyone else. According to Rowe (1974), teachers usually wait slightly more than one second. She found that when children were provided with at least three seconds of undisturbed wait-time, they responded more completely and correctly, the number of nonresponses decreased, and the number of volunteered responses increased.

Nonverbal Communication. Communication is often thought of only as a verbal process, but the important impact of nonverbal communication should also be considered, especially when teachers work with children from many different cultures. For example, a frequent type of interaction between teacher and child is the teacher's need to correct the inappropriate behavior of a child. To show respect, an Anglo child usually looks in the teacher's eyes when being corrected. The same child shows defiance by looking at the floor instead of looking the teacher in the face. Conversely, a Hispanic child often shows respect to the teacher by looking at the floor, whereas defiance is shown by looking the teacher in the eyes. What message does the teacher send by saying to the Hispanic child, "Look me in the eye when I talk to you"? In this case, the teacher might be asking the student to demonstrate defiance. This is only one of many examples of the potential for cross-cultural misunderstandings between teacher and child, even when both are behaving appropriately for their own cultures.

These nonverbal aspects of communication are a form of paralanguage, which includes many aspects of nonverbal behavior that are very useful for teachers to understand (see Table 2.2). These behaviors are the clues that tell us someone is from another culture, and sometimes even what country they are from, although we might not be able to hear them speaking. You cannot be expected to be familiar with all of the nonverbal behaviors of all of the cultures of the children in your classroom, but you can begin to reflect about the reactions of children to your nonverbal behaviors and about your own reactions to puzzling nonverbal behaviors of students. When student reactions to a teacher's behavior are counterintuitive, there is often a cultural explanation.

As children's experiences with life in the United States expand, they also begin to learn the appropriate nonverbal behaviors of the new language and culture they are acquiring. When they are successful, they are able to function comfortably in two cultures, making them bicultural. Teachers need to be sensitive to children as they go about the complicated task of becoming bicultural.

Table 2.2 Selected Components of Paralanguage

OBSERVABLE BEHAVIORS	SELECTED CLASSROOM EXAMPLES
Gestures and other movements of the body, including facial expression, movements of the eye, and posture (*kinesics*) (Pennycook, 1985)	American children often show respect with eye contact; other cultural groups of children frequently show respect by looking down.
Social distance (*proxemics*) (Hall, 1966)	Hispanic children often cling closely to the teacher and like a hug; Asian children tend to maintain a greater social distance and are less comfortable with touching.
Arm and hand movements (*haptics*) (Pennycook, 1985)	Americans indicate the height of a person with the hand held horizontally at the appropriate level; Hispanics hold the hand vertically for people, but horizontally for animals.
Nonlexical aspects of verbal communication, such as pitch variation, the use of silence, how space is filled in a conversation, e.g., *uh* in English, *este* for many Spanish speakers (*paraverbal features*) (Pennycook, 1985)	Asian children often giggle when embarrassed, such as when they are caught misbehaving.
Monochronic use of time in a linear mode in Western cultures, with sequential scheduling and tasks completed one at a time; polychronistic use of time in a cyclical mode in non-Western cultures, with less precise time commitments (*chronism*) (Hall, 1983)	*Monochronic*: Western children tend to line up to be helped by the teacher one at a time. *Polychronic*: Non-Western children often gather around the teacher's desk all wanting to be helped at the same time, unconcerned that the teacher helps each one a little bit until everyone is eventually completely helped.

Linguistic Diversity: Today's Classroom Demographics

Who are the English language learners? Where are they? Everywhere! The 2000 census revealed a significant and growing diversity in American classrooms in almost all parts of the country. Perhaps the most important aspect of this change is the number of children classified as English language learners, children who arrive in American classrooms with no English or insufficient English for learning to read and write in English. When teachers think of English language learners, they likely think of Hispanic children; indeed, Hispanics make up the largest population of English language learners. They also think first of California, Texas, Florida, and New York as the states that are most affected by the presence of Spanish-speaking English language learners. But schools in most areas of the country have begun to experience an influx of Spanish-speaking English language learners.

According to the 2000 U.S. census, the Hispanic population of the United States has nearly doubled since the 1990 census, rising from 9 percent to 12.5 percent of the total population (Campo-Flores, 2001; U.S. Census Bureau, 2000). Some of the largest percentage increases have occurred in surprising areas of the country. The meatpacking and meat-processing industry has attracted many Spanish-speaking workers and their families to such states as Nebraska, Iowa, Minnesota, Arkansas, Kentucky, Tennessee, the Carolinas, Alabama, and Georgia, accounting for major changes there.

The most dramatic difference in the growth of Hispanic populations in the 2000 census, however, was the rapid dissemination to smaller population centers and suburbs (Suro & Singer, 2002). Almost half of Hispanic population growth was in fast-growing Hispanic hubs and new Hispanic destinations; the other half occurred in established metropolitan areas.

Similar growth is seen in other language groups as well, and not only are these groups growing, but they are also appearing in states where they were not as numerous in previous years. For example, most Hmong immigrants from Laos began their American experience near Fresno, California, but many of them have moved to Minnesota and Wisconsin (University of Wisconsin–Eau Claire, 2000).

According to the National Clearinghouse for English Language Acquisition and Language Instruction Educational Programs (NCELA, 2006), almost 10 million children don't speak English at home, and about half of those don't have sufficient English-language proficiency to succeed in English in our schools. Although the vast majority of these children speak Spanish (see Table 2.3), more than 100 languages are represented.

English language learners are not a monolithic population. Some are very proficient in speaking and understanding their mother tongue, and some are literate in that language. Some became literate in their home countries; others do so in programs of bilingual education here in the United States. As a result of living in refugee camps, some upper elementary and adolescent children arrive in this country with little or no school experience at all. Some English language learners are migrant children from rural areas without educational opportunities, and others were working and contributing to the family income. Some English language learners have limited proficiency even in their mother tongue, just as some native English speakers are limited in their English proficiency. As teachers consider the challenges today's students represent, they also must think in terms of possible solutions.

BILINGUAL EDUCATION.   Perhaps the most sweeping policy change to affect the education of English language learners in recent years was the 1974 *Lau v. Nichols* decision of the U.S. Supreme Court, which ruled that equal education did not result from providing exactly the same education to all children (J. Crawford, 1989; *Lau v. Nichols*, 1974). This decision required that school districts take positive steps to overcome the educational barriers experienced by students who did not speak English. Soon afterward, the Elementary and Secondary Education Act was amended with Title VII to make limited English proficient students eligible for federal funds and to permit their enrollment in bilingual education programs.

myeducationlab
The Power of Classroom Practice
www.myeducationlab.com

Learn more about the importance of responding to individual differences by watching a video and completing the following questions in the activity "Creating a Supportive Environment for English Language Learners." (To find this activity, go to the topic *English Language Learners* in MyEducationLab and click on Assignments and Activities.)

Table 2.3 Language Backgrounds of Limited English Proficient (LEP) Students

LANGUAGE	RANK	PERCENTAGE OF LEP STUDENTS
Spanish	1	79.0%
Vietnamese	2	2.0%
Hmong	3	1.6%
Cantonese	4	1.0%
Korean	5	1.0%
Haitian Creole	6	0.9%
Arabic	7	0.9%
Russian	8	0.8%
Tagalog (Philippines)	9	0.75%
Navajo	10	0.6%
Others	—	11.45%

A 1981 court decision (*Casteñeda v. Pickard*, 1981) established three criteria for determining how programs of bilingual education were to be held accountable for meeting requirements of the Equal Education Opportunity Act of 1974. The criteria included the following:

- The program must be based on sound educational theory.
- The program must be effectively implemented with adequate resources for personnel, instructional materials, and space.
- Following a trial period, the program must be shown to be effective in overcoming language handicaps.

Although the *Lau v. Nichols* decision did not mandate bilingual education as a remedy, school districts did find it to be one of the few ways to ensure that English language learners had equal access to education, that is, education in their mother tongue while they were learning English. The No Child Left Behind Act of 2001 replaced the earlier Elementary and Secondary Education Act (ESEA) Title VII, which formerly funded programs of instruction for bilingual children and was rescinded (García, 2005). The new law, Title III, continues to provide resources for what are called English language learners. Annual assessments of English-language proficiency are mandated, as well as requirements that these children meet state academic content and student achievement standards in English (Office of English Language Acquisition [OELA], 2004). The term *bilingual* does not appear in the new law, which now stresses skills in English only. There is no federal interest in the development of academic bilingual education programs for these children.

In late 2006, the Department of Education released new regulations concerning English language learners (Federal Register, 2006). They have the effect of allowing school districts to delay the testing in reading of English language learners who have been in the United States for less than a year. Unfortunately, no evidence indicates that these children can learn English in one year, so the effect will be minimal.

ENGLISH LANGUAGE LEARNERS AND LITERACY.   Bilingual education, however, is a subject of much controversy. In recent years, initiatives in a number of states, including California, Arizona, and Massachusetts, have discouraged most bilingual education in those states. They require instead a one-year period of immersion instruction in English as a second language, although the efficacy of this approach is not supported in the

Because of the changing demographic of the U.S. population, strategies for meeting the needs of non-English-speaking students have become a focal point of discussion in many communities. (Michael Newman/PhotoEdit)

literature. In fact, abundant evidence indicates that children need two to five years of instruction in English as a second language before they are ready to learn to read in English (Thomas & Collier, 1997). An analysis of test scores from the 2002 California Stanford 9 test scores reported by the influential League of United Latin American Citizens (LULAC) (O'Leary, 2002) suggested that English language learners were not developing English fluency and that many were falling further behind in academic subjects. O'Leary reported that four years after the passage of California's Unz English Initiative, Proposition 227, more than a million limited-English immigrant students in second through eleventh grades in California still had not been mainstreamed in English-only classes, an indication of the failure of the policy.

Goodman (1986) reminds us that bilingual children are not disadvantaged in some academic way. They are disadvantaged only if their linguistic strengths are not appreciated and if schools fail to build on their strengths. The International Reading Association (IRA) has recognized the efficacy of teaching children to read in the mother tongue while they learn to understand and speak English and before they begin learning to read in their second language, English. The IRA's resolution of support includes three major elements: (1) initial literacy instruction should be provided in the child's native language whenever possible; (2) although initial literacy instruction in a second language can be successful, there is a higher risk of reading problems than beginning with a child's first language; and (3) instructional decisions should support the professional judgment of the teachers and administrators who are responsible for teaching students whose first language is not English and who oppose any restrictive federal, state, or local initiatives (International Reading Association, 2001).

Dialects of English and Literacy

English language learners, whose mother tongue is not English and whose English proficiency is limited, are not the only children whose reading instruction is affected by linguistic factors. African American Vernacular English is a dialect of English that is spoken by many urban African American children in the United States. There are other dialects, including southern regional dialect, a mostly rural dialect of both Anglo and African American children.

AFRICAN AMERICAN VERNACULAR ENGLISH.   Also known as *black dialect* and *ebonics*, African American Vernacular English is the dialect of the English language that is probably most frequently encountered in American classrooms. According to Labov (1970, 1972), African American Vernacular English is as logical and consistent as standard English, it can be reproduced, and it makes sense. It is merely different from standard English. A policy statement of the TESOL (1997) board of directors stipulates that African American Vernacular English has been demonstrated in research to be a rule-governed linguistic system that has its own lexical, phonological, syntactic, and discourse patterns and that it therefore deserves pedagogical recognition. It is not a substandard dialect of English, and it is not poor English. It is a dialect that is widely understood and spoken among many inner-city African Americans.

There are many phonological and syntactical differences between African American Vernacular English and Standard American English (Rickford, 1999). Some of those identified by Johnson and Simons (1974) are presented in Table 2.4.

These characteristics of African American Vernacular English appear so consistently that they occasionally appear in the oral reading of children who superimpose their dialect

Table 2.4 Some Differences between Standard American English and African American Vernacular English

LINGUISTIC FEATURE	STANDARD AMERICAN ENGLISH	AFRICAN AMERICAN VERNACULAR ENGLISH
Initial and final sounds of /th/ (modified)	that, these	dat, dese
	both, breathe	bof, breave
Medial /v/ (modified)	seven	seben
Medial or final /r/, /l/ (deleted)	door	doe
	help	hep
Consonant clusters (deleted)	desk	des
	told	tol
Past tense marker	I talked to him.	I talk to him.
Copula (deleted)	She is tall.	She tall.
Use of verb be (habitual)	Julie reads every day.	Julie be reading.
Subject-verb agreement	We were there.	We was there.
Double negative	Henry doesn't have a football.	Henry don't have no football.
Possessive (deleted)	The girl's dress	The girl dress
Question (reversal of subject and verb)	What is that?	What that is?

Source: Based on Johnson and Simons (1974).

over the words written on the page (Johnson & Simons, 1974). Teachers must consider whether there is a negative effect on reading comprehension or only on oral reading accuracy because both are possible, even in a single reading episode by an individual child.

ADDING STANDARD AMERICAN ENGLISH.   Teachers demonstrate that they value the language of children when they accept the way the children communicate with each other and with members of their families and communities. In classrooms, however, teachers also need to help students add a second dialect of English: standard American English, a dialect that supports the children's continuing academic learning and offers access to higher education and desirable employment opportunities. The resulting bidialectical children resemble bilingual children in that they can readily switch back and forth between dialects according to the educational or social situation in which they find themselves. Part of the process of being bidialectical is knowing when and where to use each dialect.

In schools where an ESL program is already in place for English language learners, many ESL activities will be of value for children whose home and community language environment is African American Vernacular English. Teachers can use many intermediate and advanced ESL instructional strategies to add standard American English to the children's repertoire. The children will not require instruction at the basic stages of the natural approach for English language learners (described in Chapter 15), but participation in activities at the third stage of the natural approach will be helpful because they focus on communication, not on grammar. In addition, the activities described for "sheltered English" in Chapter 15 will support and enhance the children's development of background knowledge and vocabulary needed for effective reading comprehension. In schools where such a program is not in place because there are no English language learners, an oral language development program should be provided to help children acquire standard American English in much the same way that English language learners acquire English. This is not an ESL program, but rather a program of oral language development.

Rickford and Rickford (1995) suggest a very direct approach, beginning with an agreement among students that standard American English is appropriate for classroom interaction and writing. With that understanding, teachers should provide focused activities based on language needs that children demonstrate. Delpit (1990) suggests that these include dialect contrast activities in which students and teachers agree that learning standard American English is a goal; this would probably take place in the upper elementary grades and beyond. These dialect contrasts can be incorporated into dialogue journals, class logs, and student portfolios.

LITERACY ISSUES FOR AFRICAN AMERICAN CHILDREN. The issue of mother tongue instruction has important implications for children who speak African American Vernacular English. If learning to read in Spanish while learning to speak English is the most effective program for Spanish-speaking children, then it could follow that speakers of African American Vernacular English should learn to read from materials written in that dialect while they are acquiring standard American English as a second dialect (Simpkins, Holt, & Simpkins, 1974). Indeed, some educators have advocated for this approach. There are, however, some significant barriers:

- There is not broad acceptance in the African American community for the use of African American Vernacular English as a language of instruction.
- Although some reading instructional materials have been written in African American Vernacular English through the years, they have not been broadly or systematically used.
- Limited research evidence at present supports the use of reading materials written in African American Vernacular English (Simpkins et al., 1974).
- There is a sense among some African Americans and others that the use of African American Vernacular English might be a tool for minimizing opportunities for success among African American children (Williams, 1991).

Given the highly controversial nature of the issue, there are several ways in which teachers can make effective and positive use of the presence of African American Vernacular English—and other dialects of English—in American classrooms:

- Value and acknowledge positively the communication efforts of children who use African American Vernacular English in the classroom.
- Avoid correcting pronunciation and syntactical structures from African American Vernacular English and other dialects of English used by children in their ordinary classroom discourse; such attempts betray a negative valuing of the way the children speak and, by implication, of the children themselves and of their family members and communities.
- Demonstrate valuing of the dialect by accepting it in the dictations of children in key vocabulary and language experience approach activities.
- In addition to using children's literature in which dialogue is in standard American English for read-aloud activities, incorporate children's literature that includes dialogue in African American Vernacular English and other dialects spoken by children in the classroom (Brooks, 2005).
- In activities that are designed to help children acquire standard American English, avoid references to the standard dialect as the "correct" or "better" way to speak.
- Use storytelling (Sanacore, 2004) and traditional cultural literary structures of the African American community, such as the praise song and the praise poem (Johnson-Coleman, 2001), and trickster tales, which are also a part of the Native American oral tradition. An Internet search at www.google.com will yield dozens of praise song, praise poem, and trickster tale resources.

- As an important part of the literacy program for African American children, include Afrocentric children's literature that reflects the culture and linguistic traditions of children who speak African American Vernacular English (Brooks, 2006; Sanacore, 2004).

- Ensure that phonological, morphological, lexical, and syntactical features of African American Vernacular English and other dialects of English are not used to penalize children in assessment activities, especially those that are not related to the purpose of the assessment (see Chapter 11).

Phonics and Phonological Awareness

Why do teachers need to take care that pronunciation differences among children are not penalized in assessment activities?

Delpit (1991, 2008) offers suggestions for teachers to consider in educating children of color who are too often failed by our schools. She recommends that teachers do the following:

- Teach these children more, not less.

- Provide critical thinking experiences for them (also Sanacore, 2004).

- Challenge the racist view some individuals hold that these children are incompetent.

- Recognize and build on the children's strengths.

- Use metaphors, analogies, and experiences that are familiar to the children to connect them to school knowledge.

- Ensure that the children feel cared for, as in a family (also Sanacore, 2004).

- Identify the children's needs and meet them with a variety of strategies.

- Honor and respect the culture the children bring to school (also Ladson-Billings, 2009).

- Connect the children to their community, something that is greater than themselves (also Ladson-Billings, 2009).

Differentiating Instruction for At-Risk and Struggling Readers

Another aspect of diversity in American classrooms is a more generic category that incorporates children from all groups, that of the student who is at risk of not learning to read. Through the years since the Coleman Report (Coleman et al., 1966), many terms have been used to describe students whose school achievement is below expectation, including *at-risk*, *disadvantaged*, *low-income*, and others. The constellation of factors often associated with at-risk students includes the following: low income; inner city or rural; ethnic and/or language minority; non-English speaking; nontraditional family structure, including frequent absence of father; and high rate of school dropout.

Struggling Reader

What are some of the factors associated with children who struggle learning to read?

Many students who exhibit the characteristics just listed have satisfactory or above-average achievement in school, and some students who exhibit none of the characteristics experience failure in school. But it is fair to say that these factors are strongly associated with low school achievement.

As a result of the Coleman Report (Coleman et al., 1966), a variety of federally funded efforts were initiated to alleviate the effects of these factors on low school achievement, especially in reading. These included Head Start, Title I and Title VII of the Elementary and Secondary Education Act (ESEA), and the Reading First and Early Reading First Programs. The most recent of these federally funded programs is the five-year Striving Readers Program, which sponsored eight research projects to determine the most effective ways of lowering the numbers of struggling middle and secondary readers.

The rapidly increasing influx of English language learners and other so-called disadvantaged students in U.S. schools provides a greater challenge than ever before to teachers whose charge is to promote the equitable access of all students to high-quality instruction in reading and writing. These students have generally been placed in compensatory or remedial programs, where they are expected to learn to read and write by

Teach It!

Refer to the Teach It! appendix at the end of the book for further activities you can use to reinforce concepts discussed in this chapter.

Incorporating Authentic Children's Literature

The Language-experience approach (LEA) to reading is a powerful tool for addressing culture and beginning reading that is based on the oral language of children. The approach centers on language as the vehicle for communicating thoughts and ideas. This Teach It! explores the approach with a lesson that incorporates authentic children's literature.

The first step is for the teacher to conduct a read-aloud of a piece of children's literature that is culturally appropriate—in this case, for a group of African American first graders—and that is also ideal as a stimulus for a language experience dictation. The book in this example is Patricia McKissack's *Ma Dear's Aprons* (1997), about a little boy living with his mother in a single-parent situation. In the story, David Earl's mother has a different apron for each day of the week, and David knows which day of the week it is by observing the apron his mother is wearing. Although there are seven days and seven aprons, the teacher might decide to read only up through the first three days and aprons. During the read-aloud, share the wonderful illustrations by Floyd Cooper, asking questions about the activities of the three days and the aprons that Ma Dear wears.

Then have the children dictate their brief version of the story. They might come up with something similar to the example seen in the figure. Accept the dictations of the children as stated, regardless of any cultural affectations.

In this collaborative chart story strategy, children negotiate with each other about what they want to dictate on the chart. Some children might suggest changes that result in a dictation reflecting more Standard American English than the original version. The example shows two past tense verbs, "wash" and "iron," that were written as dictated by the children because no child suggested a change. The word "next" was pronounced as "nex"; the teacher should spell it correctly according to best practice in the language experience approach. The children should have many opportunities to read the text in a shared reading mode as the dictation is recorded and after the children's rendition of the story is completed.

> On Monday, Ma Dear put on the blue apron.
> She wash the clothes.
>
> The next day she wore a yellow apron.
> She iron the clothes on Tuesday.
>
> David likes the green apron on Wednesday.
> It had a treasure pocket.
> There was candy in it.

acquiring isolated skills through interaction with incomplete fragments of language. Rarely do they emerge successfully from these programs into the mainstream; instead, frequently they leave the programs only when they leave school—all too often as early leavers or dropouts (A. N. Crawford, 1993).

COGNITIVE, AFFECTIVE, AND PSYCHOMOTOR FACTORS. Cultural and linguistic diversity are major factors for teachers to consider in planning reading instruction for children. But cognitive, affective, and psychomotor aspects of diversity also have an effect on reading.

The increasing diversity of our classrooms seems to bring with it an increase in the numbers of children who are struggling to read. Duffy-Hester (1999) examined several model reading programs for such children and found common guiding principles that should serve teachers well in working with troubled readers. Among these guiding principles are the following:

- Reading programs should be balanced, drawing on more than a single theoretical perspective. A one-size-fits-all approach to reading instruction inevitably seems to miss meeting the needs of some children. A balanced program touches on all of the learning modalities that diverse groups of children bring to the classroom.

- There should be a well-supported role for every element in a balanced reading program. Several currently popular direct instruction reading programs, for example, make heavy use of decodable text, fragments of unconnected text in which the students are to practice word recognition elements they have been studying. Yet little research supports the use of such text, whereas abundant research supports the use of connected text, especially in the promotion of reading comprehension (Allington, 1997).

- Word recognition, comprehension, and vocabulary development should be taught in the context of authentic reading and writing activities, not in isolation.

- Teacher read-aloud activities serve to build background knowledge and vocabulary, preparing children to understand their own reading of the text later.

Inclusion for students with Individual Education Plans (IEPs) is one strategy for addressing the needs of at-risk students. (Bill Aron/PhotoEdit)

- Authentic assessment provides valuable information that teachers can use to inform their instruction. Some assessment does not provide this type of information and takes up valuable time that children could use to read and write. We are reminded of a traditional dictum about assessment: "You don't fatten a pig by weighing it."

- Teachers should use their professional preparation to make instructional decisions about reading programs they use.

- Staff development activities should provide time for reflection and opportunities to share experiences about best practices.

- The learner-centered goals and strategies that are most effective for troubled readers will serve other children well, too.

Other factors can affect the plight of troubled readers. Allington (2001) offers several research-based accommodations that relate to the organization of the school. Class size is an important factor, with research demonstrating that achievement is higher when classes are smaller, especially with children from low-income families (Achilles, 1999). Allington recommends a class size of twenty. Access to appropriate instructional materials is also important. In agreement with Duffy-Hester, he feels that programs should be designed to fit children; we should not force children to fit into programs. He recommends that no more than 20 to 30 percent of instructional time be devoted to single-source materials, that is, materials that all children in the classroom use in common. A third factor is that of honoring instructional time. No interruptions of the period for teaching reading should occur, not even public address announcements from the principal's office.

Allington then turns his attention to the question of access to intensive, expert instruction. He suggests that one-on-one tutoring is the most intensive type of instruction, but that real small-group instruction (four to seven students) is much more effective than traditional large-group or whole-class instruction. He further observes that pullout remedial reading programs, such as those underwritten by federal funds, frequently offer instruction in periods that are too short, but whose course is extended over too long a time span. He recommends offering a semester of very frequent and intensive support instead of a year of less intensive support. Finally, Allington suggests expanding instruction time for troubled readers. This can be accomplished by adding a second daily lesson, providing extended-day reading instruction through after-school programs, and offering summer school reading support to minimize summer reading loss.

★ Readers Who Are Gifted

SIOP®
Sheltered
Instruction
Observation
Protocol®

Gifted children are usually not an instructional challenge for classroom teachers. Many have learned to read at home as a result of being read to, and most others very quickly learn to read in kindergarten or the first grade. But teachers often make four erroneous assumptions about gifted children:

- That gifted children don't have reading problems.

    The gifted child who is reading on grade level may have a reading problem that should be diagnosed and addressed. Ordinarily, gifted children will be reading above grade level, often several grades above their age-expected level. Teachers should identify the levels at which they need instruction and at which they can read independently without great effort, and then provide appropriate books at those levels.

- That all children will benefit from the same reading program.

    Children who already read, often far above grade level, will be bored if required to proceed laboriously through instructional content designed for children who are on grade level, or even below. Teachers should challenge such children, usually by differentiating the reading program for them and certainly by providing alternative activities when other children are learning something mastered long ago by children who are gifted or advanced in their reading abilities. This includes helping them find books of interest. Gifted children will often persevere even with difficult materials if they are of great interest.

- That gifted children have already mastered all of the basic skills.

    The fragmentation of basic skills is not unusual among gifted children. They can be integrated into reading groups that are addressing identified areas of weakness at the time an appropriate lesson or lessons are offered, even though those groups are usually working below the levels of these otherwise more capable students.

- That all gifted children speak English well.

    We should search for gifted children among English language learners and other marginalized groups of children as diligently as we search among advantaged children. Gifted English language learners and children who speak African American Vernacular English will benefit greatly from language-rich strategies such as those found in the Sheltered Instruction Observation Protocol (SIOP) (Echevarria, Vogt, & Short, 2004).

INCLUSION IN GENERAL EDUCATION CLASSROOMS. Federal law calls for inclusion for many children identified for special education services; many are now placed in general education classrooms, although sometimes for only part of the school day. They are educated, to the maximum extent possible, in the same setting as their classmates without disabilities. This means that general education classroom teachers must address the needs of some children who have intellectual disabilities, or are physically disabled, visually or hearing impaired, emotionally disturbed, or from other special needs categories.

Under provisions of the law, students are identified as requiring assessment if they have intellectual disabilities; a hearing impairment, including deafness; a speech or language impairment; a visual impairment, including blindness; a serious emotional disturbance; an orthopedic impairment; autism; traumatic brain injury; a specific learning disability; deaf-blindness; or multiple disabilities. These children's needs must be assessed, and an Individual Education Plan (IEP) must be developed for each student (Individuals with Disabilities Education Act, 1997). The plan must include the following elements:

- Current levels of educational performance
- Annual goals and short-term objectives
- Need for special education and related services
- Explanation if the child cannot be mainstreamed in the general education classroom
- Description and schedule of special education services provided
- Description of transition services provided
- Assessment of student progress, including needed accommodations

Support services from experienced special education teachers are often provided to the general education classroom teacher who is working with mainstreamed children, but they are often not sufficient or timely.

The Individuals with Disabilities Education Improvement Act of 2004 (IDEA) is carefully aligned with provisions of NCLB (NEA, 2004). Special education teachers are required to be "highly qualified"; students with disabilities are required to be assessed annually in NCLB-required assessments, with some accommodations; and students must meet the same state standards as all other students, including English language learners, with some exceptions for students with severe cognitive disability. Needless to say, these provisions in the law are the subject of much discussion in all school districts as they attempt to meet these new requirements.

There is also great concern about the overrepresentation of children from linguistic and ethnic minorities in special education classes (Hill, Carjuzaa, Aramburo, & Baca, 1993). Historically, children were often assigned to special education classes on the basis of supposed language disorders and/or intellectual disabilities that might be nothing more than limited English proficiency. Under provisions of *Diana v. State Board of Education of California* (1970) and subsequent special education legislation, such as P.L. 94-142, this is no longer permitted. Damico (1991) suggests that care be taken to ensure that referral to special education is not based on the following:

- Other factors that might explain the child's learning and language difficulties, including lack of opportunity to learn, cultural dissonance, and stressful life events, for example, among refugee children
- Language difficulties that the student has at school, but not at home or in the community
- Ordinary needs of children to acquire English as a second language or the standard American English dialect
- Cross-cultural interference
- Bias in the assessment process, including data analysis that does not take into account the child's culture, language, and life experiences

Many strategies can be used very effectively in teaching children with these needs. According to Gersten and Baker (2000), teachers should do the following:

- Build children's vocabulary and use it as a curricular anchor.
- Use visual representations to reinforce major concepts and vocabulary.
- Use the children's mother tongue as a support system.
- Adapt cognitive and language demands of instruction to the children by using sheltered English strategies. what are these?

It is not only the physical needs of these students that should be addressed in inclusion efforts, but also the content of the curriculum. If students of color or girls need to see themselves in the literature they read, then so should students with disabilities. According to Landrum (2001), this benefits not only those students, but also students without disabilities, who need to learn about and accept differences. Landrum has developed a set of criteria for the evaluation of novels that feature characters with disabilities. Among her criteria are the following:

- *Plot:* Story events are realistic, not contrived; disabled characters are active participants.
- *Character development:* Disabled characters are presented as strong and independent, not passive and dependent; the focus is on what they can do, not on what they cannot do.
- *Tone:* The text avoids using such terms as *retarded, handicapped,* and *crippled.*

RESPONSE TO INTERVENTION (RTI). RTI refers to a recent change in special education law, the Individuals With Disabilities Act (IDEA), that names reading teachers as participants in special education because more than 80 percent of identified students have difficulties with literacy (Mesmer & Mesmer, 2008/2009). RTI is a process that permits an assessment of whether a scientific, research-based intervention results in an improvement in an identified child's academic performance. This assumes that a continuing deficiency is not related to a visual, hearing, or motor disability, intellectual disability, emotional disturbance, cultural factors, economic disadvantage, or limited English proficiency.

K–3 students are screened in accordance with Reading First literacy screening instruments and procedures to determine if they are at risk of not meeting prescribed benchmarks. If students do not meet benchmarks after scientifically valid interventions are applied, the RTI models provide for interventions in small groups to provide additional assistance. The children's progress is monitored using measures that are brief, but targeted at skills the children need to attain. If difficulties continue, individualized interventions are provided. If these are not effective, then each child's case is reviewed by a team of professionals to determine if he or she is eligible for special education. According to Mesmer and Mesmer (2008/2009), the RTI process is a useful alternative to a discrepancy model.

Allington and Walmsley (1995, 2007) offer important principles that serve to strengthen programs of intervention for such struggling readers:

- All staff, classroom teachers, special education teachers, and specialists are responsible for the education of all students, with emphasis on the classroom teacher.
- All children should be provided with the same literacy experiences, materials, and expectations. Poor readers are often placed in programs that limit access to literacy because their primary focus is on low-level skill development, oral reading, and word recognition—a fragmented program.
- All children should be educated with their peers, an approach characterized by inclusion, not segregation into special classes.
- The literacy curriculum for identified students and struggling readers should contain all of the elements that successful readers encounter in their lessons, including silent reading, reading full-length material, and reading for a variety of purposes, including pleasure. Joint planning between general education classroom teachers and those who provide instructional support outside the general education classroom is needed.
- Expert teachers should provide high-quality instruction. These are usually general education classroom teachers with excellent preparation for teaching reading and writing.
- Instructional support programs for struggling readers should function as integrated wholes, rather than as a series of separately funded programs that address different issues: a single, unified instructional support program that involves all of the players in meeting children's literacy needs in an integration of remedial and special education services.

Allington (2008) adds other important elements:

- Levels of texts used must be matched to readers' reading levels.
- Reading activity must be dramatically expanded—that is, actual reading, rather than studying about reading.
- Interventions must be coordinated with the classroom curriculum.
- The focus of instruction is on meaning and metacognition.
- Expert teachers do not include paraprofessionals using workbook materials and low-level ditto sheets, a common intervention for struggling readers.

California has taken steps that reflect some of Allington's concerns about RTI. The California State Department of Education (2009) has renamed the process as Response to Instruction and Intervention Squared (RTI^2). This reflects the alignment of their curriculum, instruction, and assessment into a system that provides periodic data about student progress in core subjects. It is designed to provide high-quality instruction and to ensure early intervention for students who are struggling. Schools using RTI^2 anticipate the need for extra and early support for some students.

READERS WHO ARE BOYS. Much attention has been given to the roles of girls in literature for children in recent years—and with good effect. Whereas stories in basal readers and current literature anthologies tended to focus on boys in the most active roles in past years, there is now balance in the stories that the children read, not to mention representation of major cultural and linguistic groups as well. You might wonder why boys would be listed as a category of diversity among readers, but boys continue to have problems in reading that are out of proportion to their numbers in the population. Why do boys make up an almost overwhelming proportion of troubled readers? Among the many factors associated with this finding are the greater frequency of left dominance (left-handedness); lack of physical and emotional maturity compared to girls; greater frequency of attention deficit disorder; different cultural expectations for boys, including more physical activity and action; fewer positive reading models for boys; interest levels of books for boys; and female-dominated environment in schools, with teachers also favoring realistic fiction and character-related stories.

Teachers can take steps to ensure that boys do not continue to be overrepresented among the ranks of troubled readers:

- Provide more time in the initial stages of reading instruction for immature boys, especially those who exhibit signs of left dominance.
- Provide positive role models for boys: men and older boys who read.
- Provide books of interest to boys, such as the highly irreverent *Captain Underpants* series (Pilkey, 2000) and nonfiction informational books about nature, history, biography, and sports.
- Provide magazines and newspapers that have more real-world interest and shorter texts.
- Permit more physical movement, for example, letting the children sprawl out on the floor when reading.
- Provide structured opportunities for children to discuss the text they are reading and writing about (Young & Brozo, 2001).
- Recognize the importance of archetypes of masculinity in picture books and story books for boys (Zambo, 2007).

Instructional Conversations

Finding the Books and Materials They Want to Read

Diversity is important with respect not only to the learning characteristics of all students, but also to their need for appropriate texts to read and from which to learn to read.

The Print Environment of Students at Home

As might be expected, the print environment of the home and community is closely related to the factors of diversity described in this chapter. The newspapers, magazines, books, calendars, checkbooks, notes on the refrigerator door, website pages on the computer screen, and instructional manuals found in most middle-class homes may be absent from or less frequently encountered in the homes of children from low-income families. There might not be a tradition of reading and writing in the family, or perhaps a Bible or other religious book is the only representation of print in the home.

In a study they conducted, Halle, Kurtz-Costes, and Mahoney (1997) found that access to print was an important factor related to the reading achievement of African American children. In an international study of the relationships among reading achievement, home literacy environment, and school and public library availability of reading material in several countries, Elley (1992, 1996) reported that access to print was the most powerful factor associated with reading achievement, including the size of the school library. He found that frequent silent reading was the next most significant variable affecting reading achievement.

Beyond the presence of text to read, the need for models who read in the home is also of great importance, especially when it is recognized that men and older boys are often less likely to read than are women and girls in the family.

Besides often being a factor in the low-income home, the absence of text also characterizes the low-income communities in which the homes are located. In a study of print resources in two low-income and two middle-income neighborhoods, Neuman and Celano (2001) surveyed the availability of reading materials for purchase, such as newspapers, magazines, and children's books; the quantity of signage; public places where reading took place, such as laundromats and bookstores; the availability of books in child care centers; and the quality of services and materials provided by school and public libraries. They found an overwhelming advantage of print resources in the middle-income neighborhoods, and they concluded that children in the low-income neighborhoods would have difficulty finding books of good quality, whereas those in the middle-income neighborhoods would have difficulty avoiding them.

In addition, the provision of a full-time or even part-time librarian is often related to the income levels of students in the schools. Neuman and Celano (2001) found that there were no trained school librarians in the low-income communities they studied, whereas the schools in the middle-income communities had well-trained and highly experienced school librarians. School libraries in the middle-income communities were also open more days and hours per week than those in the low-income communities. The same disparities were found in public libraries in the communities studied.

They concluded, as did Cunningham and Stanovich (1997), that the children who are most in need of a print-rich environment are the least likely to encounter it, resulting in a spiraling down of environmental opportunities for reading in the community, which in turn results in less motivation to read and still fewer opportunities to read. Allington (1983) adds that this situation is aggravated when these same children are enrolled in public schools in which low-level programs are provided to address their reading problems, resulting in their doing less reading of text than do children who read well. These programs involve major time commitments to studying about reading instead of time devoted to reading connected text.

Getting Books, Magazines, and Newspapers into Children's Hands

Given the diversity of children in our schools, especially children who are at risk of being troubled readers, teachers should take special pains to find books and other print materials that they will enjoy, books with characters and settings with which they can identify, books in which they can see themselves in positive roles, and materials that are of high interest and have visual appeal. A valuable resource of books and other sources of connected text that reflect cultures of diversity is found in Banks's *Teaching Strategies for Ethnic Studies* (2003). Banks categorizes many dozens of books in English for teachers and for children in the following groups: First Americans (American Indians, Native Hawaiians, and African Americans); European Americans (European ethnic groups and Jewish Americans); Hispanic Americans (Mexican Americans, Puerto Rican Americans, and Cuban Americans); and Asian Americans (Chinese Americans, Japanese Americans, Filipino Americans, and Indochinese Americans).

An abundance of books available in Spanish exist for children who want and need to read in that language (Schon, 2000, 2001, 2004; Schon & Berkin, 1996). Both children who did not have the opportunity to learn to read in their mother tongue and those who have learned to read in their mother tongue in another school or country should be provided with opportunities to read more books in that language. It improves self-concept, offers evidence that the school and teacher value that language, and provides practice in reading that builds background knowledge and skills that transfer positively to reading in English later. Teachers should also be very careful about the use of so-called bilingual books that are written in two languages, usually with English and Spanish versions on facing pages. This practice ensures that children will acquire English in terms of Spanish, that is, a very ineffective translation approach. It is better for children to read a story in Spanish from one book and then read the same story in English from another book, as elaborated in later chapters. The children can use their background knowledge from the first experience to support their comprehension and learning of English in the second book.

Gifted children require a rich variety of books and other text materials to maintain their many and changing interests. They will often tackle books at a much higher level than the level at which they are reading because of their motivation and willingness to persist. Given good guidance, they can use the Internet very productively, too. Many sites are now available that are geared to younger children's reading abilities. Teacher sites like Thinkfinity (see http://www.thinkfinity.org/home.aspx) can also help teachers locate stimulating project ideas and resources for them. This is less of a problem for children in the lower grades of a multigraded school because they will find reading resources for older children in the school library. But it can be a problem for the sixth-grade gifted child in a K–6 school. This child needs access to a middle or secondary school library or an understanding teacher who is willing to check out books at the public library.

Finding materials that are high interest and low vocabulary enough for troubled readers, especially for boys, is a perennial problem for teachers. The teacher who is always conventional might have difficulty finding books that meet both criteria. A good resource for magazines is *Magazines for Kids and Teens* (Stoll, 1997), which provides descriptions of the content and the reading and interest levels of over 200 magazines on a wide variety of topics, including some that publish students' own writing.

In addition, as noted earlier, boys will enjoy recent offerings in the immensely popular *Captain Underpants* series (Pilkey, 2000): *Captain Underpants and the Invasion of the Incredibly Naughty Cafeteria Ladies from Outer Space, Captain Underpants and the Wrath of the Wicked Wedgie Woman*, and *Captain Underpants and the Attack of the Talking Toilets*. Teachers who understand and appreciate the sense of humor of nine-year-old boys will recognize the appeal of these titles and the opportunities for stimulating those boys' creative writing instincts.

School budget problems are often a factor that affects the numbers of books, magazines, and newspapers available to children in the classroom. Some sources of text that teachers can exploit to augment those supplied by the school district are the following:

- School storage rooms, where surplus books are often hidden away
- Secondhand stores, public library book sales, yard sales, and swap meets, where teachers can often negotiate low prices with vendors "for the children"; returning to vendors at the end of the day and offering to buy all remaining books for a bulk price is often an effective way to maximize scarce teacher resources (many teachers spend their own money on books for children)
- Child-made books that result from collaborative chart stories, language experience approach activities, and other student writing activities
- Local public libraries that are usually available for walking field trips and that permit children to request library cards so they can check out their own books

Teach It! 7

Making Individual Small Books

- Commercial book clubs, which offer children's books at quantity discounts, usually with paper covers instead of hard covers. Depending on the number of books ordered by the children, many book clubs provide additional books for the teacher's classroom library.
- Newspapers that often sponsor programs to adopt a classroom and also often provide newspapers at no cost
- Support from parent groups, service clubs, and other community sources
- Reading Is Fundamental (**RIF.org**), which provides sets of books to schools at no cost

Finally, teachers should ensure that a wide variety of text is readily available for children to take home to read. Too many resources are so protected from loss or abuse that they are never used.

Equity and Access to Computers

New Literacies

How can teachers use technology to help address the needs of children who range from the gifted to the struggling?

New Literacies

What is the effect of poverty on student access to libraries and technology?

As was noted, library resources for children from low-income neighborhoods are limited, and certainly the same is true with respect to access to computer technology. According to Becker (2000), only 22 percent of children of low socioeconomic status have a computer at home; 91 percent of high socioeconomic status children do.

Access to the Internet at school has improved dramatically during the past several years. According to the National Center for Education Statistics (1999), 95 percent of all public schools provide Internet access, including 90 percent of those where 71 percent of students are eligible for free or reduced-price school lunch, a frequently used measure of a school's socioeconomic status.

Even as the gap in providing access to computer technology and Internet access to all students is closing, teachers should consider the value of this access in terms of instruction in reading and writing. According to Krashen (1997), computer technology and the Internet might not have a great deal to offer in teaching children to read. He found no evidence that computer-based reading management programs such as Accelerated Reader or the IBM Writing to Read program provide any benefits to children. He concluded that funds should instead be directed to trade books for free voluntary reading, as time invested in this activity is very effective in increasing reading achievement. Becker (2000) reported that, in elementary grades from 4 to 8, most teachers who used computers in the classroom used them for skill practice games, for word processing, and to access CD-ROMs. He also reported that computers were used slightly more frequently in low socioeconomic status schools than in high socioeconomic status schools, but that their use in low socioeconomic status schools involved more traditional drill and practice activities, whereas their use in high socioeconomic status schools reflected teaching strategies that are more constructivist and innovative.

Children who surf the Net are reading, usually with high motivation. Children without access to the Internet are probably not reading something else instead of surfing the Net, the result being less practice in reading for those children, another example of the Matthew effect, according to which the rich get richer, and the poor get poorer (Stanovich, 1986). This could be a motivation to ensure that all students have access to computers with focused purposes so that even the least affluent have opportunities to sample the wealth of information on the Net.

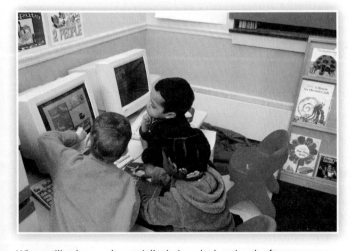

When utilized properly, specially designed educational software or access to the Internet can offer a variety of opportunities for working with all children, regardless of their needs. (Nancy Sheehan Photography)

As noted earlier, boys are much more likely to experience difficulties in learning to read than girls are. A helpful source of ideas for boys, and for other identifiable groups of children, is the List category on the Amazon website (www.amazon.com), which recently included a Gross-Out Books for Boys list. Among the irreverent books listed there were *Dragon's Fat Cat* (Dragon Tales); *Pigs Aplenty, Pigs Galore!*; *Dogzilla*; *Kat Kong*; *Captain Underpants* Boxed Set (Four Books and a Whoopie Cushion); and *Dog Breath: The Horrible Trouble with Hally Tosis*.

Teachers need to know the community of which they are a part and respect the values parents hold. Always check with other teachers and the school librarian, when there is one, before recommending any books. The lists of books recommended by the International Reading Association, the National Council of Teachers of English, and the American Library Association are good places to start. Give a book you are unsure of to some parents to review as a way of gauging their feelings. Usually, when people read the books that might be in question, the concerns dissipate.

Implications of Current Assessment Practices for Diverse Learners

In recent years, calls for increased accountability of schools for academic achievement have resulted in a number of reforms, some with positive outcomes and some with negative ones.

Tests and Standards

In almost all states, standards for reading achievement have been established, usually according to expectations for grade level. Some states have also established standards for English-language proficiency. The establishment of standards can be a positive step in that teachers, school administrators, and the school board are provided with a clear vision of what children should accomplish. Schools are held accountable for meeting children's needs. Tests are developed and adopted to assess progress in achieving established standards. But some states even adopt the dubious practice of financially rewarding schools and districts that are successful and penalizing those that are not.

Because of the priority placed on standards and the assessments derived from them, teachers need to be familiar with the standards in their states and know how their districts have designed the instructional program to reflect those standards and benchmarks. Teachers also need to review the state assessment tests and become familiar with what will be asked of students when they have to take these tests. The more teachers can help students feel comfortable with the language used in the state programs and the format of testing, the less they have to focus on specific lessons targeted to outcomes or do practice testing. It is helpful to think through your own ideas about and experiences with state or professional standards and assessments because parents will also probably involve you in conversations about them. Both positive and negative outcomes are associated with the standards and assessment movement. Positive outcomes of such practices include a clear focus on educational goals; staff development based on those goals; high motivation to improve; and the provision of data to support changes in curriculum, staff development, instructional materials, and funding. Negative outcomes include extraordinary pressure to raise test scores at all costs, dishonesty in testing programs in some areas, instruction focused on fragments of language instead of on reading connected text, and narrowing and dilution of the curriculum to teach only what is tested.

Caution About Teaching to the Test

McPhail (2005) makes a very compelling recommendation about teaching African American children to read and write. He expresses his concern about teaching low-level, basic skills and in that way placing what he calls a ceiling on their learning, however unintended. He sees great danger in the current practice of aligning the curriculum directly to the test and then teaching to the test.

Effects of a Diluted Curriculum

With respect to the last outcome, a particular concern relates to the development of students' vocabulary. When areas of the curriculum are eliminated because they are viewed as less important, students are deprived of the rich vocabulary associated with these areas. In this way, the more school-dependent students are deprived of a key tool in their own learning: vocabulary knowledge. Their knowledge of vocabulary is limited by the elimination of areas of the curriculum that are sometimes viewed as less important than reading and mathematics, and sometimes even as frills.

There are two important aspects of vocabulary development for English language learners and speakers of African American Vernacular English. One is the richness—or, often, the lack of richness—of the language that surrounds them. Students become familiar with the meanings of words when those meanings are highly contextualized, not when they are studied as isolated vocabulary words. It follows, then, that a richer language environment should result in increased exposure to contextualized vocabulary and therefore to understanding of their meanings. Teachers are often obligated to cut back or even eliminate instruction for these students, however, in the very areas of the curriculum where new vocabulary words will be offered in the most highly contextualized ways, such as science, social studies, art, music, physical education, and health. Teachers must ensure that these areas of the curriculum are present for at-risk students and presented in such a way that contextualized exposure to a rich vocabulary is promoted, including such strategies as cooperative learning, problem solving, and critical thinking.

In a related vein, Nagy, Anderson, and Herman (1987) found that a major factor in vocabulary development by third-, fifth-, and seventh-grade students was the sheer volume of reading that students did and the amount of vocabulary they were exposed to, even though the proportion of words learned was low. Stanovich (1986) elaborates this idea further in his treatment of individualized differences and the Matthew effect, the idea that those who read more (the rich) read better (get richer). Smith (1986) has added that good readers read, and poor readers take tests and do drill sheets.

For Review

This chapter considered the social and cultural contexts of literacy for children in grades K–8. Different social and cultural groups have views of literacy that reflect their own realities and needs, which might vary from the mainstream view. It is important to acknowledge the validity of the various views of literacy as instruction is planned for children from these social and cultural groups.

Teachers can often create their own cultures of literacy within their classrooms by the way they value those points of view and by their organization of the physical environment of the classroom and selection of instructional materials and trade books for their students. A shared literacy environment creates the most effective tone for extending literacy to all.

To involve parents and extended families in our shared literacy community, teachers must begin early in the school year with communications that welcome families to the classroom and request their support for classroom efforts. Teachers should also become a part of the professional community through induction activities, professional meetings, and involvement in major professional organizations, such as the International Reading Association and the National Council of Teachers of English.

Because of the diversity that is found in U.S. schools today, it is the rare classroom in which the children all come from a single cultural, ethnic, or linguistic group. A typical classroom in the coming years will have children from several cultures and ethnic groups; most will have some children who speak another language at home, usually Spanish. Most classrooms will have mainstreamed children with special needs for at least part of the school day. This diversity can be viewed as a problem, but a more healthy viewpoint is to appreciate the richness of the diversity and use it as an asset in teaching.

This diversity also provides many challenges for teachers. They must be aware of cultural differences far beyond holidays and foods. Aspects of nonverbal communication are particularly important in determining how teachers relate to their students and their families. Teachers will encounter children who speak another language or dialect of English at home and who might not be able to communicate effectively in standard American English in the classroom; recent demographic trends indicate that teachers who have not yet encountered these children in their classrooms will find them there soon.

It is clear that many children struggle to learn to read in our classrooms. Some of them are at risk of failure because of environmental factors, such as living in low-income, inner-city or rural areas and coming from ethnic or linguistic minority groups. It is sometimes tempting to address the needs of these children with one-size-fits-all approaches to literacy instruction, but their strengths and needs vary greatly, and so should the programs that are provided to teach them to read and write. Some children struggle with reading because of cognitive, affective, and psychomotor factors. Teachers must be sensitive to children with needs for accommodations that are new to them and also must be flexible to the need to work closely with colleagues from special education so that these children can have a school experience that is as similar to that of most students as possible.

In addition, it is necessary to find print materials that are interesting and culturally appropriate for children to read. Children need to see themselves in what they read. They need large numbers of books and other sources of text at many levels. This includes access to computer technology resources and the Internet for the children from many groups who have very limited access to technology.

Finally, assessment is important for planning instruction, selecting instructional materials, and making adjustments in our instruction when needed. But it is also necessary to be cautious about letting assessment become the tail that wags the dog. Assessment should emerge from the curriculum, which should in turn emerge from the needs of students and the standards established by state and local governing authorities.

For Your Journal

1. Now that you have read Chapter 2, return to the Anticipation Guide at the beginning of the chapter. What differences are there in how you would answer the open-ended questions now?

2. The true-false questions in the Anticipation Guide addressed many myths about the demographics of children in our schools and about children's learning. After you read and found answers to the questions, which one(s) surprised you the most? Why?

Taking It to the World

Now that you have considered the implications of classroom diversity, think about your classmates when you were in the third grade. In terms of diversity, how does the student population of the classroom to which you are assigned now compare to that of your own third-grade classroom? Make a list of positive outcomes that the children of today exhibit as a result of the increased classroom diversity they experience.

New Literacies Connections

1. Literacy Access Online offers connections to book and electronic initiatives for literacy access, including assistive devices and low-vision aides for the impaired. Visit their website at http://chd.gse.gmu.edu/ LiteracyAccess/prototype/resources/ and explore at least two of the listed resources. What is the primary focus of each site, and how might each help you as a teacher?

2. Visit the "Guys Read" website (www.guysread.com), a website that focuses on supporting boys' reading. How does this website help to encourage guys to explore connections to feelings through reading? Identify three books recommended by other guys as appropriate for early readers.

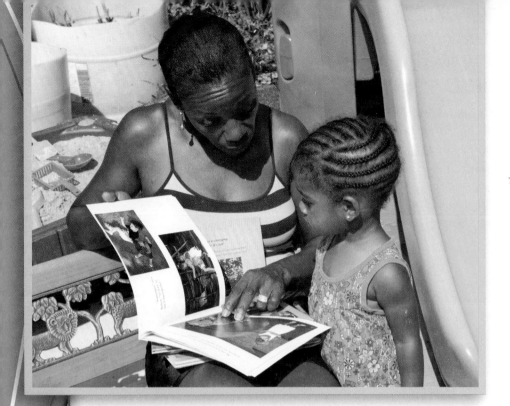

What Reading Teachers Need to Know About Language

Anticipation Guide

The following statements will help you begin thinking about the topics covered in this chapter. Answer *true* or *false* in response to each statement. As you read and learn more about the topics mentioned in the statements, think back on your answers. See what interests you and prompts your curiosity toward more understanding.

_____ 1. You study French to learn about the French language and Spanish to learn about the Spanish language. The study of languages in general is known as linguistics.

_____ 2. Chinese has an ideographic writing system; written characters relate to ideas. English has a syllabic writing system; written characters relate to spoken syllables. And Japanese has an alphabetic writing system; alphabetic letters relate to small sound units called phonemes.

_____ 3. Over the centuries, the pronunciation of English sometimes has changed more than the writing system. Many English words are spelled the way they used to be pronounced.

_____ 4. Morphemes can only be purchased with a prescription from licensed pharmacies.

_____ 5. Rimes and phonogram patterns are the same thing.

_____ 6. The words *elect* and *college* are related to each other. Both come from a Latin word meaning "to choose."

_____ 7. Vocabulary words face two ways: they are a record of what you have learned in the past, and they enable you to learn more in the future.

_____ 8. Syntax, also called grammar, cannot be learned without direct instruction.

_____ 9. We usually think of grammar at the level of sentences, but longer texts like stories have grammar, too.

_____ 10. There is not much difference in the amount of language parents use with children in families from different socioeconomic groups.

What Reading Teachers Need to Know About Language

The Sounds of Language
p. 71

How English Spelling Represents Sounds
p. 76

Vocabulary: Words and Their Meanings
p. 88

Social Variations in Language Use
p. 93

Teachers Use Linguistics

Janet Reardon feels lucky to have been assigned to this second-grade class for her observation period. She will be student teaching next fall, and she has filled a notebook with ideas she can use. Her cooperating teacher is Alan Parsons. It is exciting to watch him interact with children, and he is also generous with his time and advice, especially when Janet asks him about topics she has been studying at the university in her literacy class.

Last Friday she asked him how he assessed phonemic awareness.

"Yes, I do use the Yopp-Singer phonemic awareness test from time to time. You should try it out yourself. But the truth is, I can tell a lot about how a child is coming along in phonemic awareness by looking at her invented spelling."

"How?"

"For instance, when a child strings a lot of letters in a line without any obvious connection to sounds, I don't expect the child to have a concept of word or much in the way of phonemic awareness. But if a child writes down a few letters for a word—what is called 'early phonemic' spelling—you can be pretty sure that she has started to be aware of phonemes."

"How do you know? What does the spelling tell you?"

"Well, for a kid to invent spellings, she has to be able to break a word down into its phonemes, and then match each one of those phonemes with a letter. But there's more."

"There always is."

"You'll get used to it. When she uses 'letter name spelling,' when she writes, we know she's further along in phonemic segmentation. What's more, you can get an idea of what she knows about letter-to-sound correspondences from her early spelling. Look at this spelling: *HAK MIK*."

"Hack Mick"?

"No. 'Check mark.' That's what Andrea said when she read it back to me. She's pretty far along in phonemic segmentation. See? She spelled the beginning consonant sound, the vowel, and the final consonant on both words. But you can see from the spelling that she doesn't have a clue about digraph consonants yet—see that *H* for the /*ch*/ sound? So her invented spelling is a good indication not only of her phonemic segmentation, but also of what she knows about letter-to-sound correspondences."

"Amazing."

"Totally. Go back and tell your classmates to pay attention to linguistics. Especially to phonology."

"What's that?"

"That's for you to find out. Have a great weekend."

"Reading is talk written down," teachers say, and in many ways the statement is true. In order to read, children and young people need to know the language that print represents. And in order to teach reading well, you need to understand children's talk—children's language. The study of language, as distinct from the study of any particular language such as Japanese or Spanish, is known as *linguistics*. In this chapter we don't need to cover the field of linguistics to any great depth; we will just pay attention to those parts of language that matter the most in learning to read. The key ways that reading and writing depend on oral language are:

- **Sounds of language**, how they are made and how they relate to each other
- **The spelling system**, how the spoken language is represented in print
- **Vocabulary**, the ways that words convey meaning
- **Morphology or word structure**, the ways words are made
- **Syntax**, the grammar of sentences
- **Story structure**, the way texts are constructed
- **Pragmatics**, the way language is used, and
- **Learning processes**—the ways language is acquired by children.

Figure 3.1
Chinese Ideographs.

| 愛 | 財 | 德 | 吉 | 美 |
| Love | Wealth | Virtue | Lucky | Beautiful |

The Sounds of Language

You often hear reading experts talk about "letter-to-sound relationships," but do you think about what those sounds are? If the language is Chinese, the "sounds" are not sounds at all, but ideas. The same written character is rendered into different words, depending on the dialect of Chinese that one speaks. Hence, the Chinese writing system is called *ideographic* ("ideas written down"). (See Figure 3.1.)

If the language we spoke were Japanese, the written characters would mostly represent spoken syllables. Each character that represented a consonant would represent a vowel, too. Each consonant and vowel combination (such as *ka, ki, ke, ko,* and *ku*) gets a different graphic character. Hence, the Japanese writing system is *syllabic* (although Japanese does use some ideographic characters, called *kanji,* for content words). (See Figure 3.2.)

The English language represents sounds at a level that is one step finer than syllables. Our alphabet letters represent *phonemes,* small pieces of vowel or consonant sounds. For example, each of the three sounds that make up the word *cat:* /k/, /æ/, and /t/ is a phoneme.

If English used ideographs instead of letters of the alphabet, we would need to learn *a half million* characters for all the words in the *Oxford English Dictionary*. If English used a syllabary instead of an alphabet, we would still need to learn around 2,700 characters to represent all of our syllables (Barker, 2006). Since the English language uses an alphabet, we can get by with 26 characters—or 52, if you count upper case and lower case letters. That's a big advantage in simplicity. But there is a price to pay.

Matching a graphic image with an idea is easily done. Small children recognize the logos of their favorite soft drinks and fast foods, and soon after learn the Arabic numerals. Matching characters with syllables is harder, but still not very difficult. Middle school students who struggle to read words spelled alphabetically can be fairly easily taught to read words transcribed by their syllables (Gleitman & Rozin, 1973). But reading alphabetic writing—matching a string of characters with their corresponding speech sounds at the level of phonemes—is the most challenging of all. Many children struggle to break out phonemes in spoken words, and this difficulty causes problems in reading written words (Snow et al., 1998). That's why the economy of having the few graphic symbols in an alphabetic writing system comes at the price of having to focus on smaller bits of sound in language. Teachers can help children cope with those difficulties if they become aware of the details of the English spelling system.

Figure 3.2
Japanese Hiragana, Syllabic Characters.

sa	shi	su	se	so
さ	し	す	せ	そ
ta	chi	tsu	te	to
た	ち	つ	て	と
na	ni	nu	ne	no
な	に	ぬ	ね	の

Phonology: The Sounds of English

Since English is an *alphabetic language*, words are written by making matches between small speech sounds or *phonemes* and alphabet letters. Let's take a closer look at how we make the two kinds of phonemes: vowels and consonants.

Phonics and Phonological Awareness

How do we make the two kinds of phonemes: vowels and consonants?

HOW ENGLISH VOWELS ARE MADE.   Vowel sounds are produced when you vibrate your vocal cords and breathe across them. But what makes the difference between one vowel sound and another? That is, what are you doing when you produce the sound of "*EEEE*" as opposed to "*AHHH*"? Say those two sounds aloud, one at a time, and pay attention to what happens inside your mouth. Did you see? The answer is in how and where you hold your tongue in your mouth while you breathe past your vibrating vocal cords. The sound of "*EEEE*" is made with the tongue high in the front of the mouth, while the sound of "*AHHH*" is made with the tongue low in the back of the mouth. But there is more.

Vowels: Long and Short, or Tense and Lax?   Teachers use the terms "long" and "short" to mean the sounds represented by the letter *I* in *kite* (a "long" vowel sound) and the letter *I* in *kit* (a "short" vowel sound). But it doesn't take you any longer to say *kite* than it does to say *kit*. So "long" and "short" doesn't capture the difference between the two kinds of vowel sounds.

What does? Say *feet* and *fit* aloud, and stretch out the vowels as you pronounce them. Notice what happens in your mouth when you say each. Poke your finger firmly into the muscle under your jaw and say them again. This time you should feel your tongue muscle tense up when you say the vowel in *feet* and relax when you say the vowel in *fit*. Because of the tensing and relaxing of the tongue muscle when you make the sound of *ee* and *ih*, linguists call these vowels tense for the "long" vowel sound and lax for the "short" vowel sound.

The sounds of the vowels in *feet* and *fit* might seem completely unrelated, but that wasn't always true. During the fourteenth century, the time when Geoffrey Chaucer wrote *The Canterbury Tales*, the vowel sounds of *ee* and *ih* were spelled with the same letter. So were the vowel sounds *ay* and *eh* as in *gate* and *get*.

After Chaucer's time, the way people pronounced English words changed, so the sound that used to be pronounced *ay* changed its pronunciation to *ee*, but the sound that was pronounced *eh* stayed the same. Also, the sound that used to be pronounced *ee* was now pronounced *iy* (as in *my*), but the sound that was pronounced *ih* stayed the same. Dictionary writers could have changed the spellings to match the changes in pronunciation, but they chose not to. So the changes in pronunciation, but not in spelling, resulted in the situation we have today. Now A, E, and I each represents a pair of sounds that do not sound much like each other, and that is because the pronunciation of the tense vowels changed but the pronunciation of the lax vowels did not—although the spellings stayed the same. The change in the pronunciation of English vowels was so important that it earned a name with capital letters: the **Great Vowel Shift**.

The results of the Great Vowel Shift cause confusion when young children try to discover how to spell vowel sounds. Children find it natural to spell the sounds of *ay* and *eh* with the same letter because they sound similar, and also to spell the sounds of *ee* and *ih* with the same letter for the same reason, so they tend to write spellings like *MI FEH ES RAD* for "My fish is red." (We will say more about this later in the discussion of invented spelling.) The spelling of English vowels is also puzzling to English Language Learners, especially to speakers of Spanish, Portuguese, French, and Italian, because in all those languages vowels are grouped the way they were in Middle English, before the Great Vowel Shift.

Diphthongs and Monopthongs.   Listen to the vowels in *so* and *soil*. *So* contains a single vowel sound and *soil* contains a double vowel sound. The technical term for a single vowel sound is a **monopthong** (a term we almost never hear) and the term for a double vowel sound is a **diphthong**. The vowel sounds in *out* and *soil* are diphthongs. And that is a term you do hear more often.

HOW ENGLISH CONSONANTS ARE MADE.   We saw above that vowels are produced when you vibrate your vocal cords while you are breathing out. Consonants are made when you interrupt the flow in some way. There are many ways to interrupt the breath flow. If you completely stop it momentarily, you produce what are called *stop consonants*, such as the sounds represented by *p, b, d, t, k,* and *g*. If you buzz the breath slightly, you produce the *fricative* consonants represented by the letters *s, z, th, f,* and *v*. If you stop the air flow and then hiss it, you get *affricate consonants*, such as the sounds represented by the letters *ch* and *j*. And if you direct the airflow out through the nose, you get *nasal consonants*, such as the sounds represented by the letters *m, n,* and *ng*.

Which consonant sounds you produce depend on two more things: where in the mouth you produce the interruption and whether the vocal cords are vibrating when you make the interruption. Let's illustrate. If you stop the airflow through your mouth with the back of the tongue raised against the top of the mouth toward the rear, you get the sound of /g/ or /k/. If your vocal cords are vibrating while you do it, you get the sound of /g/. If they are not vibrating, you get the sound of /k/. Similarly, /b/ and /p/ are made by closing the lips. /b/ is *voiced* (that is, the vocal cords vibrate the whole time it is made), and /p/ is *unvoiced* (the vocal cords don't start vibrating until about 40 thousandths of a second after you start producing the sound).

Teachers of primary grades should be aware of the ways speech sounds are made, because as children begin to experiment with spelling, you will see they listen very carefully to speech sounds and their similarities, even when they can't talk about what they are hearing. For example, young children often spell the sound represented by *TH* with the letter *V*. It helps to know that the name of the letter *V* is a "buzzed" (fricative) and voiced sound that's made in the front of the mouth, just as the sound /th/ in *then* is. (The only difference is that the sound of /v/ is made with the upper teeth on the lower lip, and the /th/ sound in *then* is made with the tongue on the fleshy ridge behind the upper front teeth.) And since children expect a single phoneme to be spelled with a single letter, *V* is a natural choice for the sound of /th/, which is spelled with two letters. (More on this later.)

Consonant Blends and Consonant Digraphs.   *Consonant blends* are two or more consonants pronounced one right after the other, like the first two letters in *slip*, the first three phonemes in *split*, or the last two phonemes in *help*. In these words each of the consonants can be heard distinctly if you pronounce the word slowly.

Consonant digraphs are single consonant sounds that are spelled with two letters. The beginning consonant sounds in *then, chip,* and *shirt* are consonant digraphs. (The word *digraph* comes from two Greek words meaning "double writing"). To repeat, the difference between blends and digraphs is that in consonant blends, each of two or more consonant phonemes can be heard distinctly, but in digraphs, the two consonant phonemes cannot be pronounced separately without distorting the words in which they occur.

Why do we have digraph consonants in English? They came about because the Roman alphabet, originally developed to represent the sounds of Latin, was borrowed to write English. But English had some sounds that did not occur in Latin, so the Roman alphabet had no letters to stand for the English sounds of /sh/, /ch/, or /th/. To signal when those sounds were meant by writers, early scribes came up with the convention of writing an *H* after certain Roman letters: *SH, CH,* and *TH*. The spelling of *WH*, though, is a strange exception. The sound represented by *WH* is really a consonant blend and not a digraph. You really do hear two consonant sounds /hw/. *HW* is the way that sound was originally spelled, until scribes in the twelfth and thirteenth centuries reversed the order of the letters, to make them look like *CH, SH,* and *TH*.

Consonants and Phonological Awareness.   When children realize that words they speak are made up of small bits of sound called *phonemes*, we say they have *phonemic awareness*. Children usually show phonemic awareness in late kindergarten and early first

The World of Reading

Bring on the Linguists!

Scholars in the field of linguistics have contributed much to our knowledge of reading and writing. For instance, Professor Catherine Snow of the Harvard Graduate School of Education has authored many important works on children's language development in home and school settings. She chaired the National Reading Council that produced the influential work, *Preventing Reading Difficulties in Young Children* (Snow et al., 1998).

Charles Read, who trained in linguistics at the Massachusetts Institute of Technology, is often credited with bringing to light the fascinating practice of invented spelling in children (Read, 1975).

But Read had a great deal of help from another linguist and educator, Carol Chomsky (1971). Carol Chomsky's husband, Noam Chomsky, is the most influential linguist of the past century, and he, too, has contributed to our thinking about children's word recognition and comprehension—especially the idea that there are processes occurring "beneath the surface" of children's understanding of written language.

Michael Halliday, a linguist from Scotland, charted his son's use of functions of language, and contributed a very useful menu of ways to help children develop their ability to communicate, and later to read.

grade (Goswami, 2000). But some children have trouble with phonological awareness even into first and second grade, and if they do, it may be hard for them to learn to read. Why is phonemic awareness challenging for children? It is probably because words really cannot be spoken so slowly that each of their phonemes can be heard distinctly.

You may think it's obvious that the phonemes exist in words, but you know that fact from indirect evidence. You know it because you can substitute a /b/ phoneme for the /k/ in <u>c</u>at and get <u>b</u>at, and you can substitute an /n/ phoneme for the /t/ in ca<u>t</u> and get ca<u>n</u>. Once you began to read, you saw that letters tended to be matched with phonemes in words such as CAT, and that reinforced the idea that phonemes can be heard separately. But young learners without that experience in reading are often challenged by the task of separating or *segmenting* phonemes in words.

Note that we are not saying children cannot hear the phonemes. Of course they can. Most English-speaking three-year-olds can correctly "show you the <u>c</u>at" and "show you the <u>b</u>at." It's the task of saying slowly the three sounds in CAT that young children find difficult.

DEVELOPMENTAL MILESTONES IN PHONOLOGICAL AWARENESS Most preschool children can't show you that they know words are made up of phonemes, but most second graders can. How does that awareness develop? Hall and Moats (1999) present the pathway taken by normally developing children in kindergarten and first grade. See "Developmental Milestones in Phonological Awareness" box on page 75.

Syllables, Onsets, and Rimes

Syllables are rhythmic pulses in words. The word *final* has two of them, *fi* and *nal*, while *awareness* has three: *a + ware + ness*. In the word *awareness*, you can see that a vowel can stand alone as a syllable, but consonants cannot (at least not in English). Some languages such as Spanish, Japanese, and Kiswahili have relatively few syllables. In Spanish, roughly 50 different syllables can be combined to make most of the words in the language. The words of the English language, though, are made up of a couple of thousand different syllables (Barker, 2006). Few teachers of English would bother to have students learn groups of syllables, as teachers of Spanish, Portuguese, and Kiswahili regularly do.

English syllables can be open or closed. An **open syllable** ends in a vowel, and a **closed syllable** ends in a consonant. All three syllables in *banana* are open syllables, and both

Teach It! 12

Phonemic Segmentation with Elkonin Boxes

Developmental Milestones in Phonological Awareness

Stages of Literacy Development	Developmental Milestones in Phonological Awareness
At the end of Kindergarten:	• At the syllable level: Most children can distinguish single-syllable words from words with two syllables when they hear them. • At the onset and rime level (*p* + *at* = *pat*; *l* + *ight* = *light*—see below): Most children can match a target word with a rhyming word. • At the phoneme level: Most children can pick out words that begin with the same sound as a target word and can tell you the odd word out—the one that does not begin with the same sound as the others.
Two months into first grade:	• Given two letters on cards, most children can combine them and pronounce the word they spell (*in, on, at, it, up*) • Given a three-phoneme word, most children can say the word that is left when the beginning consonant is deleted: *bat/at, sit/it, cup/up*.
By the end of first grade:	• Most children can pronounce two-phoneme words slowly and separate the phonemes: /t/ - /oo/; /b/ - /y/. • Given longer words, most children can leave off the first consonant and pronounce what is left: *b — utterfly*. • Given three isolated phonemes, most children can combine them to make a word: /s/ /æ/ /t/ = *sat*.

Source: After Hall and Moats (1999).

---

syllables in *problem* are closed syllables. When these words are divided at the end of a line of print, the hyphen goes after the vowel in words with open syllables like *final* (*fi-nal*) and recess (*re-cess*), and after the consonant in words like *picnic* (*pic-nic*) and *knapsack* (*knap-sack*). The vowel in an open syllable often has its "long" sound, and the vowel in a closed syllable usually has its "short" sound. Compare *cable* and *cabin*; *meter* and *metric*; and *human* and *humble*.

Syllables can be broken into smaller units called **onsets** and **rimes** (Trieman, 1985). The onset is the initial consonant sound of a syllable, if there is one, and the rime is the vowel plus any consonant sound that comes after it. For example, in *cat*, the sound of C is the onset and the sound of AT is the rime. But the word *at* has only a rime, AT. Children who have experience playing with onsets and rimes—which is what we do when we recite nursery rhymes—have been shown to have an easier time learning to read words (Bradley & Bryant, 1985).

Rimes are also known as **phonogram patterns**. They are the rhyming portions of families of words such as *bug, dug, rug, tug,* and *mug,* and *bright, tight, light,* and *might*. As it turns out, the English language makes repeated use of a relatively limited set of phonogram patterns or rimes. Wylie and Durrell (1970) found a group of 37 phonogram patterns that make up many hundreds of English words (see Table 3.1).

Because so many English words share spelling patterns—call them onsets and rimes, or phonograms—wise teachers coach children to be aware of the patterns and to use them to read more and more words. Activities such as word sorting and word making help children work with phonogram patterns. You will read about those and other related activities in Chapter 4.

Teach It! 16

Word Hunts

Teach It! 20

Analytic Phonics Lesson

Teach It! 15

Word Sorting

Teach It! 17

Making and Breaking Words

Table 3.1   Phonogram Patterns, or Rimes

b**ack**	m**eat**	n**ice**	cl**ock**	d**uck**
m**ail**	b**ell**	st**ick**	j**oke**	r**ug**
r**ain**	cr**est**	w**ide**	sh**op**	j**ump**
c**ake**		l**ight**	st**ore**	j**unk**
s**ale**		**ill**	n**ot**	
g**ame**		w**in**		
pl**an**		l**ine**		
b**ank**		br**ing**		
tr**ap**		th**ink**		
cr**ash**		tr**ip**		
c**at**		f**it**		
pl**ate**				
s**aw**				
st**ay**				

How English Spelling Represents Sounds

Sometimes on a grocery store intercom you may hear advertisements for learning aids that promise to "teach your child to read simply by showing how letters spell sounds." The ads are usually accompanied by happy music and cheerful voices. But the relation between letters and sounds in English is not a simple matter. Unlike languages such as Finnish, Kiswahili, and Spanish, in which the relations between letters and sounds is nearly one-to-one, in English writing a single letter may relate to several different sounds, and a single sound may be spelled several different ways. For that reason, we say Kiswahili, Spanish, and Finnish have **shallow orthographies** and English has a **deep orthography** (Katz & Feldman, 1981). An orthography is a spelling system. A shallow orthography is a system that relates letters to sounds in a straightforward way—one letter usually represents one sound and one sound is usually spelled by one letter. A deep orthography has letters for sounds that are pronounced differently depending on the letters near them, or that used to be pronounced a different way historically (think of the Great Vowel Shift), or that are only pronounced in variations of the word—in other words, complications that keep letters from representing sounds in a straightforward way. Let's look at some examples.

Vowels in English are good examples of the complications that come with a deep orthography. First, there are "long" and "short" pronunciations. The short vowel sounds are spelled most consistently as in *get, got, fit, cut,* and *cat.* The long vowel sounds are spelled many different ways (note the way the long A sound is spelled in *way, straight, bait, fate, weigh,* and *fiancée*). Second, there are "silent letters" that may show what pronunciation to give to a vowel that is not silent. Third, there are also combinations of vowels that produce different diphthongs, as in *brow* and *oil.*

The **consonants** in English are pronounced more consistently than vowels.

- D, F, J, K, M, P, R, T, V, and Z are nearly always pronounced only one way each (although *F* sounds like V in *of*).

- B is usually pronounced as in *bet*, although it is silent in a few words like *debt*, *bomb*, *tomb*, *doubt*, and *subtle*.
- C and G have both "hard" and "soft" sounds. C can sound like /k/ in *cat*, or like /s/ in *cent*. G can sound like /g/ in *gun* or like /j/ in *gentle*.
- H usually has the sound /h/ as in *hot*, although it is silent in *oh*, *ah*, and *honest*, and it forms part of a digraph in *chip*, *ship*, and *thin*.
- K is usually pronounced /k/ as in *kit*, although it is silent in *knife* and *knot*.
- L is usually pronounced /l/ as in *loose*, but it is silent in *half* and *salmon*.
- N is usually pronounced as in *not*, but it combines with G to form a digraph in *sing* and *long*.
- Q is always followed by U, and together they have the /kw/ sound of *quick* or the /k/ sound of *unique*.
- S usually has the /s/ sound as in *sun*, but it also has the /z/ sound in *eyes*.
- W and Y are called **semivowels**, because they can function as consonants at the beginning of a word—for example, *way* and *year*; but can form diphthongs with other vowels in words such as *now* and *boy* to make vowel sounds. W is silent in *whole* and *answer*. W is also used in a consonant blend /hw/ that is spelled the reverse of the way it sounds WH in *which*, *where*, and *whirl*.

Complications in the English Spelling System

Here are the most important complications that happen between letters and sounds:

- long and short sounds of vowels, and systems for marking them
- soft and hard sounds of consonants, and systems for marking them
- consonant blends and consonant digraphs
- reduced vowels
- "family" connections between words
- historical oddities
- homophones and homographs
- loan words

MARKING VOWELS LONG AND SHORT. Teachers often tell children, "When two vowels go walking, the first one does the talking." That is often true, because the second vowel in words like *coat* and *boat* and *beat* and *seat* is a silent letter that marks the sound of the first vowel as "long." This rule works even when a single consonant comes before the first and second vowels, especially if the second vowel is E, I, or Y, as in *wade*, *trading*, and *spicy*. A silent GH is another marker for long vowels, as in *high* and *fight*. But the rule does not hold true for words like *look*, *eight*, *great*, *tool*, or *trout*—which account for more than half the words with pairs of vowels in them (Clymer, 1996).

In words like *get* and *it*, a single vowel coming before a consonant with no letter after it usually has its "short" sound. But here comes a big complication: English has grammatical endings like -ed, -er, and -ing that would mark the preceding vowel long if something weren't done to "insulate" the preceding vowel from the marking effect of the following vowel. So words like *bat* and *fib* double their final consonants before adding the endings -ed, -er, and -ing: *batted*, *batter*, and *fibbing*.

MARKING CONSONANTS "SOFT" AND "HARD." The consonants C and G change their pronunciations between "hard" sounds and "soft" sounds. In *rag* the G has its "hard" sound, but the following E (or I or Y) indicates that its sound is "soft" in *raging*, *cagy*, and *paged*. If a word has the soft sound of G before the vowels A, O, or U, the consonant is usually J: *jam*, *jog*, and *jug*. If a word has the soft sound of G at the end of a word, the G usually occurs in the cluster *DGE*, as in *badge*, *ridge*, and *fudge*. If a word has the hard sound of /g/ before *E* or *I*, the G is usually followed by *U*: *guide*, *guitar*, *guilty*.

The sound of the letter *C* is "soft" when it is followed by *E*, *I*, or *Y*. So we have *cent*, *dice*, and *lacy*. The sound of the letter *C* is usually "hard" when it comes before *A*, *O*, or *U*, as in *cat*, *cot*, and *cut*. Very few English words end only in *C* or *K*, so the sound of hard *C* is spelled *CK* in word-final position, as in *pack*, *pick*, and *lock*.

CONSONANT BLENDS AND CONSONANT DIGRAPHS. *Consonant blends*, as we saw above, are two or more consonants pronounced closely together, like the first two letters in *slip*. *Consonant digraphs* are single consonant phonemes that are spelled with two letters, like the beginning consonant sounds in *then*, *chip*, and *shirt*. Beginning readers are challenged to read two consonants together in consonant blends; and they may be baffled by consonant digraphs because they can never be "sounded out" no matter how slowly they are pronounced. In their early spelling, children often write one letter for a consonant blend (writing *SAP* for *step*, for instance). They often write a single letter with a similar sound for a consonant digraph (writing *VE* for *the*, for instance).

REDUCED VOWELS. English speakers also complicate reading and spelling by *reducing vowels*. In words of more than one syllable, vowels in the unstressed syllable are pronounced with a slightly mumbled sound called *schwa*. Schwa occurs, for instance, in the second syllable of the word *final* and in the final syllable in *syllable*. The vowel in those unstressed syllables is reduced, and the reduction presents big difficulties to spellers. How would you spell the second syllable of *fatal*? It might be spelled *-le* as in *simple*, *-ile* as in *futile*, or *-ol* as in *idol*, or *-il* as in *pupil*, or *-el* as in *label*. The trick is to think of a related word, if there is one, to the one with the unstressed syllable, in which the unstressed syllable is stressed. For example, you know that *simple* probably ends in *-le* if you think of the related word *simply*. You know that *futile* might end in *-ile* if you think of the related word *futility*. You know that *idol* might end in *-ol* if you think of the related word *idolatry*. For *fatal*, we can think of *fatality*.

To repeat, English has long and short vowel sounds spelled with the same letter, and the phenomenon of vowel reduction makes us pronounce syllables with many different vowels by the same sound, schwa. Students need much experience reading and writing English words to experience the varieties of English spellings. They also need teachers to point out patterns when several words are spelled according to the same rules.

MORPHOPHONEMICS: "FAMILY" CONNECTIONS BETWEEN WORDS. The spelling of the word *sign* makes no sense unless you consider the related words *signature* and *signal*. Then you may recognize that the spelling links words that have different pronunciations but common origins and related meanings. Those words may share a common morpheme, or meaningful word part. Being aware of common morphemes is useful in spelling, especially when vowel reduction (see above) throws the spelling of unstressed syllables into doubt.

If a child is unsure how to spell the final syllable of *simple* (is it *-ol*, *-al*, *-ile*, or *-le*?), remembering the related word *simply* can provide a helpful clue. If a child is unsure how to spell the second vowel in *photograph*, which is unstressed and reduced to schwa, it helps to remember the related word *photography*, in which that same vowel is stressed, and therefore recognizable.

HISTORICAL ODDITIES. Some words defy simple spelling-to-sound relationships because of spelling changes that happened over the centuries. For example, many words from Anglo-Saxon with *O* before following consonants pronounce that vowel as a short *U*: *brother*, *mother*, *son*, *love*, *cover*. It turns out the letter *O* was written in for the original letter *U* in many of those words by scribes in the tenth and eleventh centuries, to make them easier to read when they appeared in the Gothic script (Scragg, 1974). Medieval scribes also gave us the *B* in *doubt* (originally it was spelled without the *B*) to make the word resemble the related Latin word *dubere*. Children are unlikely to discover these things, but it will certainly help if their teachers know them and talk about them.

Table 3.2 Homophones and Homographs

HOMOPHONES. These are words that are spelled differently, pronounced the same, and have different meanings.		HOMOGRAPHS. These are words that are spelled the same, but have different meanings. Some homographs are not pronounced the same.	
too	two	dove (bird)	dove (from "dive")
new	knew	close (shut)	close (nearby)
red	read (past tense)	wind (twist)	wind (breeze)
deer	dear	read (present tense)	read (past tense)
there	they're	produce (verb)	produce (noun)
him	hymn	conduct (verb)	conduct (noun)
cent	sent	discharge (verb)	discharge (noun)
reel	real	relay (verb)	relay (noun)
Some homophones are phrases.		Some homographs are spelled the same and pronounced the same. They still have different meanings.	
I scream.	ice cream	show (verb)	show (noun)
depend	deep end	shift (move)	shift (work period)
will he	Willy	sock (verb)	sock (noun)
		bank (for money)	bank (of a river)

HOMOPHONES AND HOMOGRAPHS.   There are some different words like *deer* and *dear*, *bare* and *bear*, and *waist* and *waste* that sound the same but have different meanings. They are called **homophones** (from *homo-*, meaning "the same," and *phone*, meaning "sound"). There are other words that have the same spellings but have different meanings, like *lead* ("I will lead you to your table") and *lead* ("I put a lead weight on the line"). Sometimes homographs are pronounced the same, but still have different meanings, as in "sock someone in the arm" and "put on a sock." Several homophones and homographs are shown in Table 3.2. Homophones can be funny. Fred Gwynne's *The King Who Rained* and Peggy Parish's *Amelia Bedelia* still delight readers after many decades. Their humor hinges on homophones.

LOAN WORDS.   English contains many "loan words" from different languages, and most of them are pronounced according to the rules of the original languages: *taco, filet, wiener, fuselage, macho, chassis, chic,* and *wiki*.

How Children Navigate the System of English Spelling

Invented Spelling

Understanding speech sounds and the way words are constructed helps us to comprehend how children make sense of these sound patterns and how they incorporate that information into their reading and writing. One of the most fascinating discoveries in the past century with regard to literacy has been about children's ability to

Writing and Reading Connections

Why should teachers of reading understand speech sounds and how words are constructed?

Table 3.3   Comparing Descriptions of Spelling Development

Scribbling

	All Children Read	Gentry; Schlagal	Schlagal, 1989[1]; Bear, et al., *Words Their Way*[2]; Ganske, *Word Journeys*[3]
Mid kindergarten	Prephonemic	Precommunicative	Emergent
End of kindergarten	Early Phonemic	Early phonetic	
Mid first grade	Letter Name	Phonetic	Letter Name
End of second grade	Orthographic	Transitional	Within-Word Pattern
Late second grade through fourth grade and beyond	Morphological		Syllable Juncture
Early fourth grade through adulthood	Derivational		Derivational Constancy

[1]Schlagal, R. C. (1989). Constancy and change in spelling development. *Reading Psychology, 10,* 3, 207–232.
[2]Bear, D., Invernizzi, M., Templeton, S., & Johnston, F. (2007). *Words their way.* Columbus, OH: Pearson.
[3]Ganske, K. (2000). *Word journeys.* New York, NY: Guilford.

recognize the ways in which letters represent sounds in print and experiment with their own spellings. The discovery of invented spelling followed naturally from what was learned about the ways children learn spoken language: Children see people around them communicating in some medium (in this case, print); decide to try out their own versions of that communication; organize their versions according to rules or patterns that are logical, though incorrect by adult standards; and gradually, bit by bit or phase by phase, modify their strategies so that they grow closer and closer to the versions they hear and see adults using.

Sure enough, children appear to go through phases as they experiment with invented spellings for words (Bear et al., 2003; Gentry, 1989; Schlagal, 1989; Temple et al., 1982). Progress through the phases depends on two things: children's own developing concepts of how the English spelling system works (what we call their *word knowledge*) and the levels of challenge that system presents to them as they move through the grades.

How do we describe children's spelling development? Different writers label the phases differently. The labels we will use here are from Temple, Nathan, Burris, and Temple (1982) and they were inspired by the work of Henderson (1990), Gentry (1989), and Schlagal (1989). The phases we will use in this book are the *prephonemic phase*, the *early phonemic phase*, the *letter name phase*, the *orthographic phase*, the *morphological phase*, and the *derivational phase*. To correlate our phases of spelling development with other writers' phases, please see Table 3.3.

Learning a system of spelling phases is worthwhile for teachers, because looking developmentally at children's progress through phases of invented spelling reveals a great deal about children's knowledge of words; this is important to understand in order to help them learn to read (Hauerwas & Walker, 2004).

THE PREPHONEMIC PHASE OF SPELLING.   When children first begin to write, they often fill entire pages with a lot of unconnected letters (see Figure 3.3). Although what the child has written has no meaning, he or she has demonstrated prephonemic spelling. It is a kind of writing that uses letters without regard to their sounds. In this phase,

Teach It! 14

Beginning Sounds Picture Sorting

children write down letters at random or possibly with some early notion of how they might represent ideas.

Children at the prephonemic phase of spelling know how to make many letters (and often many more pseudo-letters). They know what writing looks like and might know how it is arrayed on the page. But children at this phase have not yet discovered the alphabetic principle: the understanding that spelling represents words by relating written letters to spoken phonemes. If this is the case, then much reading instruction in which children are expected to learn to recognize words by being exposed to them will not be effective yet. Neither will phonics instruction that focuses on learning particular letters and sounds, which requires an understanding of the fundamental idea that words are real, they consist of phonemes, and those phonemes are represented by letters.

THE EARLY PHONEMIC PHASE OF SPELLING. Figure 3.4 represents the work of a child in the early phonemic phase of spelling. This child has used letters to represent some of the sounds in words but not all of them. That is why we call this phase early phonemic: The child is just beginning to represent words by their phonemes. Children at this phase typically represent only the first and last and possibly a middle consonant in the word. They usually leave out vowels unless the whole word is a vowel, such as *A*. Children who spell in the early phonemic phase sometimes spell the first sound in a word with a sensible choice of a letter, then add random letters to make the word longer and hence make it look like a word (Ferreiro & Teberosky, 1982). But note carefully what we mean by a sensible choice. When children do use letters to represent sounds, rather than to use letters for sounds in conventional ways, they spell intuitively, matching as best they can a letter with a letter name that sounds closest to the sound they want to spell. Thus, for example, they are likely to choose the letter *H* to spell /*ch*/, and the letter *Y* to spell /*w*/.

If children are spelling in the early phonemic phase, we know that they have discovered the alphabetic principle. They are not yet very proficient, however, at breaking words into phonemes and matching them with letter sounds. Matching letters to sounds contains at least four operations: making the word hold still in the mind, breaking it down into phonemes, matching each phoneme with a letter, and writing down that letter. All of these steps may be difficult for a beginner.

Determining the number of sounds children can represent in their spelling yields important diagnostic information. Bear in mind Ehri's hypothesis that a child's memory for storing images of written words for later recognition consists of a number of "slots" (Ehri, 1991, 1997a). A child with more memory storage "slots" for word recognition will store a more complete memory of that word and will recognize it more accurately when she sees it written down.

Examining a child's invented spelling can yield clues to his or her ability to segment words into phonemes. A child who writes *HK* for *truck* (that is, the early phonemic speller) shows a limited ability to segment phonemes in words. When it comes to recognizing words in print, that child will try to say the word on the basis of very shallow processing, typically looking at the first letter and calling out a word he or she knows that begins with that letter. Because the child does not yet focus on all of the letters and phonemes in the word (Morris, 1998), he or she can easily confuse the words being read with other words that share one or two of the same letters.

THE LETTER NAME PHASE OF SPELLING. At a slightly more advanced phase, a child offers spelling like that in Figure 3.5. This child is in the letter name phase of spelling. Here, the child represents all or nearly all of the phonemes in a word, but does so intuitively. Logical judgments were made in choosing letters to represent sounds, but that logic still diverges quite a bit from the conventions of English spelling.

Children use names of the letters of the alphabet as if they were building blocks of sound out of which words could be constructed. In the case of some sounds, the letter name strategy results in spellings that look conventional; in others, the spellings

Figure 3.3
Prephonemic Spelling.

Jessie, Age 4

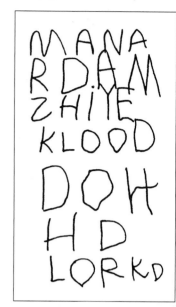

Source: Temple, Nathan, Burris, and Temple, 1992.

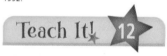

Phonemic Segmentation with Elkonin Boxes

Figure 3.4
Early Invented Spelling.

Daryl, Grade 1

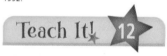

Source: Temple, Nathan, Burris, and Temple, 1992.

Figure 3.5
Letter Name Stage of Spelling.

No Name, Age 4 From Carol Chomsky.

Translation: "Once a lady went fishing and she caught Flipper."

YUTS A LADE YET FEHEG AD HE KOT FLEPR

Source: Temple, Nathan, Burris, and Temple, 1992.

can look bizarre. Especially in these cases, examining children's letter name spellings gives us a window into the ways children think about words and into the eccentricities of the English spelling system.

- **Spelling Most Consonants.** As the sample in Figure 3.5 demonstrates, many consonant letters are spelled intuitively in ways that look conventional. Note the spellings of *F, L,* and *P* in *FLEPR* (*Flipper*) and of *D* in *AD* (*and*). The spelling *K* in *KOT* (*caught*) could be correct. The names of these letters are close enough to their corresponding phonemes to make the letter name strategy successful or nearly successful.

- **Spelling Nonintuitive Consonants.** The spelling of *Y* for the /w/ sound in *YUTS* (*once*) and *YET* (*went*) reveals very clearly that the child has chosen the *Y* for the sound of its name, rather than for its conventional value. But the letter name for *W* ("double U") doesn't sound at all like /w/, while the name of *Y* ("wye") is close, so this choice of *Y* for the /w/ sound is not surprising for the child who is using the letter name strategy.

- **Spelling Digraph Consonants.** Young spellers are troubled by the spellings of digraphs, since they do not know about the conventions for spelling them. Note the invented spelling of the *SH* digraph is *FEHEG* (*fishing*) and *HE* (*she*). In both cases, the letter *H* was chosen because the name of that letter sounds closest to the phoneme that is usually spelled by *SH*. The letter *H* is often used by children in the letter name phase of learning to spell the sound of /sh/ and /ch/.

- **Spelling Ns and Ms before Stop Consonants.** As we see in the spellings of *YUTS* for *once* and *AD* for *and*, letter name spellers often leave out Ns and Ms when they come before other consonants, especially before what are called **stop consonants** (so called because they briefly stop the flow of air through the mouth) such as /p/, /b/, /t/, /d/, and /k/. The problem is not that children don't know how to spell the /n/ and /m/ sounds. It is rather that they are used to feeling the consonants produced in the mouth as they sound out the word in order to spell it (Read, 1975). When Ns and Ms are pronounced before stop consonants, you cannot feel them in the mouth, because the tongue goes to the same position to form the stop consonant anyway. Say the words *wet* and *went* aloud, and you will see what we mean: The activity of the tongue in the mouth is the same in both cases. What is different when N or M is present is that the whole syllable is pronounced through the nose. The omission of N and M in this position is prevalent in the spellings of kindergarten and first-grade children and in older children who are advancing slowly as spellers.

- **Spelling Word-Final R, L, M, and N: "Syllabic Sonorants."** The spelling of *FLEPR* for *Flipper* shows another common feature of children's letter name spelling. Unstressed syllables ending in R, L, M, and N often lack vowels when they appear at the ends of words. Thus it is common to see *TABL* for *table*, *LEDL* for *little*, and *BIDM* for *bottom* in the writing of children in the letter name phase of spelling. English has a convention that all syllables must be spelled with vowels. Even though children in the letter name phase represent most vowels, they leave them out of these words, presumably because they expect every letter they write into a word to be clearly sounded, but in these syllables, no distinct vowel sound is heard (Read, 1975).

- **Spelling Long Vowels.** As the spelling of A for A, *LADE* for *lady*, and *HE* for *she* demonstrates, long vowels in words usually "say their names"; that is, the sound to be spelled sounds much like the name of the letter we would use to spell that sound. In the spelling of *LADE* for *lady*, the spelling of the second vowel makes it clear that the child intends for the E to "say its name."

- **Spelling Short Vowels.** Spelling short vowels presents problems to letter name spellers. As was discussed earlier, short vowels do not sound very much like the "long" vowels spelled by the same letter. There are no vowel letter names that have short vowel sounds; so the speller must choose the letter name that is the best fit with that short vowel. This in practice is the long vowel sound that sounds the most like, or is produced in the mouth in the manner most like, that short vowel sound. This principle explains the spelling of E for the short vowel /ĭ/ in *fishing*. It also explains why children write A for /ĕ/ and I for /ŏ/.

Children who are letter name spellers represent nearly all of the phonemes (the smaller speech sounds) in words. But they represent those speech sounds intuitively, using a letter name strategy, rather than conventionally, using the kinds of spellings for sounds that are seen in books. Letter name spellers' ability to segment words into all of their phonemes gives them many corresponding "slots" in word memory storage for the parts of the words they see in print. Letter name spellers are usually beginning readers who are making progress acquiring sight words.

Letter name spellers have a means at their disposal to write many words, and children enjoy this freedom to create. Their spelling ability is still limited, of course. Because they spell words by relating letters to their individual sounds, they are not yet taking advantage of onsets and rimes and phonogram patterns. Nor are letter name spellers yet aware of the conventions for marking vowels "long" or "short." They also are not aware of the standard spellings of grammatical endings such as *-ing* or *-ed*, which explains why *fishing* was spelled *FEHEG* in Figure 3.5.

When it comes to recognizing words, letter name spellers often look for matches between letters and phonemes, a strategy that some researchers call *sophisticated guessing*. Letter name spellers try to sound out all of the letters in a word and sometimes produce bizarre readings such as [*ree add*] for *read* and [*lie vee*] for *live*.

Research shows that the practice of invented spelling is good for kindergarten and first-grade children. Children who are encouraged to invent spellings learn to recognize more words than children who do not use invented spelling. But children should not persist in

Figure 3.6

Spelling in the Orthographic Stage.

Stella, Grade 1. Note spelling of "nature trail"

Translation: We went to the park. We went on a nature trail. They hid the eggs. I found 7 eggs. I found candy. We ate barbeque. We had fun. We played baseball.

> Stella
>
> We went to the park
> we went on a nacher
> chrl They hid The
> eggs   I fond 7 eggs
> I fond candy   we ate
> bobyQ   we had fun
> We playd basball.

Source: Temple, Nathan, Burris, and Temple, 1992.

Teach It! 62

Word Origins and Derivations

letter name spelling much beyond the end of first grade. To help them make progress, teachers need to be careful to remind children that invented spelling is "temporary spelling"; it is the way that they can write some words before they learn the way words are spelled in books. Teachers also need to be careful to give students correctly spelled material to read and to take opportunities to call children's attention to standard spelling patterns in print.

THE ORTHOGRAPHIC PHASE OF SPELLING. Spellers in the orthographic phase are beginning readers who are becoming aware of conventional spellings for sounds. They are learning phonogram patterns (onsets and rimes) and are trying to master the marking systems for long and short vowels, although not always correctly, as seen in Figure 3.6.

Orthographic spellers may be keen observers of the English spelling system, and the difficulties they face in spelling correctly often reflect the eccentricities of the system. For example, orthographic spellers may write *LUV* and *ABUV*. The correct spellings, *love* and *above*, thwart their expectations.

Children who spell in the orthographic phase show us that they have learned many things about the way the English writing system works, and this knowledge can help them both in writing and in reading. These children show a grasp of common onsets and rimes in their writing, indicating that they should be able to use knowledge of these patterns to read unfamiliar words. Children who are aware of onsets and rimes can use the strategy of reading by analogy. For example, if they encounter the unknown word *sill*, they can recognize its similarity to the known word *pill* and will read *sill* by mentally taking away the /p/ sound and substituting the /s/ sound in front of the -*ill* rime. Such reading by analogy leads to more rapid and accurate deciphering of words than does puzzling out words letter by letter.

Spelling in the orthographic phase presents challenges that many students never move beyond. A student who has learned to spell *gate*, for example, might still be unsure how to spell *great*, *bait*, *straight*, or *eight*. It will take a habit of studying words carefully plus an act of memory to master these challenges. Of course, encouragement and reminders from the teacher don't hurt!

THE MORPHOLOGICAL PHASE OF SPELLING. Spellers in the morphological phase are able to spell in stable and correct ways grammatical endings, and prefixes and suffixes—items that linguists call **bound morphemes.** Also, the speller is able to compensate for the tendency of these word endings to give preceding vowels and consonants their alternate pronunciations.

Spellers in this phase have learned the common patterns of spelling such as the phonogram patterns and the rules for marking vowels long or short. But the spelling system of English reflects more than sounds. There are grammatical endings and prefixes and suffixes that must be spelled in certain ways, even when they may be pronounced differently from one word to another. Also, when grammatical endings and prefixes and suffixes are attached to other words, they often have the effect of marking a vowel long or short in the root word, which is another complication for a learner to take into account.

The child who wrote the piece in Figure 3.7 shows some of the difficulties posed by the morphological phase. Note his spelling of *chewed*. Note also, the effect of his South Texas accent on his spelling!

THE DERIVATIONAL PHASE OF SPELLING. Moving still further away from the expectation that letters spell sounds, learners encounter the derivational phase of spelling, in which spellings must honor the origins of words and their relationships to other words.

Figure 3.7
The Struggles of the
Morphological Phase.

Some words are derived from other "living" words, and others are derived from common ancient sources (hence the name "derivational"). Many words that are found from fourth grade up, such as *photograph*, *sign*, *doubt*, and *bomb* don't have a very obvious connection between letters and sounds, because the letters relate not so much to sounds as to word histories—or to other words from which they are derived.

When children reach the most advanced phase of word knowledge, they can recognize meaningful chunks of words called *morphemes*, and use them not just for reading and spelling but also as a clue to word meanings. In the derivational phase of word knowledge, children think of words in family relationships, and use their awareness of these relationships to write and read words.

For example, recognizing the relation between *photograph* and *photography* helps a student spell the reduced vowels in both words, because the reduced and unrecognizable second O in *photograph* is stressed and identifiable in *photography*. Likewise the A in the next to last syllable of *photography* is stressed and recognizable in *photograph*. But beyond the help with spelling, recognizing the morpheme *photo* and associating it with the meaning "light" helps unpack words like *photosynthesis*, "coming together with light." We will say more about morphemes next.

myeducationlab
The Power of Classroom Practice
www.myeducationlab.com

Analyze a student's spelling test to determine what he or she knows about spelling and phonics and the spelling patterns he or she still needs to learn in the activity "Supporting Developmentally Appropriate Spelling Instruction." (To find this activity, go to the topic *Phonemic Awareness/ Phonics* in MyEducationLab and click on Assignments and Activities.)

ASSESSMENT

Charting Children's Spelling Development

You are in your first year of teaching second grade. It's September and you know you need to find out where your children are in their spelling development. Instruction needs to get really focused, and the time is now. To do this you've already done several things.

Things Accomplished

- Started a writing workshop—children are writing nearly every day and they are using invented spelling.

- Collected several writing samples of invented spelling from each child—have written hunches about spelling on them—samples are in children's files.

- Given the children a quick five-word spelling test from Gentry's Monster Test (Bear, Invernizzi, Templeton, & Johnston, 2007).

Plans

- Study the writing samples and the results of the spelling test for three to five children each night beginning on Monday and finishing the class by Friday.

- Using this assessment data, write up a profile for each child and make a decision about approximate spelling phase. Provide two or three reasons for the decision.

- Review the assessment profiles and organize two or three small groups according to spelling development; then plan at least one data-driven lesson for the coming week for each group.

Celebrate a job well done! (Make more lesson plans; keep collecting samples.)

Morphology: How English Words Are Built

The study of the ways words are built is called **morphology.** In English, words are built in several ways. They can stand alone, like *cat*. They can be made up of two or more separate words, like *firehouse*. They can have prefixes and suffixes added to them, like *unforgettable*. And they can be built out of ancient parts, like *biology* and *biography*.

COMPOUND WORDS.   When two or more root words are combined, as in *houseboat* and *lawnmower*, they make compound words. Dictionary writers have three different ways of writing compound words:

> *Houseboat*: Words that are frequently spoken together are joined without a space. Those words are made plural by adding *-s* at the end of the last word: *houseboats*.
>
> *Mother-in-law*: Other compound words are joined with hyphens. When these words are made plural, the *-s* is added to the more important word: *mothers-in-law*.
>
> *Boa constrictor*: Some words are often said together, but are written separately.

PREFIXES AND SUFFIXES.   All of us are aware that we can add an *-s* or an *-ed* or an *-ing* onto a **root word** in English word to change its meaning. Those that are added before the root word are called *prefixes*, and those added after the root word are called *suffixes*. The general name for both of them is *affixes*. Some suffixes mark the person, number, and tense of a verb, like *fished*, and *thinking*. Others mark the plural form of nouns, like *cats*. Both of these are called *grammatical inflections*. Other prefixes and suffixes can also change the meanings of words, like *unkind, retie, underestimate,* and *likeable*. Table 3.4 shows some prefixes and suffixes that are found in children's vocabularies.

WORDS FROM ANCIENT PARTS.   Both prefixes and suffixes have less obvious forms that attach to parts of words that are not as easily recognized as root words. For example, *gradual* and *annual* appear to share the suffix *-al*, which has the meaning "in the manner of." But what do *annu-* and *grad-* mean? Both are ancient root words that came from Latin. *Annus* meant "year," and *gradus* meant "step." So in modern English, *annual* means "year by year," and *gradual* means "step by step." Ancient root words like these are called *historical morphemes.* There are many ancient prefixes and root words contained in thousands of English words. Most come from Latin and Greek. They are usually found in the

Table 3.4 Prefixes and Suffixes

PREFIX	MEANING	EXAMPLES
sub-	under	submarine, subway, substandard
dis-	not	distrust, disrespect, distasteful
mis-	not	misunderstand, misguided, mislead
inter-	between or among	interstate, international, intercity
pre-	before	preschool, pretest, preview
SUFFIX	MEANING	EXAMPLES
-er	more than	taller, shorter, quicker
-ful	containing	hopeful, wishful, bountiful
-ly	in the manner of	beautifully, miserly, shortly
-ness	state of being	goodness, highness, badness
-less	without	painless, toothless, penniless

Being a Professional Reading Teacher ★

Morphemes and Reading

Being aware of morphemes helps a person read. Even third graders use word parts to recognize words—especially in words like *hilly* and *helpful,* where the original word part is easily visible, or "transparent" (Carlisle & Stone, 2005). To read words that are typically encountered from the fourth grade up, it is more useful to be aware of the morphemes that make up words than to try to match letters with individual sounds (Reichle & Perfetti, 2003). Being aware of morphemes makes it possible to identify as many as 60 percent of unknown words that are encountered in the middle grades and above (Nagy et al., 1989). So, for example, a reader who knows

that *inter* means "between" and *planetary* refers to "planets" can figure out that *interplanetary* means "between planets." Children beyond the early elementary years who are aware of morphemes in words register better comprehension (Carlisle, 2000).

The strident emphasis on phonics—letter-to-sound correspondences—that the No Child Left Behind legislation ushered in might distract teachers from the realization that there are other important things to know about words, especially beyond the primary grades. Some of those things are the parts that make up words and where those words came from.

vocabularies of children above third grade. Knowing them can expand children's vocabularies, and can help them read and spell more words.

Table 3.5 lists some common historical morphemes. More will be found in Chapter 6.

ETYMOLOGIES: WORD ORIGINS.   In many dictionaries, you will find listings for words that look like this:

>*give. (giv). Vt gave, giv'en, giv'ing. [OE giefan]*

What do these notations mean? The part in parentheses is the pronunciation; *vt* means that the word is a transitive verb—that is, a verb that takes an object to complete the meaning. *Gave, given,* and *giving* are the past, past participle (the form used in compound verbs like *have given* or *had given*), and present participle (the form used in compound verbs like *is giving* and *were giving*). The part in brackets means that the word came down to us from an earlier word—in this case from Old English (OE). Words in English are derived from many sources. Nonetheless, it is possible to map out a rough lineage for a great many of the words you use in English. When you trace the origins of words or look at their histories, you are dealing with their etymologies.

Table 3.5   Prefixes and Word Roots from Latin

PREFIX	MEANING	EXAMPLES
com, con, col, cor	together	collect, contract, correct
e-	out of	elect, eject, emigrate
ab	from, away from, by	abstract, abrupt
ad—, al—, ac—	to, toward	admit, accord, ally

ROOT WORD	MEANING	EXAMPLES
-lect, -lege	choose	elect, collect, college
-ject, -jac	throw	inject, reject, eject, adjective
-rupt	break	interrupt, abrupt, disrupt, erupt
grad-	step	graduate, gradual, grade

The English language traces its origin to Anglo-Saxon. In the fifth and sixth centuries A.D., Germanic peoples from northern Germany and the Netherlands invaded England and pushed the indigenous Celts north into Scotland and west to Wales and Ireland. They brought their Germanic language with them, and it came to be called Anglo-Saxon (Anglo comes from Angles, the name of one of the Germanic tribes, and Saxon comes from another of those tribes). In the eighth and ninth centuries, Vikings raided from Scandinavia, and Old English became a mixture of Germanic, Norse, Danish, and Dutch words.

In 1066, the Normans from France conquered England and brought with them not only an early version of the French language but also Latin, which became widely used in the church, the government, and other places of higher culture—to the exclusion of English, which remained the language spoken around the hearth, on the farm, and in the market. Hundreds of words from Latin and Greek (Greek was read in the monasteries), as well as French, were absorbed into English in this period.

In 1477, William Caxton brought the first printing press to England and began printing books in English, giving an enormous boost to the language. The language he wrote, Middle English, had a sort of dual structure, consisting of Anglo-Saxon words and Latinate words. You can see this duality in the English words for food. The animal you call a *pig* (an Anglo-Saxon word) on the farm is called *pork* when it reaches the dining room table. *Pork* is a French word, from Latin. The *cow* (Anglo-Saxon) in the pasture became *beef* (French and Latin) in the dining room. *Sheep* on the farm (Anglo-Saxon word) became *mutton* (French and Latin) in the dining room. This all came about because English was spoken on the farm by workers, but French was spoken in the dining rooms of the ruling class. To this day, our language has a core of words that came through Old English from Anglo-Saxon. These are very often the common, basic items in our vocabulary: the words children learn first, the words you use when you are being most direct. But there is another body of words, from Latin and Greek, that are more specialized, more scientific, and more limited to educated usage. Thus, you find the Anglo-Saxon words *cat* and *dog* and the corresponding Latin words *feline* and *canine*; you also find the Anglo-Saxon word *feel*, the related Latin word *sensitive*, and the related Greek word *sympathy*. Today the English language can be described as having an Anglo-Saxon base and a Latin vocabulary. About a third of our words are Anglo-Saxon and the majority of the rest are from Latin (and through Latin, from Greek). There are also many loan words from Spanish, modern French, German, and other languages.

Vocabulary: Words and Their Meanings

Another aspect of spoken language that is important for reading is *vocabulary*. The more words children have in their spoken vocabularies, the easier it will be for them to learn to read. This is true for three reasons:

- **Having a word in the spoken vocabulary makes it possible to recognize that word in print.** Having the word in their vocabulary allows children to confirm more quickly if they have deciphered a printed word correctly. It is frustrating for beginning readers to struggle to decipher a word from its letters, only to realize that they don't know the word anyway. Having the word in their vocabulary allows children to use meaning-based strategies for word identification strategies, such as, "Think of a word that begins like this one, that would make sense in this sentence."

- **Having more words in the spoken vocabulary boosts children's language awareness.** The more children are aware of language, the better able they are to read words—to be aware of their parts and their sound (Wong-Fillmore & Snow, 2000).

- **Having words in the spoken vocabulary boosts reading comprehension.** Words are tokens for concepts. They are units of meaning. The size of children's vocabulary is a measure of their knowledge of the world. It is also a measure of their potential for understanding new information. Let's elaborate on these issues now.

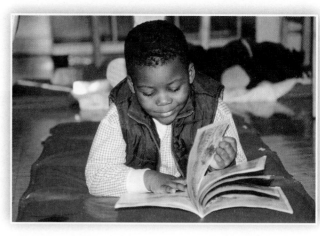

As children explore words on their own, they begin to find meaning in the words and to learn how to use words for different purposes. (Nancy Sheehan Photography)

Vocabulary is important in reading. As Carl Smith (1997) puts it, "Most people feel that there is a common sense relationship between vocabulary and comprehension—messages are composed of ideas, and ideas are expressed in words" (p. 1). Vocabulary development interacts with word recognition as children try to recognize in print words they already know—or partially know—in speech. But although younger children have most of the words in their spoken vocabulary that they are likely to encounter in print, there are still many words that occur in young children's picture books that they don't hear in speech (Stanovich, 1992). If you need convincing on this point, go reread William Steig's *Sylvester and the Magic Pebble*, where you will read that the rainfall "just ceased." By fourth grade, the vocabulary found in books is considerably richer than the words children use in speech.

Certainly, children can grow larger vocabularies from doing wide reading (Stanovich, 1992). As Nagy et al. (1985) point out, however, readers who encounter 100 unknown words will learn perhaps five of them. Children must do a great deal of reading, in at least moderately challenging texts, to learn large vocabularies from reading. But there are huge disparities in the amount of reading children do. In one study (Wilson, 1992), the top 20 percent of a fifth-grade class read 20 times as much as the bottom 20 percent. The bottom 20 percent read very little. If we count on children to learn vocabulary from reading, we will surely continue to see the huge disparities in vocabulary size described above.

Levels of Vocabulary Knowledge

What do we mean by *knowing* vocabulary? Beck et al. (2002) suggest a continuum of word knowledge that looks like this:

- No knowledge
- General sense, such as knowing *mendacious* has a negative connotation
- Narrow, context-bound knowledge, such as knowing that a *radiant* bride is a beautifully smiling happy one, but unable to describe an individual in a different context as radiant
- Having knowledge of a word, but not being able to recall it readily enough to use it in appropriate situations
- Rich, decontextualized knowledge of a word's meaning, its relationship to other words, and its extension to metaphorical uses, such as understanding what someone is doing when they are *devouring* a book (p. 10).

Family Literacy

Can you think of three ways to enlist family support in helping children's language grow?

Knowing vocabulary well means not just understanding what words in a book mean, then, but knowing words in a range of contexts, in associations with other words, and in connection with one's experience—to have words as one's own.

How Adults Support Children's Vocabulary Learning

Children benefit from having adults talk to them. It makes their vocabularies grow (Hoff-Ginsburg, 1998). This matters because the amount and quality of talk that young children get from their families varies tremendously. One research team (Hart & Risley, 1995) found that three- and four-year-old children in professional families had twice as many words spoken to them as children from working-class families, and nearly four times as many as children in families on welfare. Children in working-class families received three times as many verbal encouragements ("Good girl! See? You could do it!") as did children from families on welfare, and children from professional families received 7.5 times as many verbal encouragements as children from families on welfare. When it came to prohibitions ("Stop!" "Don't do that!" "Quit!"), the results were just the reverse. Children in families on welfare received nearly twice as many prohibitions as children in working-class families, and almost three times as many as children from professional families received. Children from families on welfare were discouraged three times more often than they were encouraged. Children from working-class families were encouraged twice as often as they were discouraged. And children from professional families were encouraged six times as often as they were discouraged (Hart & Risley, 1995, pp. 252–253).

Less talk between adults and children means less developed vocabulary. By the age of six, children from low-income undereducated families come to school with well below half the vocabulary that children from middle-class families have, and the differences continue to grow after that (Beck et al., 2002). Having a limited vocabulary—and limited structures for language—limits children's concept formation and their "world knowledge," and it certainly creates problems for children learning to read and write (Droop & Verhoeven, 2003; Snow et al., 2001).

Exploring Children's Vocabulary

The job of teaching vocabulary seems truly immense. Nagy (1985) estimates that by ninth grade, students have to cope with a total written vocabulary of 88,500 words (Nagy & Anderson, 1984). Were we to try to teach all those words, the prospect of teaching children nearly 10,000 words a year would be daunting indeed. But Beck et al. (2002) have found a useful way to break down those numbers.

- *Tier One Words.* There are many thousands of words already in children's spoken vocabulary that we won't usually have to teach. Beck et al. call these words *Tier One* words, and they include examples such as *mother, clock,* and *jump.*

- *Tier Three Words.* Then there are many more thousands of words that are so highly specialized that they are almost never used outside of the disciplines in which they are encountered. These *Tier Three* words—like *monozygotic, tetrahedron,* and *bicameral*—are best learned in the science, social studies, and other classes where they are tied to the content under study.

- *Tier Two Words.* That leaves the *Tier Two* words—the words with wide utility that most children don't have in their spoken vocabularies, such as *dismayed, paradoxical, absurd,* and *wary.* Beck et al. (2002) estimate that there may be about 7,000 Tier Two words, and even if we teach children half of them—or about 400 words a year—we will have gone a long way toward growing children's vocabularies and equalizing children's access to learning.

myeducationlab
The Power of Classroom Practice
www.myeducationlab.com

Watch a video of a second grade teacher teaching multiple meanings of the word "draw" in the activity "Teaching Multiple Meanings of Words." (To find this activity, go to the topic *Vocabulary* in MyEducationLab and click on Assignments and Activities.)

In Chapter 6 of this book we will describe ways of teaching Tier Two vocabulary, the general-purpose words many children do not know. In Chapters 7 and 13 we will share ways of teaching Tier Three words, content-specific words.

Syntax: The Grammar of English

Syntax, another term for **grammar**, refers to the set of rules that order words and their inflections meaningfully in sentences. Syntax is what enables you to read the sentence "The veterinarian bit the dog" and understand who was bitten and who did the biting. Syntax can be thought of as a kind of code that enables speakers to encode meaning and hearers to decode meaning. The "working parts" of syntax are **parts of speech**, **word order**, and **inflections**.

Parts of speech are the different grammatical functions that different words serve: *but, run, dog, the, and, across, should, a, green, very,* and *slowly* are all different parts of speech and do different things in sentences. *And* and *but* are **conjunctions**: they connect things. *Run* is a **verb** and names an action or a state of being. *Dog* is a **noun**, and names a person, place, or thing. *The* and *a* are **articles** (definite and indefinite, respectively) and introduce nouns. *Across* is a **preposition**, and shows relationships. *Should* is a **modal verb**, and shows fine shades of action or states of being. *Green* is an **adjective** and it describes a noun. *Very* is an **adverb**, and it further defines an adjective. *Slowly* is also an **adverb** and it further describes a verb. Your mind automatically knows these facts without your having to think of them. So, most likely, does whoever programmed the word processing software on your computer, which is why it lights up funny if you happen to write "I have a very dog big."

We saw *word order* in action before: For example, the noun that comes before the verb is usually the subject and the noun that comes after the verb is usually the object. *Grammatical inflections* include the past tense marker, *-ed*, and the number marker *-s* in sentences like "Yesterday the wind howl**ed**, but today it whispe**rs**."

Syntax occurs on two levels. At the conscious level, we think of syntax as the common set of rules of grammar taught in school, such as "A verb must agree with its subject in person and number." But conscious syntactical knowledge is only a fraction of what you know that enables you to produce and understand sentences. Consider, for example, the following sentences:

- *I would go bike riding if I weren't tired.* (But I won't go bike riding because I am tired.)
- *I will go bike riding if I'm not tired.* (I don't know yet if I will go bike riding.)
- *I go bike riding if I'm not tired.* (When I'm not tired, I usually go bike riding.)
- *I'm going bike riding, and I'm not tired.* (I expected to be tired, but I'm not.)
- *I did go bike riding, and I'm not tired.* (Somebody asserted that I didn't go bike riding.)

If you have ever taught English as a second language, you have surely found that although the differences in the meanings of these sentences were clear to you, it was very difficult to tell non-native speakers how to produce sentences that convey those shades of meaning. That means you have knowledge of grammar, but you cannot explain what you know. Linguists call this *tacit knowledge*—we have it, but it's not conscious—and the lion's share of children's knowledge of syntax is tacit.

Syntax and Reading

Syntax is important in reading. First, and most obviously, syntax is needed to make meaning from text. In the example sentences at the end of the previous section, a reader needs to understand the syntax to create the right shade of meaning. Syntax matters in word recognition, too. Often, teachers will ask a reader who struggles over an unknown word, "What would make sense here?" And if the child is reading the sentence, "The mother hoped the jar would contain money, but it d_____," the word *but* will help the reader figure out that the next word should say *didn't*. The conjunction *but* tells the reader to expect those words to convey a meaning counter to the beginning phrase. So the syntax of the sentence is a strong clue to the identity of the unknown word.

Syntax at a Larger Level: Story Structure

Syntax helps children learn organizing principles for longer units of language as well. Stories have been shown to have a particular order that is called **story grammar**.

Story Maps

Figure 3.8
The Frowning Princess.

The Frowning Princess

In a faraway time and a distant place, there lived a king and his daughter. She frowned. From morning to night, she frowned and frowned and frowned. Even if you saw her in her sleep, she would still be frowning.

The royal advisor worried. "This is terrible, your majesty. A frowning princess is like a cloudy day," he said. "The people will think there is something wrong with your kingdom if the princess doesn't stop frowning."

"I pay you well, so I guess you are right," said the king. "We must find a way to make my daughter stop frowning."

The king and the royal advisor told the princess every joke they knew. But kings and royal advisors are not funny people, and after they had told both of their jokes, the princess was still frowning.

They brought a dozen monkeys and three trained hyenas to the palace. Nobody got any sleep for days. The princess frowned even harder.

Then it happened that a chambermaid put her head between her legs to clean under the princess' bed. Seeing the princess from this odd position, the chambermaid discovered something. "The princess is smiling," she thought. She told the princess to stand on her head and look into the mirror. When the princess saw her reflection, she tried to turn her upside-down frown right-side up. So, of course, she smiled.

Now the princess smiles all the day long. The king, his advisor, and the people are happy. It may be that the princess is still trying to frown, but I won't tell if you won't.

STORY GRAMMAR. The most thoroughly studied of the structures of discourse (*discourse* roughly means "a body of talk") is story grammar. Consider the story "The Frowning Princess" in Figure 3.8.

Stories such as this one have a set of identifiable elements, or slots, into which the particulars of the story are placed. These slots are almost always organized in a particular order. (The terms *identifiable elements* and *particular order* are signs that one is talking about grammar or syntax.) For example, a story consists of a setting, one or more episodes, and a consequence. An analysis of the story "The Frowning Princess" using this story grammar model is found in Table 3.6.

Children as young as kindergarten age have a sense of story grammar, and they appear to use it to comprehend stories (Stein & Glenn, 1979). Teaching children story grammars improves their comprehension (Olson & Gee, 1988). Such instruction has been found to be especially helpful for children with learning disabilities (Gersten, 1998).

Social Variations in Language Use

Language and Diversity

What are three ways in which language use differs in social situations?

The focus in this chapter has moved from understanding language as a way of making meaningful utterances toward language as it is used in social situations. Three ways in which language use differs in social situations is in the use of dialects, registers, and social languages or discourses.

DIALECTS. Members of different geographic, social, and cultural groups use language in unique ways. Part of the uniqueness is captured in dialects that the groups use. Geographic dialects are reflected in the differences in the word pronunciations, word choice, and conversational styles of speakers from northern Minnesota; Goliad, Texas; or Ocracoke, North Carolina. Social dialects are reflected in the speech of people from different social classes. Ethnic dialects are reflected in the speech of people from different racial groups. Of course, all these dialects overlap, as in the speech of a professional African American family from the southern Appalachian Mountains. Differences in dialects can result in children experiencing difficulties learning to read, especially if they aren't aware of sounds in the standard pronunciations of words reflected in the spellings.

From the choice of words and the structure of sentences to the patterns in which information is presented, written language differs significantly from spoken language—so

Table 3.6 Story Grammar Applied

ELEMENTS OF STORY GRAMMAR	EXAMPLES
The **setting**, a place and time	"In a faraway time and a distant place ..."
There are **characters**	"... a king and his daughter ..."
An initiating event—something that creates a problem to be solved, and sets further events in motion.	"She frowned. From morning to night, the princess frowned and frowned and frowned."
There is one or more **episodes** that contain ...	
An **attempt** to solve the problem	"The king and the royal advisor told the princess every joke they knew."
Which has an **outcome**	"... the princess was still frowning."
Possibly another **attempt**	"They brought a dozen monkeys and three trained hyenas to the palace."
Which has an **outcome**	"Nobody got any sleep for days. The princess frowned even harder."
Possibly another **attempt**	"A chambermaid put her head between her legs to clean under the princess' bed. Seeing the princess from this odd position, the chambermaid discovered something. 'The princess is smiling,' she thought. She told the princess to stand on her head and look into the mirror."
Which has an **outcome**	"When the princess saw her reflection, she tried to turn her upside-down frown right-side up. So, of course, she smiled."
There is a **resolution**	"Now the princess smiles all the day long."
There is a **consequence**	"The king, his advisor, and the people are happy."

Source: Stein & Glenn, 1979.

The Language of School

English language learners and other students who need extra support in the classroom can be helped to learn the content of the curriculum if the right kind of scaffolding is supplied. Sheltered instruction requires that the teacher carefully think through the demands that the language of the lesson, the content of the lesson, and the learning tasks will place on the student. Then the teacher takes steps to make all three accessible. As California teacher and professor MaryEllen Vogt writes,

> For ELL's [English Language Learners] to become successful in learning content, they need to learn not only English grammar and vocabulary, but also "the language of school." … What we have learned from these students is that they need assistance with all three knowledge bases: knowledge of English, knowledge of the content topic, and knowledge of how tasks are to be completed. Together, these are the key components of academic literacy. (Vogt, 2000, pp. 335, 336)

Vogt goes on to recommend the following:

- Make the objectives of the lesson—for both the language to be used and the content to be learned—very explicit, including writing it on the board.

- Engage the students in active and meaningful activities (not just seatwork), and use various means to communicate information: graphic organizers, examples, analogies, repetitions. Communication between teacher and student and among students is frequent.

- Relate the lessons to the students' prior experiences and background knowledge.

- Choose key vocabulary for the lesson and introduce it in advance, highlight it during the lesson, and review it at the lesson's end and periodically thereafter.

- Word lessons carefully and speak clearly and distinctly.

- Explain how tasks are to be carried out, then give examples of the kinds of responses that are expected, and explain why.

- Scaffold writing assignments with graphic organizers and other outlining aids; scaffold reading assignments with study guides, written questions, and outlines for note taking.

- Encourage higher-order thinking by means of many techniques.

- Use group work, including paired work.

much so that the language of print has been called the **grapholect.** The language of books is probably closer to urban educated middle-class speech than to any other dialect. Therefore, when it comes to reading and writing, that gives an advantage to people who already speak that dialect—and a disadvantage to those who speak a different regional or social dialect.

REGISTERS.   Another way in which speakers use language differently is the many social registers all people employ when talking to people they hold in different degrees of intimacy and respect. Even a kindergarten child uses different forms of address when she is talking to another child, her mother, or her teacher. In English, different degrees of intimacy and formality are signaled by the amount of indirection that is used. Compare the following sentences:

"Hey, open the window!"
"Please open the window."
"Would you mind opening the window?"
"Don't you think we need some fresh air in here?"

Other languages signal these differences with grammatical forms. Spanish has the familiar form of the pronoun *tu*, used with close friends and family members, and the formal *usted*, used with adults. Romanian has *tu*, which is familiar, but also *dumneavoastra*, which is more formal and distant, and *dumneata*, which, as one Romanian explained, is "so polite that it's insulting." Linguists use the term *registers* to refer to the ranges of speech speakers have for expressing themselves in different social situations:

- A *ceremonial register*, used in religious functions and formal affairs such as school graduations
- A *professional register*, used in giving an explanation at school such as discussing a lesson in science or language arts
- A *polite register*, used in informal situations with people the speaker does not know well
- A *casual register*, used when telling a story or sharing jokes with close friends.

For Review

If reading is making sense of talk written down, then children need a healthy level of language development in order to read, and teachers need more than a passing acquaintance with linguistics, the study of language, in order to teach reading well.

In this chapter we explored the main areas of language knowledge, including the sound system of language or *phonology*, the grammar of language or *syntax*, and the meaning system or *semantics*. We also looked at social variations in language as well as the uses to which language is put. English uses an alphabetic writing system, so the letters of the alphabet relate to individual speech sounds. But morphemes or meaningful word roots and affixes are also important both in the structure of words and in the act of reading them.

English spelling relates to the spoken language in interesting and often vexing ways. Watching children trying to discover the patterns and rules of English spelling—that is, their invented spelling—is not only fascinating but important if we are going to understand how they are thinking about words, and help them advance their knowledge.

Teachers need to be aware of the varieties of registers and dialects of language. Dialects and registers are a great part of the richness of language; but we need to make sure all children have control of the grapholect, the "dialect" of written language. The functions for which language is used should be practiced in all their diversity. This will not only help children read a variety of genres, but also increase their awareness of the world and their ability to reflect on themselves and relate to others.

For Your Journal

1. Review the answers to the anticipation guide on the first page of this chapter. What answers would you give to those questions now that you have read this chapter?

2. If you still need proof that you have tacit knowledge of English grammar, that is, knowledge that enables you to talk and listen but of which you are largely unaware, try this exercise. Explain what is wrong with this sentence: *Ignacio is playing with a red big ball.*

State the rule that you would use in writing the sentence correctly.

3. Families from different social backgrounds think of literacy in strikingly different ways. How did you use literacy in your family when you were growing up? What materials did the people around you read? Did they share or discuss them with each other? If so, how? Was there bedtime reading? If so, what was it like?

Taking It to the World

1. Look up your own state's standards for elementary and reading teachers' knowledge of language. You can find them on your state department of education's website, usually by entering the keyword "standards." What do you think teachers need to know about language besides what is mandated in the state standards?

2. Interview a guidance counselor at a middle or high school or a counseling psychologist who treats adults.

Interview a foreman or manager at a business or manufacturing plant. With regard to their clients or the people they supervise, to what extent do these professionals find that people's problems are related to their difficulties in using language for different purposes—for self-awareness, for getting along with others, for giving and receiving directions clearly? Do these people believe that schools have a role in teaching communication for different purposes?

New Literacies Connections

The Internet has many excellent sites with information on language.

Professors Lily Fillmore and Catherine Snow have an excellent summary of language concepts for the teacher available on line at http://www.cal.org/ericcll/teachers/teachers.pdf. The work is entitled *What teachers need to know about language*, and it was originally published in August, 2000, by the U.S. Department of Education's Office of Educational Research and Improvement. This 50-page monograph is written in a question-and-answer format with chapters on oral and written language, and language and diversity. It's an excellent summary of essential knowledge about language by two distinguished scholars.

There are several sites on the Internet that provide rich examples of how sounds are made, including diagrams of the mouth, recordings of sounds, and even spectrographic displays of sound waves produced with sound.

1. Professor George Dillon at the University of Washington has a wonderful site (http://faculty.washington.edu/dillon/PhonResources/) that provides information about speech sounds and also links to numerous other sites that provide detailed information and tutorials.

2. Visit the "Vocal Vowels" exhibit at the San Francisco Museum of Science's online Exploratorium (www.exploratorium.edu/exhibits/vocal_vowels) to see how a duck call can be made to produce human vowel sounds by modifying the production chamber.

3. Noted linguist Peter Ladefoged provides a comprehensive site devoted to speech sounds at http://hctv.humnet.ucla.edu/departments/linguistics/VowelsandConsonants.

Emergent Literacy

Anticipation Guide

The following statements will get you thinking about the topics of this chapter. Answer *true* or *false* in response to each statement. As you read and learn more about the topics mentioned in these statements, think back on your answers. See what interests you and what prompts your curiosity toward more understanding.

_____ 1. When you get right down to it, learning to read is "natural."

_____ 2. The ability to tap out individual phonemes in words is normally developed by the end of kindergarten.

_____ 3. Most children understand concepts about print—such as the arrangement of print on the page or the fact that people read the print and not the pictures—without any instruction.

_____ 4. Children should never be allowed to write words incorrectly.

_____ 5. Invented spelling provides teachers with insights into children's knowledge of phonics.

_____ 6. We can teach children a lot about reading and writing through passive means, such as labeling items in the classroom.

_____ 7. When children imitate adults reading storybooks, they teach themselves important concepts about the way reading works.

_____ 8. Reading aloud to children is a waste of valuable instructional time. If it is to be done at all, it should be left up to parents.

_____ 9. Teaching reading is such a complicated undertaking that parents should be discouraged from taking any part in it.

_____ 10. Parents read to their children much more than they used to. This is true of people from all income groups.

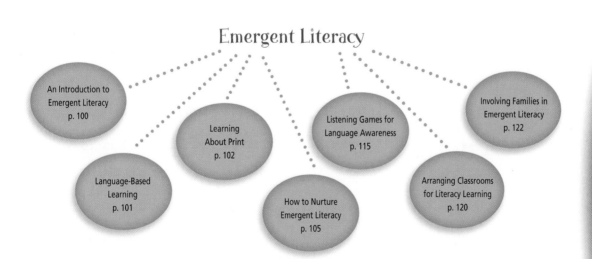

Emergent Literacy

- An Introduction to Emergent Literacy p. 100
- Language-Based Learning p. 101
- Learning About Print p. 102
- How to Nurture Emergent Literacy p. 105
- Listening Games for Language Awareness p. 115
- Arranging Classrooms for Literacy Learning p. 120
- Involving Families in Emergent Literacy p. 122

A Classroom Story

Emergent Literacy Routines in a Kindergarten Classroom

It is the second Monday in November, and Ignacio Diaz's kindergartners know the morning routine very well. As they enter, they take off their coats, stuff their lunch boxes into their cubbies, then check the job board to see who will give the weather report, who will lead the Pledge of Allegiance, and who will line the children up to go to lunch. Then they go to the task board and see what their rotations are for the language block. Their names are pasted in quadrants with symbols, indicating who will go to the independent study center, who will work with the teacher in the reading circle, who will write, and who will have reading time. Charmaigne enters the room and hands her teacher a book baggie, a plastic bag that holds a book and a group of games and activity sheets.

"Mama said she liked the drawing I did of Toad. Or maybe it was Frog. … How do you tell them apart again?" she says. "And she said to tell you we finally figured out how to do the alphabet game."

Ignacio laughs and puts the book baggie into a bin to be repacked for another child to take home.

As children come in from various buses,

Charmaigne wanders to the library corner and begins reading a little book about frogs. It is one of her favorites, written by Henry, the boy who taught them all to draw cartoons. Henry's penciled letters make dubious spellings that flow across the page in pencil, but Charmaigne focuses on the neat black letters her teacher has written with a felt-tipped pen. She can read some of the words, and she likes finding the ones she knows. Henry's drawings always make clear what is going on in his books, so when Charmaigne wants to, she can hold the book up and tell the story aloud as if she were reading it, even though she does not yet know many of the words.

The class is all here, and Charmaigne's time has come to lead the Pledge of Allegiance. She knows what a flag is, but the word *flag* is taped underneath it anyway. It begins with *F*, just like the title of Henry's book, *Frogs*. Now Mr. Diaz calls the children to the rug in front of the chart stand.

"Who knows what today is?" he asks.

"Monday," says Henry.

"Right," says Ignacio. "And I'm going to write 'Today is Monday' right here on the

chart. Let's say that sentence: 'Today is Monday.' "

"Today is Monday," chants the class.

"What's the first word I need to write?"

"Today," Charmaigne offers.

"Good. I'm going to start writing up here," and he points to the upper left-hand corner of the sheet. "What's the first sound we hear in 'Today'?" Some children, including Charmaigne, chant the *tuh* sound, over and over. After a moment's hesitation, other children join them.

"Aw, you're champions. Now, what letter will we use to spell the *tuh* sound?" With the children and Mr. Diaz taking turns offering up sounds and naming letters to spell them with, the morning news is written on the chart. It covers four lines. Ignacio is careful to show the children that he begins writing over on the left side, then writes across to the right, then returns to the left but down one line, and continues writing to the right again.

The children read the sentences through three times as Ignacio points to every word with his "Harry Potter wand," the stick he uses for pointing to words.

An Introduction to Emergent Literacy

If they grow up in a community where others read and write, children learn a great deal about literacy years before they meet their first teacher. They learn by their own efforts, and they employ an amazing capacity to look closely at language, tease out its patterns, and work their way toward competent use through a succession of more and more sophisticated stages, or layers of strategies. We now realize that children depend on adults to "put literacy in their way"—to surround children with print, read to them, and set up opportunities for children to try out their own versions of reading and writing. These opportunities are a hidden advantage for children, and they allow them to start right into reading instruction with understanding and enthusiasm. But we also have learned that while some children get thousands of hours of early experiences with literacy at home, other children get few. So teachers of children in preschool and in the early school grades have a lot of work to do to prepare all children to make a good start in learning to read and write. We call this whole enterprise **emergent literacy.** It's a mix of what children first discover for themselves and what adults help them learn about literacy.

Emergent literacy means:

- a period in children's experience between the time when they first notice print and wonder what people are doing when they work with it, and the time when they can read words.
- the early informal and formal teaching that children receive in preschool and kindergarten at the hands of careful teachers who make sure that all children understand what reading and writing are and what they are for, so they can benefit fully from reading instruction.

Because print represents spoken language, children learning to read must be familiar with the features of print, and also have an adequate control of spoken language. A group of scholars commissioned by the U.S. government, the National Early Literacy Panel (2008), concluded from a review of the research that these factors predicted the success of children five years old and younger in learning to read:

- a set of spoken language factors—vocabulary, grammar, and the ability to hear sounds in words—and
- a set of print factors—knowing the letters of the alphabet, knowing the ways print is arranged on the page, and being able to write their own name and other words.

Learning about language, learning about print, and learning how print and language go together in reading and writing are the main aspects of emergent literacy that will be explored in this chapter.

Language-Based Learning

With our speech, we can pledge love, declare war, or forecast heat waves or blizzards—rarely having to think about the language we use to do these things. When children learn to read, though, they have to be conscious of language. Because print represents spoken language, emergent readers need to be aware of the words from which language is built. They need to be aware of the syllables and sounds that make up words. They also need to be learning about print—beginning with some general ideas about what it is and what its main features are, and going on to the letters that make it up.

The Concept of Word

The concept of word (Morris, 2005) has two parts to it. One is knowing that a frantically uttered expression such as "MamacomequickYvonneseatingmycandy" is actually made up of the words "Mama, come quick. Yvonne's eating my candy." This is not an easy feat. Even adults can have trouble separating the speech stream into word units. Another aspect of the concept of word is knowing that words in print are clusters of letters separated by spaces.

Not being aware of words in speech puts children at a disadvantage when they are learning to read. Instead of focusing on each word as they say it in their minds, children who do not have the concept of word might scan their eyes across a whole line of text, or

Teach It! 4

Language Experience or Group Dictated Story

Short periods of dedicated instruction can help struggling readers improve their reading skills. (Lindfors Photography)

they might look at only a single letter, or they might confuse written words with spoken syllables. A child who doesn't have the concept of word and isn't looking at the correct word unit is not likely to learn to recognize any new written words during a reading activity. But the child who has the concept of word, who looks at the written words at the instant each is read aloud, will likely have made matches between some of the written versions of the words with the spoken versions. That child may be able to recognize some of those words in the future.

An instrument for assessing children's concept of word may be found in Temple, Crawford and Gillet, *Developmental Literacy Inventory* (2008).

Phonological Awareness

Beyond the level of words, there are other levels of speech of which emergent readers must be aware. These are *syllables, onsets and rimes,* and *phonemes*. As we saw in Chapter 3, **syllables** are the pulses of language. They are the "beats" we hear in *elbow* (two syllables), *love* (one syllable), and *popsicle* (three syllables). In that chapter, we also discussed that onsets and rimes are the next largest parts of syllables: The **onset** is the beginning consonant sound (if the syllable has one), and the **rime** is the vowel sound plus any consonant sound that follows. In *cat*, the onset is /c/ and the rime is /at/. In *step*, the onset is /st/ and the rime is /ep/. As the smallest speech sounds in language, **phonemes** roughly correspond to letters. *Dig* has three phonemes: /d/, /i/, and /g/. *Clam* has four phonemes: /k/, /l/, /a/, and /m/. (Note that we conventionally represent phonemes with slashes on either side.)

A good deal of research (e.g., Adams, 1991; Snow et al., 1998) has shown that children who are aware that words can be broken into phonemes are more likely to learn to read words successfully than those who lack this awareness. We know that if children are aware of sounds in words, they will have an easier time matching letters and sounds when they begin to read. We also know that even short periods of instruction in phonemic awareness can improve children's word reading (Blachman, 2008).

An instrument for testing children's awareness of phonemes is found in Temple, Crawford, and Gillet, *Developmental Literacy Inventory* (2008). Several exercises to help emergent readers become aware of language—from words to syllables to onsets and rhymes to phonemes—are presented later in this chapter.

Phonics and Phonological Awareness

Why must emergent readers be aware of syllables, onsets and rimes, and phonemes?

Learning About Print

Now let's look at the print side of things. As we said, children's emergent literacy is partly knowing about language and partly knowing about print. Print awareness includes:

- having concepts about print: a set of ideas about what print is and how it works
- understanding the alphabetic nature of writing: the idea that, in languages such as English, German, Spanish, and Kiswahili (but not Japanese or Chinese), writing works by using units of letters to represent language at the level of phonemes
- alphabet knowledge: being able to recognize and produce many letters of the alphabet
- orthographic concepts: an understanding of the rules that relate letters to sounds

Concepts About Print

New Zealander Marie Clay (1975) offers us this account of a novice teacher giving a reading lesson to a group of beginning readers:

> Suppose the teacher has placed an attractive picture on the wall and has asked her children for a story, which she will record under it. They offer the text, "Mother is cooking," which the teacher alters slightly to introduce some features she wishes to teach. She writes: Mother said, "I am baking."
>
> If she says, "Now look at our story," 30% of the new entrant group [children who are just beginning reading instruction] will attend to the picture. If she says, "Look at the words and find some that you know," between 50 and 90% will be looking for letters. If she says, "Can you see Mother?" most will agree that they can, but some see her in the picture, some can locate M, and others will locate the word Mother.
>
> Perhaps the children read in unison, "Mother is ..." and the teacher tries to sort this out. Pointing to said, she asks, "Does this say is?" Half agree that it does because it has s in it. "What letter does it start with?" Now the teacher is really in trouble. She assumes that the children will know that a word is built out of letters, but 50% of the children still confuse the verbal labels word and letter after six months of instruction. She also assumes that the children know that the left-hand letter following a space is the "start" of a word. Often they do not. (pp. 3–4)

As this example shows, there are many concepts about print that children must have in place so that in a reading lesson, they can orient themselves properly to a book and direct their attention appropriately. These concepts include knowing the layout of books; knowing what the print and the pictures do; knowing how print is laid out on the page; knowing the terms used in reading instruction, such as "the beginning of the sentence," "the end of the sentence," "the first word," "the top of the page"; knowing what a word is; knowing what a letter is and that uppercase and lowercase letters are different versions of the same thing; and knowing at least some marks of punctuation.

An instrument for testing children's concepts about print is found in Temple, Crawford, and Gillet, *Developmental Literacy Inventory* (2008).

Big Book Lesson

Alphabet Knowledge

Alphabet knowledge is an important part of a child's emergent literacy. Some children learn to recognize most letters of the alphabet before they enter kindergarten, and all are expected to recognize and produce all 26 letters by the beginning of first grade. Knowing all of the letters does two things for a child: it gives teachers an idea of how much exposure to print a child has had (Walsh, Price, & Gillingham, 1988), and it helps that child learn to read (Morris, 2007).

An instrument for testing children's knowledge of the alphabet is found in Temple, Crawford, and Gillet, *Developmental Literacy Inventory* (2008).

LETTER-TO-SOUND CORRESPONDENCE: LEARNING PHONICS. A child realizes that language is real and comes in units of words, syllables, and phonemes. The child can now produce not just letter-like forms, but also many actual letters. The child has learned to orient himself or herself to books. The child realizes that ours is an alphabetic writing system that works not by showing pictures of things, not by representing syllables, but by matching letters with phonemes. Now what?

Now comes the process of discovering the system by which writing spells words, and letters and clusters of letters represent sounds or groups of sounds. This kind of knowledge is called **phonics**. It is also called *orthographic knowledge* and *letter-to-sound relationships*. The patterns that relate letters to sounds are complex. They come in layers that are peeled back, essentially in stages, by the child who is encouraged to be an active explorer of written language.

Phonics and Phonological Awareness

Phonics is the system by which letters and clusters of letters represent speech sounds.

Working with Names to Teach the Alphabet

Analytic Phonics Lesson

The World of Reading

The Development of Storybook Reading: Language and Print Together

A line of development that combines both language awareness and concepts about print is children's progress in storybook reading. Researcher Elizabeth Sulzby (1985) has shown us that having children pretend-read a favorite storybook can be a very useful way to observe their concepts of what reading is about and how language is captured in print. When we read a storybook to children at the age of four or five, they often ask to have it read again. A storybook that is read to a child three or more times, especially when it is requested, can be said to be a favorite storybook. What happens if we ask the child to read that favorite storybook back to us? With a little encouragement, most children will pretend-read the book; when they do, they are demonstrating for us their conception of what reading is. Sulzby has observed hundreds of children rereading favorite storybooks and has documented stages or advancing strategies that children use to read books. Her stages are repeated by other children so reliably that watching for them can give us a developmentally based assessment tool.

- **Picture naming.** At the earliest of the book-reading strategies, the child points at the picture, shouts the name of the depicted object, then points to the next page and does the same thing. As Sulzby notes, such a child is repeating a ritual he or she has been through many times with a parent or other adult reader, who often opens a book, points to a picture, says, "What's that?" waits for the child's answer, then says, "Right! That's a _____!"

- **Verbal storytelling with conversation.** Slightly later, some time around the age of four or five years, the child will point to the pictures and then weave an oral story around them in a conversation with the adult. This is not a stand-alone story yet, as it still relies on an adult for support. It also is cued by the pictures rather than by the print on the page or the exact words the child remembers from the adult's reading.

- **Verbal storytelling without conversation.** At a slightly later time, often around age five, a child will tell a story while paging through the book from picture to picture. The story is clearly a told

story, and if the child pretend-reads this book more than once, no attempt will be made to keep the wording the same.

- **Talking like a book.** Still later, the child will use a singsong, rather distant voice that sounds like a reader's—sometimes even complete with stumbling over words—while creating a monologue to accompany the pictures. Amazingly, the child is still not actually reading the words, which you will note when the monologue bears little resemblance to what is on the page.

- **Refusal to read.** At a still later stage when asked to read the book aloud, the child will become troubled by the request. Why? Because the child doesn't know how to read the words. This is actually a breakthrough. Not knowing the words did not prevent pretend-reading of the book before. But now the child seems to have realized that to read a book, one has to look at the print and know how to pronounce it as spoken language.

- **Reading a word or two.** Still later, when asked to pretend-read the book, the child will look for known words and read them aloud.

This fascinating sequence of strategies shows the child moving from a series of isolated verbal responses to pictures to a woven verbal text—first with the support of conversation and then without support, followed by a phase of talking like a book and then leading to the realization that to truly read, one must know how to bring to life exactly the words that are written on the page. Once that last discovery has been made, the child is ready to match the expected words with the words on the page (and doubtless bringing into play other knowledge, such as the concept of word and knowledge of letters) and read a few words aloud. The child has gone from playful imitation of the whole of reading to a careful study of the details. Bit by bit, especially if given books written on an accessible level, the child will be able to return to the whole while reading the entire book aloud.

Allowing children to act out stories encourages interpretive imagination, and the active involvement adds fun.

INVENTED SPELLING AND WORD KNOWLEDGE.   One of the best ways to observe children's growth in the ways letters and sounds go together is through their invented spelling (see Chapter 3). When children spell words they have not been taught, their invented spelling gives us a window into the complicated issues of how children understand the relationships between spoken words and written symbols, also known as their **word knowledge**. Looking at children's invented spellings can help to answer questions like these:

- Does this child appear to have a concept of word? Can the child make words "hold still" in his or her mind while examining their parts and deciding how to spell those parts?

- Can this child segment words into phonemes, and match letters to phonemes? Which ones?
- Which principles of the English writing system does this child understand? Letters-to-sounds? Onsets and rimes? Marking of long and short vowels? Grammatical endings? Word families?

How to Nurture Emergent Literacy

Moving children along toward literacy—and giving thoughtful extra boosts to those children with gaps in their awareness of reading and writing—is the teacher's task in the phase of emergent literacy. Teachers use two kinds of strategies here: logistic strategies (those that develop many skills at once), especially reading aloud, shared reading, and shared writing; and activities directed at specific skills, such as alphabet learning, hearing sounds in words, phonics, and comprehension. The classroom environment is suffused with literacy, including learning centers that encourage drawing, literacy-centered play, a classroom library, listening centers, charts and posters, and technology.

Emergent writing samples offer insight into the concepts about print and knowledge of letters and sounds held by an individual student. Complete the Building Teaching Skills and Dispositions activity "Analyzing Emergent Writing for Emergent Literacy Understandings" to develop your skills in assessing what a child knows and needs to learn. (To find this activity, go to the topic *Emergent Literacy* in MyEducationLab and click on Building Teaching Skills and Dispositions.)

Reading Aloud to Children

Reading aloud is one of the most useful, active things adults can do to nurture children's literacy growth. Many of the abilities that are considered essential to literacy can be developed as children listen to a book read aloud by a parent or teacher. Among the main benefits of being read to are the following:

Reading Aloud

- **It expands their vocabulary.** As Stanovich (1992) has pointed out, there are words that are more commonly encountered in books—even children's books—than in conversation or from watching television. Listening to books being read aloud helps children learn a literate vocabulary.
- **It develops their ability to comprehend written language.** Research on reading comprehension tells us that it involves component skills that include perceiving main ideas and supporting details, making inferences, venturing predictions and confirming them, and visualizing in the mind's eye what the words suggest. Children have the opportunity to develop all of these abilities from listening to a book being read aloud and discussing it.
- **It encourages enthusiasm for literacy as they participate in the teacher's excitement.** When children first learn to talk, parents slow down and exaggerate their speech and their gestures as if to say, "This is how language works. This is how we show excitement and interest. This is the way we soothe each other." Similarly, when adults read books aloud with expression, they have the opportunity to show children how written language conveys the full range of emotions. This not only will make literacy appealing to children, but also will show them how to derive meaning and associate emotions with the language of print.
- **It makes them aware of the structure of stories and of other kinds of texts.** Skilled readers learn to find questions and pursue answers according to the structure of whatever text they are reading. A story shows characters in settings, along with the problems they have and how those problems are solved. Expository writing frames questions about topics and goes about answering those questions. By reading texts aloud and commenting on them, a careful teacher can help students to become aware of the recurring structures of different texts and use them to guide their comprehension.

Reading aloud two or three times each day should be a regular feature of every classroom from preschool through the primary grades and on through the elementary grades. Even when children are learning to read, it is not until fourth grade that many children's reading ability approaches the speed and fluency with which teachers can read to them. Many children's reading rate will take much longer to develop. Therefore, the teacher's reading aloud is a necessary source of language, of stories, and of information for children. Please see the Teach It box for detailed guidance on reading aloud to children.

Teach It!

Refer to the Teach It! appendix at the end of the book for further activities you can use to reinforce concepts discussed in this chapter.

Reading Aloud

You certainly do not need advanced training to read a book aloud successfully with children! Nonetheless, good preparation is rewarded by a more satisfying experience all around. We suggest following these steps when reading aloud to children:

1. **Prepare to read the book.** Read the book through yourself before you read it to children. Decide whether it is suitable for this group. Does it have enough excitement or depth to hold the interest of a whole group? If it is suitable, decide how you want to read it—with humor, with drama, with questions to whet curiosity? If there are voices to bring to life, decide how you want to make each one sound. If you decide to stop reading to ask for predictions or discussion, decide where the stopping places should be. If there are any words or ideas that will be unfamiliar to the children, make a note to pronounce them carefully and explain them to the children.

   If the book has illustrations large enough for the children to see, practice reading the book through while you hold it in front of and facing away from you, where the children will be able to read it.

2. **Prepare the children.** Make sure the children are seated comfortably where they can see and hear you. Most teachers prefer to have the children sit on a carpet or cushions in front of them. Remind the children, if you need to, of the behavior you expect of good listeners: hands to themselves, eyes on the teacher, and ears for the story.

3. **Begin to read.** Show the children the cover of the book. Ask them what they know about the topic. If you want to arouse more curiosity, quickly show them some other pictures in the interior of the book (but not the last pages, keep the children in suspense about those). Ask the children to make predictions about what will happen or what they expect to find out in the book.

   Turn to the title page. Read the author's name and the illustrator's. Talk about what each contributed to the book. It might help to point out

that if only one name is given, then the illustrator and author are the same person. Otherwise, the children should know that the author and illustrator both have important things to do to bring the book into being. (Publishers usually pay authors and illustrators equally and usually encourage them to work independently of each other.) Remind the children of any other books they know by this author or this illustrator.

4. **While reading.** As you read the book through the first time, ask for comments about what is going on. How is the character feeling? What is the character's problem? What do they think the character can do to solve the problem? Ask the students to predict what will happen. Read a few pages, then stop again. Ask how things look for the character now. What is the character doing to solve the problem? How is it working? What do the children think will happen now? Why do they think so? Stop right before the end and ask for last predictions. You can add to the suspense if you take an obvious quick look at the last page, but don't let the children see it. Then ask the children to predict what will be on the last page.

5. **Follow up the reading.** Ask the children whether the book turned out the way they thought it would. What made them think it would turn out that way, or why were they surprised? What did they like about the book? How did it make them feel? Why?

6. **Reread the book.** Read the book a second time through. This time, you might want to take more time to look at the ways the illustrator pictured the action. If there are any chants given in the book, ask children to repeat them. If there is time, ask questions about characters, motives, and other things you and the students find interesting about the book.

7. **Leave the book available to the children.** Put the book on display in the library corner, and encourage children to read it later during scheduled time in the reading center or between other activities. The children might especially enjoy taking turns reading it to each other.

Extending Reading Experiences for Younger Children

The meanings of books can loom larger in children's imaginations by providing them opportunities to respond to the books in various ways. Although children of all ages can talk about what they read (Morrow & Gambrell, 2004), younger children find it most natural to respond to books with their whole bodies: by getting up and moving around, by chanting chants, by acting out parts, and by drawing key scenes (Hickman, 1992). English language learners have more opportunities to participate if meaningful responses to stories are encouraged through drama, music, and art rather than through discussion only.

USE CHANTS.   A very engaging form of response to a story is to repeat a key phrase or chant every time it occurs in a book. English language learners profit from repeating shorter chants, which become nuggets of remembered language that are useful models of grammar and good for pronunciation practice.

USE DRAMA.   Many children's books have clear patterns of actions that are easy for children to act out. Some books, such as Michael Rosen's *We're Going on a Bear Hunt* (2003) and Frances Temple's *Tiger Soup* (1992), are already scripted for children to act out. Both have chants and movements that the children will enjoy. *The Three Billy Goats Gruff* is not scripted as a play, but it has simple, repeated actions and chants that are easy for children to practice and perform. The whole story can be rehearsed and staged in a single class period. Single scenes of longer stories can be acted out, too, if time is short.

Acting involves interpretation. You can encourage children to interpret stories imaginatively as they rehearse the dramatizations: "How does the little goat feel when he sees the troll? How might he look at that point? What would his voice sound like?" Props help children get into character. In *The Three Billy Goats Gruff*, horns made of construction paper bring the goats to life, and a robe and a club add to the troll's fierceness. Construction paper masks indicate which character is Tiger and which one is Anansi the Spider in *Tiger Soup*.

USE ART.   Drawing is a favorite way for children to respond to a story. The drawings may be extended by asking the children to leave space at the bottom of their papers and think of one line they want to dictate to the teacher. The children can rehearse reading these lines and then take them home to read to family members. Another activity, "Sketch to Stretch" (Short, Harste, & Burke, 1996), is a wonderful way to add interpretation when children draw in response to a story. After they have listened to a story, the children draw their favorite part or the most important part. Then one child is invited to be the artist and display his or her work for the critics (classmates) to interpret. After the critics have noted the features in the drawing and commented on what they think each one means, the artist then gets to interpret his or her own work, telling the critics why the story was depicted as it was.

Making Individual Small Books

Allowing children to act out stories encourages interpretive imagination, and the active involvement adds fun. (Lindfors Photography)

Dialogic Reading

When working with individual children, one approach to reading with children called **dialogic reading** helps put the child in the active role as a storyteller and not just as a listener. Dialogic reading has shown gains in children's language acquisition and growth in concepts about print (Whitehurst & Lonigan, 2001).

Emergent Readers

SIOP®
Sheltered
Instruction
Observation
Protocol®

Emergent literacy faces in two directions. In one direction, it focuses on the concepts about reading, writing, and written language that children have acquired at home. The teacher can build on those and make a bridge that connects what children are figuring out for themselves with the formal reading curriculum. In another direction, emergent literacy helps us realize the concepts and abilities that some children have not developed yet—concepts and skills they will need to be successful in learning to read and write. These children will need to

- Be read to, to boost their vocabulary and their familiarity with books.
- Explore print, as in giving dictations and having someone read them back.
- Learn the letters of the alphabet.

These are critical experiences, but fortunately it is not such a long list. One way to make sure children get these experiences is to recruit and supervise volunteers. The U.S. Department of Education provides funding for college students to be paid from work-study funds to serve as tutors. Many colleges and high schools have service learning classes in which students are required to perform some kind of community service. Student volunteers can offer effective help to young readers who need it. The key to the success of such efforts is the teacher's supervision. Tutoring is far more effective when a teacher assesses the children in advance to see exactly what they need, and orients and supervises the tutors to make sure they provide the right help (Morris, 2005).

Dialogic reading is intended to be used by parents, teachers, and volunteer tutors, such as college students working in special literacy programs such as America Reads or Jumpstart. In some communities, training in dialogic reading is available through family literacy programs offered by public libraries. The training is supported by twenty-minute videotapes (Whitehurst, 1994). Adult readers are taught to read interactively with the child. Two acronyms, PEER and CROWD, are used to remind the adult readers of the steps. PEER is a mnemonic for a strategy used to nurture language development with younger children as they read a book together with an adult. The letters stand for:

Prompt the child to name objects in the book and talk about the story.

Evaluate the child's responses and offer praise for adequate responses and alternatives for inadequate ones.

Expand on the child's statements with additional words. Then,

Repeat by asking the child to repeat the adult's utterances.

For more advanced children, a more involved form of dialogic reading called CROWD is used. The acronym CROWD identifies five kinds of questions adults ask:

Completion prompts. Ask the child to supply a word or phrase that has been omitted. (For example, "I see a yellow duck looking at ___.")

Recall prompts. Here the child is asked about things that occurred earlier in the book. ("Do you remember some animals that Brown Bear saw?")

Open-ended prompts. Here the child is asked to respond to the story in his own words. ("Now it's your turn: You say what is happening on this page.")

Wh- prompts. The adult asks what, where, who, and why questions. ("What is that yellow creature called? Who do you think Brown Bear will see next?")

Distancing prompts. Here the child is asked to relate the content of the book to life experiences. ("Do you remember when we saw a yellow duck like that one swimming in the lake? Was it as big as this one?")

Helping Literacy Emerge

Approaches for helping children's literacy emerge include lesson strategies (Shared Reading, Shared Writing, and Guided Reading), skill instruction (teaching the alphabet and raising children's awareness of sounds), learning centers and games, and embedding literacy in the classroom environment.

Shared Reading

Shared Reading (Booth & Schwartz, 2004; Holdaway, 1979) is a strategy for guiding the students' attention through the reading process. It is also very effective for introducing the concepts of print and word to children. It requires a "big book": a book large enough so that all can easily read the print, an easel to place the book on, so the teacher's hands are free for pointing, and a pointing stick.

Seat a group of up to ten children close enough so that they can see the text and also feel a sense of community. With the book on the easel, use a pointer stick (a ruler or something more exotic, like a Harry Potter wand) to point to each word as you read it. But read the words smoothly and fluently, keeping in mind that you are modeling fluent reading.

Big books (Holdaway, 1979) are very large versions of children's books with print and illustrations that can be read by a group of children. While teachers sometimes make big books themselves, many publishers are producing big book versions of simply written picture books, especially those with highly patterned texts that are especially good for emergent and beginning readers.

Big books can be used to show children the layout of books and also to practice reading and rereading text. In a typical lesson with emergent readers, the teacher reads the book twice.

On the First Reading

- Put the big book on an easel and call the children's attention to the cover. Point to the title and have the students read it aloud with you. Ask the students to say what they think the book will be about, given the title, and invite their ideas and predictions.

- Point to the cover illustration and invite the students to say what they see. When they think of the title and consider the picture, what do they think will happen in the story?

- Open to the title page and point to the author's name. Make sure the children understand that this is the person who wrote the book. Do the same with the name of the illustrator. Do the children know any other books by either one of them?

- Now turn to the first page of text and read it aloud, pointing to the words as you go. Read several more pages this way, pausing to discuss a picture or to comment on an action.

- Ask the children to make predictions, even predictions about what will happen on the other side of a page. Sometimes rhyming books have a phrase on one page that ends in a word that is matched with a phrase on the next page ending in a rhyming word. You might pause at the page turn and ask the children what will come next. For example, on one page of John Langstaff's *A Hunting We Will Go* are the words:

Using big books is a valuable way to introduce students to reading and to help them become familiar with all the elements in books. (Ellen B. Senisi)

A hunting we will go
A hunting we will go
We'll catch a fox

Before turning the page, pause and ask the children to predict what comes next. The text continues:

And put him in a box
And then we'll let him go.

On the Second Reading
Now get the children to help you read the book.

- Go back to the beginning of the book, and invite the children to read it again with you. Using a stylus or something similar, choral-read a page with the children.
- Still pointing to the words, echo-read the next page with the children.
- Silently point to the words in a repeated phrase, and invite the children to read them.
- Finally, invite individual children to come up and read a line of text as you point to the words.

On a Third Reading
To teach a lesson using the text, you may:

- mask a word with your hand or with a piece of tag board, and ask students to guess it from context, or from context with only the first letter showing, or the first two letters, and so on.
- write four or five sentences from the text on strips of paper, and have students arrange them in order in a pocket chart.
- cut apart a sentence and have a student or students arrange the words in order in a pocket chart.
- pass out word cards and have students match them to words in the text, or with words that begin with the same letter, or that rhyme with them, or that contain the same syllable.
- pass out cards with lowercase letters on them and have students match them with uppercase letters in the text, and vice versa.
- point to capital letters at the beginnings of sentences and explain why they are there.
- point out the function of punctuation.
- ask students to point to words that show how something looked, or how someone felt, or what someone did, etc.

You may have a discussion of the book. Ask the students about their favorite parts of the text. Also ask open-ended questions that connect to the students' backgrounds and experiences, and even to other books they have read.

Following the reading with the group, leave the big book available for children to read individually and to each other.

THE LANGUAGE EXPERIENCE APPROACH.   The Language Experience Approach, or LEA (Crawford et al., 1995; Stauffer, 1975), has long been considered a "natural" way to introduce children to literacy because it uses the student's oral language to teach written language. Like shared reading, it is especially effective for introducing the concepts of print and word to children. There are many variations of the LEA approach. The following is a step-by-step process we recommend. Use it with a small group (six to ten children) or when working with one child.

First Lesson   In the first twenty- to thirty-minute lesson, complete these three steps.

Step 1: Discussion. Talk with students about their experiences (e.g., their favorite foods or birthday parties). Respond positively, be curious about their stories, and value their input. Let the children know that you will write down some things from their stories that they can all read together. In later LEA lessons the discussion topics could be about science or current events.

Step 2: Dictation. Ask the children what to write, select some of their responses, and write them on large chart paper, an overhead, or a computer screen. Be sure everyone can see your writing. Make teaching points about where to begin writing as you think appropriate. Read each sentence and ask them to read it back to you.

Step 3: Reading the Text. Now it's time for the children to read their text. But first read it to them again and guide them to watch the words as you run your finger or pointer under them. Then have the children read along with you, and finally they read on their own.

To extend the lesson, give the children copies of the text and have them practice in pairs or alone. Emphasize that this is just practice; give the children time and support to engage deeply in reading their own language.

In this initial two-day cycle of LEA, the first lesson consists of motivation and discussion, dictation and reading, and shared reading, as just described. On the following day, there are several additional steps.

Second Lesson

Step 1: Reading the Text. Read the text again and prompt careful watching of the words as you point to them. Then have the children read with you. Practice this as much as needed. When reading sounds somewhat fluent, have the children take turns reading on their own. Include everyone. Every child can read even if it is only a word or two with your support.

Step 2: Reassembling the Text. Before beginning step 2, make copies of the sentences on sentence strips in the order they appear on the original text. Begin the lesson by having the children look at the whole text and then have them look for the first sentence. As children point out each sentence, put them in a sentence strip holder or adjustable pocket chart one at a time and practice reading them together. Each time, read the sentence and then read the entire text. Again, children can take turns reading individually as they are able. You can also ask children to point at the sentence that tells [fill in blank]. This two-day cycle is repeated once or twice every week with a new theme for each set of lessons. Children will not learn all the words at first, but keep developing new charts for them to maintain interest. Be sure to keep copies available so children can practice. When you notice that children have learned to recognize a number of words, usually after several weeks, you can add a third lesson on sight vocabulary and move on to a three-day LEA cycle.

Third Lesson

Step 1: Reassembling the Words into Sentences. Before beginning step 1, cut each sentence strip made for the second lesson into individual words. Place the words in the pocket chart or even on the chalk rail. Place them in a random order and support the children in reassembling the words into sentences. Have the original story nearby so they can refer to it as needed. Build independence by asking children, "If you don't know a word, can you find it in our story? Now read the sentence. Can you read the word?" As sentences are reassembled, guide the reading of the whole text from time to time.

Finally, you can implement other word activities. Here are a few ideas:

- Give word cards from the sentences to the children, and ask them to find the words in the text.
- Say, "Here is the word _____. Find the same word in the text."
- Make a large chart paper copy of one of the texts with some words left out. Tell the children that some words are missing and ask if they can identify them. Read with the children, pausing when you come to a missing word. Support them in "guessing the missing word" and write it in.
- Guide the children to write and keep a personal file collection of the words they learn. Begin with a few words and encourage building the collections and game playing with the word cards.

Teach It! 18

Making and Using Word Banks

For further support of word recognition, you might color code sentence strips and word cards. Or various colors might be marked on the back of cards. Word cards are inevitably mixed up as children work with them at their desks or tables. They are easily sorted back into word groups of original sentences according to the colors on the reverse side.

Several weeks or even a few months after the third lesson activities are added, children will likely show signs of recognizing using letter/sound correspondences in words. This is a signal to add a fourth day to the cycle, a day for word analysis using the context of words the children now recognize at sight.

Fourth Lesson

Step 1: Word Recognition Study. The children read the story, they find words that begin alike, and you support their learning to associate letters and sounds using words they already know. Guide the children to draw conclusions, that is, phonic generalizations out of their observations of letters and corresponding sounds. Continue to use the written language, the words, sentences, and whole texts that have evolved from the children's oral language dictations. This makes powerful use of their background knowledge and helps them to extend their knowledge of sounds and letters in known words to new words. You can also bring out old LEA charts from time to time for review lessons and practice.

Repeated readings develop fluency and automaticity (when children recognize words automatically). As word recognition becomes easier and easier, they are able to focus attention on comprehension (Samuels & Farstrup, 2006).

Guided Reading with Little Books

Little books are short, patterned, and predictable texts supported by pictures and written at carefully graduated levels of difficulty. The lowest difficulty levels include one or two words on a page, with an illustration that strongly suggests what the words might be. Several titles are available on each level so that all readers, even struggling readers, can practice reading in material that is accessible. The difference in challenge between levels is so slight that children can find progressively more difficult material within their reading competence.

Different publishers of little books use different systems for indicating levels. Table 4.1 shows how several of these publishers' systems relate to each other.

Commonly used reading assessment instruments employ somewhat different systems for indicating levels of students' reading ability and the challenge levels of books. See the table and the discussion on pages 342–344 of Chapter 11 for information on the Lexile

Table 4.1 Systems of Leveling Books for Young Readers

BASAL READING LEVELS	SUNSHINE BOOK STAGES	SUNSHINE BOOK LEVELS	READING RECOVERY LEVELS
pp–p	Early emergent	Levels A B C D	1–10
1 to 2–1	Upper emergent	Levels E F G H I J	11–12
2–2 to 3–1	Early fluency	Levels K L M N	13–20
3–2 to 4	Fluency	Levels O P Q R S T	

System, the Developmental Reading Assessment system, and the *Developmental Literacy Inventory*, by two of your present authors.

To make sure the book matches the child's reading level, preview a book with a child and then ask the child to read it through. If the child misses at least one but no more than two words in twenty, the book is at the appropriate instructional reading level for the child to read with supervision. At this level, the child experiences moderate challenges and learns to read new words and practice new strategies without being overwhelmed by difficulty.

The Guided Reading strategy, developed by Irene Fountas and Gay Su Pinnell (2001) is done with small groups of children, usually containing between four and seven students. The children are grouped by their reading level, and the lesson is carried out with a book that is moderately challenging—that is, one in which children can read about nine words out of ten without help. Ideally, the children are seated at a crescent-shaped table with the teacher inside the arc, close to each child.

The lesson begins by previewing the book, both to arouse interest and also to pre-teach a few key words the children might need. The teacher may do a picture walk through the text—that is, weave a preview version of the text while paging through and pointing to the pictures—to support the children's understanding. The book should be introduced in a way that connects with and builds on the children's prior knowledge. "Hmm . . ." you might say, "This looks like a story that could be about a friendship; see, it says (pointing to the text) *Lost and Found* by Oliver Jeffers (2005) and if we look at the picture, the boy and the penguin are hugging. What do you think it's about?"

After children have the opportunity to talk with the teacher and with one another, instruction may then shift to looking at some key vocabulary words from the text that have been put on word cards. Remember, too many words can overwhelm children, so just do a few, perhaps only two. When showing the words, pronounce them and discuss their meanings. This is an opportunity for word study to begin, but don't focus on that aspect yet. Rather, the next step is to read the story.

The teacher then reads aloud the first page or two, thinking aloud about the characters and their situation, and asking questions to engage the students. Once the teacher decides the students know enough to continue reading on their own, he or she invites the children to "whisper-read" to text—reading just loudly enough for the teacher to hear and monitor their reading, but not enough to bother their neighbors.

As the children read, younger children—kindergarten and first graders—are invited to point to each word as they read. (They will be asked to stop pointing once their reading becomes less halting.) The teacher listens for children having problems, and leans in and offers encouragement, corrects a reading, or invites a child to reread a line.

Following the reading, the teacher invites children to have a discussion about what they read, in order to make sure they see that getting the meaning is the purpose of reading.

Later the teacher may go back and teach a lesson from the text. The lessons are similar to those we saw under Shared Reading (see pages 109–112 above).

Finally, the books may be set out for the children to reread with a buddy, to practice reading for fluency.

Teach It! 19

Word Wall Activities

Shared Writing

Teach It! 52

Shared Writing

In Shared Writing (Tompkins, 2000), the teacher and the children produce a text together. The text can be inspired in many ways:

- A counting text based on a theme: "One hungry lion, two scared gazelles," etc.
- A story, perhaps based on a children's book, such as *Frog and Toad* or *Corduroy*.
- Seasons or months.
- Special things about each student.

Depending on the children's needs and the teacher's objectives, the teacher can carefully emphasize the spelling, the way the words are arranged on the page, the punctuation, or the choice of words ("Let's use words that make the readers see what we mean!").

A sample lesson in shared writing might go as is shown in the Teach It! Box.

Writing Workshop

Beginning in kindergarten, many teachers conduct writing workshops three or four days per week. (Writing workshops are described in greater detail in Chapter 10.) For emergent readers and writers, teachers begin by reminding children of the topics they want to write about. Children who are reluctant to begin writing immediately might draw a picture of their topic. The teacher reminds the students to leave space at the bottom of the drawing for their writing. The children then have a period of ten to fifteen minutes for writing and drawing at their seats. Those who have drawn pictures write captions underneath their drawings. Then, one at a time, they take the page to the teacher and read it aloud to her or him. The teacher writes the words correctly above the child's words and

Teach It!

Refer to the Teach It! appendix at the end of the book for further activities you can use to reinforce concepts discussed in this chapter.

Sample Writing Lesson

After discussing an exciting event with his students, a teacher gathers kindergarteners around an easel and invites them to help write about the event. First they agree on a short sentence they want to write:

A fireman came to school.

They practice saying the sentence several times so that everyone is aware of the words. The teacher then tells the students that they will write the first word and asks, "Who can tell us what letter we need to write?"

A child suggests the letter *A,* and the teacher accepts it, writes it slowly on the easel, and then says, "We wrote *A.* Now what's the next word we want to write?"

After someone says, *"Fireman,"* the teacher says, "Right. It's *fireman.* That's a new word, so I'm going to leave space between the word *A* and the first letter of this new word."

The teacher puts his finger after the *A* to identify the space and says, "What is the first sound we hear in *fireman?"*

When the students identify the first sound, the teacher asks, "What letter are we going to use to write the *fuh* sound in *fireman?"*

The teacher pauses for responses and then says, "Right. It's *F.* Who can come up and write the letter *F* for me?"

This process continues as the group works through the entire sentence. When they are finished, the teacher might end up with

A FIRMN CAM TO SKOL.

The teacher concludes by saying, "This could say *A fireman came to school.* Later on, I will show you another way to write it."

The teacher recognizes that these kindergarten children—most of whom are prephonemic or early phonemic spellers—will not be ready to focus on the silent letters in *fireman* and *came* or on the uncommon spelling of *sch* in *school.* Later, when the children can produce letter name spellings, the teacher will show them where silent letters and other conventional spellings would be added to these words to show the students the next challenges they will need to master. But for now, matching letters with phonemes is a sufficient challenge for these children. Shared writing lessons can be conducted almost daily with a class. In the meantime, children should be encouraged to use writing every chance they get.

might take this opportunity to show the children how letters represent sounds. During sharing time, children share their works with the rest of the class.

The writing workshop should have a period of time set aside for focused lessons that show students how to handle particular aspects of writing.

Teaching Phonological Awareness

Phonics and Phonological Awareness

How will you teach children to be aware of speech sounds in spoken words?

As we noted earlier in this chapter, children who are aware of the sound constituents of language have an advantage when it comes to reading words because they will sense the elements of words that are matched with letters. The National Reading Panel (NRP) (2000) recommends that teachers teach phonological awareness in kindergarten through grade 2. This teaching may occupy a short part of each day—six or seven minutes—to yield the 20 hours a year of phonological training that the NRP recommends. Activities to boost phonological awareness can take place at several levels.

LISTENING GAMES FOR LANGUAGE AWARENESS.   Children need to pay attention to language—to listen for words, to move their bodies in response to words, to clap along with the rhythm of language, and to notice rhymes. A number of enjoyable listening activities can help them develop these skills.

Listening for Special Words.   From Mary Hohman (2002) comes the suggestion of using "Magic Words." Say a word like *hotdog,* and tell the children that you are about to tell a story that will have the word *hotdog* in it—they should clap their hands when they hear the word. Start telling the story. For instance, you could say, "Last summer I went down to the park. I was really hungry, so I walked up to the food counter and ordered a—hamburger. The waitress said 'We don't have hamburgers. I'll have to make you a hotdog.' "

Make up several stories with the word *hotdog.* Then ask the children to give you a "magic word," and then you make up a story that has that word in it. The children can take turns making up stories of their own with "magic words" in them, and tell them to others.

Next, you can raise the level of challenge of the magic word game by asking children to listen for two words together. If those words are "ironing board," for instance, you might

Being a Professional Reading Teacher

Children's Reading Levels

The point of providing children with little books on many levels of reading difficulty is to invite them to "ramp up" their reading skills gradually and even delightfully, with colorful and fun books that are just within each child's level of competence. There are a couple of issues here for the teacher to be mindful of, however.

One concern is that the teacher should be aware of each child's instructional and independent reading levels. The instructional level, which will be discussed at length in Chapter 11, is the level of challenge that is just hard enough, but not too hard for a child. This is the level of text that is recommended when the child is working with the support of a better reader. The independent level, as the name implies, is the level

where the child can read on his or her own without support. Even when they are reading at their independent levels, it is recommended that children read the highest-level books that they can read independently.

The other issue is that children should be given books that are as substantial as possible, even when they are written on low levels. With a little searching, a teacher can find simply written books that give students something to talk about: such as Chris Rashka's *Yo, Yes!,* Arnold Lobel's *Frog and Toad* stories, and Nancy Shaw and Margot Apple's *Sheep in a Jeep.* Learning to read fluently is important, but children should also learn from the very beginning that the point of reading is to explore meaning.

say, "My father was ironing his shirt. He was ironing it on the table, but the table got too hot. He was ironing it on the floor, but the floor was too dirty. 'Daddy,' I said. 'I know. Why don't you try ironing on the ironing board that's in the closet?' "

You can also have children listen for one word repeated two times, such as "Short short."

> "There was a girl named Short. But Short wasn't short. Short was tall. Her friend Gladys was short. One day Gladys asked Short, " 'If you were short, Short, your name would match you better.' "
> (Temple & MaKinster, 2005)

Clap Out Words. You can make clapping games that range from the simple to the elaborate. Clapping their hands to the words you pronounce is an easy game. Clapping in a sequence adds more challenge: hands together, hands on knees, hands on chest, hands on sides of thighs. Have children clap to the words as you say these words with emphasis:

> "When—I—go—to—Lu's—big—house
> I—like—to—play—with—Lu's—pet—mouse."

SONGS, CHANTS, AND POEMS. Songs and chants are a natural way to get children to pay attention to rhymes—and also to memorize words, phrases, and sentences that will aid language development. Songs, chants, and poems are also a lot of fun to learn and repeat.

A song like this one invites hand claps and close attention to the rhymes:

> *Miss Mary Mack*
> *Dressed in black*
> *Silver buckles*
> *Up and down her back*

The lyrics are available in book form. Tutors and new teachers are advised to seek out collections of songs, especially those with tapes. The following are good bets:

Cole, J. (1990). *Miss Mary Mack*. New York: Morrow.

Beall, P.C., Nipp, S.H., & Klein, N.S. (2002). *Wee Sing 25th Anniversary Celebration*. New York: Price Stern Sloan.

Delacre, L. (2004). *Arrorro Mi Nino: Latino Lullabies and Gentle Games*. New York: Lee and Low.

Graham, C. (2004). *Let's Chant, Let's Sing*. New York: Oxford University Press.

Jenkins, E. (1997). *Ella Jenkins Songbook For Children*. New York: Music Sales Corp.

Milnes, G. (1999). *Granny, Will Your Dog Bite?* Little Rock, AR: August House.

Orozco, J.-L. (1994). *De Colores And Other Latin American Folk Songs For Children*. New York: Dutton.

_____. (1997). *Diez Deditos And Other Play Rhymes And Action Songs From Latin America*. New York: Puffin.

_____. (2002). Fiestas: A year of Latin American songs of celebration.

Swasos, E., & Cepeda, J. (2002). *Hey You! C'Mere! A Poetry Slam*. New York: Arthur Levine.

Silberg, J., Schiller, P., & Wright, D. (2002). *The Complete Book of Rhymes, Songs, Poems, Fingerplays*. Lewisville, NC: Gryphon House.

All of these are valuable additions to a teacher's personal collection. Also, you can learn many other songs from experienced teachers. Songs for transitions, songs that introduce tasks, songs to celebrate special people—all of these are essential for a teacher's repertoire. When you find a teacher who knows these songs, write them down! And also, bring along a small tape recorder so you can capture the tunes.

To build language awareness at the syllable level, these strategies are available:

- Children can clap along to the syllables in their names—"Bet-ty," "Ta-kee-sha," "Da-vid."
- Children can raise their hands when the teacher says a word with one syllable, two syllables, or three syllables.
- When the teacher says "One syllable!" a child must say a one-syllable word; when the teacher says, "Two syllables!" and calls on a child, that child says a word with two syllables; and so on.

To build language awareness at **the onset and rime level:**

- Children are asked to supply rhymes to complete couplets such as the following:

  Ding, dong, dell
  Kitty's in the _____ (well)
  Ding, dong, dasement
  Kitty's in the _____ (basement)
  Ding, dong, dimming pool
  Kitty's in the _____ (swimming pool)

- The teacher says a target word, such as *boy*, and the children raise their hands when they hear a word that rhymes with it from a list of words the teacher reads such as *"tea, tock, tack, toy."*
- The teacher says a word such as *bat* and then pronounces the sound /k/; then the children say a new word that begins with the sound /k/ and rhymes with *bat: cat*.

To build language awareness at **the phoneme level,** there are three kinds of tasks that are generally used. One is **phoneme segmentation**. Segmentation means to break something into small parts. Phoneme segmentation tasks have children take spoken words and break them into their individual sounds.

- A spoken exercise goes like this: "If I say dog /d/ /o/ /g/, you say *cat*, *ball*, and *foot* the same way."
- The children place letter markers into boxes as they pronounce each letter sound. Then they say the word that is formed by the sounds (Elkonin, 1973). (See Figure 4.1, and also Chapter 12.)
- Once children begin to learn letter sounds, they can practice pushing tokens marked with letters. For example, given a card marked with three boxes, and the three letter chips, *l, e,* and *t,* the child places each letter into the box, pronouncing its sound at the same time: *ull, ehhh, tuh* and then saying the whole word *let.*

A second way children become aware of phonemes is to combine phonemes into words, or **phoneme combination**. For example,

Word Hunts

Watch the video showing a kindergarten teacher working with a small group on developing phonemic awareness for beginning sounds in the activity "Teaching Phonemic Awareness to Young Children." (To find this activity, go to the topic *Phonemic Awareness/Phonics* in MyEducationLab and click on Assignments and Activities.)

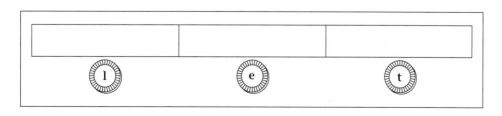

Figure 4.1
Elkonin Boxes.

- The teacher asks, "What word do I get if I add the sounds of *ih* and *tuh*? or *suh* and *ay*? or *cuh, uh,* and *puh*?"

A third way that children become aware of phonemes is to delete a phoneme from a word and say what word is left over, or **phoneme deletion**. For instance,

- The teacher asks, "What word do I get if I take off the sound *suh* from *slot*? Or if I take off the sound *duh* from *find*?"

Games that work with phonemes can be playful, of course. For example, the children can sing a song that substitutes the vowel sounds:

I like to eat, eat, eat, apples and bananas
I like to eat, eat, eat, apples and bananas.
I like to oot, oot, oot, ooples and bonoonoos
I like to oot, oot, oot, ooples and bonoonoos
I like to oat, oat, oat, oples and bononos
I like to oat, oat, oat, oples and bononos.

Teaching the Alphabet

"Whole-part-whole" is the mantra of many seasoned teachers. It means *begin by showing students how larger chunks of language are used meaningfully. Then call their attention to the parts. Then have them use the parts in the context of the whole.* That suggestion can be applied to teaching the alphabet. Children pay closer attention to the letters of the alphabet after they have come to notice writing as a holistic display; and they learn the letters as they use them when they are trying to write and read messages.

WORKING WITH NAMES. Cunningham and Allington (2003) wisely suggest that teachers call children's attention to the alphabet by focusing on their names. A teacher writes each child's name on a piece of tagboard and puts all of the names in a box. Each day the teacher draws out a name, and calls that child forward and interviews him or her—asking about favorite pastimes, pets, games, and so on. Then the teacher puts the child's name on the bulletin board and explains that this word is a name. The teacher can point to the letters, reading left to right, and have the children count the letters. Then the teacher can call attention to the letter that begins the name. If the name is *Nancy*, the teacher can ask if the children can spot a small letter that looks like the big letter that begins the name *Nancy*. The teacher can ask if other children have *Nancy*'s letter N in their name (each child has her name taped to her desk, of course). Every day another child's name is drawn from the box, that child is interviewed, and the teacher calls the children's attention to the letters in this new name. As this activity is carried on day after day, the children are naming more and more of the letters of the alphabet, including the other letters that make up each name, both upper- and lowercase.

ALPHABET BINGO. Another way to help children recognize letters of the alphabet is to pass out cards with the letters of the alphabet written on them where the numbers would be written on a Bingo card, as in Figure 4.2.

The order of the letters may be scrambled. All upper- or lowercase letters may be used in the beginning, and then a mixture of the two is used, as children are able. The children are given cardboard chips just the size of the cells on the Bingo card. As a letter is called out, each child places a chip over the letter. The child may call BINGO! when she has a row of chips arranged up or down, side to side, or diagonally.

JUMPING LETTERS. From Patricia Cunningham's energetic teaching (Cunningham & Allington, 2003) comes an idea that associates letters with sounds in children's minds. The teacher (or the teacher and the class) thinks of a movement or action that can be paired

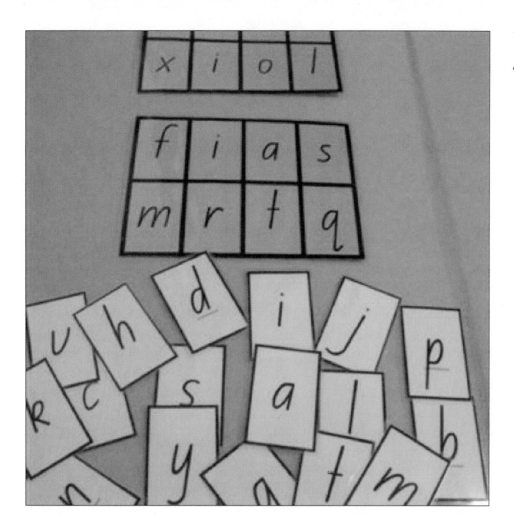

Figure 4.2
Alphabet Bingo.

with each letter of the alphabet. Then the children shout the letters and make the movements: JUMP! for J, LEAP! for L, SING! for S, and so on. The class may go out on the playground to practice these first, to give them an air of excitement, and later the letters may be acted out a little less exuberantly in the classroom. It can be great fun to call the letter and ask children to perform the action, or demonstrate the action and have children shout the letter.

LETTERS ON THE WEB. There are many fine programs on the Internet that help children learn the alphabet. As you know, such sites can come and go quickly, but as of this writing, the following were good bets.

- "Alphabet Action" from Learning Planet.com shows the letters in order on the page. When the child clicks on a letter, he hears the name of the letter pronounced, and a picture of a word that begins with the letter.
- "Mrs. Alphabet," at mrsalphabet.com, offers songs and chants for every letter of the alphabet, and many other activities.
- "Haunted Alphabet" from Kaboose.com presents a spooky picture with letters of the alphabet hidden in it. A child clicks on a letter and it is magically transported up to its place in the alphabet. If she clicks on a shape that is not a letter, she hears screechy laughter (which some children will find to be more fun!).

Entering "Alphabet" in a search engine will turn up dozens of activities that can be accessed at no charge, including interactive games children can play on the computer and downloadable worksheets that can be duplicated for the class.

Arranging Classrooms for Literacy Learning

To promote literacy, reading and writing is made part of the classroom environment. The classroom itself should demonstrate both the importance of literacy and the way literacy works while also providing many opportunities for children to observe and use written language. There are many ways in which classrooms can be arranged passively to immerse children in print.

LABELS. Label objects around the classroom with written letters that are readable from far off. Every several days, take time to "read the room" together with the children (Fountas & Pinnell, 1996) as you or a student points to the labels with a pointer or ruler. Remind students to listen for the first sounds in the words, such as in *door* and point out that the first letter in *door* is D.

LITERACY PLAY. Make props readily available to support children's dramatic play. Some of these props might include reading and writing. For example, the doctor's office has an eye chart and a pad for the doctor to write prescriptions. Shelves in a grocery store center might have labels (*fruit, soup, bread*) where the grocer would stock the items and pads handy for the customers to use for writing grocery lists.

CLASSROOM LIBRARY. Create a classroom library in a corner of the room. It should have a carpet and comfortable chairs (such as beanbag chairs) for creating an inviting reading environment. Include a space for displaying books so that children can see their covers, and change the books on display every few days to catch the children's attention. Books should accommodate a range of tastes, from informational books with bright illustrations to simple patterned books. On a regular basis, read a book or part of a book aloud and then place it on display in the library corner to entice children to look it over. The classroom library should include books written by individual classroom authors and books written or dictated by the whole class—perhaps books of favorite jokes and riddles, books about animals, and books about the seasons.

CHARTS AND POSTERS. Display on the walls around the classroom posters of children's books and pictures of authors. You can solicit these directly from children's book publishers. Children know authors such as Rosemary Wells, Dr. Seuss, Arnold Lobel, Cynthia Rylant, and Alma Flor Ada, and they will be excited when the teacher announces that the class has a new book by one of these authors or another author they know and like. You can also display charts of interesting things, such as volcanoes and maps of the town or neighborhood with the children's street names labeled. You could also include autobiographical posters with each child's name and something special that each child has dictated. Children love to see their own works posted.

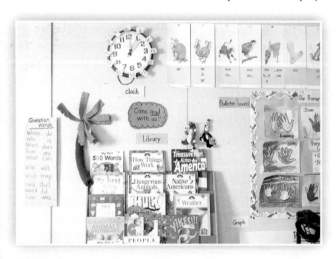

Taking time to "read the room" labels provides an opportunity for children to observe and use written language. (Michael Newman/PhotoEdit)

CLASSROOM POST OFFICE.   Include in your classroom a post office where children can mail letters. Each child could have a mailbox (constructed from three-inch cardboard tubes) for receiving mail. Have children write each other letters at least once a week; the teacher should also make a point of writing something to put in each child's box every few days.

WRITING CENTER.   Create a writing center with paper, markers, and pencils. Include magazines as sources of pictures that can be cut out and glued to attach them as illustrations for children's compositions.

Displaying Print

Even as you invite children to write inventively, including mock-writing, or read aloud to them and show them print, you also need to show them individual letters and demonstrate how the letters are formed. There are many ways of doing this:

- Alphabet letter cards can be posted around the room, with pictures of objects that feature that letter.
- Games for matching letters, coloring letters, and tracing letters can be arranged for children to play with at center time.
- Magnetic letters and link letters (cardboard letters with edges cut like jigsaw puzzle pieces) can be placed in centers, so children can arrange them to match words printed on tagboard, including their classmates' names. (Note that for beginners, letters all of the same color are preferable to letters of mixed colors.)
- Children can practice writing letters at their desks as the teacher writes a model. They may use large-ruled paper for this or individual slates and chalk. Later, they may practice writing letters with a grease pencil on a transparency film overlaid on sample words with large letters.
- Alphabet strips can be taped to children's desks. A strip of tagboard with the letters of the alphabet carefully printed in lowercase can be attached to each child's desk in front of the pencil tray. Such strips are available commercially, or they can be produced by the teacher or by an aide.
- The teacher can teach children the alphabet song, pointing to the letter cards on the wall as the children sing the song slowly.
- Children's names can be written on cards and taped to their desks, with the first letter of the first name written in a bright color. Then the children can practice saying, "A is for Ana, B is for Bart," and so on.
- Sandpaper letters on cards can be used in centers for children to trace with their fingers.
- Letter cards can be sent home so that parents can play letter recognition games with the children.
- Alphabet books can be made. Prepare a blank book for the class and print a letter on the top of each page, A to Z. The children think of objects that begin with the sound of that letter and take turns drawing pictures of those objects on the appropriate page.

Teaching Resources

CLASSROOM-PRODUCED BOOKS.   Classroom-produced books provide a useful and enjoyable way to showcase children's authorship and to enable them to share their works with each other. Single-author books typically are written or dictated by a child (if written, they have corrected text pasted or written in by the teacher or parent volunteer)

Making Individual Small Books

and, of course, are illustrated by the child-author. Composite books are collections that all of the children in a class contribute to. The range of such books is very broad, but for emergent readers, the following are recommended. These can be written by the children themselves (with corrections written in darker ink) or simply dictated. Remember that because the books are intended to be read repeatedly by children, the text should be spelled correctly.

- **Alphabet books:** Every child is assigned a letter and writes a word that begins with that letter and draws a picture of it.
- **Counting books:** A group of children are assigned numbers 1 through 10. They draw pictures of 1, 2, 3 (and so on) of something and then write the name of the things (e.g., birds, pennies, cars) next to or under each drawing.
- **Riddle books:** Children contribute individual riddles. The riddle is written on one side of the page and the answer on the other.
- **Joke books:** The jokes of five- and six-year-old children are funny, if only for their lack of obvious humor. Individual children can contribute jokes to a whole-class book.

Concept books: Concept books focus on one or a few specific topics, such as kinds of animals, sports, famous people, things to be thankful for, or images we associate with each season. Ideas for topics are limitless.

Explore how a kindergarten teacher creates a print-rich environment by completing the activity "Creating Purposeful Environments for Emergent Readers and Writers." (To find this activity, go to the topic *Emergent Literacy* in MyEducationLab and click on Assignments and Activities.)

Involving Families in Emergent Literacy

Family Literacy

How can teachers help parents celebrate their children's entering kindergarten, and form lasting partnerships with parents?

The day a child leaves home to enter kindergarten is a poignant one for families. Many parents feel the shock of having well-meaning strangers take over much of their child's upbringing; for parents who feel "different" from the school because of language, culture, or income, the feeling of estrangement can be particularly pronounced. Kindergarten and first grade are especially important times for teachers to reach out and invite parents to take part in their children's education.

Keeping parents involved in their children's education is important for the children, too. Parental involvement in school is linked to everything from children's academic achievement to good behavior (they will be less likely to be disruptive); and it even reduces the risk that they will use drugs later on (National Center for Educational Statistics, 1999, 2002). Of course, parents help children's literacy learning at home, too; and the amount of time parents devote at home to reading to their children, telling them stories, and teaching them songs is clearly related to the gains children make in literacy. Likewise, a child's level of reading ability in English is related to the mother's reading ability in English.

Parents' involvement in school, like parents' support of their children's literacy at home, varies with income and level of education. And the differences are large. The government's statistics show that children from the poorest 20 percent of families leave kindergarten with lower reading scores than children from the better off 20 percent enter with (NCES, 2006).

But there is good news here, too. Over the last dozen years there have been big gains in the amount of support families give their children in reading—with the biggest increase by far in the poorest families. These increases in par-

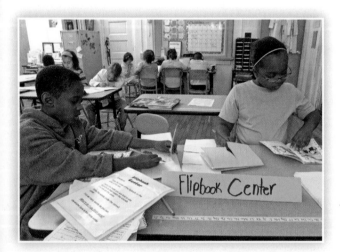

Classroom produced books enable children to share their work with each other. (Ellen B. Senisi)

ent involvement are the result of enormous efforts by the schools, the public libraries, and even social services—often working together.

For emergent readers, families can be involved in their children's literacy instruction in two ways: in the school and at home.

In the Classroom

First, it is desirable for parents to come into the classroom and take part in activities. They can help move instruction forward by reading to children, taking dictation, and helping publish and bind books. They can also tell stories, especially family stories, and they can demonstrate family traditions and crafts. In this latter way, they can make their families' lives part of the curriculum.

Some parents might be more willing than others to come into the class and participate. Parents of children who have been through Head Start might well have been involved in classroom activities already and might have been trained to conduct activities such as reading aloud. For other parents, special invitations and special orientations will probably be required. The National Center for Family Literacy has developed a program to recruit and orient parents to help out in classrooms. A description of the program, called PACT (Parents and Children Together), can be found on the center's website at www.Famlit.org.

At Home

Family literacy initiatives can also be reinforced at home by sending parents materials and ideas for helping develop their children's literacy. Two good examples of home-directed family literacy initiatives are home books and book baggies.

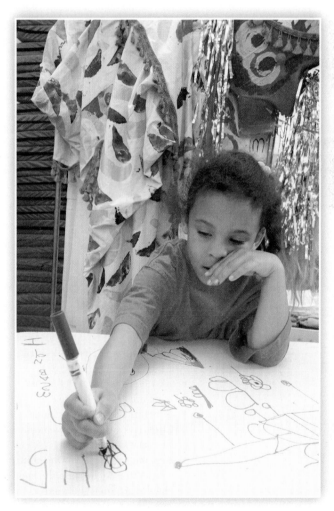

HOME BOOKS. Simple books with very short and predictable texts can be written and sent home for children to read aloud to their parents. Eight-page home books can be made from one sheet of paper, printed on both sides, and assembled with the two double pages stapled one inside the other. Pictures are added to remind the children of what the text says. A sample text for a home book is shown in Figure 4.3.

The teacher reads the book through twice with the children before they take it home so that they will be able to read it on their own. Instructions go home with the book for parents to read the book with their children—many times, if possible. Home books can go home once a week. They provide useful practice in reading and help children to acquire concepts about print and even sight words.

BOOK BAGGIES. A book baggie consists of a simple paperback book in a bag with an accompanying activity sheet (such as instructions to draw a favorite character, a word hunt, or an alphabet matching game) and perhaps a recording of the book on tape. Parents are encouraged to read the book with the child and take time to do the accompanying activity. Children should be told how to take care of the book bags when they go home. A book bag may spend

Family involvement in education is associated with children's academic and social success on many levels. (Ellen B. Senisi)

Developmental Milestones
Emergent Literacy

Stages of Literacy Development	Developmental Milestones	Teaching Strategies
Exploring Print (Beginning Kindergarten)	• May tap out syllables in most words, but not phonemes • Holds a book the right way up and can point to the front. • May know that print "talks" and not pictures. • May recognize some letters and may be able to write a few of them. • Writing shows no relation between letters and sounds. P2X = "little." • After memorizing a short text, cannot voice-point to the words accurately. • When listening to stories, some will respond to parts of them with movements and chants; others will follow the plot with displays of expectation, suspense, and relief. • Can make up a story while paging through a familiar picture book. • May draw pictures and tell you about the scene he or she is describing. • May write captions to pictures or other compositions, using invented symbols and random letters.	• Read-alouds—teachers read daily to children, thinking aloud and emphasizing plot structure (who the characters are, what the problem is, what they do to solve the problem, what happens, how things are at the end). The same story is reread several times and children are later invited to pretend-read it themselves. • Sing-alongs and rhyming games. • Morning message: The teacher asks children to take turns helping introduce and write up the day, date, month, and weather, as well as the day's activities. Rebus symbols are used for weather and names of activities. • Assignment charts: Children's names printed on tagboard are divided among slots in a pocket chart according to their tasks and center assignments for the day. • Shared reading—the teacher carefully points at large print while pronouncing words. The teacher carefully names aspects of reading—"letters," "words" "direction," "top of the page," "bottom of the page," and calls attention to individual letters and words that are repeated. • Teaching the alphabet. • Incorporating print in play activities—post office, grocery store, etc. • Writing Workshop: Children have opportunities to communicate with pencils and colored pencils; encouragement to write captions; opportunities to share what they have drawn and written.
Becoming Familiar with Print (Late Kindergarten) Logographic Reading	• Can begin to tap out phonemes. • Can provide rhyming words. • Still can't confidently voice-point at word units. • Knows way around books. • Can write own name. • Uses invented spelling to write words or phrases as captions to pictures. • Invented spelling begins to represent sounds in words, but only a few: LL = "little." • May recognize most letters and associate upper- and lowercase letters. • Sometimes writes letters and lines of print backwards, unless shown where to start writing. • Less pretend reading—the child often refuses to read, because she knows she doesn't know the words; or reads only the few words she knows.	• Read-alouds—teachers continue to read two or three times daily to children, thinking aloud and inviting the children's comments and predictions. At least one book per day is reread several times and children are invited to pretend-read it themselves. • Children are invited to reenact stories using drama, puppets, or flannel boards. • Sing-alongs and rhyming games. • Morning message: The teacher asks children to take turns helping introduce the day, date, month, and weather, as well as the day's activities. Rebus symbols are used for weather and names of activities. • Assignment charts: Children's names printed on tagboard are divided among slots in a pocket chart according to their tasks and center assignments for the day. • Alphabet teaching activities. • Shared reading, with the children reading lines after the teacher. • Sharing the pen writing. • Writing Workshop: Children have opportunities to communicate with pencils and colored pencils; encouragement to write captions; opportunities to share what they have drawn and written.

Stages of Literacy Development	Developmental Milestones	Teaching Strategies
Beginning Finger-Point Reading (Beginning First Grade) Early Alphabetic Reading	• Can tap out phonemes. Many can combine phonemes to make new words: *s + top = stop*. • Many children can voice-point at word units. • Those who can voice-point are learning some words from encounters with print. • Writes with invented spelling, and includes letters for most sounds that are heard. A few high frequency words are spelled conventionally. • LDL = "little." • Still makes active responses to stories, like chanting and moving. Is increasingly following the plot and other patterns, too, as demonstrated by predictions and comments.	• Read-alouds—teacher continues to read two times daily to children, thinking aloud and inviting the children's comments and predictions. The teacher emphasizes parts of the book: the title, the author, the illustrator. • Children are invited to reenact stories using drama, puppets, or flannel boards. • Sing-alongs and rhyming games. • Morning message uses longer sentences and introduces new words. • Charts for tasks and center assignments are still used. • Shared reading, with the children reading lines after the teacher. The teacher calls attention to the title, the author, and the illustrator and introduces other terminology as needed, such as "first word," "bottom of the page," etc. The teacher teaches lessons on letter sounds and word recognition. • Sharing the pen writing teaches letter-to-sound correspondences and conventions of capitalization and punctuation. • Language Experience Approach. • Guided Reading: In small groups, children are led to finger-point read simple texts. • Word study activities (see Chapter 5). • Writing Workshop: Children have opportunities to communicate with pencils and colored pencils; encouragement to write captions; opportunities to share what they have drawn and written
Finger-Point Reading (Mid First Grade) Alphabetic Reading	• Can more easily tap out phonemes, and can combine phonemes to make new words: *s + top = stop*. • Can more easily produce rhyming words, in games like "Ding, dong, dell…" • Is able to finger-point read simple predictable books with strong picture support. • Continues to acquire sight words from reading activities. • Is able to sound out predictably spelled words, letter by letter. • May write messages of two or three lines. Invented spellings are mixed with more conventionally spelled words. • LEDL or LETL still spell "little." • Is able to take highly predictable books home to read aloud.	• Read-alouds—teacher continues to read two times daily to children, thinking aloud and inviting the children's comments and predictions. The teacher emphasizes parts of the book: the title, the author, the illustrator. • Children are invited to reenact stories using drama, puppets, or flannel boards. • Sing-alongs and rhyming games. • Morning message uses longer sentences and introduces new words. • Charts for tasks and center assignments are still used. • Shared reading, with the children reading lines after the teacher. The teacher calls attention to the title, the author, and the illustrator and introduces other terminology as needed, such as "first word," "bottom of the page," etc. The teacher teaches lessons on letter sounds and word recognition. • Sharing the pen writing teaches letter-to-sound correspondences and conventions of capitalization and punctuation. • Taking dictation; using the Language Experience Approach. • Guided Reading: In small groups, children are led to finger-point read simple texts. • Word study activities (see Chapter 5). • Writing Workshop: Children have opportunities to communicate with pencils and colored pencils; encouragement to write captions; opportunities to share what they have drawn and written. • Focused lessons are offered on both the conventions of writing and strategies for composing (see Chapter 10).

Figure 4.3

A Typical Home Book.

Where is my dog?	In the yard?
No.	In the closet?
No.	In the kitchen?
No!	He is under my bed!

several days at a time with each child and then be repacked with a new activity sheet and passed along to a different child.

Help with Family Literacy

A parent who was a regular volunteer in a Head Start classroom worried aloud because her child was going into kindergarten the next fall.

"But you can still volunteer in the kindergarten," the teacher pointed out. "They will be happy to have you."

"Me? Suppose they hand me one of those school books to read?" the troubled mother said.

Like this mother, there are parents who do not volunteer to help in school and do not read to their children because they cannot read well themselves. For those parents, the agencies that used to provide adult literacy services are now offering family literacy programs, in which parents who are English learners are taught basic English and parents who need help with reading are taught to read to their children. These programs can be quite successful, since the imperative of helping the children can serve as a motivation for parents to improve their own literacy skills, and the stories they practice to read to their children can be appropriate fare for developing their own reading fluency. For information on programs that offer literacy services to parents, contact the following organizations:

- Literacy Volunteers of America at www.literacyvolunteers.org
- The Barbara Bush Literacy Foundation at www.barbarabushfoundation.com
- The National Center for Family Literacy at www.famlit.org
- The Even Start program at www.evenstart.org

For Review

Children's literacy begins to emerge at home, well before they enter school. Once they enter kindergarten and first grade, their literacy develops through a combination of children-driven discoveries and experiences orchestrated by a teacher. A successful teacher of reading and writing in the early years must be part psychologist—a kidwatcher (see Chapter 11), a careful observer of what children have discovered and are discovering for themselves—and part bridge builder, carefully constructing experiences that will lead children from where they are to where they are going as readers and writers.

Although all children develop concepts about print before they enter school, the amount of experience they have with literacy varies widely. A teacher of kindergarten and first grade must provide lavish opportunities for children to learn about print and target help for children to learn what they need to know. The teacher can also reach out to the home, both to invite families to contribute material from their lives—family stories and traditions, for example—and to enlist the help of parents in helping children practice their literacy.

Emergent literacy refers to the period from early childhood through the first year of school in which children learn about language and print and about reading and writing. In recent years, scholars have come to recognize the role of the child's own discoveries in learning to read and write, and research in literacy has identified aspects of literacy that teachers can help children to develop.

Children must learn about the features of print and how print works. Marie Clay has provided a set of concepts about print that children must honor in their reading. The English writing system is alphabetic—letters of the alphabet represent words by their smallest sounds, called phonemes. This concept, too, must be discovered or otherwise understood by children. Once children recognize the alphabetic principle, they are ready to figure out how letters represent sounds, or phonics. On the writing side, they may discover the mirror image of phonics as they invent ways to use writing to represent words. Understanding children's invented spelling yields valuable insights into their word knowledge — the knowledge they use to read and to spell words.

Teaching for emergent literacy should support and encourage children's processes of discovery, call children's attention to details, and give them guided and independent practice in reading and writing. Parents are children's first teachers, and careful teachers include parents in the school's efforts to help children's literacy emerge. Technology is available to help develop emergent literacy concepts, too. Children's literacy development at this stage deserves special attention. It is not easy to compensate for uneven background experience in language in the early years. But because it is much harder to help children get back on track in later grades, after years of confusion has been built on a shaky foundation, teachers should make the extra effort now to familiarize children with key concepts about language and print.

For Your Journal

1. Take a moment to review your answers to the questions on the Anticipation Guide that opened this chapter. Has your thinking changed? If so, write about the changes in your journal.

2. Some teachers and literacy experts expect children to learn much of what they need to know about literacy from their own discoveries: from being surrounded by books and charts, being read to, and having chances to read and write on their own level. Others rely less on discovery and plan to teach virtually all the skills of reading. If you could think of these teachers placed along a continuum, where along this continuum would you place yourself?

Taking It to the World

1. What are your first memories of reading and writing? Can you remember not being able to read and write? Were you curious about these activities? What things did you do to teach yourself about them?

2. Visit a preschool—a Head Start program, if possible. Ask the teachers what they do to support children's early literacy. How and when are reading and writing used during the day? How have their approaches to supporting children's early literacy changed over the last ten years?

3. To learn about efforts to involve parents in supporting children's literacy, interview an elementary school teacher or administrator. How are parents' ideas and volunteer efforts brought into the classroom? What things are sent home to help parents assist their children? What special efforts are being made toward increasing family literacy?

4. Continuing with the interview in item 3, how are English learners being supported as they learn to read and write? How is the school working with their parents?

5. Speak with a kindergarten or first-grade teacher about how he or she assesses students' concepts about print and what types of screenings are used to assess students' reading skills.

6. Visit the Jumpstart website (www.jstart.org/about/) to determine whether there is a Jumpstart program near your community. What are some possible ways in which you might be able to volunteer some time?

New Literacies Connections

1. Visit the literacy homepage of the North Central Regional Educational Laboratory at www.ncrel.org/litweb and do a search for "emergent literacy." Examine the numerous articles and connections to useful information and materials.

2. The National Right to Read Foundation (www.nrrf.org) provides thorough information and support on phonics instruction. The site also raises a number of concerns about issues such as emergent literacy and invented spelling. Visit the "Topical Essays" page to read the critiques of these and other topics.

3. The Center for Research in Early Reading Achievement is a federally funded consortium of five universities. Its website (www.ciera.org) might be the single best site on emergent literacy, with research reports, book reviews, news of conferences, and links to other sites.

myeducationlab

PEARSON

Now go to MyEducationLab (www.myeducationlab.com), where you can:

- Find learning outcomes for the topics covered in this chapter, along with the national standards that connect to these outcomes.

- Complete Assignments and Activities that can help you more deeply understand the chapter content.

- Engage in Building Teaching Skills and Dispositions exercises, in which you can apply and practice core teaching skills identified in the chapter.

Chapter

5

Phonics and Word Knowledge

Anticipation Guide

The following statements will help you begin thinking about the topics covered in this chapter. Answer *true* or *false* in response to each statement. As you read and learn more about the topics mentioned in these statements, think back on your answers. See what interests you and prompts your curiosity toward more understanding.

_____ 1. Teaching children to read words in Japanese may be easier than teaching them to read in English.

_____ 2. *Sight words* are words that are not decoded, but that are recognized instantly.

_____ 3. As they learn to read words, children most naturally learn first to read letters, then syllables, then whole words.

_____ 4. *Phonics* is an umbrella term for a variety of explicit, implicit, and systematic ways to show children how the print-to-speech/speech-to-print system works.

_____ 5. Decoding requires the skill of transforming written words into spoken words. Spelling requires exactly the same thing.

_____ 6. If you pronounce any English word slowly enough, you can distinctly hear each one of its constituent sounds, its phonemes.

_____ 7. A consonant digraph is a single sound— one in which two separate consonant sounds cannot be heard—even though it is spelled with two consonant letters.

_____ 8. Knowing where a word came from makes little difference in reading that word.

_____ 9. Word walls are groups of words, usually arranged in columns, written on chart paper and hung on the wall.

_____ 10. The English spelling system is so irregular that looking for patterns in it is a complete waste of time.

Phonics and Word Knowledge

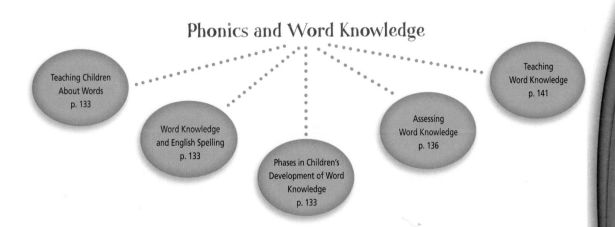

Teaching Children About Words
p. 133

Word Knowledge and English Spelling
p. 133

Phases in Children's Development of Word Knowledge
p. 133

Assessing Word Knowledge
p. 136

Teaching Word Knowledge
p. 141

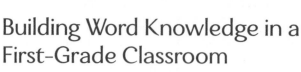
A Classroom Story

Building Word Knowledge in a First-Grade Classroom

First-grade teacher Ms. Gupta has students who range from emergent to beginning readers. This afternoon she sits at her desk planning a lesson on word recognition for some of the children who are struggling to read beginning consonant blends. The lesson will use words from the book *The Eensy Weensy Spider* (Hoberman, 2000) to focus on a limited number of initial blends. She gathers sets of "/gl/ /gll/ as in *glue*" word cards she made for a previous lesson and constructs a set of cards featuring "/sl/ /pl/ *sp* as in *spider*" so that the children can compare and contrast the different blends. She also sets aside some of the more challenging cards such as /sl/ /tl/ /rl/ for the more advanced readers. She makes matching target word cards on small pieces of acetate to show on the overhead projector. She sets up two large charts and puts the book *The Eensy Weensy Spider* on her desk. Now she is ready.

The next morning, Ms. Gupta calls the children who will *not* take part in her phonics lesson to the writing center and helps them get started on their choice of two writing activities. She then asks the others to turn around in their chairs so that they can see the overhead screen clearly and says, "Children, do you remember reading *The Eensy Weensy Spider*?" *PK*

The children nod yes and then read along as Ms. Gupta points to each of the words in the poem on the "spider chart," a three-foot tall version of *The Eensy Weensy Spider* text. She demonstrates how fluent reading sounds and asks the children to reread some lines more fluently. Because she knows the importance of fluent reading, Mrs. Gupta demonstrates how it should sound. She then emphasizes how reading sounds when it's not fluent, something that always brings humor into the lesson and provides a nice comparison and contrast. She then asks the children to

practice reading fluently with her. Following the reading, the children and Ms. Gupta sing the poem and do the finger-play for *The Eensy Weensy Spider*.

Ms. Gupta then calls the children's attention to the words *water* and *spout*. "If you *Vocal* think you know what a *spout* is, whisper it in your neighbor's ear," she says. The children do *Social* so eagerly. With a vocabulary teaching point in mind, Ms. Gupta goes to the chalkboard and *Visual* sketches a waterspout pipe that carries rain away from a house. The children whisper their ideas to one another and then state their guesses aloud.

"Did you picture in your head what it would look like for a spider to climb up a *Visualization* pipe? Good readers make pictures in their minds when they read; they really think about what they are reading."

"Here is something else I've noticed about some of the words in the spider poem," Ms. Gupta continues. "With what two letters does the word *spider* begin?" Ms. Gupta writes the word *spider* in large letters on the board and points to the *sp* blend as children say the letters. "And how about *spout*?" She writes, *Explicit Phonics* points, and the children respond again. Ms. Gupta draws a line under the *sp* in each word and says, "This *s-p* is a blend. Blends are letters that work together to make a beginning or ending sound in a word. When you say the blend, *sp*, it sounds like /sp-/. Try it with a partner—remember to whisper."

The children practice saying the *sp* blend, and Ms. Gupta reviews. "Blends are interesting spelling chunks. Even though they work together, you can still hear each letter sound if you listen carefully. For today's word sort, we will work mostly on beginning blends, although some of you may have some ending blends, so watch carefully."

Ms. Gupta continues to talk as she puts the word *spider* on the overhead and under-

lines the *sp*. With several blank transparency cards nearby, Ms. Gupta asks the children to *authentic* think of some words that begin with the *sp* *child* sound. The children's responses, guided as *driven* needed by her prompts and questions, are written on the transparency cards and placed under the word *spider*.

Drawing the discussion to a close, Ms. Gupta reviews: "Excellent thinking. You've come up with *spell, spend,* and *spot*, and we found out that *see* and *snow* won't work. And why is that?" Children respond by talking about the differences, and Ms. Gupta confirms. She adds, "I also made the words *spill* and *space* [she shows each of these word cards on the overhead projector], and you have these words in your new word sort bags."

Ms. Gupta has some of the children help her make cards for each of the words the class provided and adds them to the word sort bags. She then has the children get started on word sorts by having them work in pairs to compare and contrast words, and to watch for the target blend.

As the children begin working on their word sorts, Ms. Gupta checks on the students at the writing center and then moves quietly around the room, speaking to and questioning the children as she guides them toward success. To complete this lesson, she will have the children self-assess their consonant blend word sorts using classroom checklists that have the correct sorts listed. When the children are finished, Ms. Gupta will assign as homework fifteen minutes of reading for pleasure (or being read to) and a minimum of five to eight minutes of adult/child word sorts (or longer if the child is having a good time).

At various points throughout the lesson, Ms. Gupta jots down some assessment notes about the children's responses to the lesson. Later, she will elaborate on these notes and put them into children's individual files.

Teaching Children About Words

This chapter is about what children need to know in order to read words, and how we can teach them. It assumes that the children have reached the point at which:

- They know most of the letters of the alphabet.
- They realize that spoken words can be broken down into smaller units of sound.
- They are looking for ways that print represents spoken words.

Now they are ready to learn to work their way toward a reasonable competence with the English system of spelling, so they will be able to read the words they encounter daily in print and write words without embarrassment. It's going to be a pretty long road, though. Getting comfortable at reading and writing English words can take up all of the elementary school years and last on into middle and high school.

Word Knowledge and English Spelling

The relations between letters and sounds in English are understandable, but they are certainly not simple. In languages with spelling systems that have **shallow orthographies**, where one letter spells one sound and vice versa, word recognition and spelling are simple matters. But over the centuries English has developed a **deep orthography**. The spellings of many of our words don't have very much to do with their sounds, but rather with their histories and their relations to other words. In English, we don't just teach children which letters make which sounds. We teach them layers and layers of word knowledge.

Phonics and Phonological Awareness

How would you describe the relation between word recognition and phonics?

Phases in Children's Development of Word Knowledge

Over the years as students learn to read and spell words, there are two kinds of development happening. One is children's growing awareness of the structure of words. Another is that, at higher levels, the words themselves become more sophisticated.

Let's look now at phases of word recognition and the kind of instruction that can help children at each phase. Please bear in mind that the ages assigned to each phase are approximate, and many children will be found ahead of or behind these estimates.

WORDS AS WHOLES: THE LOGOGRAPHIC PHASE.   Children who are just beginning to notice words in their environment tend to recognize familiar words as whole displays. These children, usually preschoolers and kindergartners, may recognize the word *look* by associating the two O's with eyes. They may identify the same word with different but related names, calling a Crest toothpaste label at one time "Crest" and at another time "toothpaste" (Harste, Woodward, & Burke, 1984). They are not yet reading the letters in the words, but are trying to find any identifiable feature that will help them remember the words, almost as if the words were faces.

Children in the **words as wholes** or **logographic phase** of word reading often give no response at all when faced with a word they do not know. They do not yet have a strategy for sounding out words. Marsh et al. (1981) called this phase of word recognition "glance and guess" because children look at a word and call it by the few names of words they know, or say nothing at all. They have no means yet to begin to recognize words by working through their letters.

Frith (1985) and Goswami (2000) called readers in this phase **logographic readers,** which is just a Greek way of saying they are reading word by word, without looking at the parts. When they are writing with invented spelling, children who are logographic readers may produce one or two memorized words—usually their names—and also symbols such

Word Wall Activities

Shared Writing

Word Sorting

as heart shapes or sun shapes. They will also produce *emergent spelling*: strings of letters that might resemble words, but whose letters have no phonetic value (see Chapter 3).

Teachers of logographic (word by word) readers focus first on having the children amass many words that they can read (Cunningham & Stanovich, 1998; Juel, 1988; Lehr, Osborn, & Hiebert, 2006). They may use the strategies of labeling things in the classroom, doing shared reading (see pages 109–110) and language experience (110–112). The teachers call children's attention to letters, starting with the consonant sounds that begin words. But the main emphasis is on having children amass several dozen **sight words**, words they can recognize easily.

LETTER BY LETTER: THE ALPHABETIC PHASE.   More advanced children—usually in early first grade—begin to read words by their letters, but not by very many letters. The reader who is early in the letter-by-letter or alphabetic phase might read the first consonant of a word and call it by the name of another word she or he knows that begins with that sound. It is as if a word such as *ball* appeared to children like this: **bxxx.** They might correctly read the word, especially if they are helped by the context, but they might readily confuse it with *bat, bark,* or *beep* (Morris, 2006).

As writers using invented spelling, alphabetic readers produce what we call *early phonemic spelling* (see Chapter 3); that is, they write a few letters to represent only the most salient sounds, usually consonant sounds. Thus they might write LDL for *little* and BT for *boat*.

As they advance through the middle of first grade and into early second grade, most children begin to read more and more letters in words. When they attempt to read a word, rather than calling out the name of another word that begins the same way, a child might sound out every letter, even if it means pronouncing something that doesn't make sense. A child might say, "We went to the fire sta-ty-on" instead of "fire station." With practice, students produce fewer nonsense word readings and read words more accurately.

Children are acquiring a growing body of sight words, which they can read accurately and quickly. This rapid word identification occurs after a period of sounding out the words, or **phonological recoding**, as linguists call it. Ehri (1991) suggests that the earlier practice of reading words alphabetically—figuring them out letter by letter—lays down pathways to the memory that makes it easier for children to recognize the words when they see them later. She explains,

> When readers practice reading specific words by phonologically recoding the words, they form access routes for those words into memory. The access routes are built using knowledge of grapheme-phoneme correspondences that connect letters in spellings to phonemes in the pronunciation of words. The letters are processed as visual symbols for the phonemes, and the sequence of letters is retained as an alphabetic, phonological representation of the word. The first time an unfamiliar word is seen, it is read by phonological recoding. This initiates an access route into memory. Subsequent readings of the word strengthen the access route until the connections between letters and phonemes are fully formed and the spelling is represented in memory. (p. 402)

As writers using invented spelling, readers who are further along in the letter-by-letter phase may produce examples of what we call *letter name spelling*. Now children's spellings represent all or most of the phonemes in a word. Yet, because they focus on matching one letter to one sound at a time, they are not aware of silent E's or other ways of marking vowel letters long or short. Thus BET can spell either *beat* or *bit*. Children usually do not spell consonant digraphs either; they might write HIP for *chip* and VE for *the*. In fact, because their reading exposure is still very limited, they are only gradually noticing conventional ways in which letters represent sounds in spelling (Read, 1975; Temple et al., 1992).

Frith (1985) and Goswami (2000) called readers in the early part of this phase *transitional alphabetic readers* and those toward the end of the phase *alphabetic readers*. In both cases, the important point is that the readers are looking at the relations between individual letters and individual sounds.

Teaching letter-by-letter or alphabetic readers focuses first on teaching children the common letter-to-sound matches—beginning with consonant sounds, and then moving on to long and short vowel sounds, and consonant digraphs and consonant clusters. Teachers use shared writing (see pages 145–146), word sorts, and word walls (page 144) for this purpose.

Teach It! 17

Making and Breaking Words

CHUNKING: THE ORTHOGRAPHIC PHASE.   By late first grade and on into the middle of second grade, most children are looking beyond one letter to one sound, and focusing on spelling patterns, such as *-at, -ock, -ake,* and *-ight.* Children are visually separating words into **onsets and rimes** as Trieman (1985) calls them. (We also call them **phonogram patterns.**) They can read by analogy; that is, if they can read *bake* and *take,* they can also read *rake* and *stake.*

Reading by chunking means that children can read letters in clusters and also begin to recognize that some groups of letters have a long vowel sound and some have a short vowel sound, depending on the ways the vowels are marked, such as *bit* and *bite.*

Children's spelling now passes into the transitional spelling phase. They are spelling words in conventional ways, although not always correctly. For example, they might write *baisball, fase,* and *trane.*

Frith (1985) and Goswami (2000) call this phase of word reading **orthographic** (which is a Greek way of saying "writing by the rules") because the children are looking beyond letter-to-sound relations to rules that relate to larger units of sound and spelling. (This was the last of Frith and Goswami's phases of word recognition. But we have more. Read on!)

Teaching readers at the chunking or orthographic phase focuses on the common rimes or phonogram patterns (see pages 71–72). Teachers use word sorts (see pages 146–148), word walls (page 144), and making and breaking words for this purpose.

MEANINGFUL WORD PARTS: THE MORPHOLOGICAL PHASE.   From second or third grade and up, normally advancing readers enter a phase of word recognition that we call reading by **meaningful word parts**. There are three main kinds of word parts at play at this phase.

One kind of word part is seen in compound words such as *fireman* and *birdhouse.* Readers from late first grade and second grade are recognizing the "small words within the big words," as many teachers put it.

Another kind of word part children are recognizing are grammatical morphemes, such as plural markers and verb tense endings: the difference between *bird* and *birds,* and *want* and *wanted.* These grammatical markers raise difficulties in their spelling, because the E in *-ed* and the I in *-ing* also serve as vowel markers: They can mark the preceding vowels long in words like *bat* and *sit* (which must therefore be spelled *batted* and *sitting* and not *bated* and *siting*). This is a lot for a young writer and reader to think about!

A third kind of meaningful word part includes prefixes and suffixes such as the *un-* in *unkind,* the *-ful* in *helpful,* and the *non-* in *nonsense.*

If this no longer strictly sounds like phonics, you're right. As word knowledge advances, many more considerations go into reading and writing words than just letter and sound relations.

Teaching readers at the **morphological** phase, the phase of meaningful word parts, should include explicitly teaching them about those word parts. Teachers continue to use word sorts, word walls, and making and breaking words and other word-building games. Children also need to be encouraged to read a great deal. They need to see many words—thousands of words—used meaningfully in interesting text, and also have their attention called to the structures of words.

WORD HISTORIES AND FAMILIES: THE DERIVATIONAL PHASE.   From about fourth grade up, students who read with at least average proficiency can recognize that words like *telegraph, telephone, biology,* and *biography* contain word parts that they recognize. They may notice that *telegraph* and *graphic* (as in graphic novel) have something in common: Both contain the word part *-graph,* from a Greek word meaning "to write."

They may notice a shared part in *telephone*, *telescope*, and *telepathy*: *tele-*, it turns out, comes from another Greek word meaning "at a distance." Proficient readers are aware that *sanity* is related to *sane*, *grave* (as in "a grave look") is related to *gravity*, *sign* is related to *signal*, and *sympathy* is related to *pathetic*. We call this phase **reading for word histories and families**, or the **derivational phase**. We say *derivational* because, as you can see, words like we just saw were derived from the same older sources. Word reading at this phase is going farther away from a matter of recognizing letters and sounds. It combines something of word recognition and vocabulary.

Teaching readers at the derivational phase again includes explicit teaching about word families and word histories. Teachers need to make an interesting subject out of the study of words. Students should have ready access to dictionaries with word histories or etymologies. They can be assigned projects in which they research word origins and see how the histories of words relate to their spellings and connect them to other words. Students need to be encouraged to read prolifically, and to talk about interesting words at the same time they discuss other aspects of texts.

Word knowledge is a term that captures more than one kind of learning. It includes what children need to know in order to recognize words and to spell them—especially words they don't have stored in memory. The table "Milestones in Children's Development of Word Knowledge" shows the phases through which children's word knowledge passes. In it you will notice that different scholars have used different terms to refer to the same phases.

Teach It! 62

Word Origins and Derivations

Assessing Word Knowledge

Teachers need to have an idea what level of word knowledge a child is operating within so that he or she can give that child the best instruction. There are two main ways to do this. The first is to observe the child while reading words. The second is to analyze the child's invented spelling.

CATEGORIZING WORD RECOGNITION ERRORS.   Once teachers have become accustomed to thinking about children's development through phases of word knowledge, they can observe a child's reading errors and estimate the level or phase of word knowledge. This can be done in a structured way. Ask a child to read 100 words of text written at her instructional level—that is, a piece of moderately challenging text of which the child misreads about one word in ten. Then write down the errors, with the target word (the word the child was attempting to read) next to it. Compare the errors to the responses in the chart in Table 5.1 on page 137. If half of a child's errors fall within a phase, according to the chart, this is a reasonable indication that the child is reading words using strategies from that phase.

ASSESSING WORD KNOWLEDGE THROUGH INVENTED SPELLING: *THE MONSTER TEST*.   Another way to assess children's word knowledge is by analyzing their spelling errors: their invented spelling. A widely used measure for assessing spelling errors is Richard Gentry's **Monster Test** (see Table 5.2 on page 137). The Monster Test is intended for young readers: kindergarten through second grade. It consists of only ten words, and is simple to administer.

To give the test, you begin by telling the students that you want to see how they spell. You know that the words are too difficult for students their age to spell correctly, so you want them to invent their own spelling, to show how they think the words might be spelled. The activity won't be graded right and wrong; it will be used to see how the children think the words might be spelled. Let the children know they are helping their teacher do her work so she can teach better.

Read the spelling word and then the explanatory sentence. Give lots of encouragement; keep the atmosphere playful and fun.

Table 5.1 Word Knowledge Levels by Error Type

LEVEL OF WORD KNOWLEDGE	TARGET WORD	TYPICAL ERROR	DESCRIPTION OF THE ERROR TYPE
Logographic Reading	plant right	*Larry. He has L.* ———————	Student typically looks at one letter and calls out any word it reminds her of.
Alphabetic Reading	plant right	*pal ?* *rye gut?*	Student reads through words one letter at a time, making a sound for each letter. Early in the phase, only a few letters are read.
Orthographic Reading	plant right	*pl, pl, ant, plant!* *ruh, ruh, -ight, right!*	Student begins to see words as clusters of onsets and rimes.
Morphological Reading	ticked surprising unfed	*tiked, tick-ed, ticked!* *surprise, surprising!* *oonfd, oonfeed, unfed!*	Student begins to recognize prefixes, suffixes, and grammatical endings—and to see that they have consistent spellings even when they have different pronunciations.
Derivational Reading	*assign*	*assigg—No, assign!*	Student recognizes that the target word is derived from a familiar word.

To interpret the results, read over the descriptions of spelling phases provided in Table 5.3.

Compare your student's spellings to the samples given in the chart. If half or more of the child's errors can be matched to any one phase, it is likely that this is the child's phase of spelling development. But now what? Table 5.4 shows the phases identified by the Monster Test as they correspond to the phases we have been discussing.

For more information on the Monster Test and teaching procedures that are recommended from it, please see Gentry, 2007. For further instructions on administering and scoring the test, including a video, please see Gentry, 2008.

Table 5.2 The Monster Test

By J. Richard Gentry, Ph.D.

monster.	The boy was eaten by a monster.
united.	You live in the United States.
dress.	The girls wore a new dress.
bottom.	A big fish lives at the bottom of the lake.
hiked.	We hiked to the top of the mountain.
human.	Miss Piggy is not human.
eagle.	An eagle is a powerful bird.
closed.	The little girl closed the door.
bumped.	The car bumped into the bus.
type.	Type the letter on the typewriter.

Source: Adapted from "You Can Analyze Developmental Spelling" by Richard Gentry. In *Teaching/K–8*, May 1985.

Developmental Milestones
Children's Development of Word Knowledge

Phases of Word Knowledge	Other Names for This Phase	Developmental Milestones	Teaching Strategies
● Mid-kindergarten			
Word knowledge: just beginning to show signs of the *words as wholes* or *logographic phase*. **Invented Spelling:** *Prephonemic phase.*	Gentry[1]: **Precommunicative;** Schlagal (also Bear et al., *Words Their Way* and Ganske[2], *Word Journeys*) **Emergent** Ehri[3]: **Pre-alphabetic.**	● May recognize own name ● May recognize a few other words by their visual appearances, but not letter by letter ● Won't attempt to decode unknown word ● Spelling mixes symbols such as hearts with nonsense strings of letters	● Focus on having the children amass many words that they can sight read. ● They may use the strategies of labeling things in the classroom, shared reading, language experience approach.
● End of kindergarten			
Word knowledge: *words as wholes* or *logographic phase*. **Invented Spelling:** *Early phonemic phase.*	Gentry: **Early Phonetic;** Schlagal (also Bear et al., *Words Their Way* and Ganske, *Word Journeys*) **Emergent.** Ehri: **Partial alphabetic.**	● Can pay attention to first and last consonant, and few other letters in a word ● Writes a few letters to represent only the most salient sounds, usually consonant sounds. Thus they might write LDL for little and BT for boat.	● Focus on having the children amass many words that they can sight read. ● They may use the strategies of labeling things in the classroom, shared reading, language experience approach. ● Begin to call children's attention to letters, beginning with the consonant sounds that begin words. ● Writing workshop
● End of kindergarten; early first grade			
Word knowledge: *Letter by Letter: The alphabetic phase.* **Invented Spelling:** *Letter name phase.*	Gentry: **Phonetic;** Schlagal[4] (also Bear et al., *Words Their Way* and Ganske, *Word Journeys*) **Letter-Name.** Ehri: **Full alphabetic.**	● Reads an unknown word by sounding out every letter, even if it means pronouncing something that doesn't make sense. ● Children's spellings represent all or most of the phonemes in a word. ● Children are not aware of silent *e*'s or other ways of marking vowel letters long or short. Thus *BET* can spell either *beat* or *bit*. ● Children usually do not spell consonant digraphs; might write *HIP* for *chip* and *VE* for *the*. ● Children use the *lettername strategy*: use a letter in spelling for similarity between the sound of its name and the sound they wish to represent.	● Teach children the common letter-to-sound matches—beginning with consonant sounds, and then moving on to long and short vowel sounds, and consonant digraphs and consonant clusters. ● Use shared writing. ● Use word sorts. ● Use word walls. ● Use shared reading and guided reading, to teach word parts in the context of meaningful reading and writing. ● Writing workshop

Phases of Word Knowledge	Other Names for This Phase	Developmental Milestones	Teaching Strategies

● Middle to end of second grade

Phases of Word Knowledge	Other Names for This Phase	Developmental Milestones	Teaching Strategies
Word knowledge: *Chunking: The orthographic phase.* **Invented Spelling:** *Orthographic phase.*	Gentry: **Transitional;** Schlagal (also Bear et al.[5], *Words Their Way* and Ganske, *Word Journeys*) **Within-Word Pattern.** Ehri: **Consolidated alphabetic.**	• Children can separate words into **onsets and rimes** or **phonogram patterns:** *b + at, d + ock, b + ake,* and *l + ight.* • Children can read by analogy: that is, if they can read *bake* and *take*, they can also read *rake* and *stake.* • Children begin to recognize that some groups of letters have a long vowel sound and some have a short vowel sound, depending on the ways the vowels are marked, such as *bit* and *bite.*	• Use word sorts for rimes (phonogram patterns). • Use word walls and word wall chants. • Use word building strategies. • Continue to use guided reading to teach word parts in the context of meaningful reading and writing. • Writing workshop

● Late second grade through fourth grade

Phases of Word Knowledge	Other Names for This Phase	Developmental Milestones	Teaching Strategies
Word knowledge: *Meaningful word parts: The morphological phase.* **Invented Spelling:** *Morphological phase.*	Gentry: **Transitional;** Schlagal (also Bear, et al., *Words Their Way* and Ganske, *Word Journeys*) **Syllable Juncture.**	• Reader is learning to recognize compound words like *fireman* and *birdhouse.* • Reader is noticing grammatical morphemes, such as plural markers and verb tense endings: the difference between *bird* and *birds*, and *want* and *wanted.* • Reader is noticing prefixes and suffixes such as the *un-* in *unkind*, the *-ful* in *helpful*, and the *non-* in *nonsense.*	• Teachers teach about word parts. • Continue to use word sorts, word walls, and making and breaking words and other word-building games. • Children also need to be encouraged to read a great deal; need to see many words—thousands of words—used meaningfully in interesting text. • Children need to have their attention called to the structures of words.

● Fourth grade and beyond

Phases of Word Knowledge	Other Names for This Phase	Developmental Milestones	Teaching Strategies
Word knowledge: *Word histories and families: The derivational phase.* **Invented spelling:** *Derivational phase.*	Gentry: ———; Schlagal (also Bear et al., *Words Their Way* and Ganske, *Word Journeys*) **Derivational Constancy.**	• Children recognize shared word parts (historical morphemes) in words like *telegraph, telephone, biology,* and *biography.* • Recognize "family" relationships between words that may be pronounced differently, such as *sanity* and *sane*, *grave* and *gravity*, *sign* and *signal*, *sympathy* and *pathetic.*	• Teachers make an interesting subject out of the study of words. • Students should regularly consult dictionaries with word histories or etymologies. • Students can be assigned projects to research word origins and relate histories of words to their spellings and their connections to other words. • Students should be encouraged to read prolifically. • Students should talk about interesting words (their meanings, spellings, and histories) at the same time they discuss other features of texts.

[1]Gentry, J. R. (2008). *Step-by-step assessment guide to code-breaking.* New York: Scholastic.

[2]Ganske, K. (2000). *Word journeys.* New York: Guilford.

[3]Ehri, L.C. (1995). Phases of development in learning to read by sight. *Journal of Research in Reading, 18,* 116–125.

[4]Schlagal, R. C. (1989). Constancy and change in spelling development. *Reading Psychology, 10*(3), 207–232.

[5]Bear, D., M. Invernizzi, S. Templeton, and F. Johnston (2007). *Words their way.* Columbus, OH: Pearson.

Table 5.3   Interpreting the Results of the Monster Test

Analyze the Spellings

Table 1 will help you analyze the spellings. Before going further, think about the features that you will look for at each developmental level.

PHASE 1   *Precommunicative spelling* is the "babbling" stage of spelling. Children use letters for writing words, but the letters are strung together randomly. The letters in precommunicative spelling do not correspond to sounds. Look for spellings such as OSPS for *eagle* or RTES for *monster*. This is Level 1 writing.

PHASE 2   *Semiphonetic spellers* know that letters represent sounds. They perceive and reliably represent sounds with letters in a type of telegraphic writing. Spellings are often abbreviated, representing initial and/or final sounds. For example, EL for *eagle* and MTR for *monster* are semiphonetic spellings. Only some of many possible semiphonetic combinations are represented in Table 1. This is Level 2 writing.

PHASE 3   *Phonetic spellers* spell words like they sound. The speller perceives and represents all of the phonemes in a word, though spellings may be unconventional. EGL for *eagle* and BODM for *bottom* are good examples of phonetic spelling. This is Level 3 writing.

PHASE 4   *Transitional spellers* think about how words appear visually; a visual memory of spelling patterns is apparent. Spellings exhibit conventions of English orthography, such as vowels in every syllable, e-marker and vowel digraph patterns, correctly spelled inflectional endings, and frequent English letter sequences. Transitional examples include EGUL for *eagle* and BOTTUM for *bottom*. To distinguish between phonetic spellings (influenced by sound) and transitional spellings (influenced by visual conventions) ask the question: Was this word spelled like it sounds (phonetics) or is its spelling analogous to a visually recalled spelling (transitional)? This is Level 4 writing.

Table 1   Possible Test Responses

Word	Precommunicative	Semiphonetic	Phonetic	Transitional	Conventional
1. monster	random letters	MTR	MOSTR	MONSTOR	monster
2. united	random letters	U	UNITD	YOUNIGHTED	united
3. dress	random letters	JRS	JRAS	DRES	dress
4. bottom	random letters	BT	BODM	BOTTUM	bottom
5. hiked	random letters	H	HIKT	HICKED	hiked
6. human	random letters	UM	HUMN	HUMON	human
7. eagle	random letters	EL	EGL	EGUL	eagle
8. closed	random letters	CD	CLOSD	CLOSSED	closed
9. bumped	random letters	B	BOFT	BUMPPED	bumped
10. type	random letters	TP	TIP	TIPE	type

Conventional spellers develop over years of word study and writing. Conventional spelling can be categorized by instructional levels; for example, correct spelling of a general corpus of commonly used words that can be spelled by the average fourth grader would be fourth grade level conventional spelling. Place a given test response in this category if the word is spelled correctly. In words of more than one syllable, if one syllable is spelled at one level and another syllable at a different level, classify the word at the lower developmental level.

Source: Adapted from "You Can Analyze Developmental Spelling" by Richard Gentry. In *Teaching/K–8*, May 1985.

Table 5.4 Phases of the Monster Test

MONSTER TEST PHASE	WORD KNOWLEDGE LEVEL
Phase 1	_____
Phase 2	Logographic or Early Alphabetic
Phase 3	Early Alphabetic or Alphabetic
Phase 4	Early Orthographic
Conventional	Orthographic
_____	Morphological
_____	Derivational

Teaching Word Knowledge

In the sections that follow, we make suggestions for teaching word recognition. Before we begin, note that children at different phases in their development of word recognition need different kinds of instruction. When it comes to teaching word recognition, one size does not fit all. In word recognition, as in other aspects of reading instruction, children need differentiated instruction.

Teaching the Whole Word, or Logographic Reader (K–Grade 1)

Children at the logographic phase of word recognition are emergent readers. They are just learning to recognize words as wholes, so we encourage that. As children increase the number of words as wholes that they can recognize, they will begin to pay more attention to the letters that make up those words.

WHOLE-PART-WHOLE TEACHING.   Begin word study at all levels by paying attention to words in the context of meaningful sentences before you focus attention on individual words and their parts. The few minutes of extra time that are required to pay attention to the context may well keep some children from becoming confused. It also will make it more likely that children will apply what they learn from the word study sessions when they are reading words in connected text. Several models of whole-part-whole teaching follow here: shared reading, the language-experience approach, and guided reading.

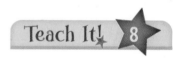

Modified Reading Recovery Lesson

Reading Words in Context.   Children who are getting familiar with words need structured opportunities to focus their attention on a written word at just the instant they hear it spoken, so they can build a connection in their memories. There are two tried-and-true teaching methods that accomplish this. One is the **shared reading method** (Booth and Schwartz, 2004; Holdaway, 1979 and the other is the Language Experience Approach. Both were presented in Chapter 4 [see pages 109–112]).

Using either the shared reading method or the language-experience approach, you can extend the children's word learning by using **word banks.**

Making and Using Word Banks

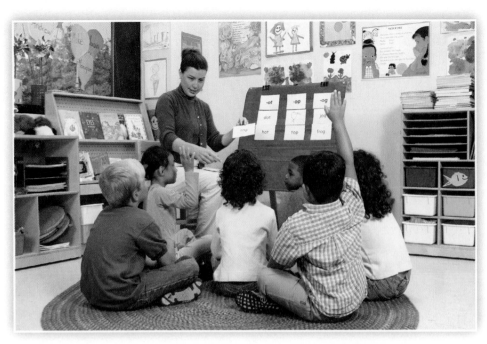

A teacher using a pocket chart in class. (David Mager/Pearson Learning Photo Studio)

Word Banks.   Once a student has demonstrated she has learned to recognize a word that is separated from other words, write that word on a piece of thick paper or tag board. Give the card to the student to put into her **word bank**, a personalized collection of words in a container such as a zippered plastic bag, or an index card box. Students should practice reading the words in the word bank every day or every other day. They can

- Read the words to partners or to parent volunteers.
- Group the words into categories, such as things, actions, animals, etc.
- Group all the words that begin with the same letters.
- Do "word hunts": look for the same words in children's books.

Try to find time to review each child's word bank every week or ten days. If there are words the child cannot read correctly, take them out of the word bank and put them in a special envelope inside or beside it. The child can practice reading those words later, and if they are read correctly, the words go back into the bank.

Morning Message.   As a technique for getting students to understand written language and to focus on words, morning message (Kawakami-Arakaki, Oshiro, & Farran, 1989) gets high marks. Use chart paper or a pocket chart, and write the words in handwriting large enough for all of the children gathered in front of you to see. A typical morning message says,

> *Today is Wednesday, October 17th.*
> *The weather is snowy.*
> *We have art today.*
> *Surprise! Today is Janisha's birthday!*

Ask the students what words you should write. If a child says "Today," ask which letter it should begin with. If she volunteers "T," ask if it will be an uppercase or a lowercase T. A child can come forward and write some of the letters for you. The other children can "air write" (make gestures of writing in the air) while one child writes on the chart.

Write some of the words that are often repeated on separate pieces of thick paper. Either tape them to the bottom of the chart or arrange them in a lower pocket of the pocket chart. Invite children to come forward, find the proper word, and either tape it onto the chart (the tape is already placed on the back of the word) or place it where it should go in the pocket chart. Have the child read the sentence aloud before placing the word in the sentence, and then read the sentence with the word in place.

Next, have all of the children practice reading the lines of print as you follow along beneath the words with a pointer: First they read the lines aloud as you point, then they choral-read the text, then they echo-read, and then different groups of children are invited to read.

Finally, ask individual children to come forward and point to any words they can read alone (that is, in isolation). Bracket each word with your hands as the child reads it. If he or she is successful, write the word on a small piece of thick paper and present it to the child. The word then goes into the child's word bank for later practice.

Labeling the Room. Each child's name should be printed in big letters on her or his desk. The important items around the classroom should be labeled, too—the blackboard, the clock, the door, the window, the books, science center, the sink—with cards bearing letters 3 inches high so they can be read from anywhere in the room. In time, children will be able to write or trace the labels you prepare. Take time every other day to "read the room": first as a whole class, then in small groups taking turns to read the signs together. Every few weeks, change some signs around (so that the label "sink" is over the door, for instance) and ask who notices anything wrong. Ask the children to move the words to the correct locations.

Words that are used as labels can be put in students' word banks, too, if the students can read them correctly.

Teaching the Letter-by-Letter or Alphabetic Reader (Grade 1)

As alphabetic readers, children are beginning readers who have learned several dozen words and are paying attention to the letters in words and associating them with sounds. The goal of our instruction with these children should be to help them notice more and more letters and the sounds with which they are associated. It will also help to call students' attention to sounds in words.

PICTURE SORTS. Make sets of 1 × 2-inch cards with pictures on them, depicting objects that begin with different sounds. For example, *sun, sandal, sail, sand, soda; can, candy, cat, cart, calendar; dog, dart, dish, diaper, diamond; goat, girl, gorilla, guitar, gun.* Place one member of each group side by side on the table. Scramble the rest of the pictures, and then ask a child to name the picture aloud and then place the picture cards one at a time in a column below the appropriate picture. Once children become proficient at this, substitute a card with a letter as the guide card at the top of the column.

Picture cards can be downloaded for free at:

- http://www.kellyskindergarten.com/picturecards/picturecards.htm
- http://pals.virginia.edu/pdfs/activities/beginning-sounds/picture_sorts.pdf

Commercially prepared picture sort cards are available from these companies:

- Teaching Resource Center (http://www.trcabc.com/)
- ReallyGoodStuff.Com (https://www.reallygoodstuff.com)

PLASTIC LETTERS. Gather two to five students in front of you. Using sets of plastic letters (some are sold in toy stores with magnetic backs to stick to refrigerators), make a word such as *band*. Say the word aloud, and then take the letter S. Exaggerate the sound of /s/, and tell the students to watch what happens when you substitute the S for the B. You get *sand*. Demonstrate this several times, and let some of the children make the same substitution. Then hold up the letter H and ask who can tell what word we will have when we substitute the letter H for the S in sand. Then follow with l. Pairs of children can follow up by playing this game themselves. On other days you can introduce other phonogram patterns and other beginning consonants.

RHYMING GAMES.   Chants and songs are good for rhyming games, and rhyming games help call children's attention to sounds in words. The Mother Goose rhyme, "Ding, dong, dell/Kitty's in the well," can be used to play with rhymes:

> Ding, dog, doset
> Kitty's in the _____ (closet)
> Ding, dog, dimming pool
> Kitty's in the _____ (swimming pool)
> Ding, dog, didewalk
> Kitty's on the _____ (sidewalk)

Or try the popular children's song, "Willoughby, Wallaby, Woo":

> Willoughby, Wallaby, Woo
> An elephant sat on you,
> Willoughby, Wallaby, Wee
> An elephant sat on me.
> Willoughby, Wallaby, Wonna
> An elephant sat on _____ (Donna)
> Willoughby, Wallaby, Walan
> An elephant sat on _____ (Alan)*

WORD WALLS.   Word walls (Cunningham, 1995; Cunningham, Hall, & Sigmon, 2007) can provide strong support in children's learning and teachers' systematic instruction. Word walls consist of words that children are learning arranged alphabetically on the walls of the classroom in ways that allow the words to be easily seen and accessed. Word walls should be interactive, made and used by the teacher and the children. Much good instruction can spring from various kinds of words on walls, including serving children's self-assessment needs. Here is a brief description of two types of word walls and how they be might be used (see also Bear et al., 2007; McGee & Richgels, 2003; Pinnell & Fountas, 1998):

- **A picture-word wall:** Post the words from favorite books, inquiry units of study, and words and pictures with the letters of the alphabet. It is nearly always best if words are put on the wall during the teaching process.
- **A literature-based picture-word wall:** This type of word wall can be used with both young children and older children. For example, if the class has read *Lilly's Purple Plastic Purse* (Henkes, 1996) or *Lilly's Big Day* (Henkes, 2006), you can introduce the word wall by showing an enlarged picture or colorful sketch of Lilly on the wall with Lilly's name under it. Ask for suggestions about other words children want to add from the book. Write their words in full view, leaving space for the pictures that will come. Ask the children to remember their favorite word. Next, have them draw a picture that depicts or explains their word and write the word and explanation. Talk the children through some examples of what they might write.

As children's development progresses, word walls change from picture-word walls to word-only walls. Word hunts and word sorts expand the word study. Books are reread to keep a focus on meaningful reading and reading for enjoyment. Imagine the word walls on science and other inquiry work you can have with middle and upper grades!

---

*"Willoughby, Wallaby, Woo" from *Alligator Pie* by Dennis Lee (Macmillan of Canada, 1974, Key Porter Books, 2001). Copyright © 1974 Dennis Lee. With permission of the author.

SIGHT WORDS. Sight words are learned primarily through sheer exposure. Repeated readings are key. Children should reread their favorite books while they also select challenging books from several the teacher recommends. Importantly, sight word knowledge helps children progress in reading to the point that reading is easy and joyful. With enough sight words in their memory, students read with less effort and are better able to concentrate on meaning and reading comprehension.

Sight word walls contain high-frequency words that are posted as the children encounter them in their reading and in lessons. The teacher should engage children in practicing reading sight word walls regularly (Cunningham et al., 2007). When word walls are used daily in the course of reading, writing, and spelling, they are embedded in authentic literacy practice. This is how you can create and use a sight word wall:

- Add words gradually (about five per week).
- Make words highly accessible by putting them where all students can see them, writing them in large print with big black letters, and using colors for words that are often confused, such as *for, from, that, they,* and *this.*
- Select only the words children encounter most frequently in their reading and the words they use most frequently in their writing. Do not overwhelm them or yourself with too many words. Nothing succeeds like success!
- Practice the words by saying, spelling, and writing them ("do the wall").

WORD WALL CHANTS. From Joe Fuhrmann's amazing website (http://www .k111.k12.il.us/lafayette/fourblocks/word_wall_chants.htm) come these suggestions for word wall chants. As the children and the teacher review the words on the word wall, they use different and engaging ways to spell out the letters and then read the word. Some of the chants can be done with the children at their seats:

- "The chicken": Flapping your arms up and down as you say each letter
- "The movie star": Blowing kisses, like a starlet on awards night as each letter is said
- "The opera singer": Singing each letter, and finally the word, in an operatic voice
- "The volcano": Saying each letter louder and louder, until you shout the word
- "The nose": Holding your nose as you say the letters and the word

Other chants can be done standing up and moving around:

- "Dribble and shoot": Dribbling each letter and shooting the word
- "Mexican Hat Dance": Chanting letters as each foot goes forward
- "Pumping iron": Pretending to hoist a heavy weight as you say each letter, then pretending to put the bar back on the frame as you say the word with an exhausted voice
- "Frog jump": Beginning standing up, and crouching a little lower as you say each letter, then leaping as you say the word

SHARED WRITING. Shared writing is a way for the teacher to demonstrate how spoken words are broken into their sounds and spelled with letters. It is also a means of engaging children's participation in writing. After sharing a poem or discussing an event that is exciting to the children, the teacher gathers students around an easel and invites them to help him write about what they just heard. First children agree on a short sentence they want to write, for example, "A firefighter came to school." The children practice saying the sentence several times so that everyone is aware of the words. Then the teacher says, "Now we're going to write the first word, 'A.' Who can tell us what letter we need to write?" A child suggests the letter A. The teacher accepts it and writes it slowly on the easel. Then he says, "We wrote A. Now what's the next word we want to write? Right. It's 'firefighter.' That's a new word, so I'm going to leave space between the word A and the first letter of this new word. [He puts his finger after the A to demonstrate the space.] What is the first sound we hear in 'firefighter'? Right: it's 'fuh.' What letter are we going to use to write the 'fuh' sound in 'firefighter'? Right: It's F. Who can come up and write the letter F for me?" A child comes up and writes the letter. The teacher proceeds in this way, having the children supply the letters they can, and adding the sounds himself that the children do not hear. If a child makes an error in writing, the teacher puts a piece of wide correction tape over the error and helps the child write the correct letter.

It is important to conduct shared writing lessons with the class almost daily when children are in the alphabetic phase of writing. In the meantime, encourage the children to use writing every chance they get.

Guided Reading and the Four Blocks Approach

GUIDED READING.   As you saw in Chapter 4, guided reading is done with a small group of children or as few as two children to support children's progress in reading development, including fluency, comprehension, and word knowledge. The texts used in guided reading gradually become more and more challenging (Fountas & Pinnell, 1996). Even when you want to use guided reading to emphasize word study, it is important to create a meaningful context for the words. Thus you begin the lesson with a focus on meaning before proceeding to word study. Detailed steps for Guided Reading are presented in Chapter 4, pages 112–113. See also the Four Blocks Model in Chapter 1, page 18.

Teaching the Reader at the "Chunking" Phase: The Orthographic Reader (Grades 2 to 3)

Children in the "chunking" or orthographic phase of word reading are starting to pay attention to spelling patterns, or what linguists call *onsets* and *rimes*. At the beginning of this period, they are ready to understand that if they can read *hit* and they know the sound represented by the letter S, they can also read *sit*. Toward the end of this period, they must learn how to cope with two-syllable words, homophones, and other challenges English orthography poses to the reader. Teaching activities at the orthographic phase should work extensively with patterns of spelling.

WORD SORTS.   Word sorting activities include sorting words by spelling or phonogram patterns—for example, words that are spelled like *rock*. Word sorts also may focus on the concepts that words represent—for example, sort all the weather-associated words in one row (*rain, snow, . . .*), and sort all the cooking-associated words in another row (*stove, bowl, . . .*). Word sorting by affixes and whole words provides sound practice and the kind of hands-on activity that older children appreciate.

Sorting instruction encourages children to see words as objects that they manipulate and own by organizing and classifying them. Jerry Zutell (1999, p. 105) notes, "Organizing objects, events, and experiences into categories and classes is a fundamental way we make sense of the world around us. The act of sorting makes words concrete objects of study."

The first time children do word sorts, it is good to begin with a small group demonstration. After children have had a lively experience with a text—whether by reading a big book, reading back a dictated story, or reading a trade book—the teacher calls their attention to a small group of individual words. These words are chosen because they share patterns that can be generalized to other words. By *generalized*, we mean that once children have noticed a pattern in one word, they can apply that pattern to help them read other words. For example, the words *sit* and *cub* can be chosen for children who are early orthographic readers, because they introduce patterns that other words share (see below). The teacher writes these words on cards made of thick paper or tag board. If they will be used in front of a small group of children, use 3" × 5" cards.

Now the teacher creates more cards with several words that share the same phonogram patterns as *sit* and *cub*. For example, he writes *fit, bit,* and *kit*; and *tub, rub,* and *sub*.

The teacher then puts the two original cards on the table or in the top pocket of a pocket chart, side by side. He reads both words several times, pointing to each word, to make sure that all of the children can read them. Next the teacher scrambles the remaining cards. Then he draws one of the remaining cards—let's say it is *rub*—and holds it up for the children.

"Where does it go?" he asks. "Should I put it in the column with *sit* or the column with *cub*?" Note that he doesn't read the word he drew yet.

The children say it goes in the column under *cub*. Then the teacher says, "Let's read down the column. *Cub* and *rrrrrrr*—. . ."

The children say "*Rub!*" The teacher congratulates them, and then he stresses the point that once they could read *cub*, and they saw that the new word began with *r*, they could read it: "*rub*."

Now he invites children to come up one at a time to choose words from the scrambled set and place them under the guide words, *sit* or *cub*. Later the teacher can add another group of words to the sets: *dad, sad, mad*, and *had*.

After the children demonstrate that they understand how the activity works, they may practice in pairs. Once the procedures for word sorts have been taught to the class, pairs or trios of students can play word sort games with groups of words that have been prepared in advance. The procedures for the game work are the same as in the group lesson just described.

- Write groups of words on 1 × 2-inch cards, about the size of a business card.
- Prepare four to five examples of each spelling pattern.
- Make sure that each student can read at least one word from each group. These words should be used as the guide words. They should be placed at the top of the column, and during the word sorting game, the other words should be placed one at a time underneath them.
- Leave the other cards face up and scrambled.
- One at a time, have each child choose a card from the scrambled pile, place it in the column beneath the guide word, and read down the column of words.

A memory game can now be used to give children more practice with the patterns. Once the students have sorted the words into their respective columns, they can put the cards face down on the table in front of them, arranged in rows (see Figure 5.1). Taking turns, one student turns over two cards. If they match (that is, if they share the same phonogram pattern), that student gets to keep those cards. Students continue playing in turns until all of the cards are paired with other cards and taken off the table.

Further practice with the patterns can be provided with board games. Groups of cards arranged into patterns make good board games. In the "Race Track" game, a board with fifteen to twenty blank spaces is drawn up. Sets of word cards that share spelling patterns are shuffled and dealt to two to four payers. One player rolls one die and moves her marker piece (similar to marker pieces in a Monopoly game) the number of spaces showing on the die. If she is the first to land on a space, she may put down one card on the space. The next player who lands on that same space must put down a word with the same spelling pattern or forfeit a turn. The game continues until all cards are exhausted. Note: It can add a welcome element of chance if you add some wild cards to the stack: "give two cards to the person to your right" etc. (see Figure 5.2).

After children become accurate with word sorts, they can extend their expertise by seeing how quickly they can sort, using speed sorts. This activity supports fluency and healthy competition in a game-like task. (Sixth to eighth graders really like them.) Like so many developmentally appropriate activities, speed sorts build intrinsic motivation and provide that all-important sense of satisfaction!

A speed sort is done as follows:

- Use a timer of some type. Egg timers really help and are quiet!
- Children sort as fast and as accurately as they can.

Figure 5.1
The Memory Game.

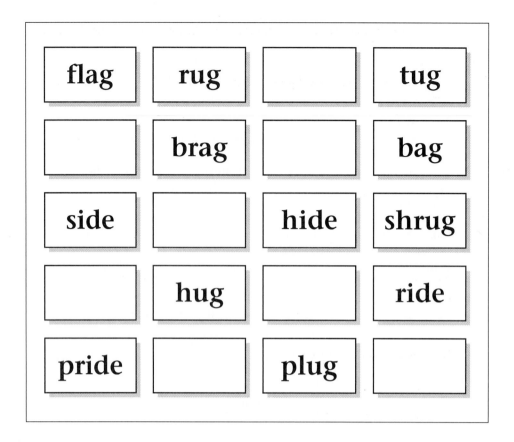

flag	rug		tug
brag		bag
side		hide	shrug
	hug		ride
pride		plug	

- Children self-assess the sorts with a rubric alone or with another child. If they encounter any uncertainty, they skip the word and later get help with it.
- Children may chart the number of words sorted correctly in *the designated amount of time*. Once the activity has been taught well, a teacher-made charting sheet aids children's independent charting. Learners thrive on healthy competition with themselves.

The order of words used in word sorts matters. We work in this order:

- **Start with single beginning consonants.** For demonstration purposes, we can begin with *M* and *S*. Why those two? Because you can stretch out the pronunciation of the sounds (try stretching out the sound of *T*, if you don't believe us!), and also the two sounds are nicely contrasted. Then you can add **L** and **N** because those, too, can be stretched out. Later, you can add **B, D, F, H, P,** and **T**. Those letters usually represent a single sound each. Choose the most different letters to introduce together. Avoid grouping **B** and **D** because they look similar;

Figure 5.2
Board Game for Word Sorts.

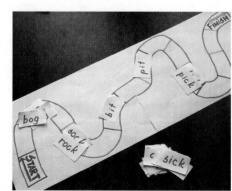

and also avoid **D** and **T** because they sound similar. Beginning consonants are introduced with picture sorts, and later you can substitute letters on cards for the pictures.

- **Then introduce short vowel phonogram patterns.** Use words with these short vowel patterns:

  -an, -ad, -ap, -at

  -ed, -et

  -it, -ip, -id

  -ot, -ob, -op

  -up, -ub

  -ill, -ell

  -ack, -eck, -ick, -ock

  -ank, -ink, -ump

- **Now make groups of words with the same short vowel, in different spelling patterns:**

  For example, *cap, bad, sack, stab,* and *sank* as a group contrasted with

  jump, pup, cut, stub, rut, and *duck.*

- **Introduce *r*-controlled vowels:**

  -ar, ur, -ir, -or

- **Introduce words with *-all.***

- **Introduce consonant blends at the beginning of words:**

  dr-, tr-, cl-, pl-, st-

- **Introduce long vowel patterns:**

  -ate, -ake, -ail, -ame, -ain, -ay

  -eat, -eal

  -ice; -ide

  -ool

- **Introduce patterns with *-ook* and *-ull*; and *wa-.***

- **Then two-syllable words,** such as *mother, table, kitten,* and *happy.*

- **Then compound words,** such as *into, cowboy, steamboat,* and *football.*

- **Then words with inflectional endings,** such as *-er, -est, -ing,* and *-ed.*

WORD HUNTS. Word hunts help children make connections between spelling the words and reading them. This is important because some children do not automatically apply what they learn in word study activities when they are trying to read words in texts (Ehri, 1997). Word hunts also incorporate children's literature, poetry, or other whole texts. The Teach It! box shows a sample lesson that uses a word hunt based on a poem.

Teach It! 16

Word Hunts

WORD WHEELS. On a piece of thick paper or tag board, write a phonogram pattern such as *-an, -it,* or *-ock.* Leave space to the left of the pattern. Then cut out a round piece of the same material, and write consonant letters such as *F, S, H,* and *P* (for *-it*) facing outward around the edges of the circle. Attach the circle to the slip of paper with the phonogram pattern using a brad, as shown in Figure 5.3. Children can rotate the circle until a beginning consonant lines up with the phonogram pattern, and then pronounce the resulting word.

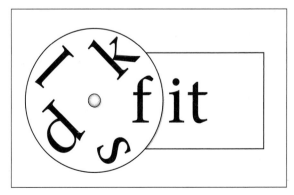

Figure 5.3

The Word Wheel.

FLIP CARDS. Instead of a circle with consonants as in the word wheels, cut out a set of short cards (1 inch × 1 inch), write consonant letters on them, and staple them to a longer card (1 inch × 3 inches)

Teach It!

Refer to the Teach It! appendix at the end of the book for further activities you can use to reinforce concepts discussed in this chapter.

Word Hunts

In the fifth week of school, student teacher Breanna demonstrates a word hunt for her children. She works with eight to ten children at a time. Breanna reads the poem "Books, Books" by Ritsa Tassopoulos (Personal communication, April 10, 2002) to the children from a large chart and then says, "Now, let's read it together."

Books, Books

Books, books fun to read
Books, books just what I need
Books, books fill my head
Books, books in my bed
Books, books morning noon and night
Books, books make me feel just right.

The children follow along well. After reading, the children reread together in partner groups. Breanna then says, "What do you notice about some of these words?"

Children talk. They share their observations and volunteer to read rhyming words (times and rhymes).

Breanna says, "Now I'm going on a word hunt. I want to find two words that don't rhyme."

Thinking out loud about rhyming and non-rhyming words and how they sound and look, she lists two words—*head* and *need*—in separate columns. Breanna organizes the group of children into pairs and asks them to work together. She says, "Copy these two words onto your papers and make them look like this (pointing to the columns). Find rhyming words to match the top word in each column. The words can be new ones you think of, words from our word walls, and words in this poem. Get ready to talk about what you've found. This is just practice. No one has to get everything right; it's practice. Don't worry, we'll have fun talking about what makes words rhyme."

with a phonogram pattern written on it, as shown in Figure 5.4. Children can fold back the short cards to pair up different beginning consonants with the phonogram pattern and then read the resulting word.

Word Sorting with Two-Syllable Words

Children in grades 2 through 4 must learn what happens when syllables meet. This is more of a challenge for spelling than for reading, but readers must be aware of the problems raised by the vowel marking systems of English. For example, the spelling pattern of *bat* is fairly easy to learn. But when *bat* adds the grammatical ending *-ed* or *-ing*, the consonant must be doubled. If it were not doubled, the E or the I would have the effect of marking the vowel in *bat* long, giving it the pronunciation *baited* or *baiting*. Conversely, the final two consonants in *sing* are enough to insulate the vowel from the lengthening effect of *-ing*, so nothing need be added to its final consonants. And here is an oddity: Because the *x* in *ax* is made up of two sounds, it insulated the vowel from the lengthening effect of any following vowel, so we write *axes* and *axing*. But words that contain a long vowel already do not need to double the final consonant: *dream, dreaming; cool, cooled*.

Children can be taught when they should and should not double consonants when endings are added to single-syllable words. To teach children to sort for two-syllable words, begin by making groups of words that double the final consonants before adding an ending *-er* or *-ing*. For example, the guide words might be *batted* and *dreaming*. The "scrabbled" words can be *call, steal, sit, start, run,* and *cut*. Children place each word under a guide word depending on whether the word doubles the final consonant when the ending is added.

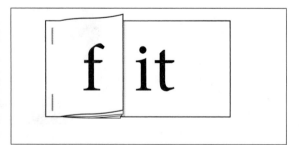

Figure 5.4

Flip Cards.

FAMILY AND COMMUNITY. Home support by families or caregivers can be built from nearly any lesson that is taught at school. For example, easy word sorts can go home for five- to seven-minute practice sessions; word sort games can be especially fun when played with a loved one. Simple turn-taking and charting progress or keeping score (with the little ones winning!) create a game. Include for the adults one page of simple and limited suggestions for conversations about words with take-home sorts. Ask for a "read around the house" adventure. Adults help children read any and every word they find in the kitchen, bathroom, or elsewhere. Groups of parents, caregivers, and children who play together or attend community functions will benefit from getting together to support their children in literacy play. Some thoughtful adult structure and guidance can help regular play groups move into literacy games and activities.

Family Literacy

Suggest a lesson plan that might encourage support from families.

NEW LITERACIES. For home and school technology materials, look into word recognition software programs. A good program that is very popular with young children is *Wiggle Works* from Scholastic Publishing and the Center for Applied Special Technology. *Wiggle Works* focuses on emergent, early, and fluent language development using reading, writing, speaking, and listening. It contains a variety of creative activities that entertain while also building skills. Additional programs can be found online at Superkids.com (www.superkids.com), where teachers and parents can check out various programs and read reviews of their efficacy.

New Literacies

Do an online search for a good word recognition program.

Teaching the "Meaningful Word Parts" or Morphological Reader (Grades 3 and 4)

Children in the "meaningful word parts" or morphological phase of word reading are coping with compound words, grammatical endings, and prefixes and suffixes. There are places for explicit teaching—explanations of how words work—extended exploration of words, and also copious reading for students to learn what they need at this phase.

STRUCTURAL ANALYSIS. Structural analysis is the activity of examining the parts of a word to help arrive at the meaning of the whole word. This procedure works when (1) the word is a compound word, or is made up of root words and prefixes and suffixes, and (2) the students understand the meanings of those affixes.

As we pointed out in Chapter 3, English words are built from other words. **Compound words** are built three different ways. Knowing whether to write two words together, like *motorboat*, to join them with a hyphen, like *mother-in-law*, or write them separately, like *fire truck*, is a challenge for spelling rather than for reading. But readers can find long words like *grandmother* or *grasshopper* to be daunting, so teachers often give the advice, "Find a little word that you know in that big word," and we hold our thumb over part of the word to focus their attention on the other part of the word.

Make 3 × 5 cards with these words on them: *foot, ball, basket, ball, rain, coat, lawn, mower, mother, in, law, see, saw, ninety, six, ice, cream, paper, boy, all,* and *right.* Also, make five hyphens ("–") on cards. Place these in the bottom rows of a pocket chart. Have the students help you assemble words to make compound words. Which ones are joined together without spaces? Which ones are joined with hyphens? Which ones are written separately? For more movement in the classroom, write the words and the hyphens on tablets. Pronounce the words aloud and have teams decide if the students holding the words should stand shoulder to shoulder, have a hyphen between them, or stand apart.

To work with **prefixes and suffixes**, make 3 × 5 cards with these prefixes and suffixes on them: *dis-, inter-, re-, un-, under-, -able, -al, -ant.* Place these on the bottom row of a pocket chart. Make another set of cards with these root words: *trust, do, act, stand, nation, contest,* and *consider.* Place these word cards on the next-to-bottom row. Then have the students help you combine root words, prefixes, and suffixes into words that you place on the upper rows of the pocket chart. (As an alternative, you can write the prefixes, suffixes, and root words on small pieces of acetate and have the students build words on the

Being a Professional Reading Teacher

Taking a Broad Perspective on Phonics

Phonics, the teaching of letter-to-sound relationships, has long been the most controversial aspect of reading instruction. As we saw in Chapter 1, over the past forty years, several large-scale summaries of research in reading instruction have tried to answer the question of which works best: teaching phonics explicitly or teaching phonics implicitly (by showing words that share spelling patterns and asking children to derive a generalization about the ways spellings represent sounds). Research has fairly consistently favored teaching phonics explicitly.

But that does not mean phonics instruction is all children need in order to read. Catherine Snow and her colleagues (2005) recently made that point very clearly: "A focus on phonological awareness, phonemic awareness, and phonics is essential for poor readers but not enough—instruction must also address key areas such as comprehension, vocabulary, the identification of irregular words, and fluency" (p. 166).

Teachers receive plenty of advice on teaching word recognition from all sides. Not only has the federal government come down firmly on the side of teaching explicit phonics, but many states have, too. Laypeople also offer plenty of advice on the subject, as we saw in the example of the phonics programs for sale in the grocery store.

Professional reading teachers should stay informed on this issue. One good way is to read the publications of the International Reading Association, especially *The Reading Teacher*, and to attend the regional and national conferences.

Word knowledge instruction with older students focuses more on structural analysis and understanding word derivations. (Lindfors Photography)

overhead projector.) For follow-up, make a word wall of words with prefixes and another word wall of words with suffixes.

Word Journals. A useful way to have students record and recall words from word-sorting and word-building exercises is to have them keep a word journal. A word journal is a medium-size spiral notebook, with sections labeled according to the groupings of words it contains. These groupings might contain all the categories into which words have been sorted during word-sorting activities. To record compound words, have the students divide a page with two vertical lines to make three columns. In the left-hand column, they can write compound words that have the parts written together; in the central column, words joined with hyphens; and in the right-hand column, words written separately. For words with prefixes and suffixes, students set aside half a page each for words with *un-, re-, inter-,* and *-dis, -ant, -ful,* and *-able.* They add words to those pages from time to time as they come across them from their reading. The teacher reminds the class to share aloud some of their new entries. These also can be added to the word wall.

Teaching the Reader of "Word Histories and Families" or the Derivational Reader (Grade 4 and Up)

At the phase of derivational reading, the challenges of reading words have to do with

- Understanding how words are built from historical spare parts from languages that are no longer spoken
- Thinking of relationships between words that have common ancestors
- Reading words whose spellings honor their histories rather than their present-day pronunciation

Table 5.5   Prefixes and Suffixes of Latin and Greek Origin

PREFIX OR SUFFIX	MEANING
con-, com-, col-, cor-	together
ab-	from, away from, by
ad-, al-, ac-, at-	to, toward
de-	down from, off
dis-	lack of, not
e-	out, out of
re-	back, or again
-ure	state of
pre-	before

We use the term *derivational* for this phase because the most common challenge is reading words derived from other words.

WORKING WITH WORDS WITH PARTS FROM ANCIENT SOURCES.   Most of the words in the English language are made up of ancient parts from Latin and Greek. We mean words like *fortunate, masculine, ignition, sensitive, symphony,* and *microscope.* As you can see from the examples, those words are considered more mature vocabulary items, though, so children don't read very many of them before fourth grade, unless they are precocious readers. From that point on, however, readers encounter more and more of them, and it is very useful for students to recognize their parts, know their range of meanings, and be able to figure out at least roughly how the words should be pronounced as well as what they mean.

Teach It! 23

Connect Two

STRUCTURAL ANALYSIS WITH LATIN AND GREEK PARTS.   Make 3 × 5-inch index cards of the Latin and Greek prefixes in Table 5.5. Display them in a pocket chart for the students. Explain that they came from two languages, Latin and ancient Greek, that are no longer spoken, but that contribute to most of the words in the English dictionary. Then discuss their meanings.

Then make 3 × 5-inch index cards of the word roots in Table 5.6. Display them in a pocket chart for the students, and discuss their meanings, too.

Have the students help you join prefixes and stems to make words. Discuss what you think the words mean. Then check the meanings in a dictionary to be sure. (Note: Some possible words are *collect, college, elect, object, dejected, eject, reject, conjecture, abrupt, erupt, disrupt, corrupt, revolve, evolve, devolve, contain, detain, retain, attain, contort, distort, retort, torture.*)

Make smaller sets of word cards and have pairs build words with them. Make a word wall on which to display sets of these words. Have students record them in their word journals. For more on structural analysis (with roots), see Freppon (1987).

Teach It! 62

Word Origins and Derivations

WORD REPORTS.   Assign students to teams that will research words that share common roots. Give each team a historical root word, such as *grad-, -meter, bio-, -graph, -tele,* or *miss-.* Have them look through dictionaries and find all of the words that contain their word root. They may prepare a chart of their findings, and present their work to the class.

Table 5.6	Roots of Latin Origin	
ROOT	**MEANING**
-lect, -lege	choose
-ject, -jac	throw
-rupt	break
-tort-	twist
grad-	step
-volt, -volve	turn, roll
-tain	have, hold
dict	say or tell
-mit or -miss	send

Family Literacy

How will you encourage all families to raise their children's curiosity about words?

FAMILY AND COMMUNITY.   As we stated earlier, the importance of family or care-giver involvement in children's word learning does not decrease with the child's age. An easy and interesting mall walk creates a discovery game for older students. It involves giving the child a list of Greek root words: *aero* (means "air"), *bio* (means "life"), *geo* (means "earth"), *log, logy, or logue* (means "word" or the study of something), *meter* (means "measuring"), *phone* (means "sound"), *therm* (means "heat"), *photo* (means "light"), *hydro* (means "water"), and so on. The child and adult(s) identify words in the mall signs that have a Greek root and do a structural analysis of each word. For example, a father spots "log" in a word on a store sign, the child reads "logo," and the father and child read the sign: "T-Shirt Logos in One Hour." Many word games are created once adults and older children begin to play them.

Teach It! 5

Language Experience with Authentic Children's Literature

Helping Students Read Words in Context

When teaching children to learn and recognize words, it is very important to help them connect the words they've studied with similar words they come across in reading various texts. You can help children of all ages become more keenly aware of this in many ways.

Effective teachers know that demonstration and modeling provide a good beginning. For example, recall the opening classroom story of this chapter that featured Ms. Gupta's lesson with the words *spider* and *spout* and the focus on *sp* blends. In this lesson the children studied several words including *spider, spout, spell, spend,* and *spot.* They also generated words such as *see* and *snow* that didn't work for *sp* blends. This was a way to model and demonstrate connecting "studied words" with new ones.

Now picture Ms. Gupta's extending her teaching by presenting a lesson that used a sample of new text with similar words (e.g., some new *sp* blend words and some that did not fit the *sp* blend pattern). In such a lesson Ms. Gupta builds on the previous lesson and even more explicitly shows students that they can and should pay attention to words in their reading that are similar to words they know and are studying.

In conducting such demonstrations you model your thinking out loud to show the children that this is the kind of thinking they should also do. Imagine yourself reading a text on a large chart or in a big book in view of the children. The conversation goes something like this.

Teacher: Humm. . . . I'm not sure about this word (silently draw your finger under the word *motorcar*), but it looks like one I know because we did a word sort with *motorboat* in it. And this story is about driving to the store. What do you think, children?

A few children respond that they see *C-A-R* and almost immediately some respond in unison saying, "car!"

Teacher: Nice observation! I like the way you watch carefully and connect words you know with new words. And you are thinking about what is going on in the story. Good thinking, you used the context!

Once children have been taught through teacher modeling, remind and support them by teacher talk to connect known words to unknown words using everything they know to figure out more and more words. Watch like a hawk and seize opportunities to affirm children's accomplishments in acquiring word knowledge in their reading.

Word learning strategies discussed in this chapter such as word hunts can also be adapted and expanded. Rather than hunting for the same studied words in books, children hunt for words that are similar to those in a list of known words given to them by their teacher or that they write on their own.

Also, as noted earlier in this chapter, word walls built from social studies, science, or literature units provide words that are similar to studied words. Call children's attention to comparing and contrasting such words to their studied word walls and invite them to find similarities.

A powerful teaching tool for any instruction is your classroom talk and use of language (Johnston, 2004). Often, instead of directly telling students something, asking them questions provides strong motivation. Consider a seventh-grade teacher observing a student puzzling over the word *periscope* in a book about submarines. Because in this class they study Greek and Latin roots, the teacher initiates the following conversation.

Teacher: Is there a word you know that looks like this one?

Student: It looks a little like *telescope*.

Teacher: Yes. We've had that one. Do you know any other words that are similar to this one [pointing to *periscope*]?

Student: Well, we also had *microscope* in science the other day.

Teacher: Hmm. . . . what's this book about?

Student: Submarines. Is it *periscope*?

Teacher: How did you know?

Student: I remembered the scope part. And the "up periscope" I saw in a movie.

Teacher: Great thinking!

Here you saw the teacher guide the student to use multiple cues to get the unknown word. As so often is the case, use of multiple cues supports children's literate thinking. Importantly, this teacher's talk attributed competence to the student. This is a wonderful way of building independence and students' awareness that they are in charge of their word learning.

For Review

Throughout the elementary grades, children need systematic, frequent, and flexible opportunities to learn words. They must have word knowledge instruction that is grounded in reading as a sense-making and meaningful activity. Many word-learning activities may be used successfully from grades 1 to 8 in exclusive practice time periods of about ten to fifteen minutes. About thirty minutes of word work in context and in exclusive teaching and practice usually works for most children. Use a whole-part-whole approach in highly contextualized word instruction, especially in exclusive word study. That is, always return to word, sentence, and whole text meaning. It is recommended that you teach children the relation-ships between letters and sounds, beginning with individual letters and individual sounds and soon moving to groups of letters that spell parts of syllables, that is, onsets and rimes.

This chapter focused on word knowledge, what it contributes to the reading process, and why it is important. It highlighted phonics and how to handle teaching word recognition. We saw that phonics is not a one-time thing, though: children's word knowledge, and the challenges of reading and spelling English words, changes dramatically as children move from kindergarten through middle school.

For Your Journal

1. Imagine a grade level you wish to teach or are teaching. Make a list of what you need to know about teaching words. Jot down any related concerns or frustrations you have at this point or anticipate having later.

2. Try this on your own, or work with a partner. Review "The Eeensy Weensy Spider" lesson described in the chapter-opening classroom story. Consider the levels of word knowledge in this chapter: logographic, transitional, alphabetic, orthographic, morphological, and derivational. What phase or phases were Ms. Gupta's children in? Why do you say so?

Taking It to the World

The debate about whole-word versus phonics instruction as ways of teaching children to read has never been as simple as people often make it sound. Virtually all teachers read to children, invite children to write, and give them opportunities to explore meaningful print; and virtually all teachers point out letter-to-sound relationships to children. But there are differences in the emphasis that teachers put on these activities.

1. Either alone or with a partner, interview two or three first grade and two or three second grade teachers about their approaches to teaching reading. What things do the teachers at the same grade level have in common? What aspects of teaching are approached differently?

2. Ask them, also, to what extent their reading approaches are left up to their own decisions and to what extent their approaches are guided by reading coaches at the school level or district level.

New Literacies Connections

1. Visit Freereading.net for free lesson plans for teaching word study:
http://www.freereading.net/index.php?title=Word-Form_Recognition_Activities.

2. Read Ron Cramer's suggestions for using the Language Experience Approach here:
http://www.literacyconnections.com/Cramer.html.

PEARSON myeducationlab

Now go to MyEducationLab (www.myeducationlab.com), where you can:

- Find learning outcomes for the topics covered in this chapter, along with the national standards that connect to these outcomes.

- Complete Assignments and Activities that can help you more deeply understand the chapter content.

- Engage in Building Teaching Skills and Dispositions exercises, in which you can apply and practice core teaching skills identified in the chapter.

Helping Readers Build Fluency and Vocabulary

Anticipation Guide

The following questions will help you begin thinking about the topics covered in this chapter. Answer *true* or *false* in response to each statement. As you read and learn more about the topics mentioned in these statements, think back on your answers. See what interests you and what prompts your curiosity toward more understanding.

_____ 1. Fluency and vocabulary are both considered key areas of reading ability by the U.S. government.

_____ 2. Reading fluently consists entirely of reading quickly.

_____ 3. Children who read fluently tend to understand what they read.

_____ 4. Teachers should never model fluent reading for children, for fear of discouraging them.

_____ 5. An average reading rate for a third grader is about 30 words per minute.

_____ 6. Vocabulary is knowledge of words and word meanings.

_____ 7. All children enter school with very nearly the same number of words in their vocabularies.

_____ 8. Having a word for something in your vocabulary makes it more likely that you will notice that thing, or quality, or situation.

_____ 9. Vocabulary knowledge is one of the best predictors of reading comprehension.

_____ 10. Research suggests that while it helps to teach vocabulary, we don't need to teach all of the words children need to know.

Helping Readers Build Fluency and Vocabulary

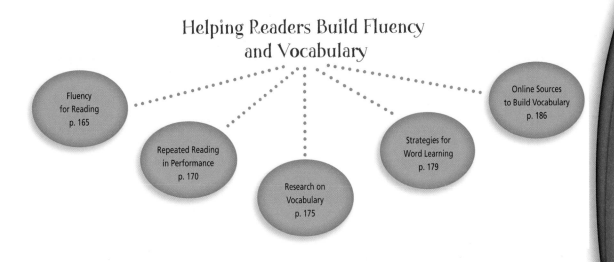

Fluency for Reading p. 165

Repeated Reading in Performance p. 170

Research on Vocabulary p. 175

Strategies for Word Learning p. 179

Online Sources to Build Vocabulary p. 186

Volunteer Tutors Help Children Develop Fluency

Katie Flowers directs a tutoring project for a small liberal arts college. The program has worked continuously for thirteen years, and is very popular with college students. Nearly one hundred of them volunteer each term to go out to a local school and work one on one with a first-, second-, or third-grade student who has been recommended by a teacher for extra help.

At the beginning of each semester, the students are given a couple of hours of training. Then the students go out to a local school two times each week, both before and after school. Each time the students go out, they follow a lesson plan with five parts. The lesson plan was borrowed from Darrell Morris's *Howard Street Tutoring Manual* (2006):

1. Read an easy book to develop fluency.
2. Read a harder book to help the children learn new words.

3. Do a word study task—phonics or vocabulary.
4. Have the child write something.
5. Read aloud to the child.

Katie asks the teachers to fill out feedback forms at the end of each term. Last spring, one teacher reported that over the year a third-grade student progressed from reading 58 to 153 words per minute. Another teacher reported a big increase in a child's Lexile score on a commercial reading test. These and other comments from teachers attest to the success of the students' tutoring, but they also reveal something else. The teachers' comments nearly all emphasize the aspects of reading that are stressed under the federal No Child Left Behind legislation: phonemic awareness, phonics, word recognition, fluency, vocabulary, and comprehension. Over the past dozen years these aspects of reading have always been stressed in the

tutoring program, just as all of them have been emphasized in Morris's Howard Street model. But Katie realizes she should adjust the emphasis of the tutoring on some of these aspects, at least to make sure the tutoring "stays on the same page" with where the teachers are now placing their emphases.

Two areas that call for more attention are fluency and vocabulary. Katie sets about making sure her first training session this fall will show her student-tutors how to do repeated reading, readers' theater, and choral reading. She thinks to herself that the tutors and their young charges will need to work in groups some of the time in order to do these fluency activities—and that will bring some welcome variety to the tutoring sessions. She also plans to show the tutors how to lead Word Conversations, and also how to use semantic maps, semantic feature analysis, and some other vocabulary building activities.

Both **reading fluency** and **vocabulary** are important areas of children's reading ability. As we will demonstrate in this chapter, if children are to read well, they must read fluently: with appropriate rate, automatic word recognition, and meaningful phrasing. Reading fluency can be taught, and it should be. Vocabulary, which can be thought of as a growing storehouse of tokens of meaning, is also critically important for students of all ages to develop. Students must learn tens of thousands of words during their school years, and most of them will be learned through reading. There is much that teachers can do to help students learn words and their meanings.

Part I: Fluency in Reading

"Dance like nobody's watching, . . . sing like nobody's listening." That advice from Mark Twain is true whether we are dancing, singing, swinging at a baseball, or reading. Conscious attention to the act itself takes concentration away from the purpose of the activity, and makes our performance stiff, self-conscious, and unsuccessful. With regard to reading, it has been demonstrated that those who are lacking in reading fluency have diminished comprehension: The more they're thinking about pronouncing the words, the less they're thinking about the meaning (Foorman & Mehta, 2002; Perfetti, 1985; Samuels & Farstrup, 2006).

Thus reading fluency has two parts to it: effortless efficiency at word recognition and also rendering the text expressively so that it sounds like it makes sense. Here is the National Reading Panel's (2000) definition of reading fluency:

> *Fluency is the ability to read a text accurately and quickly. When fluent readers read silently, they recognize words automatically. They group words quickly in ways that help them gain meaning from what they read. Fluent readers read aloud effortlessly and with expression. Their reading sounds natural, as if they are speaking.* (p. 22)

Fluency is not just word recognition. Children can score well on word recognition tests without being able to read smoothly, accurately, and with expression in connected text. Fluency is not just comprehension. Children can demonstrate comprehension skills without performing the rapid acts of understanding that characterize fluency; however, we know that unless children read fluently, their comprehension is likely to be impaired (Pinnell et al., 1995).

Between the component skills of word recognition, vocabulary, and comprehension on the one hand, and the ultimate goal of successful reading on the other, reading fluency stands in the middle, serving as the driving force that orchestrates those skills and puts them to work in reading text, so that with experience over time, learners will acquire the large vocabularies, the versatility with sentence and text structures, and the background knowledge they need to become successful readers. Jay Samuels (2006) compares learning to read fluently with learning to drive a car. Fluent reading, like fluent driving, requires the orchestration of many tasks at once. A beginning driver can only focus on one task at a time, but a fluent driver can change lanes, obey signals, watch for traffic, and choose which route to take, all while carrying on a conversation or listening to a talk show on the radio.

Drivers learn to drive with some training and a great deal of practice. Readers need practice, too. But most young readers don't get enough of that practice. One careful study of fifth graders' reading showed just how scant that practice can be (see Table 6.1).

According to this study, the average fifth grader reads less than five minutes a day. That prompted one of the researchers to observe, "If you walk into a typical elementary school today, you would have to say that you were among non-readers" (Wilson, 1992). The good news is that 14 minutes of reading per day amounts to a million words read in a year, so efforts to increase children's time spent reading need not change children's lives dramatically to have some results. But such efforts will not soon close the gap between good readers and poor readers. In one year, the top six readers read as much as the bottom six readers would read in 54 years, and the top three readers read as much as the bottom three readers would read in two centuries.

On the positive side, we know that some of children's favorite moments in reading instruction come as they listen to the teacher reading aloud to them fluently and with animated expression, and also when they themselves perform fluent reading aloud brilliantly in front of their classmates (Ivey & Broaddus, 2002). As a second grader who participated in a study of oral reading exclaimed to Martinez, Roser, and Strecker (1999), "I never thought I could be a star, but I was the best reader today."

Fluent reading was itself elevated to star status among the five main emphases in "scientifically based reading instruction," the approaches that are sanctioned under the federal No Child Left Behind Act. That means that reading programs that hope to receive government funding need to show that reading fluency is a priority. It also means that reading experts consider an emphasis on reading fluency to be a best practice in reading instruction.

Table 6.1	Differences in Amounts of Independent Reading by Fifth Graders	
PERCENTILE RANK	**MINUTES OF BOOK READING PER DAY**	**WORDS READ IN BOOKS PER YEAR**
98	65.0	4,358,000
90	21.1	1,823,000
80	14.2	1,146,000
70	9.6	622,000
60	6.5	432,000
50	4.6	282,000
40	3.2	200,000
30	1.3	106,000
20	0.7	21,000
10	0.1	8,000
2	0.0	0

Source: R. C. Anderson, P. T. Wilson, and L. G. Fielding, "Growth in Reading and How Children Spend Their Time Outside of School," *Reading Research Quarterly*, 23(3), 285-303. Copyright 1998 by International Reading Association (www.reading.org). Reproduced with permission of International Reading Association via Copyright Clearance Center.

Tim Rasinski (2003) suggests that teaching reading fluency should include these four emphases:

1. Model good oral reading.
2. Provide oral support for readers.
3. Offer plenty of practice opportunities
4. Encourage fluency through phrasing.

Modeling Fluent Oral Reading

As a five-year-old, one of the author's daughters loved to pretend-read books. Once she picked up Bill Martin's *Brown Bear, Brown Bear, What Do You See?* and read, "Wuh, wuh, wuh once . . . thuh, thuh, thuh, there . . . wuh, wuh, wuh, was . . . a buu, buh, buh, bear . . ."

"Annabrooke," I said. "What in the world are you doing?"

She beamed and said proudly, "I'm reading like a first grader!"

The anecdote should make us pause to ask, do our students know what fluent reading sounds like? Many students may not, if most of the reading they hear around them is the word-by-word struggles of other neophyte readers.

Teachers should be careful to provide models of fluent reading for their students. We mean this in two senses. First, teachers should actually demonstrate the concept of fluent versus disfluent reading. Second, teachers should frequently read aloud to students and entice them with examples of rich language read well.

Reading Aloud

Reading Aloud with Expression

When you read aloud to children, you are pointing out for them what is important and interesting in books. You convey enthusiasm and paint events with importance using your voice. Your voice is a marvelous instrument, capable of communicating joy, drama, humor, excitement, and importance. If you do not have very much experience reading to children, or even if you do, it is worth taking the time to become a charming and charismatic reader.

QUALITIES OF VOICE.   Have you ever watched a golf coach demonstrate the proper way to drive a ball? The coach will slow down and exaggerate the swing, to give the learner time to watch the grip of the hands, the planting of the feet, the rotation of the hips, and the swing of the arms. Reading aloud to children is like that: You slow down and exaggerate the swings of the voice from fast to slow to high to low; you add pauses to create suspense; you read the action as if you were seeing it and the dialogue as if you were hearing it. Listen to a recording of a professional actor reading a children's book. Note the way the actor gives life to characters, creates suspense, moves the story quickly along in spots and slows it down for dramatic effect in other places. All of these are techniques that you can imitate, and they will add power to your reading aloud.

BRINGING CHARACTERS TO LIFE.   When books have more than one character in them, it helps animate the reading if you read each character's lines in a different voice. Younger characters might get higher voices; older characters lower ones; and wiser characters slower, more thoughtful voices. As a rule of thumb, try to portray personality styles—clever, lazy, humorous, haughty—in the different voices, rather than the character's ethnicity or region of origin—since doing the latter may be offensive to some.

Readers' Theater

Choose Texts for Reading Aloud

Your school librarian, or the local children's librarian, will have good recommendations for read-alouds. There are printed sources you can rely on for suggestions as well. The International Reading Association annually sponsors the children's choice contest, in which teachers across North America ask children to select the books they enjoy most from each year's new publications. *The Reading Teacher* publishes the results. The American Library Association's monthly journal *Book Links* publishes reviews of books with curricular tie-ins. And the *Hungry Mind Review* publishes suggestions of books that are especially provocative and interesting for young people.

Teach It!

Refer to the Teach It! appendix at the end of the book for further activities you can use to reinforce concepts discussed in this chapter.

Demonstrating Fluent Reading

To show students what fluent reading looks like and sounds like, begin by reading a passage to the students two ways. First read it haltingly and uncertainly, in a voice that suggests you are concerned with slashing your way through the words and getting a disagreeable experience over with. Then read the passage again, but this time with your voice full of expression and interest, with pauses and emphases. Show that you are enjoying the message of the text and not simply struggling to pronounce the words: That is to say, read fluently. Then ask the students which reading they preferred and why. In the discussion that follows, call attention to the qualities of fluent reading:

- The reader is thinking about the message and not just about pronouncing the words.

- The reader varies her voice between loud and soft, and between faster and slower.

- The reader groups words meaningfully.

- The reader may show emotion—enjoyment, surprise, and excitement—as she reads.

Later, read aloud to the students again, reading as fluently as you can, and "thinking aloud" as you read, that is, pausing to explain to the students a decision you just made—such as where to pause, what words to group together, or how to read a character's voice—in order to read fluently.

When you read aloud to students, you can point out what is important and interesting in books, and convey enthusiasm, joy, drama, humor, and excitement. (Lindfors Photography)

Read books from parallel cultures often. American children are truly fortunate to have books available that reflect the lives of all of our children, from every cultural group. As Rudine Simms Bishop (Simms Bishop, 1999) reminds us, books from parallel cultures can serve as *windows and mirrors*: as *windows* into other cultures that are different from the readers' own, and as *mirrors* of the readers' own culture, to give those readers reflections of their own experience. Best books each year about African American children's experience compete for the Coretta Scott King Award. Best books about Latino children's experience compete for the Américas Award.

Don't overlook informational books—especially books about science and social studies topics—when choosing books to read aloud. Children enjoy hearing about the real world, too. Informational books for young people are written with as much skill and artistry as fictional works, but listening to them and understanding them exercises different kinds of concentration and comprehension (Duke & Bennett-Armistead, 2003). The National Science Teachers Association's journal *Science and Children* recommends good titles for children in their field. The National Council for the Social Studies' journal, *Social Studies and the Young Learner*, also recommends good books on topics from the social sciences for young readers. Finally, articles from the excellent specialized journals on scientific, geographical, and historical topics—from *Ranger Rick*, *National Geographic World*, and *Cobblestone*—can make excellent read-alouds as well. Remember, a key to a good read-aloud is that you, the teacher, have surveyed the text and determined where to put emphasis and how to read orally.

Teach It! 26

Fluency Oriented Oral Reading

Engage the Students as You Read

When you read a text aloud to your students, you should take steps to call attention to your fluent reading. Make sure to point out to students how you:

- Match the emotional qualities of the passages—serious, humorous, exciting, urgent—with your tone of voice.
- Stress the important words in the passages.
- Honor the punctuation—pausing at commas, stopping at periods, and raising your voice at the ends of sentences with question marks.
- Read the dialogues as if people were actually talking.

Your reading will be more successful if you take steps to engage the students as you read. These steps include previewing the text, pausing to raise suspense before important parts of the text, asking for predictions, inviting the students to read repeated parts of the text with you, and rereading the text to invite the students to read more of it with you (see the discussion of reading aloud on pages 162–163).

Extend the Meaning of the Text

After reading a text aloud to the students, you may further engage them with the meaning of the text with follow-up activities. These include dramatizing the students' favorite parts (see pages 211–212), posing reader response questions (see pages 193–197), having the students do a free-write (see page 164), or having them do a "Sketch-to-stretch" activity (see page 209) or fill out a four-way response chart.

FOUR-WAY RESPONSE CHART. To create a four-way response chart, the students each take a sheet of paper and divide it into four panels. In one panel they write an important quote they remember from the text (younger readers write just a few words). In another panel they draw a picture of an important character or scene. In a third panel they write or draw what the text reminded them of or made them think of. In the last panel they write what they liked about the text (adapted from Preece, 2000).

Supporting Children's Reading for Fluency

There are at least three general approaches to supporting children's reading for fluency:

- Sustained silent reading
- Directed activities, such as repeated reading
- Artistic means, such as readers' theater and choral reading with voice choirs

DROP EVERYTHING AND READ AND SUSTAINED SILENT READING. Drop Everything and Read (DEAR) and Sustained Silent Reading (SSR) are reading activities that are scheduled during times set aside during the day for children—as well as teachers, school principals, librarians, custodians, and parents—to pick up a book or magazine and read it for a fixed number of minutes—usually fifteen to thirty minutes.

Teachers still may set aside time for sustained silent reading, especially if they take steps to keep the students on task, and provide opportunities for students to report on what they have read so that they encourage others to try those books. Books that are read during sustained reading time should be those written at each child's independent reading level—that is, the children should be able to read them without a more fluent reader's help. Nonetheless, students can be encouraged to read more interesting and challenging materials within their independent reading levels.

There are few rules for sustained silent reading, except that:

- Everyone should choose what to read—the material is not assigned—but students should choose material at their independent reading level.
- Games, television, videos, and similar distractions are out of bounds for students; grading papers and getting other work done is not allowed for teachers.
- The reading time should be followed with a discussion, such as having students give synopses of what they read and recommend it to others.
- Teachers may wish to keep track of what students read in the classroom. Students can write their responses, evaluations, and recommendations—or two or three students can be asked to share these orally at the end of each reading session. You can ask parents to keep track of what children read at home, when they are reading under the guise of DEAR or SSR. Students can write their responses to their independent reading in a reading journal.

REPEATED READING. Repeated reading is a method of having a child practice reading the same moderately challenging passage repeatedly up to four times until she or he can read it at a predetermined level of speed and accuracy. To carry out repeated reading, select passages of between 50 and 500 words, depending on the reading rates of the children. The passages should come from different sources, but they should be running text and not poetry or lists. Informational text should be mixed in with fiction. Find a text written at each student's instructional level—that is, the student should be able to read the text with about 95 percent accuracy—making one error for each twenty words. If the text seems a little difficult for the student, offer support, such as *echo reading* (you read a line and the child reads a line).

Sit next to the student in a quiet place, and listen as the student practices reading the text repeatedly. Keep a copy of the text yourself on which you can mark the student's reading errors. Errors are words that are omitted, or for which other words are substituted, or which are mispronounced. If the student does not say a word, wait two seconds and say

Practice identifying the components of effective fluency instruction in different teachers' classrooms by completing the activity "Fostering Reading Fluency." (To find this activity, go to the topic *Fluency* in MyEducationLab and click on Building Teaching Skills and Dispositions.)

The World of Reading

Is Sustained Silent Reading Effective?

Because there have been few experimental research studies that have measured the effects of sustained reading, the National Reading Panel (2000) did not endorse this practice in its survey of recommended instructional strategies to improve reading.

The National Institute for Literacy discourages the practice of sustained silent reading because they don't find sufficient support for it in research. The NIFL website says this:

No research evidence is available currently to confirm that instructional time spent on silent, independent reading with minimal guidance and feedback improves reading fluency and overall reading achievement.

. . . Research . . . has not yet confirmed whether independent silent reading with minimal guidance or feedback improves reading achievement and fluency. Neither has it proven that more silent reading in the classroom cannot work; its effectiveness without guidance or feedback is as yet unproven. The research suggests that there are more beneficial ways to spend reading instructional time than to have students read independently in the classroom without reading instruction.

The Institute's web page goes on to recommend:

Rather than allocating instructional time for independent reading in the classroom, encourage your students to read more outside of school. They can read with an adult or other family member. Or, they can read on their own with books at their independent reading level. Of course, students might also read on their own during independent work time in the classroom—for example, as another small group is receiving reading instruction, or after they have completed one activity and are waiting for a new activity to begin.

http://www.nifl.gov/partnershipforreading/publications/reading_first1fluency.html

What's wrong with sustained silent reading? Some critics worry that poor readers won't get much done during sustained silent reading time; they may need support from the teacher in order to stay on task and learn to read more fluently (Kuhn & Stahl, 2003). Others worry that, left to their own devices, students may choose material that is too easy to increase their fluency by much (Shanahan, 2002).

We would argue that in order to become fluent, students certainly do need to read material that is written at their **independent reading level** (see Chapter 11)—material that they can read without help. And in order to learn new words and structures, and to become able to read more challenging material, of course they also need to read materials at their **instructional reading level**—materials in which they encounter occasional words they don't know or structures that are less familiar, and for that they will need the support of the teacher or some other more fluent reader.

Given the amount of time children spend reading outside of school (see Figure 6.1), just fifteen minutes of sustained silent reading per day *triples* the average fifth grader's accomplishment. It amounts to *twenty times* the reading done by the least avid five readers, and *150 times* that of the two or three least avid readers. That's a lot of bang for fifteen minutes of instructional time.

Encouraging children to read outside of school is important to do, and all teachers should work with book clubs, participate in reading incentive programs, encourage children to get library cards, and make other efforts to get children reading outside of school. But since we know from research that the average child does very little reading outside of school and some children do virtually none, we would not recommend giving up on encouraging reading during the school day, especially if it is well-supervised, and if children are given regular opportunities to talk about what they are reading and encourage other children to read what they did.

In order to improve their reading fluency, children need guided support in reading challenging texts, too—material that is written at their instructional reading levels. In order to read at those levels, the children will need the support of the teacher or some other capable reader. Techniques that provide that support include the method of repeated reading and other similar strategies.

Watch a video of a second-grade teacher administering a fluency assessment and answer the following questions in the activity "Assessing Students' Reading Fluency." (To find this activity, go to the topic *Fluency* in MyEducationLab and click on Assignments and Activities.)

the word yourself, and count that as an error. Time the student's reading for exactly sixty seconds, then stop the student, count the total number of words read, and subtract the errors from the total. The child should practice reading the text several times—preferably until she reaches the criterion score for her grade level (see Table 6.2). WCPM means "words correctly read per minute," that is, the total number of words read, minus the words read incorrectly.

Once the child has reached the criterion score, assign her another text of equivalent or greater difficulty to practice reading. From time to time, ask the child to read a passage she has not prepared, and measure the reading rate for an independent comparison.

Keep a record of the child's efforts on a log such as the one in Figure 6.1.

Figure 6.1
A Chart for Recording
Repeated Readings.

Child's Name:				
Name of Passage	Dates Read	Date Ended	CWPM	Comparison Text Rate

Instructions: Record the name of a new text the student is working on, and enter the dates that he or she reads the text. In a separate row, you may enter the date of each day the student reads the same text, and enter the CWPM ("Correct Words Per Minute") attained that day. When the child reaches the criterion score, enter the date of that achievement. Occasionally (at least every two weeks) have the child read a text of similar difficulty that she or he has *not* prepared. Enter the name and date in the first two columns, and enter the fluency score (in CWPM) in the right-hand column.

Practicing Fluency without the Teacher's Guidance

The method of repeated reading requires that the teacher set aside the time to listen to individual students reading. Rasinski (2003) recommends setting aside time each day for repeated reading instruction. If that recommendation is followed, the teacher of a moderate-size class might reach each child for a few minutes each week. What should the students do when they are not with the teacher? Four suggestions are *paired reading, buddy reading, recorded reading,* and *Radio Reading.*

PAIRED READING.   In **paired reading** (Topping, 1987), a fluent reader is matched up with a less fluent reader. They work together on a passage that is chosen at the less fluent reader's instructional reading level. The more fluent reader begins by reading the passage

Table 6.2   Average Reading Rates

GRADE LEVEL	TARGET NUMBER OF CWPM
Second half of first grade	60 CWPM
Second grade	90 CWPM
Third grade	100 CWPM
Fourth grade	110 CWPM
Fifth grade	120 CWPM
Sixth grade or higher	140 CWPM

Source: Rasinski, 2003

aloud to the less fluent reader. Then the two read the passage through several times in unison. Then the less fluent reader takes over the reading, while the more fluent reader monitors the other child's reading. The more fluent reader corrects the other's errors by saying the word correctly, and by having the less fluent reader reread the sentence in which the error occurred. The fluent reader might say, "Read that sentence again and make it sound like you're talking to me." The "more fluent reader" in this method might be a parent volunteer, a tutor from the local university, or even an older student.

Labbo and Teale (1990) suggest having a less fluent reader from an older class pair up with a younger reader who needs support and carry out the paired reading procedure. Research shows that the activity can be beneficial to both.

RECORDED READING. A fine way to have students read the same passage repeatedly for fluency is to give that student a small tape recorder and ask him or her to read a passage. When the tape is played back, the student can evaluate his or her reading—was it smooth, the right speed, with interesting phrasing, with voices read in character, conveying excitement? The student can be encouraged to record the text over and over again until it sounds the way he or she wants it to.

RADIO READING. Radio Reading (Tierney and Readance, 2000) combines thoughtful oral reading and questioning in a way that merges reading fluency and comprehension. Students working in groups of four or five are assigned a reading of one or two pages. They all read the passage through silently first, and then are each assigned a passage of a paragraph or two to prepare to read aloud. Each student also prepares a question about her or his passage to ask the others. Then the rounds begin: a student reads her passage and puts her question to the group. They answer quickly. Then the turn passes to the student with the next passage to read and ask a question about.

Family Literacy

The paired reading procedure and other related methods can be carried out by parents with their own children. During a parents' night at your school, you can give parents an orientation in the method of paired reading. Begin by pointing out the importance of reading fluency. Show the parents the statistics on children's book reading (see page 162). Parents will be surprised to learn how even 10 or 15 minutes a day of support for their child's reading can greatly increase the amount of reading the child might otherwise do. Point out the benefits that can be gained from this: as many as a million words read, with accompanying boosts in vocabulary and understanding.

Show parents how to carry out the steps of the paired reading procedure. Remind them to keep the tone encouraging.

Send home passages that are on the child's instructional level for the parent to read with the child. Send notes of encouragement to the parents who carry out the procedure, and recognize them at school.

Some parents might be interested in offering to support students' reading fluency by using these methods with other students in the community—or they might be persuaded to come to school and volunteer to read with children in the classroom.

BUDDY READING. Buddy reading is another way for students to practice reading for fluency without the teacher's devoting time to individual students. At its simplest, two students take turns reading paragraphs of the same text to each other. A more elaborated version begins with the teacher reading from a big book or a text projected on an overhead projector, while running his hand under the words and using a fluent delivery. Then pairs of students take turns reading passages from the text (Koskinen & Blum, 1986). How are the pairs formed? In one approach, the teacher divides the students into four groups of readers, from the most fluent (group 4) to the least fluent (group 1). Students from group 4 are paired with students from group 2, and students from group 3 are paired with stu-

Family Literacy

How can you demonstrate most attractively a strategy to promote reading fluency so that parents will want to do it with their children at home?

Paired Reading

In paired reading a fluent reader is matched up with a less fluent reader. (Ellen B. Senisi)

dents from group 1. Some teachers find that students spend more time on task if they are allowed to choose their own partners.

FLUENCY ORIENTED ORAL READING (FOOR). This strategy combines group instruction with paired study. FOOR (Kuhn & Schwanenflugel, 2008) proceeds in a three-day cycle. The teacher assembles a group of students who are on roughly the same instructional reading level. Copies of the text are provided for the students and the teacher.

- **Day 1:** The teacher fluently reads a passage aloud to the students. The teacher may "think aloud," and call attention to the way he reads the words in groups, and how he provides emphasis with his voice to important words (see pages 162–163 for discussions of fluent reading). The teacher may discuss the meaning of the passage and invite comments. Then teacher and students echo read the text; that is, the teacher fluently reads a line, and the students read the same line. They take turns echo reading the entire text.
- **Day 2:** The students pair up and take turns reading the text—each one reading a sentence or a paragraph.
- **Day 3:** The students come back together in the original group with the teacher. Now they choral read the text—that is, they all read the text as if with one voice. The students may take turns reading parts of the text in dramatic fashion, following the ideas of readers' theater (see pages 170–171 below).

New Literacies

The National Reading Panel (2000) recommends two kinds of activity to help students learn to read fluently: modeling fluent reading and guided repeated reading, with monitoring and feedback offered to the student. The latter of these activities ordinarily takes one-on-one attention from a competent adult. But computer-based programs have been able to provide much of this support. Consider Fluent Reader©, developed by Renaissance Learning (http://www.renlearn.com), for a good example. On a computer screen, students are offered texts to read from fiction, poetry, and informational genres, and the passages are organized at seventeen difficulty levels. While reading the passage for the first time, the student clicks on each difficult word, and also clicks on the last word read after one

New
Literacies

Would students rather practice fluent reading with a computer or with an adult? What is the best balance to keep them motivated?

minute. The program then computes the student's reading and accuracy rates, and sets a target score. Both the student's present score and the target score are presented to the student on a bar graph. Then the student reads the text again, while listening to the recorded voice of a fluent reader. On the screen the lines are highlighted as the recorded voice reads them. The recorded voice can be set to different speeds, so that the student can listen to the words spoken slowly and clearly at first, and then again read at a normal speaking rate. After reading the text several times, the student can be tested again by the program, and again his or her speed and accuracy scores are recorded and presented on a bar graph. The teacher may print out a version of the text the student is working on, too, either to enable the student to practice reading the text at home, or to free up the computer for another student to use while the original student practices reading the paper version. The program records the student's voice, so the teacher can listen to it later for assessment purposes. It also compiles assessment information for each student, including the passage she or he is working on, the student's speed and accuracy rate, and the number of repetitions it has taken for the student to reach the target score.

Embedding Repeated Reading in Performance

Language education is about more than skill development. Teachers want to cultivate children's appreciation for language and broaden the variety of literature that children can enjoy. So it is recommended that teachers use literary performance as another approach to teaching children to read fluently. Two such activities are readers' theater and choral performance.

READERS' THEATER. Readers' theater combines an emphasis on fluency, meaning, drama, and rhetoric, as students practice reading texts aloud, using their voices to convey the meaning of the text. Performing in readers' theater is much like acting on a stage, except that instead of speaking memorized lines, the students read them; and instead of moving dramatically around the stage, the students convey meaning with the sound of their voices and their facial expressions. Readers' theater is most commonly used with fictional works, and when it is, the readers must decide what the characters are like, what is at stake for the characters at each point in the text, and thus how the reading should sound. On the other hand, if the piece is informational or persuasive, the readers must decide what the text is saying, what the important points are, and what kinds of emotions the readers should convey. In either case, students need to practice reading the same passages many times to "get them right." Thus they are doing repeated readings naturally, with the emphasis on meaning.

As they prepare to read a fictional text with readers' theater, players should discuss the setting of the text, who the characters are and what they are like. Then they should read portions of the text several times in order to read the lines fluently and with the expression that is called for. It helps if the teacher offers coaching, asking the students some of the following questions:

- "What is your character feeling right now? How do you sound when you feel that way? Should your voice be loud or soft? Fast or slow?"
- "What might your character think about what the other character is saying? How will your character sound, then?"
- "What is going on at this point in the story? How is your character reacting to it?"
- "How is your character changing as the story proceeds?"

As they prepare to read an informational or argumentative text, readers decide what the message of the text is and how they feel about it. Then they decide what points to read with greater emphasis, where to put pauses for suspense, what parts should be said quietly, what parts loudly, and what parts to hammer home. They think about how the beginning and the end of their piece should sound. The teacher's side coaching helps the students make these decisions.

Both the teacher and the other students can offer comments and suggestions after each practice reading.

Selecting Texts for Readers' Theater. Fictional texts for readers' theater can be found in picture books and chapter books, and in the many commercial sets of readers' theater scripts now available. Some of these even have different levels of reading for particular parts so differentiation can occur within the same production. The best choices are those that contain a good deal of dialogue. For example, *White Dynamite and the Curly Kid* by Bill Martin, Jr., and John Archambault is written entirely as dialogue. Frances Temple's *Tiger Soup* contains a readers' theater script in the dust jacket. Chris Raschka's *Yo! Yes?* is a simple dialogue between two little boys and has a multicultural theme. When using longer books, choose dialogues taken from pivotal scenes in the plot. *Roll of Thunder, Hear My Cry* by Mildred Taylor contains many scenes in which confrontations between people of different races is thoughtfully handled. Kate DiCamillo's *Because of Winn-Dixie* contains many poignant encounters between characters. Informational or argumentative texts should be interesting and powerful. News stories of historical events make good texts for readers' theater. So do speeches, such as Martin Luther King, Jr.'s "I Have a Dream" speech.

To prepare texts for a readers' theater, do the following:

1. Make a photocopy of the text you plan to use for readers' theater.

2. Read through the text and mark the parts that should be read by different readers. Create a code for different readers, such as a capital letter to represent the name of each different character, and a capital N followed by a number for narrator number 1, 2, 3, and so on.

3. Put brackets [ ] around the parts that will be read by each reader, and write in a letter over each section to indicate who should read it (Carrick, 2006).

4. Strike through any parts that do not need to be read. Often "He said," "she replied" and similar phrases can be eliminated without affecting the meaning.

5. The text can be duplicated and distributed with the marks just described—but it will be easier for students to read if you type it out with each character's name by his or her part.

Scripted texts for readers' theater are available in which roles are identified for readers of different levels of fluency. Following are some books that contain readers' theater scripts:

Braun, W., & Braun, C. (1995). *Readers' theater: Scripted rhymes and rhythms.* Calgary, Alberta: Braun and Braun Educational Enterprises.

Coleman, M., Farley, J., & Holliday, S. (2001). *Readers' theater level 1.* Columbus, OH: McGraw-Hill. (grade levels 2–5)

Crawford, S. A., & Sanders, N. I. (1999). *15 irresistible mini-plays for teaching math.* New York: Scholastic.

Farley, J., & Sishton, J. (2001). *Readers' theater level 2.* Columbus, OH: McGraw-Hill. (grade levels 3–7)

Glassock, S. (1995). *10 American history plays for the classroom.* New York: Scholastic.

Glassock, S. (2001). *10 Easy-to-Read American history plays that reach all readers.* New York: Scholastic.

Hoberman, M. A. (2001). *You read to me, I'll read to you.* Boston: Little, Brown.

Haven, K. (1996). *Great moments in science.* Englewood, CO: Teacher Ideas Press.

Pugliano-Martin, C. (2000). *25 just-right plays for emergent readers.* New York: Scholastic.

Pugliano-Martin, C. (1999). *25 Spanish plays for emergent readers.* New York: Scholastic.

Worthy, J. (2005). *Readers' theater for building fluency*. New York: Scholastic. (grade levels 3–6)

Websites with scripts for readers' theater that are available for free include:

Blau, L. *Monthly scripts readers' theater language arts ideas*. www.lisablau.com/freescripts.html

Lansky, B. *Classroom theatre*. www.fictionteachers.com/classroomtheatre/theatre.html

Shepard, A. *Readers' theater (Readers' theater: Free scripts)*. www.araonshep.com/rt.rte.html

When you assign roles in readers' theater, you can give all the students roughly equal chances to participate. There can be several narrators. Students can read the lines for more than one character (although if they do, they should read the same characters' lines consistently—and they might develop different voices for different characters). The same script can be read by more than one group, and the "readings" (as in interpretations) can be compared afterward. Another way to involve more students is to choose different scenes from a longer work, and assign each scene to a smaller group of students.

CHORAL READING IN VOICE CHOIRS.   Choral reading is another performance-oriented way of practicing reading for fluency. As in readers' theater, where readers are reading and rereading to get just the right sounds to convey meanings and emotions, in choral reading the practice of repeated reading is imbedded in a meaning-driven activity. Choral reading can be done with poetry, or with speeches or other texts. When they are choral reading poetry, readers should practice over and over again to get the sounds right. What are the possible variations of sound? Texts may be read:

- By the whole chorus, by individuals, by pairs, or by two alternating sections
- In loud or soft voices
- Rapidly or slowly
- Melodiously, angrily, giggling, or seriously.

Prepare the children to choral read a text by discussing the circumstances or the context in which it might be said. For example, the following poem, "The Grand Old Duke of York," has a martial rhythm. Invite the children to imagine they are a platoon of soldiers marching along a road. From a single vantage point they are very quiet when they are heard from a distance, then louder as they approach, then very loud when they are right in front of the person, then quieter until they are very quiet. Have them practice reading the poem in unison, going from very quiet to VERY LOUD to very quiet again.

The Grand Old Duke of York (Traditional)

The Grand Old Duke of York
He had ten thousand men.
He always marched them up the hill
Then he marched them down again.
And when they were up they were up.
And when they were down they were down.
And when they were only halfway up
They were neither up nor down.

"Come Play Catch?" by Bucksnort Trout can be read by two individual children, or by two groups. One group takes the words on the left and the other takes the words on the right. The children should practice reading the poem until they can keep up the rhythm perfectly.

"Come Play Catch?"

Hey, Cousin Kenny, can you come play catch?
   Can you catch come, come? Can you come play catch?
Whatcha say, Cousin Kenny, can you come play catch?
   Can you come catch, come play catch—huh?
Hey, Aunt Jody, can you come jump rope?
   Can you rope jump, jump? Can you come jump rope?
Whatcha say, Aunt Jody, can you come jump rope?
   Can you rope jump, come jump rope—huh?
Hey, Uncle Harry, can you come hop scotch?
   Can you scotch hop, hop? Can you come hop scotch?
Whatcha say, Uncle Harry, can you come hop scotch?
   Can you scotch hop, come hop scotch—huh?
Hey, gorilla, will you put me down?
   Will you down, put, put? Pretty please, down, down?
Whatcha say, gorilla, will you put me down?
   Will you down put, put me down—huh?

This country poem, whose author is anonymous, can be said as a round, with up to three parts. When they are performing the poem, have each group begin reading right after the group before it completes the first line. Have each group read the poem through two times fully. On the second time through, the first group repeats the last line while the second group reads it, and then the first and second groups repeat the last line as the third group reads it.

Can you dig that crazy music?
Can you dig it, Can you dig it, Can you dig it, Can you dig it?
Can you dig that crazy music?
Can you dig it, Can you dig it, Can you dig it, Can you dig it?
Oh, look. Here's a chicken come struttin' down the road.
Now, now. There's another on a barbed wire fence.
Ma-ma! Ma-ma!
Get that son-of-a-gun off my porch!

Encouraging Out-of-School Reading

Children need to read to become readers, and there is nothing quite so motivating as having their own book in their hand to take into a corner and read. Commercial book clubs like Scholastic (http://teacher.scholastic.com/clubs/) distribute catalogues periodically to classrooms (Scholastics come every month) and children can choose to purchase books at below-retail prices. Some companies also hold book fairs in the school, in which they make attractive displays of books that children can purchase.

Reading Is Fundamental (http://www.rif.org/about/programs/default.mspx) is a well-established program that gives new books for free to children and families, especially in lower income communities, including migrant workers' camps. RIF also sponsors community-based literacy activities.

Public libraries conduct many activities to interest children and their families in reading. The children's divisions in libraries often hold special events after school, on weekends, and during the summer to get children in the habit of using the library. The American Library Association (http://www.ala.org/) is a valuable ally of reading teachers. Their Association for Library Services to Children (http://www.ala.org/ala/alsc/alsc.htm) links 4,000 children's librarians around the country. Their website gives a window onto their activities to promote reading among children.

Some community-minded organizations have put their resources behind the goal of encouraging children to read. Notable among these is Pizza Hut, whose Book It! program rewards millions of children across the United States who meet their reading goals by giving them personal pan-sized pizzas and other prizes (see their website at http://www .bookitprogram.com/).

Part II: Helping Readers Build Vocabulary

Knowing vocabulary is essential to comprehending what one reads (Blachowicz, Fisher, Ogle, & Watts-Taffe, 2006; Davis, 1944). For nearly a century, research has stressed the relationship between vocabulary knowledge and text understanding (Baumann, Kame'enui, & Ash, 2003; Blachowicz & Fisher, 2000; National Reading Panel, 2000; Whipple, 1925). In this section we will outline what research tells us about vocabulary and how it can be taught and learned. The following sections describe the major components of good vocabulary instruction.

What Is Vocabulary?

Vocabulary is knowledge of words and word meanings (Lehr, Osborn, & Hiebert, 2006). This is not as simple as it sounds. That definition implies that vocabulary has two parts: the word and the meaning that the word stands for. Since a word is a sign for a concept, a student may or may not have the concept that an unknown word labels. For example, children may not know the word *interrogate*, but they do know what it is to have someone question them in order to find out if they did something wrong! On the other hand, many children will lack both the label and the concept behind the word *ennui*, because few of them will know what it is for a person to be sated over a long period of time to the point where nothing is capable of exciting that person.

In addition to consisting of words and their meanings, vocabulary also varies between being either receptive or productive. **Receptive vocabulary** refers to the words students can understand when they hear or see them, and **productive vocabulary** refers to the words they can use themselves. And, of course, words can also be received and produced in speech or in print.

Receptive vocabulary is usually larger than productive vocabulary, either in speech or in print; that is, most people can understand more words than they feel confident enough to use. And most students' spoken vocabulary is larger than the number of words they can recognize or use in print, at least until after fourth grade, when the gap is largely closed (Loban, 1976). That means that for teachers of the primary grades, "vocabulary" is as much an issue of helping students recognize the printed form of words they already understand in speech as it is of expanding children's knowledge of unfamiliar words and their meanings. For teachers of older students, the issue of "vocabulary" is particularly about helping students learn challenging content words that they neither know in speech nor in print (Lehr, Osborn, & Hiebert, 2006). It is also the time when students need to learn how words are formed and modified by affixes and bases. The changes in word usage over time and the multiple meanings related to individual vocabulary terms are also parts of what exploration of vocabulary entails.

Besides consisting of signs and the concepts they represent, being receptive or productive, and occurring in speech or in print, words vary in some other ways, too. Many words have multiple meanings—like *bank, root, staff, vessel, glass, row,* and *star*. Some words have completely multiple meanings—like the *bank* of a river and a savings *bank* (although the meanings were originally much closer). And some words have much closer multiple meanings, like a *glass* window and a drinking *glass*.

Words have denotations and connotations, too. **Denotations** are the literal meanings of the words, and **connotations** are the associations we have for those words. So the word *tyrant* has the denotation of someone who governs with little regard for the governed, and the connotation of a terrible, brutish person.

Words differ in their degree of **formality** and **informality**, as well as their **propriety** and **impropriety**. Informal and formal words with roughly the same meaning are "Hi" and "Greetings," and "automobile" and "ride." Propriety adds a different dimension and refers to words that are not permitted on school grounds, or for which our grandmothers sometimes threatened to wash our mouths out with soap.

What Does the Research Say About Vocabulary?

Over the last decade there have been several excellent reviews of the research on vocabulary. Together they make clear how important attention to vocabulary is and the contribution good vocabulary knowledge makes to reading comprehension.

Perhaps most importantly, vocabulary knowledge is one of the best predictors of reading comprehension (Davis, 1944, 1968). This may relate to the fact that vocabulary knowledge can be used as a measure of general verbal ability that underlies learning (Terman, 1916). It is also true that the ability to make inferences is a critical component both in reading comprehension and in learning the meaning of new words (Sternberg & Powell, 1983). Both explanations have strong support in the research literature. In addition, text meanings are conveyed by the words authors choose; to understand the meanings requires knowledge of the words.

We also know that there are great differences in students' vocabularies. One factor contributing to these differences is related to economic conditions in the home. Hart and Risley's (1995) long-term study of vocabulary development in children during the first years of life revealed significant differences strongly related to parental income and welfare status. Children in economically disadvantaged households were exposed to significantly fewer words and to less oral engagement. These conditions affected the children's breadth of vocabulary use as well as their rate of vocabulary growth during these formative years. Hart and Risley found that when these economically disadvantaged children enter school, they possess only about half the vocabulary of their more advantaged peers and so begin their school careers at a disadvantage.

Another factor contributing to the size of students' vocabularies is the amount of reading they do. Keith Stanovich (1992) demonstrated that children who were avid readers had much larger vocabularies than children who did not read so much, even when the children had the same levels of general intelligence. Perhaps a big reason for this is that written language is a far richer source of vocabulary than either speech or television. As Figure 6.2 on page 176 demonstrates, even a children's book has a richer vocabulary than a prime-time adult television show, even more sophisticated vocabulary than the conversation of college-educated adults. The best way to get a bigger vocabulary is to read.

Research studies have also demonstrated that vocabulary knowledge is a critical factor in the school success of English language learners (Carlo, August, & Snow, 2005; Folse, 2001; Nation, 2001). Knowledge of English vocabulary is one of the strongest correlates associated with the discrepancy between the reading performance of native English speakers and English language learners. This correlation remains despite the fact that many English language learners possess a large vocabulary in their native language (Garcia, 1991; Goldenberg, Rezaei, & Fletcher, 2005; Verhoeven, 1990).

The impact of readers' vocabularies is most clear in the comprehension of academic content. While most students, including the disadvantaged and those who are English language learners, do well with conversational English, it is when they engage in more academic topics that the differences emerge. Cummins (1980) describes these differences as basic interpersonal communication (BIC) and cognitive academic-language proficiency (CALP). For learners to be successful in school they need to become increasingly competent with academic language. This is clearly an ongoing process. Teachers need to be sensitive to the fact that the more dense materials are with content-specific terminology, the more support students will need in making sense of the materials. Stories and literature are much less dependent on specific terms used by authors than informational texts used in science, social studies, and mathematics. There are two kinds of academic terms that are essential for all learners: the procedural terms used to give directions and structure

myeducationlab
The Power of Classroom Practice
www.myeducationlab.com

Students who are English learners face the challenge of learning a new language while also trying to master content area material. The video clip shown in the activity "Teaching Content Vocabulary to English Language Learners" presents strategies to help students understand content specific vocabulary. (To find this activity, go to the topic *English Language Learners* in MyEducationLab and click on Assignments and Activities.)

Figure 6.2

On the "Richness" of Vocabulary from Different Sources.

	Rank of Median Word	Rare Words Per 1,000
I. Printed Texts		
Abstracts of scientific articles	4,389	128.0
Newspapers	1,690	68.3
Popular magazines	1,399	65.7
Adult books	1,058	52.7
Comic books	867	53.5
Children's books	627	30.9
Preschool books	578	16.3
II. Transcripts of Television Shows		
Popular prime-time adult shows	490	22.7
Popular children's shows	543	20.2
Cartoon shows	598	30.8
III. Adult Speech		
Expert witness testimony	1,008	28.4
College graduates, friends, spouses	496	17.3

The "rank of median word" refers to how common or rare the word is. For instance, "the" is common and has a low score. "Antidisestablishmentarianism" is a rare word and has a high score.
Source: Hayes and Ahrens (1988).

learning tasks and academic "content terms," words with precise meanings that are often central to content area understanding and differ from general meanings of even the same terms (for example, "borrowing and sets" have very specific meaning in mathematics). These academic terms and their specialized meanings often pose the greatest challenges for English learners (Graves, 2006; Marzano, 2004).

There are also numerous studies indicating that vocabulary can be improved by good instruction. In their summary of this research, Blachowicz, Fisher, Ogle, and Watts-Taffe (2008) explain that good vocabulary instruction:

- Takes place in a language- and word-rich environment that fosters the word consciousness, the motivation, and the ownership that support incidental word learning.
- Includes intentional teaching of selected words, which provides multiple sources of information and opportunities for repeated exposure, use, and practice.
- Includes the teaching of generative elements of words and word-learning strategies in ways that give students control over their own strategic behaviors.

How Do We Teach Vocabulary?

Efforts to teach vocabulary can be organized around these principles:

1. Motivate students to be open to learning words by promoting a respect for language.
2. Create a language-rich environment in which students can learn words through general acquisition.
3. Teach specific words (during language arts and during specific content study).
4. Teach students strategies for learning new words.
5. Use assessment to monitor students' vocabulary learning.

Promoting Respect for Language

A fire inspector for the Hartford Insurance Company and amateur linguist named Benjamin Whorf used to spend his summer vacations among Native American peoples of the southwestern United States, paying attention to the language they used and the ways they thought. Later, he announced a radical conclusion about thought and language that is nicely summarized in this quote:

> Every language is a vast pattern-system, different from others, in which are culturally ordained the forms and categories by which the personality not only communicates, but also analyzes nature, notices or neglects types of relationship and phenomena, channels his reasoning, and builds the house of his consciousness. (Whorf, 1964, p. 252)

Put simply, he meant that each culture makes sense of reality in its own way, and uses language to pass on to its members its way of understanding reality. Put still more simply, language gives shape to thought.

Having a word in our vocabulary means we can notice something. Each word is a flashlight that illuminates another corner of our experience (Patterson, 1984). In psychological research, it was demonstrated years ago that we most readily recognize what we have a name for (Brown, 1958). This point was recently made in a classroom setting, too, by Mary Cowhey (2006):

> During my first year teaching, I estimate I lost twenty to thirty minutes of instructional time each day dealing with post-recess conflicts, long tearful renditions of who did what to whom, fraught with passionate contradictions and denials . . . The following summer I took a workshop in Second Step, a "violence prevention curriculum." . . . I was surprised when some students really couldn't identify emotions such as disgusted, scared, and angry in photos of children. Before I began teaching Second Step lessons, I observed a couple of boys "joking" with some other children. They didn't notice when one of the other children became upset, and continued "joking" even when the other child began to cry. When I intervened, the jokers said "We were just having fun." I asked if they thought Patrick, who was crying, was still having fun. They said yes. (p. 40)

As Mary Cowhey's example makes clear, having a word in one's vocabulary means that one understands the word and can connect it to experience. Indeed, she goes on to say that her lessons about emotions

> . . . explicitly teach children to read facial expressions, body language, and tone of voice to name the emotion being expressed, to recognize cause and effect, and to realize that two people can have very different feelings about the same situation. (Cowhey, 2006, p. 40)

But without the word, there is nothing to anchor the experience in consciousness, and nothing to enable one to communicate about it to others.

Creating a Language-Rich Environment

Reading Aloud

A cornerstone of classrooms rich in language is teachers reading aloud to students from a variety of books just beyond the students' own reading levels. Most of the vocabulary students will want and need to learn can be introduced naturally through the oral reading or "read-alouds" by the teacher. Teachers at every grade level can entice students into developing interest in words and language as they read aloud. Pausing over interesting terms and phrases, thinking aloud and elaborating on words, exploring the images created by text passages, and savoring particular words are all ways teachers can help students develop interest in words and build their vocabularies. Teachers can also ask students to listen for interesting, beautiful, curious uses of language and then take time after an oral reading to discuss what students noted. It is useful to write these words and phrases on the board so all students, particularly English language learners, have the advantage of both hearing and seeing the terms.

In the intermediate and middle grades students also take great pleasure in word play and jokes. Reading humorous pieces and challenging students with riddles and jokes can connect with students' developing explorations of the richness and complexity of language. (For example, Nothing succeeds like success/no – recess.; I've heard of trade schools, and I'd like to. ; What's black and white and red/read all over? – A newspaper.) Teachers often have bulletin boards devoted to multiple-meaning words or confusing phrases.

The classroom also is enriched when teachers make available a collection of books that explore and play with language. Students enjoy reading books like *Miss Alaineus* (Frasier, 2000), *A Chocolate Moose for Dinner* (Gwynne, 1988), and *Baloney* (Scieszka, 2001). In addition, books with puzzles and word games, rhymes and riddles, and magazines that introduce varied topics in inviting formats encourage language exploration. Critical to these classroom collections on language is a good set of dictionaries; there should be enough so that each student can have one, and the classroom also should contain more adult and larger dictionaries for reference. Making available and teaching students how to use both dictionaries and classroom thesauruses provides them independent tools for expanding their language. In classrooms with English language learners, some bilingual dictionaries are also important. The whole class can enjoy exploring how different words are expressed in each language and can learn when the different forms of the words are displayed in the classroom.

"Word Conversations" for Primary Grades

General Vocabulary Development and Content-Specific Terms

At the primary level, teachers informally expand students' vocabularies through their oral language use and by their reading to students. By the time students are in the intermediate grades, teachers become more specific in their attention to vocabulary learning. Both in literature and in other content areas, specific terms are needed to ensure comprehension of text materials. By attending to specific terms, teachers can also build the vocabulary knowledge students will need for school success. The less students are stimulated at home with rich oral language contexts, the more important it is that at school teachers focus on and reinforce vocabulary development.

Teachers are often unsure about what words they should teach directly. Yet, there are good sources of help in making those decisions. Most basal reading programs now include a vocabulary strand and highlight some key words that are essential to the selections. Focusing students' attention on a small set of words prior to reading a literature selection will help them notice these words as they read. These vocabulary words can then be discussed after the reading and students can practice using the terms in their own speaking and writing. The same is true in most science, social studies, and other content area curricula. Textbooks often identify key terms that are basic to the content. Teachers can highlight these and ask students to Rate Your Knowledge (Blachowicz, 1987). Figure 6.3 shows a Knowledge Rating chart of terms that was used as a pre-reading activity.

Semantic Feature Analysis

If we attempted to teach all of the words children need to learn, we couldn't do it. Nagy and Anderson (1985) put the number of words in "printed school English" at 88,500. And that was just through ninth grade! There is no way to teach 10,000 words a year. Most of these words will have to be learned from experience, especially from reading. But teaching helps, too.

Beck and her colleagues have come up with a way of approaching the seemingly enormous task of teaching vocabulary (Beck, McKeown, & Kucan, 2002). As we saw in Chapter 3, they identified three "tiers" of words. The first tier of words are common, everyday words that most of us know. The second tier of words are those that we encounter frequently in school and in reading and that are used in a variety of situations; knowing these words provides a foundation for many kinds of learning. These are words worth teaching in language arts and reading. The third tier of words are the specialized vocabulary terms connected to particular content. They have specific meanings that need to be honored. These terms are only taught as they are needed for specific content development. (See Chapter 3, pages 84–86, for further discussion.)

Figure 6.3
Rate Your Knowledge Chart.

These are words we are going to be using during this unit. Mark how familiar you are with them as we begin. Those that are not so familiar are words to put in your learning journal so you can build your understanding of them during our study.

Key Words	New to Me	Have Seen	Know Well
mummy			
pyramid			
scribe			
artisan			
pharaoh			

Another useful guide for content words is the one developed by Marzano (2005). He and his colleagues collected all of the academic terms needed for students to be successful with state and national standards and then sorted them by school levels. The Academic Vocabulary List includes key words for eleven subject areas including science, mathematics, language arts, history, social studies, the arts, and health. These words are then organized according to four levels (level 1 = grades K–2; level 2 = grades 3–5; level 3 = grades 6–8; and level 4 = grades 9–12). These lists provide a good reference for teachers who want to assess and then develop students' vocabularies for academic reading and learning.

A final important source for words is the students themselves. Some researchers have demonstrated that involving students in selecting the words to be studied is a productive strategy (Fisher, Blachowicz, & Smith, 1991; Haggard, 1985). Students are able to self-select important terms that are similar to and equally valuable to those the teachers select. And, when students self-select terms, their involvement has the added benefit of motivating them to learn the terms more deeply (Fisher, Costa, & Pozzi, 1993).

Teaching Strategies for Word Learning

Students need to develop independent strategies for dealing with the new words they will meet both in school and in other areas of their lives. The goal is that when they encounter unknown words, students can examine the context for general clues, look at the structure and morphology of the word itself (the internal context) for clues, or consult a reference, if needed. They will also determine if the word is one they want to add to their general vocabulary. If it is, then they will employ a strategy to help them retain the word by creating a word card, making a personal association and practicing it, or using some other memory device.

Teachers can do a great deal to help students become active language learners. For students to maximize their opportunities to expand their vocabularies, they need to be actively engaged in their own learning. They need to be helped in developing some awareness of how they can learn new words and exploring strategies for attending to words and rehearsing them. It is important that teachers not give the false impression that word learning is memorizing definitions for terms on a list they supply. Teachers do students a big disservice when they pass on this traditional and ineffective approach to word learning. Rather, teachers need to guide students to understand that word learning is an ongoing

myeducationlab
The Power of Classroom Practice
www.myeducationlab.com

In the video clip shown in the activity "Fostering Independent Word Learning" a literacy coach teaches her students strategies to learn new words. Watch the video and answer the following questions. (To find this activity, go to the topic *Vocabulary* in MyEducationLab and click on Assignments and Activities.)

Figure 6.4
Concept of Definition Map.

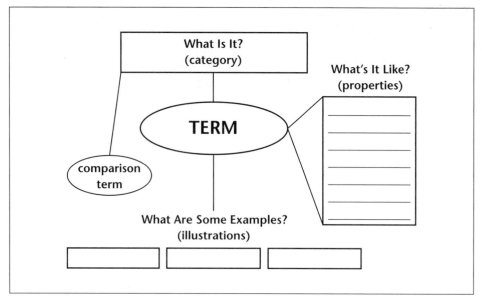

Source: R.M. Schwartz and T.E. Raphael, "Concept of Definition: A Key to Improving Students' Vocabulary," *The Reading Teacher, 30*(2), 198–205. Copyright 1985 by the International Reading Association (www.reading.org). Reproduced with permission of International Reading Association via Copyright Clearance Center.

and cumulative process. We start with a kernel of meaning for a new term and then keep expanding our understanding of how that term is used in varied situations. Each time the term is encountered in print or in oral language, learners can check out their own understanding against the new input and then modify their association network for the term.

A graphic format that helps students understand the ways an understanding of new terms is built is the "Concept of Definition" map (see Figure 6.4) that highlights the relations among words and their meanings (Schwartz & Raphael, 1985). On the "Concept of Definition" map, the new term is listed in the center. Above the term the student indicates the larger class of word to which the new one is related. Then the student elaborates the description of the term with more categorical and semantic information related to the word's definition, along with examples and nonexamples. Some variations of the map also ask students to draw an example of the term. By building this kind of association web around the new term, students can develop a better concept of what word learning entails.

Semantic feature analysis is another activity that helps illustrate semantic relationships among words. Semantic feature analysis provides a graphic display that focuses on the features that distinguish words in a particular category from one another, such as various types of vehicles or human relatives. The teacher creates the matrix either as a model or with students during a unit of study. (See Figure 6.5 for an illustration.)

The students then determine which features each of the terms possesses and finally can compare and contrast similar terms. In their research to determine the effectiveness

Figure 6.5
A Semantic Feature Analysis.

	Bear live young	Have gills	Cold-blooded	Have milk
SHARKS				
DOLPHINS				

of various approaches to vocabulary learning, Bos and Anders (1989, 1990, 1992) compared the effectiveness of three semantic relatedness techniques (mapping, semantic feature analysis, and semantic/syntactic feature analysis) to definition study with students of various ages and abilities. They concluded that all three of the interactive techniques were more effective than the traditional approach of having students write and study definitions.

More recently an added component has been included in word learning: having students create visual diagrams or pictures of the targeted terms. In his six-step process for helping students learn new academic terms, Marzano (2005) includes the component "Students create a nonlinguistic representation of the new term." After the teacher provides a description of each term to be learned, students first write their own explanation of the term and then represent the term in a graphic organizer, picture, pictograph, or cartoon form. In this way English language learners and students with nonverbal strengths can build personal associations with new terms.

Showing Relationships among Terms and Word Parts

Students benefit when teachers guide them to understanding the relationships among words and the various aspects and attributes of terms. The more students use new terms, the more likely it is that they will retain them and incorporate them into their working vocabularies. You can give students points or credit when they use the new terms either in oral class discussion or in their written work to reinforce the continuing attention word learning requires.

Another important component of a word-learning strategy is for students to identify key word parts. The intermediate grades are the years to focus students' attention on how words are formed and modified. Identifying morphemes, particularly derivational morphemes (see pages 82–84 in Chapter 3) and common affixes helps students determine word meanings. Activities that involve students in brainstorming and creating word splashes of related terms focus attention on related terms and how meanings can be deduced from partial knowledge (i.e., disrupt = *dis* (apart) + *rupt* (break up). Then students can connect the morpheme *rupt* to other words they may know like *interrupt* and *corrupt*. Students can take the prefix *dis* and brainstorm other words with the same prefix, or even the prefix used as a stand-alone slang word, "Don't *dis* me." (See Chapter 3, page 82.)

Word Origins and Derivations

DIFFERENTIATED INSTRUCTION

English Language Learners

SIOP®
Sheltered
Instruction
Observation
Protocol®

In a case study focused on using visual enhancements with English language learners and other reluctant readers (Ogle, 2000), struggling, less-than-enthusiastic science students became much more eager learners when their teacher developed a vocabulary card deck for her students. Each week there were eight terms to be learned, for which students were given 4" x 6" note cards. On one side the student wrote the term and a description based on information provided by the teacher. On the other side the students drew a representation of that term. During the week students were given five minutes at the beginning of each science class to test their friends on the word cards. Each student would show the pictures to another student, who would have to guess what term was being illustrated. The increased motivation and

learning were apparent. Students who had barely contributed to class became eager to see if their drawings would elicit the accurate connection for the class terms. José turned out to be a fairly gifted artist, and soon other boys were calling on him to help them more creatively illustrate terms. He also provided suggestions for depicting some of the more abstract concepts. A nearly invisible student became a central resource to the class with this artistic talent; in the process the teacher also learned that he had more to contribute about science than she had expected. While he hesitated to speak in class, he didn't hesitate to illustrate ideas. (See Figure 6.6 for an example of one student's word cards.)

Figure 6.6
José's Word Cards.

Charting Students' Word Learning

Teachers struggle with how to evaluate students' vocabulary learning because word learning is not a one-step process. Words are learned gradually over time as more and more associations with terms are experienced. Yet, it is also important for teachers to find out how much of the vocabulary needed to comprehend particular texts is known by students before the texts or materials are used. If students lack a significant number of key terms, then more pre-reading and concept building needs to be done. Teachers also need to determine what strategies students possess so they can figure out new terms in context as they read. If students can use context effectively and know how to identify combining forms and affixes, they have good tools to help as they read.

However, teachers also need to know how supportive the texts are in helping students access new terms. Supportive texts will provide meanings for important terms through restatement, illustrations, and examples. The terms may be identified in boldface type or in italics. Some texts define terms in the margins. Other texts or text sections may not provide these scaffolds and key terms may remain opaque; then students will require outside support for the vocabulary to become meaningful.

Before asking students to read a text or begin a unit of study, teachers can easily identify students' familiarity with key terms. Several informal activities provide good starting points. Using a Rate Your Knowledge chart of the terms, students can indicate their levels of familiarity with the terms before reading. As students are completing the activity, teachers can move around the class making an informal assessment of how the students are responding. Teachers can also ask students to "Connect 2–3 of the Terms" and write a sentence using the terms as an initial assessment. The students who struggle to create interesting and accurate sentences can be noted and more vocabulary work can be provided. An alternative activity is to have students sort new terms into concept groups and then to label the groups. Each of these informal activities provides a way for teachers to get an initial assessment of students' familiarity with key terms and concepts needed for learning.

These same activities can be used at the completion of the study, also. Changes in levels of knowledge of terms, ability to write using the terms accurately, and ability to cluster similar terms by concept are expected from focused learning. Both students and teachers can compare the beginning and ending knowledge levels and evaluate growth together.

If the study permitted focus on particular combining forms or affixes, the same kind of pre- and post-assessments can be given. Creating an activity in which students are asked to divide several key content words into their parts (prefix, base, suffix) and provide meanings for each is a quick way to determine how comfortable students are with using word parts. Any unfamiliar word part can then be included on a study list, with students searching for other similar words and groups creating lists of families of terms. At the conclusion of the unit students can be asked to create a list of related terms, to define some unknown terms with the familiar parts, or to engage in using the word parts in some creative way.

By focusing assessment on specific terms that are used in the stories, informational texts, or general unit concepts, teachers and students can take the word-learning journey together. Specific targeted words and word-learning tools are valuable to monitor and the concreteness of the gains motivates students to continue their learning.

Introducing and Focusing Attention on New Vocabulary

WORD CONVERSATIONS FOR K–1.   When young readers (kindergarten and first grade) are learning new words, Beck and colleagues (2002) suggest that teachers conduct a rich discussion of words that includes these six steps:

1. Contextualize words, one at a time, within a story. For example, with kindergartners, the teacher could use Don Freeman's perennially popular *Corduroy* (1978) as a pretext for introducing the words *insistent*, *reluctant*, and *drowsy*. The teacher says, "In the story, Lisa was reluctant to leave the department store without Corduroy [her new teddy bear]."

2. Ask the children to repeat the word so as to make a phonological representation of it.

3. Then explain the meaning of the word in a child-friendly way: "*Reluctant* means you are not sure you want to do something."

4. Now provide examples of the word in other contexts: "I am reluctant to go swimming in the early summer when the water is cold."

5. Next ask children to provide their own examples: "What is something you would be reluctant to do?"

6. Finally, ask the children to repeat the word they have been talking about, so as to reinforce its phonological representation.

Word conversations are not as easy as they look. Teachers need to do the following:

- Choose books carefully to provide a meaningful context for introducing the vocabulary.
- Think carefully about the words, and formulate child-friendly explanations of the word meanings.
- Plan questions to relate the words to the children's experience.
- Remind the children of the words they are studying, giving them several opportunities to pronounce the words. (See Beck et al., 2002, for further discussion of this approach.)

Activities to teach vocabulary should relate words to a meaningful context, to other words, and to the students' own experiences. The following activities satisfy these requirements by making connections (to self, personal stories, and other books); collaborating with peers (interpersonal dynamics through all the language arts); exploring meaning (asking questions, making statements, interpreting higher-level thinking such as application, synthesis, and evaluation); and participating as an active reader (summarizing, predicting, confirming, and clarifying).

- **Vocab-o-gram.** Terms that are important to a piece of fiction can be highlighted for students through the use of a vocab-o-gram. The terms are listed and the students are asked to sort the terms according to the story elements of plot, setting (time and location), characters, conflict, and resolution. Words that just don't seem to be clearly identified with the elements can be placed in the mystery category (see Figure 6.7).

- **Semantic Webs.** A semantic web is a way to organize information graphically according to categories. There are several ways to use semantic webs. The most open-ended way is to draw a circle on a page and write a topic word in it. Then, together with the students, the teacher thinks of aspects of the topic and comes up with examples or aspects of that subtopic.

Cumulative Semantic Map

Figure 6.7

Vocab-O-Gram.

Before we read the Japanese folktale, see what you can predict about how these terms will be used. Put each term in the box with which you think it is connected. Words: bitterly cold, weaving, reed hats, empty cupboards, New Year's Day, kind old man, stone statues, fortunate, Jizo, guardian god of children, old woman, hungry, no coal, sack of food, thank you, village, gift.

Characters	Setting	Problem
Feeling/Tone	Solution	Other Words

One approach to semantic webs is the character web, in which the name of a character is written in the circle in the middle of the display. Then words that describe the character are written as satellites around the character's name. Examples that illustrate each attribute are then written as satellites around the descriptive words. Figure 6.8 depicts a semantic web on dolphins.

- **Webbed Questions.** Schwartz and Rafael (1985) suggest guiding the students' responses to a semantic web and asking them to offer answers to three questions asked about the target word, as shown in Figure 6.9.

  What is it?

  What is it like?

  What are some examples of it?

- This beginning web can then be turned into the more formal **Concept of Definition Map** in the upper grades. (See Figure 6.4 for an example.) In creating the map, students extend their attention to new terms by asking themselves to describe the term and find examples of it. Some teachers have added a section for students to illustrate the term and/or use it in a sentence. In both the basic semantic webbing and in creating maps, students learn to think of words as related to larger concepts. They also begin to look for associations and attributes for the terms being learned.

Teach It! 22

Semantic or Concept Web for Upper Grades

Figure 6.8

A Semantic Web.

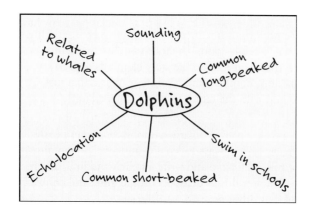

Figure 6.9
Mapped Questions.

- **Concept Ladders.** Concept ladders (Gillet & Temple, 2003) provide yet another way for children to organize their thinking and to categorize, thus supporting comprehension. The concept ladder shown in Figure 6.10 would be useful in a study on volcanoes and earthquakes. It also helps students think of new terms as having important attributes that distinguish each from other similar terms.

- **The Frayer Model.** Another graphic organizer for laying out words for a concept in relation to other words is the Frayer Model (Buehl, 2001). The Frayer Model directs students to think of essential and nonessential characteristics of a concept as well as examples and nonexamples of it. The model is best used to name a common concept that has many characteristics and examples. That way the students get to consider a larger number of words in context. (See Figure 6.11.)

Teachers can do a great deal to build students' interest in words and language by having newspapers, magazines, and books from other languages in the classroom and referring to them periodically. Listening to music from other countries and cultures is another way to develop sensitivity to languages and vocabulary different from our own. Because so many of our academic terms come from Latin and Greek origins, it is often interesting to compare forms of the words we use with those in Spanish and other languages of the students in the classroom. For example, during the political elections in the fall, or during school elections it would be interesting to put the terms on the board and ask students to supply the equivalent terms in their home languages. What would *election, candidate, voting, campaigning,* and *party* look like in Spanish, French, or Farsi? Asking the question and taking the time to compare languages is another way to expand students' flexibility with words and the ever-expanding corpus of words in English.

Figure 6.10
A Concept Ladder.

What kind of thing is this?	What is it a part of?	What causes it?
_____ _____	_____ _____	_____ _____
What are the kinds of it?	What are its parts?	What does it cause?
_____ _____	_____ _____	_____ _____

Using Online Sources to Build Vocabulary

Teachers can stimulate students' interest in words by using the online resources on vocabulary websites. Some have a new word each day that can be shared. Others are great for providing word histories and noting new words that come into our language. There are dictionaries, so terms can be looked up and the definitions and references compared. One of the easy ways to help students explore language is to introduce them to the resources now available on the web. The tools are particularly useful for English language learners since they can use the online resource to look up words that they don't know in English and get helpful hints on what other sites are useful. There are several fun sources for words. General vocabulary and interesting information about words are available at:

www.eduplace.com/kids/hmsv/
www.wordsmith.org
www.vocabulary.com
www.funbrain.com/words

Spanish-English dictionaries are available at:

http://www.spanishdict.com/
www.yourdictionary.com
http://www.my-spanish-dictionary.com
http://education.yahoo.com/references/dict_en_es/

Figure 6.11
The Frayer Model.

Creating Acrostics

Getting to know your students is made interesting and enjoyable by asking each student to create an acrostic poem of their name. Each letter in the student's name is written vertically down the left side of the page of paper. The students select descriptive words that begin with the letters of their name and these terms then create the poem. For example, Diedra created her poem in the following way:

Daring
Interested
Explorer
Doing
Rambunctious
Activities

It is very easy to identify some of the things that Diedra may be interested in doing given the window on her personality and interests she opens. Each student's poem is distinctive; even those who are shy generally reveal that aspect of their selves, too. Teachers can use this activity as a way to build awareness of the value of selecting words carefully. By involving students in several steps, they are more likely to find good terms. Begin by brainstorming lots of words that begin with each letter of students' names. Then give students thesauruses and have them search for additional words that may be even more illustrative of what they want to say about themselves. Model this with your own name if they seem unsure of how to proceed. The dictionary can also be helpful in leading students to just the right words. These resources make it more likely that they will find just the right terms to describe themselves. Finally, before the poems are completed, have students check their acrostics with a partner for a final review. The final poems can be read orally, posted in the room, and combined with lists of students' favorite music, books, and activities. It certainly is a good way to focus students' attention on the value of words and the connotations and nuances each word we use contains.

For Review

Traditionally, reading instruction focused on word recognition and comprehension. Now we realize that reading fluency needs our attention and so does vocabulary. These two aspects are included in the five Building Blocks for Literacy that are identified for special attention by the National Institute for Literacy.

Reading fluency is not just reading rate. In fact, sometimes children read *too* fast. Reading fluency includes an easy and natural rate, appropriate to the material, along with intonation and proper phrasing. Fluency can be learned, and that means that attention to teaching children to read this or that text fluently will carry over to their reading of other texts. Reading fluency aids comprehension: The more naturally and fluently a child reads, the more attention that child will have left over to think about the text.

Approaches to teaching reading for fluency include:

- Model good oral reading.
- Provide oral support for readers.
- Offer plenty of practice opportunities.
- Encourage fluency through phrasing.

In this chapter we showed techniques such as repeated reading, and also approaches embedded in performance, such as choral reading of poetry and readers' theater.

Vocabulary, too, is getting more attention in reading instruction than in the past. Vocabulary is a big divider: Some children have at least twice as many words in their vocabulary as others, and the vocabulary size affects their understanding, not only of text, but of the world around them. Words are labels for concepts, and the more concepts we have, the more easily we can notice things and think about experience. There is a vast vocabulary to learn, so teachers must prioritize. One way is to focus on useful words that children don't yet know (as opposed to words they are learning anyway, or words that are included in disciplinary study). Several suggestions for teaching vocabulary were included in this chapter, including encouraging respect for words, teaching relationships between them, and teaching their parts. Also, children can be helped to recognize words in context. A key to developing vocabulary is creating classrooms that are alive with talk and curiosity about vocabulary. Teachers who encourage children's explorations with words and provide tools for them to use give their students a good start.

For Your Journal

Fluent reading means reading with expression and not just reading quickly. Fluent reading is a skill that many adults need to work on, especially if we are going to be models for children.

Find a well-known children's book with rich language. J.R.R. Tolkien's *The Hobbit* is a good choice. Or Kate DiCamillo's *Because of Winn-Dixie*. Practice reading passages of it aloud. Then go to the library and check out the audio book versions of the books. Listen carefully to the professional readers.

Choose one reader and listen for two minutes. Then write in your journal: What makes this person's reading so interesting to listen to? How many of the qualities of reading fluency that were described in this chapter are present in the readings? How does the reader group words? How does the reader use intonation—make his or her voice rise or fall at certain points? How does the reader bring characters to life?

Finally, try reading the text yourself the way the professional reader did it. Try tape recording your reading, and analyze it the same way you did the professional reader's. Afterward, decide what aspects of good oral reading you do well. Decide what aspects you want to work on. Write these things in your journal. And be sure to practice.

Taking It to the World

How much does vocabulary matter to people? Sit down with two or three classmates and make a list of as many ways as you can that vocabulary matters in people's lives. It might help get the conversation going to recall the self-help books published for adults that promise them more successful careers if only they will master a larger vocabulary or the vocabulary items on the SAT test.

Think also of times—in films or in the discourse of our politicians—when having a larger vocabulary is held up as a sign of snobbery.

After making a list of both kinds of situations, try to reach a conclusion. What are the advantages of having a large vocabulary? What caveats should be kept in mind about using the right words at the right time? How will you use these conclusions in your teaching?

New Literacies Connections

1. Many software packages are now available that purport to help build children's reading fluency. Consider the aspects of reading fluency we have explored in this chapter—automatic word recognition, reading rate, and expressive reading. Then look up "reading fluency software" on a search engine. Review the descriptions of three or four programs. How many of the above-mentioned aspects of reading fluency are built into them?

2. Go to the SuperKids! Website at http://www.superkids.com/aweb/pages/reviews/vocab/ and look up several of the vocabulary building software programs that are reviewed there. To what extent are the five principles of vocabulary listed in this chapter (see page 176) taken into account in these programs?

PEARSON
myeducationlab

Now go to MyEducationLab (www.myeducationlab.com), where you can:

- Find learning outcomes for the topics covered in this chapter, along with the national standards that connect to these outcomes.

- Complete Assignments and Activities that can help you more deeply understand the chapter content.

- Engage in Building Teaching Skills and Dispositions exercises, in which you can apply and practice core teaching skills identified in the chapter.

Comprehension: Understanding and Responding to Narrative Texts

Anticipation Guide

The following questions will help you begin thinking about the topics covered in this chapter. Answer *true* or *false* in response to each statement. As you read and learn more about the topics mentioned in these statements, think back on your answers. See what interests you and what prompts your curiosity toward more understanding.

_____ 1. Comprehension, or understanding what you read, is mostly a process of memorizing the details of the author's message.

_____ 2. Schema theory holds that readers understand what they read by using what they already knew to interpret the new information.

_____ 3. Readers vary considerably from one another in what they understand and take away from a text.

_____ 4. Comprehension is the aspect of reading that has traditionally gotten the most attention in classrooms.

_____ 5. Good teachers show how readers read with comprehension, by "demonstrating their own thought processes when they read."

_____ 6. Good comprehension lessons have three parts: consolidation, building knowledge, and anticipation, in that order.

_____ 7. The structure of the text helps the reader make sense of what is written.

_____ 8. Students who are good observers of nature tend to notice and remember details in what they read.

_____ 9. Struggling readers need an entirely different kind of instruction in comprehension than more able learners.

_____ 10. Drama has no place in the teaching of reading comprehension.

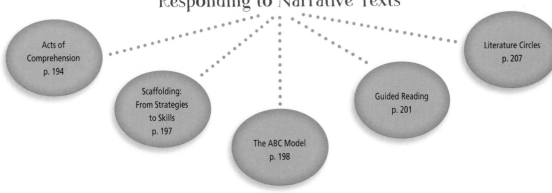

Comprehension: Understanding and Responding to Narrative Texts

Acts of Comprehension p. 194

Scaffolding: From Strategies to Skills p. 197

The ABC Model p. 198

Guided Reading p. 201

Literature Circles p. 207

A Classroom Story

Reading Activity in a Fourth-Grade Classroom

The students in Hank da Silva's fourth grade at North Street Elementary School can predict the day's events in broad outline, but not completely. They know that after the morning class meeting, they will talk about their topics in social studies. They have been reading about the settlement of the Great Plains in their social studies text. At the same time, they have been reading Patricia McLachlan's *Sarah, Plain and Tall* and Laura Ingalls Wilder's *The Little House on the Prairie*. Mr. da Silva reads to them from *Letters from a Woman Homesteader,* a work of nonfiction told in the form of letters a feisty single woman wrote home during the 1880s. He has also bookmarked and assigned three Internet sites where students will find information about the settlement of the Great Plains by European Americans.

The class has written dual-entry diaries every day about their readings. They have also created a Venn diagram comparing what skills people have to have if they move to a new place now compared to what skills people

needed in the days of the homesteaders. Figure 7.1 shows what the class has come up with.

This morning, Mr. da Silva is conducting a discussion of a couple of pages of the social studies book. He begins by pointing out that sometimes textbooks do not make their meanings very clear.

"Take right here, for instance," he points out. "The text says, 'Westward expansion gave the new country a constant sense of excitement, of new possibilities.' What do you suppose the author means by that sentence? Let's start with 'Westward expansion.' What do you suppose he means by *expansion*? If the author were here, what do you think he would say about that?"

After lunch, Mr. da Silva has reading workshop. According to the rotation chart on the wall, some students read independently. Today those students are doing something special: They are writing self-assessments about their reading comprehension, which they will later give to Mr. da Silva. A group of six students who are reading Phyllis Reynolds

Naylor's *Shiloh* meet with Mr. da Silva for a literature circle; each of the six students is conducting a part of the discussion, according to a role she or he has been assigned. Mr. da Silva takes part in the discussion, but he also is taking occasional notes. He writes about how the discussion is going. He writes a note to remind himself to have the students to ask more questions of each other in the literature circle rather than just reporting on what they think. He also makes a note that four of the students do not seem to make the connection between the boy's asking the shopkeeper for stale bread to feed the dog he has hidden away and the food that people in the community begin leaving for his father, a mail carrier. In other words, they are not making inferences. In the course of the next week, Mr. da Silva will make a point of reading with each one of these students to see what they know about reading comprehension. He will also teach a mini-lesson on making inferences during reading workshop tomorrow.

The goal of reading instruction is for all students to read with comprehension—understanding what they read. Comprehension in reading is also a sort of thermometer measuring the intellectual life of a classroom. True, teaching children to read with understanding is partly a matter of teaching them a special set of reading skills. But it is also a matter of exposing students to literature, cultivating their knowledge about a range of subjects, stimulating their habits of inquiry, helping them make connections between ideas, and inspiring in them a broad range of interests. Researchers tell us that reading comprehension has too often been left to chance, as if understanding would happen if only children could read the words. Surveys of reading instruction in elementary schools, from thirty years ago (Durkin, 1978–1979) and more recently (Pressley, 1999), have found that word recognition instruction is common enough, but it is rarer to find teachers trying to develop their students' comprehension.

In this chapter, we talk about ways to help students understand narrative texts. Chapter 8 is devoted to teaching readers to understand informational text. Chapter 9 moves beyond reading comprehension into critical literacy.

Understanding Reading Comprehension

What do people do when they understand something they read? Many reading specialists' favorite explanation of the act of comprehension is *schema theory*. Schema theory (Anderson & Pearson, 1984) holds that readers understand what they read by finding clues in the text that lead them to summon up frameworks of stored knowledge from their memories. These frameworks have been called **schemas**. Schemas give readers a "big picture" that helps them make sense of details. At the same time, the details give readers the data that flesh out the schemas.

Schema theory is a powerful way of understanding comprehension. It shows us that students' prior knowledge (or their schemas) is important to their reading comprehension. It also shows us that to understand something, the reader must be active. Readers do not passively absorb meaning from the page; they construct meaning by trying to make sense of details according to the schemas they already possess in their memories. Hence schema theory supports a **constructivist approach** to reading comprehension because it suggests that readers construct meaning.

When it comes to interpreting works of fiction, the **reader response theory** (Bleich, 1978; Iser, 1978; Rosenblatt, 1978) goes further in explaining how individual readers construct different readings of a text. Since a text has no meaning without a reader to whom it means something, and a reader needs a text to guide her imagination in constructing a work, reading is described as a **transaction** in which an experience of meaning is created from the suggestions planted by the author and the ideas and sensations evoked in the reader by those suggestions. The experience of meaning thus created is a bit different for every reader. But such differences come about in real life, too. For example, polls taken after a debate between candidates in a presidential election usually show that viewers see the same debate differently, depending on the political persuasions they brought with them. Classrooms should be safe and respectful places where students can talk freely about what texts mean to them, and are asked to explain their reasoning and explore their differences. Such environments turn out to be laboratories of democracy (Temple, 2000).

Dual-Entry Diary

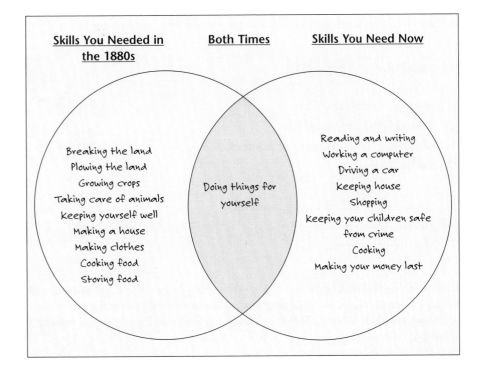

Figure 7.1

What You Need to Live in a New Place.

The World of Reading

Reader Response in Action

Diane Barone (1992) reports on a second- and third-grade class in which the teacher was having her students record their reactions to each chapter of Roald Dahl's *Danny the Champion of the World* (1998) in a kind of response journal called a *dual-entry diary* (see page 206). An early chapter in the book describes the cozy days enjoyed by Dahl's protagonist, living in a gypsy wagon with his father. After reading this chapter, a student in the class wrote that he was expecting the woman to come into the story at any time. The teacher was puzzled, because the only woman who had been mentioned in the book was the boy's late mother, who had died before he was born. But in entry after entry, her student registered his worry that the woman might come into the story on the very next page. As it turned out, this young reader had lived a cozy existence for some time alone with *his* own father—until the father found a female companion. For the little boy, the woman really did come along, and the boy no longer had an exclusive claim to his father's attention.

The boy created a poem out of *Danny the Champion of the World* that was about the almost-too-good-to-be-true bliss of a boy's living alone with his father and his feeling of dread at its loss. The boy's concerns had led him to write responses that seemed bizarre at first. Yet it serves as a good example of how stories can evoke different responses from different people, children included. Teachers need to be aware of this critical piece of information.

As the boy's reading of *Danny the Champion of the World* suggests, there can be striking variations in the interpretations or poems created by different readers. That is why David Bleich (1970) urges teachers to think of literature discussion groups as interpretive communities. *Interpretive communities* are places where readers share their responses to works of literature so that communities of understanding can be formed. The sharing of individual responses not only contributes to a larger understanding of a work, but also promotes students' awareness of each other's thinking. Becoming aware of others' thinking is of particular value when the students come from different social and cultural backgrounds.

It takes special approaches on the teacher's part to set up an interpretive community. Merely asking students to answer literal questions will not do it. What is needed is to create a risk-free environment and to conduct—or let students conduct—discussions that invite personal responses to questions such as "What did you notice in the text? What did it make you think of? How did it make you feel?"

Acts of Comprehension

What are key strategies and skills that children and other readers use to comprehend text? Researchers have agreed on several. This list, derived from Pressley and Afflerbach (1995), captures the issue nicely. Comprehending a passage well involves the following:

Engaging prior knowledge

Imaging

Knowing vocabulary

Following the patterns of texts

Asking questions and pursuing answers

Noting details

Recognizing main ideas

Summarizing and rehearsing main ideas

Making inferences

Monitoring comprehension

Teach It! 30

Terms in Advance

ENGAGING PRIOR KNOWLEDGE. When they begin to read, good readers focus on the topic of the text, decide what they already know about it, and make predictions about what they are likely to learn. As they read, they go back and forth between what they knew about the topic and what they are finding out. When they are finished reading, they might reexamine what they knew or thought they knew and take note of how their knowledge has changed on account of the reading they have done. Not all readers do this fully developed version of engaging prior knowledge and checking new information against it, but readers should at least sense the topic of the reading and be reminded of what they already know about it.

Families can support children's development of comprehension by keeping up their contributions to children's background knowledge and supporting children's voluntary reading. Teachers can remind parents of the importance of taking their children to the library and museums and of putting informative children's magazines on their children's gift lists. *Ranger Rick* (www.nwf.org/rangerrick/index.html), the nature magazine, features enticing photographs of animals in the wild and articles on wildlife that fascinate children ages seven and up. *Cobblestone* (www.cobblestonepub.com) magazine features interesting articles on historical topics that appeal to children ages nine and up. *National Geographic World* (www.nationalgeographic.com) features highly illustrated articles on everything from undersea exploration to mountain climbing, and *Sports Illustrated for Kids* (www.sikids.com) follows teams and players and talks about the basics of the sports.

For general reading, including stories to read, *Cricket* magazine (www.cricketmag.com) for children ages eight and up and *Ladybug* for slightly younger children feature material that makes good reading by well-known and aspiring children's authors. *Highlights for Children* (www.highlights.com) also features stories and interesting informational articles, as well as riddles and games.

Family Literacy

How can families support children's development of comprehension?

IMAGING. In creating works of fiction, authors take pains to describe events so that readers can create images in their minds and be drawn into the scene, or in Langer's term, "step into the envisionment." Frances Temple (1996) begins *The Beduin's Gazelle* with these rich images:

> *Halima sat with her chin resting on her knees, close enough to touch her kinspeople, yet with her mind far away. The singsong of the storyteller's voice lulled her. The lanterns threw a soft glow on the dark wall of the tent, on the red and brown embroidered cushions, on the familiar faces of the listening women and children. Halima played with her bangles, her mind drifting with the story.* (p. 1)

The author's words appeal to many of the reader's senses. Some words name sounds: *The singsong of the storyteller's voice* . . . Others evoke the sense of touch: . . . *sat with her chin resting on her knees, close enough to touch her kinspeople . . . played with her bangles . . .* And others refer to sights: . . . *lanterns threw a soft glow on the dark wall of the tent, on the red and brown embroidered cushions.* Together, these words and phrases invite readers to create images of the inside of a beduin's tent in North Africa, where the events of the novel will soon unfold. It's no wonder we speak of being "lost in a book." Having their senses evoked can take readers out of their seats and into other realities. But not all readers allow words on the page to evoke sensory images. Part of teaching comprehension is guiding readers in imaging, and reminding them to participate in a book's imagery when they read.

Visualization

KNOWING VOCABULARY. Words are building blocks of understanding. A good reader has a vocabulary in her mind that nearly equals the vocabulary she encounters when reading. She also has strategies for inferring from the context a rough approximation of words she doesn't know. But making those inferences ties up concentration that might be used to comprehend the meaning of the text. Having an adequate vocabulary makes comprehension easier. Measures of comprehension usually include measures of readers' knowledge of vocabulary—often both the word meanings they have stored in memory and also their ability to infer word meanings from context.

New Literacies

How is the structure of a web site different from the structure of an article?

Story Maps

Directed Reading-Thinking Activity

Character Clusters and Character Maps

FOLLOWING THE PATTERNS OF TEXTS.   Texts come to us in patterns arranged for a purpose. The purposes are usually to narrate, explain, describe, persuade, or express. The patterns include:

For stories:	Plots, or story grammars
For explanations:	Cause and effect, comparison and contrast, taxonomy (categories of relationships)
For descriptions:	A system of aspects of the topic plus describing words
For persuasion:	Arguments
For expression:	Topic plus feelings about the topic
For Internet-based text:	Entries are linked to other entries, in a chain or a web

Reading by the pattern can help to guide the reader beyond a line-by-line understanding to a deeper logical structure of the text. Readers who know how to follow the patterns of text when they read learn to raise questions and search for answers according to the way the text reveals its contents. When they are reading a story, readers can identify the problem that the character has and try to anticipate the solution to the problem. When they are reading a problem-and-solution explanation, readers can identify the problem and look for solutions.

ASKING QUESTIONS AND PURSUING ANSWERS.   Once they are aware of the topic, good readers become curious about what they will learn, and they actively seek answers. They monitor what they are learning from the text to see if it is what they were expecting. When good readers read a story, they are led by the plot to wonder what will happen, sometimes make predictions, and experience satisfaction or surprise as those predictions are confirmed or not by what happens. In fact, authors count on readers' acts of prediction to evoke readers' emotional experiences of suspense, surprise, and completion as patterns of events raise expectations and sometimes thwart and sometimes satisfy them.

NOTING DETAILS.   Writers have an obligation to their readers to be truthful and to be relevant: to tell readers things that are important. For their part, readers have an obligation to pay attention, even to details. Sometimes details are important because readers need them in order to construct the big picture. At other times, details are important in their own right—like the way the big friendly giant met Sophie in Roald Dahl's popular book *The BFG*, or the way volcanoes are formed, as explained in an informational book such as Anne Schrieber's *National Geographic Readers Volcanoes!* It may be, as teacher Emily Kissner (2008) asserts, that children who notice details in life notice details in books and also give us interesting details in their writing. It is certainly true that paying attention to details is a useful habit.

RECOGNIZING MAIN IDEAS.   Readers who are aware of the argument of the text can separate out the main ideas from the small details. Consider, for example, a child reading this passage from *Charlotte's Web*:

> *On foggy mornings, Charlotte's web was truly a thing of beauty. This morning each strand was decorated with dozens of tiny beads of water. The web glistened in the light and made a pattern of loveliness and mystery, like a delicate veil. Even Lurvy, who wasn't particularly interested in beauty, noticed the web when he came with the pig's breakfast. He noted how clearly it showed up and he noted how big and carefully built it was. And then he took another look and saw something that made him set his pail down. There in the center of the web, neatly woven in block letters, was a message. It said:*
> *SOME PIG!*
> *Lurvy felt weak. He brushed his hand across his eyes and stared harder at Charlotte's web.* (White, 1952/1980, p. 77)

There are many details in this passage about the way the spider's web looked. But a reader who gets the main idea will focus on the fact that the spider has written words, and they describe her friend Wilbur the pig. The child who has been following the plot of the story will realize that Charlotte's writing is a possible solution to the main problem of the book because it is meant to impress Wilbur's human owners so they will spare the little pig's life.

Readers who can distinguish main ideas are following the argument of the text. They understand the problems the text is setting out to solve, and they are aware when information answers the questions or solves the problems posed by the text: Such information is a main idea.

SUMMARIZING AND REHEARSING MAIN IDEAS.   Once they identify main ideas, good readers might slow down, reread the passage that contained them, and rehearse the ideas so that they will remember them later (Pressley & Afflerbach, 1995). Following the reading, the readers might retell the main ideas to themselves, or they might reread important passages aloud to a friend. Good readers might reread the key passages in the text to make sure the main ideas were stated the way they remembered them. In this way, good readers hope to store the main ideas in memory and learn from the reading.

MAKING INFERENCES.   When readers have to reach judgments that are not directly stated in the text, they are making **inferences**. "BK + TC = I" is how Harvey and Goudvis (2005) put it: Background knowledge plus textual clues add up to an inference. Making inferences means taking details from the text and reasoning from them to a conclusion. Consider. For example, Harry Allard and James Marshall's popular picture book *Miss Nelson Is Missing* (1977), about a too-sweet school teacher who is replaced by a very mean substitute teacher. When they see the illustration that shows an ugly black dress hanging in Miss Nelson's closet underneath a box with the word WIG written in upside-down letters, most readers infer that the mean substitute teacher was Miss Nelson in disguise.

Sometimes inferences draw heavily on the reader's prior knowledge, in combination with details from the text. When we read that a character in a book is "dabbling with drugs," we usually assume the "drugs" are not treatments for athlete's foot, but mind-altering substances. We may also assume that the character is at risk of losing judgment and self-control and possibly of falling into dependency. That assumption would soon be confirmed by more information from the text.

MONITORING COMPREHENSION.   Good readers are aware when a text is making sense, and they notice when it does not. Perhaps they have misread a word, or they have assumed the text was going to say something that it did not. Then the breakdown in their comprehension leads them to go back and make a "repair." They reread the misinterpreted word or reconsider where the argument is going so that they again have the feeling they understand the text. Comprehension monitoring, then, assumes that readers think on two planes: They think about what the text means, and they are also aware of their own understanding or lack of it.

Scaffolding: From Strategies to Skills

Once you are aware of the different strategies that comprise reading comprehension, you can teach readers to cultivate them until they become internalized, that is, until they become skills (Duffy & Roehler, 1989).

Skilled and struggling readers use the same processes to read with comprehension that we just described. But struggling readers might need more support to make sure they use all of these strategies and orchestrate them into fluent reading with comprehension. Kame'enui (1998) recommends that teachers of struggling readers employ these steps:

1. **Make strategies explicit.** Through modeling, think-alouds, and regular reminding, show the students how to carry out each of the comprehension strategies we described in the previous sections.

Struggling Reader

How can we help struggling readers read with comprehension?

myeducationlab
The Power of Classroom Practice
www.myeducationlab.com

Learn how to deliberately teach readers to use comprehension strategies and skills over a period of time by completing the activity "Scaffolding Reading Comprehension." (To find this activity, go to the topic *Comprehension* in MyEducationLab and click on Building Teaching Skills and Dispositions.)

Teach It! 40

Story Maps

2. **Supply scaffolding.** Scaffolding is temporary support for students as they learn to do a task or apply a skill. Scaffolding may be used temporarily and be withdrawn when students can function independently. An example of scaffolding is a story map, in which students are asked to identify the character, setting, problem, and solution in a story they are reading. (See Figure 7.5 on page 213.)

3. **Connect ideas.** Remind students of ideas they find in a text that they have seen on a field trip or in a lesson in another subject. Struggling readers might be so preoccupied by the act of making sense of what they read that they do not think about the larger ideas. They need the teacher to point out to them the relatedness of ideas.

4. **Provide background knowledge.** Struggling readers might not have the background knowledge they need to make sense of what they read. A story about an early twentieth-century immigrant's journey from Europe to America will make little sense to a student who does not realize that Europe is a continent that lies thousands of miles across the ocean from America or that until a few years ago, travel from Europe was so difficult and expensive that people who made the trip could not go back.

5. **Review skills and ideas often.** Struggling readers need to be reminded of both the skills they have learned and the ideas they have gained. They need to be reminded of both, and they need to apply the tasks and ideas in new settings.

Teaching for Comprehension

Teaching for comprehension and response is not just a matter of teaching skills. Although it is important to develop children's reading strategies and support the strategies until they become skills, it is also important to develop children's familiarity with literature as well as their knowledge and interests. In the pages that follow we present several methods and strategies for teaching reading comprehension and response to text.

Organizing Instruction for Comprehension and Response: The ABC Model

Children should have many opportunities to read for meaning and for pleasure in personally chosen books that are not used for instruction by the teacher (Block & Pressley, 2001). Children should also have lessons in which the teacher guides them through aspects of comprehension so that the students will internalize those aspects and practice them when they are reading independently. Teaching comprehension successfully requires that teachers engage students' thinking and invite students to keep their minds appropriately active throughout the reading process. The ABC model offers instructional choices for guiding comprehension—for activities to be used before reading (in the *anticipation* phase), during (in the phase of *building* knowledge), and after reading (in the phase of *consolidation*) after Vaughn and Estes (1986) and Steele and Meredith (1997). The ABC model is flexible. Within its three parts or phases, the teacher can make many choices. So, eventually, can the students, because they need to internalize the pattern of thinking captured by this model and use it when they read independently.

FOR THE ANTICIPATION PHASE.   Before they read, readers should think about the topic, and then recall their prior knowledge about it. If they don't have very much prior knowledge about the subject or if their thoughts are disorganized, the teacher might want to spend some time telling the students more about the topic and organizing their thinking about it. Readers should wonder how their present knowledge about the topic might relate to the text they are about to read. If they are to read an informational text, what do they still want to know about the topic that they might learn from this text? If it is a fictional text, what other works do they know by this author or in this genre? What does their prior knowledge lead them to expect from this reading? This preliminary phase of the lesson is called **anticipation**.

Teaching goals in the anticipation phase are to prepare the students to read with comprehension. We want them to do the following:

- Connect the topic (or the genre, or the author) of the text they are about to read with their prior knowledge.
- Raise questions about the text they are about to read and set purposes for reading.
- Know the vocabulary they will need to make sense of the text.

How does the think/pair/share activity encourage anticipatory reading? (Mary Kate Denny/Stone/Getty Images)

Several teaching approaches can be used to achieve these goals.

Focusing Questions.   Questions that make a connection between what the students already know and what the reading will cover are valuable ways to prepare for a reading. In keeping with the goal of encouraging principled knowledge, it is advisable to steer questions toward the main ideas of the passage.

For example, a group of fifth graders are reading Pam Conrad's *Pedro's Journal* (1992), a fictional account of Columbus's historic voyage. Before the students begin reading the first chapter, the teacher asks, "If you were about to sail three ships across the Atlantic Ocean in 1492, at a time when nobody knew for sure what was on the other side of the ocean, what three pieces of advice would you give yourself?"

The students might discuss the question as a whole group, or use the think/pair/share procedure (see below). Doing so activates thoughts and ideas that will help students make sense of and appreciate what they will encounter as they read the book.

Think/Pair/Share.   Focusing questions can be still more effective when a mechanism has been provided for all students to consider and answer them. Think/pair/share (Kagan, 1997) is a cooperative learning activity in which the teacher puts an open-ended question to the class, preferably by writing it on the chalkboard. Children are given two minutes to respond to the question individually. (Often they are asked to do this in writing.) Next, each child turns to a partner, and they share their answers with each other. Finally, the teacher calls on two or three pairs to share their answers with the class. Then the class begins reading the text. In a think/pair/share activity, every student—even in a class of thirty or more students—is motivated to think about the topic and to discuss it with someone else.

Anticipation Guide.   Anticipation guides are used with fiction or with informational text. In using an anticipation guide (Vaughn & Estes, 1986), the teacher prepares a set of questions with short answers (usually true/false answers) that tap important aspects of the topic of the text. The questions are distributed to children on a worksheet, and the children are asked, individually or in pairs, to answer the questions as best they can before reading the assigned text. After reading the text, they return to the questions at the end of the class to see how their thinking has changed. Figure 7.2 provides an example of an anticipation guide.

Paired Brainstorming.   When factual information will be shared, older students can be asked to make personal lists of the facts they know or think they know about the topic of the reading (Vacca & Vacca, 1986). After two minutes, they turn to a classmate and combine their lists. The teacher can make a master list of the class's ideas on the chalkboard or on a piece of newsprint so that the students can compare them to the ideas they have after they have read the text.

myeducationlab
The Power of Classroom Practice
www.myeducationlab.com

Watch a literacy coach supporting students' comprehension in the activity "Supporting Meaningful Thinking and Talk About Text." Reflect on the lesson and answer the questions following the video. (To find this activity, go to the topic *Comprehension* in MyEducationLab and click on Assignments and Activities.)

Figure 7.2

Anticipation Guide for *Pedro's Journal.*

Instructions: Before reading *Pedro's Journal,* answer these questions *true* or *false* on the left-hand side. After reading the book, enter new answers on the right-hand side.

Answer Before   *Answer After*

_____   1. Columbus was well liked by his crew.   _____

_____   2. Columbus prepared his ships to sail in front of the wind.   _____

_____   3. Columbus's captains were very loyal to him.   _____

_____   4. The first people Columbus met lived in a city.   _____

_____   5. Columbus was very respectful of the people he met.   _____

_____   6. Columbus seemed very interested in finding gold.   _____

Terms in Advance.   A teacher may display a set of key terms that will be found in a reading and ask students to ponder their meanings as well as the relationships among the terms. The students are asked to predict how this particular set of terms might be used in the passage they are about to read. For example, if they are about to read *Miss Nelson Is Missing,* the terms might be as follows:

kind teacher	mean substitute	police inspector	return
misbehave	make faces	homework	disguise

Teach It! 45

Graphic Organizers

Graphic Organizers.   Graphic organizers are diagrams that guide students to make their ideas visible. Graphic organizers come in many forms. A **semantic map** or a **cluster** puts a topic in the middle and surrounds it with aspects of the title, arranged like satellites. Semantic maps can be used with a wide range of text types, both fictional and nonfictional. A particular kind of semantic map used with stories is the **character cluster** (see pages 213–214). Another kind of graphic organizer used with narrative texts, the **story map** (described on pages 211–213; see also Figure 7.3), guides students' attention to the parts of the plot. As anticipation activities, graphic organizers are used to draw out prior knowledge or preliminary thoughts from a class of students. Either as they read a text or afterwards, students will return to the graphic organizer and add new ideas to it. 7.4 shows a kind of graphic organizer called a spider map. The topic is written in the circle in the middle, main ideas or aspects of the topic are written along the diagonal lines, and details are written on the horizontal lines.

FOR THE BUILDING KNOWLEDGE PHASE.   Once students have had their expectations raised for what they are about to read, they are ready for activities that will help them construct meaning from the text—what we are calling **building knowledge**.

As they read and build their knowledge, students need to do several things:

- Think about what they are reading and sense its organization (the way the text is revealing its information)
- Make sure they understand details
- Identify the main points
- Reflect on what the text is meaning to them personally and fill in any blanks in the text—that is, make inferences about what the text says
- Compare their expectations with what they are learning from the text, and be able to revise their expectations or raise new ones as the text reveals more information, suggests more questions, or plants more clues.

Several strategies for helping students to build knowledge are described next.

Figure 7.3
A Story Map.

Once upon a time in

_____

a character named

_____

wanted

_____

but

_____

so

_____

and at the end,

_____

which goes to show you that

_____

GUIDED READING. The guided reading procedure (Fountas & Pinnell, 1999) introduced in Chapters 4 and 5 provides an excellent opportunity to teach comprehension. When guided reading is used to emphasize comprehension, you may use these three steps.

Teach It! 9
Guided Reading

1. **Prepare the children to read with understanding.** Your purpose in the introductory phase is to create curiosity about the book to be read, connect with the children's prior knowledge, and deal with vocabulary and other details they may need to be aware of in order to understand. Here are some strategies you can use.

   • **Preview the text.** Show the children the cover illustration, the title, and some of the pictures inside. "Think aloud" and speculate on what the text might be about. You might discuss the author and the kinds of books she or he writes.

   • **Introduce the genre.** Explain that we may expect different things to happen in the text depending on whether the book is a folktale, a biography, tall tale,

Figure 7.4
Spider Map.

A teacher using Guided Reading offers needed support as students read. (Ellen B. Senisi)

Teach It! 21

"Word Conversations" for Primary Grades

Teach It! 47

Know-Want to Know-Learn (K-W-L)

a work of realistic fiction, or an informational book. Which genre is this book? What does that genre lead us to expect to read in it?

- **Go over vocabulary.** Tell the students that they will meet some interesting words in this text. Name them one at a time and write them on the board.

- **Teach other skills.** Depending on your objectives for this lesson, introduce a brief focused lesson on the skills you want the students to practice as they read the text. For example, if you want the students to pay attention to the plot of a story, you can prepare them to fill out a **story map,** such as the one found in Figure 7.5 on page 213. Show the whole group how to fill out a story map, and later have them fill out a story map themselves after they have read the story.

- **Read the text to them.** If the story is challenging for some of the students, you may choose to read aloud the first few pages.

- **Begin a K-W-L (Know/Want to Know/Learn) or Directed Reading-Thinking Activity (DRTA).** Comprehension strategies that ask children to discuss what they know and what they think they will find out can be introduced now.

2. **The students read the text.** The students may read the text on their own or in pairs.

- **If you are conducting a DRTA or a K-W-L,** they read to an assigned stopping place and have questions to guide their search for information.

- They may *buddy read*, that is, take turns reading paragraphs or pages.

- They may use the *Paired Reading/Paired Summarizing* technique (Crawford et al., 2005). That is, one student reads a paragraph aloud and summarizes it. The other student asks questions about the passage that both answer. Then they change roles with the next paragraph, and so on.

- They may read with *text coding* (Crawford et al., 2005). That is, the teacher helps students think of a set of four to six questions or issues they wish to track as they read the text. For example, if they are reading a passage about acid rain, they may be asked to look for passages that say where it occurs (W), others that say what its sources are (S), others that describe the chemical reactions that make it happen (CR), others that talk about the damage it does (D), and still others that talk about possible preventions of the problem (P). As they read, the students pencil in the letter indicating which kind of information they have found.

3. **The group reviews what they have learned.** After the students have read the text, the teacher brings them back together to discuss the text and to consolidate what they have learned.

- **Discussions** can use many of the formats described in this chapter. These methods include Sketch to Stretch, shared inquiry, dual-entry diaries, Save the Last Word for Me, the discussion web, and dramatization.

- **Review by revisiting the skills you introduced.** Assuming you began the lesson with certain skills in mind—understanding characterization, following the plot, getting the main idea, and so on—you will revisit those skills now. Have the students or pairs of students explain how they read and what they discovered, and make sure everyone understands and can carry out the practice you introduced.

Save the Last Word for Me

The Directed Reading-Thinking Activity. The **Directed Reading-Thinking Activity,** or DRTA (Stauffer, 1975), uses the dynamic of prediction and confirmation to create interest and excitement around a reading assignment, provided that the text is a work of fiction with something of a predictable structure. The DRTA is normally done with a group of six to ten students; this size is large enough to yield a range of predictions but small enough for everyone to participate. It is advisable that the students be roughly matched for reading ability, because all students must wait for the slowest one to finish reading each section.

The DRTA can be used by itself, or it can follow one of the activities we introduced in the anticipation phase. Some teachers precede the DRTA with the terms-in-advance procedure or with the anticipation guide.

The teacher prepares for a DRTA by choosing four or five stopping places in the text, yielding more or less same-sized chunks of text. The stops should be placed right at points of suspense, places where the reader has been given some information and is wondering what is going to happen next (in other words, where the commercial break would be placed in a television thriller). One of these is normally right after the title. The Teach It! box demonstrates the DRTA process.

In a DRTA, the questions are worded in a very open way. The teacher asks, "What do you think will happen? Why do you think so?" More specific questions from the teacher would take some of the initiative for making predictions away from the children, and the point here is for children to learn to ask their own questions about what they are reading.

There are a number of ways to scaffold a DRTA to make it more accessible to students. One is to read the text aloud instead of having the students read it. This variation of the method goes by a different name: the directed listening-thinking activity. Another is to think aloud yourself. If the predictions are slow in coming or seem to be going too wide of the mark, the teacher can offer a choice. For *Miss Nelson Is Missing*, the teacher might say, "I'm wondering if Miss Nelson has gone away to teach in another school where the kids are better behaved, or if she'll come back to her same class. Which one do you all think will happen?" Finally, in third grade and above, instead of a teacher-directed activity, a DRTA can be done by individual students or pairs of students.

Instructional Conversations. Teacher Nancie Atwell (1989) remarked that her goal in discussing a text with her students was to recreate a kitchen table. By that she meant the enthusiastic environment she enjoyed with friends while discussing a book around her own kitchen table: everyone thinking hard, saying what they think, building on each other's ideas, and sharing responsibility for keeping the conversation going. How can we recreate those circumstances in the classroom? Tharp and Gallimore (1991) worked out procedures, which are more like guidelines, that teachers can use to create and support conversations that achieve many of Atwell's goals.

Teach It!

Refer to the Teach It! appendix at the end of the book for further activities you can use to reinforce concepts discussed in this chapter.

Conducting a DRTA

The directed reading-thinking activity is a sound strategy for helping students build knowledge as it helps create interest and excitement around a reading assignment. Following are the steps in a DRTA:

1. Tell the students that you are about to read a story together, using the method of prediction. The activity should be enjoyable, but it is necessary that they follow your instructions closely. You will tell them to make predictions about what they are going to read. Then you will have them read short passages of the text and stop. It is very important that they stop reading where you tell them to and not read ahead until asked.

2. Tell the students the genre of the story: realistic fiction, tall tale, folktale, etc. After naming the genre, ask them what kinds of characters they expect to meet. Ask what kinds of events they expect to happen.

3. Read the title, and show the students the accompanying picture, if there is one. Ask them what they think will happen. Remind them that it will not be possible to know for sure, but ask them to stretch their imaginations and take a guess. Press for the most specific answers you can get. Write some of these on the chalkboard. (Remember to leave room to write three more rounds of comments.)

4. Before the students read on, ask them to consider the predictions they have heard and silently choose the one they think is most likely to hap-

pen. Then ask them to keep their predictions in mind as they read to the next stopping place.

5. Now they should read (silently) to the stopping place and turn their books over when they have finished.

6. At the stopping place, review several of the predictions and ask the class whether the predictions seem to be borne out by the text or contradicted. Ask for proof from the text: Which predictions are coming true? What evidence do the students find in the text that makes them think so? You can put check marks on the board next to the predictions that are coming true, minuses next to those that are not, and question marks beside those that are uncertain. Ask the students how things look now in the story.

7. After some discussion, ask the students to make more predictions, choose the most likely ones, and read ahead as in step 4.

8. When the students have reached the end of the story, review the predictions, and ask the students what it was that made them guess what turned out to be the correct predictions. What was it about the characters, the plot, or the genre of the story that helped to guide their predictions?

When engaging students in an instructional conversation, the teacher first selects meaningful chunks of the text for discussion. A good conversation can last half an hour or longer, which is enough time to discuss a theme or topic to some depth, but not more than one theme.

Next, the teacher decides on the theme or issue for discussion. It should be something that students can relate to, that is likely to engage them. And it should be framed in such a way that it invites different responses—it is not a "read my mind" invitation, but a real issue that real people might wonder about.

Some teachers conduct instructional conversations with an entire class, but there is more chance for participation if the group is kept down to under ten. That way, too, the students may be homogeneously grouped so that the text being discussed can be read and understood by everyone in the group.

To begin, the teacher explains to the students that they will have a conversation about the text they are reading, and that everyone will be invited to think hard and share ideas. They won't need to raise hands, but they should be respectful of each other, and wait for others to finish before contributing.

The teacher throws out a question to start, and asks students what they think about it. The teacher takes care to relate the question to things the students already know about, tapping into their interests and background knowledge. As the conversation proceeds, the teacher keeps the conversation loosely focused on the theme, and while he may explore ideas that a student raises, he will tactfully steer the conversation back to the main topic.

As needed, the teacher will explain points that are not clear and provide background information the children do not have—being careful to keep from lecturing. Likewise, the teacher will ask a student to support her ideas with references to the text: "Find the place in the text that gives some evidence for what you're saying." Likewise, the teacher will invite a student to express something more clearly, and occasionally offer up a word that conveys an idea a student is groping to express—all with the quiet goal of supporting more sophisticated thinking and expression.

The Directed Reading Activity. The Directed Reading Activity (DRA) is a strategy that gives the teacher a broad opportunity to guide students' thought processes toward the aspects of comprehension that were discussed earlier in this chapter. The steps to the procedure are described below.

Before the lesson begins, the teacher will have chosen four or five stopping points in the text for each class period in which it will be discussed. Then, to begin the activity, the teacher does a pre-reading introduction of the text, pointing out the title, the author, and the genre, showing pictures if there are any, and inviting students to venture what they think the text may be about. The teacher may use think-alouds to model how to make predictions and comments.

Before the students read the first marked-off section, the teacher puts a question to them, to establish a purpose for their reading. "Read this section to see who this story is going to be about, and what kind of situation she is in," the teacher might ask. The students read to find answers to the question. After they have finished, they share their answers. The teacher may challenge them to go back and reread the passages on which they based their answers.

Before they read the next section, the teacher asks them to read to find the answer to another question, and the reading proceeds in this scavenger hunt fashion.

What kinds of questions should the teacher ask?

In the Directed Reading Activity, teachers may ask questions that follow the **format and genre** of the text. That is, the questions should help readers follow the presentation of information that is particular to the kind of text the students are reading.

If the students are reading a narrative text, it would usually contain a predictable set of elements: the **setting,** the **characters,** the **problem, attempts at solutions,** the **consequences of the actions**, and the **theme or message** of the story.

- Questions about **settings** may lead students to notice what sensory words the author used to evoke images: "Read this next section and pay attention to what the author wants you to hear, see, smell, and feel." Students may also be asked to predict what kinds of events might happen in such a setting.

- Questions about **characters** similarly call attention to how the author helps the reader know the characters, sense the tensions between the characters, and understand the kinds of problems the main character might have and what kinds of actions he or she might engage in.

- Questions about the **problem,** the **attempts at solutions,** and the **consequences of the actions** can guide readers to follow the plots of stories. Readers can be asked to note the main character's problem and to predict how she or he will attempt to solve it, given what they know about the character (and what they could predict from the kind of story they are reading). They can also be asked about the consequences of the actions, and how the situation at the end of the story differs from the situation at the beginning.

- Questions about the **themes or messages** of stories may be asked in several ways. Students may be asked what the story meant to them. They may also be asked why they would or would not agree with the message the story seems to convey—because many popular stories suggest ways of living to which we shouldn't readily subscribe—that one must be beautiful or very aggressive in order to be successful, for instance.

Teachers also may ask questions when using the Directed Reading Activity with other genres of text, such as informational and persuasive texts.

Table 7.1 Activities for Consolidation

	TEACHING APPROACHES	
OPEN RESPONSE	**FOCUSED APPROACH**	**ANALYTIC APPROACH**
"Save the Last Word for Me"	Shared inquiry	Story maps
Literature circles	Discussion web	Character clusters
Value line	Debate	Character maps
Sketch-to-stretch		Dramatic roles
Dual-entry diary		Structured opposites

FOR THE CONSOLIDATION PHASE.   By the **consolidation** phase, the students have gone through the text and have at least begun to comprehend it. They need to go further, though, and do something with the meaning. They need to summarize it and be able to interpret and debate the meaning while applying it to new situations and creating new examples of it.

Students need to practice higher-order thinking with the issues from the text. After they read, students should be able to think back over the material and summarize the main ideas. They should compare what they found out with what they thought about the subject when they first approached the reading. If the ideas are not transparent, students should be able to interpret them. If the text is evocative in some way, students might be able to make personal responses to the ideas, such as applying them to the way they normally think or to the realities of their own lives. Students should also be able to test out the ideas—using them to solve problems or to think up other solutions to the problems posed in the text.

Several teaching approaches are available to assist teachers with guiding students to consolidate and extend their ideas about what they have read. For fictional texts, teachers can use activities that allow students fairly free responses, some techniques that guide their attention to different aspects of the text, or more analytic approaches that help students to take a close look at particular aspects of the text. Table 7.1 identifies various activities with the appropriate approaches.

Dual-Entry Diary.   The dual-entry diary (Berthoff, 1981) is a kind of journal students use to record responses to readings. To make a dual-entry diary, the students draw a vertical line down the middle of a blank sheet of paper. On the left-hand side, they write a passage or image from the text that affected them strongly. Perhaps it reminded them of something from their own experience. Perhaps it puzzled them. Perhaps they disagreed with it. Perhaps it made them aware of the author's style or technique.

On the right-hand side of the page, they write a comment about that passage: What was it about the quote that made them write it down? What did it make them think of? What question did they have about it?

There are a number of ways in which these journals may be treated next. Students can exchange them and comment on each other's quotes. The teacher can take them up (a few each day) and comment on them. Or the children can bring them to a discussion group in which students are reading a common book and offer their comments to the discussion.

Save the Last Word for Me.   Save the Last Word for Me (Short, Harste, & Burke, 1996) provides a framework for a small-group or whole-class discussion of a text. The procedure is especially good for encouraging children to take the lead in discussing their reading. The steps of the strategy are as follows:

1. After being assigned a reading to do independently, students are given note cards and asked to find three or four quotations they consider particularly interesting or worthy of comment.

2. The students write the quotations they have found on the note cards.

3. On the other sides of the cards, the students write comments about their chosen quotations. That is, they say what the quotations made them think of, what is surprising about the quotations, and why they chose them.

4. The students bring their quotation cards to discussion groups. The teacher calls on someone to read a card aloud.

5. After reading the quotation on his or her card, the student invites other students to comment on that quotation. (The teacher might need to help keep comments on the subject of the quotation.) The teacher also may comment on the quotation.

6. Once others have had their say about the quotation, the student who chose it reads his or her comments aloud. Then there can be no further discussion. The student who chose it gets to have the last word.

7. That student can now call on another student to share his or her quotation and begin the process all over again. Not all students will be able to share their quotation if the whole class takes part in the activity, so the teacher will need to keep track of who shared quotes and make sure other children get chances to share their quotes the next time.

Literature Circles. *Literature circles* (Short & Kauffman, 1995), *grand conversations* (Eeds & Wells, 1989), and *book clubs* (Raphael et al., 1995) are all terms for literary discussions in which students' curiosity about the text is allowed to play a directing role.

Students in such discussions typically have read the same work; that work might be a short text they have already read or heard, or it might be a longer work that is discussed while students are still in the middle of it. The choice of texts for literature circles is critical because not all works are equally effective in evoking interested responses. Those that are successful often have a core mystery, elements that invite more than one interpretation, and a clear connection to issues that matter to the students.

These discussion groups may initially be conducted with the whole class until students have grown familiar and comfortable with the procedure. Then they may be held in smaller groups of four or five students meeting simultaneously. Literature circles meet several times a week. Early in the year, they might last no more than twenty minutes, but

Literature circles can result in fascinating discussions. (Ellen B. Senisi)

as students gain experience and confidence talking about literature, they might run for up to forty minutes, not counting the time it takes to read the text. Everyone is free to offer comments and questions in literature circles, and students are reminded that they are free to address their comments and questions to other students and not always to the teacher.

The role of the teacher in a literature circle is mainly to be a spirited participant; however, Martinez (in Temple et al., 2010) points to four additional roles teachers play:

1. **The teacher is a model.** The teacher might venture her or his own questions or responses to get a discussion going. The teacher is careful to speak as one seeking insights and not as a lecturer. The teacher's statements might begin, "I wonder about . . ."

2. **The teacher helps students learn new roles in a literature circle.** Although all students know how to have conversations, they might need reminding of ways to participate in conversations in a classroom. These include rules such as:
   - Sit in a circle so that everyone can see each other.
   - Only one person speaks at a time.
   - Listen to each other.
   - Stay on the topic.

3. **The teacher moves the conversation forward.** Without dominating the discussion, the teacher might invite other students to comment on something one student has said. The teacher might ask a student to clarify an idea. Or the teacher might pose an interesting open-ended question that she or he has thought about in advance. (Such interpretive questions are discussed in the section on shared inquiry later.)

4. **The teacher supports literary learning.** Lecturing about literature is not an adequate substitute for having students think and talk about it; nonetheless, it helps if teachers supply students with concepts and terms they can use to give form to ideas they are trying to express or insights they are struggling to reach. A student might notice that there is a point in a story where tension is highest because the main question in the story is about to be answered. The teacher tells the student that this is a *climax*. Researchers have noted that students' discussions go deeper when they have literary terms available to them (Hickman, 1979, 1981).

When conducting cooperative learning activities, the teacher might need to assign students particular roles to play in a group. Over time, as individual students learn to play the many roles of encourager, timekeeper, facilitator, recorder, and summarizer, they eventually learn all of the aspects of group behavior because a good participant may practice most of these roles at once.

Literature circles often function better when students have particular roles to play. Also, by performing designated roles, students may exercise the many tasks that are carried out by an effective reader and discussant of literature. Table 7.2 outlines roles that students may play in a literary discussion (Daniels, 1994, 2001). Five suggestions make the use of these roles more successful:

1. Teach the roles to the whole class, one at a time. The teacher might read or tell a story, then introduce one of the roles—for example, the connector. The teacher might then call attention to a connection between something in the text and something in real life. Then the teacher will invite several students to do likewise. Over several days, many of the roles can be introduced in this way before students use them in an extended discussion.

2. Encourage students to ask questions from their roles rather than to say what they know. For example, the character interpreter might invite the other students to construct a character map or a character web about a character and venture his or her own ideas only after the other students have shared their own.

Table 7.2 Roles in a Literary Discussion Group

- *Quotation finder:* This student's job is to pick a few special sections of the text that the group would like to hear read aloud.
- *Investigator:* This student's job is to provide background information on any topic related to the text.
- *Travel tracer:* When characters move from place to place in a text, this student's job is to keep track of their movements.
- *Connector:* This student's job is to find connections between the text and the world outside.
- *Question asker:* This student's job is to write down (in advance of the discussion) questions for the group to talk about—questions he or she would like to discuss with the others.
- *Word finder:* This student's job is to find interesting, puzzling, important, or new words to bring to the group's attention and discuss.
- *Checker:* This student's job is to help people in the group do their work well by staying on the topic, taking turns, participating happily, and working within time limits.
- *Character interpreter:* This student's job is to think carefully about the characters and to discuss what they are like with the other students.
- *Illustrator:* This student's job is to draw pictures of important characters, settings, or actions so that the other students may discuss the pictures.
- *Recorder:* This student's job is to take brief notes on the main points raised in the discussion.
- *Reporter:* This student's job is to report on the group's discussion to the teacher or to the whole class.

3. Choose only the most useful roles for a particular discussion. Sometimes four or five roles are sufficient.

4. Rotate students through the roles. Each student should play many roles over the course of several discussions. The accumulated experience of playing many of these roles adds dimensions to each student's awareness of literature.

5. Be careful not to stress the roles more than the rich discussion of the literary work. Having students carry out the roles is a means to the end of sharing their insights about a work. Once the conversation is under way, the teacher should feel free to suspend the roles and let the conversation proceed.

Sketch-to-Stretch.   An ingenious device for having students of all ages respond together to a literary work is *Sketch-to-Stretch*, from Short et al. (1996). After the students have read and thought about a poem or a story, they are invited to draw pictures that symbolize what they believe are the main ideas or central themes of the piece. One student shows his or her drawing to a group of students, and they interpret the picture, saying what they think it means and how its images relate to the literary work. After the other students have had their say, the student who drew the picture is invited to give his or her own interpretation of the picture.

Shared Inquiry Discussion.   The Great Books Foundation developed the shared inquiry method to accompany their literature discussion program (see Plecha, 1992), which has been conducted in thousands of schools and libraries for more than thirty years. Shared inquiry is a procedure by which the teacher leads a deep discussion into a work of literature. It is best done with a group of eight to ten students, to maximize participation but allow for a diversity of ideas. The procedure follows these steps:

1. Before the discussion takes place, choose a work or part of a work that encourages discussion. Such a work should lend itself to more than one interpretation

(not all works do this well) and raise interesting issues. Folktales often meet these criteria surprisingly well.

2. Make sure that all of the students have read the material carefully. (The Great Books Foundation insists that students read material twice before discussing it. But in our experience, a reading using some of the comprehension methods just described can make the students very aware of the contents of the reading selection.)

3. Prepare four or five discussion questions. These should be what the Great Books Foundation calls **interpretive questions**, and they have three criteria:

   (a) They are real questions, the sort of question you might ask a friend as you walk together out of a provocative film.

   (b) They have more than one defensible answer. (This criterion guarantees a debate. If it is not met, the discussion won't be a discussion but a "read my mind" exercise.)

   (c) They must lead the discussion into the text. (A question such as, "Why was the giant's wife kinder to Jack than his own mother was?" leads the children to talk about what is in the text first, even though they might then comment on what they know from experience. A question such as "Have you ever done anything as brave as Jack?" leads the discussion away from the text and out into twenty-five different directions.)

4. Write the first question on the chalkboard, and ask the students to think about the question and then briefly write down their answers. (If the children are so young that writing answers is laborious, allow plenty of time before calling on anyone. This allows them time to think about their answers.) As you invite students to answer, be sure to invite reluctant speakers to read what they wrote as well. Encourage debate between students, pointing out differences in what they say and asking them and other students to expand on the differences. Press children to support their ideas with references to the text or to restate ideas more clearly. However, avoid correcting a child or in any way suggesting that any one answer is right or wrong. Finally, do not offer your own answer to the question. Keep a seating chart of the students' names with a brief record of what each one has contributed. When the discussion of a question seems to have run its course, read aloud your summaries of the students' comments and then ask whether anyone has anything to add.

5. Once the discussion gets going, follow the children's lead and continue to discuss the issues and questions they raise.

Even when they don't use the whole approach, many teachers use aspects of the shared inquiry procedure in conducting book discussions. For example, they might ask students to write down ideas to bring to a discussion, they might take notes during the discussion, or they take care to draw out the students' ideas and not dominate the discussion themselves.

Other Kinds of Questions. The shared inquiry approach uses interpretive questions. The Directed Reading-Thinking Activity makes simple requests for predictions. And the Directed Reading Activity asks questions that follow the plot, or other contours of the text. Another approach to questioning gives us the Text-to-self, Text-to-text, and Text-to-world questions, developed by Keene and Zimmerman (1997).

Text-to-self questions ask the reader to compare characters, situations, and events in the story to their own lives. The teacher might ask,

- "How is this situation like something that has happened to you, or to someone you know?"

- "How is this situation different from something that has happened to you, or to someone you know?"

Text-to-text questions ask the reader to compare characters, situations, and events in the story with those in other stories they know. Here the teacher might ask,

- "Do the characters, situations, or events in this story remind us of something we have read in other stories? In which ones? How are they the same?"
- "And how are they different in this story?"

Text-to-world questions ask the reader to compare characters, situations, and events in the story to what they know about the world. The teacher may ask,

- "Think of the characters and situations that we meet in this story. How are they like characters and events in the real world? Are there really people like that? Who? Is anyone really living situations like the ones we are reading about? Who? In other words, although this is a story, what is true to life about it?"
- "In what important ways are these characters **unlike** people or situations in the real world? That is, in what ways is this story not a reliable guide to real life?"

Lively discussions can result from asking these questions, as students explore the meaning of texts. **Text-to-self** questions invite personal responses to the texts. **Text-to-text** questions invite students to explore similarities and share these between texts, an activity that theorists call **intertextuality**. And **text-to-world** questions invite students to locate the truths that emerge from fictions, and also help students to realize that stories may or may not be reliable guides to living in the world.

Drama in Response to Stories.   James Moffett (1976), a brilliant teacher of the language arts, pointed out many years ago that forms of literature differ in the degree to which they move closer to or further away from actual events. An essay about human nature is *abstract* (the word comes from two Latin roots that mean "drawn away from"), far removed from actual events. A story is more concrete, getting closer to events. Still, by putting events into story form, an author summarizes them, compresses actions, and leaves out much of what might really have happened. Drama, however, is live action: It is about as close to the real events as we can get because it plays the events out in real time for us so that we can see, hear, and feel them as they unfold. Here is Moffett's shorthand way of stating these points:

- Drama shows what is happening.
- A story tells what happened.
- An essay tells what happens.

Dramatizing a story, or a part of a story, can be a very effective way for children to unpack its meaning. Dramatization should be done after the children have read or heard a story and have had a chance to air their first thoughts about it. The Teach It! box on page 212 demonstrates a procedure for dramatizing a story.

The teaching approaches that we have considered up to now encourage discussions of stories or enactments of them. It is also useful to lead students in activities that teach them particular aspects of stories.

Story Maps.   As a rule, students read with better comprehension when they are asked questions that conform to the main arguments or developments of a text. When it comes to reading fiction, it helps if students are encouraged to raise questions along the lines that the stories are organized, and that usually means following the plot. The *plot* is a structured

What can students learn by acting out a story? What does it mean to "unpack" the meaning of a story? (Mary Kate Denny/Stone/Getty Images)

Teach It!

Refer to the Teach It! appendix at the end of the book for further activities you can use to reinforce concepts discussed in this chapter.

Dramatizing a Story

Dramatizing a story allows children to take a closer look at a story by getting a real feel for the action. The procedure for dramatizing a story is adapted from the works of Viola Spolin (1986) and Dorothy Heathcote (Wagner, 1999).

Immerse students in the story. You need to make sure the students get the story on a literal level—that they know what happened. This might mean reading the story to them or asking them to reread the part you are going to dramatize.

Warm them up to do drama. There are many warm-up activities that work well to prepare students to act with more expression:

1. Stretches: Have the students stand in a circle. Now tell them to stretch their arms as high as they can as they spread their feet apart and make very wide faces. Now tell them to shrink up into tiny balls. Then stretch out big again. Have them do the same with their faces: Lion face! (expansive expression). Prune face! (shrunken expression).

2. Mirrors: Have students stand opposite each other. One is the person, and the other is the person reflected in the mirror. Have the person move (slowly) as the other mirrors the person's movements. Then switch roles.

3. Portraits: Have students get into groups of four or five. Have them think of something to depict that uses all of them as parts. For example, to depict a skier, children can act as poles, skis, and the person.

4. Superactions: This activity is more complex. Explain to the students that when we do things with other people, we often act on two levels: what we are doing and what we mean by what we are doing. For example, when we pass somebody we know in the hallway, having just seen the person a short time before, we might nod and say, "Hi." But when we see a friend in the hallway who has just come back to school after a long illness, we might say "HI!" with more exuberance. In both cases, the action is the same: to greet the friend. But the *superaction* is different. In the first case, it is just to show the person that we know he or she is there; in the second case, it is to show that we are surprised and delighted to see the person. Now practice dramatizing superactions by setting up brief situations, such as a waiter taking a customer's order. Write superactions on small pieces of paper, and give one privately to each actor.

Have different pairs of students act out the same scene, with the same actions but with different superactions, leaving time for the other students to guess what they thought the superaction was and say why they thought so.

Choose critical moments. It can be particularly useful to dramatize just a few choice scenes from a story, especially the turning points when the most is at stake. In "Jack and the Beanstalk," such a scene might be when Jack first approaches the Giant's castle, knocks on the door, and is greeted by the Giant's wife.

Segment the situation. Now assign students to take each of these roles. Invite other students to join them as they think about the situation from each character's point of view. What must be on Jack's mind when he approaches the huge door? What do the door and the walls of the castle look like? How large are they in proportion to Jack? What does Jack hear around the place? What does he smell? How does the place make him feel? What makes him pound his fist on the door? What is at stake for him? What are his choices? What will he do if he *doesn't* knock on the door? Why does he decide to do it?

Do the same for the Giant's wife. How does the knocking sound to her—thunderous or puny? What does she think when she sees the small but plucky boy at her door? What thoughts go through her mind, knowing what she knows about her husband? What are her feelings as she looks down at Jack?

Ask the actors to focus their minds on a few of these considerations as they prepare to act out the scene.

Dramatize the scene. Use minimal props and minimal costumes to help students think their way into their roles. Ask the other students to watch carefully and see what the actors make them think of.

Side coach. As the director, don't be passive, but take opportunities to make suggestions from the sidelines that will help children act more expressively. You might ask, "Jack, do you feel scared now or brave? How can you show us how you're feeling?"

Invite reflection. Ask the other students what they saw. What did they think was on the characters' minds? It is worthwhile to invite several groups of students to dramatize the same scene and have the class discuss the aspects of the situation that each performance brings to light.

---

way in which authors organize places, people, actions, and consequences to make all of those things meaningful for the reader. The elements of a plot are as follows:

- *The setting:* the time and place the story happened
- *The main characters:* the persons the story is about

- *The problem*: the challenge the main character faces, which is his or her goal to solve
- *The attempts*: the effort or series of efforts the character makes to solve the problem, along with their outcomes
- *The solution*: the attempt that finally pays off in solving the problem or the event that otherwise puts an end to the action
- *The consequence*: how things are for the characters at the end, including what the events of the story meant for them

For many years, researchers have noted that students down to age five and even younger use something like a plot or a story grammar to understand and tell stories (Stein & Glenn, 1978; Sutton-Smith, 1981). You can help students use the plot consciously in understanding a story by using a story map, a chart that invites them to identify the key parts of a story (see Figure 7.5). The process builds their responsiveness to the structures of story plots. For students younger than second grade, it might be preferable to use a simpler version of a story map consisting of only the setting, the characters, the problem, and the solution.

Character Clusters.   Not only are stories developed through plots, but characters come to life in them, too. Literary critic Roland Barthes (1975) suggested that characters are mostly just bundles of attributes that authors put into situations and play off against each other to show us what happens. In essence, writers ask themselves, "What would happen if a person like X got stuck in a situation like Y with people like Z?" Children's comprehension and appreciation of stories can be enhanced by showing them some ways to think about characters.

One way is the **character cluster**, which is a kind of graphic organizer: a semantic web with the character's name written in the middle, main features of the character written as satellites around the character's name, and examples of those features written as satellites around the features. Figure 7.6 shows an example of a character cluster.

As when using other graphic organizers, you need to teach the whole class how to create a character cluster first. Then they can use it on their own as a guide to thinking more deeply about characters.

Figure 7.5   A Story Map.

Setting	Characters	Problem	Attempts	Solution	Conclusion
In . . .	there was	who wanted	so she . . . , but . . . And she . . . but . . .	Finally, she . . . and . . .	In the end . . .

Figure 7.6
A Character Cluster.

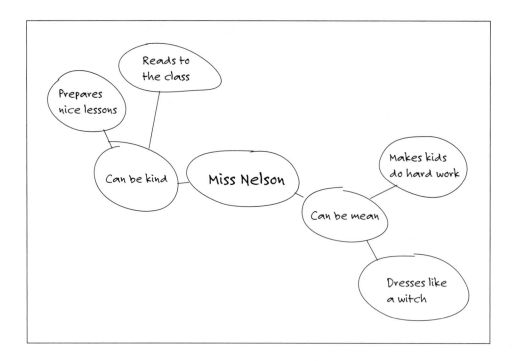

Character Maps. When characters in stories interact with other characters (which is most of the time), students might need some way of keeping track of them and the relationships between them. **Character maps** are a way to guide students' thinking about relationships between characters. In a character map, you write the names of two or more characters in their respective circles. The circles should be spaced widely apart on the page. Then draw arrows between the characters. Along the arrow that points from Character A to Character B, write about how Character A feels about Character B. Along the arrow that points from Character B to Character A, write about how Character B feels about Character A. An example of a character map for two characters in Mildred Taylor's *Roll of Thunder, Hear My Cry* (1997) is found in Figure 7.7.

Figure 7.7   A Character Map for *Roll of Thunder, Hear My Cry.*

Placing Students in the Proper Level Material

If a student is especially interested in a topic, or if he already knows a lot about it, he will be able to read a more challenging text about that topic than he might otherwise. Nonetheless, a student's reading level is a normally good indicator of the level of text that student should be expected to read. Many times in this text we have referred to the independent level as the level of a text easy enough for a student to read with accurate word recognition and sufficient understanding that the student will not require help. In measurement terms, that means the child should read with 90 percent comprehension, which is to say that he can answer at least nine questions out of ten or retell nine important points out of ten. If he is to read a text with the support of a teacher, then a rate of comprehension between 70 or 75 percent and 90 percent would be expected.

Once students have been assessed, they should be placed in text material that is at the proper reading level for the instructional task, even if that means moving a student up to more challenging material or down to less challenging material.

Figure 7.8   A Language Chart.

Books by William Steig	What Was the Problem?	What Was the Solution?	How Were Things Different at the End?
Sylvester and the Magic Pebble	Sylvester got turned into a rock.	His parents found the magic pebble and wished him back to his old self.	Sylvester was happy to be normal.
Caleb and Kate	Caleb got turned into a dog.	Kate said the magic words and changed him back.	Caleb and Kate were glad to be together.
The Amazing Bone	Pearl was going to be killed by a fox.	The bone said a charm and shrank the fox.	Pearl was glad to be home with her family.

The Language Chart.   As a way to motivate children to think more deeply about themes and other features of books, you might choose three or more books that share similarities and construct a language chart as a means of comparing them. A **language chart** (Roser & Hoffman, 1995) asks the same question about all of the books, as shown in Figure 7.8.

Children discuss these and other questions at the time they read each book. Then the teacher records a summary of their answers in the space provided on the chart. After they have read two books, they compare them according to the questions. Using a language chart has been shown to lead even young children into more analytical thinking about what they have read.

Assessing Comprehension

We have seen in this chapter that reading comprehension is a complex activity that includes readers'

- Prior knowledge and their willingness to use it to generate questions about what they are reading
- Ability to seek answers to questions and construct meaning
- Ability to follow the pattern or structure of the text
- Metacognition—thinking about their understanding and rereading to repair their understanding when it fails
- Making mental images of what is described in the text
- Getting the main idea and supporting details
- Making inferences
- Connecting the meaning to other texts and to issues outside of the text

There is no simple way to measure all that. The most thorough approaches to the assessment of comprehension are observations of the reader's attempts to comprehend. In addition, you may wish to use a more quickly administered device, recognizing that such a device will yield an incomplete picture of a reader's comprehension.

Approaches to assessing comprehension include the following:

- *Observational assessments:* You observe and assess students' comprehension behaviors as students demonstrate them in real reading tasks.
- *Self-assessments:* You ask students to observe and critique their own use of comprehension strategies. Self-assessments have the advantage of teaching students to be mindful of reading strategies and deliberate about their use when they read.
- *Quantitative assessments:* Periodically, you might gather data that allow you to compare students' performance against some standard, such as grade-level expectations.

Observational Assessments

One kind of observational assessment is simply to keep a folder for each student into which you place observations that you write down every few days. The observations consist of whatever strikes you as being worthy of note.

A more systematic way of making observational assessments is to keep a checklist of reading behaviors—in this case, comprehension behaviors. Schedule an eight- to ten-minute period every week to read with each child, individually or in a group of no more than four, and record observations on a checklist such as the one shown in Figure 7.9.

Student Self-Assessments

Self-assessments (see Figure 7.10) are recommended because they not only give the teacher some information about how the child is reading but also make the child aware of what she or he should be doing while reading. In other words, self-assessments teach at the same time that they assess reading behaviors.

Students will need to be taught what each of the questions on the self-assessment instrument mean. Each question can be presented in a mini-lesson and added to the self-assessment instrument after it has been taught. This means that the self-assessment instrument will get longer and more elaborate as the year goes on and as more component strategies of comprehension are taught and then added to the instrument.

Students can be given self-assessments to complete every two or three weeks. It is helpful to review the assessment instrument with the students just before they complete a reading assignment and have them fill out the assessment afterward. Discuss with the students how the strategies they indicate they are using help them to understand what they read. Talk over the strategies they still need to learn to use, and teach those strategies if necessary.

Quantitative Assessments

Teachers and students also need to know how well students are reading in comparison with their grade-level group. As we noted in Chapter 1, teachers and grade-level teams can focus attention on aspects of teaching that need improving, but only if they have evidence that tells them where the strengths of their instructional program are as well as the areas in which they need improvement.

Several kinds of assessment devices are available. For the purpose of getting a close look at readers' strengths and areas of need, probably the most informative are informal reading inventories. Informal reading inventories must be administered one at a time, so they are time consuming. But the fact that they yield both quantitative results (in terms of reading levels) and detailed portraits of most areas of students' reading abilities makes them worth the investment of time.

Informal reading inventories (IRIs) are thoroughly discussed in Gillet, Temple, and Crawford's *Understanding Reading Problems* (2007).

Although teachers can make their own IRIs, most teachers prefer to use commercially available ones. Here are some recommended informal reading inventories:

Temple, C., Crawford, A., & Gillet, J. (2008). *Developmental literacy inventory: Emergent reading through high school.* Boston: Allyn and Bacon.

Lauren, L., & Caldwell, J. (2005). *Qualitative reading inventory-4.* New York: Pearson Education.

Burns, P. C., & Roe, B. D. (2006). *Informal reading inventory: Preprimer to grade twelve.* Boston: Houghton Mifflin.

Silvaroli, N., & Wheelock, W. (2003). *Classroom reading inventory.* New York: McGraw-Hill.

Applegate, M. D., Quinn, K. B., & Applegate, A. J. (2003). *The critical reading inventory.* New York: Pearson Education.

For more information on IRIs, see Chapters 10 and 12. Other procedures for assessing reading comprehension, including the Cloze procedure and the Lexiles Framework, are discussed in Chapter 10.

Figure 7.9   Observational Checklist for Assessing Comprehension.

Student's name: _____ Date: _____ Observer: _____

Material read: _____ Level: _____

1. Before reading

a) The reader demonstrated familiarity with the topic (or the author or the genre) of the text before reading.

No prior knowledge shown	*Some prior knowledge shown*	*Much prior knowledge shown*

b) The reader raised questions about the content of the text before reading.

No questions offered *even when asked*	*Vague questions raised when* *asked to by teacher*	*Precise and informed* *questions offered*

c) The reader was able to make predictions about what was coming in the text.

No predictions offered *even when asked*	*Imprecise or illogical predictions* *made when asked for by teacher*	*Made logical predictions* *spontaneously*

2. During reading

a) The reader read aloud with animation that honored the meaning of the text.

Expressionless reading	*Sometimes showed emphasis* *and drama*	*Consistently showed proper emphasis* *and reflected the dramatic contours of the text*

b) The reader knew the vocabulary in the text.

Did not know many key words	*Knew most key words; used context* *for some but not all others*	*Knew almost all key words and was able* *to use context to figure out others*

c) The reader continued to ask questions and make predictions.

No questions or predictions *even when asked*	*Some questions and predictions when* *asked by the teacher*	*Asked insightful questions and made* *reasonable predictions*

(Continued)

Figure 7.9   Continued.

d) The reader found answers to questions or confirmed predictions.

Seldom	Sometimes, when asked	Consistently

e) The reader was able to make inferences.

Unable to, even when asked	Occasionally, when asked	Consistently, and picked up on subtle nuances

f) The reader monitored comprehension.

Frequently misread text without self-correction	Occasionally misread text and made some self-corrections	Rarely misread text or always self-corrected

3. After reading

a) The reader could retell or summarize the text.

The retelling had major gaps	The retelling was fairly complete	The retelling was complete, and the reader summarized the main points

b) The reader could interpret the text.

Offered limited response or interpretation when asked	Offered responses to aspects of the text	Offered personal response to or interpretation of the main point of the text

Figure 7.10 Student Self-Assessment.

Your name: Today's date:

What you read: Pages:

	Not at all	A little bit	A lot
Before Reading			
I thought about what I knew about the topic of the reading.			
I thought of things I wanted to find out.			
It was a story. I tried to predict what would happen.			
While Reading			
I read with expression to make it sound real.			
I thought about what I was finding out.			
It was a story. I predicted what would happen next.			
I was able to figure out words I didn't know from the words around them.			
I was able to tell what was going on, even when the author didn't come right out and say it.			
After Reading			
I thought back over what I had found out so I would remember it later.			
I thought about what it meant to me.			
I thought about why the author wrote this text and what he or she was trying to say.			

For Review

Reading comprehension is using the knowledge we already have to understand the new information we find in the text. It is an active process in which we quest after new knowledge and make meaning in the process. Responding to literature, too, is an active process in which we bring our own expectations and associations to the words the author has strung along the pages of the text.

Comprehension has several components: knowing the vocabulary of a text and being able to follow the text's structure, visualizing it, making predictions about it, summarizing its meaning, getting the main ideas in it, making inferences within it, interpreting it, arguing with it, and monitoring one's comprehension of it.

To encourage students to carry out that activity, there are teaching techniques we can use before, during, and after the reading or during the phases of a lesson we have called anticipation, building knowledge, and consolidation. In the anticipation phase, we remind students to think of what they already know about a topic, raise questions about what they are about to read, and otherwise prepare for reading. In the building knowledge phase, we guide students in using strategies to set expectations and meet them and to clarify meanings. In the consolidation stage, we have a host of methods for having students think back over what they have gained from the reading, respond to it, interpret it, critique it, apply it, and debate it.

In this chapter, we also stressed the importance of assessing students' comprehension. The three general approaches we discussed were observations, self-assessments, and quantitative assessments.

For Your Journal

1. Return to your answers to the anticipation guide that opened this chapter. Look at the items for which your answers remained the same. In your journal, explain how you came to know the answers. Look at the items to which your answers changed, and explain how your thinking has changed.

2. What do you think the main differences are between teaching students to comprehend and respond to fiction and teaching them to do this for informational text?

3. Recall the vignette of Hank da Silva's classroom that began this chapter. He used a combination of strategies for teaching students to read with comprehension. Think of a class you have taught or might teach. Describe the combination you might choose from the reading comprehension strategies you have seen in this chapter. How would you make them work together?

Taking It to the World

1. When they observed skilled teachers teaching reading comprehension, Michael Pressley and his colleagues (1996) found that they usually taught their students to do the following:

   - Make predictions of what was to come in the text based on their prior knowledge
   - Generate questions about issues in the text
   - Seek clarification about confusing parts
   - Form mental images of what they read
   - Relate what they already knew to what they are reading in the text
   - Make summaries of what they have read

   Alone or with a group of your fellow students, observe three reading lessons in a primary grade school. Do these six activities capture what the teachers are doing by way of helping the children read with comprehension? Do they do other things as well, such as encouraging students to make inferences or debate about what they read?

2. Go to a school, and practice a shared inquiry lesson (see pages 209–210). Make sure you use a text that has a core of mystery to it (many folktales work fine), and prepare your questions carefully according to the criteria given on page 210. Before you put the questions to the children, though, write out your own best answers to your questions. How do the students' answers compare to yours? Are you surprised? If so, what surprises you and why?

3. Using the text you employed in your shared inquiry lesson, try the dramatic activities described on page 212 with your classmates. Then try the activity out in an elementary school. What different insights about the text come to light when you dramatize it rather than discuss it?

New Literacies Connections

1. Online programs are available to teach reading comprehension. Early versions were often criticized for being little more than electronic worksheets. New versions are much more sophisticated. Using a search engine, explore *Kid Biz* and *StarFall*, along with two other computer-based systems. Learn all you can about them. What kinds of texts do they use? How do they match the level of difficulty with the young reader? What is their teaching strategy? That is, what do they do before, during, and after the child reads a passage? What is gained from using such a program? What is sacrificed?

2. Examine the free sites for teaching reading comprehension that are turned in by a search engine when you enter the keywords "Teaching comprehension." Do a quick survey of the six most popular sites. (Those are usually the first ones that come up.)

PEARSON
myeducationlab

Now go to MyEducationLab (**www.myeducationlab.com**), where you can:

- Find learning outcomes for the topics covered in this chapter, along with the national standards that connect to these outcomes.

- Complete Assignments and Activities that can help you more deeply understand the chapter content.

- Engage in Building Teaching Skills and Dispositions exercises, in which you can apply and practice core teaching skills identified in the chapter.

Comprehension: Understanding and Learning with Informational Texts

Anticipation Guide

The following statements will help you begin thinking about the topics covered in this chapter. Answer *true* or *false* in response to each statement. As you read and learn more about the topics mentioned in these statements, think back on your answers. See what interests you and prompts your curiosity toward more understanding.

_____ 1. There has been a big shift from fiction reading to informational reading by adult readers in the United States.

_____ 2. Primary children get too confused with the different formats of nonfiction texts. Instruction in using nonfiction should wait for third grade and above.

_____ 3. Teachers in the United States have changed their teaching practices to show students how to comprehend informational material.

_____ 4. One of the best ways to show students how to read informational text with comprehension is to read an informational text yourself and discuss it with your students.

_____ 5. Having prior knowledge helps students to comprehend, but one kind of prior knowledge is about as useful as another.

_____ 6. Students who have had an extensive introduction to a topic are likely to be more motivated to learn about it than are those with only superficial knowledge.

_____ 7. Just as stories have a "grammar" that readers can follow to understand the story, informational texts have recognizable structures.

_____ 8. Reading strategies for informational texts are the same as those for fiction.

_____ 9. Informational texts have so many different structures that there is little point in teaching students the parts of an informational text.

_____ 10. When it comes to teaching vocabulary, teachers should stress only the words the authors of the text prioritize.

Comprehension: Understanding and Learning with Informational Texts

Comprehending Informational Texts
p. 227

Teachers Guide Instruction
p. 229

Student Engagement
p. 232

External Features of Informational Texts
p. 233

Internal Organization of Informational Texts
p. 238

Active Reading of Informational Text
p. 243

Reading to Learn in a Primary Classroom

Teacher Debbie Gurvitz likes to introduce her first- and second-grade students to informational reading through integrated units of study. In the spring, she develops an expanded science unit that involves real problem-based inquiry. It serves as a way of expanding students' reading skills in nonfiction and of teaching some science standards. Recently, Ms. Gurvitz focused the unit on pond life and the relationship between the quality of the water for animals and the human community. To introduce the unit, she invited a naturalist from the local nature preserve to speak to the students. When the naturalist showed the students some of the animals from the pond, they became fascinated with the mutant frog he included. "Wow, that's weird!" "That doesn't look like the frog I have at home. Who did that to it?" "What happened?" The children's questions came naturally and quickly. Garth, one of the first graders, expressed the feelings of the whole group when he said, "Ms. Gurvitz, we really have a problem!"

Ms. Gurvitz took her lead from the children and helped them to focus their study of the natural environment on the frog problem. They began by framing the problem—exploring what facts and information they already knew and identifying the questions they had. On a large piece of chart paper they made a list of what they knew about frogs. She helped them write questions for research; these also filled a sheet of chart paper and were hung on the wall. As a result of these discussions, she divided the class into smaller groups that searched for information to help

solve the problem. In this case, it was a very real problem. Scientists do not understand why so many frogs in the area are being born with strange-looking body parts. This created an authentic study full of the kinds of ambiguities that are found in most scientific research.

Ms. Gurvitz was careful to make sure she could locate the kinds of reading texts the children could read. She wanted some that would be at an independent level for all the children and some that would be good instructional-level texts for her guided reading groups. After collecting the books, she leveled them to ensure that she could accommodate the whole class with appropriate materials.

In considering the language arts and reading objectives she wanted to address, Ms. Gurvitz focused instruction on helping students find answers to questions they posed. She wanted them to learn to use the table of contents and the index in books to locate the information they needed. She knew this would be a good opportunity for them to learn to make decisions about what sections of a text they would read and to gain control over information searching as contrasted with fictional reading. She also wanted the children to learn to make notes about what information they were collecting so that those notes could guide their reporting. To do this, she made copies of the Amazing Fact Sheet (see Figure 8.1) and put them in a shoe box on the inquiry table so students could take one whenever they wanted to save some interesting or important information.

As she introduced this way of making notes, Ms. Gurvitz used one child as a model. Side by side at the overhead transparency, she and Andrew made a note card of the information he wanted to remember.

"Andrew, what do you want to write?" Ms. Gurvitz asked.

"It says that frogs lay lots of eggs in water," Andrew replied.

Ms. Gurvitz encouraged him, "So, can you write that on your Amazing Fact Sheet?" As Andrew began to write on a transparency, the other children watched. When he tried to write "water," he hesitated.

"What is giving you trouble with that word?" Ms. Gurvitz asked. "Can you find it written somewhere?"

With that nudge, Andrew turned to the book again and located the word; without any further help, he finished his writing. Ms. Gurvitz reminded him to list the book title, the author, and the page that contained the fact on his note. Finished, he then signed the note on the Reporter line.

Ms. Gurvitz praised his efforts: "Good work, Andrew."

She concluded the mini-lesson by reminding the children that when they found interesting information, they should write that on an Amazing Fact Sheet and put it in the Amazing Facts Box on the counter. Each morning, Andrew and other children read their cards during the morning share time and used them to build their knowledge.

To be human is to be a learner. Young children are full of questions, so many that parents and teachers are sometimes amazed by the depth and breadth of children's curiosity. As we grow, we continue to be curious about the world around us and ask questions. To find answers to these questions, we read informational materials—from textbooks like this one to websites, newspapers and magazines, cookbooks, travel guides, biographies, and self-help and diet books. To be successful learners in school, students must learn to read and study about concepts that society considers important. These are generally elaborated on in textbooks and other reference materials. Therefore, it is important for teachers to prioritize helping young readers develop the joy in and ability to read a wide range of materials. They need guidance so they can become confident and flexible readers empowered by the variety of strategies they have developed to navigate the wide range of materials and formats in the informational materials they encounter daily. They also need to learn to study new material and find strategies that will help them retain that material.

Why Does Reading to Learn Matter?

Much of the reading we do is to learn. Schools require students to use textbooks and a wide variety of other resource materials throughout the grades. Unfortunately, too often we just assume that students will develop good strategies for using informational materials and knowing how to prioritize what they need to remember. Most schools also spend little time teaching students how to use text materials effectively for answering their own questions and for creating reports. Yet this kind of reading becomes increasingly important as students progress through the grades. Most content courses still depend heavily on textbooks, but they won't be used well unless teachers show students how to use these resources effectively. Most middle and secondary school teachers also expect students to engage in independent research and to write informational essays and reports. The skills needed to be successful learners can be introduced in the primary grades and developed throughout the grades. (See the Standards and Literacy box.)

What we read outside of school also underscores the importance of knowing how to read and use informational materials. Recent research studies on the reading habits of adults reflect the shift away from fiction to informational reading and nonfiction sources (Smith, 2000). We read newspapers and magazines to find out about the world around us and our favorite activities. We browse the Web to gain in-depth information and alternative points of view. We read self-help books and books on health and fitness because we

---

AMAZING FACT SHEET

An amazing fact about frogs is that

_____

_____

Found in (provide the source of your information)

_____

Written by _____ p. _____

Reporter _____

Figure 8.1
Amazing Fact Sheet.

Standards and Literacy

Content Area Standards

The standards of many states now include expectations that students be able to read and learn from informational texts. Although traditional reading instruction has focused on story reading, a real shift is occurring, and both fiction and informational reading are being highlighted. Standards such as the following are frequently found:

- Use information to form questions.
- Summarize content using text organization.
- Use table of contents.
- Use information presented in simple tables, pictures, and charts.

Standards for teachers also may specifically address the importance of teaching content reading. For example, Illinois now has a reading strategy standard for all content area teachers. Check to see what you will be expected to know and be able to do as a teacher helping students with reading to learn. Then examine the instruction provided to elementary students in your schools. Do students have regular opportunities to engage with informational texts and build their confidence by reading a wide range of materials?

want to improve our health and lifestyle. We read spiritual and religious books to reflect on our beliefs and deepen our quality of living.

As a society, we are shifting from a nation of fiction readers to a people who read a preponderance of **informational texts.** We want to know as much as possible—about ourselves as well as the rest of the world. Publishers recognize this shift in interests and are publishing more and more informational texts, both printed and electronic. The wide range of magazines being published reflects the wide range of reader interests. Just check a magazine stand for the hundreds of specific topics that are available to address particular interests and tastes of readers. The best-seller lists generally have one section for fiction, another for nonfiction, and often a third for self-help books. One of the real transformations in the last decade has been the explosion of materials available for us to read on an enormous range of topics on the Web as well as in more traditional publishing venues.

Knowledge Standards and High-Stakes Assessment

The current focus on knowledge standards and measuring what students learn each year puts pressure on teachers to cover more content. This means that students are asked to read more and remember what they are taught. In this climate of rising expectations, students who have read widely possess the background knowledge that enables them to remember new material and deepen their knowledge schemata. Instead of diminishing, the demands on learners as readers are increasing.

Another implication of the current accountability climate for teachers is that the assessments of students' reading abilities are now balanced between reading for literary purposes and reading to learn. These assessments reflect the fact that for students to be successful as readers throughout schooling and life, they need to read for a variety of purposes from a variety of materials. Reading fiction for pleasure is only one of many forms reading takes. More important for school success across the curriculum is the ability to read informational texts and learn from them (Ogle & Blachowicz, 2001). Standardized tests, state performance assessments, and the current international tests (Donahue et al., 2001; Organization for Economic Cooperation & Development, 2000; Sainsbury, 2001) all incorporate a variety of materials and purposes. Reading for information is as important as reading for literary purposes. Like many state assessments, the new framework for the National Assessment of Educational Progress (NAEP) has an equal proportion of literary and informational items at fourth grade and 55 percent informational items at eighth grade (National Assessment Governing Board, 2008).

Instructional Priorities

Elementary teachers are being challenged to provide more informational reading. Publishers have responded with new core reading programs and have made many short, highly visual informational books available for young readers. These programs make it easier for teachers to focus students' reading in informational materials. Using them also helps children understand the value of learning to read as a key to acquiring new information and a way to unlock new interests. By integrating instruction, teachers can develop both literacy and content learning and improve learning in both areas (Pearson, 2008).

In their planning, responsible teachers provide a broad range of instruction in reading strategies and purposes and make students comfortable negotiating a variety of text types. Because purpose has such a powerful effect on individual reading habits, it is important to provide opportunities for many purposes, from learning new information to performing tasks to recreating experiences and representing them in new ways. Teachers can prioritize the importance of reading to learn by instructing students in how to locate and synthesize information in textbooks as well as the reference materials that are used heavily in schools. This kind of reading ability often determines whether students will be successful throughout their schooling.

Informational reading does not develop automatically and deserves concerted attention by teachers. In an electronic environment where we have access to a world of information, students must learn to use this new source of informational materials as they engage in inquiry and report writing. Reading across texts, comparing authors and ideas, and evaluating materials are important priorities. Students' abilities to read, write, and think critically are important, especially with the range of unedited ideas available on the Internet. Today's elementary and middle school classrooms can be alive with the kinds of experiences that help students develop these skills.

Understanding Comprehension in Informational Texts

Learning from reading is an active, ongoing process that can be described by what we do before, during, and after engagement with a text. Just as we do with reading literature (see Chapter 7), we follow the simple ABCs of reading to learn. We begin by anticipating what we want and need to learn. Then we build knowledge as we read and engage with authors. Finally, we consolidate the ideas with what we previously knew, sometimes modifying those ideas and sometimes expanding on them. This ongoing process is also a recursive one. That is, with each new set of ideas we read, we rethink what we knew, ask new questions and set new purposes, and build on the ideas that are freshly ours. Some essential aspects that undergird active reading to learn include the following:

- Assessing schemata or prior knowledge
- Assuming a metacognitive orientation
- Setting one's own purposes and asking questions
- Actively seeking information and making notes so that it can be retained for connecting and organizing ideas
- Forming interpretations of what is read

- Consolidating new information and ideas
- Analyzing and evaluating the sources and adequacy of information
- Creating a synthesis and representation of the learning that can be shared
- Reaching conclusions about and finding applications of what has been learned

As students develop their own control over reading to learn, all of these aspects of the process need attention. How teachers introduce learning tasks to students and give students instructional tools to use as they learn will determine to a great degree students' success at becoming learners. Planning carefully across each year, beginning with initial assessment of what students already know and can do and then structuring good teaching and guided practice activities will lead both teachers and students to success.

The Importance of Background Knowledge

Reading is always an active, constructive process during which students need to activate what they know to make sense of text. As we noted in Chapter 7, readers comprehend by having the details in the material they are reading lead them to evoke relevant knowledge **schemata.** Then they use these schemata to give meaning to the details and, ideally, to understand the meaning of the whole passage. There are at least four kinds of background knowledge that readers need in order to comprehend well. The first is knowledge of the vocabulary. The second is knowledge of text structure. The third and fourth deal with content knowledge, both topical and principled.

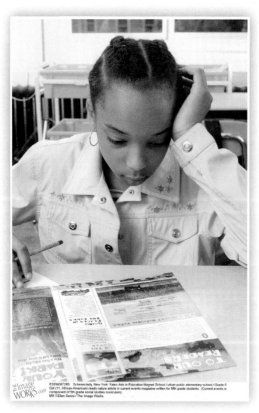

The layout of a book or magazine can either encourage or impede the understanding of the content. What would the design of a textbook need to look like to be attractive to middle school students? (Ellen B. Senisi/The Image Works)

VOCABULARY.   One of the most important tools in understanding content is having a grasp of how the key terms are used in a specific content. Vocabulary represents the knowledge of words and their meanings. In reading, the issue of vocabulary knowledge ranges between word recognition and comprehension. In word recognition, children may labor to recognize a word in print, but once they recognize it, they may or may not know the spoken word and its meaning. Obviously, a reader must know the meanings of most of the words in a text to read it successfully.

KNOWLEDGE OF TEXT STRUCTURE.   The structure of a text is a little like the grammar of a sentence. Because you understand the grammar of a sentence such as "The man bit the dog," you know who was bitten and who did the biting. In the same fashion, if you understand the structures of stories, you know how to follow a plot. If you can understand the structure of explanations, you know how to find the questions and get the answers to them. If you understand the structure of persuasive writing, you know how to spot the claim and weigh the support for it (Goldman & Rakestraw, 2000). The more you know about the way informational articles and texts are generally organized, the more you will be able to predict and read actively. This knowledge of structure also helps you retain what you read, because you can organize the ideas into major categories for memory.

TOPICAL CONTENT KNOWLEDGE.   The term **topical content knowledge** represents a fairly shallow level of knowledge, consisting of little more than some passing familiarity with the subject of the reading. For example, assume that while reading a little girl is faced with a scientific passage about ducks. If she has seen a Donald Duck cartoon (and realizes that the character of Donald is based loosely on a real duck), she will have some topical knowledge about ducks. She will realize ducks have beaks, two wings, and two webbed feet and that they make quacking sounds. This amount of knowledge will not help much when reading a scientific text about ducks, but at least it will help her picture what is being talked about.

PRINCIPLED CONTENT KNOWLEDGE.   In contrast to topical content knowledge, **principled content knowledge** is knowledge of a deeper kind. It consists of familiarity with the topic as well as an understanding of its parts, its causes and effects, and other issues related to it (Gelman & Greeno, 1989). For example, readers who have learned about geese and know something about the lives of migratory aquatic birds will have principled knowledge with which to understand a scientific passage about ducks. Readers with principled knowledge are better prepared to understand challenging passages than readers who have only topical knowledge. Their curiosity is likely to be deeper, and their expectations will conform more closely to the unfolding presentation of information in the text. The reader with topical knowledge, by contrast, might recognize isolated parts of the information in the text but will be less prepared to make sense of the flow of information or the more important ideas in the text.

The Teacher's Role in Guiding Instruction

The choices teachers make in determining instructional focus and the kind of guidance they provide greatly influence the way students think as they read and make a difference in the kinds of knowledge students gain about the subject matter in the curriculum. Too often, content reading becomes frustrating for both students and teachers. To prevent this, teachers need to take care to focus instructional time on the most important aspects of comprehension development. As we already noted, a key is to ensure that students have an understanding of how the content or text they are reading is organized. This framework provides a structure within which students can distinguish key ideas from those of lesser importance. During instruction, teachers have several important tasks. These include modeling and guiding engagement with text, teaching skills and strategies, eliciting students' own interests and motivation, and providing adequate time for students to explore ideas and concepts in depth.

DEVELOPING PRINCIPLED KNOWLEDGE.   The kinds of knowledge students gain about the subject matter in the curriculum is very important. In reading to learn, the content-specific information needs attention, something that is not a priority when reading fiction. A key to comprehending a text is having the ability to link ideas presented within and across sentences to create a sense of a whole text. Teachers influence students' knowledge formation in two important ways: by the questions they ask and by the depth of study they encourage with their students.

Anticipation Guide

The Questions Teachers Ask.   The ideas to which you call children's attention, by means of your questions or comments, influence the course of the children's thinking about what they read and study. You can direct students' attention toward important ideas or trivial ones. When reading a story, it makes a difference whether you dwell on minor details or ask questions that call attention to the deep structural elements of the story: the character's problem, goal, conflicts, and solutions to problems or the author's message or theme in the story. When reading informational text, it matters whether you call attention to minor details or to important ideas such as chronological development, cause and effect, or hierarchical relationships between ideas.

The Depth to Which Teachers Lead Children to Study a Topic.   You can encourage children to gain deeper knowledge about topics by staying with subjects for more than brief periods. You also can enhance children's understanding by looking at topics through many different disciplines. For example, look at a historical phenomenon such as immigration through fictional works in addition to the social studies text. By seeing phenomena through the eyes of fictional participants, students have more possibility of connecting with, visualizing, and interpreting the concept. Lengthy discussions, especially those that make connections between the subject of study and the children's own experience, also make it more likely that children will form deep, principled knowledge about a subject (see Allington & Johnston, 2002).

SKILLS AND STRATEGIES.   In addition to some background knowledge with which to understand text, readers need skills and strategies. **Skills** are processes that readers use habitually. **Strategies** are the processes by which they use their skills under conscious control. Teachers need to know what skills and strategies students possess and consciously develop a strong repertoire in all students.

When children first learn to read, they may be taught to perform comprehension activities consciously as reading strategies. For example, when they come across a word they do not know, the teacher might urge them to read to the end of the line to get a sense of the meaning of the sentence, then go back and guess the unknown word. This strategy is known as the *reading ahead/reread activity*. Later on—possibly much later on and after continued support from the teacher—when the readers habitually use the context to figure out unknown words, the behavior has become a skill.

When students are working with difficult material, however, or when they want to be especially careful in their reading, skilled readers often employ some reading strategies consciously (Pressley & Afflerbach, 1995). For example, even when their reading skills are adequate for comprehending a reading in a social studies text, readers might consciously choose to apply the strategy of summarizing and rehearsing main ideas to remember them for a discussion the next day.

INTEREST AND MOTIVATION.   Performing acts of comprehension takes some effort, and exerting effort takes will. No wonder children are more likely to take the trouble to do what they need to do to understand what they read when the topic is interesting to them. This fact, although not always honored in school curriculum offerings, has been recognized for the better part of a century (Beane, 2002; Dewey, 1913; Guthrie & Davis, 2003). But readers may be interested in a topic in different ways, and these differences have consequences. In the chapter-opening vignette, as Ms. Gurvitz began her unit on the pond, she had a naturalist speak with the children and show them samples of the frogs that were deformed. This piqued their interest. Readers might be interested in a topic because it has been presented in an engaging way—with exciting illustrations or dramatic writing and explanation points. Or they might be interested because they have some reason to find out more about a topic and they want to know more about the line of inquiry the text is following. For example, because you want to know how to help your present or future students read with comprehension, you might find this textbook of particular interest. You likely don't need movie poster-like illustrations to draw you into the ideas presented here. If you pick up the Sunday magazine in your newspaper, however, it might take an interesting picture with a curiosity-provoking caption to get you interested in reading about something that is new to you.

These individual **motivations** for learning correspond to the kinds of prior knowledge readers have about a topic. Readers who have principled knowledge about a topic tend to be interested in adding to and deepening that knowledge, whereas readers with shallower, topical knowledge might not be motivated automatically to learn more about something through reading. Research has shown (Alexander, 1998) that readers with these different kinds of background knowledge notice different things in a text. Readers with only topical knowledge might focus on flashy or exotic details to the exclusion of main ideas and arguments, whereas those with principled knowledge might do just the opposite.

THE "MATTHEW EFFECT": ASPECTS OF COMPREHENSION ARE INTERRELATED.   What we have just considered as separate aspects of comprehension—prior knowledge, strategies and skills, and interest—are in fact interrelated. Although it is true, as Duffy and Roehler (1989) and others have shown, that children can profit from being taught to carry out comprehension strategies, it is also true that reading comprehension develops as a conglomerate of achievements (Alexander et al., 1994). For example, engaging prior knowledge can be helped along by teaching; however, for this teaching to be successful, children must have some prior knowledge of the topic to call on. Moreover, children are more likely to have deep enough interests in the topic to use the strategies of applying prior knowledge, making predictions, arguing with the text, or finding main ideas, unless their prior knowledge is deep and principled. To carry this point further, if their prior knowledge about a topic is deep and principled, then their interest in the topic will also extend below the surface to main ideas and structures of argument.

The process is cyclic and is an example of what researcher Keith Stanovich (1986) called the "Matthew effect" in reading. If young readers have deep and principled knowledge, they will have deep interest; if they have deep interest, they will use thoroughgoing strategies of comprehension; and if they use thoroughgoing strategies, they will gain more principled knowledge (see Figure 8.2). The cycle works the other way, too. A reader might lack deep knowledge, not habitually use thoroughgoing reading strategies, or have only superficial interest in the topics being read. These factors may interact to prevent satisfactory comprehension. The best teaching for comprehension, then, includes attention to all these aspects:

- Creating a learning environment in which students can become immersed in a topic over time and explore it deeply
- Guiding students' attention to the way the texts they read are organized
- Helping students develop principled knowledge by encouraging them to consider ideas deeply, and pointing them toward the main ideas and the underlying structures and issues
- Teaching thoroughgoing, powerful strategies for comprehending and remembering and then supporting and reinforcing these strategies until they become habituated into skills
- Engaging children in deep discussions of what they read and getting them to think about, write about, and respond to what they read so they will understand issues deeply and extend their curiosity to other meaningful topics in their world

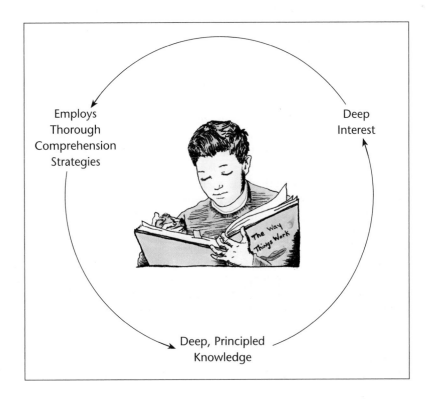

Figure 8.2

The Matthew Effect in Reading Comprehension.

- Focusing their attention on the vocabulary of the topic or area so they develop a more precise way of thinking and differentiating ideas
- Encouraging students' questions and taking their inquiry seriously, weaving their deep-seated interests into the very fabric of the school day

Student Engagement

Although the teacher's role in developing a thoughtful class is critical, students play equally important roles as learners. Right from the beginning of the school year, teachers need to take time to observe how students approach learning. How involved and aware are students of what learning entails? They need to be active—and interactive—if they are going to be successful learners. People learn best when they do so strategically. That means taking charge of their own reading with a clear purpose. Just as in reading fiction (see Chapter 7), students need to be actively engaged while reading and learning from nonfiction and other content materials. Because content material is usually dense with ideas to be learned, the following strategies are especially important.

Think-Pair-Share

ANTICIPATING.   Students need to anticipate—to ask what they want to learn from the reading. They do this by first assessing what they know and what the task demands are and what needs to be accomplished. For young students, this initial orientation is modeled in the K-W-L framework discussed later in this chapter. As students begin their engagement with a new topic, watch them and discuss with them how they begin. Do they skim through the material and activate what they know and make connections with the text? Do they look closely at diagrams or pictures and think about their meaning?

Once students have assessed their starting point in learning, they then need to develop a plan for how to proceed in order to accomplish their goals. This includes knowing that there are options for how to proceed. Students too often think that all they can do is read and then reread. Rather, they need to know they can use a variety of tools to guide their acquisition of knowledge. They are going to want to make notes when they encounter new information that is important or use some form of marginal notation if they can keep the materials. Stick-on notes serve wonderful purposes in helping students keep track of what they want to learn. These notes can be grouped later to chunk information in a way that will give the student a more coherent sense of what is to be learned. Some students learn best when they can create a graphic network of ideas or draw diagrams of what they learn. Being active during the process of learning is essential. It takes little time to check whether students are using active strategies when they read informational material that is full of important concepts and main ideas. (Several strategies that support students' active engagement are discussed later in the chapter.)

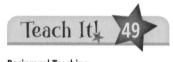

Reciprocal Teaching

BUILDING KNOWLEDGE.   Students build knowledge as they deal with the ideas they are reading about. That means monitoring what they are thinking and learning, asking questions as they go, and creating summaries of ideas for themselves. Some students like to think aloud, others make notes in the margin or on sheets of paper, some prefer drawing key ideas to represent the text's main ideas, and some like to share with another person what they are getting out of a text as they read. Teachers need to model each of these approaches to building new learning. Asking students to put stick-on notes in their text material as they read is an easy diagnostic of how they attend to important elements of these texts. As you expand their options for engaged reading and help them practice these strategies frequently, your students will become better equipped to make decisions about which strategies work best for them in particular situations.

Graphic Organizers

CONSOLIDATING WHAT THEY LEARN.   As students continue to build their knowledge and understanding as a result of reading, they also consolidate what they are learning. That means going back and thinking again about how the ideas fit together and what they mean. Students can create a new graphic representation of what they have learned. They might write an outline and then elaborate on it in a summary, or they might want to talk to someone about the ideas they have gained. If students are using a textbook or a guide from a teacher, they can return to the questions or talk about the main objectives. If students are going to retain important ideas, they need to do something actively with them—by summarizing or extending what the authors have presented. Most elementary students need sustained teacher guidance and support to develop the habit of rehearsing what they are learning. Several graphic organizers discussed later in this chapter can help students to organize their thinking and provide good visual reviews of content. If they transform the ideas they are learning into a new form, students have a greater chance of remembering them. Simply asking the question "What did that mean to me?" helps students to stay active metacognitively. Strategies for working together to read, question, and reflect can be used with even the youngest students, who can learn to pair and ask each other what they have learned (Pressley, 2002).

Finally, good readers engage in evaluation of both the materials they read and their accomplishment. If the text seems unclear or lacking in information, they might decide to read other sources of information to clarify ideas or to confirm accuracy and currency. Good readers also assess the achievement of their own purposes. Returning to their questions or categories that were unclear, good readers make sure they understand and have met their own purposes. They know that learning takes effort. Those who are not confident learners often feel disadvantaged when there are intense content expectations. You can help them to realize that they can learn new material, but it is a process that takes time and active involvement on their parts. It is essential to give insecure learners and second-language learners models of process learning and time to rehearse and clarify ideas. They need to understand that reading a text once is never enough if the material is new and important. Studies of effective fourth-grade teachers (Allington & Johnston, 2002) revealed that they often help students to engage in rehearsing the same materials many times as a tool to their learning. Regularly modeling and reinforcing a process of anticipating, building knowledge, and consolidating learning will create active, confident readers (Pressley et al., 1998).

The Nature of Informational Texts

Reading to learn is linked generally to reading informational materials, not pieces of fiction or poetry. Successful reading for the sake of learning requires readers to develop specific strategies to use magazines, trade books, newspapers, primary documents, and Internet sites. For example, readers of informational texts will notice that they don't have to start on the first page and read to the end of the material. Rather, by using the table of contents and index, they can find a pertinent section without reading the whole text. Or they might be able to skip parts that are less essential to their purposes. The first thing they might observe about informational material is that it is organized differently from fiction both internally and externally.

Developing Familiarity with External Features of Informational Texts

One of the first things we notice when we pick up nonfiction or informational materials is that they generally have a format different from fiction, with many external aids to help readers negotiate them. These aids include the following:

Table of contents

Chapters

Headings and subheadings

Illustrations (e.g., maps, graphs, diagrams, pictures, cartoons)

Captions

Index

Vocabulary noted in italics or other graphic ways

Glossary of terms

References

In surveying the features of books, we note that in addition to a table of contents, these books generally include a glossary and index. The chapter titles are worth some attention because they are often key indicators of how the author has organized the information. Within each chapter, there is likely to be a further breakdown of information with headings and subheadings designed to guide our reading to important content or main ideas. Many books and articles also highlight key vocabulary with italic or boldface type or in marginal notes that provide explanations of the terms. A well-organized informational piece includes several of these external features that help us locate the part of the text we want to read when we have particular questions we want answered. In addition, because timely, accurate information is important, readers need to be aware of both the copyright date and the author's qualifications.

Books for very young readers are just now becoming more complete, so looking for chapter divisions is important before books are selected for primary students. Check to see whether the pages are numbered because it is hard to locate and return to information without some pagination. As you help children use informational books, be sure you have high-quality books available for them. Sometimes the color photographs are stunning, but the rest of the important book features are inadequate or missing.

Some books now display graphics in a wide variety of places on the pages and often on a two-page spread. The captions are often placed variously, too. Sometimes the captions are beneath the picture; at other times, they are beside or even above the illustrated material. Only by carefully studying the individual pages and mapping the positions of text, graphics, and captions can their relationships be determined. It is important to share with the children that process of exploration and what readers must learn about the text layout. Without support from teachers, young readers can overlook much of the richness of these new informational texts. When you introduce a new informational text or textbook, it is useful to do a picture and visual walk through the text. Each new text deserves attention because there are so many different formats and organization is highlighted in so many ways.

Watch the video included in the activity "Previewing Nonfiction Features and Structures" to see a teacher previewing text structure with her students. Reflect on the lesson by answering the questions following the video. (To find this activity, go to the topic *Comprehension* in MyEducationLab and click on Assignments and Activities.)

FOCUS STUDENTS' ATTENTION ON FEATURES. As a way to reinforce the special nature of informational books, you could have students complete a nonfiction book report using the checklist shown in Figure 8.3. The book report might ask students to tell what they liked, what they learned, and what would make the book better. When their attention is drawn to these features of the text, students begin to use them more regularly and think of them as resources (adapted from D. Gurvitz).

Intermediate-grade teachers also can have children preview expository texts they are using both as textbooks and as other resource materials. At the beginning of the year, it is always good to refresh students' use of all the ways information is available. Reading aloud to students from magazines and books and consciously thinking aloud provides further opportunity to focus their attention on illustrations, captions, and other presentations of information. Viewing a transparency of the first one or two pages in a chapter or article with the class lets you talk with the students about what they do when they navigate a page of informational text. In fact, informational texts are similar to the computer programs with which many students spend a great deal of leisure time. Students can have fun exploring the similarities and differences in materials presented in these two formats. After such a comparison, encourage students to add diagrams and other visuals or links from their textbooks to other sources. They can become active in making materials more accessible. Rather than feeling overwhelmed by texts, students need to develop confidence in using texts and in going beyond single texts when these are not clear.

Figure 8.3 Nonfiction Book Checklist.

Title _____	
Author _____	
Nonfiction Book Checklist	Something I liked about this book:
_____ 1. Table of Contents	
_____ 2. Index	
_____ 3. Photographs	
_____ 4. Realistic, accurate illustrations	
_____ 5. Maps	
_____ 6. Diagrams	
_____ 7. Captions—bold lettering	Something I learned from this book:
_____ 8. Glossary—words and definitions	
_____ 9. Page numbers	
_____ 10. Other	

Predict Tables of Contents. Intermediate-grade students should begin to anticipate how informative expository material is organized. By third grade, most students should be able to predict what might be in the table of contents of an animal book (e.g., description, habitat, food, family). Before studying regions of the earth in fourth grade, some students should be able to identify possible topics that will reoccur with each region studied (e.g., plants, animals, geography, human life). Fifth graders need to know that biographies have some common topics that are used to organize information (e.g., early life, education, hardships, accomplishments). One way to assess students' awareness of these expert ways of organizing content information and then using it to prepare for reading and learning is to have them create a possible table of contents alone or with a partner. In this way, teachers can help students to think more deeply and to begin to develop principled knowledge (see the Teach It! box).

Create Chapter Graphic Organizers. At the middle-grade level, some teachers have students identify and use the external structure of chapters in textbooks and magazines to make notes. They skim through the chapter and create a graphic organizer or map of the chapter with the title in the center and each of the main headings on one spoke of their spider map (see Figure 8.4). This graphic organizer is then used while students read to help them understand how the information is related. This mapping of the text can also be used as an interactive guide for reading. The students can brainstorm what they know about each section before reading; write those ideas on the map; highlight the areas that are least familiar and that will require slower reading, note making, and possible rereading; and then make notes on their map of new information as they read. This active engagement helps students to focus and retain information as they read.

Jigsaw Text Sections. Another strategy teachers employ to help students utilize the external structure of articles and chapters is to have a chapter read in cooperative fashion using a type of "jigsaw" cooperative learning strategy. The class first previews the text and identifies the major sections, which the teacher writes on the board. Then the class is divided

Figure 8.4

A Chapter Graphic Organizer.

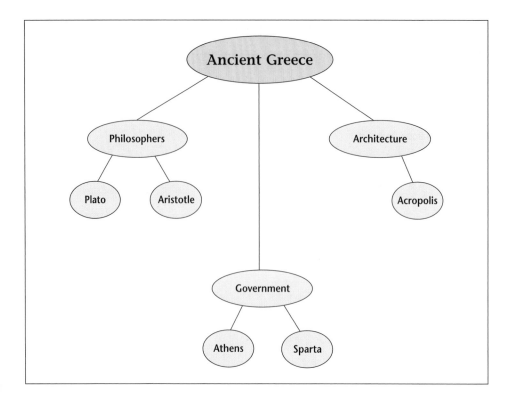

into teams, with one team assigned to each major section. Each team of students reads and creates a visual report of the key ideas of their one section of the text. Because many of the informational chapters and articles have such a heavy load of information, asking students to learn just one section from reading makes it manageable. Each group then reports on their section. Serving as "teachers" for the rest of the class both enhances the students' engagement in reading and creates a shared environment for learning.

Teach It!

Refer to the Teach It! appendix at the end of the book for further activities you can use to reinforce concepts discussed in this chapter.

Using the Table of Contents to Predict

There are many ways to help students become familiar with the structure and organization of informational materials. One of the easiest is to predict what content a book might contain and then check the table of contents to see how the authors have organized the text. For example, before beginning an oral reading of a book on polar bears, a first-grade teacher asked her students what they thought they might learn as they listened to her read this interesting book. One eager boy blurted out, "How they fish for their food!" Soon other children volunteered their ideas: why they are white, how they take care of their babies, and more. The teacher praised the children for their ideas and then turned to the table of contents of the book. She ran her finger down the list of chapters or sections and said, "Um, yes, the book begins with 'An Arctic Home'—that must tell about where they live. 'A Fight for Food'—that must tell us about how they get their food." In this way she modeled for the students the way they can

begin to think like experts—and build the foundation for principled knowledge of polar bears.

With older students, skimming through the headings of an article or chapter can provide an overview of the authors' organization. When these reader aids do not indicate the text structure, students can do a quick read and use stick-on notes to label the text parts as they occur. Then students can create a graphic organizer to guide their reading of the material. Many teachers have found that having students learn to create graphic organizers of informational texts (articles, chapters, or books) provides a good road map for reading materials that might seem so dense that readers are in danger of getting lost in details.

Refer to your Teach It! booklet for further activities you can use to reinforce concepts discussed in this chapter.

USE VISUAL AND GRAPHIC INFORMATION. Information presented visually in pictures, diagrams, and graphics is also critical in many informational texts. Think of an informational book you have recently read or a children's book such as *My Season with Penguins* (Webb, 2000) with its maps, drawings, and journal format. Today, good informational books, textbooks, and magazines use more pictures and visuals to enhance engagement and help readers understand the concepts than ever before. Much of the information, in fact, is often presented in the pictures, graphs, diagrams, maps, cartoons, and their captions. This visual information is often essential to understanding the content. Teachers need to help students read this information and integrate it into the rest of the narrative textual content.

There are several ways in which you can guide students' use of these texts to learn. First, you need to assess how students attend to pages of busy text. Informally ask students individually to describe how they read a two-page spread in a book or magazine. As they share, make notes of their approaches. Where do they start? Do they read the visually presented information? When do they read it? Do they integrate the visuals and the running text? Do they read captions on graphs and pictures? Are they aware of how they approach reading when the materials are presented in a variety of formats? Do they integrate these different sources in notes they make or in summaries they create?

Questions such as these can help you to assess students' engagement with text materials. From this assessment, you can develop your instructional focus. A good starting point is modeling how to approach busy text by doing think-alouds, such as the following, with groups of students. Make a transparency of one or two pages of text. Using an overhead projector, demonstrate how you survey the page, noting the different layout of information and graphics and raising questions that are stimulated by the text. Start by looking at the title of the chapter or section and note the way the sections are marked—with boldface print or words in capital letters, for example. Then focus on the visuals, such as pictures, diagrams, or notes in the margins. You might ask, "Why did the author/s use this cartoon? What is its role in this section? Let's see, the caption says . . . Oh, yes, I bet it is an example of . . ." You can also cover the text on the transparency and ask students to survey the graphic information. From this survey, ask them to predict what content they think is being highlighted and what questions they think will be answered on the next page or two. In this way, the importance of using the visually presented material may become clearer to them. In fact, sometimes this kind of preview can reduce the actual reading time considerably.

When you take time to think aloud about how to approach informational texts, students begin to think metacognitively about their own approaches to texts. Adults use many of these strategies automatically when appropriate. Students, by contrast, often need to hear another person's thinking before they understand how active they need to be as readers.

UNDERSTANDING THE ORGANIZATION OF INTERNET SITES. Internet websites have an external structure just as informational print texts do. The organization is different from print but has some of the same elements. A key to deciding if a site is worth reading is knowing who has created the website. This information is located on the initial page of each site and is required by law. It may be under the heading, "About Us" or "Home." This is an important first step in surveying a website. It is like looking for the author, illustrator, and publisher of a book. Additional information about the site can often be found in the section on Sponsors and in links that are provided. Just as students may find it useful to draw the layout of a page of a printed textbook, they also can learn a great deal about website layout by sketching the various sections on two or three web pages and then comparing them. See Figure 8.5 below for a general frame for this evaluation.

Evaluating Sites. Websites are often selected by teachers or through adult supervision. However, it is also good to teach students how to identify good websites themselves. A step that precedes going to the website itself often comes as students use a search engine (AolKIDS, Yahooligans, AwesomeLibrary, etc.) to locate possible sources online. The URLs tell a great deal about the site authors and can help in the selection of a good website. Sites that are government- or university-sponsored are generally more reliable than

myeducation**lab**
The Power of Classroom Practice
www.myeducationlab.com

Watch the video included in the activity "Using Think-Aloud to Model Effective Reading Comprehension" and see a teacher modeling reading informational text for her students. Reflect on the lesson by answering the questions following the video. (To find this activity, go to the topic *Comprehension* in MyEducationLab and click on Assignments and Activities.)

Figure 8.5

Analyzing Internet Sites.

Home	About Us	Connect	How to ...	Programs

those that come with a ".com" address. Teachers can help students in site selection by writing a sample set of URLs on the board as students begin the study of a particular topic where they will use online sources. For example, as they began researching information about the building of the Statue of Liberty, the teacher wrote these URLs on the board and asked students which ones they thought would provide the best, most reliable information:

1. www.nps.gov/Elis (National Parks Service)
2. www.nyctrip.com (travel company with tours to the site)
3. www.statueofliberty.org (private organization supporting the statue)
4. www.wikipedia.org
5. www.NYDN.com (*New York Daily News*, with stories written by subscribers)

In the discussion that followed, students thought about the impact of site sponsors and promoters on the information presented; these insights helped the class become more critically aware of how to look for information. The teacher followed up this initial part of the search for sites by showing students how they could also cross-check information by using encyclopedias that are online or checking print sources and textbooks that are edited before being made public.

Once a few websites are selected, students need to learn to navigate the sites themselves. The organization of web pages varies considerably and the best formats keep evolving. Some have key categories and options listed in ways that make them easy to use; others can be cluttered and take several steps to navigate. Taking the time to walk through website structure using an LCD projector and to "think aloud" about how to scan the various parts of the visual layout can be very helpful to young users. Research by Leu and others (2007) indicates that all too often, students don't explore websites in enough depth to make the most of the resources that are available. Knowing how material is organized and which categories are the most general are important keys to using websites. So, too, is interpreting the visually presented information. Some of the same attention to how students scan and interpret pictures and visuals in texts can be used as they look at web pages.

Developing Understanding of Internal Organization

Another key to reading and learning from materials written to inform is becoming familiar with the way the writer has organized the ideas. As readers of narrative stories, we have learned—often first by listening to stories our parents read to us—that fiction has a predictable pattern. We read to find out who the characters are, what problem they encounter, and how they go about resolving it. Then we savor their victory at the end. No similar single pattern characterizes informational texts. They are written with different internal organization patterns. The most common ways of organizing ideas include the following:

Description (main ideas and details)

Compare/contrast

Problem/solution

Cause/effect

Sequence of events

These varying patterns can make predicting and organizing ideas more difficult for novice readers; therefore, it is all the more important that teachers provide guidance so students can learn to identify these internal structures. As they do, their ability to write informational pieces and reports more effectively also will improve. Here again, graphic organizers can help students recognize the underlying organization of texts. Figure 8.6 shows some simple models.

COMPARE TEXTS.   One way to introduce internal patterns of texts is by collecting several books on the same topic and guiding students to compare their internal structures. By introducing the reading of the book in this way, you engage the students to think in terms of the big picture about what an author is trying to accomplish in a text. An easy way to create varieties of texts is to download articles from online encyclopedias and Internet articles and compare their organization. This can be a starting place for contrasting and comparing longer articles and books (see the Being a Professional Reading Teacher box on page 241).

WRITE TEXTS.   A good way to help students apply their knowledge of text organization is to have them write their own books using the structure of one they have studied. For example, during a unit on insects, third-grade students used Brown's (1949) *The Important Book* as a model for their writing. Each student wrote about his or her chosen insect and used the book structure as a guide. They took the text predictable pattern,

The important thing about _____ is that _____. They have _____, _____, and _____, but the important thing about _____ is _____,

and wrote about insects. One child had studied bees and wrote, "The important thing about a bee is that it stings. It is true that a bee has two pairs of wings and collects honey, but the important thing about a bee is that it STINGS!" Each child used this same pattern to write about his or her insect and the teacher then collected the pieces into a class book, *Important Insects.* This experience helped students focus their attention on simple, predictable text structures. Later the teacher introduced other structures used by authors of informational books they were reading. With this concrete experience in writing, the students were more attuned to organization and the structure of ideas.

Being a Professional Reading Teacher

Collecting Books for Reading Aloud

Teachers model good reading for their students. One way you can prepare for your role is to build a collection of texts that you can read to your students. You probably remember some special books that teachers read to you. You may also remember teachers who read aloud to you from the newspaper or current magazines. Begin collecting informational materials you can share with your students. Find good biographies and autobiographies that you can use to entice students into reading about real people and events. (For example, Barak Obama has written a very accessible autobiography, *Dreams from My Father: A Story of Race and Inheritance.*) Locate books about special holidays like the Mexican Day of the Dead, the Muslim religious month of Ramadan, and the American holidays of Halloween and Fourth of July. With increasingly diverse student populations in our schools, all students can learn about important traditions. These make good read-aloud texts.

If you read magazines like *National Geographic* and the *Smithsonian,* start making a file of good articles that you can read to students to entice them into expanding their own interests. As you visit schools, talk with teachers about the magazines they bring in to share with their students and start making a list of resources that can deepen what you can bring to your future students. Reading aloud to students from informational texts is an important part of building students' familiarity with these resources and expanding their interests.

Figure 8.6   Graphic Organizer Models.

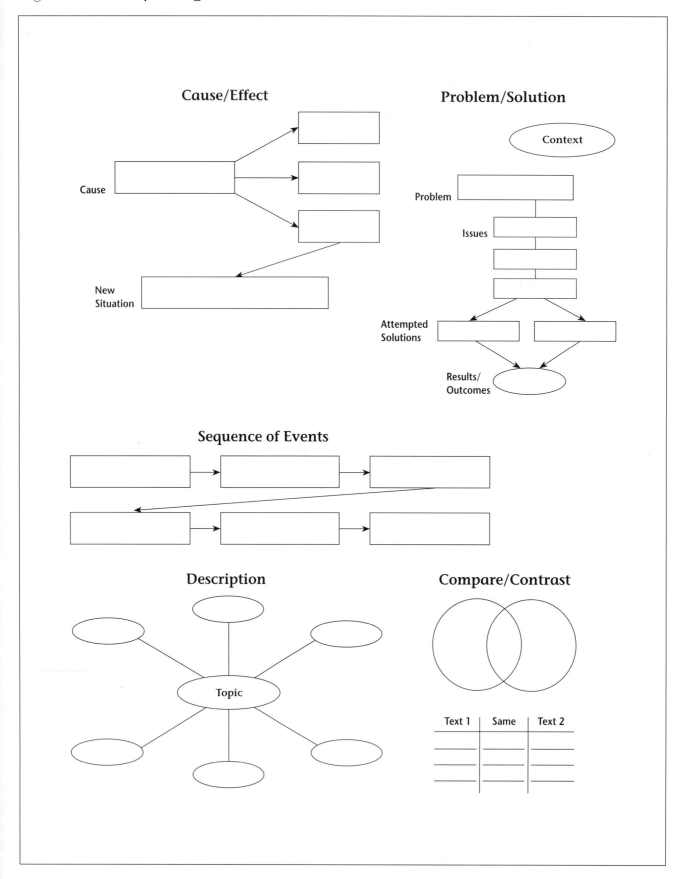

ATTEND TO VOCABULARY AND CONTENT-SPECIFIC TERMINOLOGY. A key to learning content material is to give attention to vocabulary that conveys key concepts. Again, the differences between reading for one's own purposes and reading to learn are dramatic. When one reads for oneself, unfamiliar vocabulary can be ignored. In fact, good readers attend only to information that they know is helpful in comprehending. As a result, they skip unfamiliar terms. In reading to learn, however, this practice can hinder comprehension. The unfamiliar terms are often exactly what the reader needs to attend to. Therefore, you need to help students develop the habit of attending to key terms that are content carriers. There are three important components to vocabulary learning in content materials:

Teach It! 23

Connect Two

- Words the authors prioritize (e.g., with boldface, italics, marginal definitions, or illustrations)
- Teacher-highlighted key new terms
- Students' own monitoring of what words are new and need to be learned

The first place to start in attending to vocabulary is by noting what the authors have already indicated as important. Without teacher guidance, students often overlook these aids. Because authors often assist readers by highlighting these terms, helping students to preview material to find these indicated words can be a great support to later reading and learning.

Teachers can help students note key words, too, by creating a list of key terms and then giving students some activities to focus their attention on these terms. One easy way to do this is to ask students to connect two (or three) of the terms and create new sentences using them (see Chapter 6 for an example of this activity). Even if the students do not know much about the words, they can have fun anticipating what they mean. Working with partners to create new sentences gives children a chance to use the words orally, too, thus increasing their awareness of the words both visually and orally. A more sophisticated activity is to ask students to chunk new words into categories and then label the groups and justify them to the class. The children now are attuned to these words and will definitely notice them as they read. (See the Differentiated Instruction box for ideas to use with English language learners.)

myeducationlab
The Power of Classroom Practice
www.myeducationlab.com

Watch the video included in the activity "Intentional Vocabulary Instruction" to hear educators discuss the importance of learning new words in context. Reflect on the video by answering the questions that follow. (To find this activity, go to the topic *Reading and Writing in the Content Areas* in MyEducationLab and click on Assignments and Activities.)

Being a Professional Reading Teacher

Develop Interest in Informational Reading

As children develop their abilities to process information through reading, expository text becomes a very important source. What are the major differences between processing expository text and processing narrative text? What strategies are most effective?

Reading Comprehension in Expository Text

- Why is background knowledge such an important factor when students are reading informational text? How can we tap that knowledge before and during reading?

- How are vocabulary and text structure factors in understanding expository text?

- Name some effective strategies for reading informational text. Compare and contrast them with strategies for reading narrative text.

Text Features

What text features do authors of expository text use? How can they be useful to students reading this textbook? How would the appearance of this textbook change without them?

Reading Comprehension: Understanding and Learning with Informational Texts

SIOP®
Sheltered
Instruction
Observation
Protocol®

Many students who speak languages other than English in their homes do very well with conversational English, and teachers may be unaware of the need to provide specific instruction when it comes to the academic vocabulary needed for content area reading and learning. Yet this is an area deserving particular attention. Research studies have highlighted the fact that there is a great difference between conversational English and academic English competence. Teachers can do a lot to help English language learners be successful in this area of academic learning by focusing on vocabulary development.

Begin by assessing students' depth of understanding of key academic terms. For example, if the unit in social studies is about the westward movement of European pioneers across the continent, then terms like *pioneer, covered wagon, wagon train, trails, obstacles,* and *hardships* will probably be needed. These are terms that students would not encounter in normal conversational contexts. They are academic terms needed for this particular unit of study. In a similar way, as a unit in science on light is initiated, teachers highlight terms that will be used and check to see if academic terms like *opaque, translucent, transparent, reflection,* and *refraction* are familiar to students. Because these are words not used in

regular conversational English, they need to be highlighted and taught specifically.

It is often helpful to English language learners to make a list of key terms and then compare them with the same terms in their home language. Because there are many Latin-based cognates used in English, this can make the learning task much easier. For example, the science terms can be listed on one side and the Spanish terms on the other.

Opaque	opaco/a
Reflection	reflexión
Refraction	refracción
Translucent	translúcido/a
Transparent	transparente

English language learners will be much more successful if teachers focus on key academic terms and provide them with extended opportunities to practice these words and phrases. It is in academic English that these English language learners deserve our help.

New
Literacies

How can your use of specific vocabulary help students develop their interest in precise language?

Teach It! ★ 24

Semantic Feature Analysis

In addition to noting key words from the subject matter, the teacher can be alert to important words from the text that are not content-specific. Words from academic discourse that are not limited to a single subject area but are also not much used in everyday speech are sometimes called **Tier Two words** (Beck, McKeown, & Kucan, 2002; see Chapter 6). For example, *cotyledon* is a word that is specific to biology or botany; and *differentiate* is a word that is used in many contexts, but not normally in speech. Tier Two words are helpful for students to know because they are often encountered in their reading.

The website **Word Sift** (www.wordsift.com) will let you paste in a passage of text and have it scanned to distinguish the easier words from the more challenging words—many of them Tier Two words. The program highlights the words; then, if you click on one, it will display a semantic map with words related to the target word. It will also show photographs of the words.

Students need to follow their initial search for terms with some active ways of retaining them. You can model this process by keeping a list of key terms on the board or on a word wall. This list can include both the words you introduced and ones the students identify as important. Then students can find more examples of these words being used in other places in their reading and listening and build a more elaborate meaning for the words. Asking students to draw their own images of the terms also helps to lock new words in place. Elaborating associations with new words through drawings and personal examples will help students to retain the words. Concept maps for the terms can also be used (see Chapter 6, page 180 or Figure 8.7). In this way, students learn that terms have meanings, associated examples, and attributes. Specific terms are critical in content learning. Marzano (2004) has provided an excellent summary of the key academic terms students need to know and use to meet the content standards in each of eleven academic areas. Some school districts are now identifying key terms in each grade level that students should know and be able

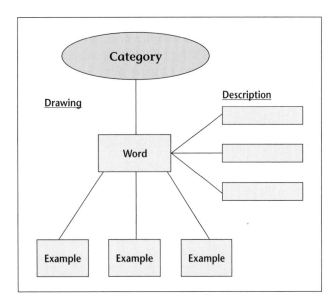

Figure 8.7
Concept of Definition
Map.

to use. This is one way they are highlighting the importance of specific academic language in learning. With the importance of vocabulary in informational materials, students need to develop their own metacognitive control over what words are new to them, and they need to develop ways to retain those particular terms. Individual student vocabulary notebooks and word cards are good tools for students to use to rehearse and practice these words. Making new vocabulary a part of the oral talk of the classroom is an essential component in this process. Some teachers employ a reward system to encourage usage, such as giving students points when they hear and note a new word being used by a fellow student. This highlights oral as well as written vocabulary recognition and provides an internal incentive as well.

"Word Conversations" for Primary Grades

Strategies for Active Reading of Informational Text

As students become familiar with the structure of informational text, they must develop ways to engage actively with the authors of those texts and think about the content. There are some basic strategies worth practicing to the extent that students can use them on their own. They have been developed independently but often work well when used together.

Prereading Preparation

Until students are able to take control of their learning by finding their own questions and level of knowledge, it is unlikely that they will retain much of what is studied. Therefore, the time spent activating personal and class interest is important.

K-W-L. Students become much more engaged in reading when they and their interests are the starting point for new inquiry and learning. K-W-L (Ogle, 1986, 1991) is a group process in which the teacher models and guides active engagement with informational texts. It uses the knowledge and information students bring to help each other build a better starting place for learning and for sharing the results of their reading. The adept teacher weaves together what some class members know (either topical or principled knowledge) and stimulates questions for all to pursue as they read to learn. The process also helps students who lack confidence in both reading and writing because the teacher is the first one to write on the board. This permits children to see the written forms of key terms they will encounter later in the text. It also models what the students will write on their own guide sheets (see Figure 8.8) or in their learning logs.

Teach It! 43

Paired Brainstorming

What We Know.   The teacher and students begin the process of reading and learning by brainstorming together what they *know* (the **K** in K-W-L) about the topic. The teacher guides students to probe their knowledge statements and find conflicting or partial statements of what they know. For example, as a group brainstorms what they know about the desert, one student says, "Nothing much lives there." Another volunteers, "That's not true! I know lots of insects live there. I just read a book about tarantulas." The teacher can encourage more student engagement by continuing the thinking: "Does anyone else know something about what lives in the dry, barren lands of the desert? Can anyone frame a question that may help us find out more?"

Another student chimes in, "We'd better find out what animals can survive there with little water or food." The teacher writes on the blackboard, overhead, or computer what the students ask as their own questions and what they volunteer they think they know, writing down their ideas just as the students volunteer them (see Figure 8.9). The teacher does not correct or evaluate, but encourages and stimulates students to think broadly about what they bring to the study. Through this brainstorming process, some questions or uncertainties generally surface.

The teacher's role is to help students activate their knowledge and develop interest in the topic. Some basic rules are established at the beginning:

- All ideas are acceptable.
- Say what first comes into your mind. These ideas will be checked and edited or revised later.
- Listen to each other, but do not judge the quality of ideas.
- The goal is to get as many different ideas out as possible in the time allotted.

As ideas are voiced and written down, they might seem random and unconnected. At this point, you need to make a decision. If the group is engaged and ready to think a little more deeply, ask the students to think of ways in which the experts organize information on this topic. This move to a deeper level of thinking (to principled knowledge) can begin by first focusing on categories of information about which the children already have some intuitive knowledge. You can initiate reflection: "Look at what we listed in the 'Know' column. Are any of these items connected? For example, I see three items about animals that live on the desert. I also see some plants. Can you find other items that go together in a category? What are the basic categories of information we are likely to need to use?" In this case, the categories might be those shown in Figure 8.10.

The teacher might also begin simply by asking students to step back and think about the topic generally: "If you were going to write a table of contents on this topic, the desert, what would you include?" The ideas that students volunteer can be listed at the bottom of the "Know" column.

What We Want to Know.   With a variety of ideas being shared, the teacher can easily ask what the students *want* (the **W** in K-W-L) to know. Again, it is the students' responsibility to think of real questions as you write down what they say. These questions form the second column on the worksheet or blackboard. If students are not familiar with the process of generating their own questions, you might need to model some questioning at the beginning. You might be able to extend comments made by class members into questions.

For example, if the class is beginning a unit on the desert region and someone has listed cactus as a plant in the desert, you can extend this by suggesting, "I wonder whether there are any uses people make of cactus in the desert?"

Figure 8.8 K-W-L Guide.

1. K – What We Know	W – What We Want to Learn	L – What We Learned and Still Need to Know

2. Categories of Information We Expect to Use:

A.   E.

B.   F.

C.   G.

D.   H.

3. Where We Will Find Information:

1.

2.

3.

4.

Source: D. Ogle, "K-W-L: A Teaching Model That Develops Active Reading of Expository Text," *The Reading Teacher, 36*(6), 564–570. Copyright 1986 by International Reading Association (www.reading.org). Reproduced with permission of International Reading Association via Copyright Clearance Center.

Figure 8.9

What We Know about Deserts.

You can write this in the "We Want to Know" column and continue to guide students to find questions, suggesting, "Is there anything else we might want to learn about the animals that live on the desert? Do we have to be careful of any of them? If we were hiking, should we watch out?"

This process puts the students right in the center of any new study. Rather than beginning with a text and previewing it, the students and the teacher become active listeners and recorders. This group-focusing effort helps students think about the range of ideas that they and others already have on the topic. It should also help them make new connections and become intrigued by what they don't know. Listening to each other can stimulate new vocabulary and associations; the writing done by the teacher often helps more reluctant readers begin to make associations between oral language and the written forms of words they will encounter as they read.

Once the students have discussed the topic, they are more ready to begin their own reading. It might be useful to have students write down on their own worksheets or learning logs the pieces of information they individually think they know and the questions they want to know more about. In this way, both the group and the individual are respected. You could have students work in pairs to do both the writing and reading because this is more stimulating and supportive of some children who lack confidence in writing and taking risks.

What We Learned. You can diagnose from this discussion what texts will be most useful to the students. It might be that what you thought would be adequate turns out to be inappropriate. Rather than reading the planned text, the class can collect other materials and even write some of their own materials as needed. This is where the Internet can come in handy as a resource. Look up a few sites, and bookmark them for the class. If the text or texts in the classroom and school library are appropriate, students can read and make notes on their own of what they *learn* (the **L** in K-W-L)—both answers to their questions and unexpected information they think is interesting and/or important. Many teachers create large bulletin boards with sections for the "What We Know," "What We Want to Learn," and "What We Learned" sections of the K-W-L. Students can keep adding information and questions to the class chart as they study. Small index cards work well for this kind of class activity. You can also make photocopies of material or graphics that students find and want to have shared.

K-W-L+. After years of working with students in content areas, teachers know that even with motivation and engagement, students will not remember much of the new information the first time they encounter it. Therefore, the "plus" in K-W-L+ (Carr & Ogle, 1987) extends this learning process by asking students to do more reorganizing of what they have learned by making a semantic map or graphic organizer of the key information (see Figure 8.11). Students select the major categories and list facts under those categories, thus rethinking what they are learning.

Finally, they write what they have learned in an essay, summary, or more personal form (see the example in Figure 8.12 on page 248). The cognitive activity needed to use ideas they have been learning in a new written format deepens memory and provides an additional opportunity to consolidate their learning. Engaging actively in this variety of learning gives the students a sense of how they can become active learners on their own, even when the teacher is not present. Reorganizing and rehearsing new knowledge and

Figure 8.10

Categories of Information.

Categories of Information:

A. animals   C. location   E. physical features
B. climate   D. plants

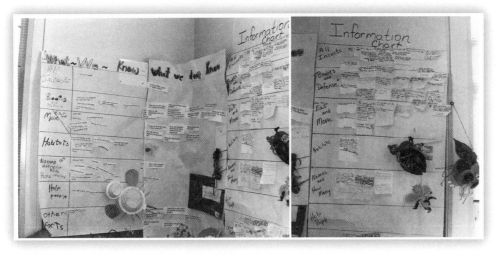

K-W-L charts provide a good strategy for motivating students' interest in new topics.

connecting it with what was previously known establishes for students the effort needed in learning and reinforces their personal self-esteem because they possess a productive process for school tasks (see the Assessment box on page 250).

I-CHART.   Using multiple sources of information is an important way to help students find texts that meet their own levels of knowledge and interest, discover answers to their own questions, and compare and contrast authors' points of view. It encourages the critical thinking so needed in the world today. Yet many students have a difficult time using more than one source effectively. Hoffman (1992) has developed a very useful tool in the **I-Chart** (see Figure 8.13 on page 249), which helps students take important questions,

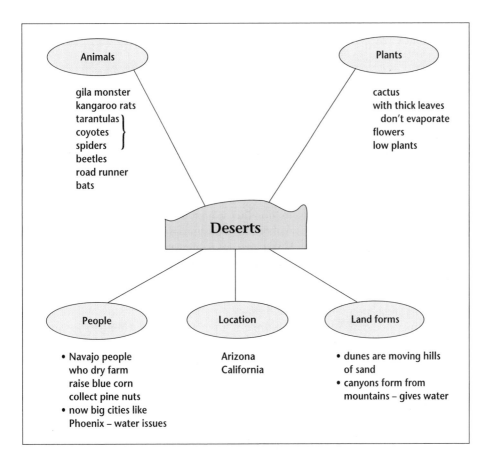

Figure 8.11

K-W-L+ Semantic Map.

Figure 8.12
K-W-L+ Essay.

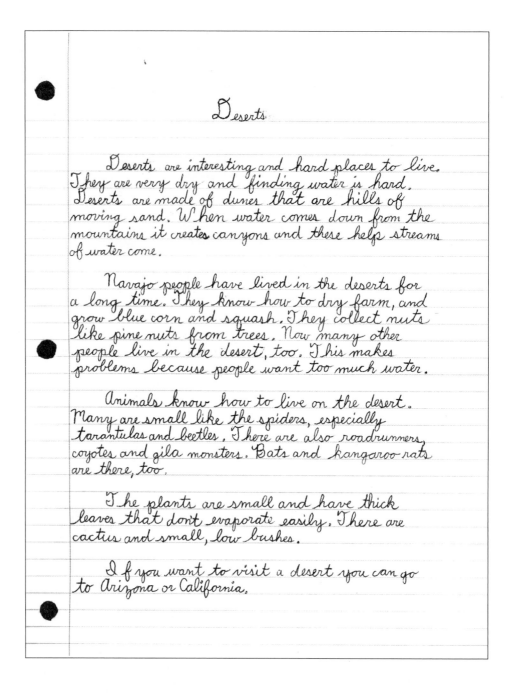

Deserts

Deserts are interesting and hard places to live. They are very dry and finding water is hard. Deserts are made of dunes that are hills of moving sand. When water comes down from the mountains it creates canyons and these help streams of water come.

Navajo people have lived in the deserts for a long time. They know how to dry farm, and grow blue corn and squash. They collect nuts like pine nuts from trees. Now many other people live in the desert, too. This makes problems because people want too much water.

Animals know how to live on the desert. Many are small like the spiders, especially tarantulas and beetles. There are also roadrunners, coyotes and gila monsters. Bats and kangaroo rats are there, too.

The plants are small and have thick leaves that don't evaporate easily. There are cactus and small, low bushes.

If you want to visit a desert you can go to Arizona or California.

select three to four sources of information they want to use to explore those questions, and then come to their own conclusion about the questions they framed initially.

Once students have used the K-W-L process to activate their knowledge and interest, they select some key questions for more in-depth research they can do together. The class or small groups can decide on the questions they want to concentrate on and write these on the chart. Then the best sources of information for the questions are selected, usually with teacher help and guidance, and they are also listed across the top of the chart. This simple framework establishes that multiple sources are needed when seeking answers to questions.

The practice of summarizing the information and answering their own questions scaffolds the process of inquiry well. Using the I-Chart establishes a simple framework for a systematic search for information. The chart also includes a column for interesting information, pieces that do not fit the basic questions but still are relevant to the students' inquiry. This often becomes an important way to take notes on ideas that can be shared with the class later—ideas that are full of potential for more reading.

Questions	What We Know	Text 1	Text 2	Text 3	Summary
1.					
2.					
3.					
Interesting new info./ New questions					

Figure 8.13
I-Chart.

Reading Strategies

K-W-L and the I-Chart are frameworks through which teachers can engage students personally and cooperatively in thinking about their relationship to a content area to be studied and in setting a course for learning. The frameworks do not show students how to actually engage with the text as they read it, however. That is where one of the following strategies is most useful.

RECIPROCAL TEACHING.   One of the most researched strategies for engaged reading of informational text is **reciprocal teaching**. Developed by Palincsar and Brown (1984, 1986) to help less able readers handle the demands of expository texts, reciprocal teaching includes four different strategies that students learn to use. You first model each of the strategies and then turn the teacher's role over to the students. The students apply what they are learning by becoming teachers for their classmates and guiding the continued reading of small portions of text. The four basic strategies are as follows:

1. Summarize what has just been read.
2. Think of two or three good questions about the passage.
3. Clarify any ideas or information that was not clear.
4. Predict what you think will be in the next part of the text.

In conducting a reciprocal teaching exercise, decide in advance how large the chunks of text will be that the students will read before you engage them in thinking about that portion. The text units should be short enough that the students can discuss each in five to seven minutes. Tell the students you will be the first discussion leader and that the students should pay attention to how you conduct the discussion, not just focus on answering the questions.

Model reading a short section of text and creating a summary of the main ideas. Depending on the group and the amount of time needed to teach each of the four strategies,

Involving Students in Self-Assessment

As children move into the intermediate and middle grades, they should be involved in monitoring their own growth as readers. Having students maintain Reading Logs helps them become more self-conscious about their reading habits, preferences, and strategies. Asking them to keep a record of all the books and articles they read along with their responses to the pieces is an easy starting place. Periodically, it is helpful to ask all students to record their responses to particular texts. In this way you can compare how students respond and what focus they reflect. Asking students to share their responses with each other is a good way to stimulate a discussion of the various ways readers attend to and construct meaning from texts. Reading Logs can provide an ongoing record of engagement and help teachers know if students need to be encouraged to expand their range of readings. Some students tend to stay in one genre or with very easy books.

Another way learning can be made visible to students is to have them keep samples of texts that they have marked with marginal notes or sticky notes during the four quarters of the school year. They can return to earlier text notations and analyze changes. If students are engaged with several units and reading many informational texts over the course of the year, there should be changes in depth and range of responses they can look for. For example, students can track the number of times they make comparisons across texts, as well as the times they question authors' inferences, ask questions of a text, and visualize ideas presented. The K-W-L sheets can be a good component of this kind of activity, too. Students can evaluate the quality of their questions, the extent to which they fulfill their desires to learn new content, and the graphic organizers and summaries they create.

you might spend several sessions on a single strategy, or you might model more than one at a time until all four strategies become part of the readers' response to each paragraph or segment. Students learn to ask good questions about the text through this process. They also learn to identify problems that hinder comprehension—vocabulary items that are unfamiliar, for example, or references that are confusing, or other unclear aspects—and ask questions to clarify these problems posed by the text. Finally, they learn to make predictions about where the text is leading. Students then assume the teacher role for each segment of text so that during a class period, many students have had the opportunity to lead their fellow students in considering the meaning of a common text. You can create a visible chart of the four strategies to help students understand the process. This becomes a guide for students when they lead the discussions.

This form of guided and shared reading has been effective in helping less able readers make sense of dense text material. The combination of good interactive strategies with group-oriented teaching and a shared learning approach helps students to maintain interest and focus on the material they are studying. The Teach It! box provides an example of how one teacher used reciprocal teaching in his classroom.

It is not easy to generate increased interest or to give students a sense of power when dealing with difficult and dense reading material. Both reciprocal teaching and the teaching strategy—Questioning the Author—(see pages 284–286 for a detailed discussion) give teachers and students supportive alternatives to round robin reading, a still overused way to have students read content texts.

METACOGNITIVE GRAPHIC ORGANIZER. Although several variations have emerged in recent years (Radcliffe, Caverly, Hand, & Franke, 2008), the key to the metacognitive graphic organizer strategy is that students create their own graphic organizer as they preview a chapter of text and use this visual as a guide for their reading. The term **metacognition** refers to the process in which learners are self-aware of their own learning needs and can monitor and adjust to the demands of the text. Students place the title of the chapter or article in the center of a sheet of paper and then add the major headings from the chapter as they survey the material. After doing this, they return to the text and look at the visual information in charts, diagrams, and the like. They put key ideas from these visuals on the graphic where appropriate under the headings. They can add subheads if necessary to make the flow of the text clear. Once the author's structure and visuals are clearly framed, students return and do the metacognitive check by asking themselves which sections are familiar (✓), which are unknown or unfamiliar (?), and which seem interesting (+). Sections that seem most necessary for the course, if that is the purpose of reading, can be highlighted with an asterisk (*). In this way, readers create a personal guide for reading and study. Then while reading, students can make additional notes on the outline or on sticky notes.

When they have finished reading, students review the graphic and the notes they made and decide whether to revise the graphic, add to it, or write some extended notes to rehearse the important ideas. The final step of note making is designed to encourage student reflection and learning. What an individual student does depends on how much detail needs to be absorbed to achieve the learning goal. It might be that the actual organization of the text is different from what the student initially drew and requires creating a revised text graphic. It might be that there are many new ideas, and the student needs to write a summary explaining the meaning of the ideas. Students monitoring their own learning can adjust this final stage of learning to their own needs to retain the content.

Personal graphic guides are very helpful to many students. They combine attention to the text and to the learner at the same time. In longer chapters, they help students maintain their focus on how all the ideas and sections fit together. They also provide a great tool for review and rehearsal later.

Teach It!

Refer to the Teach It! appendix at the end of the book for further activities you can use to reinforce concepts discussed in this chapter.

Reciprocal Teaching

George Mead and five of his fifth-grade students are reading a short informative text on crocodiles and alligators. Mr. Mead is still modeling the reciprocal teaching process with these troubled readers because they have had only a few experiences with the process. He has decided in advance that this text is best read in units of paragraphs. These students are very unconfident about their abilities as readers and the text is dense.

Mr. Mead announces that he will be the discussion leader for the first paragraph. He advises students not only to pay attention to the paragraph and participate in the discussion, but also to observe carefully how he conducts the discussion. They know that each of them will play the role of the discussion leader when the next paragraphs are read. Mr. Mead has prepared a chart that lists the steps that are taken after each paragraph is read. He refers the students to the chart to help them follow the procedure he is using as he leads the discussion. Mr. Mead asks everyone to read the first paragraph silently. When they are finished, he gives a verbal summary of the paragraph and looks around at the students to ask if they would summarize the passage in the same way or if they have something to add. Next, Mr. Mead formulates a question. He takes care with the question because as well as eliciting their ideas, he is demonstrating the art of questioning for the students. He asks, "What are the easiest ways to tell the differences between alligators and crocodiles?" He draws out the students' ideas on this question and affirms their suggestions. When Matt volunteers that the shape of the mouths might be easier to notice than either how their teeth fit together or whether the animal has sensory pits, especially if one was coming at you, he gets a nod.

Next, Mr. Mead attempts to clarify parts of the paragraph that are unclear to the students. He notes that the word *crocodilian* is used for the whole group of reptiles that includes crocodiles, alligators, and caimans. He asks whether someone can clarify when to use *crocodilian* and when to use *crocodile*. As the students try to differentiate the uses of the terms orally, Mr. Mead knows that they are becoming more familiar with these words in both their reading and their speaking. To help them as they clarify, he writes the words on the chalkboard as one student explains that *crocodilian* should be above the other three words, *crocodile, caiman,* and *alligator,* because they are all examples of this group of reptiles. Then Mr. Mead goes on to make a prediction, suggesting that the text will probably tell how these different reptiles survive. Finally, he assigns the next section of the text.

After that paragraph is read, Mr. Mead takes another turn as discussion director to make sure the students fully understand how to carry out the steps in conducting a discussion before it becomes their turn. Mr. Mead often refers to the chart as he conducts each step in the discussion. He knows that if the students do not clearly understand how to conduct the procedure, he will have to intervene later, which will undermine the students' autonomy and confidence. Before the third passage is read, Mr. Mead points to the student on his left and asks her to lead the next discussion. After that student has had her turn, the role of discussion leader passes to the student on her left, and so on.

Questioning

Before we close this section on learning, it is valuable to address the role of questioning for both teachers and students. Asking and answering questions are major parts of the life of schools. Each of the active strategies described here requires both teachers and students to become good at asking important and thoughtful questions. Questioning is an important active thinking activity that learners use while reading and trying to make sense of text. It is a central part of comprehension for students and teachers. Therefore, it is valuable to spend time both in analyzing the questions you ask and in developing students' sensitivity to what constitutes good questions and good questioning. A starting place is to discuss with students what role questioning plays in learning and what they think good questions are. Direct the discussion to include the realization that some questions ask for very specific and direct information (e.g., "What was the pharaoh's role in religion?"), some for more abstract interpretations or conjectures (e.g., "What effect did the caste system have on how people treated each other?" or "What similar situation have we had in our country?"), and some are very personal (e.g., "What do you think or how do you feel?").

You also need to tape yourself during class discussions and to analyze periodically how you use questioning. Traditionally, and continuing into today, many teachers have used questions to find out how well students have comprehended what they read. The teacher asks the student a question, the student answers, and the teacher gives some evaluative feedback. Researchers (Mehan, 1979) refer to this form of school dialogue as **I-R-E** (initiation, response, evaluation) and conclude that the process helps teachers test students more than it aids student comprehension. To encourage students to ask good questions and engage in metacognitive self-monitoring, you need to model good thinking when sharing ideas out loud and questioning students.

You can use questioning to model the process of thinking before and during reading. Begin a lesson or introduce a story by asking students what they already know about a topic. This kind of questioning activates students' own thinking. Most teachers use questions to help students connect ideas, consolidate what they have read, and reflect on ideas. However, you can ask much more thoughtful and reflective questions by first considering how you want to focus students' reflections about what they have read. Think about how you can involve students in reflecting together to deepen their responses to questions you or texts pose.

Reading specialist Marge Harter (2000), who has worked with teachers in her school to develop better questioning, suggests making the process of questioning very explicit with teachers. In her teacher workshops, she has helped them to focus on and identify good questions and has developed a chart (see Figure 8.14) based on the reciprocal teaching strategies for teachers to use in planning lessons. One group of teachers developed their own guide called "Questions Teachers May Ask to Help Students Clarify Text." In the guide, they suggest these options:

- Does anyone need anything clarified?
- Please share words or phrases you're uncertain of.
- What do you think this means? Can anyone add to what has been given?
- What other resources might we use to help us clarify and answer our questions?
- Where did this information come from? If you used the textbook, what part was most helpful?

As Harter worked with the teachers, they also discussed ways to help their students become more aware of their questions. She encouraged the teachers to discuss with their students the role of questioning in thinking and learning. The students in one middle-level classroom made a chart of what they thought constitutes good questions.

A Good Question:

1. Cannot be answered "yes," "no," or have a one-word answer
2. Requires a researcher to give more information that is focused or directed to a concept

Teach It! 51

ReQuest Procedure

Figure 8.14   Content Questions.

PREDICTING

What is your prediction for this passage?

What strategies will you use to help your students predict?

CLARIFYING

What words, phrases, or ideas do you need clarified?

What words, phrases, or ideas do you think your students may need clarified?

What strategies and responses will you use to help clarify those parts of the text?

SUMMARIZING

Write your summary for this passage.

How will you help your students summarize?

QUESTIONING

What "Quality Questions" are you asking your students?

1.

2.

3.

Why are these questions "Quality"?

Answer these questions on the back of this sheet.

Source: Harter (2000).

The World of Reading

Using Taxonomies in Questioning

As we take time to consider the role of questioning in learning, we need ways to categorize and analyze the nature of our questions. There are some commonly used frameworks that can be used to help us in this activity. The most widely used is probably one developed by Benjamin Bloom and his colleagues in the 1950s. Bloom's taxonomy was not really developed for use by teachers but was developed as a taxonomy of educational objectives to measure school goals and assessment. However, teachers saw its value and have used it as a tool to help us reflect on our classroom questioning patterns. The taxonomy has seven levels of questions: memory, translation, interpretation, application, analysis, synthesis, and evaluation.

In research studies of classroom talk, it is not uncommon to see analyses of the levels of teacher questions. In some descriptions of reading comprehension and reading assessment, Bloom's seven levels have been chunked into three or four levels. For example, one common way of describing reading is by thinking of literal, interpretive, applied, and critical levels of comprehension to define kinds of questions in relation to text.

Raphael (1986) has helped students to think about sources of information for questions they are to answer by creating four categories:

- Right there: Questions that can be answered directly from the text
- Think and search: Questions that require more than one piece of information from the text
- Author and you: Questions that go beyond the text
- On your own: Questions that rely on the reader

The whole strategy is called Question-Answer-Relationships and provides very practical definitions that make it easy for students to become more involved in both planning their strategies for responding and becoming aware metacognitively of the range of responses they need to be able to make to the text.

Taxonomies provide a helpful language to think about questioning and the kinds of thinking we want to help stimulate in students. Some teachers keep the levels of questions in their teacher manuals or put them on the bulletin boards so that both they and students are more aware of the need to go beyond the literal or memory level. Other teachers do not like to use taxonomies to evaluate comprehension. Rather than conceiving of them as a hierarchy, these teachers see taxonomies as an array of options that are available to use as appropriate.

---

3. Uses the following possible beginnings—Describe, How, Why, Compare, Explain

The teacher then puts this chart on the board so that the class could refer to it regularly. Both students and teacher became much more conscious of their questions as a result of this activity.

Some teachers extended their attention to questioning by engaging students in discussing what kinds of questions are most interesting to have answered and how much elaboration is needed in answering well. From an initial discussion of questions, teachers expanded students' understanding of kinds of questions and appropriate responses. Writing questions on the board and making them visible led to a good discussion of the significance of the questions and helped students to understand the value of voicing their own uncertainties.

Many educators focus on the nature of the process of constructing meaning and argue that questions should ask students, "What do you predict will happen?" "What else could have been done?" and "What does this remind you of?" They argue that the reader–text interaction should be the focus of attention and that questions should derive from those interactions. Do readers connect and respond personally to what they read? Can they establish a purpose and fulfill their own purpose? This focus leads to another range of questions about text construction or engagement. Some students never seem to connect text to their own lives or to the reality around them. Thinking of this dimension of questioning can be helpful in planning for activities so that students see school learning as part of their own world (see the World of Reading box).

Because the process of asking and answering questions is a critical part of teaching and evaluation, some focused attention to questions is necessary. By considering the nature of the questions they ask and the questions in the materials they give students, teachers can make the questions as valuable as possible. Modeling and attending to questioning provides the context for students to become more aware of their own questioning and encourages them to develop questioning skills that are useful to their own learning. Two strategies to use while students are reading that help them apply their knowledge of good questions are ReQuest and paired reading/paired summarizing.

ReQuest PROCEDURE.   The ReQuest procedure (Manzo, 1969) is best suited for use with informational texts. In this procedure, two students read through a text, stop after each paragraph, and take turns asking each other questions about it, which the other student must try to answer. It helps if the teacher serves as a partner when the technique is first introduced. Because one goal for teaching comprehension is to develop principled knowledge of the topic, the teacher's questions serve as valuable models of ways to inquire about the important ideas in a text.

For an example of the ReQuest procedure in action, assume you have assigned the students in the class to pairs. Amalia and David are reading a text together. After they both read the first paragraph silently, Amalia asks David three good questions about that paragraph. She asks questions about main ideas. She asks questions that probe beneath the surface. She asks what importance some item in this paragraph might come to have later in the text. David answers those questions as well as he can. After David has finished answering Amalia's questions, they both read the next paragraph. Now it is David's turn to ask Amalia questions about the new paragraph, and Amalia has to answer them. When both students have brought to light the information in that paragraph, they read the next one, and Amalia gets the first turn at asking David several good questions about that paragraph, and so on.

The ReQuest procedure can be used well with a whole class, too. One way is for the class to read one or two paragraphs from the text. Then the students pause and close their books, and take turns asking the teacher all the questions that come to mind. Following that, they read a new paragraph and the roles are reversed: The teacher asks the students several good questions, taking care to model not just factual questions but also those that probe concepts and implications. After several such exchanges, the teacher might shift the activity to ask students to predict what the rest of the assignment will be about and state why they think so (Vacca & Vacca, 1996). Another variation for a whole-class use of the ReQuest procedure is to assign students to teams of three and have them take turns asking and answering questions.

PAIRED READING/PAIRED SUMMARIZING.   Paired reading/paired summarizing is an elaboration on the ReQuest procedure that introduces more comprehension processes into the mix. In paired reading/paired summarizing, students pair up and read a text together and then divide the text into chunks of one or two paragraphs. The first student reads a chunk aloud as the other student reads along silently. Then the first student summarizes what the passage said. The second student then asks questions about the passage to probe its meaning. Both students attempt to answer the questions. The students exchange roles for the next passage. Like the ReQuest procedure and reciprocal teaching, students will play their roles more effectively if the teacher first demonstrates what is meant by making an effective summary and by asking good questions.

Engaging in Research

An important part of study reading is learning to conduct research and write reports. This skill is often left for the middle grades, where teachers demonstrate a semiformal approach to research. However, when primary-grade teachers engage students in content reading and study, the process can be scaffolded so that by the time students reach

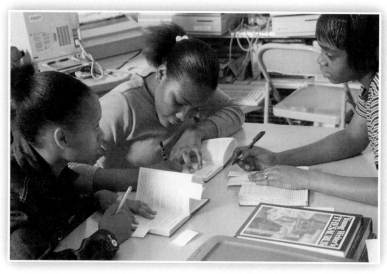

Taking notes while reading can help the reader identify the details of information content and organize them for understanding. (Lindfors Photography)

the middle grades they are already confident in the skills that permit them to conduct good research. Think back to the activities that have been described already. Research requires the following:

- *Asking good researchable questions.* Learning to narrow one's topic is a basic skill that needs to be developed. When children use K-W-L and I-Charts, they become experienced in finding good questions.

- *Locating good sources of information.* Integrated units that are framed around students' questions develop their abilities to find the materials they need and to locate within the texts the sections that will answer their questions.

- *Making notes of important ideas.* Children who get in the habit of writing Amazing Fact Sheets have already learned how to make good notes. The use of graphic organizers and journals also helps students build good note-making skills.

- *Critically evaluating information.* Students who have regularly read several texts on the same topic know the importance of evaluating the sources of information they use and cross-checking them for accuracy and currency. They learn to check the authors of websites for their expertise and biases. They also know that textbooks and encyclopedias are good, reliable backup sources for their use.

- *Organizing information.* When students learn to chunk ideas as part of the K-W-L process, when they cluster new vocabulary, and when they learn to look for and use internal text organization in their reading and writing, they develop skills in organizing ideas into interesting and coherent texts. The more writing they do throughout the elementary grades, the more confident they become in creating interesting and meaningful texts.

- *Presenting information visually and graphically.* Students who have studied how authors and illustrators present visual information and weave it together with the connected texts are more able to create their own. The computer tools and digital cameras that schools now possess make this task an exciting one for young students.

Look back over the different strategies that help to engage students actively as learners across the content areas. All of these taken together prepare students to be active, thoughtful learners. With this foundation, doing research and writing reports and even creating a more formal research paper is not difficult.

As we think of learning new material and conducting research, writing becomes an essential part of the ongoing literacy curriculum. (Refer to Chapter 10 for many ideas on how to develop a good writing program in the classroom.) When children write regularly, they develop their skills and fluency as writers. Regular writing, just like regular reading in a variety of genres for a variety of audiences and purposes, creates confident and capable learners. The more students can engage in their own inquiry on topics and questions of their choosing, the more they will want to write and share what they learn. The more they write, the more comfortable they will become with informational texts and the more able they will be to consider alternative ways authors can present information to connect with their readers. These experiences also prepare them for the focus of most of the writing they will be asked to do throughout their schooling: reports, summaries, and expository and persuasive essays.

Look at Classrooms for Learning

As teachers take seriously the importance of helping children become confident readers and learners with informational materials, the greatest challenges are finding the time and structuring the learning experiences properly. Two general approaches are often used. The first is to think of teaching reading as finding a balance between the reading of fictional literature (for literary purposes) and the reading of informational material (to learn). The second approach is to create integrated units of instruction and combine standards and strategies for both literacy and content learning. If your school has basal readers, check to see that there is a balance of literary fiction and nonfiction and informational selections. Many of the newer basal reading programs include more varied selections, recognizing that students need to become familiar with these texts. You also need to provide experiences in integrated content units so students learn the value of using a range of informational resources in their learning.

Involving English Language Learners

Integrated content units provide an open framework in which teachers can involve students at all levels of language competence in classroom learning experiences. Because the unit model provides for a range of materials and activities, students with little English can participate using resources in their own language and can begin their learning in their first language. Helping English language learners to create vocabulary lists with words in both English and their first language makes their participation in the general classroom activities more possible.

Teachers and other students can often gain from the English language learners' knowledge about the topics of study. Often, their experiences have been rich in the content of focus. For example, students from South America might have personal experiences with some varieties of frogs we consider exotic and might have a sense of their value that is different from the sense of urban dwellers in North America. Children from North Africa can contribute much to the study of civilizations that have derived from ancient Egypt or of studies of deserts. All children bring with them their experiences, language, and folktales and stories that can enrich any unit of study. Think of the potential resources represented by diversity in the classroom, and seek out what your students and their families can bring to each other.

During the development of the units, English language learners also can participate in ways that go beyond verbal learning. They can take major roles in creating the visual displays and the graphic representations of the topics, as in the development of the murals

Language and Diversity

How could such a class chart be used to stimulate interest in word histories?

What particular benefits come from
using online resources for second
language learners?

of the frog issue. If some dramatic presentation of content is part of the unit, these students can build their English skills by memorizing parts and participating in group presentations.

Using Computer Resources

Units of instruction provide an ideal place to introduce the use of computer resources. A number of excellent websites exist that can be resources to learning. With the help of the instructional media or technical support team in a school, specific and appropriate web resources can be bookmarked for a class, and students can participate in learning from these resources. Many also contain great visual content, so students with limited English proficiency can learn in easy ways.

The computer also makes the development of reports easier for all. Digital cameras make it possible to dress up reports (e.g., by importing pictures of direct explorations during science units) and clip art and free photographs on the web help students create impressive reports. By the middle grades many schools help students create Podcasts and movie trailers as part of their research reporting. The ease with which corrections can be made on the computer gives students more freedom to compose their own reports and not fear misspelled words or poor handwriting. Students take great pride in producing reports with great graphics and print quality that reflect their best work. Knowing that their work can be turned into high-quality products serves as an incentive to many students. For primary students, the support of parent helpers or older-grade aides in the classroom can make the computer accessible and not consume all of the teacher's time.

Planning Instruction: A Reflection

You can build a strong reading to learn curriculum in both of these ways—by creating a balance between fiction and informational material in the reading block of the day or by integrating reading to learn instruction with content units. Our experience has been that for new teachers, it is easier not to do all the instruction through integrated blocks initially but to first be sure there are resources for the range of reading and learning needs of students in your class. What is critical is that you pay attention to what students bring with them in skills and strategies for reading informational texts and provide instruction so students develop increasingly sophisticated knowledge of how to read to learn in a variety of materials and for a variety of purposes. Reading to learn from science content is different from reading to learn from social studies materials. Both are different from reading that is taught as if a selection of text was sufficient just to be read and enjoyed.

For Review

Students are eager to learn about the world around them. Your job is to provide the scaffolds so they can do so successfully. This chapter began with an explanation of why teaching students to use informational texts is so important. Then the ABC model of active reading was applied to reading for information. Four kinds of background knowledge were identified: vocabulary, text structure, and content knowledge, both topical and principled.

Many children have little experience with informational materials. Therefore, specific features were explained that you need to introduce to students. These include external features like chapter headings and subheadings, captions, illustrations, the glossary and index, and even the table of contents. The internal structures of informational texts are also important for students to identify so they can determine what is important information and retain it. The use of graphic organizers, having students jigsaw the reading of sections of texts, and having

them write using the pattern of the authors were suggested as ways to highlight text organization.

This chapter introduced two frameworks and several instructional strategies that help students become aware of and utilize these features and become active questioners and thinkers. K-W-L and I-Charts help frame students' inquiry. Reciprocal teaching, questioning the author, metacognitive graphic organizers, and ways to develop good questioning through paired reading/paired summarizing and ReQuest help students build their knowledge as they engage actively with text ideas.

Finally, the chapter concluded by highlighting the importance of helping students develop their abilities to engage in research and establishing a rich classroom environment where students' inquiry can be nurtured with print and technological resources.

For Your Journal

Keep a record of all the reading you do for one or two days. Note the material you read, the time you spent, and how you engaged yourself in the materials, including what you thought and felt as you read. Try to remember your school experiences, and write about what kinds of materials you were taught to read. What tips did you learn for reading and comprehending informational material?

Taking It to the World

1. Most children are curious about the world around them. Yet sometimes teachers get very busy meeting all the curricular demands and overlook students' interests as a natural connection point to content. Visit a school library or a public library and become familiar with some of the excellent magazines available for young readers. Sit down and talk with some children about which of the magazines they enjoy most. Then see whether the library has a service that permits you to search the magazines by topic so you can use articles in the future as you develop your own teaching units and extend readings on key topics in the curriculum.

2. Try out your skills in eliciting from students what they know about a topic and helping them articulate good questions to extend their knowledge. The K-W-L process is an easy way to start. Ask a teacher to allow you to teach a lesson with a small group of students around some topic of current interest, such as an item in the news or some community event. Have two or three short texts with you so you can read to the students to help them answer their questions after the first two steps in the K-W-L are complete. Keep a copy of the chart you create so you can reflect on the students' knowledge and interests after the session.

New Literacies Connections

Visit the National Geographic Kids Website (www.nationalgeographic.com/kids/), and investigate what it has to offer young children. How does it utilize graphics to enhance the information? Is the layout organized in a way that is easy to follow? What options are available to help students search for more information about specific topics?

Critical Thinking and Critical Literacy

Anticipation Guide

The following statements will help you begin thinking about the topics covered in this chapter. Answer *true* or *false* in response to each statement. As you read and learn more about the topics mentioned in these statements, think back on your answers. See what interests you and what prompts your curiosity toward more understanding.

_____ 1. Even primary grade children can think deeply about texts if they are asked good questions.

_____ 2. Critical thinking is the process of reasoning and reflecting in order to decide what to believe or what to do.

_____ 3. Critical literacy is concerned with the social or political purpose of messages and the contexts in which they are understood.

_____ 4. The structures of stories are usually very different from one another, to keep them from being boring.

_____ 5. To find ways stories influence readers, don't look at just one story, but at many— the effects of stories accumulate.

_____ 6. The **monomyth** is a large stone carving in South Dakota.

_____ 7. A **Socratic Seminar** is a form of debate only practiced by the Cincinnatus Society of Ohio.

_____ 8. Good arguments usually consist of claims, reasons, and evidence.

_____ 9. It is not good to teach children to be skeptical of some things they read. It will make them bitter people if done too early.

_____ 10. Fortunately, all arguments students read before they reach high school will be logically formed and honest.

Critical Thinking and Critical Literacy

What Do Critical Thinkers Do? p. 264

Critical Thinking and "The New Literacies" p. 266

Thinking Critically About Texts p. 267

Critical Thinking: From Understanding to Teaching Practice and Back p. 275

Suppose *Beauty* Had Been Ugly?

Midge Burns's combined class of second and third graders have just finished listening to her read Marianna Meyers's version of *Beauty and the Beast*.

"I'm wondering about something," says Mrs. Burns. Second grader Connie smiles. It is April of the year, and Connie knows Mrs. Burns always begins an interesting discussion with those words.

"Suppose Beauty had been ugly. Do you think the Beast should have married her?"

"That would be sort of no fair if he wouldn't," says Abigail, looking unsure.

"What do you mean?" asks Mrs. Burns.

"I mean, the Beast shouldn't expect Beauty to love *him* if he's not willing to love *her* . . . I mean . . ."

"They're both ugly, so they should get along," says Daniel.

"I think there's like a moral to the story," says Michael.

"And what's that?" asks Mrs. Burns.

"I think it's saying 'Don't judge the book by the outside . . .' "

"Don't judge the book by its cover," offers Phillip.

"That's right," says Connie. "They called her Beauty, but that just meant she was kind and gentle and she looked out for other people. 'Cause you don't marry people just 'cause they look good."

"Then let me ask you something else," continues Mrs. Burns. "Suppose Beauty had been a boy in this story, and the Beast had been a girl." (A whoop goes up from the children.)

"That would be a problem," says Laurinda.

"Why is that?" asks Mrs. Burns.

"I saw it on TV that the girls asked boys to the prom. I don't think that's right. Besides, suppose the woman in the story was older than the man?" Laurinda clearly looks troubled.

"Why do we care?" demands Michael. "We don't know how old Beauty or the Beast is. The story doesn't say. But you should be free to marry whoever you want."

"My Mom says it's not OK for a girl to ask a boy to marry her. That's what my Mom says. I'm not sure if that's true," says Harriet.

"It doesn't matter," repeats Michael. "But I'll tell you what bothers me. In these stories, the guy marries this woman he doesn't even know."

"That's true. And I wish the woman would say, 'How can I marry you? I don't even know you. I don't even know what your *attitude* is,' " says Connie.

"I know," says Harriet. "In these stories, the people are marrying complete strangers. They don't even know if they change their underwear . . ."

What Do Critical Thinkers Do?

In this example Midge Burns is inviting her students to practice critical thinking. We know that she's encouraging critical thinking because of several things she does:

- **Her questions take a critical attitude.** Not only do they stem from the assumption that students are capable of coming up with their own responses but also they imply that the meanings suggested by the text can be scrutinized and challenged, and possibly rejected in favor of better ideas.

- **Her way of conducting the discussion shares the responsibility for making meaning.** She spreads responsibility for making meaning by expecting the students to provide ideas. And while she sometimes says things to help students express themselves more clearly, she doesn't put herself in the position of the evaluator of their ideas, or as the authority on the story's meaning.

- **She treats the meaning-making as a social activity.** She encourages students to interact with each other, sometimes to build on each other's ideas and other times to critique them, but at all times to work toward more sophisticated thinking.

- **She has thought hard about the text herself.** She has examined the text for the issues it raises that might be important to the students and the attitudes and assumptions it conveys. Even though she doesn't plan to share her own insights, she has constructed a general idea of ways the discussion might go.

The students are thinking critically, too. We can see that because they:

- **Offer insights and not just recycled facts.** They are aiming to think through what the text might mean, and what they can do with the meaning.
- **They behave as if they feel free to question and to doubt.** They don't passively accept the suggestions made by the text.
- **They follow the ramifications of ideas.** They "try ideas on for size" in real life, and they make connections to other things they have read and heard.
- **They offer support for their assertions.** They can find evidence in the text or in reality to support their claims.
- **They listen carefully to each other and build on each other's ideas.** They don't just passively agree, though; they are willing to question each other's assertions, and venture alternatives.

Defining Critical Thinking

Philosophers usually define **critical thinking** as a process of reasoning and reflecting that is done in order to decide what to believe or what course of action to take. Critical thinking is usually done in response to something: a problem in real experience, something we read, or an argument we hear (Fisher, 2001). But a philosopher's definition can miss a lot of what children and teachers do when they think critically in classrooms. Young critical thinkers like those in Midge Burns's class do several things well.

- They read, watch, and listen as if the meaning of the text were the starting point in their pursuit of greater awareness and not the end point. They ask not only "What does the text mean?" but also "What can I do with the meaning?"

Value Line

- They make meaning by constructing interpretations of what they hear and read, and supporting those interpretations with evidence from the text.
- They use reading and discussions of reading as opportunities to know what their classmates think, even joining their ideas with those of others to create more sophisticated insights.
- They look below the surface of texts, and use their knowledge of literary structures and genres as they construct meaning and venture interpretations.
- They hold texts up to scrutiny, sometimes questioning their messages and the purposes of those behind the messages.

Defining Critical Literacy

Critical literacy takes place when readers examine the social, political, and cultural purposes and values that the texts reflect. Critical readers may ask who is behind the text

Good teachers press students not just to understand, but to think deeply about material that is presented to them. (Ellen B. Senisi)

and why the argument is being made. They may ask whose voices are missing from the text. They may "talk back" to the text, and construct different readings of it. When they do this, they are becoming "text critics" (Freebody & Luke, 1990). Critical readers learn that texts are powerful tools that can influence readers. That is why teachers like Midge Burns help students examine the unstated value messages behind texts.

Critical Thinking and "The New Literacies"

New Literacies

What do you consider "new" in the literacies in your life?

The importance of developing students' stance as "text critics" has become all the more urgent with the growth of the Internet as a source of communication and information. The electronic texts that come to us through the Internet are quite different in one important respect from materials that are usually encountered in print. Books, magazines, and newspapers more often than not are accountable for what they publish, and are screened for accuracy before they are released to the public. Texts on the Internet are mostly unedited and, while they may look "authoritative," they are often filled with strongly biased and misleading information. As Leu and his associates (2010) explain,

> *Whereas critical evaluation is important when reading offline information, it is perhaps more important online, where anyone can publish anything; knowing the stance and bias of an author become paramount to comprehension and learning. Determining this in online contexts requires new comprehension skills and strategies. For example, knowing which links take you to information about who created the information at a site (and actually choosing to follow these links) becomes important. So too, is knowing how to check the reliability of information with other information at other sites. Students do not always possess these skills. In one study (Leu, et al., 2007), 47 out of 53 higher performing online readers in 7th grade believed a site designed to be a hoax was reliable* (Save the Endangered Pacific Northwest Tree Octopus: http://zapatopi.net/treeoctopus/), *despite that most students indicated in an interview that they did not believe everything they read online. Moreover, when told the site was a hoax, a number of students insisted it provided accurate and reliable information.* (p. 4)

Defining New Literacies

Leu and his colleagues have taken the lead in arguing that teaching students to read must involve teaching them the "new literacies" of online reading. In the twenty-first century, the dominance of the Internet as an information source and as a communications facilitator makes their argument strong. These literacies are not static; in fact, it seems that there are new forms of Internet literacies emerging regularly. That is why Leu chooses to call them "literacies" and not literacy. Some of the emerging options such as blogs, Twitter, YouTube, and nings stimulate more student-to-student exchanges and help students create their own visual and verbal messages. The flood of websites makes a nearly overwhelming amount of information available; it is important that students learn to navigate the Web and use it properly for many different purposes. Schools bear responsibility to provide guidance for students, particularly since students from less affluent families often lack regular access to the Internet at home.

In describing the essential functions teachers can help students develop for online literacy, Leu (2009) includes five essentials:

1. Identifying important questions
2. Locating information online

3. Analyzing information (sources and content)

4. Synthesizing information

5. Communicating information

Leu and colleagues (Coiro & Dobler, 2007; Leu, 2009) explain that although those skills just listed are similar to the literacy skills required to read print on paper effectively, literacy functions work differently when the information is online. In fact, some students who do very well comprehending online materials have been very poor comprehenders in traditional text tasks. The reverse is also true.

It is important that teachers help students learn to think deeply and comprehend whether they are reading printed text on paper or viewing messages online. Online literacy is more interactive and more engaging for many students. The strong use of visual information may support comprehension in distinct ways. Clearly, the new literacies that have come with new technology warrant the attention of those of us who are concerned with children and young people's literacy.

Thinking Critically About Texts

Even preschool children encounter persuasive messages. Saturday morning television shows abound with advertisements that attempt to persuade children to want to buy things. Children shower arguments on each other, sometimes primitive, sometimes not. Although some adults might wish to hold off on discussing persuasive messages with children—especially dishonest messages—more and more teachers are deciding that children should learn to understand and—if necessary—to protect themselves from such messages in the elementary grades. In the rest of this chapter, we will first take a broad view of how texts work—beginning with narratives, then examining informational and persuasive texts, and finally considering what happens when students read several texts on the same topic—sometimes even texts from different genres. We will conclude with a presentation of teaching strategies for guiding students' reading and thinking about different kinds of texts for different purposes. Some of the strategies may encourage critical thinking; others may encourage critical literacy. In this chapter, as in real classrooms, we will often mix the two.

Looking Closely at the Structure of Literature

Even the most familiar stories such as "Cinderella," "Beauty and the Beast," or "Jack and the Beanstalk" may influence young readers' and listeners' attitudes and beliefs in subtle ways. We will examine two kinds of influence fictional texts have on readers. The first point is that fictional texts often relate symbolically to people and actions in the real world. A single text, or more likely, a collection of texts, may have the effect of conveying certain attitudes toward groups of people, certain actions, or certain values. The second point is that the structure of a particular text may lead the reader to a certain attitude toward characters and events, and these same attitudes may carry over into readers' beliefs about the real world.

THE WEB OF NARRATIVE AND "THE WAY IT IS."   Anthropologists sometimes look at the many stories or other texts that are circulated in a society and note that they constitute a common story, a sort of web of narrative. This may be called the *mythos*: Whether it is a story or a series of stories, or even a series of advertisements or a string of video games, the collection of texts becomes familiar and understandable because they say the same things again and again. The *mythos* may consciously or unconsciously relate to a kind of logic of "the way things are." Anthropologists call this unspoken understanding of the social order the *logos*, a tacit understanding of "how things are" and "how things work." For example, traditional fairy tales spin a narrative web that portrays males as active heroes who go on quests, and females as passive creatures who wait to be rescued and become prizes to be won by the bold masculine heroes. Male heroes often strive aggressively or violently against those who are cast as foes. Females use extreme kindness and self-denial—not to achieve their goals, because in traditional stories females are often punished if they have goals, but to have things turn out well.

Even though they are "just stories," through much repetition the web of narrative normalizes a certain understanding of "the way things are." In traditional stories told in European and American culture, "the way things are" is that only aggressive males and self-denying females have things turn out well. The winners, usually males, are solitary figures who triumph over others, and have no sympathy for those who stand in their way.

Of course the *mythos*—that is, traditional Western stories taken as a whole—teaches a *logos* that may be far out of touch with society as it is today. For instance, can you imagine having a class of boys and girls—or teaching in a school faculty of men and women—who behaved that way? This is a big reason children need to think critically about stories.

DRAMATIC ROLES. Looking more closely at the structure of individual narratives shows how a story shapes readers' reactions to it. From experience with hearing and reading stories and watching media, readers construct what has been called a *story grammar* (Mandler & Johnson, 1977; Stein & Glenn, 1979): a set of rules that help them make sense of who is doing what and what the actions mean.

Character Clusters and Character Maps

One version of a story grammar assigns roles to characters (Souriau, 1955; Temple, Martinez, & Yokota, 2010). A character in a story may be the hero or the protagonist, the person whose needs give rise to the actions in the story and with whom readers most strongly sympathize. Another character may serve as a rival, a person against whom the hero competes to get what he wants. Yet another character may be the helper, who supports the hero. Readers sense who is playing what role, and their loyalties are directed accordingly: They cheer the hero (and may forgive his aggression), they spurn the rival (and may give him little sympathy), and they appreciate the efforts of the helper (but don't give her much consideration beyond what she does for the hero).

Authors don't often tell readers who is playing what role—readers intuit those judgments themselves. But once readers assign characters to roles, their affections may be strongly shaped: Once we decide that Jack is the hero of "Jack and the Beanstalk," we cheer him through his adventures, and we may forgive his thievery, and even murder. Once we cast the giant as the rival, we don't much sympathize with him, even as he is robbed and killed. And once we think of the giant's wife as a helper, we don't give her another thought after she has helped Jack for the last time.

CHARACTERS AS STAND-INS FOR OTHER PEOPLE. Characters in stories have special meanings for us in our own lives. For example, we can say the story of "Cinderella" is about what happens when a deserving but overshadowed young person like Cinderella competes for recognition against overprivileged people like Cinderella's haughty stepsisters. Kate DiCamillo's *Because of Winn-Dixie* is about what happens when a troubled child (Opal) who is searching for community reaches out to the people around her, who are also suffering and lonely, but powerless in their isolation.

Cinderella and Opal are like many other people we know. We speak of "Cinderella" sports teams, who have these same attributes of being deserving but overlooked until one day they burst into glory. And many a youngest child, feeling that other siblings get all the breaks, has identified with Cinderella. Opal in *Because of Winn-Dixie* reminds us of Maniac Magee (in Louis Sachar's book by that name) because Maniac, too, is a kid who lacks a normal support group and who ultimately creates community. In real life, they both remind us a little bit of other peacemakers, like Mother Teresa and Martin Luther King, Jr. But they also remind us of some children in dysfunctional families, who must do more than their fair share to make things right for the others in their surroundings.

The dynamics of identifying characters with other characters works like this: We look at characters in stories both horizontally and vertically. We look horizontally at the relationships between characters, and once we see who occupies the slots in those relationships, we look vertically at categories of people like that. The horizontal dimension is akin to the grammar of a sentence, and the vertical dimension is akin to the parts of speech.

One shorthand way of capturing the relations between characters in stories and characters in the real world is to chart them horizontally and vertically. We use the horizontal dimension to depict the relationships between characters within a story, and once we see who occupies the slots in those relationships, we use the vertical dimension to show categories of other people in the real world who relate to each other in similar ways. The horizontal dimension is akin to the grammar of a sentence, and the vertical dimension is akin to the individual parts of speech.

For example, in plotting the relationships we might arrive at a diagram like this:

Others like Jack	Jack	◆ relates to ◆	The Giant	Others like the Giant
David	small		huge	Goliath
Harry	weak		strong	Voldemort
Roadrunner	modest		arrogant	Coyote
Serfs	poor		rich	Barons
	on his way up		"Over the hill"	

This brings us back to the question of how stories have meaning for us. We can ask of "Cinderella": When do we feel overlooked and underappreciated? What do we do at those times to find relief? Especially if we don't have fairy godmothers? And doubly especially if we don't want to wait for a prince to come calling? We recognize the problems presented in these stories and check to see if we find part of ourselves in those problems. Then we critique the solutions offered by the stories. If we don't buy the story's solution, then we can decide upon a better one.

Thinking Critically About Texts Other Than Stories

Attempts at persuasion are everywhere in our society. Commercial interests bid for children's attention and loyalty even in the lunch room. Political parties are quick to tell anyone who will listen why just about any piece of news is proof that they are the ones who should lead us, while the others are incompetent. Sometimes messages that would persuade us come in the form of structured arguments. When they do, readers can use strategies like the ones outlined just below to decide if those messages are arguing fairly. More often, though, the messages use more subtle means than claims, reasons, and evidence to win over their audience. This latter kind of messages will need other strategies, outlined later in this section.

EXAMINING ARGUMENTS. When faced with a message that seeks to persuade us or even inform us, students can learn to look closely at the ways in which the arguments are made. Teachers can help younger students approach arguments in a simple way. Let's assume students are given a piece of persuasive writing such as the following.

Dogs make better pets than cats. There are two good reasons. First, dogs are good companions. Second, they guard your house and keep you safe.

Dogs make good companions because dogs are friendly animals. The ancestors of dogs hunted in groups, so they had to learn to get along with others. The ancestors of cats hunted alone, though, so they never had to learn to get along with others.

The World of Reading

The Hero Cycle

Stories abound of people who start out underappreciated, then are challenged to do something that requires strength and courage and that benefits other people, and finally reach some triumphant state by the end of the story. *Holes, Hoot!, Because of Winn-Dixie, Harry Potter,* and *The Lord of the Rings* follow this pattern. Joseph Campbell wrote a famous description of this kind of plot in his book, *The Hero With a Thousand Faces* (2008). The plots of many hero stories are so similar, wrote Campbell, that they are telling the same story: the **monomyth, or hero cycle** (see Figure 9.1).

Campbell's monomyth begins with an unlikely **hero** (not yet recognized as such) who resides **at home**, neglected, underappreciated by those around.

The hero hears a **call to adventure**. Sometimes it literally is a call, as when the hero is sent on a quest to find something that will eliminate a threat and restore order at home (think of *The Hobbit,* or *The Lord of the Rings* trilogy). Sometimes the quest is more figurative—the hero must survive an ordeal and develop his own strength (as in *Hatchet*) or restore his family's reputation (as in *Holes*), or bring harmony to a community (as in *Because of Winn-Dixie*).

The hero must cross a **threshold** into a special place where the full range of her or his powers may be at play, a place that Campbell calls the **land of adventure.** The threshold may be impossible to cross; in myths and folktales, it will take magical aid for the passage to be possible. The hero may face and pass **tests** in order to gain (sometimes magical) assistance from a **helper** in order to cross this threshold. In "Jack and the Beanstalk" something of a joke is made of these tests, but they are enough to win magical aid for Jack in the form of beans from the helper, the strange little man that Jack meets on his way to market. Crossing the threshold into the land of adventure is serious business, though. In "Jack," had it not been for those magical beans, no otherworldly beanstalk would have bridged the distance between earth and the sky, just as few people idly make their way into Narnia, or Never-Neverland, or Oz, or Hogwarts.

Once the hero has made it over into the land of adventure, he or she goes through a death-like experience. Campbell likens this to descending into **the belly of the whale**, recalling the story of Jonah from the Old Testament. Here a person's childlike self dies away so the adult can be born. When the young protagonist of the hero story emerges from the belly of the whale, he or she has adult-like powers. In "Jack and the Beanstalk" perhaps the Belly of the Whale is the copper cooking pot where he hides from the giant. The Belly of the Whale in "Hansel and Gretel" may be the witch's house.

The hero must prove himself or herself against a stern father figure. Is the young person capable of being taken seriously as a hero? Only the ultimate test against the supreme authority figure will decide the question. Campbell called this competition with the authority figure **father atonement.**

At the height of the journey, the hero seeks a prize, a magic potion, a key that will have some benefit to those who are waiting back on earth. The hero must win it or steal it, in a move that Campbell calls **the elixir theft**. In older stories and those derived from them the elixir, which means "medicine," is often an actual item—the Holy Grail, the Golden Fleece, the magic hen and magic harp, the Firebird; or the sorcerer's stone, or the Ring. In modern stories it may be something more abstract, like harmony and engagement among the people of Naomi, Florida, in *Because of Winn-Dixie*.

Following the theft of the elixir the hero often has to make a dramatic escape or **flight** from the father figure, back across the threshold from the land of adventure into the real world, where the hero once again finds himself or herself **at home.** But, of course, when the hero is at home at the end of the story, unlike the beginning—when the hero was all unrecognized potential, the hero is now a fully developed human being, with all of her or his talents expressed to their fullest.

What value does knowledge of the monomyth have to those of us who want to discuss literature with children? The monomyth provides a ready means of comparing stories, to make text-to-text comparisons. It provides a way to compare current TV and video heroes such as the popular power rangers and Japanese magna heroes to those from literature. It also helps us question the basic assumptions of how the stories unfold: Why is the character a male in most classical tales? What about *Mufaro's Beautiful Daughters*? Do individuals have to take these journeys alone?

Dogs protect your house because they want to protect the place they live. They are friendly to people and other dogs they know, but they want to keep strangers away—at least until they know them. Cats won't protect your house. They mind their own business when people come around.

Wouldn't you rather have a cuddly dog than a snobby cat?

Students ask these questions:

- **What are you saying?** What claim or suggestion is the message making?
- **What are your reasons for saying it?** What reasons does the message give about why we should accept that claim or suggestion?

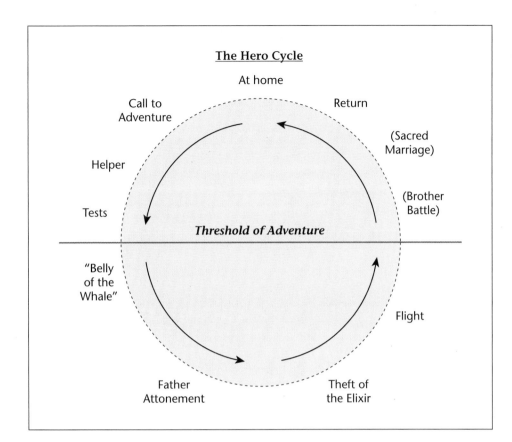

Figure 9.1

The Hero Cycle.

After J. Campbell (2008).

The Hero Cycle

- At home
- Call to Adventure
- Return
- (Sacred Marriage)
- Helper
- (Brother Battle)
- Tests
- *Threshold of Adventure*
- "Belly of the Whale"
- Flight
- Father Attonement
- Theft of the Elixir

- **What evidence do you have?** What evidence does the message give that would make us believe each reason?

With regard to the example, we can answer the questions as in Figure 9.2.

A good argument will make clear claims, with clear reasons, and ample evidence to support each reason.

WHAT IF THE TEXT DOESN'T PERSUADE FAIRLY? Many texts don't argue fairly, of course. To understand how misleading arguments work, more tools are needed. Students can be led to ask four questions such as the following to look below the surface of misleading arguments:

- **What's missing?** A statement may seem perfectly valid with its claims and reasons and evidence—until we realize what it has left unsaid.

- **Is this for real?** Are there "facts" in the text that we might have reason to doubt?

What are you saying?	*Dogs make better pets than cats.*
What are your reasons for saying it?	*First, dogs are good companions. Second, they protect your house and keep you safe.*
What evidence do you have?	*Dogs make good companions because dogs are friendly animals. The ancestors of dogs hunted in groups, so they had to learn to get along with others . . .* *Dogs protect your house because they want to protect the place they live. They are friendly to people and other dogs they know, but they want to keep strangers away . . .*

Figure 9.2

Looking at Arguments.

Figure 9.3
A Further Look at
Arguments.

What's missing?	The argument about dogs and cats doesn't mention that dogs are more costly to keep and are sometimes aggressive toward innocent people.
Is this for real?	What proof, beyond simply saying so, does the text offer that dogs have always been gregarious and cats have always been
What's in the words?	Using the word "snobby" to describe cats is unfair because it goes beyond the evidence. The text hasn't proved that cats believe themselves too good to spend time with others, as the word "snobby" suggests.
Who cares?	The text assumes that everyone wants a companionable pet. But many readers may prefer their pets to be more independent and to require less frequent attention.

- **What's in the words?** What loaded words are used? "Loaded" words are terms that pass judgments without making arguments.
- **Who cares?** Texts often argue as if all readers wanted a state of affairs that we don't necessarily value.

For an example of these questions' being asked of the topic of dogs and cats, see Figure 9.3.

WHAT IF AN ARGUMENT DOESN'T LOOK LIKE AN ARGUMENT?   Many of the messages children see in a day are intended to persuade them. But few of them take the form of well-formed arguments, with claims, reasons, and evidence. See Figure 9.4 for an example.

There are four "scans" (based on Alan Luke and Peter Freebody's "Four Resources Model of Reading") that we can give such texts to figure out: (1) what they are and how they work; (2) what they mean; (3) what we will do with them; and (4) what they're doing and why they're doing it.

1. **What *is* this thing? How does it work?** On the first scan, we try to determine what kind of text we are looking at. Is it a story, a piece of information, an advertisement, or something else? We should be alert to texts that pretend to be one thing, but turn out to be something else—entertainment that is selling something, or is some other kind of promotion.

Figure 9.4
Persuading Without an
Argument.

Stay ahead of the pack
On a Bronwyn bike

Once we know what it is, we can also ask how it works. Each type or genre of text has its own code, its own set of rules. A story has a plot (characters, setting, problems, solutions, and consequences). A persuasive essay has logic (claim, reasons, and evidence). An informative piece has its structure of presentation (cause and effect, steps in a procedure, chronology, taxonomy, comparison and contrast). An advertisement has its rhetorical strategy (an ideal state of affairs that can be won by Joe or Jane Average if he or she will only consume a certain product). Once we are aware of the rules of a genre, we can use them to decipher its meaning.

2. **What does this text mean?** Texts can have meanings on many levels. Once we identify the meaningful parts of a text, we can ask what associations those parts bring to mind. We can ask how those parts work together to create meaning. And we can generate one or more readings for the text.

3. **What can I do with this text?** Once we have arrived at some meanings of the text, we can choose what to do with it. There are many ways to read a text. We can read to be entertained. We can read to be informed. We can read to be persuaded, or to have our views reinforced. If we decide to be critical, we read to reveal what effects the text is trying to have on its readers. In some cases, readers may decide to take direct action: they may write letters to advertisers, they may speak for change at a school or community meeting, or they may create a civic project to bring about change.

4. **What is the text doing, and why is it doing it?** Once we adopt a critical stance to the text, we can ask what the text is trying to do to us. We can ask about the motives of those who wrote it. We can question whose views and interests are advanced by the text, and whose views and interests are left out.

With regard to the simple advertisement in Figure 9.4, we might see responses like those in Figure 9.5.

New Literacies

What questions can encourage students to check multiple sources for their information?

READING ONLINE WEBSITES. The set of questions Luke and Freebody developed are excellent to use when reading websites. In addition, when using Web resources, a preliminary step needs to be included that asks the question of who sponsors a site and what their authority and purpose is. Too many students approach Web information in the same way they approach printed texts: If it is there, it must be true. As you recall in our earlier example, even when Leu (2007) informed students about the inaccuracies in a website, they continued to respond that "if it is there, it must be right"—a real call for action in our giving more attention to critical literacy.

These questions about website sponsorship also are connected to the purposes for which we seek information. If I want to get a range of ideas for how to clear my garage of spiders, I may try some sites that are from government health offices and some that are from individuals or blogs. In this case the authorship may be varied. If I want to learn more about the relationship between Ponce de Leon and Christopher Columbus, I am going to want only reliable sources, not speculation or opinions. Then the URLs I use should end in ".edu," or I should consult a reliable student-oriented search engine such as "Ask." The democratization of the World Wide Web means that even elementary students need to learn to think critically about what they are seeing and reading online. Before asking, "What does this text mean?" it is helpful to ask, "Who is sponsoring this site and why?" Beginning with this question makes students better and more productive learners. They can decide if they want to read further, and if they do, they will be able to more easily respond to the question, "What is the text doing, and why?"

Online formats are becoming more varied all the time; it is good to help students identify the variety of forms of online communication they will encounter. Some elementary classrooms use discussion formats so students can share their own ideas with other students in distant locations; some connect students to adults for book discussions (e-bookchats). These are good ways to help students develop their persuasive abilities. Asking questions of the sources of these communications and knowing whose voices are being expressed is

The effective use of technological resources and media to enhance learning is essential in today's classrooms. Learn more about judiciously using technology by completing the activity "Using Electronic Texts and Media to Help Students Learn Essential Concepts and Evaluate Their Own Learning in Content Area Subjects." (To find this activity, go to the topic *Media/Visual Literacy* in MyEducationLab and click on Building Teaching Skills and Dispositions.)

Figure 9.5

Four Ways of Looking at a Questionable Text.

1. What *is* this thing? How does it work?	This thing looks like an advertisement. Advertisements work by showing an idealized person who looks like a mirror image of the reader. Since the person in the image is exaggerated happier and more successful than the reader, the reader wants to know how he or she can be like that idealized person. Then the reader notices that the idealized person is using the product being advertised, and is led to conclude that by using the product he or she too will be as happy and successful as the person in the image. Bingo!
2. What does this text mean?	Associations? The boy on the bicycle in front is smaller than the others. He looks like he is in competition with them, and he is winning. They look frustrated, which confirms this interpretation. Since the lead boy's bicycle is shown more clearly and colorfully than the other clunkers, the advertisement suggests that the bicycle is the key to the boy's success and happiness. The caption confirms this. Thus the meaning of the whole advertisement seems to be that if you buy this bicycle, you will stay in front of the other boys who are your competition. But maybe the boy on the lead bicycle is trying to escape from the boys behind him. That's another possible reading of the advertisement. Either way, discerning readers may decide that the text is setting up an unhappy division between the boy in front and the boys behind him. Hmm. A more expensive bicycle may help you get ahead of your friends. But it may also keep you from having friends.
3. What can I do with this text?	Readers might be persuaded by the advertisement, and hound their parents to buy them a Bronwyn bike. Or they may choose to question the advertisement, and reject its message.
4. What is the text doing, and why is it doing it?	The text is trying to persuade readers to buy a Bronwyn bicycle. Surely the people who paid for the advertisement want to sell bicycles. Whose voices are left out? People who worry about consumerism being pushed onto children. Also, people who would like information about products, and not just imagery.

foundational. The more students use online exchanges, the more they become aware of how differently they can respond to the same issues and texts; this can whet their appetite to listen more actively for varied perspectives and interpretations.

Texts That Take Different Approaches to the Same Topic

Debate

Different texts may take different approaches to the same topic without expressly arguing with other texts. For example, a health textbook warns preteens not to get hooked on consumerism, particularly when it comes to clothing and cosmetics. An article in a magazine that is largely sponsored by the clothing and cosmetics industry shows preteen girls how to buy just the right products in order look glamorous. For younger readers, a book chapter may emphasize a live-and-let-live approach to all living things, including bees and spiders. Another book chapter may warn of the dangers of spider bites and bee stings.

In fictional works, different stories may show the same issue from very different perspectives. Many of the books of Roald Dahl, such as *Matilda*, *The Witches*, and *George's Amazing Medicine* show adults as oppressive despots, and delight in the child protagonist's triumphing over them. Other works, such as Vera Williams's *A Chair for My Mother* or Kate DiCamillo's *Because of Winn-Dixie*, show adults as so preoccupied with their own problems that they are largely helpless, and the child protagonist makes generous and heroic efforts that bring comfort to the adults as the child grows in her awareness of adults' emotions and motives. Such different works don't explicitly argue with each other. Nonetheless, children may be confused by their differing messages if teachers don't help them make sense of the differences.

Critical Thinking: From Understanding to Teaching Practice and Back

Now that we have surveyed some ways of thinking through how texts do their work, it is clear that readers have a choice: They can read texts actively or passively. They can take control of the understandings they derive from the experience of reading them, or they can allow the text to have the effect on them that the author intended, almost without realizing it. Teachers can make the difference in the ways students approach texts. In the following sections, we will share techniques for helping students read while engaging their critical faculties. The chart in Figure 9.6 relates teaching strategies to the descriptions of critical thinking and how texts work that we have just described.

General Strategies to Encourage Discussion and Debate

In this section we present several teaching strategies that encourage discussions to lead students into critical thinking and critical literacy.

THE DISCUSSION WEB. The discussion web is a cooperative learning activity that involves all students in deep discussions of readings. The discussion web proceeds with the following steps:

1. The teacher prepares a thoughtful binary question—one that can be answered "yes" or "no" with support. For example, in discussing "Jack and the Beanstalk," a binary discussion question might be "Was Jack right to steal from the giant?" For Louis Sachar's book *Holes*, the question might be "Did Stanley succeed in the end because of his personal qualities, such as being strong and good, or was it because the luck of his family finally changed?"

2. The teacher asks pairs of students to prepare a discussion web chart that looks like the one in Figure 9.7. Those pairs of students take four or five minutes to think up and list three reasons each that support both sides of the argument.

3. Next each pair of students joins another pair. They review the answers they had on both sides of the issue and add to each other's list. Then they argue the issue through until they reach a conclusion, that is, a position they agree on, with a list of reasons that support it.

4. At the conclusion of the lesson, the teacher calls on several groups of four to give brief reports of their position and the reasons that support it. The teacher can invite groups to debate each other if they took different sides of the argument.

DEBATES. With students in third grade and up, it is often useful to follow the discussion web activity with a debate. The purpose of the debate is not to declare winners and losers, but to help the students practice making claims and defending them with reasons, even when others defend different claims. Working with claims, reasons, and arguments and debating ideas without attacking people—these are key elements in critical thinking.

Figure 9.6
Matching Strategies to Purposes in Critical Literacy.

A View of Critical Thinking and How Texts Work	Corresponding Strategies for Teaching
Establish purposes and identify authorship and credibility.	Develop purpose-setting questions and plans. Check site sponsorship.
Responding and Articulating a Position in Relation to the Text	The Discussion Web Debates Value Line

Looking Closely at the Structure of Texts
Structure of folk and fairy tales
    Mythos and *logos*
    The Hero Cycle
Informational and persuasive structures
Propaganda techniques
Visual and graphic components
	Graphic overview of text structure
	Analysis of text arguments and evidence
	Evaluating a Web page
	Creative Dialogue
	Reading for structured opposites
	Matrix of story comparisons

Thinking Critically about Literature and Informational Texts
    Examining Arguments
    What If the Text Doesn't Persuade Fairly?
    What If an Argument Doesn't Look Like an Argument?
	Analyzing propaganda tools
	Anticipation/Reaction Guide
	Questioning the Author
	Socratic Seminar

Figure 9.7
Discussion Web.

Was it wrong for Jack to steal from the giant?

1. In pairs, list 3 or 4 reasons to support a "yes" answer to that question, and 3 or 4 reasons to support a "no" answer. Write those reasons in the spaces provided.

YES!	NO!
_____	_____
_____	_____
_____	_____
_____	_____
_____	_____
_____	_____
_____	_____

2. Now, each pair joins another pair. First, share all of your reasons to support a "yes" and a "no" answer. Then, discuss the question to reach an answer you can agree on. Write it in the space provided.

Conclusion:

_____
_____
_____
_____
_____
_____

To have a debate, you need a binary question (since the discussion web we examined above also uses binary questions, you can follow the discussion web with a debate). Here are the steps:

1. Think of a question you believe will truly divide the students' opinions, and put the question on the chalkboard for all to see. If you are not sure the question will divide the students roughly equally, ask for a show of hands on each side of the issue before going forward.

2. Give students an opportunity to think about the question and discuss it freely.

3. Ask students to divide up: Those who believe one answer to the question is right should stand along the wall on one side of the room, and those who think the other is right should stand along the wall on the other side. Those who are truly undecided (that is, after thinking about it, they believe that both sides are partially right or neither side is right) should stand along the middle wall.

4. Explain or review the two ground rules:

    (a) Don't be rude to each other. (You might have to explain and demonstrate what this means.)

    (b) If you hear an argument that makes you want to change your mind, walk to the other side (or to the middle). Here is a hint to the teacher: As the debate proceeds, you can model the behavior of changing sides with a pantomime, by looking thoughtful for a moment after someone offers a good argument and moving to that student's side.

5. Give the students on each side three or four minutes to put their heads together and decide why they are on that side. Ask them to come up with a sentence that states their position. Then ask them to appoint someone to say that sentence.

6. Begin the debate by asking one person from each side (including the undecided group) to state that group's position.

7. Invite anyone on any team to say things (counterarguments or rebuttals) in response to what the other team has said or give more reasons in support of their own side.

8. Monitor the activity to make sure the tone stays away from negative attacks. Ask for clarification. Offer an idea or two as necessary from the devil's advocate position. Change sides. Encourage the students to change sides if they are persuaded to.

9. When the debate has proceeded for ten or fifteen minutes, ask each side to summarize what they have said.

10. You may follow the debate with a writing activity: Ask each student to write down what he or she believes about the issue and why, and then write out their position in the form of an essay.

VALUE LINE. A cooperative learning activity that is an extension of the debate procedure is the value line (Kagan, 1991). The value line is well suited for questions that have more than two good answers, and students might have a range of answers along a continuum. Here are the steps:

1. Pose a question to the students on which answers may vary along a continuum. For example, after reading Beverly Cleary's *Ramona and Her Father*, you might ask the children, "Do you think Ramona's parents really understand her?"

2. Give the students three minutes to consider the question alone and write down their answers.

Good teachers encourage students to develop and express original interpretations. (Ellen B. Senisi)

3. Now stand on one side of the room and announce that you represent one pole, or extreme position, on the argument. You might say, "Yes, I think Ramona's parents understand her perfectly, 100 percent of the time." Invite a student to stand at the other end of the room to represent the other pole of the argument. The student might say, "No, I don't think Ramona's parents understand her. Not at all. Never."

4. Now invite the students to line up between the two of you in places along the imaginary value line between the two poles of the argument. Each stands at a point in the line that reflects his or her position on the question. Remind the students to compare their views with those of the students immediately around them to make sure they are all standing in the right spots. After hearing others' answers, some students might elect to move one way or another along the value line.

5. Students may continue to discuss their responses with the students on either side of them.

6. Identify three or four clusters of students who seem to represent different views on the question. Invite them to prepare a statement of their position and to share it with the whole group.

7. As an option, the formed line may be folded in the middle so that students with more divergent views may debate their responses.

8. You might want to follow this exercise with a writing opportunity in which students write down what they think about the issue and why. In this way, the value line serves as a rehearsal for writing an argumentative or persuasive essay.

CREATIVE DIALOGUE. Based on the work of Paolo Freire, Alma Flor Ada and Isabel Campoy (1998) developed the Creative Dialogue as a way of having students investigate issues in a story and relate them to their own lives. "Creative" is used in the sense of "constructive," emphasizing the student's activity of constructing meaning from a story. Creative Dialogue can be used with first grade children up through middle school and beyond.

Many works of fiction have implications for ways students should understand and live their own lives. Teachers need means of exploring the implications of the stories, and how students might use the meanings.

Creative Dialogue can be done with a whole class, but a group size of no more than 12–15 allows for better participation by each student. Creative Dialogue needs a "told" or written story to discuss. The story should have relevance for the children's lives, and should directly or indirectly raise issues that will be important to them. The activity usually takes 20 to 30 minutes or longer.

To carry out the Creative Dialogue activity, find a text that raises an important issue in the children's lives. The story may be contemporary or classical—it may be a folktale. The important thing is that it should raise an issue or a theme that can lead to a lively discussion.

The teacher prepares questions ahead of time for discussion. Questions for the Creative Dialogue are asked on four levels. The authors of this method insist that each level of question be used one after another, since there is a natural progression to them. The four levels of questions are presented in Figure 9.8. As the teacher leads the discussion, the format may follow other formats described elsewhere in this book, such as Shared Inquiry (see Chapter 7) or Socratic Seminar (see pages 285–286). Remember that the teacher's role in the Creative Dialogue is to encourage participation. This is a time for personal storytelling, reflection, and decision making on the students' part. The teacher's role is to be a friendly and respectful host and facilitator.

As a follow-up to the Creative Dialogue discussion, students may write in their journals about their own goals and resolutions. The teacher may provide further instruction and discussions to help the students act on the ideas that arise during the Creative Dialogue.

Teach It! 36

Shared Inquiry

Figure 9.8   Creative Dialogue on Four Levels.

Level	Purpose	Typical Questions Include
Descriptive Level	Questions at the descriptive level are meant to get the important points of the story on the table so they can be discussed by the group.	What do you like or not like about the story? How would you describe _____? (one of the main characters in the story) Why do you think that _____ (main character) made that decision? What do you think is the major difficulty that _____ (main character) faces? Why is that so hard for him or her? Why do you think that _____ (main character) changed during the course of the story? What do you think that this story is about, and why? What do you see as the moral or teaching of this story?
Personal Interpretive Level	At this next level the students should relate the story to their own experiences, and ways of seeing the world. We want to make the connection as personal as possible, because we want the children to see the relevance of reading to their own lives, and also see the classroom as a place that is friendly to them as persons.	Do you know of (have you seen, felt, or experienced) something like this in your own life? Have you ever seen (done, felt, thought, wanted) something similar? How is what you saw (did, felt, thought, wanted) different from what happened in the story? What would you have done (said, thought) if you were in that person's place? How might someone in your family responded?
Critical Level	At this level the students go back to the story, and look more deeply into it. They entertain alternative actions, and make decisions about those actions that derive from their own values.	Why do you think this decision is or is not fair? Why do you think this was or was not a good decision? Why would this be a fair decision in all circumstances? In what circumstances might it not be a fair decision? Who benefits by this decision, and how do they benefit? What do you think will be the results of this decision? What alternatives do you see to this decision? What might have been the consequences if the character had chosen an alternative course of action?
Creative, Transformative Level	Here, say Ada and Campoy (1998), ". . . our goal is to develop children's critical awareness so that they are able to make decisions that will enrich their own lives and improve the world around them." "[T]he purpose of the dialogue is to help children think about the aspects of their lives that they can improve, and to encourage them to make decisions with that purpose in mind."	What kinds of problems in your own life do you want to solve, like _____ (main character) in the story? What can you do to make your dreams and wishes come true, like _____ (main character) did in the story? In what ways do you want to cooperate with others, just like _____ (main characters) worked together to reach their goals? What kind of help from others do you want to ask for in your own life, like _____ (main character) asked for help? What do you want to do in your own life when you have feelings like _____ (main character) did? In what ways can you help others, the way that _____ (main character) helped others in the story?

Strategies That Unpack the Structures of Narratives

FOLLOWING DRAMATIC ROLES.   As French drama critic Etienne Souriau (1955) pointed out many years ago, a large part of the way we understand characters in stories is by the symbolic roles they play in the plot. That is because, whether we are watching sports or reading fiction, it is normal for us to cheer the hero, boo the rival, and have a warm place in our hearts for the trusty helper. Authors of stories wittingly or unwittingly use these propensities to shape the reader's reactions to characters: assigning one the role of protagonist or main character, another the role of helper, and another the role of rival or enemy.

Making children aware of the roles characters play in stories can help them interpret the stories and, eventually, better understand how stories work. Following are common roles that occur in stories:

- The *hero* is the person whose desires and needs drive the story forward. In "Jack and the Beanstalk," to use that story as an example, the hero is Jack.
- The *goal* is the hero's main need or desire. In "Jack and the Beanstalk," Jack's goal seems to be to get money or to get some independence and not be thought of as a dolt.
- The *rival* is the person who stands between the hero and her or his goal. The rival in "Jack and the Beanstalk" is certainly the giant.
- The *helper* is a person or persons in a story who helps the hero achieve his or her goal. In "Jack and the Beanstalk," there are a couple of candidates for the helper: the mysterious old man who sells him the beans and the giant's own wife.

The teacher can use dramatic roles in several ways to help students think about stories. One way is to have students nominate candidates for each of the roles and discuss their choices in small groups or as a class. These discussions can become lively, because not all role assignments are obvious. Is the helper in "Jack and the Beanstalk" the mysterious old man or the giant's wife? If it is the giant's wife (and the giant is the rival), why should she help the person who is striving against her husband? Is Jack's goal to obey his mother, to get money, to satisfy his curiosity, or to prove himself? Or is it all of these things? Discussing these issues takes students deep into the story.

Another way of using dramatic roles is to help students take different perspectives on a story. The teacher does this by asking students to take a character who seems to be playing one role and ask how the story would proceed if we imagined that character playing a different role. For example, in "Jack and the Beanstalk," suppose the giant's wife were the hero; that is, suppose we saw things from her perspective. What is her goal? Who is her rival? Exploring these questions can lead to some very interesting discussions of stories; this process also exercises the comprehension strategies of inferring and interpreting.

EXPLORING THE HERO CYCLE.   Many myths, religious legends, and folktales from the Western tradition follow the Hero Cycle or Monomyth structure we described on page 270. Many contemporary heroic tales also closely follow the pattern: *The Hobbit, The Lord of the Rings, The Dark Is Rising, Harry Potter, The Prydain Trilogy, The Golden Compass* (maybe), and many others. The original *Star Wars* film was expressly written to fit the pattern of the Hero Cycle. The Canadian critic Northrop Frye (1951) argued that all (Western) literature shares a common genealogy, and that contemporary stories reflect themes and structures from older stories. To the extent that this is true, it can be an interesting exercise to compare stories children are reading to the Hero Cycle.

We suggest that you introduce the Hero Cycle by having the students read and discuss several relatively short stories that follow the pattern fairly closely. One might be "Jack and the Beanstalk." Others might be novels such as *Because of Winn-Dixie, Maniac Magee,* and *Holes.*

After reading and discussing each story, construct a **Language Chart** (Roser & Hoffman, 1992) graphic organizer like the one shown in Figure 9.9. Use it to record summaries of the discussions of each story. Discuss the patterns that the stories have in common, too. These questions can help organize a discussion of the pattern:

What were all of these heroes like at the beginning of their stories? What did those heroes think of themselves then? How did others think of them?

What were those heroes like at the end of their stories? In what ways did they change?

What qualities did the heroes show in order to meet their challenges successfully? Why were *they* the ones who had those qualities?

What did the heroes win? Why were these things important?

Why do you suppose older people told younger people stories like these, generation after generation after generation?

How might these patterns play out in your own life? How will *you* be a hero? What talents and qualities will you develop that are uniquely yours to help you succeed? What challenges might you face to prove your worth? What might you achieve that will be worthwhile to others?

Once the students have a clear sense of the Hero Cycle pattern, you can discuss other works that fit the pattern more indirectly, or don't fit it at all. For an example of the latter, it is striking to examine African American tales such as "Wiley and the Hairy Man," "The TailyPo," and "Barney McCabe," as well as Afro-Caribbean tales like the "Anansi" stories, that differ from the pattern in that the characters are no better off in the end than they were in the beginning.

Contemporary realistic stories tend not to pit their characters against such daunting challenges as do the folktales, nor do they win such exaggerated rewards. Nonetheless, the characters face important social and psychological challenges, and achieve rewards that matter in their lives. Psychological critics such as Bruno Bettelheim (1975) and Maria Von Franz (1996) argue that these amount to the same thing, since the challenges and rewards of the folk and fairy tales were symbolic of the social and psychological challenges that are named as such in contemporary literature.

Students can discuss contemporary works they have read in terms of a shortened version of the hero cycle, as shown in Figure 9.9.

BEHAVIOR AND REWARDS. People who worry about violence in the media point to the number of violent acts that go unpunished, as well as the frequency with which those acts win for the perpetrators what they wanted. Critics correctly worry that this is a formula for influencing viewers:

"The characters commit X deed, and get what they want.

Therefore, young viewer, you should commit X deed to get what you want."

But there is a more subtle formula at work in literature that children read, especially the traditional literature, where different kinds of characters get different results for different kinds of actions.

In stories like "Cinderella" or "Beauty and the Beast," for example, it is clear that men get different rewards from women for the same actions. Consider the chart in Figure 9.10.

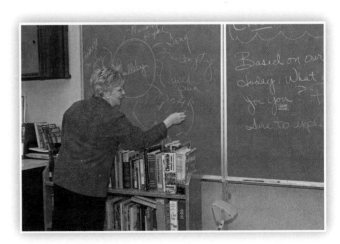

Graphic organizers may look simple, but they are tools students can use to think deeply about topics. (Ellen B. Senisi)

Figure 9.9 A Shorter Version of the *Hero Cycle.*

	"Jack and the Beanstalk"	*Maniac Magee*	*Holes*	*Because of Winn-Dixie*
Character in the beginning				
Challenge				
Great struggle				
Achievement				
Character at the end				

You get the idea. The "yes-yes-yes's" are all successful: They're the males who go after what they want. So are the "No-no-yes's": They're the females who don't go after what they want. The ones who fail, and who are often horribly punished, are the "No-yes-no's": the females who go after what they want. For females to go after what they want seems to be forbidden in Western folktales.

Constructing a chart like this with students can be a helpful exercise—but only if there is plenty of time for the students to question whether these patterns make sense in their own lives.

READING FOR STRUCTURED OPPOSITES.   A useful way of interpreting stories is to look for their contrasts, ask what things are similarly contrasted in other stories, and then find parallel contrasts and tensions in our own lives (Levi-Strauss, 1970). A method for

Figure 9.10
What They Wanted and What They Got.

	Is this character a male?	Did this character actively *seek* what she or he wanted?	Did this character *get* what she or he wanted?
Beauty	No	No	Yes
Beauty's sisters	No	Yes	No
Beast	Yes	Yes	Yes
Cinderella	No	No	Yes
Cinderella's sisters	No	Yes	No
Cinderella's prince	Yes	Yes	Yes
Sleeping Beauty	No	No	Yes
Sleeping Beauty's prince	Yes	Yes	Yes
Snow White	No	No	Yes
Snow White's stepmother	No	Yes	No
Snow White's prince	Yes	Yes	Yes

Jack	The Giant
Young	Old
Poor	Rich
Small	Huge
"Plucky"	Dull
Seems weak	Seems strong
"On his way up"	"Over the hill"

Figure 9.11

Looking at Relations Between Characters Horizontally.

doing that is called **reading for structured opposites**. A folktale works very well for introducing this method and could be taught like this:

1. Ask the students to think of the two characters in the story they are reading who are most unlike each other or most opposed to each other. For example, if the story is "Jack and the Beanstalk," the two characters might be Jack and the giant.

2. Write the names of those two characters at the heads of two columns (see Figure 9.11). Ask the students to come up with contrasting descriptive words about those two characters. That is, ask for a word that describes one character; then ask for an opposite word that describes the other character.

To take "Jack and the Beanstalk," those might be Jack and the giant, obviously. Let's begin with Jack and the giant. What words would we use to describe each of them? Each of these columns—a bundle of features with a name at the top—can be called a **category**. We will do more with the categories in a moment.

The dynamics between these characters can be called a **relationship**. In this case, it's a relationship of rivalry—Jack wants what the giant has, and the giant wants to keep what he has and eliminate Jack as a threat (eat him, if possible).

Now who else do we know who could occupy the same **category** with Jack, or occupy the other category with the giant—paradigms that are partially defined by their relationship with the other—in this case, the rivalry of the young, poor, underprivileged one who is on his way up, and the older, bigger, richer one who is desperately clinging to his or her privilege? We will nominate a few and write them in the outer columns to the left of Jack and to the right of the giant (see Figure 9.12).

Wow. It now seems that Jack and the giant are actually more than mere characters in a story. They are bundles of features with names attached—characters who remind us of other characters. Who are other candidates who share these paradigms, and occupy the same categories with each other? (See Figure 9.13.)

Others Like Jack	Jack	The Giant	Others Like the Giant
David	Young	Old	Goliath
Marty (in *Shiloh*)	Poor	Rich	Judd Travers (in *Shiloh*)
Peter Pan	Small	Huge	Captain Hook
Robin Hood	"Plucky"	Dull	Sheriff of Nottingham
	Seems weak	Seems strong	
	"On his way up"	"Over the hill"	

Figure 9.12

Looking at Relations Between Characters Horizontally and Vertically.

Figure 9.13   Looking Further at Relations Between Characters Horizontally and Vertically

Others Like Jack in Real Life	Others Like Jack in the Arts	Jack	The Giant	Others Like the Giant in the Arts	Others Like the Giant in Real Life
Serfs	David	Young	Old	Goliath	Nobles
Slaves	Marty	Poor	Rich	Judd Travers	Owners
People	Peter Pan	Small	Huge	Captain Hook	Tyrants
Workers	Robin Hood	"Plucky"	Dull	Sheriff of Nottingham	Sweatshop managers
Children		Seems weak	Seems strong		Bullies
		"On his way up"	"Over the hill"		

There. You may have noticed that in exploring the contrasted characters and their characteristics in this story—in both their categories and their relationships—we have explored text-to-text relationships and text-to-life relationships.

QUESTIONING THE AUTHOR.   In the Questioning the Author teaching strategy, also called QtA (Beck, McKeown, Hamilton, & Kucan, 1997), the teacher does three things.

First, the teacher reminds students that authors are people like themselves, with their own ideas, experiences, foibles, and prejudices. When authors communicate with audiences, they sometimes tell readers exactly what they need to know; but often they take too much for granted and leave out needed explanations. Or they may slant their message to suit their own beliefs, without inviting the reader to disagree. In classrooms where students write and share their works with each other, students are not surprised when their peers make points that aren't clear, or state positions with which they disagree. They find it natural to question their peer-authors at those times. The teacher tries to evoke that same confidence in questioning an author when students are faced with a work by a published author, not a peer.

The second step is for students to have an imaginary dialogue with the author, and ask about things that are not clearly stated, points where more information is needed, or claims with which they disagree. Here are some basic questions students might ask:

- What is the author trying to say here?
- How can we restate this idea, in words we all can understand?
- Why is the author telling us this now?
- What does the author want us to believe? Why?
- What is the author's point of view?
- How might someone with a different point of view have explained this point?

The third step, which is usually combined with the second, is to invite the students to provide the answers they might expect an author to supply to their questions. A group of students is usually able to do this, because their collective ideas may be more comprehensive than their individual ideas.

Reading to Follow Arguments

Students from fourth grade and up are ready to look at the ways persuasive texts and media make arguments. When they are given guidance, they can become quite expert at asking about evidence for perspectives they read and view.

Teach It!

Refer to the Teach It! appendix at the end of the book for further activities you can use to reinforce concepts discussed in this chapter.

Socratic Seminar

With students in late elementary and middle school, nearly any topic to be interpreted or explored from different points of view can be used in the Socratic Seminar. The purpose of the Socratic Seminar is to empower students to conduct discussions on their own. The teacher provides a structure that usually leads to successful discussions, but after the teacher models the process by leading the first few discussions, the students are the ones who ask the questions and conduct the discussion. A Socratic Seminar is not a debate. The ideas offered do not compete with each other. Rather, they often build on each other to reach a mutually constructed and deeper understanding of an issue. Asking good questions and developing ideas in concert with others is good practice in active learning and critical thinking. Taking responsibility for preparing the questions and conducting the discussion intensifies the experience for the students.

Socratic Seminars are done with the whole class. If the group is larger than twelve (and it usually is), a fishbowl arrangement is used. That is, between eight and twelve students sit in a circle conducting the discussion, and the other students array themselves around that group, close enough to hear the discussion.

The Socratic Seminar requires no particular resources other than a text or a topic that students can discuss. It helps if the seating is treated flexibly; that is, either the chairs are moved into a circle, or students sit so they can face each other in a circle. The seminar itself usually takes forty minutes. Twenty minutes or more will be needed to introduce the idea, and then students will need time to prepare for the seminar.

To conduct the Socratic Seminar, the teacher first immerses students in an interesting topic. The topic can come from literature, social studies, art, science, or any topic of which there are layers of understanding, different interpretations, or diverse implications. One of the easiest ways to introduce the Socratic Seminar is to discuss a piece of literature that the whole class has read. A seminar is also productive midway through a unit of study where students have acquired a significant amount of information on a topic or theme.

The teacher prepares the students to formulate questions for discussion. The Socratic Seminar requires that everyone discuss good questions. Eventually, students may formulate the questions, but for the first couple of sessions the teacher may prepare them, and use his or her questions to model for the students the kinds of questions that are preferred. A suggested approach to formulating questions worthy of deep discussion is Grant Wiggins's and Jay McTighe's (2005) concept of essential questions. Essential questions usually:

Lead into the heart of a topic and its controversies

Invite many answers from different perspectives

Invite rethinking of old knowledge in a new light

Lead to discovery and "uncoverage" vs. "coverage"

Encourage deeper interest in the subject; students keep on questioning

Are framed in a provocative and enticing style.

In practical terms, you may use the set of suggestions following:

A Socratic Seminar is a time to have a good discussion. To have a good discussion, you bring up things you are curious about, things you think are important. To have an even better discussion, you ask your classmates questions—but real questions—questions you don't know the answer to. Those can serve as guidelines. To prepare for a Socratic Seminar, you should plan some real questions that ask about things you are interested in, that you think are important. And the questions should be real in the sense that you don't already know the answers. ("Read my mind" questions are not allowed!)

Often these questions point in either of two directions, as we see in Figure 9.14:

The teacher explains the ground rules for the seminar. One set of suggestions are these.

Be prepared to participate.

Don't raise hands—just find a good time to speak and jump right in.

Invite others in the circle into the discussion.

Refer to the texts or other resources that have been studied.

Make comments that are appropriate, respectful, and focused.

Listen to and build on one another's comments.

Be sure it's OK with others before you introduce a new question.

Ground rules are introduced at the beginning of a seminar. It is best if the group is reminded of them often. If a student does an excellent job of adhering to a ground rule, the teacher may point that out, since positive reinforcements will make students feel more responsible than criticisms will.

Participating students (between eight and twelve of them) sit in a circle. The other students gather around what is called the "fishbowl" (so called because their discussion will be observed by the others—see the next section for instructions).

The teacher may invite a student to throw out a question and ask the other students to respond. The other students share their thoughts about the question, and also refer both to each other's answers and to the material being discussed.

When the responses to a question seem to have run their course, another student may raise a new question, or an aspect of an old one. It is considered polite for that student to ask if anyone had more to say about the previous question first, and to wait for any more responses before raising a new question.

After the teacher gives the signal (usually after five minutes), students who are observing from outside the group may "tap into" the group. That is, one student at a time approaches a student in the circle, and taps that student gently on the elbow. Then the new student takes that student's place in the discussion group. The new student should respond first to what the group has been talking about before introducing a new question. From

(ccontinued)

time to time the teacher can invite a student to sum up the positions that have been heard, and ask if there are more ideas.

Following the Socratic Seminar, students are asked to evaluate their participation. They can be asked to write responses to questions such as:

What did you learn from this seminar?

How did you feel about this seminar?

How would you evaluate your own participation in this seminar?

What can improve your participation in the next seminar?

The teacher "debriefs" the discussion by reviewing the ideas and arguments that came to light. Or she may ask each student to write a journal entry or a personal essay, writing down what he believes about the issue and why.

Students can be asked to bring "Entry Sheets" to future Socratic Seminars. On these sheets they should write at least three questions for the others to answer, as well as their own thoughts on those questions. Another device for structuring the seminar will be to pass out small pieces of paper to each student, have them write their name and their class period on it, and ask them to write a short entry each time they offer a question or a response to one. These can be given to the teacher at the end of the class period to keep track of the students' participation.

Figure 9.14   Questions About Stories.

Questions That Focus *In* (on the article or topic)	Questions That Focus *Out* (to the world outside the text or topic of study)
1. If the question is about a story, you can ask about: A character's motives. ("Why did she agree to do that?") The relationships between characters ("Do you think he is a good influence on her?") What is going to happen (if we haven't finished reading it yet). Why the author wrote the story. ("What did this author want us to see or to understand?") What the action had to do with the setting. ("Can you picture this story happening anywhere else? Why not?") Why the author used certain words, or a certain style of writing. ("Why do you think the author said it that way?") Something the author has done particularly well. ("What do you think is the best feature of this story?") 2. If it is an informational topic or work of nonfiction, you might ask: What are we learning from this that we didn't know before? Is this argument convincing? What other points of view have we learned about? Is there more to be said about this topic?	1. If the question is about a story, you can ask about: Whether the characters made good choices. ("Would you have done what he did? What is another way to solve that problem?") Whether the behavior pictured in this story should serve as a model for us in real life. ("Is that the way boys should really behave with girls? Suppose she was your sister?") The consequences of the actions. ("What do you suppose happened to each one of those characters after the story was over?") About connections to other stories and to real life. ("What other stories does this remind us of? Who or what does this remind us of in real life?") 2. If it is an informational topic or work of nonfiction, you might ask: Do we think this is true? How do we know? What is the most important idea? If we believe what this text says, what should we do?

Discussion Web

PRODUCING ARGUMENTS.   One good way to prepare students for this kind of thinking is to have them produce arguments of their own—and a lively way to do that is to:

- Engage students in issues.
- Have each student take a position on the issues.
- Have students debate with others from their position.
- Have students write about their position.

A graphic organizer such as the one in Figure 9.15 may be used to help students form their brief position essay.

I think . . .	
because . . .	
Evidence for that is . . .	
Also because . . .	
Evidence for that is . . .	

Figure 9.15

Structuring an Argumentative Essay.

ANALYZING ARGUMENTS IN TEXTS.   After the students can confidently write out their own arguments according to this structure, they are ready to outline the arguments of others. Note that it is best to begin with short, simple, and clearly structured arguments such as the essay on dogs and cats found on pages 269–270. Teachers may write their own sample essays to give students practice, making sure those essays (1) state a claim clearly, (2) offer two or three reasons for the claim, and (3) immediately support each reason with evidence. It is advisable to use the words "reason" and "evidence" right in the essays, to help students identify them.

Then the students take notes about the essay in a graphic organizer such as the one in Figure 9.16.

Once the arguments are laid out this way, the teacher and students can discuss whether the reasons logically support the claim, and whether the evidence really supports the reasons.

Some students may be ready to move beyond tracking the simple form of arguments, and pay attention to one or more of the following:

- missing information (MI)
- loaded words (LW)
- faulty assumptions about what the world needs (FA)

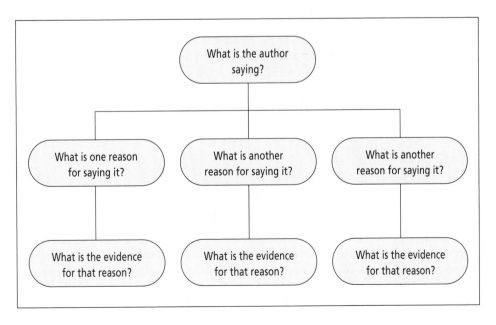

Figure 9.16

A Graphic Organizer for Arguments.

Figure 9.17
Words and Their Connotations.

Negative	Neutral	Positive
Shack	House	Palace
Cowardly	Cautious	Prudent
Sluggish	Slow	Guarded
Oversized	Large	
Fat		
		Confident
	Casual	

The students can locate and mark places where these problems occur, underlining the offending phrases and putting the corresponding letters in the margins near the problem phrases.

Semantic Feature Analysis

WORDS AND THEIR CONNOTATIONS. For an exercise on loaded words—words that carry judgments that have not been justified, teachers sometimes use an exercise like the following. The teacher shows students a chart with rows of words divided into three columns. In the middle column goes the most neutral word. In the left-hand column goes a positive word—a word with positive connotations—and in the right-hand column goes a negative word—a word with negative connotations (connotations are the other things a word means beyond its literal meaning, especially the value judgments a word conveys). The students may fill in the blanks in a chart like the one in Figure 9.17; and later create charts of their own.

LOOKING AT ARGUMENTS THAT DON'T SAY THEY ARE ARGUMENTS. Not all of the messages that seek to persuade people state their claims clearly and offer reasons supported by evidence about why we should accept those claims. So it can be valuable for students to learn how to do a little detective work before they let themselves be persuaded by something they read, see, or hear. The graphic organizer in Figure 9.18 is adapted from Luke and Freebody's "Four Resources Model of Reading" (Luke & Freebody, 1999) that was discussed on pages 272–273. Teachers may practice asking the question about a simple text first—even a text as simple as a stop sign. Then the class can move on to another kind of text, such as an advertisement.

Strategies That Compare Multiple Texts with Common Themes

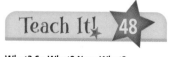

What? So What? Now What?

COMPARING TEXTS. Primary as well as upper grade teachers introduce students to the value of reading multiple texts and thinking about how texts function when they create thematic and inquiry units. These units usually begin by posing some question for exploration such as, "How should we treat the insects in our environment? Should we use insecticides and try to kill them or are there some insects that are useful to us?" or "How important is it to share with others what we have?" Teachers collect an array of materials that are accessible to students (at their reading levels and that capture their levels of inter-

1. What *is* this?	Decide what kind of message this is.	
	Then decide how we should read it.	
2. What does it mean?	Now, list some of the words or images in the message that caught your eye—What do they make you think of?	
	Next, say what you think the whole message means.	
3. What is it for?	Decide what you can do with this text.	
	Say what you think others may do with it.	
4. Who is behind the message?	Explain what you think the text is trying to do.	
	Say who you think might want the text to do that, and why.	
	Then say whose point of view you think is left out.	

Figure 9.18
Looking Critically at Messages.

est and knowledge). These materials represent a range of genres and formats so students can compare and contrast how authors present ideas and information.

USING INFORMATIONAL TEXTS.   Many classes begin their inquiries with a group K-W-L in which the teacher creates a chart of what the students think they already know about the topic. During the discussion that ensues, the teacher also helps students generate questions that will guide their initial inquiries. Once the students are reading, viewing, and searching for information, the teacher can bring them back together to formulate key questions that can then be put on the class Inquiry Chart (Hoffman, 1992). The teacher also selects some of the best texts for students' use in this class activity. Small groups of students can take turns examining the texts and recording what they learn from the authors. The groups can either record their information and ideas on 8 × 11 inch record sheets or put what they learn on sticky notes to be included on a large class I-Chart.

Teach It! 47

Know-Want to Know-Learn (K-W-L)

As students read from different sources of information, their awareness increases about how authors have to select and leave out information. The ways authors explain ideas and provide visual information also vary considerably. Students attend to these characteristics and teachers can guide them to make comparisons about which texts are most useful and which could use revision to be more "considerate" to them as readers. See an example of an I-Chart that the teacher used as students completed their unit in Figure 9.19. As part of the culmination of this unit, groups of students wrote their own books and took time to consider the structure, the ways they would present information, and the themes they wanted to communicate. The children developed a deeper understanding of the relationship between texts and readers throughout this process.

Children are often amazed by the amount of partial information and misinformation contained in some of the documents. As one group of second graders exclaimed, "These two books are confusing—one says there aren't brown recluse spiders in the middle part of the country; the other says they can be found everywhere in dark, damp areas. One makes spiders sound like they are really helpful; the other tells about a woman who almost died when a brown recluse bit her while she was rocking in her chair and shows an ugly picture of an arm of someone bitten."

Figure 9.19 Inquiry Chart.

Topic:	Guiding Question 1	Guiding Question 2	Guiding Question 3	Guiding Question 4	Other Interesting Facts and Figures	New Questions
WHAT WE KNOW						
Source 1						
Source 2						
Source 3						
Summary						

Source: J. Hoffman, "Critical Reading/Thinking across the Curriculum: Using I-charts to Support Learning." *Language Arts*, 69(2), 121–127. Copyright 1992 by the National Council of Teachers of English. Reprinted with permission.

READING MULTIPLE VERSIONS OF THE SAME STORY. Another way to help young students understand how texts function in social contexts is to read and examine several texts written by different authors using the same basic story. One of the easiest to use is the Cinderella tale. Almost any library will have several versions of this tale available. Teachers can read some tales to students and have them chart their similarities and differences, their structure, their characters, the challenges faced, the ways the problems are solved, and the underlying message the author seems to want readers to accept. For example, after reading the classic French version of Cinderella, students who read *The Rough-faced Girl* (American Indian tale) and *Mufaro's Beautiful Daughters* (West African tale) can discuss the different challenges faced and the ways the girls are able to overcome their hardships. The pictures or drawings are also worth examining critically to see how the context and characters are represented. Children may want to create their own illustrations or locate others online or in other books. Figure 9.20 shows an example of how one first-grade teacher helped her students think deeply about various versions of the folktale, "Stone Soup." This activity led students to analyze the major story elements and then compare the ways the authors developed the basic story theme in a variety of settings.

Teach It! 40

Story Maps

Figure 9.20 *Stone Soup:* A Single Story from Multiple Perspectives.

Title	*Stone Soup* M. Brown, 1947	*Stone Soup*, T. Ross, 1987	*Nail Soup*, Zemach, 1964	*Group Soup*, B. Brenner, 1992	*Stone Soup*, Muth, 2003
Characters					
Setting Genre					
Problem					
Resolution					
Theme or Lesson Learned					

For Review

This chapter has focused on critical thinking and critical literacy. It is difficult to say exactly at what age children can read (or listen, or view) deeply. Vivian Vasquez (2004) has demonstrated how it is possible to encourage even preschool children to look deeply into the messages they are exposed to, and to challenge some of them. When even young children are working with ideas they are deeply immersed in, including stories, they are capable of sophisticated thought. This chapter described some kinds of thinking that texts evoke. It began by examining what is meant by critical literacy and why that is so important in the twenty-first century. It argued that students need to read carefully to understand the structure of texts, to connect with the texts, to ask questions about authors' purposes and to discern and question the example texts set out for readers to follow. Then the chapter discussed some ways of analyzing the structures of stories for the ways they guide readers' responses, including structured opposites, and what were called "categories and relationships." Further on in the section that described conceptions of reading, the chapter looked at the logic of argumentative texts, and then at ways of examining texts that weren't clearly argumentative, but still seemed to have persuasive intentions.

The second half of the chapter set out methods for guiding students' reading through different kinds of texts. First strategies were presented for helping students develop an understanding of how similar texts can be structured very differently and thus communicate different messages, then techniques were provided for examining and weighing arguments, and finally suggestions were offered for looking at all kinds of messages that seek to influence readers.

For Your Journal

1. Take a moment to review your answers to the questions on the Anticipation Guide that opened this chapter. Has your thinking changed? If so, write about the changes in your journal.

2. Read the story "The Ugly Duckling" by Hans Christian Andersen. There is a version online at http://www.ivyjoy.com/fables/duckling.html. Does this story have an uplifting message for everyone? Think through this story using the four scans of Luke and Freebody described on pages 272–273. Write down your conclusions and share them later with your class.

Taking It to the World

1. Watch an hour of mainstream children's television one Saturday morning. Pick any one of the frameworks of analysis presented earlier in this chapter, such as "The Web of Narrative and 'The Way It Is'" or "Behavior and Rewards." Write up your insights using a Dual Entry Diary format.

This Is What a Dual Entry Diary Looks Like	
In this column indicate the section from the show that made you pause.	In this column, write your comment on it: What was striking about it?

New Literacies Connections

1. Explore the University of Connecticut's website on the New Literacies at this address: http://www.newliteracies.uconn.edu/team.html.

Read a research article or two and be prepared to summarize it for your classmates.

Now go to MyEducationLab (**www.myeducationlab.com**), where you can:

- Find learning outcomes for the topics covered in this chapter, along with the national standards that connect to these outcomes.

- Complete Assignments and Activities that can help you more deeply understand the chapter content.

- Engage in Building Teaching Skills and Dispositions exercises, in which you can apply and practice core teaching skills identified in the chapter.

Chapter

10

Teaching Children to Write

Anticipation Guide

The following statements will help you begin thinking about the topics covered in this chapter. Answer *true* or *false* in response to each statement. As you read and learn more about the topics mentioned in these statements, think back on your answers. See what interests you and prompts your curiosity toward more understanding.

_____ 1. In general, children never write until they have been carefully taught how.

_____ 2. When we speak of a writing process, we mean a process by which many successful adult writers as well as schoolchildren produce written compositions.

_____ 3. The goal of writing instruction is to teach children to write everything once and write it correctly.

_____ 4. Children can help each other learn to write.

_____ 5. It is generally better for teachers to assign writing topics than to let children choose their own.

_____ 6. Children need different levels of support as they learn to write. Some children flourish in the open atmosphere of the writing workshop, but others need more explicit guidance.

_____ 7. It is important for teachers to write in front of children and demonstrate writing as a studio craft.

_____ 8. The difference between editing and revising is that editing is done only by professional writers.

_____ 9. There is no such thing as different levels of support that teachers can give to writers at different ages. Writing is a sink-or-swim affair.

_____ 10. Reading helps children learn to be writers because it shows them the choices that writers make in crafting language into print.

Teaching Children to Write

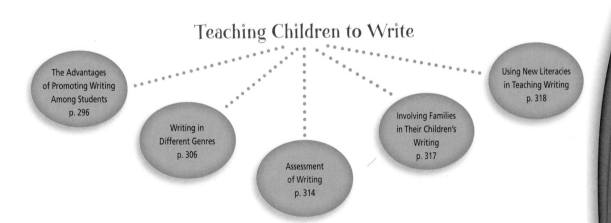

The Advantages of Promoting Writing Among Students
p. 296

Writing in Different Genres
p. 306

Assessment of Writing
p. 314

Involving Families in Their Children's Writing
p. 317

Using New Literacies in Teaching Writing
p. 318

The Writing Process in a Third-Grade Classroom

At West Street School in Geneva, New York, Anne Bergstrom is trying a new approach to her third graders' study of African geography. The school's experience has corroborated what the National Assessment of Educational Progress has found: Not only do elementary students need to know more geography, but they also need to know how to think with geographical information. So this spring, because their student teacher from last fall, Sarah Barry, is studying in Dakar, the capital of Senegal, Ms. Bergstrom has arranged to conduct an inquiry lesson on Senegal via the Internet.

In the fall, the students located Senegal on a map and discussed its tropical climate and its history as a slave state and as a colony of France. They read material about Senegal from the National Geographic website, and also did their best to make sense of the U.S. State Department's Web-based information. In December, the students thought of questions they wanted Sarah to investigate, wrote them on a piece of chart paper as part of a K-W-L chart (see Figure 10.1), and sent them to Sarah in an e-mail.

Sarah wrote the students an e-mail from Senegal and asked them how they wanted her to find answers to their questions: "Who do you want me to talk to? What do you want me to ask?" The students took turns writing e-mails to Sarah on the classroom computer. But Sarah realized that there were fascinating things about Senegal that the students did not know to ask about. So she sent them occasional transmissions that she called "mysteries," intriguing photographs with questions attached. The students took turns writing to Sarah about the mystery; they sent guesses or questions they wanted to ask her. In a way, Sarah became an extension of the class—their remote-control anthropologist.

In the spring, Ms. Bergstrom had the students prepare write-ups of what they had learned. The students used the writing workshop to focus on their topics, write a first draft, revise their drafts, edit them, and prepare them for publication. Later, the class collaborated on a joint composition: the script for a class play about aspects of life in the West African country of Senegal, which they performed for an audience of the whole school.

The Advantages of Promoting Writing Among Students

Even preschool and kindergarten children are eager to write—that is, if we accept making communicative marks on paper as "writing." As we saw in previous chapters, writing down ideas word by word and sound by sound helps young learners take a close look at the language they speak and the system of print that represents it. But emphasizing writing has other advantages, too:

- Writing makes students more observant, both of their own inner experiences and of the outside world.
- Being writers makes students closer readers of other writers. Young writers are sensitive to language and style, and writing can make them feel like "workers in the same vineyard" as the Kate DiCamillos and Gary Sotos whom they admire.
- Writing makes students more reflective as they record an idea, examine that idea in print, and maybe come up with a further idea.
- Writing builds community. As students work hard to capture and communicate their thoughts and experiences and as they listen to their classmates' efforts to do the same, students reveal themselves to each other and come to better understand each other.

The First Questions We Have

1. Do they go swimming?
2. What is the population?
3. Do they know about King's fight for freedom?
4. How do they talk?
5. What do they eat?
6. How hot does it get?
7. What are their houses made of?
8. What do they do in their spare time?
9. Was it a slave trading place?
10. What do they celebrate?
11. What games do they play?
12. What kinds of animals do they have?
13. What are their religions?
14. How do people treat each other?
15. What kind of jewelry do they wear?
16. Does anyone have piercings or tattoos?
17. Do they trade? What do they trade with other countries?
18. Does everyone have a job?
19. Are there homeless people?
20. How do they dispose of trash?
21. Do they brush their teeth, and if so, with what?

Figure 10.1
The First Questions We Have.

- Applied to literature and to other subjects in the curriculum, writing responses and other kinds of inquiry also serve as a powerful learning tool.

In this chapter we will present many ways teachers can help children learn to write. We begin by outlining the well-known "writing process," a set of activities through which writers create works. Then we will look in more detail at many ways of teaching and supporting writing.

The Writing Process

A model of the **writing process** was put forward nearly thirty years ago by Pulitzer Prize-winning journalist and writing teacher Donald Murray (1985) and language arts specialist and researcher Donald Graves (1982). That model is now used widely both within schools and in other contexts to describe what people do when they write, and also to guide teachers of writing. According to their writing process model, thoughtful writers may go through five steps or phases as they produce their works: rehearsing, drafting, revising, editing, and publishing.

REHEARSING.   During this phase writers prepare to write by gathering information and collecting their thoughts. Student writers think of what they might like to write about, they survey what they know about the topic, and they begin to plan a way to write about it. Several strategies are available that can teach students to rehearse their ideas before writing:

- *Brainstorming and clustering.* Children can jot down a list of their ideas about a topic before embarking on writing about it. As a more elaborate version of the brainstorm, they can create a graphic organizer, such as a cluster or semantic web, with the topic listed in the center connected to "satellites" of related ideas around it (see Figure 10.2).
- *Interviewing each other to find the story.* Students can interview a partner. Regardless of whether a writer has already prepared a cluster, it often helps if another student asks questions about the topic to help the writer "find the story." The student asks questions such as the following:

"Why did you choose this topic?"

"What most interests you about the topic?"

Teach It! 45

Graphic Organizers

Figure 10.2
A Cluster.

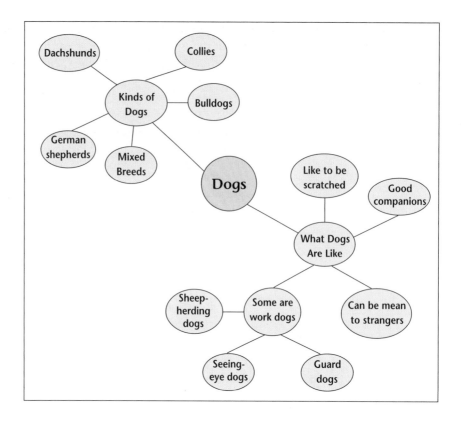

Teach It! 59

Form Poems

The student also asks questions about details, things that the writer might not realize other people will want to know.

- *Making class collaborations.* In introducing a new kind of writing, such as a poem or a fairy tale, it might be best to ask the students to compose one work together before writing their own piece. This is especially helpful for younger students. The teacher can contribute as well to help steer the work in positive directions. If the students have difficulty beginning, offer them a series of choices:

Where does the story take place? In a big city or a small village?

Who should be the main character? A young girl or an old magician?

A young girl? Okay. Then who can describe her? And what is her problem?

- *Researching the topic.* Students are often able to write stories or papers about personal experiences off the tops of their heads, but when they are writing about the real world beyond themselves, they will soon run out of things to say unless they collect information about their topic. They might need to read up on it or interview experts about it, or they might observe carefully and collect details about it. Lucy Calkins and her colleagues in the New York City Writing Project (1992) suggest having students keep notebooks for gathering observations.

DRAFTING. Drafting involves setting ideas out on paper. Drafting is tentative and experimental. Students write down their ideas so that they can see more of what they have to say about their topic; often their best ideas do not occur to them until they begin committing thoughts to paper. The phase of drafting is not the time to be critical about spelling and handwriting. Such mechanical concerns are better dealt with later; this is the time for students to focus on getting their ideas onto the page.

Young writers do not yet have the habit of writing more than one version of a paper. Proficient writers, however, know that good writing is rewriting. Teachers can encourage students to think of writing as drafting in a number of ways:

- Stamp the papers DRAFT or use the backs of recycled office paper. Both actions make it clear to everyone that these versions of the papers are not final.

- Have the students write on every other line. This leaves room for them to add material they think of later on.

- Show students how to use arrows, carets (^), and stapled-on sections to indicate on a draft how it should be rewritten. Unless they are shown, students will not know how to physically mark up and modify a draft and use it to plan the next version of the paper.

- Remind students not to worry too much about spelling, handwriting, and mechanics at the drafting stage. A large advantage to writing more than one draft of a paper is that it frees writers to concentrate on their ideas at first and worry about form and correctness later. This should be explained to students at the start, and the treatment of their early and later drafts should be consistent with it. Be careful, however, that you do not encourage students to be messy. Bromley (1999) advises against calling an early draft of a paper a "sloppy copy."

REVISING.   After their thoughts have been written out in draft form, students need to think about stating the ideas more clearly. Most students need to be shown ways that writing can be improved: by having clear beginnings, middles, and ends; by finding a topic and sticking to it; by showing and not telling; and the like. Teachers can teach these points through focused lessons (discussed later in this chapter) and help young writers internalize them by means of conferences. Teachers use two main kinds of conferences in teaching writing.

Teacher-led Conferences.   Conferences allow the teacher to help students clarify their writing and also to model for the student ways to ask helpful questions that will help encourage other struggling writers—their peers. The teacher needs to ask questions that teach, pulling solutions from the students themselves and always respecting the students' ownership of their writing. The teacher asks students questions to help them focus on areas to improve their writing and provides checklists of things to watch out for.

Peer Conferences.   Once the teacher has modeled the process, students can hold conferences with each other. Because many conferences will be going on in the room at one time, it helps if students understand their tasks clearly. The teacher can put together a checklist of good questions for the students to ask each other as they review their works-in-progress, such as the following:

- Did my opening lines interest you? How might I improve the beginning paragraph?

- Do I need more information anywhere? That is, where could I be more specific?

- Do you ever get lost while reading my draft?

- Do I stay on topic?

- Do I come to a good conclusion?

EDITING OR PROOFREADING.   Once a paper has been drafted and revised, it needs to be reviewed for mistakes. Naturally, proofreading is held off for last because whole paragraphs might be cut or added in the revising stage. The habit of proofreading must be taught. It consists of three things:

- Caring that the paper is correct

- Being aware of particular errors

- Knowing how to set those errors straight

A caring attitude toward writing is probably best developed by publishing what students write. Students are most likely to care about correctness once they realize that writing is not simply done for a grade; their works also must pass the scrutiny of others, who will be distracted from their ideas if the papers are marred by flaws in spelling, grammar, and handwriting.

Children should be made aware of errors through focused lessons that demonstrate one or two writing errors at a time. Focused lessons treat errors that one or more students are actually making in their writing. Areas in which children make errors might include the following:

- Beginning each sentence with a capital letter and ending it with terminal punctuation (a period, a question mark, or an exclamation point)
- Making each sentence express a complete thought, avoiding sentence fragments and run-on sentences
- Spelling correctly

After clearly teaching students to be aware of different kinds of errors and how to repair them, the next step is to get the students to proofread their own work. Give them a checklist to guide their proofreading, such as the one shown in Figure 10.3. Each point on the checklist should be carefully introduced, explained, and practiced before students are sent off to use it on their own. Several versions of the checklist might be introduced during the year as new points for correction are added to the students' repertoires. Once the checklist has been introduced, students should practice using it with a partner to go over each other's papers before they are ready to use the checklists by themselves.

PUBLISHING.   Publishing is the final stage of the writing process and actually drives the whole endeavor. The prospect of sharing what they have to say with an audience makes many students want to write, rewrite, and smooth out and refine, especially if they have seen other students' work received with appreciation and delight. Publishing also lets stu-

Figure 10.3
Proofreading Checklist.

Source: Reprinted with permission from *Classroom Strategies That Work: An Elementary Teacher's Guide to Process Writing* by Ruth Nathan, Frances Temple, Kathleen Juntenen, and Charles Temple. Copyright © 1989 by Ruth Nathan, Frances Temple, Kathleen Juntenen, and Charles Temple. Published by Heinemann, Portsmouth, NH. All rights reserved.

1. Did I spell all words correctly?

   (Underline words you are unsure of. Try looking some of them up.)

2. Did I write each sentence as a complete thought?

   (This is an incomplete thought: "On the street." This is a complete thought: "The little puppy stood all alone on the street." Note: Sometimes writers use an incomplete sentence on purpose—to create a certain effect. For example: "Not me!")

3. Do I have any run-on sentences?

   (Here is a run-on sentence: "The little puppy stood all alone on the street and he couldn't find his mother and he was so, so frightened that he thought he would die and so he looked around to find a friend and he didn't find one so he walked on and on." This is a run-on sentence, too: "I don't have a pet at home do you?")

4. Did I end each sentence with the correct punctuation?

   (Here is a sentence that has the wrong punctuation at the end: "Could the puppy find his mother." The sentence needs a question mark, not a period.)

5. Did I begin each sentence with a capital letter?

6. Did I use capital letters correctly in other places?

   (Names, days of the week, months, titles, etc.)

7. Did I use commas, apostrophes, and other punctuation correctly?

   (Commas are used between words in lists, before a conjunction introducing an independent clause, after salutations, etc. Apostrophes are used with possessive forms [Jimmy's shoes, the boys' lockers] and in contractions [can't, it's—for "it is"].)

8. Did I indent each paragraph?

   (Whenever you start a new idea, you need a new paragraph. Dialogue [talk between two or more people] also requires a new paragraph each time a different speaker talks.)

dents see what others are doing. A good idea is contagious; anything from an interesting topic, to a plot structure, to a way to use dialogue, to the habit of taking risks with spelling may be shared from one student to another through the process of publishing. How refined should published works be? Not all writing that is published in the classroom has to be perfect. Age level matters here. If they are to be kept in the classroom community, younger children's publications may be less than completely perfect; if they are going "public" such as out in the hallway, that writing should be corrected up to your grade level standards.

How to Organize and Manage a Writing Workshop

A popular approach to teaching children to write is the **writing workshop**, in which students are shown how to use the writing process and are given regular opportunities to produce many kinds of writing. Teachers who teach writing successfully work three elements into their teaching:

- *Time.* Writing workshops should be scheduled at regular intervals so students know when they will have opportunities to write. When students know that they will have these opportunities, they are more likely to collect ideas during their daily lives that they can write about during writing workshop.

- *Emphasis on communication.* It matters a lot whether students are writing for the teacher (to demonstrate skill or to get a grade) or writing because they want to say something to people who will be interested in hearing it. When writing is real communication, students may engage more of their powers of expression. Students should have opportunities to choose their own topics or—when the topics are assigned—to decide on their own approach to a topic. When conferences are conducted to help students improve writing, their ownership of the work— that is, what they mean to say—must still be respected.

- *Demonstration and direct instruction.* Teaching writing is a studio craft, with attention to the process of creating. The teacher should demonstrate every phase of the process so that students will know how writing is done. The teacher should also teach skills of writing, from organization to correct punctuation, but should do so in the context of writing for communication so that students will actually come to use these skills.

How often writing workshops are conducted and how much time they are given varies from one teacher to another. Figure 10.4 shows one plan for managing the time in a writing workshop. This writing workshop lasts an entire 60-minute class meeting, perhaps three days a week, with time set aside for five distinctive activities.

Minutes in the Period

0–2	10	30	50	60
Sense-of-the-class meeting	Focused lesson	Writing time	Conferences	Sharing

Figure 10.4
Daily Schedule of a Writing Workshop.

SENSE-OF-THE-CLASS MEETING. Assuming that the students are already engaged in writing tasks, the period begins with a brief sense-of-the-class meeting (Atwell, 1986) to find out who is working on what writing topic. Students keep a list of writing topics in a journal or a writing folder; if they do not have a work in progress, they should already have a topic ready to be written about. By finding out and recording several interesting things about each child at the beginning of the year, the teacher can have a lively suggestion ready if a student comes up empty.

Descriptive Writing

FOCUSED LESSONS. The goal of writing workshops is to encourage students to write about things they care about for real audiences and to improve their writing so that it communicates more and more effectively. It is essential to give students time, models, and opportunities to write. But students also need careful instruction on all aspects of writing—from how one carries out the writing process to proper punctuation. Focused instruction helps children in the rehearsal and drafting stages by showing them strategies for writing, and it helps them in the revising and editing stages by giving them criteria or working standards for making their writing better. In the past, focused lessons were called *mini-lessons*, and teachers tried to hold their length to five to seven minutes; now the preferred term is *focused lessons*, to give due attention to the importance of writing instruction (Bromley, 1999; Routman, 1996).

Focused lessons may relate to any aspect of writing, from mechanical issues such as spelling and punctuation; to word-choice issues such as showing, not telling, for clear and vivid expression; to composition-related issues such as ways to write strong introductions and closings. Focused lessons also may highlight the writing process itself, showing students how writers get ideas and narrow them, how writers put ideas into words, how writers go back and make the work better, and how writers share their work and learn from their peers' comments.

The goal of all focused lessons is for students to internalize the main points and use them while they are reviewing their peers' papers and their own. In other words, the writing teacher tries to work himself out of a job. It is important to conceive of focused lessons not as teaching about writing in the abstract, but rather as providing guidance to the children's own writing and editing processes.

Focused lessons follow a four-part model for teaching skills in context: demonstration and immersion, attention to detail, guided practice, and independent use. In the writing workshop, focused lessons use those four parts in the following ways.

1. **Finding a text that demonstrates a point or skill you want to teach.** For example, if you want to show children how to write vivid beginnings to stories by jumping right into the action, read the beginning of *Charlotte's Web*:

"Where's Papa going with that axe?" said Fern to her mother as they were setting the table for breakfast.

"Out to the hoghouse," replied Mrs. Arable. "Some pigs were born last night."

"I don't see why he needs an axe," continued Fern, who was only eight.

"Well," said her mother, "one of the pigs is a runt. It's very small and weak, and it will never amount to anything. So your father has decided to do away with it."

"Do away with it," shrieked Fern. "You mean kill it, just because it's smaller than the others?" (White, 1952/1980 p. 1)

2. **Sharing the example and calling students' attention to the skill it demonstrates.** E. B. White could have begun his story by describing the setting and the characters, but he didn't. He started right in with the action. He decided to have Fern ask that question, hear that terrible answer, and get upset. After just these few lines, it is evident that the main problem of the story will be saving the little pig's life, and readers will want to know what can be done to solve this problem.

You might ask the students how the beginning made them feel and what it led them to expect. What advice do they suppose E. B. White gave himself that made him begin the story that way? Discuss this example until the point is clear that a good way of beginning a story is to start right in with action that shows readers a problem and makes them care about what will happen in the story.

3. Providing the students with guided practice using the skill. Ask the students to take out a draft of a story they are writing. Have them rewrite the beginning of the story so that it starts right in with action or dialogue that leads the reader directly into the main problem of the story. Have the students pair up and take turns explaining to a partner the changes they made to their paper.

4. Encouraging students to use the skill in their independent writing. So that the points taught in the focused lessons enter students' repertoire of writing skills, you might add each point to a writing rubric or editing checklist or to your guidelines for good writing. You can also add that point into rubrics used to evaluate students' writing or into the checklists they use to edit their own and each other's drafts.

WRITING TIME.   During much of the writing workshop, all of the students are writing. This is quiet time. The teacher writes for the first five minutes as well, to help establish an atmosphere for quiet independent work. For the next ten minutes, the teacher might move around to individual students, to encourage them as they write. Nathan and colleagues (1988) advise that the teacher go first to those who appear to be having trouble writing.

CONFERENCES.   After the students have written for a period of time, conferences begin. The teacher can conduct a conference for the whole class, with one student, or with a small group.

Students may confer with a partner or with a small group. Conferences were discussed in detail earlier on page 299. Students who wish to continue writing during this time may do so.

SHARING.   The last ten minutes of the workshop are reserved for sharing. The students chosen to share should be those who are far along in a draft or whose work displays an interesting issue. Different students should share each time because only one or two can normally participate in a ten-minute period. Some teachers extend sharing time to get in three students a day; that way, every student gets to share every other week.

Effective teachers of writing must consider how they present author's craft to their students so that their students will not only understand the strategy, but will also be able to apply it in their own writing. Analyze the effectiveness of teachers' lessons in the activity "Teaching a Mini-lesson on Author's Craft in Writing." (To find this activity, go to the topic *Writing* in MyEducationLab and click on Building Teaching Skills and Dispositions.)

Different Levels of Support for Writing

The writing workshop model assumes students are capable of a fair amount of self-direction and that they understand at least the rudiments of how ideas are put down on paper. It is true that children as young as kindergarten age can participate in writing workshops in some fashion. But teachers find that many young writers—and not just the youngest—sometimes need more explicit support as they learn to write. Fountas and Pinnell (1996) and Tompkins (2000) suggest that teachers prepare to give different levels of support for young writers and provide a range of activities for doing so. Those activities that give higher levels of support put the teacher in the role of demonstrator and explainer.

Activities that give lower levels of support maximize the children's initiative and put the teacher more in the role of coach and guide. Five kinds or levels of writing support are modeled writing, shared writing, interactive writing, guided writing, and independent writing. Figure 10.5 shows examples of the kinds of activities that are conducted at each level of writing support. Although some of the activities at the more highly supported end of the scale are intended for young children, it is not the case that only younger writers need more support and only older writers need less. At one time or another, writers of all ages can use both support and freedom to create.

Figure 10.5   Writing Instruction with Different Levels of Support.

High				Low
Teacher Input and Support				
Kind of Support	Modeled Writing	Shared Writing	Interactive Writing	Guided Writing	Independent Writing
How many?	*Group*	*Group*	*Group*	*Group*	*Solo or buddy activity*
Whose ideas?	*Teacher composes*	*Teacher and students compose*	*Teacher and students compose*	*Students compose*	*Student composes*
Who writes?	*Teacher writes*	*Teacher writes*	*Teacher and students write*	*Students write*	*Student writes*
Sample activities	*Demonstrations*	*K-W-L charts; dictations*	*Daily news; songs, poems*	*Class collaborations form poems; formula books; concept books; riddles, etc.*	*Writing workshop; journals; plays; free compositions*

Source: Adapted from Tompkins, 2000.

MODELED WRITING.   In **modeled writing**, when students need to be shown some aspect of the writing process, the teacher models the approach for the class. For example, if you wish to introduce the writing process to young students for the first time, you might proceed as follows:

> *Gathering the children in front of you, announce that you are going to write about something important. Explain that you are first going to draw your ideas as you talk about them and that you will then write in a space below the picture. Take a piece of chart paper, and fold it horizontally so that the crease is about a third of the way from the bottom. When the paper is flattened out, the crease will mark off the space for writing. Now think aloud by naming and talking about your topic: your aging family dog. Using a page of chart paper, draw a picture as you talk, and demonstrate how you can use drawing as a way of rehearsing or thinking out your ideas. Then think of one line you want to write about the dog in the space you left for writing underneath the picture.*
>
> My dog is old.
>
> *You say the sentence to yourself several times and then announce that you're going to write the first word, "My," which you pronounce slowly.*
> *"What sound does it begin with?" you ask.*
> *"Muh," you say, "and what letter makes that sound?"*
> *"M," you say and write M on the board.*
> *You then pronounce the next sound and spell it, and you write the other words in the same way. When you are finished, you have the children read the sentence with you and discuss the picture. Ask the children to identify one thing that interests them about the picture and writing and to ask one question. Post the composition on the wall for the children to look at later, and remind the children that they can write down their ideas in the same way.*

SHARED WRITING.   In **shared writing**, the teacher not only models acts of writing but also engages students in composing the writing. When shared writing is used, the topic needs to be one that both the teacher and the students know about and are excited about. Such a topic might be a shared experience such as a field trip, a story that all are reading, or a topic that is under investigation by the class. Completion of a K-W-L chart offers a

Teach It! 4

Language Experience or Group Dictated Story

natural occasion for shared writing. Another kind of shared writing activity is group dictation. Here the writing activity is preceded by some kind of activity that excites the students and stimulates talk about it. The teacher leads a discussion and helps students find things to say, then asks the students to offer comments about the topic and writes these down on a piece of chart paper. The teacher might lead the students to sound out some of the words and to offer spellings for them.

INTERACTIVE WRITING.   This procedure was developed to help emergent and beginning readers and writers explore the writing system in its details. Developed by Moira McKenzie at the Ebury Street Centre for Language in London, interactive writing has been incorporated into Fountas and Pinnell's guided reading program because "Interactive writing provides an authentic setting within which the teacher can explicitly demonstrate how written language works" (Fountas & Pinnell, 1996, p. 33).

Interactive writing works very much like taking a dictated account except that the teacher and the children "share the pen." The procedures follow these steps:

1. The teacher and a group of six to twelve students share an experience and agree on a topic. The topic might be a retelling of a story, a poem, or a song; the daily news; or an idea that the class is studying.

2. The students offer a sentence about the topic. The teacher has the students repeat the sentence many times and even count the words to fix them firmly in their minds.

3. The teacher asks the students for the first word, then pronounces that word slowly, writing its letters.

4. The teacher now asks for the next word and invites a child up to write the whole word, a few letters, or a single letter. The teacher fills in letters the students miss. Each time a word is added, the whole text is read back by the students, with the teacher pointing to the words.

5. To help the students orient themselves to the text and add letters, the teacher might write blanks where the letters should go.

6. The teacher uses correction tape to paste over letters that are poorly formed.

7. The teacher talks about words and print as the lesson progresses, reminding students of words they know or almost know, reminding them of spelling patterns they have seen before, and reminding them to leave spaces between words and to add punctuation.

GUIDED WRITING.   When teachers instruct students to create a particular pattern of writing or use a particular strategy, compose a sample piece as a group, and then produce their own writings according to the form or the strategy—either individually or in pairs—they are guiding student writing. **Guided writing** is used when students can handle the rudiments of writing—making letters and spelling words—but still need to know some strategies for organizing their ideas on the page.

Many of the kinds of writing lessons described in the next section on writing in the genres lend themselves to guided writing. For example, the form poems of cinquains and list poems can be done as class collaborations and then individually by students as guided writing activities.

INDEPENDENT WRITING.   Writing in journals, self-initiated writing of all kinds, and writing done in writing workshops are all forms of **independent writing**. It is important that students of all ages have regular chances to write independently. Doing so allows children to exercise many of their ideas and strategies for writing—from letter formation

Phonics and Phonological Awareness

How do writing activities support development of phonemic awareness?

myeducationlab
The Power of Classroom Practice
www.myeducationlab.com

Watch a video showing kindergarten teachers helping students form a reading-writing connection in the activity "Making the Reading-Writing Connection Explicit for Kindergarten Students." Reflect on the video by answering the questions that follow. (To find this activity, go to the topic *Writing* in MyEducationLab and click on Assignments and Activities.)

myeducationlab
The Power of Classroom Practice
www.myeducationlab.com

Think about the supports available for the range of students for whom English is an additional language while watching the video clip in the activity "Supporting English Language Learners' Writing Development Through Guided Writing." Reflect on the video by answering the questions that follow. (To find this activity, go to the topic *English Language Learners* in MyEducationLab and click on Assignments and Activities.)

Enthusiasm for writing differs among children, but it's an important part of literacy that goes beyond just learning how to put words on a page. (Lindfors Photography)

Helping Struggling Writers

SIOP®
Sheltered
Instruction
Observation
Protocol®

The writing workshop is a wonderful forum for many children's creativity, but it has not always served all children well. There are some students for whom the self-direction afforded by the writing workshop seems almost tantamount to neglect, particularly children whose home culture and language differ significantly from those of the school (Delpit, 1996). One explanation of the difficulty is offered by Collins (1998), who points out that writing is a secondary form of discourse normally based on speech, which is the primary form of discourse. If the kind of discourse a child sees in books and is expected to produce with a pencil fairly closely resembles the kind of discourse that is spoken in his or her home environment, then the task of learning to write is largely one of discovering or acquiring the relations between speech and writing—that is, to figure out the strategies that enable us to put down on paper what we say in speech. The kind of writing workshop described earlier should serve this child well, for as Collins (1998) tells us,

> When literacy activities involve language forms and functions that are close to one's primary discourse, they can be achieved through a balance between acquisition and learning which favors acquisition. The typical writing workshop shows this balance in favor of acquisition, owing to its pronounced student-centered methods, including student-generated topics and genres for writing, multiple drafts to gradually improve writing, and supportive feedback from teachers and peers. When literacy activities involve ways of using language substantially different from one's primary discourse, the balance shifts in favor of learning. (p. 6)

As you might recall from the discussion of language acquisition and language learning in Chapter 3, *learning* refers to formal, teacher-directed, explicit instruction. *Acquisition* means learning by discovery and inference from being immersed in writing activities. Moving the balance toward learning means explicitly teaching students what they need to know to carry out the processes of writing. Struggling writers do not need to be taken out of writing workshops and given skill sheets to fill out. It is still possible for teachers to give students strategies for writing that they can use to express themselves to an audience of their peers (Harris & Graham, 1996).

Strategies are explicit procedures. Strategies relate to every aspect of writing, from choosing a topic to deciding which parts of the topic to include and which to leave out, to organizing ideas on paper. Strategies may be taught in two ways. One is by means of focused lessons. In a focused lesson, the teacher makes it very clear to the students when and how to use a particular technique in writing, whether it be a beginning + middle + ending organization for a paper or the way to punctuate dialogue. Another means of teaching a strategy is by using writing guides or graphic organizers. For struggling writers, having a graphic organizer to follow, such as a story map or an outline for a persuasive essay, helps to make the writing strategy explicit. After the students understand the steps to the strategy, the teacher gives them guided practice using the strategy and provides feedback on their use of it. After they have learned to use the strategy, they will no longer need to use the graphic organizer.

to the direction of print on a page, to spelling, to the use of illustrations, to the arrangement of ideas in a composition. Good writing ideas are contagious. If you observe students who have spent extended time in writing workshops, you will see that many more ideas emerge and are passed from student to student than the teacher would have time to think up and teach during more structured writing time.

Some students will produce writing on their own, but many will not. That is why the writing workshop is so useful: It combines teacher example and direction with encouragement of children's peers to get them writing. But what about students who find writing difficult? See the suggestions in the Differentiated Instruction box.

Writing in Different Genres

A writing **genre** is a form or pattern of writing related to a purpose. Writing expert Lucy Calkins (1994) suggests that teachers immerse students in genre study, in which they read several published works written in a particular genre and then try their hands at writing in that genre. The format for teaching lessons of genre study is similar to that of focused lessons and is demonstrated in the Teach It! box. Different kinds or genres of writing pose different challenges to writers. The main genres of writing include the following:

- *Journals* are personal accounts of events or ideas whose purpose is to record experiences and help writers remember them and think about them deeply.
- *Stories* are fictional accounts of characters who attempt to overcome problems in various settings. The purpose of stories is to provide outlets for writers' inventiveness and to entertain others.
- *Poems* are compositions that capture and convey emotions and insights while taking liberties with sentence and paragraph construction.
- *Expository accounts* are intended to be careful descriptions or explanations of things in the world.
- *Persuasive essays* convey writers' views of real issues in their lives and try to influence their readers' views.

These genres include important subtopics: A play is a kind of story; a song is a kind of poem; an observation report in science is a kind of expository account, as are biographies and autobiographies; and an advertisement is a kind of persuasive essay. They may also be mixed with each other; sometimes writers describe or explain to persuade readers or to tell them a story. Fictitious journals can be a form of storytelling, as Pam Conrad (1992) ably demonstrated in her novel *Pedro's Journal*, a fictional day-by-day account of the voyage of Christopher Columbus.

Journals and Other Personal Writing

Journal writing consists of writing down thoughts, feelings, and impressions that are close to the writer and are addressed to the writer herself or himself as the audience. Such writing usually comes fairly naturally to young writers because it has few formal demands. Nonetheless, the kind of personal expressive writing used in journals is important for students to use because it serves as a sort of playground or laboratory for the imagination (Britton, 1970). Students may begin ideas in journals that they later turn into more formal pieces.

DUAL-ENTRY DIARY.   Journals have other important pedagogical uses, too. Response journals are used to encourage students to reflect on their reading and their learning. A simple but powerful approach to response journals is the **dual-entry diary** (Barone, 1992; Berthoff, 1981). In a dual-entry diary (DED), the students are asked to divide the page down the middle with a vertical line. On the left-hand side, they record phrases that they found striking, important, or puzzling. On the right-hand side, they write comments on the passages. DEDs can be used to respond to literature or a host of other topics. After the students have written their DEDs, the teacher may write comments in them or may ask the students to share their entries in a discussion group.

Dual-Entry Diary

DIALOGUE JOURNALS.   In this form of response writing in journals, students are assigned to pairs by the teacher. After they have read a part of a book or participated in some other learning event, they write their impressions of it in their journals. Later, they have conversations in writing with each other. One writes a comment and ends with a question for the other. The other writes an answer to the question, makes a comment as well, and writes another question for the partner, and so on.

Stories

Most students enjoy writing stories, and because they are surrounded by stories, they find it natural to do so. Yet the structure of stories is fairly complicated, so some instruction in writing stories is helpful. There are many ways to show students how to write stories.

IMITATING AN AUTHOR.   In the genre study approach, you might read the children several stories by the same author and then ask them to write a similar story. For example, second- and third-grade children delight in writing their own episodes about Amelia

Teach It!

Refer to the Teach It! appendix at the end of the book for further activities you can use to reinforce concepts discussed in this chapter.

Teaching Students to Write in Genres: Descriptive Writing

Writing expert Lucy Calkins (1994) suggests that teachers immerse students in genre study, in which they read several published works written in a particular genre and then try their hands at writing in that genre. The format for teaching lessons of genre study is basically the same as that for focused lessons.

In the following sample lesson, teacher Paul Darion has decided to immerse his students in descriptive writing.

- *Sharing a sample of the writing form.* To demonstrate descriptive writing, Mr. Darion selects the opening paragraphs from Frances Temple's *Tonight, By Sea* (1995) and makes copies of them for his students. He plans to call the students' attention to the author's skill at writing vividly. In this case, the writer has carefully observed a process and shown it to the reader, step by step, and has put the reader in the picture by naming sights, sounds, smells, and tactile sensations.

- *Calling attention to the features of the writing form.* Mr. Darion reads the passage aloud as the students read along. Then he invites the students to say aloud what they experienced in reading the passage. He invites one student to retell the process of lighting a fire. Then he invites several more students, one at a time, to name a detail the writer has given and say whether that detail is a sight, a sound, a smell, or a feeling. Mr. Darion has also decided to pass out different colored pencils and ask students to use different colors for words that appeal to different senses. This part of the lesson ends with the students saying aloud how the writer achieved vivid descriptive writing: "Descriptive writing names things exactly, and uses words for sights, sounds, smells, tastes, and feelings."

- *Providing guided practice in using the writing form.* Sometimes, the next thing Mr. Darion does is to have the students observe something carefully in the classroom and describe it in writing. Today, however, he pulls out a mystery bag he created beforehand. It is nothing more than a paper bag containing an object (such as a chess piece, a spark plug, a sewing thimble, or a Christmas tree light bulb). Mr. Darion invites the students, one at a time, to reach into the bag and touch the object. The students then describe it on paper, with the understanding that they must thoroughly describe the object before they name it.

- *Making a poster explaining how to write in that genre.* Mr. Darion has the students create a poster that names the kind of writing, provides an

example of it, and includes a graphic organizer that makes clear the instructions for writing in that form or genre. The students will now be able to refer to the poster as they complete their own writing.

- *Encouraging the students to write in that genre during their independent writing.* Mr. Darion reminds the students of what they know about descriptive writing and encourages them to describe things carefully with words that appeal to the senses. The term *descriptive writing* enters the students' vocabulary, and the reminder to "use words that name sights, sounds, smells, tastes, and feelings" is commonly heard among the students themselves.

Kneeling in the sand, Paulie shredded dry seaweed and fluffed it into heap between the three black cooking stones, half forgetting that she had no food to cook. She broke palm fronds over the seaweed, then propped two pieces of driftwood with their tips just above the palm. Raking the sand together with her fingers, she built up a ring around the outside of the stones, careful to make room for the air to blow in and give life to the fire, a little and not too much.

Paulie leaned back, still kneeling, circling her upper arms in her hands to warm them. Night had come. The tree frogs stopped singing all at once.

"You got matches, Uncle?"

Paulie's uncle was washing in seawater from a bucket, pouring it down his back to get off the sweat and the sawdust, rinsing his arms.

"All the matches gone, Paulie."

"Go see if you can borrow a coal," her grandmother said. Sitting on the steps of her house, a cloth around her thin shoulders, Grann Adeline leaned toward the fire as if it were already lit. She frowned, slapped at a mosquito on her ankle. "Go on, girl. Ask sweetly and somebody bound to give you an ember."

Paulie wandered down the sand path. The small houses clustered under the trees were mostly dark. She could hear voices talking softly, a baby crying. A thin dog came out and sniffed at the backs of her knees. Paulie looked for the glow of a cook fire, smelled the breeze for one. She could feel the sea air, and hear the waves coming in, but it seemed like nobody was cooking.

Source: From *Tonight* by Frances Temple. Scholastic Inc./Orchard Books. Copyright © 1995 by Frances Temple. Reprinted by permission.

Bedelia (Parish, 1992), James Marshall's character Fox (Marshall, 1994), or Russell Hoban's character Frances (Hoban, 1995).

Teach It! 58

Story Maps for Writing

STORY MAPS. Story maps are outlines that give shape to stories. In Chapter 7, story maps were used as devices for calling children's attention to the parts of a plot. In writing, story maps can be used as frameworks like the one shown in Figure 10.6. In using a story map as a way of planning to write a simple story, students fill in the blanks on the right-hand side of the chart. The parts in parentheses are filled in when a story has more than

Figure 10.6
A Story Map.

There was a person . . .
who wanted . . .
So she . . .
but . . .
(and she . . .)
(but . . .)
And then she . . .
And finally, . . .
So . . .

one episode. After the students have filled in the chart, they write the story out, adding details and whatever other twists occur to them. No one would maintain that a story written to a formula will be interesting to read, but children can use story maps during the rehearsal stage of writing as they think and talk through—individually or with a partner— where their story might go.

DIALOGUE STORIES. A simple but effective pattern for structuring stories is the dialogue story. Students can be shown an example of a dialogue story, such as John Archambault and Bill Martin, Jr.'s *White Dynamite and the Curly Kid* (Archambault & Martin, 1989). Then ask the students to write their own story in dialogue form. As a rehearsal step, have two students make up an oral story together and each write their own version of it later.

Poems

Styles of poems range from those that put an emphasis on form to those that stress ideas and let form take care of itself. We will discuss three different approaches to writing structured poems. Even though the form is tightly prescribed, children write poems that are lively and surprising with these frameworks to support them. To teach children to write a form poem, follow these steps:

1. Show the students an example of a well-written poem that follows the form. (You might need to write this yourself or save it from a previous class.)
2. Have the students help you create a poem as a group. Discuss each choice they make so they understand the process well.
3. Have individuals or pairs write their own poems.
4. Share several of the poems, and discuss their qualities. Also call attention to the ways in which the poems followed the structure.
5. Make a wall chart in which you feature several of the students' poems; also outline the procedures for writing a poem with the structure in question.

ACROSTICS. Acrostics can be used simply, as when they spell a person's name. Students write a name in capitals vertically down the left side of a page and then go back and insert a word that begins with each letter. Here is one:

Persistent
Energetic
Never dull
Native of the mountains—
Yes, you will like this person.

On a more ambitious level, students can create acrostics with whole phrases, rhymed or unrhymed, but still having the first letter of the first word of each line spelling a word when read from top to bottom:

Alicia lived through long, cold days
Like an old unnoticed stone
Off the path, far from the crowds
Never seen,
Ever.

In their wonderful book, *Ways of Writing with Young Kids*, Sharon Edwards and her colleagues (2003) explore many ways of using acrostics. A particularly interesting way is to have a poet read her acrostic aloud to the class twice: first as a poem, with attention paid to the sounds, the images, and the tone, and then to uncover the mystery word that is spelled by the poem.

CINQUAINS.   Christmas tree–shaped poems that look like the following are called *cinquains*:

Harry
Young, charmed
Studying, flying, surviving
What an unlikely hero!
Wizard

Cinquains are surprisingly useful means of encouraging students to think about a concept. They follow a simple pattern:

- The first line names the topic.
- The second line contains two describing words.
- The third line has three action words ending in *-ing*.
- The fourth line is four feeling words, which may be written as a phrase.
- The fifth line is a one-word synonym for the name in the first line.

LIST POEMS.   Throughout the ages, many fine poems have been developed around the idea of lists. Take this medieval prayer, for example:

From Ghoulies
And Ghosties
And long-legged Beasties
And Things that go bump in the night:
Good Lord, deliver us.

Writers can use the idea by listing all of the things that are:

dark

lonely

round

scarce

The effect is heightened when writers include in their list both concrete and abstract things. For example,

> A pebble in the pond
> a policeman's beat
> the moon's halo
> subway tokens
> surprised eyes
> a ghost's mouth
> and the world—
> are round.

Expository Writing

Expository writing includes works that describe or explain. Young writers can be helped to write expository works by focused lessons that share good examples from literature and encourage their imitation. Graphic organizers serve as valuable tools for helping to write descriptive and explanatory prose. A number of graphic organizers are popular with children from second grade up and have been discussed at various points in the book. As you might recall, graphic organizers are important learning aids in comprehension (see Chapters 7 and 8) as well. This reinforces an important theme of this book about the close connection between the teaching/learning of reading and writing.

Graphic Organizers

CLUSTERS. Clusters, also called *semantic webs*, are linked circles that show relationships between ideas. The writer starts by naming the topic of the writing in a circle in the center of the page and then writes subordinate topics in satellite circles around the main circle. Aspects of each subordinate circle are written in still more satellites (see Figure 10.2, on page 298). After the details about a topic have been set out in the form or a cluster, the writer can refer to them in writing out an essay.

VENN DIAGRAMS. Venn diagrams are helpful planning aids when writers want to compare and contrast two items, and they consist of two interlocking circles (see Figure 10.7). In the outer left-hand circle is listed everything that is true about Topic X but not Topic Y. In the outer right-hand circle is written everything that is true about Topic Y but not Topic X. In the overlapping part in the middle is written everything that is true about both Topic X and Topic Y.

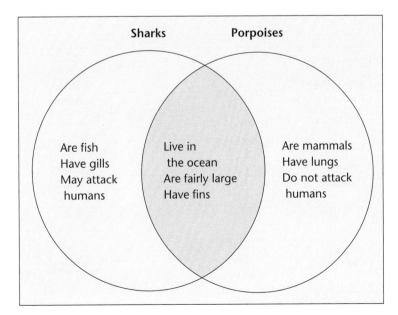

Figure 10.7
A Venn Diagram.

Figure 10.8
A Framework for a
Descriptive Essay.

I'm going to write about . . .		
Here is a word that describes my topic:	Here is one example of that word	
	Here is another example	
Here is another word that describes my topic:	Here is one example of that word	
	Here is another example	
Here is another word that describes my topic:	Here is one example of that word	
	Here is another example	
This is how I feel about my topic:	Here is the reason I feel that way	

DESCRIPTIVE ESSAY FRAMES. Frames can lend more structure to a piece of writing, by providing boxes that prompt writers to collect and organize their thoughts before writing out an essay. Like all writing frameworks, though, they should be used sparingly: They can become a crutch when relied on too much, and they may take the place of the student's own voice and originality. Figure 10.8 shows one example of a frame for structuring a descriptive essay.

CAUSE-AND-EFFECT CHARTS. When students plan to write about cause-and-effect chains, they may organize their ideas before writing using a cause-and-effect chart. Causes are listed in separate boxes on the left-hand side of the chart with effects listed on the right. A cause-and-effect chart may have few or many boxes. Several causes may contribute to a single effect, which may simultaneously be the cause of several other effects. The chart in Figure 10.9 shows the many causes of air pollution and their related effects.

Persuasive Essays

Teach It! 47

Know-Want-to-Know-Learn (K-W-L)

There are many ways to help students produce arguments and shape them on paper into persuasive essays. A popular procedure for helping students formulate their ideas for a persuasive essay is the K-W-L strategy (Ogle, 1984), discussed in Chapter 8. By constructing

Figure 10.9
A Cause-and-Effect
Chart.

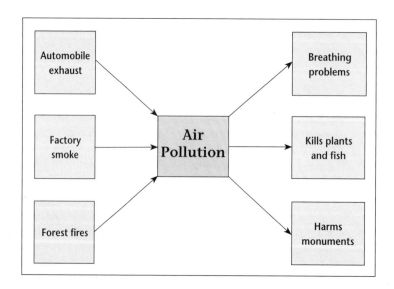

Figure 10.10   What? So What? Now What?

What?	So What?	Now What?
Pollution from automobiles and industrial pollution causes global warming.	Global warming is bad for plants and animals, including humans.	We should reduce automobile pollution by driving less and reduce industrial pollution by using less fossil fuel.

a K-W-L chart, students consider what they already know about a topic, formulate questions that say what they want to know about it, and later list what they learned about the topic. Having done this activity, you can then construct a new chart labeled like the one in Figure 10.10 that will guide the students to think about and take positions on actions that should follow from those findings.

After the students have completed the chart, they might think about ways to use their entries in an argumentative essay. One way in which the essay can be structured is to enter the information into another kind of format, like the one shown in Figure 10.11.

Writing should be integrated into the reading program early and children should write every day. How can we accomplish these two goals?

Figure 10.11   Framework for a Persuasive Essay.

What do you believe should be done about _____?	We should reduce automobile pollution by driving less and reduce industrial pollution by using less fossil fuel.
What is one reason why that should be done?	Pollution from automobiles and industrial pollution causes global warming.
(What is a second reason why that should be done?)	Global warming is bad for plants and animals, including humans.
(What is a third reason why that should be done?)	We are ruining our environment by warming the whole planet's climate.
So, say again what you believe should be done about _____.	Therefore, we should reduce automobile pollution by driving less and reduce industrial pollution by using less fossil fuel.

MIXING GENRES: RAFT.   A writing-to-learn strategy that calls attention to genres even as it mixes them up is the RAFT procedure, developed by Carol Santa (1988). RAFT is an acronym for **Role, Audience, Format,** and **Topic.**

Once a **topic** has been established in a lesson, students are invited to adopt different **roles** of people or other characters who have a stake in the issue. For example, if the **topic** is protecting dolphins (see Chapter 13), the **roles** might be fishermen, conservationists, the state wildlife protection people, and (with a little imagination) the dolphins themselves. Once each student (or team of students) has chosen a role, the students decide who the **audience** is—the people or characters to whom the message will be addressed. For example, conservationists might want to send a message to fishermen on the topic of protecting dolphins. But now the question is what **format** the message might use. Conservationists could write persuasive letters, editorials for the local newspaper, billboard advertisements, or catchy jingles, to name just a few formats. Once the four aspects of the RAFT are decided on—the Role, the Audience, the Format, and the Topic—the students create their works.

As an added twist, Alan Crawford (Crawford, et al., 2005) suggests using **Reciprocal RAFT,** in which the original messages are distributed to students in the class, who then adopt the role of the audience and respond to the messages.

YOUR PORTFOLIO.   It is always useful to include writing samples of your students in your portfolio. Sometimes it is difficult to convince students to part with their best work, but you might be able to photocopy pieces of writing that they want to keep in their own portfolios.

In addition, think about including samples of your own writing. Here are some examples that you might consider: a letter to the editor of your local paper or a magazine, a poem submitted for publication, or a short piece of work submitted for a college class. Your reflections about artifacts in your portfolio and your statement of philosophy of education are also examples of your own writing that might be included in your portfolio.

Finally, think about including a photograph of your author's chair. The more it looks like a place of honor, the more importance children will attach to it!

TEACHING RESOURCES.   There are many very useful writing strategies in this chapter. As you read the chapter, make a list of strategies and note where they are used most effectively in lessons—as anticipation activities, such as quick-writes; as knowledge-building activities, such as constructing a story grammar while reading; or as consolidation activities, such as the written retelling. Of course, some writing activities are just that, opportunities to write using different styles and conventions. As you begin teaching, refer to the list and make an effort to use each strategy. Your students will appreciate the variety of approaches, and they will not grow weary of the same tired strategy used over and over.

Assessment of Writing

Various parts of this chapter have focused on teaching children to revise and edit their own work. Revising and editing are basic forms of assessment of children's writing. Assessing students' writing and providing ongoing feedback are critical in encouraging students to write. However, in assessing students' writing, keep in mind some valuable principles:

- Not everything should be assessed. Most of children's writing should be for communication and not be graded.
- Assessment should teach; that is, children should learn about writing from the assessment.
- The criteria for assessment should be explicit and clear.
- Children should be involved in their own assessment.
- Assessment should show strengths and progress as well as needed improvements.

Using Rubrics

Rubrics are detailed presentations of quality criteria. Rubrics address several aspects of writing at once, and they explain clearly what constitutes a good job. Rubrics may be constructed by the teacher or by the teacher and the students together. Rubrics should be closely connected to the qualities of writing that have been stressed in the focused lessons and any checklists that have been used to guide the students' revising and editing. Students should be fully aware of the meaning of each criterion (aspect of quality) on the rubric before they produce the work that will be assessed. Figure 10.12 illustrates a sample rubric for middle elementary grades, which was adapted from the Six Traits writing evaluation.

Figure 10.12

A Rubric for Assessing Writing: Six Traits Writing Evaluation Sheet.

Ideas and Content:

Clear ideas. It makes sense.

The writer has narrowed the idea to a manageable topic.

Good information—from experience, imagination, or research.

Original and fresh perspective.

Details that capture a reader's interest. Makes ideas understandable. _____

Organization:

A snappy lead that gets the reader's attention. _____

Starts somewhere and goes somewhere. _____

The writer continually makes connections within the work. _____

Writing builds to a conclusion. _____

The writer creates a memorable resolution and conclusion.

Voice:

Sounds like a person wrote it.

Sounds like this particular writer.

Brings topic to life.

Makes the reader respond and care what happens.

The writer has energy and is involved. _____

Word Choice:

Words and phrases have power. _____

Word pictures are created. _____

Thought is crystal clear and precise. _____

Strong verbs and precise nouns. _____

Sentence Fluency:

Easy to read aloud.

Well-built sentences.

Varied sentence length. Some long sentences, some short.

Conventions:

Looks clean, edited, and proofread.

Free of distracting errors. _____

Easy to read. _____

No errors in spelling, punctuation, grammar and usage, capitalization, and indentation. _____

Following are the steps for using rubrics:

- Choose four to eight qualities of writing to assess. (Consider having the children suggest qualities of good writing.)
- Make sure the qualities of writing you assess have been carefully explained.
- Describe good work according to each quality. You may also describe fair and poor work.
- Share the rubrics with the students before they write the works that will be assessed.
- Use the rubrics often so that students learn what they mean and are able to use their criteria to guide them when they write.

Six Traits Assessment, a popular evaluation tool, is featured in the Assessment feature "Six Traits Writing Evaluation." It's important to stress that, whatever assessment tools you use to evaluate children's writing, it is imperative to use the same terms in your instruction as you use in evaluation. For example, if you evaluate on children's use of written dialogue, you must be sure you have carefully taught them how to write dialogue (Spandel,

Six Traits Writing Evaluation

The Six Traits model for writing assessment meets all of the principles just identified. Developed by Vicki Spandel and her associates (1996, 2000) at the Northwest Regional Education Laboratory, the Six Traits model seeks to direct teachers' and students' attention to six aspects of writing: ideas and content, organization, voice, word choice, sentence fluency, and conventions.

1. *Ideas and content* amount to the quality of having something to say and saying it clearly to the reader. They include having found out something about the topic before writing about it and having an original point of view. They can include providing details that lend an eyewitness feel to the paper.

2. *Organization* refers to the paper's having a beginning, a middle, and an end. It may include supporting main ideas with details, sticking to the topic, and making clear transitions from one point to another.

3. *Voice* describes the quality of reaching for words that express ideas well, even when this means writing words one has not been taught to use or to spell. A paper with a well-developed voice approaches the writer's oral fluency and expressiveness.

4. *Word choice* is the quality of showing the writer's meaning with precise words and specific details, and using fresh ways of expressing ideas, avoiding clichés.

5. *Sentence fluency* means a reader can easily read the work aloud. There are sufficient numbers of sentences to convey the meaning, and the sentences are varied in their length and form.

6. *Conventions* include spelling, capitalization and punctuation, and grammatical correctness. In later grades, conventions may refer to allocating separate ideas to separate paragraphs.

Children of different ages and levels of development naturally will be more or less advanced in their performance within each trait. Spandel and her associates have listed behavioral descriptors at four levels of development:

- *Exploring writers* are young writers who are experimenting with the whole enterprise of making meaning with graphic communication. Thus, within the trait of ideas and content, exploring writers might use pictures and scribbles to express ideas.

- *Emerging writers* are still young writers, but they have advanced to the point at which they are starting to work the features of conventional writing into their graphic productions. Thus, within the trait of ideas and content, emerging writers may use pictures or both pictures and mock writing in such a way that a reader might be able to guess an approximate meaning.

- *Developing writers,* through a mix of their own inventions and discoveries and overt teaching, can produce written messages that convey clear meaning, with the beginnings of formal organization and attention to some of the conventions of spelling and capitalization. Thus, within the trait of ideas and content, developing writers create stand-alone messages that are more readily decipherable. Their works show some attention to detail.

- *Fluent/experienced writers* express meanings more eloquently in print and take advantage of many features of fluent writing within all six traits. Thus, within the trait of ideas and content, fluent writers create works that show advancing mastery of qualities of writing, including the ability to say things clearly and in fresh and interesting ways, honoring more and more of the conventions of writing.

2008). Use the same terms in your instruction such as "dialogue"; avoid switching to terms like "write like talking." And make sure your writing lessons and writing workshops are filled with teacher-to-children, teacher-to-child conversations about writing and writing terms. Make sure your students are familiar with the rubric that will be used to judge them. Read the rubric together and have it available in the classroom.

Spandel's text on Six Traits writing assessment (Spandel, 2008) includes many examples of student writing at various grade levels that correspond to each trait, such as word choice, sentence fluency, and punctuation. Direct "how to do it" teacher guidance is provided that shows appropriate instruction to correct various aspects of student writing, such as when a student overuses words such as "things," writes a series of choppy sentences, or doesn't use adequate punctuation.

Work Sampling

Another effective approach to evaluating writing is work sampling. One way to sample work is to choose representative pieces of each child's writings at intervals during the year, but at least once per month. Sit down with the child and discuss the improvements you both see. Ask the child to take the lead in pointing out the improvements. If the child needs help, you might comment on the following:

- The length of each piece
- Organization: sticking to a topic and saying interesting things about it
- The appearance of new features, such as description or dialogue
- Attempts to write in a new genre, such as persuasion or description
- Attention to mechanics, such as spelling, punctuation, and handwriting

Before ending the conversation, ask the child to set goals—writing improvements to make in the next month. Write these down, or have the child write them, with a copy for yourself and a copy for the child. Provide regular reminders of the goals.

Involving Families in Their Children's Writing

Families can be partners in all stages of children's growth as writers. Research has shown that children who are drawn into family literacy activities, and especially into letter writing activities, make more progress as readers and writers (Clay, 1987).

Family Literacy

How can you recruit the help of families in supporting students who are learning to write?

Family Writing for Young Children

When children in kindergarten and first grade begin to explore the writing system, it helps if parents give them reasons and opportunities to practice their early writing, even when it bears only a slight resemblance to adult writing. As discussed in earlier chapters, children make progress both as readers and as writers if they are allowed to produce pretend versions of writing. Indeed, with a little training, it is possible to ensure that important concepts about print are discovered and practiced through early writing experiences, even scribbling and invented spelling. Families of younger children can invite children to write some of the following:

Greeting cards to relatives
Grocery lists

Children feel encouraged to write more when they receive letters—in one way or the other. (Ellen Senisi/ The Image Works)

Captions on their drawings
Refrigerator notes to the rest of the family

New
Literacies

What is the "digital divide" and how
can we avoid it?

You might need to explain to parents the importance of encouraging young children to write even before they have learned to do so conventionally. Many parents may worry that early untutored writing could reinforce incorrect habits. Assure them that this is not the case. However, you must then observe some safeguards in your classroom, such as making sure that the materials displayed for children to practice reading are written conventionally.

Family Writing for Older Children

When children are able to spell words and write sentences, they should be encouraged to do meaningful writing at home. Writing at home might include the following:

- Writing up family stories to share on special occasions, as in family letters to relatives
- Letters to friends and relatives
- Writing to a safe circle of friends via a computer-based instant messaging service

Children will be inspired to write if they see family members writing. Some families make a custom of compiling and writing down family stories that occur during the year: the most outrageous camping trip, the funniest family event, and so on. These can be a fine addition to a family photograph album scrapbook, and can be written by all—children included.

Using New Literacies in Teaching Writing

It is in the area of children's writing that new literacies play one of their most useful roles in children's education. Technology—computers, e-mail, and the Internet— provides a powerful invitation for children to write. Anyone who is a regular user of e-mail knows how much more writing is done when you can communicate with friends online. The same is true for children of all ages. But as Larry Cuban (2001) warns, in most cases, children use computers more frequently and more imaginatively at home than they do at school. This raises the specter of a technology gap, or **digital divide**, between families that can afford computers and the monthly fees levied by Internet service providers and the many families who cannot or do not spend their money in this way.

Communicating via Computers

Because communication via computers is still mostly done by typing on a keyboard, computers elicit a great deal of writing from children when they write to others via e-mail or instant messaging or in chat rooms. Children can communicate via computers in several ways.

INDIVIDUAL E-MAIL ACCOUNTS. Conventional e-mail allows users to read and send messages from and to people all over the world. E-mail systems save the messages that one receives and sends, and they enable the user—at the click of the mouse—to reply to messages, send messages to many people at once, and even to block senders of messages. Regular e-mail is not well suited for carrying on a conversation, however, because there may be delays of many minutes between the time a note is sent by one person and when it is received by another, and the reply might not come for hours or days.

INSTANT MESSAGING. Instant messaging software is supplied by AOL, Microsoft, and others. It enables people to have nearly instantaneous conversations with a limited group of "buddies." Users typically sign up using a fictitious name—a fact that can, in some cases, invite people to write to others without the sensitivity they would normally maintain if their identities were known to each other. It is worthwhile to talk to students about the etiquette of chatting by instant messaging and in chat rooms (see Figure 10.13).

CHAT ROOMS. Similar to instant messaging are Internet-based chat rooms, in which people may log in and exchange messages with many parties at once. Like instant messaging, chat rooms usually offer the option of signing in under a pseudonym. Chat rooms are sometimes moderated by someone whose job it is to screen out offensive messages. Children should be warned to avoid chat rooms that are not especially moderated to keep them safe for children.

Figure 10.13
Etiquette for Electronic Conversations.

1. Let your parents know each time you go online. Tell them where you are going and with whom you are communicating. Let your parents participate in the conversations.

2. If anyone says something offensive to you online, log off and alert an adult—don't answer the message.

3. Don't write something online that you would not say to someone in person—in short, be polite.

4. Don't say unkind things about others online. Once they leave your computer, messages may "stay alive" and circulate to people other than those to whom you sent them.

5. Don't reveal personal contact information—not your last name, or your home address, or your telephone number. The person you are talking to might not be who you think that person is.

6. Limit the amount of time you spend in computer-based chats. Other people in your house may need to use the computer.

PEN PALS AND OTHER EXCHANGES. In the 1920s, an inspired French educator named Celestin Freinet (Temple, 1994) devised ways of having his elementary-grade students study geography and climate by corresponding with other students from around Europe and the world. Freinet's students asked about other children's surroundings, their weather, and their climate and how these affected their activities. Freinet's lessons were very popular with his students because investigating distant places by talking to the children who lived there was far more concrete, vivid, and engaging than reading dry facts from a book. Yet to pull off this innovative style of inquiry, Freinet's students used what computer savants today contemptuously call "snail mail." Their exchanges took weeks. With the use of e-mail and the Internet, pen pal networks have a global reach, and exchanges can be completed in a matter of days or even hours.

Today, many pen pal networks are available to students. Some central sources link individual children as well as whole classrooms in many countries around the world. Most of the sites have safety procedures, including moderators, to keep children out of contact with unseemly sorts, although caution is still in order. One such site is the Kids on the Web, at www.zen.org/~brendan/kids-pen.html.

Protecting Children from Harmful Material Online

Websites, mailing lists, and chat rooms enable children to leave their own neighborhoods and communicate with others around the world who share the same interests. But this infinite mobility has a negative side. As psychologist James Garbarino (2000) points out, in some mailing lists and chat rooms, young people may find communities of a harmful sort. In an actual community, for example, a young person who has violent fantasies is not likely to find like-minded companions for encouragement, but in the virtual community of a chat room, this young person can easily find the support of others.

Parents should be reminded to monitor their children's e-mail and Internet use, just as teachers and librarians do when children are in school. Online services and software companies such as Norton and McAfee market programs that give families the ability to screen out whole categories of websites, such as those with prurient or violent content. Most e-mail software can be set to block undesirable e-mail messages, but only if the name or e-mail address of the sender is known. The problem of children's vulnerability to undesirable contacts through the Internet gets a lot of discussion these days. One group that is a good source of suggestions for keeping children safe while online is Wired Safety, whose web address is http://www.wiredsafety.org/.

Using Computers for Writing Reports

One of computers' greatest strengths is as a learning aid when it comes to children writing papers. The ease with which young writers can add, delete, and move their words around makes computers the ideal support for the writing process described earlier in this chapter. Computers give children control over design capabilities that only layout artists could manage years ago. Now they can arrange their writing in columns, experiment with different typefaces and even colors of fonts, and add artwork from software archives. All of this adds great appeal to the whole enterprise of writing.

With access to the Internet, children can download and paste into their papers photographs as well as text from a nearly infinite array of sources. Having control over so many variables expands children's creative potential, but it also sets them up to be scavengers of the fruits of other people's creativity unless teachers set clear guidelines for what constitutes original work. Strategies such as the I-Chart (see Chapter 8) are recommended when children are writing reports because the I-Chart format invites children to write a narrative of their investigation and then report their findings. Several online services are available to children for their review and to inform their research:

- Scholastic, Inc., has a website at www.scholastic.com that includes a Research Starters section. There, students can find illustrated presentations on a growing list of topics (e.g., Pilgrims, dinosaurs, Native American cultures) that are designed to whet their curiosity and give them enough information to begin inquiries that will take them beyond what is presented there.
- The Public Broadcasting Service offers a children's page (www.pbskids.org) (grades 4 and up) with links to interesting online articles.
- The National Geographic Society operates a website for children that is accessible through their main site at www.nationalgeographic.com.
- Classics for Young Children (www.ucalgary.ca/~dkbrown/storclas.html) is a large set of links to scores of complete works for children, many of them illustrated, that are in the public domain. The works include the E. Nesbit books (e.g., *The Treasure Seekers*), Frank Baum's *Wizard of Oz* books, Frances Hodgson Burnett's *The Secret Garden*, works by Mark Twain, and many others.

For Review

This chapter focused on both the process and the products of writing. The process was described as one of interlocking, usually sequential activities: rehearsing, drafting, revising, editing, and publishing. Students as young as kindergarten age can learn to use some version of the writing process. They are helped to do so by a writing workshop, a regular period of class time set aside for students to receive focused lessons on one aspect of writing, do some writing, have conferences with the teacher and with each other, and share their works.

The products of writing are arranged into genres. Genres include expressive writing such as journals, stories, poems, expository writing, and persuasive essays. Suggestions were given for helping students write in each genre. Children sometimes need more explicit support than the writing workshop gives them. Different levels of support for children's writing include modeled writing, shared writing, interactive writing, guided writing, and independent writing. The special problems of struggling writers were also addressed, and it was suggested that strategies for writing be introduced to them through focused lessons and graphic organizers and be regularly practiced. Assessment is an important part of teaching children to write.

Assessment should teach, by employing means that communicate clearly what the children are doing well and what needs work and by involving the children in assessing their own work.

Families have a role to play in supporting students' writing, and suggestions were given for families of younger children and older children. Instructional technology can play a valuable role in children's writing. More and more children in later elementary grades find it natural to communicate via e-mail or in chat rooms. Once the difficulty of keyboarding has been overcome, using the writing process to compose papers is ultimately easier on a computer than with a pencil. The variety of formatting possibilities on a computer is also a draw. That said, there are concerns about children's use of computers. Plenty of material is available on the Internet that is not suitable for children, and although schools have screening software, not all homes do. Also, although the Internet (and electronic encyclopedias) give report-writing students ready access to a wealth of material on virtually any subject, the challenge for teachers is to help students navigate past merely downloading other people's material and teach them to use this information to inform their own reports.

For Your Journal

1. Try out the writing process for yourself with the assistance of a partner, although you can do this activity alone.

   - Make a list of five topics you might write about. These should be topics you might share with children in grades 1 through 5.
   - Ask yourself or have a partner ask you what interests you about each topic. Find your story!
     - Write a draft of your paper. Write for eight minutes without stopping.
     - Read back over your paper, or have a partner read it, and consider areas you need to revise.
     - Write about this writing experience in your journal. Reflect on what happened in the process: How did you feel about writing this way? Is it different than previous writing you've done?

2. In helping children learn to write, where do you think the proper balance can be found between the need to encourage children to feel ownership for their writing and take initiative for their learning and the need to teach them to write better—that is, more coherently and correctly?

Taking It to the World

1. The writing process described in this chapter—rehearsing, drafting, revising, editing, and publishing—is often described as the way professional writers create. But is it? Find and interview at least two writers. If possible, look for writers of fiction and poetry as well as writers of nonfiction. Ask them what they do when they write. (*Hint:* Don't mention the writing process or talk about the steps. See whether they mention those themselves.) Compare your notes with those of your classmates. Do the writers do similar things as they write? Does the process they use seem to depend on whether they are writing fiction or nonfiction? Do their processes resemble the process described in this chapter?

2. The writing workshop described in this chapter is widely regarded in the educational literature as a valuable development. Many teachers use the workshop approach successfully and many children seem to have internalized the steps of the writing process, but maybe not as many as reading the literature might suggest. Visit an elementary school, and ask the teachers whether they use writing workshops with their children. If so, how often? What do they like about it? Does it work for all students? If not, what modifications must they use for the children who struggle? If they don't use the writing workshop, why don't they? What approach to writing instruction do they use?

New Literacies Connections

1. Visit the websites of Cyber Patrol (www.cyberpatrol.com) and Net Nanny (www.netnanny.com), and compare the services each company has to offer parents for protecting their children from gaining access to offensive sites. Which site would you recommend to parents? Why? Does either service offer the option of blocking undesirable e-mail messages?

2. Check out the online magazine for writing for and by children called Cyberkids (www.cyberkids.com). Investigate the Creative Works gallery. How might you be able to use this site to help you teach children to write?

PEARSON myeducationlab

Now go to MyEducationLab (**www.myeducationlab.com**), where you can:

- Find learning outcomes for the topics covered in this chapter, along with the national standards that connect to these outcomes.

- Complete Assignments and Activities that can help you more deeply understand the chapter content.

- Engage in Building Teaching Skills and Dispositions exercises, in which you can apply and practice core teaching skills identified in the chapter.

Assessing Literacy

Anticipation Guide

The following statements will help you begin thinking about the topics covered in this chapter. Answer *true* or *false* in response to each statement. As you read and learn more about the topics mentioned in the statements, think back on your answers. See what interests you and prompts your curiosity toward more understanding.

_____ 1. Assessment of literacy is done at different times and for different purposes. At the beginning of the year, screening assessment is done, followed by diagnostic assessment for those who need it. Throughout the year, all students are subjected to monitoring assessment, and at the end of the year, most face outcomes-based assessment.

_____ 2. High-stakes assessment has so alarmed and angered the American public that it probably won't be around by the time this book makes it into print.

_____ 3. The concepts of validity and reliability are not only of interest to researchers; teachers also need to be concerned with the validity and reliability of the instruments they use.

_____ 4. Informal assessments are only given on weekends, preferably at a cookout with everybody dressed in old clothes.

_____ 5. An important piece of information yielded by assessment concerns children's independent, instructional, and frustration reading levels.

_____ 6. It is usually harder for a child to read words in the context of a meaningful passage than it is to read them off lists.

_____ 7. The online management and reporting of children's assessment data are becoming something of an industry in the United States.

_____ 8. All assessment should be done using scientifically tested instruments.

_____ 9. Readability measurement is an exact science. It is possible to pinpoint precisely the level of challenge any piece of text will pose to any reader.

_____ 10. Assessment is for children. There is no earthly reason why teachers should ever assess themselves.

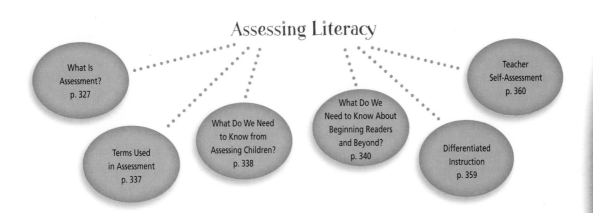

Assessing Literacy

- What Is Assessment? p. 327
- Terms Used in Assessment p. 337
- What Do We Need to Know from Assessing Children? p. 338
- What Do We Need to Know About Beginning Readers and Beyond? p. 340
- Differentiated Instruction p. 359
- Teacher Self-Assessment p. 360

A Classroom Story

Assessment Drives Teaching Decisions

John Samuels teaches first grade at a small elementary school in a farming community in western New York state. Of his twenty-seven students, seven speak Spanish at home. The parents of eight of the children, including two of the Spanish-speaking families, are scientists at a nearby agricultural experiment station. Some children are from families of farm workers, and others are from families on public assistance. John believes very strongly that his job as a teacher is to help all of his children be as well prepared for a happy and successful life as he can make them.

At the beginning of the year John, the school's reading teacher, and the three other first-grade teachers in his school administer a screening test of early reading abilities to the entire first grade. They test the children's letter knowledge, their concept of word, their phonemic segmentation and phonics skills (through an invented spelling task), and their recognition of both environmental print and decodable words. The results for John's class are given in Table 11.1 on page 327.

Family Literacy

How is John partnering successfully with his students' families?

John and the other three teachers look through all of the scores together. They decide that the top scoring readers in John's groups are probably beginning readers already. The middle group still needs a moderate amount of support in emergent literacy skills and concepts. The group with the lowest scores will need special intervention to help them profit from reading instruction during the year.

During the first two weeks of the school year, John gives further diagnostic tests to his students. The children with the lowest scores have their concepts about print assessed as well as their awareness of phonemes in words. The early screening already showed him which letters of the alphabet each child still needs to recognize and be able to produce, and their other scores suggested that they will need a holistic introduction to reading, with lots of listening to read-alouds, lots of dictation and shared book reading, and shared writing. They will need the whole sequence of systematic phonics instruction.

But John is also a good "kidwatcher." He observes the children carefully as they participate in his early lessons. He is pleased to see them singing along to "Down By the Bay" and smiling as they clap along to the rhythm. He watches to see whom they interact with on the playground.

He has already visited with their families before school started. The parents want their children to learn, and they make it clear that they are counting on his suggestions for ways to help their children. One of the fathers and two of the mothers are unemployed. They seem skeptical when John suggests that they might come into the classroom to help out, but John thinks at least the father and one of the mothers can be persuaded.

John finds time to read a simple book with each of the top- and middle-scoring children, and he keeps a running record of their abilities. He has learned to be a little skeptical of test scores, and he watches carefully to see if their performance in a real reading task lives up to what the test predicted. He is "roaming around the known," as Marie Clay puts it (1993). Soon he has found a reading level for each one and is ready to place them in their first group for guided reading.

Struggling Reader

What is John doing to support his struggling students?

As he makes running records of the middle-scoring children's reading, he finds levels of books they can read at the instructional level, too. He notes that they have developed some sight vocabulary and are developing some phonics skills. They are not fluent readers—they read word by word, without inflection. He will see if he can match them up with tutors from the nearby college's service learning project to remedy that.

Assessment is an essential part of doing anything well, including the teaching of reading. The topic of assessment is getting more attention in reading instruction now than ever before. With the current emphasis on "research-based reading instruction," educators are paying more and more attention to how children are learning, what works and what doesn't, and why.

What Is Assessment?

Assessment in reading means gathering, analyzing, and interpreting information to tell how well a student reads. Assessment covers everything from informal observations of a student's reading to the use of commercial tests. Assessment practices include:

- Deciding what we need to know about the reading ability of a child or a group of children.
- Determining which measures will tell us what we want to know.
- Gathering information.
- Interpreting the information.
- Making decisions on what to do next, based on this new information.

Why Do We Assess?

There are different purposes for assessment, and also different audiences for the information that assessment brings to light.

1. **We assess to guide our instruction.** We may assess to:
   - *Determine reading levels* (independent, instructional, and frustration) so that we can place students in materials at the right level.

Table 11.1 Scores of First Graders on the Early Reading Screening Inventory

STUDENT	ALPHABET KNOWLEDGE (%)	CONCEPT OF WORD (%)	INVENTED SPELLING* (%)	WORD RECOGNITION (%)
High-scoring group				
Janice	100	100	92	80
Ephraim	92	100	88	75
Ignacio	98	100	90	80
Topaz	96	90	92	82
Middle-scoring group				
Peter	70	80	65	50
Carla	65	88	60	55
Laticia	68	80	70	60
Low-scoring group				
Juana	52	40	35	20
George	55	45	30	24
Alexia	40	40	20	10
Amanda	30	30	16	5

*Includes phonemic segmentation and early phonics.

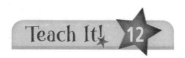

Phonemic Segmentation with Elkonin Boxes

- *Determine children's readiness or prior knowledge* before starting instruction. Many aspects of learning to read and write are developmental, and in order to give the right instruction, teachers need to know where learners are in their development. For example, as we saw in Chapter 4, children need to acquire the ability to segment phonemes and also develop a concept of word before more advanced phonics lessons will make sense to them.

- *Locate children's strengths and areas of need* to direct our instruction. In the previous chapters, we have covered many aspects of children's literacy development. Children need encouragement in all of them, and if there are a few or several aspects in which they are not progressing adequately, we need to locate those so we can offer specially tailored help. For example, a child may have learned many sight words, but have low reading fluency. We must monitor that child's reading so we can identify the need to work on the student's fluency.

- *Identify children's literacy strategies* so that we can strengthen them. For example, good readers preview texts and set purposes for reading to help themselves understand better. Does each child know how to do this?

2. **We assess to monitor the success of instructional approaches.** Approaches vary in their success with individual children, or with whole classrooms of children. We assess to:

Guided Reading

- *Find out if a teaching approach or set of materials is working for a child.* For example, to build reading fluency, teachers may use "buddy reading" (see page 168) or a computer program. But does the child know how to take advantage of these activities? Or in teaching word study, the teacher wants each child to be given words to study that are at his or her level of development of word knowledge. Is this the case? In guided reading, we want children to read some texts that are moderately challenging and some texts that are easier. Is this the case for each child?

- *Find out what strategies seem best suited to whole groups of students.* Research shows that the most effective schools for helping all children learn to read and write are those in which teachers monitor how well instruction is working, and then use this information as they work with other teachers to find ways to improve instruction (Cunningham & Allington, 1999; Taylor, et al., 1999). Teachers may monitor a host of factors, from classroom routines and management strategies, to teaching methods, to materials, to ways of working with instructional aides and parent volunteers, to ways of assessing children.

3. **We assess to give feedback to students and their parents.** Findings from assessments should be communicated to children and their parents so that both can work toward the children's success. We assess to:

- *Show students what they are doing well and what they can do better* by communicating information in a way that helps them understand and purposefully reinforces those strategies they are using successfully, and that can point the way toward improvements.

- *Help students set goals for better performance* and monitor their progress toward meeting those goals.

- *Help parents understand how their children are performing* in learning to read and what the parents can do to help.

4. **We assess to make decisions on the placement of students in special instructional services.** All children in the United States are entitled by law to special education services as they need them, and they are also entitled to special support to learn the English language, if necessary. Parents may request that their children be screened for such services, but teachers may also identify students who need more support than what is likely to be available to them in the regular classroom. In either case, special screening is called for, including specialized tests

that are normally administered by school psychologists. But the teacher's own observational records and assessment results play a useful role in these decisions.

5. **We assess to make sure all students are meeting state standards for learning.** The federal No Child Left Behind law that passed in 2002 mandated that every child in America be tested in reading from grades 3–8. The tests are developed by the individual states. Because the tests have considerable consequences, many teachers are giving more frequent assessments throughout the year to monitor their students' progress toward meeting the standards on which their state tests are based.

6. **We assess ourselves as teachers or as teachers-to-be.** We make sure our professional knowledge is up to date, and that our practices are serving our students as best they can. We assess our professional knowledge, both to keep ourselves current and to meet teaching licensing requirements.

Approaches to Assessment

Let us look further at these and other kinds of assessment approaches that are used to measure and investigate children's reading and writing abilities.

NORM-REFERENCED TESTS.   Standardized or norm-referenced tests of reading compare children's performance with that of large numbers of other students. For example, tests such as the Stanford Achievement Test and the California Achievement Test report children's reading performance in comparison to other students at their grade level. The tests are given under rigorously controlled conditions so that the results will be comparable. Norm-referenced tests are typically used, along with other information, to inform decisions about placing a child for special reading services. But these tests traditionally have lacked an obvious connection with any school curriculum, so it is difficult to tell what aspect of a school's instruction has contributed or failed to contribute to the children's performance.

STANDARDS-BASED TESTS.   Standards-based tests have been developed in recent years as individual states have set standards for achievement in reading and other subject areas at each grade level. This is required by the federal No Child Left Behind Act (http://www.ed.gov/admins/lead/account/saa.html#peerreview). Standards vary from state to state, but in most states they are specific enough to guide teaching. In California, for example, first graders are expected to meet English language content standards, of which the following is a small sample:

Reading

1.0 Word Analysis, Fluency, and Systematic Vocabulary Development
Students understand the basic features of reading. They select letter patterns and know how to translate them into spoken language by using phonics, syllabication, and word parts. They apply this knowledge to achieve fluent oral and silent reading.

Concepts About Print
  1.1. Match oral words to printed words.
  1.2. Identify the title and author of a reading selection.
  1.3. Identify letters, words, and sentences.

Phonemic Awareness
  1.4. Distinguish initial, medial, and final sounds in single-syllable words.
  1.5. Distinguish long- and short-vowel sounds in orally stated, single-syllable words (e.g., *bit/bite*).

1.6. Create and state a series of rhyming words, including consonant blends.

1.7. Add, delete, or change target sounds to change words (e.g., change *cow* to *how*; *pan* to *an*).

1.8. Blend two to four phonemes into recognizable words (e.g., /c/ /a/ /t/ = *cat*; /f/ /l/ /a/ /t/ = *flat*).

1.9. Segment single-syllable words into their components (e.g., /c/ /a/ /t/ = *cat*; /s/ /p/ /l/ /a/ /t/ = *splat*; /r/ /i/ /ch/ = *rich*). . . .

Source: California Department of Education, 2009.

Standards-based tests are meant to assess each student's performance on the standards set by the states. Students may be promoted to another grade or held back, depending on their performance, and schools may suffer sanctions if they do not make "adequate yearly progress." Standards-based tests are sometimes called **high-stakes testing**, because a child's performance on such a test can determine whether she or he is promoted to the next grade. The performance of many children can decide if a school is achieving or underachieving (see the Standards and Literacy box).

Standards and Literacy

High-Stakes Testing

The U.S. Constitution left the governance of education up to the individual states, but with the passage of the No Child Left Behind Act in 2002 the federal government greatly increased its leverage over the states by mandating the requirement that states adopt standards-based education. As a result of this initiative, most states have set performance standards for children, and by the year 2006, most states developed tests for those standards. There is some variety from state to state in what children are expected to learn and what teachers are expected to teach. Some states have specified fairly explicitly what is expected, while others have left more room for the teachers' discretion.

The No Child Left Behind Act requires that schools report "disaggregated scores" for male, female, white, African American, Hispanic, Asian, Native American, limited English proficiency (LEP), special education, and economically disadvantaged students (those on free or reduced payment lunches). As former President Bush said, the legislation attempts to fight the "soft prejudice of low expectations." Talking about the different achievement rates of poor versus economically better off children, girls versus boys, and majority versus minority students is a beginning. But society must muster the will to do something about it.

Although the federal government has not required a single set of tests for use nationwide, connecting results with federal monies through the No Child Left Behind Act has placed great pressure on states and schools to comply. But that does not mean that everyone agrees with the standards movement. Richard Allington (2000), a prominent reading expert and leader in the International Reading Association, has noted two major omissions from the government's list of required areas of focus. One is the habit of reading. Allington argues that no

amount of skills instruction is as effective as simply motivating children to read a lot, and children will not become proficient readers unless they read. The other is the absence of what Allington calls thoughtful reading: reading to solve problems, to generate ideas of one's own, to think critically, and to think interpretively. Allington points out that, although not required by the federal government, many state standards do include these two concerns. For example, New York State expects every student to read twenty-five books a year at grade level.

Another issue is what to do if children do not pass the state tests. In what has been called high-stakes testing, many states have ruled that children will not be promoted to the next grade, and that schools may be placed on deficiency lists—and parents will therefore be encouraged to transfer their children out of those schools or apply for publicly funded tutoring services—if enough pupils' scores fail to meet the standards. Many observers have complained that these are severe consequences to base on a one-time event such as an examination, and as of this writing there appears to be growing resistance to many of the mandates of the No Child Left Behind Act in many parts of the country. For example, Utah and Connecticut, two states with different demographics and levels of funding for education, have both threatened not to comply with the testing requirements of No Child Left Behind. A growing body of literature has exposed the legislation to serious critique (Meier, 2004; Peterson & West, 2003).

Nevertheless, from the time the legislation was passed, polls showed that a majority of parents support having standards and the tests that go with them (Public Agenda On-Line, 2002), and that support continues among a majority of families five years later (Public Agenda On-Line, 2006). Learning standards and some sort of standards-based testing are probably here to stay, and those who teach must be mindful of them.

CURRICULUM-BASED MEASUREMENT (CBM). As the term *high-stakes testing* implies, by the time a student takes a standards-based test, it is usually too late for the teacher to do anything more for the student that year. To ensure that children are making good progress toward meeting the standards measured on the high-stakes tests—and indeed, to better teach children to read—many educators are turning to the practice of **curriculum-based measurement** (Fuchs, Deno, & Mirkin, 1984; Shinn, 1989), a set of practices and instruments that have been borrowed from the special education field. These measures are normally based on the skills students are expected to acquire according to the state standards for learning, but they have the advantage of being given repeatedly—sometimes as often as weekly—throughout the school year so the teacher can still take corrective action as needed. Curriculum-based measurements are very brief samples of behavior, deliberately so, because a teacher may have to test twenty-five or more children individually several times during the year. To test oral reading, for example, a teacher may have a student read three passages aloud for one minute each and average the speed and accuracy of the reading. Nonetheless, even such brief measures of oral reading have been shown to predict students' later performance on different states' high-stakes standards-based tests. Although curriculum-based measures have many uses, among the most promising is that they facilitate continuous monitoring of a student's performance in reading throughout the year to ensure both the student's learning strategies and the teacher's instruction are working well.

Repeated Reading

Curriculum-based measurements may be designed by the teacher (see Jim Wright's guide on CBM at http://www.jimwrightonline.com/pdfdocs/cbaManual.pdf), or they may be purchased commercially. For grades 5–8, Timothy Rasinski and Nancy Padak (2005) offer a series of *Three-Minute Reading Assessments: Word Recognition, Fluency, and Comprehension.* School districts in many states are using DIBELS, the Dynamic Indicators of Basic Early Literacy Skills, and some studies have shown scores on DIBELS predict later performance on the standards-based tests of some states, including Arizona (Wilson, 2005), Florida (Buck & Torgesen, 2003), North Carolina (Barger, 2003), and Oregon (Shaw & Shaw, 2002).

New Literacies

Research DIBELS online and describe what you've found.

DIBELS was created with public funds, and it is available without cost on the Internet (at http://dibels.uoregon.edu/index.php). For a fee the providers of DIBELS offer an electronically based data management and reporting service that keeps track of each child's scores on each part of the test, follows the child's progress on each of several indicators over time, and makes available a number of verbal and graphic ways to display results.

The Developmental Reading Assessment (DRA) was developed by a commercial company. It, too, provides a range of assessments for screening, diagnosis, and monitoring. It also enables teachers to manage the test scores online and perform a number of tracking, comparing, and reporting functions—for a fee, of course. The Web address of DRA is http://www.pearsonlearning.com/dra/.

Some caveats are in order, however. The main advantage claimed for these brief measures is that they save time (Rasinski & Padak, 2005), and thus they afford teachers a feasible way to monitor children's progress toward meeting the state's or the locality's learning standards in reading. However, before serious educational decisions are made about a child—such as the placement of students in special educational services or the recommendation of whether a child should be promoted to the next grade—more extensive assessment procedures should be used. Response to Intervention (RTI), as described in Chapter 2, provides guidelines for the process of assessing a student's strengths and needs for the purpose of providing special education services.

INFORMAL READING INVENTORIES. Informal Reading Inventories (IRIs), developed more than 60 years ago by Emmett Betts (1946), are comprehensive measures of students' reading ability. IRIs are administered to individual children to measure their word recognition, fluency, comprehension, and overall reading levels. In contrast to standardized reading tests, IRIs have not been normed by elaborate field testing with hundreds or thousands of children. They are created from samples of grade-level texts, either taken from basal readers at ascending grade levels or Lexiles, or written by the test authors and

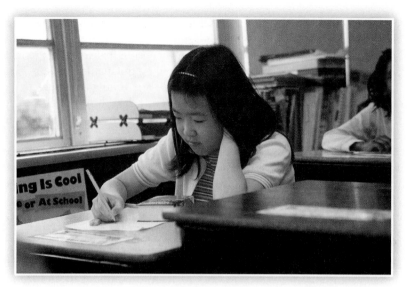

Thoughtful assessment procedures should be used before serious educational decisions are made about a student. (Lindfors Photography)

matched to grade levels according to readability formulas. Hence, they are called "informal" reading inventories. IRIs consist of lists of words and text passages of graduated levels of difficulty—usually from early first grade or *preprimer* through grade 8 or higher.

Teachers may create their own IRIs, and there are several good ones commercially available, including *The Developmental Literacy Inventory*, written by some of this book's authors (Temple, Crawford, & Gillet, 2009). It combines an Informal Reading Inventory with assessments of emergent literacy. Another is the *Qualitative Reading Inventory* (Leslie & Caldwell, 2005). A major section of this chapter is devoted to the use of the informal reading inventory. See also Chapters 13 and 14, "Putting Effective Literacy Instruction into Practice: Grades 3 to 5" and "Putting Effective Literacy Instruction into Practice: Grades 6 to 8," for further discussion of IRIs.

myeducationlab
The Power of Classroom Practice
www.myeducationlab.com

Consider the rationale behind administering an IRI by completing the activity "Analyzing the Purposes Behind Informal Reading Inventory Procedures." (To find this activity, go to the topic *Assessment* in MyEducationLab and click on Assignments and Activities.)

THE READING MISCUE INVENTORY.   Also called the RMI or miscue analysis, the Reading Miscue Inventory (Goodman & Burke, 1972, 1987; Goodman, Watson, & Burke, 2005) derives from the belief that reading errors should not be dismissed as matters of ignorance. Rather, like children's original utterances as they are learning to talk, reading errors are signs of children's efforts to understand, to find meaning, and to gain competence in written communication. Hence, the term *miscue* is used instead of error, because if the child says something different from what is written in the text, the written word has *cued* a different response from the child than what was expected. According to the thinking behind the Reading Miscue Inventory, those cues can usually be categorized as having to do with the strings of letters on the page (*graphophonic cues*), the context provided by the grammatical structure of the sentence or text (*syntactic cues*), or the context of the meaning of the passage (*semantic cues*).

To administer a Reading Miscue Inventory, the teacher chooses a moderately difficult text that is long enough to elicit at least 25 errors. The student's reading is tape-recorded for later analysis, during which each error is subjected to nine different questions to evaluate which sorts of cues the reader is using and how. Lessons are then developed to improve the child's reading based on the findings. The Reading Miscue Inventory is time-consuming to administer—fifteen to twenty minutes is required for the testing and another hour for the analysis—but many teachers value the information it yields.

RUNNING RECORDS.   Developed by Marie Clay (1993) to support her Reading Recovery Program, running records are teacher-made assessment devices administered to individual students to monitor their fluency, word recognition accuracy, and reading levels. Running records are partially based on the Reading Miscue Inventory (discussed previously), but are simpler to administer. Running records are usually carried out with younger readers in the first two grades, with whom they may be used every month or more frequently, both for diagnostic testing and for monitoring. The teacher chooses simple texts that he or she suspects are at several difficulty levels for the child: one moderately challenging, one easy, and one more challenging. Clay suggests that an easy book be one that the child has read before with the teacher, and of which the child can read more than 95 percent of the words. A moderately challenging text would normally be one that the child had seen before but not studied with the teacher, and whose words the child can read with 90 to 95 percent accuracy. A difficult text would be one the child had not seen, and whose words the child could read with 80 to 89 percent accuracy.

The teacher's role is to observe carefully and record what the child says as she or he reads the book. It is best to construct a form for recording the student's performance, like the one shown in Figure 11.1, but, in a pinch, you may sit close enough to the child to see the words as they are read and make notes on a piece of paper.

The running record shown in Figure 11.1 allows the teacher to observe the following:

- The error rate
- The self-correction rate
- The kinds of miscues (incorrect word identifications) that the child makes: visual, structural, or meaning-based
- Other behaviors, such as the direction in which the student reads, the number of repetitions of words, and so on

Characterizing miscues as *visual, structural,* or *meaning-based* is intended to bring to light the kind of information a child is tracking in a text. Clay writes:

> **Meaning:** *Does the child use meaning (M)? If what he reads makes sense, even though it is inaccurate, then he is probably applying his knowledge of the world to his reading.*
>
> **Structure:** *Is what he said possible in an English sentence (S is for syntactically appropriate)? If it is, his oral language is probably influencing his responding. If it is not . . . [he] is paying close attention to detail, or to word by word reading. . . .*
>
> **Visual information:** *Does he use visual information (V) from the letters and words or the layout of print? [In a footnote, Clay adds, "Whether the child is relating visual information to sounds (phonological information) or to orthography (information about spelling) is a refinement of using visual information not distinguished in this analysis at this time."]* (Clay, 1993, p. 31)

A running record is a quick way to verify that a particular book is written at a child's instructional or independent reading level. It should be supplemented by other kinds of assessments when you want more detail on a child's word knowledge. Running records are used most often with beginning readers; however, when children reach a level of reading where both fluency and comprehension become issues—and teachers are rightly becoming concerned about both of these, even with young readers—you will want to use measures for both fluency and comprehension. Many teachers follow a running record with a retelling task (i.e., the child is asked to retell what he or she just read, and the teacher may tick off items from a pre-prepared list of main ideas and details) (see the World of Reading box).

AUTHENTIC ASSESSMENT. Sheila Valencia and her colleagues (Valencia, Hiebert, & Afflerbach, 1993) popularized the idea of the *authentic assessment* of literacy. Authentic assessment addresses the problem that most assessment methods have students perform contrived tasks that are not very much like what they do when they are actually reading and writing. Contrived tasks may not yield the full picture, including how the students think about literacy, their interests and motivations, and their preferences, strategies, likes,

myeducation**lab**
The Power of Classroom Practice
www.myeducationlab.com

Watch a reading specialist conduct a running record with an elementary student in the activity "Analyzing and Interpreting Running Record Data." Listen to the student's reading to learn about his reading strengths and needs. After watching the video, return to the activity and answer the questions that follow. (To find this activity, go to the topic *Assessment* in MyEducationLab and click on Assignments and Activities.)

Figure 11.1   Running Record Sheet.

Name: _____   Date: _____

School: _____   Teacher: _____

Text Titles	Running Words Errors	Error Rate	Accuracy	Self-Correction Rate
Easy (100%–95%)		1:	%	1:
Instructional (94%–90%)		1:	%	1:
Hard (89% and lower)		1:	%	1:

Analysis of Errors and Self-Corrections

Information used or neglected [Meaning (M), Structure or Syntax (S), Visual (V)]

Easy: _____

_____

Instructional: _____

_____

Hard: _____

_____

Teacher Observations:					
Analysis of Errors and Self-Corrections					
				Information used	
Page	E	SC	E		SC
			MSV		MSV

The World of Reading

The Three-Cueing System

Both the Reading Miscue Inventory and running records highlight the importance of the **three-cueing system** in children's word recognition. The three-cueing system is the idea that children use visual (or graphophonic), structural (or syntactic), meaning-based (or semantic) information to recognize new words.

There is no doubt that readers use the surrounding context to help identify a word. For example, any time you administer an Informal Reading Inventory you expect students to recognize more words when the words appear in the context of meaningful passages than when they appear in isolation, such as on lists (see Table 11.2).

The argument arises over *when* the context matters. In the early days of the Reading Miscue Inventory, its advocates thought readers read words by sampling enough visual information from the text to create a sense of the meaning. Once they had a sense of the meaning, they needed only to sample the print to confirm or disconfirm what they thought the text must be saying. As long as they could assume what the text must be saying from the meaning that was forming in their heads, they had a reduced need to take in the visual information (the strings of letters) from the page. When it was unclear what the text was saying, they focused on more of the letters in the words.

But that view of reading aroused a chorus of criticisms. Penfetti (1985), for example, found that readers always read the words and the letters, and the most fluent comprehenders were the best at word recognition, because fluent word recognition freed up the brain's available attention for making sense of the text.

All of this matters because if you believe readers should rely heavily on context to read words, you are more likely to emphasize that approach as you help struggling readers. And if you believe that well-developed word identification skills, including decoding ability, are the key to successful reading, you are more likely to teach accordingly.

The National Reading Panel (2000) clearly endorsed the view that reading requires the reading of words, and not guessing words from context, and readers need to know the relations between letters and sounds to help them read words. Marilyn Adams (1998), a member of the National Reading Panel, has elsewhere expressed doubts about the idea of the three-cueing system, first because so many educators seem to follow it yet nobody is sure where it came from and, secondly, because the model doesn't underscore the primary importance of reading words or give much guidance to the teacher on what kind of correction is best if a child depends too much on one cueing system versus another.

Other educators strongly argue that the larger context of information should be kept in mind when teaching reading (see Margaret Moustafa's summary of these articles at http://instructional1.calstatela.edu/mmousta/) (please note that in the preceding URL, the word "instruction" is followed by the letters "al" and the numeral "1").

So when you pick up a Reading Miscue Inventory or a running record, or nod your head when you read an article about the three-cueing system, controversy may be lurking just around the corner.

---

and dislikes. Authentic assessment thus involves both *informal* and *structured observations* (sometimes called **kidwatching**) and *work-sampling*, including *portfolios*. Authentic assessment also includes the use of *rubrics*.

KIDWATCHING.   Kidwatching is a term coined by influential literacy educator, Yetta Goodman (Goodman, 1985; Owocki & Goodman, 2002) to refer to a set of observations, ranging from impressions quickly captured on sticky notes, to home visits, to more formal assessments.

Table 11.2 Scoring Word Recognition on an Informal Reading Inventory

	INDEPENDENT READING LEVEL	INSTRUCTIONAL READING LEVEL	FRUSTRATION READING LEVEL
Word Identification in Isolation	90% +	70%–89%	Below 70%
Word Identification in Context	97% +	90%–96%	Below 90%

Kidwatching Is Informed.   Teachers learn more from observing children in the daily life of the classroom if they know a good deal about language and literacy processes, as well as how children talk, read, think, investigate, and interact with each other and the world.

Kidwatching Is Nonjudgmental.   Teachers record events or pieces of language as they occur, without filtering them through judgments. Planning what to do on the basis of the collected evidence will happen later, preferably after many different kinds of information have been collected. Here is an example of one kidwatcher's observation:

> *Notes on Erin (11/19) age 5½ in the library corner: Erin is turning the pages of* Fruits Good to Eat *in order, at a regular pace. She gets to the page with a pineapple on it, looks at it closely, turns to Robin, and asks, "Is this a pineapple?" Robin replies, "I think so, but let's ask Ms. B." They come to me. I ask Erin what she thinks, and she says, "I think so, but what does this say [pointing to the print]?" When I ask her what she thinks, she says, "I think it says pineapple because that's in the picture and there's a p."* (Goodman, 2006)

Note that this kind of written observation is also called an *anecdotal record.*

Kidwatching Uses Diverse Sources of Information.   Goodman (2006) writes, "Kidwatchers use a variety of tools to document their observations, including informal conversations, formal interviews, check sheets, observation forms, field notes, portfolios, and home visits." Using many sources of information, including not only the teacher's observations but also the child's and the family's points of view, as well as more formal assessments, allows teachers to make small adjustments—and sometimes larger ones—to instruction and classroom procedures.

Dual-Entry Diary

PORTFOLIOS.   Portfolios are collections of children's works gathered according to the objectives of the teacher's instruction. They may be maintained by the teacher as a way of keeping a diverse collection of artifacts related to a child's progress in learning to read and write. But usually they are maintained in collaboration with each child. The teacher and the child should decide in advance the sorts of items that should be kept in the portfolio. These might include

- Lists of books read
- A reading journal
- Repeated reading score sheets
- Written works chosen as indicative of the child's best work and range of work during a particular time period
- A list of topics for the child's writing
- Learning logs
- Running records

Periodically—at least once a month or once each marking period—the teacher schedules a conference or interview with the child. Ahead of the conversation, both the child and the teacher should look through the portfolio to find signs of progress and areas that need work. During their conversation, the child describes what he or she has learned during this period and sets goals for improvement during the next period. The teacher may ask questions to find out what things the child likes and doesn't like to read, what strategies he or she is using in reading, and aspects of the reading instruction that might be changed. The teacher makes suggestions to help the child learn.

RUBRICS.   According to Andrade (2002),

> *A rubric is a scoring tool that lists the criteria for a piece of work, or "what counts" (for example, purpose, organization, details, voice, and mechanics are often what count in a*

piece of writing); it also articulates gradations of quality for each criterion, from excellent to poor.

Rubrics have the advantage of allowing teachers to observe and evaluate an authentic performance, such as a child's oral reading, or a piece of writing created for a real purpose other than testing. They also have the advantage of teaching. Especially when they are shared with a student before he or she carries out a task, the rubrics tell the child how to do a task well.

Rubrics may be already designed by educational experts, such as the Multidimensional Fluency Scale in Table 11.5 in this chapter and the Six Traits rubric for evaluating writing discussed in Figure 10.13 in Chapter 10. Rubrics may also be developed by teachers, or even by the students themselves. When students participate in designing a rubric, they may become more strategic in reading—that is, they have a better idea how they should try to perform.

It helps to think of a rubric like a chart. Each row names an important aspect of performance on a task, and in the boxes under each column are descriptions that range from unsatisfactory to satisfactory to excellent performance on that factor.

Terms Used in Assessment

Students' performance on norm-referenced tests is usually reported three ways. First, they are given *raw scores*, which simply report the number or the percentage of items on the test they answered correctly. Raw scores mean little, however, without the understanding of how a particular child's score compares with those of other children in the same age group. Therefore, scores are presented in two additional ways. *Percentile scores* are based on a ninety-nine point scale, and they tell a child what percentage of the children in a comparison group received a lower score than his. *Stanine scores* may also be used to report performance on a test, especially when they are also used to eliminate the fine distinctions reported in percentiles that don't mean much. Stanine scores are reported in whole numbers on a nine-point scale. The spread of scores represented by each number is based on a normal curve of distribution. Scores of 4, 5, and 6 are average. Scores of 1, 2, and 3 are below average. Scores of 7, 8, and 9 are above average. **Grade-equivalent scores** are what they sound like: indications of what grade-level material an average reader would read at an instructional or independent level based on his or her performance on this test. Thus, if a fourth grader's grade equivalent score on a reading test is 7.5, that means he scored the way an average seventh grader would have scored on the material in that test. (But that doesn't mean the child is ready to be promoted to seventh grade; that he read material on a test intended for fourth graders like an average seventh grader would doesn't necessarily mean that he will be able to read seventh-grade materials like an average seventh grader.)

Tests are often described in terms of their validity and reliability. *Validity* refers to the extent that they measure what they claim to measure. Because all tests take a sample of a child's performance and claim to generalize from that sample to the child's more global level of performance, it is important to know if the test really does tell you what it claims to evaluate.

Educators often speak of different kinds of validity.

- **Content validity** is the degree to which a test measures what it claims to measure. If a test of reading comprehension asks students to answer questions about a passage after reading it, that test can be said to have content validity because answering questions is a reasonable demonstration of comprehension. But if the test asks students to locate all the words in a passage beginning with *B*, it would not have content validity as a test of comprehension.
- **Predictive validity**, also called *assessment-criterion relationship validity* (Linn & Gronlund, 2000), refers to the power of the test to predict the student's future

performance on related tasks. Predictive validity is important when we are doing screening assessments and monitoring assessments because at those times we wish to use students' present performance on reading tasks to predict their future reading performance. Note, too, that the predictive validity of a test may depend on when—that is, with what age child—it is used. For example, a test of phoneme awareness given to five-year-olds is not a very good predictor of future reading performance (Snow, Burns, & Griffin, 1998). The same test given in first grade may have greater predictive validity because a greater number of six-year-olds versus five-year-olds display some phonemic awareness.

- **Reliability** has to do with the likelihood that the results of the test are stable and dependable: that is, if the same test were given to the same child by two different people, or on two different days, would the results be similar? The different ways reliability is thought of include:

  - *Test-retest reliability*, in which the same students are given the same test within a short interval, to see if the results are similar
  - *Split-half reliability*, in which samples of a student's performance on different items of the same test are compared with each other
  - *Inter-rater reliability*, in which an instrument such as a rubric is used by different raters to assess the same student, and the results are compared

The terms *validity* and *reliability* are usually applied to standardized tests, but they are worth considering regardless of the kind of assessment being done. The No Child Left Behind Act requires that assessments be scientifically validated, which often means that assessment instruments have demonstrated validity and reliability. But a caution is in order—many valuable ways of collecting and making judgments about children's reading and writing do not have demonstrated validity and reliability. Informal observation of students' reading is one; all types of informal reading inventories (IRIs) are another.

What Do We Need to Know from Assessing Children?

We need to assess and monitor many things with respect to what children are learning about literacy.

Emergent Readers

Phonics and Phonological Awareness

Why is it important that children understand what literacy is about, and what books are for?

Emergent readers are usually preschool, kindergarten, and first-grade children who are developing concepts about language and print and knowledge of the alphabetic writing system that form the foundation on which later reading is built. As we saw in Chapters 3 and 4, children develop all these at different rates and to varying extents. Giving children special, finely tuned intervention early on can help many of them avoid reading failure and make progress as readers and writers. Assessment of children's early literacy is essential. So what do we need to know? Effective early literacy assessments focus on:

- **Concepts about print and awareness of what books are and what they are for.** The more developed holistic sense children have of what literacy is about, the better they will be able to focus their attention on the details they must understand in order to read. Without an orienting sense of what literacy is for (reading and writing that makes sense) and what books are for, early literacy instruction may be confusing for some children.
- **Awareness of sounds in language.** Writing represents spoken language, and in English, writing represents language at the level of words, onsets and rimes, and

phonemes, as we saw in Chapter 3. The problem is that in speech, children can use language without thinking about it. But when they learn to read and write, children must be conscious of words, rimes, and phonemes. Those things must be real for young learners, because young learners will need to think hard about the relations between spoken units of spoken language and units of print.

- **Knowledge of the alphabet.** Children must know many letters of the alphabet to begin to develop the ability to read. Knowledge of the alphabet is an indicator of the amount of print exposure they have had (the more letters they know, the more print they are likely to have seen). But knowing letters is also important in itself because the more letters they know, the more successfully they can explore how print and speech go together. There is a difference between letter identification and letter retrieval. Because some readers with disabilities have difficulty naming letters quickly (Katzir & Pare-Blagoev, 2006), some assessments of early literacy include a timed letter identification task.

- **Knowledge of some words.** Virtually all children in America are exposed to print before they begin formal reading instruction. Many of them learn to identify some words: their own names, names of fast food restaurants, words from favorite book titles. The number of words they can identify while still prereaders is a sign of emergent literacy.

- **Listening comprehension.** Children need to have receptive language developed to the degree that they can follow books read aloud to them by the teacher and also comprehend texts themselves when they become readers. Some, but not all, emergent literacy assessment instruments include measures of listening comprehension.

- **Knowledge of letter-to-sound correspondences (phonics).** Children need to develop ideas about the relations between letters and sounds to learn to read. As we saw in the discussion of invented spelling (Chapter 4), most children don't wait to be taught. With even a little encouragement, however, they will begin to speculate actively on what those relationships are. Children's understanding of letter-to-sound correspondences can be assessed beginning in kindergarten and continuing through first grade. (Phonics knowledge will continue to be assessed in beginning readers and in older struggling readers.)

Phonics and Phonological Awareness

When can children's understanding of letter-to-sound correspondences begin to be assessed?

Watch a teacher administer a concepts about print assessment to her student in the activity "Assessing Emergent Readers and Writers." What does the assessment tell her? (To find this activity, go to the topic *Emergent Literacy* in MyEducationLab and click on Assignments and Activities.)

Contemporary assessment of early literacy, then, tracks the development of concepts about print, awareness of sounds, awareness of letters, knowledge of words, and (sometimes) listening comprehension. Note that we do not concern ourselves so much with children's ability to recognize colors or shapes, to repeat numbers back, or to distinguish a ringing bell from a chirping bird. Some educators do concern themselves with general indicators like these of children's readiness to learn. But, when assessing early literacy, it is best to focus on literacy-related factors because they more reliably predict children's future success as readers than the more general measures of learning readiness (Snow et al., 1998). Also, because teachers need to assess and monitor children's emergent literacy repeatedly during the school year and because children must be assessed one at a time, they need to focus on aspects of emergent literacy that are most important. Note, too, that many factors, not just one, should be assessed. In practice, however, concepts about print tend to develop before the other factors do, so a teacher may stop assessing those concepts after children have shown that they have them and keep focusing on the other factors.

Measures of Emergent Literacy

Teacher-made measures of emergent literacy can be fashioned after the Early Reading Screening Inventory (Morris, 2000) and the Print Concepts Assessment (after Clay, 1999). The Early Reading Screening Inventory, as the name implies, has been widely used to identify young readers in early first grade who will need additional help to learn to read. Other emergent literacy assessment programs are in use around the United States, some

Emergent readers can be young children who are developing a foundation upon which later reading is built. (David Mager/ Pearson Learning Studio)

of them promoted by individual states. The Phonological Awareness Literacy Survey (PALS) (http://pals.virginia.edu/) is provided to school districts in Virginia and is widely used elsewhere as both a screening and a monitoring tool. The Illinois Snapshot of Early Literacy is promoted by that state as a screening tool. The Texas Education Agency developed the Texas Primary Reading Inventory (http://www.tpri.org/About/), with versions for kindergarten through third grades that can be administered as a screening, diagnosis, and monitoring tool.

At the University of Oregon, the Dynamic Indicators of Basic Literacy Skills (DIBELS) was developed with a federal grant and is available to teachers without cost online. This test, which can be used as a screening, diagnostic, and monitoring tool, begins with a preschool version that assesses initial sounds or *onset fluency*. At the kindergarten level, there are added tests of phonemic segmentation fluency, letter naming fluency, and nonsense word reading fluency. These continue through first grade, where an oral reading fluency measure is also added. It continues through third grade. These are called fluency tests because children's responses are timed, and the speed of the child's responses is noted in addition to accuracy (see http://dibels.uoregon.edu/measures.php).

"ROAMING AROUND THE KNOWN." How accurate are all of these measures? According to Snow et al. (1998), the correlations between the component measures listed earlier in this section and children's later success in learning to read are in the 30- to 50-percent range. Scores in this range suggest that the factors are important in reading, but there is a very real chance that a child will be more or less successful in learning to read than these tests predict. With these limitations in mind, prudent teachers avoid making important decisions about children's education on the basis of one of these tests alone. Many use the practice of following the testing with "Roaming around the Known" (Clay, 1993); that is, taking the findings from the assessments as suggestions only, and teaching the child for several days to see how she or he responds to actual instruction—in other words, teaching with the idea that the assessments may very well be wrong.

What Do We Need to Know About Beginning Readers and Beyond?

Beginning readers are starting to read words in connected text. Just as it is important to know that they have their emergent literacy concepts and abilities in place, it is also critical to know if each child is making progress in all aspects of beginning reading. These aspects include word recognition—including having a *sight vocabulary* stored in memory, *decoding skills* so that the child can read a word he didn't know before, and the ability to *use context* to help identify words. Children's reading *fluency*—their accuracy, rate, and intonation—needs to develop apace as well. Their *vocabulary* should be growing by thousands of words each year, and they will need to learn vocabulary from reading—reading widely. *Comprehension* is the ultimate goal of reading, and we want to know how this ability is growing, too. As we saw in Chapters 6 and 7, comprehension is a complex of many factors including having and using world knowledge, getting main ideas, making inferences, having metacognition or cognitive monitoring—that is, knowing if the text is making sense—and following the patterns of different kinds of fictional and informational texts to construct meaning. We also care about their attitudes toward reading and what kind of text and how much of it they read. But one measure that combines all of these factors is their reading levels.

Reading Levels: Independent, Instructional, Frustration

It is possible to measure students' *reading levels*, the levels of text they can read for different purposes. To talk about reading levels implies two things: that texts have levels of difficulty and that readers have levels of ability. To speak of levels of difficulty of texts implies that some are written on a first-grade level, some on a second-grade level, and so on. These levels of difficulty are referred to as **readability**, and we will say more about that later. When we speak of the reading levels of individual readers, it helps to ask what the reading task is: Will they be studying a book in a group under the teacher's supervision, reading a textbook for homework, or reading for pleasure? Depending on the answers to those questions, it is proper to speak not of one reading level but three: the *independent level*, the *instructional level*, and the *frustration level*.

INDEPENDENT READING LEVEL.   If the student is to read material on his or her own, without the support of a teacher or other more skilled readers, then the material should fall within the student's independent level of reading ability. In material written at the student's independent level, the student should encounter no more than three or four unknown words in a hundred and should enjoy nearly total comprehension.

Books that fall within students' independent level include books students choose to read for pleasure and textbooks they use independently for homework. Regardless of a student's grade placement, if the books are above the student's independent level, then the student should be given easier books or should be offered support for reading such as buddy reading, study guides, or recorded text. Conversely, teachers sometimes have to prod students to read more challenging material that falls within their independent level.

INSTRUCTIONAL READING LEVEL.   In the classroom, teachers often work with students using material that is moderately challenging for them so they will learn from the supported practice. Material used for this purpose should fall within the student's instructional level of reading ability. Such material presents the student with unknown words at a rate of up to one in ten, and language and concepts that are not fully comprehended—at least not at first. The intention is that with guided practice in materials written at the instructional level, students will learn the unknown words and come to comprehend the once-challenging language and concepts. The instructional level corresponds to what Vygotsky (1976) called the *zone of proximal development*, the area of moderate challenge that is just at the threshold of a reader's growing abilities. It is here that teachers most often practice *scaffolded instruction*, providing temporary support, including teaching strategies that will help the student learn on his or her own in the future.

Again, a particular student's instructional level often falls above or below that student's grade placement level. Because of the value of working in moderately challenging materials when teaching a student to read, it is very important to locate a student's instructional level wherever it may be.

FRUSTRATION READING LEVEL.   If the material is too challenging—that is, if it contains more than one unfamiliar word in ten, and language and concepts that substantially resist comprehension—the material is said to be written at the student's frustration level. The frustration level is not actually a reading level because students do not practice successful reading there. It is used rather to define the limits of a student's instructional level. Teachers can assign reading material during closely supervised instructional tasks that approach, but do not cross into, the frustration level.

As the name implies, frustration level text is so challenging to a student that the challenge of reading it is burdensome and disagreeable. Students will actually progress faster in learning to read and learning to spell when they are placed in instructional-level text, even though that is easier than frustration-level text.

It is often possible to determine through observation that a student is reading at frustration level. The student exhibits some or all of the following behaviors: laborious word-for-word, or even letter-by-letter, reading with flat intonation; pointing behavior, especially when that is not observed in easier passages; squinting or moving the text very close to the eyes; and rocking back and forth, perhaps kicking the chair or table. Think about what your own physical behaviors would be if you were asked to read aloud from a quantitative chemistry text that you did not understand at all.

Students' reading levels are often determined by administering an Informal Reading Inventory (IRI). When an IRI is used, it will normally tell you how many errors a student can make in each part to be independent, instructional, or frustrated at that level. If an IRI is not used, you can still get a rough idea of a student's reading level if you know the reading levels of several short texts. Have the child read a passage of at least 150 words. Mark each reading error as an *omission* (leaving out a word), a *substitution* (reading a word other than the word supplied in the text or misreading the word in the text), or an *insertion* (adding a word or words that were not in the text). Each counts as one error every time it occurs. *Proper names* that are misread count as one error, regardless how many times they are misread. *Reversals* (reading two words in the wrong order) count as one error. Repetitions do not count as errors, and neither do self-corrections or long pauses.

Using those criteria, here is how the scores are interpreted:

Independent level: 97 to 100 percent of the words are read correctly.

Instructional level: 90 to 96 percent of the words are read correctly.

Frustration level: Fewer than 90 percent of the words are read correctly.

These criteria are taken from Betts (1946).

READING LEVELS AND READABILITY.   Applying the concept of reading levels that was just presented, a teacher might test a particular third-grade student and find that his independent level is second grade, his instructional level is third grade, and his frustration level is fourth grade. For this information to be useful to the teacher, we must assume that reading material is available that is written at the second-, third-, and fourth-grade reading levels. This is a reasonably safe assumption, but there are some problems with it. Most important, we now know that whether a reader comprehends a particular text depends to some extent on what is already in the reader's head and not solely on what is in the text (Alexander, 2000; Pearson & Anderson, 1985). Two third-grade readers may read a text about a game of basketball. Even though they have equivalent reading abilities, if one happens to be a passionate player of the game, that student may understand the text better than the other student.

The determination that a text is written at a particular grade level is usually based on surface features of the text, such as the length of the sentences and the number of syllables in the words. The readability level might also be determined by trialing the text with a group of sample readers of different ages. Either way, a particular reader may have a harder or easier time reading a particular text, depending on that reader's background knowledge of, and interest in, the topic of the text.

Measuring Readability

In the 1940s an Austrian immigrant to the United States wrote a doctoral dissertation in which he showed a mathematical formula for estimating the readability level of written language. Soon Rudolph Flesch's formula and many others like it were being used to help publishers adjust the level of difficulty of their products, be they textbooks for children, newspapers and magazines for the general reader, or government publications aimed at special audiences such as farmers, cooks, or sanitation workers. Now readability formulas are available for many of the world's languages.

One of the simplest readability devices for English was developed by Edward Fry, now emeritus professor of literacy at Rutgers University in the United States. Fry's procedure is to take three separate 100-word samples from a work to be studied, and to count the number of sentences to the tenth place, and to count the number of syllables in that sam-

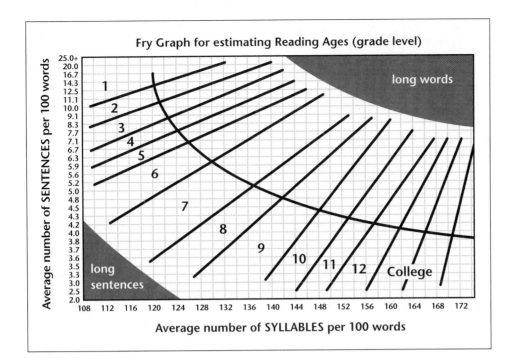

Fry Graph for estimating Reading Ages (grade level)

Average number of SENTENCES per 100 words

25.0+
20.0
16.7
14.3
12.5
11.1
10.0
9.1
8.3
7.7
7.1
6.7
6.3
5.9
5.6
5.2
5.0
4.8
4.5
4.3
4.2
4.0
3.8
3.7
3.6
3.5
3.3
3.0
2.5
2.0

108 112 116 120 124 128 132 136 140 144 148 152 156 160 164 168 172

Average number of SYLLABLES per 100 words

long words

long sentences

Figure 11.2

Fry Readability Graph.

Source: Edward Fry, Elementary Reading Instruction. Copyright 1977 by The McGraw-Hill Companies, Inc. Reprinted by permission.

ple. The sentence counts and syllable counts are averaged, and the results are plotted on the graph presented in Figure 11.2.

Fry's graph resembles other formulas in that it considers the length of sentences and the length of words as the variables that affect readability. The logic here is that longer sentences tend to be more grammatically complex, and more grammatically complex sentences are harder to read. Longer words tend to be more sophisticated, rarer, and encountered later in schooling. Combining the two measures of sentence length and word length yields a more reliable estimate of readability than one measure alone (see the Teach It! box).

Other readability formulas are Flesch-Kincaid (which is folded into most versions of Microsoft Word [go to Tools → Spelling and Grammar → Options → Check Readability Level]), Dale-Chall, and SMOG ("simplified measure of gobbledygook").

Teach It!

Refer to the Teach It! appendix at the end of the book for further activities you can use to reinforce concepts discussed in this chapter.

The Fry Readability Graph

Try the Fry readability graph on a sample of this text. For a short exercise, instead of taking three 100-word passages and averaging the results, you can take just one 100-word passage. Count off 100 words, then count the number of syllables in that sample. Count the number of sentences to the tenth place. Plot the results on the graph. Are you surprised at the results? Try the readability graph on a children's book. Try it on an article from your daily newspaper. If you can, find a memorandum to parents from a local school and try it on that. Try it on the warranty statement of the next electronic item you buy, or on the user's agreement of the next software program you download.

If you are in a classroom, have students bring in some written materials that come in the mail at their house (with their parents' permission, of course!). Have them look at the fine print on an application for a credit card. Or have them go online and look up information on applying for U.S. citizenship through the U.S. Immigration and Naturalization Service. In pairs or triads, have them compute the readability levels.

What conclusions can you draw about the reading demands faced by citizens in your community? What levels of reading ability allow people to understand which kinds of communications? What are some of the consequences of having a low reading level?

A now widely used system for establishing readability level is the Lexile Framework (Lennon & Burdick, 2004). The Lexile system, developed with federal funds by Metametrics, Inc., measures both readability of text and reading ability of readers. Readability measures are based on semantic (word-based) and syntactic (sentence-based) features of the text. The semantic score is calculated from the frequency or commonality of the words in the text and the length of the sentences. A computer program compares the words in a particular text to a dictionary that has a score for the frequency with which each word is typically encountered ("the" would be a common word and "indefatigable" would be a less common one). The syntactic score is based on the average length of sentences in the text, and the two factors together yield a Lexile score of between 200 (for a very easy text) and 1,700 (for a very challenging one). The Lexile Framework is also used to assess a reader's ability to read a text. Using Lexile scores to match readers with books can be more accurate than establishing a child's reading ability in grade equivalents, and then matching the reading score with the readability score of a book. Students with a Lexile score of 300, for instance, would be expected to read with 75 percent comprehension a book with a Lexile score of 300. Information about the Lexile Framework is available online at www.lexile.com. Reading difficulty of text is now measured in grade equivalents, Lexiles, Reading Recovery levels, Fountas and Pinnell levels, and others (see Table 11.3).

Somewhere between a readability formula and a comprehension test is the cloze procedure (Taylor, 1953; Bormuth, 1968). The cloze procedure tests a reader's ability to read a particular text at the independent, instructional, and frustration levels. Thus if you are fairly sure of the difficulty level of the text, you can use the cloze procedure to get an idea of the reader's independent, instructional, and frustration levels. And if you are fairly sure of the reading ability of the group of people who take the test, you can use their performance on the cloze procedure to get an indication of the readability level of the text.

To conduct the cloze procedure, select a passage of more than 260 words. Leave the first sentence intact. Go through and mark every fifth word thereafter until you reach fifty words marked. Then leave the sentence after the fiftieth word intact. Retype the passage, and replace every word you marked with a blank of equal length. Have the students read the passage and fill in the blanks. Cloze tests are scored as follows:

The independent reading level = 60 percent and greater correct responses (30+ words)

The instructional reading level = between 40 and 59 percent correct responses (between 20 and 29 words)

The frustration level = fewer than 40 percent correct responses (fewer than 20 words)

More information about readability is available on the Internet. For a good introduction and links to other sites, you might begin with the article in *Wikipedia*, the free encyclopedia, at http://en.wikipedia.org/wiki/Readability.

Assessing Word Recognition

Phonics and Phonological Awareness

What's the difference between sight word reading and decoding?

As we noted in Chapter 5, word recognition has several aspects to it:

- **Sight vocabulary.** These are the words a reader has stored in memory that can be recognized instantly. Sight words are learned from reading. Words that may initially be decoded or figured out from context become sight words after repeated exposures.

- **Decoding ability.** Young readers frequently encounter words they do not have stored in memory. One way they can read them—which the National Reading Panel and the No Child Left Behind Act have indicated is the most important way—is to *decode* the word, or work out its identity by matching its letters and its sounds. Children differ in their ability to decode, and a task of assessment is to measure their ability to do it.

Table 11.3   Comparing Readability Levels

Several different systems provide ratings of the difficulty levels of texts. Readability formulas such as the Fry, the Dale-Chall, and the Flesch-Kincaid report scores in terms of grade level equivalents. Most informal reading inventories report results as grade level equivalents, also. Recently, other systems have proliferated. In addition to Lexiles, which range between 200 and 1700, Reading Recovery (Clay, 1993), Fountas/Pinnell (2005), and Developmental Reading Assessment or DRA (from Pearson Education http://plgcatalog.pearson.com/program_multiple.cfm?site_id=2&discipline_id=807&subarea_id=1000&program_id=23661) provide fine gradations of difficulty for readers in the primary grades. This chart shows how scores from the different systems compare to each other.

GRADE LEVEL	INFORMAL READING INVENTORY SCORES	FOUNTAS/PINNELL GUIDED READING LEVELS	READING RECOVERY LEVELS	LEXILES	DRA LEVELS
K		A	A, B		A
			1		1
		B	2		2
	Pre-primer 1	C	3		3
1.1	Pre-primer 2		4		4
	Pre-primer 3		5		
		D	6		6
			7		
1.2		E	8		8
			9		
	Primer	F	10		10
		G	11	200–299	
			12		12
			13		
	Grade 1	H	14		14
			15		
		I	16		16
2	Grade 2	J	18	300–399	20
		K	19		
		L	20	400–499	28
		M			
3	Grade 3	N	22	500–599	30
		O, P	24	600–699	34
					38
4	Grade 4	Q, R, S	26	700–799	40
5	Grade 5	T, U, V	28	800–899	44
6	Grade 6	W, X, Y	30	900–999	
7	Grade 7	Z	32	1000–1100	
8	Grade 8	Z	34		

Source: After Salt Lake City School District, 2006

- **Identifying words from context.** When unrecognized words occur in meaningful texts, readers have two other ways besides decoding to figure out what they are. One is the syntax of the sentence. For example, if we read, "Give me the _____," we can be pretty sure that whatever fills that blank is a noun, or something that can function like a noun. But suppose the text said, "It was midnight. The safe cracker had opened the safe and taken the money. Just as he reached the door, the lights went on and a voice said, 'Stop. Now turn around slowly. Give me the _____.'" Now we would probably guess that the missing word was not only a noun, but *money*, because the meaning of the text limits our choices to that word. Both of these examples go under the name of *using context to support word identification*. However, Marie Clay's *running records* procedure keeps track of each kind of context support by distinguishing *structural cues* from *meaning-based cues*. Both of those are distinguished from *visual* or graphophonic cues.

Assessing Word Recognition and Phonics

There are several ways to assess word recognition. Assessments of reading fluency in the repeated reading task measure students' accuracy in word recognition. If you know the reading level of the book, and you know the student's accuracy score on at least a 100-word passage (the score, in percentages, is derived by dividing the number of errors by the total number of words), you can compute the student's level of word recognition in terms of grade equivalents as follows:

Independent: 97–100 percent correct

Instructional: 90–96 percent correct

Frustration: Below 90 percent correct

Word recognition rates can also be measured by means of an Informal Reading Inventory. Many IRIs measure word recognition three ways. First, they give a measure of a child's *sight vocabulary*, the words a child has stored in memory and can recognize instantaneously. They do this by "flashing" (exposing very briefly between two index cards) words from a list (see the Assessment box on pages 348 and 349).

Second, they give a measure of a child's *decoding*. They do this by giving a long exposure of any words the child could not recognize instantly, and allowing the test administrator to compare the difference between the "flashed" and the "untimed" scores. The difference in favor of the untimed score shows the power of the child's decoding ability because it shows how many words he could not recognize instantly, but could sound out given the time to do so.

IRIs also give a measure of children's power to recognize words in context. The child reads aloud words from a text passage as the teacher listens carefully and records and scores the errors. The percentage scores of words correctly read in context are interpreted using the same criteria used in the fluency measure.

Assessing phonics knowledge can also be done by carefully observing the kinds of errors children make when they are recognizing words. In Chapter 5 we showed a system of categorizing errors that showed if a child's word reading was in the logographic, alphabetic, orthographic, or derivational stage.

Some tests, including DIBELS (the Dynamic Indicators of Basic Early Literacy Skills) and the Woodcock-Johnson-III Basic Reading Battery, assess phonics knowledge by testing children's reading of nonsense words, like *VAJ, KOL, NAK*, and the like. The advantage to having children read nonsense words is that we are assured they have never seen them before, so the words must be read by pure decoding. The disadvantage is that, because they are nonsense words, the children don't have the normal self-correction to them that comes from arriving at a word they know in their speech. Another disadvantage is that some of the nonsense words do not conform to English orthography. For example, DIBELS uses *doj*, *ol*, and *huf*, even though there are no single-syllable words in English that are spelled that way.

Another test of phonics knowledge is done by means of children's spelling. The assessment inventories built into Kathy Ganske's (2000) *Word Journeys* have children spell challenging words, and then give teachers advice on (1) analyzing the spelling error to assign the child to a probable level of invented spelling and (2) pinpointing the aspect of phonics knowledge that the child needs to learn.

Assessing Reading Fluency

Reading fluency has moved from being a neglected skill (Allington, 1983) to an area of intense interest. In *Put Reading First*, Armbruster, Lehr, and Osborn (2001) define reading fluency this way:

> *Fluency is the ability to read a text accurately and quickly. When fluent readers read silently, they recognize words automatically. They group words quickly in ways that help them gain meaning from what they read. Fluent readers read aloud effortlessly and with expression. Their reading sounds natural, as if they are speaking. (p. 22)*

Assessing reading fluency is most simply measured by counting the number of words children read per minute minus their errors. This yields a measure called words correct per minute (WCPM), which is calculated using this formula:

$$\frac{(\text{Total words read, minus words read incorrectly}) \times 60}{\text{Reading time in seconds}} = \text{WCPM}$$

Thus, for example, if a third-grade student reads 125 words in one minute but makes five reading errors, we would calculate her fluency rate of WCPM as:

$$\frac{(125 - 5) \times 60}{60} = \frac{120 \times 60}{60} = 120 \text{ WCPM}$$

According to Table 11.4 on page 350, this would be an acceptable reading rate for a mid-year third grader.

Reading fluency consists not only of speed and correctness, however, but also of **prosody** (reading with expression and with proper phrasing) (Miller & Schwanenflugel, 2008). Zutell and Rasinski (1991) developed the Multidimensional Fluency Scale (see Table 11.5 on page 351) to help teachers observe several dimensions of fluency at once. Those factors are expression and volume, phrasing, smoothness, and pace. The scale is a rubric to guide teachers' judgment. To carry out the procedure, the teacher selects a passage of at least 100 words that should be written at the student's grade level or a year below. The student reads the passage and the teacher tape records it. The teacher then plays the tape back and evaluates the student's reading for each of the factors of accuracy, phrasing, smoothness, and pace.

Assessing Vocabulary

Vocabulary development is recognized more and more as a critical variable in learning to read. But how do we know how many words a child knows? As we saw in Chapter 4, it depends on what we mean by "know." Does the child have a vague idea about what the word means? Can the child understand the word when reading it or hearing it, but not when using it? Does the child know all of the meanings of it? These questions show what a complicated thing it is to **assess vocabulary**. Vocabulary has often been assessed as part

Writing and Reading Connections

Why has reading fluency become an area of such intense interest to educators?

Word Recognition Inventory

The word recognition inventory has two parts: a display list, which is shown to the child one word at a time, and a recording sheet for the child's answers.

To administer a word recognition inventory, you have two options. You can simply point to the words one at a time and have the child read them, putting a checkmark on the recording sheet for each word that is correctly identified. You may record what the child says when he or she misreads a word if you want to study those errors later. Count the number of words read correctly, and multiply by five points to yield a percentage score.

As an alternative, you can hold two index cards over the word and *briefly* expose the word (expose for about a quarter of a second) to the child. If he or she reads the word correctly, place a checkmark in the "flashed" column of the record sheet and go on to the next word. If the student fails to read the word correctly, record whatever he or she says in the "flashed" column and then open up the cards to expose the words. If she now reads the word correctly, place a checkmark in the "untimed" column; if not read correctly, record whatever the student says, or enter a zero if he or she says nothing. Calculate the scores for both columns by multiplying the words correctly identified by five points.

The scores can be used as follows to identify the child's independent, instructional, and frustration levels, as follows:

Independent level: 90 to 100 percent correct
Instructional level: 70 to 89 percent correct
Frustration level: Below 70 percent

Display List

cards	station
above	ought
library	idea
brave	coach
instead	type
dear	damp
press	elbow
popcorn	mystery
pretty	yourselves
monkey	midnight
feather	motorcycle
become	insect
grandfather	study
hair	easier
people	headache
kept	match
mountain	quit
pass	alive
seem	moment
anyway	range

Recording Sheet

	Flashed	Untimed		Flashed	Untimed
cards			station		
above			ought		
library			idea		
brave			coach		
instead			type		
dear			damp		
press			elbow		
popcorn			mystery		
pretty			yourselves		
monkey			midnight		
feather			motorcycle		
become			insect		
grandfather			study		
hair			easier		
people			headache		
kept			match		
mountain			quit		
pass			alive		
seem			moment		
anyway			range		
Total Errors:			**Total Errors:**		

0–2 errors = independent level
3–6 errors = instructional level
7 + errors = frustration level

Source: From C. Temple, A. Crawford, and J. Gillet (2009). *Developmental Literacy Inventory: Reading and Spelling from Emergent to Mature Levels.* Published by Allyn and Bacon, Boston, MA. Copyright © 2009. Reprinted by permission of Pearson Education.

Table 11.4 Oral Reading Fluency Norms

GRADE	PERCENTILE	FALL WCPM*	WINTER WCPM*	SPRING WCPM*
2	75	82	106	124
	50	53	78	94
	25	23	46	65
3	75	107	123	142
	50	79	93	114
	25	65	70	87
4	75	125	133	143
	50	99	112	118
	25	72	89	92
5	75	126	143	151
	50	105	118	128
	25	77	93	100

*WCPM is words correct per minute.
The 50th percentile for upper grades is 125–150 WCPM.
Source: From Curriculum-Based Oral Reading Fluency Norms for Students in Grades 2 Through 5, by J. Hasbrouck and G. Tindal, *Teaching Exceptional Children, 24*, 1992, p. 42. Copyright 1992 by The Council for Exceptional Children. Reprinted with permission.

of an IRI and other reading tests. But with the advent of No Child Left Behind and Reading First, teachers are being called upon to assess children's vocabulary knowledge more systematically.

When states specify that teachers use scientifically based tests of vocabulary—that is, tests with proven validity and reliability—the choices are rather limited. A group commissioned by the U.S. Department of Education to approve assessment instruments for use with federally funded programs yielded a very limited list of approved instruments for assessing vocabulary at the points of screening, diagnosing, monitoring, and outcomes-based assessment.

According to the *Final Report: Analysis of Reading Assessment Instrument for K–3* (http://people.uncw.edu/kozloffm/rfassessmentexecsummary.pdf), one instrument, the *Peabody Picture Vocabulary Test-III*, was approved for all purposes for levels kindergarten through grade 3. This test costs $450. Other tests such as the *Expressive One-Word Picture Vocabulary Test*, the *One-Word Picture Vocabulary Test Revised*, the *Texas Primary Reading Inventory*, and the *Expressive Vocabulary Test* were approved for limited applications in certain grades.

Teachers who wish to construct their own vocabulary tests would do well to follow the advice of Barone, Hardman, and Taylor (2006) and construct devices that ask children to:

- Select the meanings from a set of possibilities when a target word is given.
- Select a target word from a set of possibilities when a meaning is given.
- Classify words into categories.
- Tell which word from a group of words does not belong.
- Use visual and contextual clues to understand difficult words in sentences.
- Choose the correct word meaning, an antonym, or a synonym from a set of possibilities.

Table 11.5   Multidimensional Fluency Scale

	1	2	3	4
Expression and volume	Reads in a quiet voice as if to get the words out. The reading does not sound natural like talking to a friend.	Reads in a quiet voice. The reading sounds natural in part of the text, but the reading does not always sound like talking to a friend.	Reads with volume and expression. However, sometimes the reader slips into expressionless reading and does not sound like talking to a friend.	Reads with varied volume and expression. The reading sounds like talking to a friend with voice matching the interpretation of the passage.
Phrasing	Reads word-by-word in a monotone voice.	Reads in two- and three-word phrases, not adhering to punctuation, stress, and intonation.	Reads with a mixture of run-ons, mid-sentence pauses for breath, and some choppiness. There is reasonable stress and intonation.	Reads with good phrasing, adhering to punctuation, stress, and intonation.
Smoothness	Frequently hesitates while reading, sounds out words, and repeats words or phrases. The reader makes multiple attempts to read the same passage.	Reads with extended pauses or hesitations. The reader has many "rough spots."	Reads with occasional breaks in rhythm. The reader has difficulty with specific words and/or sentence structures.	Reads smoothly with some breaks, but self-corrects with difficult words and/or sentence structures.
Pace	Reads slowly and laboriously.	Reads moderately slowly.	Reads fast and slow throughout reading.	Reads at a conversational pace throughout the reading.

Source: Zutell and Rasinski (1991).

- Show an understanding of root words, prefixes and suffixes, historical morphemes, or grammatical endings.
- Choose correct meanings for homophones (words that sound the same but have different meanings: *read a book*; *a reed in a pond*) and homographs (words that are spelled the same but have different meanings: *lead the singing*; *a lead pipe*).
- Complete a sentence with a correct word choice from alternatives.
- Demonstrate dictionary skills.

Assessing Comprehension

Reading comprehension consists of several abilities. Students' prior knowledge (sometimes called world knowledge) is needed to contextualize the new information they gain from the text. And students need to read actively, using their prior knowledge and clues from the text to set purposes and raise questions to answer while reading. They need the ability to find main ideas and supporting details and recall them later. They also need to be able to make inferences to construct meanings when ideas are not explicitly stated. They need to be able to follow the patterns of different kinds of texts, both fictional and informational, as guides to constructing meaning. And they need to keep building their inventory of vocabulary. They must do all this while reading aloud and silently.

That is a lot for a teacher to assess! In practice, when teachers want to observe this many factors, they often rely upon IRIs because they provide comprehensive measures.

Assessing Comprehension with an Informal Reading Inventory

Informal Reading Inventories allow teachers to **assess comprehension** by means of meaningful text passages written at ascending levels of difficulty. Questions are asked before and after the reading, and the child's behaviors are closely observed during reading.

Before reading a passage on an IRI, students may be asked a set of optional questions to ascertain what they know about the topic, to get an indication of the extent of their *prior knowledge* about the topic. Some examples, all taken from Temple, Crawford, and Gillet (2009), are in the following paragraphs.

After they have read the passage, students are asked a series of questions of different kinds. Some questions may also ask a student to summarize a main idea that has been stated in the text. For example, in a second-grade passage, the text says:

> *Jan lives in the city. The city has many big buildings. People work in some of the buildings. People shop in other buildings. Some buildings have apartments. . . . There are many cars, trucks, and buses in the city. They make a lot of noise. Many people walk on the street. Some people ride on the bus. There are many people on the bus.*

The question asks: *What did this story say that it was like in the city?*

Some of the questions require the recall of important details. For example, the text says: *In Israel, the birthday girl or boy gets a beautiful crown of flowers. The mother places the royal crown on her child's head.* The question asks: *According to this passage, in what country does the birthday child wear a crown of flowers?*

Questions may require that readers make inferences to construct meaning where ideas are not stated explicitly. In narratives, some inferences require that the readers infer motives for behavior. For example, in a sixth-grade passage, the text says:

> *"Cast near the trunk. Watch out for the branches."*
> *"I know, Dad," said Paco. But his first cast landed on top of the trunk. Without commenting, his father paddled the canoe to the other side of the dead tree, pried the lure from the bark, and gently tossed it into the water.*

The question asks: *How did Paco feel about his father's advice? How do you know?*

When the text is informational, inference questions can require readers to derive an answer by applying logic to pieces of information that are given, although the answer to the question is not explicitly stated. For example, in a middle school level passage, the text says:

> *Industries like the textile industry have had to shut down because of increased competition. They could no longer compete in the global economy. Increased competition often leads to lower prices for consumers. But lower prices can sometimes cause lower profits for industries.*

The question asks: *From what the article said, do you think you pay more or less for a shirt now that we have a global economy?*

Questions may assess *vocabulary*, too. One kind of vocabulary knowledge is the knowledge of words and their meanings that is stored in memory. Another kind is the ability to infer word meanings from context. As an example of assessing words and meanings stored in memory in a second-grade passage, the text says, *Jan lives in the city. The city has many big buildings. People work in some of the buildings. People shop in other buildings.* The question asks, *When the text said "People shop in other buildings," what does "shop" mean?* As an example of assessing a child's ability to infer vocabulary meaning from context, in a fourth-grade passage the text says, *The wings quiver as they slice through the turbulent air.* The question asks: *In the sentence, "The wings quiver as they slice through the turbulent air," what does "turbulent" mean?* A student who did not already know that the word meant "stormy" or "stirred up" might infer the meaning from the context because it is obvious that *turbulent* refers to air that an airplane is flying through, and it is a condition that makes the wings of the airplane tremble.

For the purpose of scoring, correctly answered questions are counted as a percentage of the total number of questions the child is asked. The scores are interpreted as follows:

Independent reading level = 90 and greater percent correct responses

Instructional reading level = 70 to 89 percent correct responses

Frustration reading level = below 70 percent correct responses

Most IRIs contain both narrative and informational texts, so teachers can assess reader success in dealing with all of the factors just mentioned in different patterns or genres of text. For example, the inference question we saw before from the narrative passage about Paco fishing with his father relied upon the reader's prior knowledge of relationships between parent and child to make a successful inference. The inference question regarding the informational passage about globalization, however, requires the reader to consider information about a generalized situation (cheap labor brings down prices on consumer goods) and to draw a conclusion about the way it affects the reader personally (how much he will pay for a shirt).

IRIs also allow teachers to assess students' listening comprehension in contrast to their reading comprehension. In the case of developing readers, listening to a text is usually easier than reading it—the activity of recognizing written words and constructing understanding from them is less practiced than listening to speech and constructing meaning from it. In reading assessment, testing listening capacity offers an indication of readers' potential for comprehending a text, and may serve as a goal against which their reading comprehension of a text can be measured (see Figure 11.3).

How to Administer and Score the Informal Reading Inventory

An Informal Reading Inventory offers the opportunity to observe in a single sitting a student's reading behaviors under many different conditions. While teachers value the opportunity to observe the student's reading, they are also careful to use consistent procedures when they conduct the assessment with several students, or with the same student at different times, so the scores can be compared.

ADMINISTERING THE INFORMAL READING INVENTORY. The IRI should be administered at the beginning of the school year, when the teacher is planning instruction, selecting textbooks and trade books for the class, and grouping children with similar needs. Because children are often grouped for instruction on the basis of the outcomes of the IRI, it is desirable to administer an IRI once or twice during the school year. Children have spurts of achievement gain, and groups that are formed at the beginning of the school year should not be so rigid that children never have the possibility of moving from one to another. It might not be necessary to administer an IRI systematically to every child at the same time later in the year, as is done at the beginning of the year, but children should be reassessed when the teacher observes a change in a student's achievement, whether positive or negative.

An IRI is an individual test, and although a substantial investment of classroom time must be dedicated to the process of assessing each child, it is time well spent. A skilled teacher can administer an IRI to an entire class within several hours, and the process goes faster with experience. Each child needs ten to fifteen minutes of uninterrupted time with the teacher. It is tempting to begin assessing on the first day of school, but classes are often reorganized because of rapid changes in enrollment during the first week. Therefore, it

Figure 11.3

Word Recognition in
Context and
Comprehension.

Narrative 2nd Grade Level (2.2): Anita and the Airplane

Introduction: Teacher says: *"Can you imagine what it would be like to fly in a small airplane? Read to find out what happened when Anita went flying in her Uncle Albert's small airplane."*

Anita and the Airplane

Anita's Uncle Albert was a pilot. He had an airplane. "Why don't you come flying with me, Anita?" he asked.

"OK," she said. Little did she know what she was getting in for!

They were sitting in the tight cockpit. Uncle Albert looked at some dials and pulled some knobs. He said something into the radio. A voice came back on the radio. "You're clear for take-off," it said. The engine roared, and the airplane sped down the runway. Suddenly, trees looked like bushes. People looked like ants.

When they were high in the air, Uncle Albert showed Anita how to steer the plane. He showed her how to make it go left and right. He showed her how to make it climb and dip. Then he let Anita hold the steering wheel. She was flying!

Uncle Albert nodded, then he nodded again. Then he snored. His chin fell on his chest. Her uncle went to sleep!

"Wake up!" said Anita. But Uncle Albert just snored, so Anita flew the plane.

Uncle Albert suddenly opened his eyes. "Where are we? Oh, my goodness. I went to sleep," he said. "I shouldn't have done that."

Anita was glad he was awake. Uncle Albert saw the runway and made the plane go down. "Hold on tight," he said. They landed. And do you know what? It was the wrong airport!

Record the time at the end: _____.

231 Words in Passage   Errors in Oral Reading Accuracy: _____

Scoring Guide for Oral Reading

(Circle the boxes that correspond to the Student's Score)

	Oral Reading Accuracy
Independent level:	9 or fewer errors
Instructional level:	10 to 23 errors
Frustration level:	24 or more errors

might be wise to delay this process until enrollments in the school settle down late in the first week. You will need to provide activities for the children who are waiting their turn for assessment and for those who are already finished. It is also important that children not be able to hear the assessment of their peers on this oral procedure. A paraprofessional or a parent volunteer can be invaluable in supporting the quiet environment needed during each child's IRI.

On the basis of widely accepted percentages of accuracy and comprehension, the teacher needs to decide what levels to administer, and the answer will be different for each child. Most teachers administer a grade level below their estimate for the child that is based on test scores and information on the cumulative record from the teacher of the previous year. For example, a third grader who was reading at grade level the year before would usually begin with an IRI passage on the second-grade level. The child should feel successful on the first passage. Children know when they have failed, and they are often reluctant to continue to another level, even if that level is lower—perhaps especially if that level is lower.

Explain to the child that he or she will be reading some passages out loud to you and will then respond to some questions about what has been read. The child then reads a passage aloud to you as you record the oral reading errors made by the child. Then take the passage back from the child and ask the questions that accompany it. On the basis of the child's performance, another passage will be administered, as described later.

INTERPRETING THE OUTCOMES.   As we saw earlier, the IRI yields three levels: frustration level, instructional level, and independent level. The most important are the instructional and frustration levels. The instructional level is the level at which the teacher should target instruction and for which instructional materials should be selected. As mentioned earlier, it corresponds to Vygotsky's zone of proximal development (Vygotsky, 1978). Some call it the Goldilocks level—not too difficult, not too easy, but just right.

In determining the instructional level of a child, the frustration level is determined at the same time. Children are asked to read and respond to questions from passages at various levels until they fail to meet criteria for **instructional level**, which are above 90 percent accuracy in oral reading and above 70 percent in comprehension. They should not have seen or read the passages before the assessment. The level at which the child fails to reach the criteria is the **frustration level**. The next level down—that is, the highest level where the criteria are met—is the instructional level. The percentages for accuracy are focused on a base score of 100 percent, each oral reading error resulting in the loss of two percentage points, for example, on a 200-word passage. The types of errors are as follows (Temple, Crawford, & Gillet, 2009):

Substitution: The student substitutes a different word for a word in the text.

Insertion: The reader inserts a word that is not in the text.

Omission: The student omits a word or phrase.

Words given by the examiner: After giving the reader time and encouragement to try the word, the examiner supplied the word. Pauses, however, are not scored as errors.

Self-corrections made by the reader without help from the examiner are not scored as errors, although they provide insights into students' thinking about reading. Neither are repetitions or ignoring punctuation counted as errors. When a student commits a series of errors that are related, only a single error is counted. The 70 percent criterion for comprehension is based on answering approximately six of eight comprehension questions.

This complex process is best understood with an example. The teacher assessed a fourth-grade student who, according to the previous teacher and cumulative records, was

Age of student _9_ Gender _M_ Grade level _4_ Home language _English_

Level administered	Accuracy	Comprehension
_2_	99%	100%
_3_	97%	75%
_4_	95%	75%
_5_	89%	25%
Frustration level***	5	
Instructional level*	4	
Independent level**	2	

*Highest grade level with 95% accuracy, 75% comprehension
**Highest grade level with 99% accuracy, 100% comprehension
***Next level more difficult than instructional level

Figure 11.4

Informal Reading Inventory (IRI) Results.

reading at grade level last year. The teacher therefore administered a third-grade passage to begin, using the form shown in Figure 11.4 to record results. The child was successful in reaching at least 90 percent accuracy and 75 percent comprehension, indicating that his instructional level was at least third grade. On the fourth-grade passage, he also met the criteria, but not at the fifth-grade level. The frustration level was at fifth grade, indicating that the instructional level was fourth grade.

The **independent reading level** is the level at which the child can read without support. It is generally one to three years lower than the instructional level. It is the highest level at which the child reads with 99 percent accuracy and 90 to 100 percent comprehension. In the example in Figure 11.3, the teacher had to drop to the second-grade level to determine the independent level. If the student had achieved less than 99 percent accuracy and 100 percent comprehension on the second-grade passage, the teacher would have dropped to a passage at the first-grade level.

Determining the independent level can dramatically increase the time it takes to administer and interpret an IRI, and the extra information might not be useful enough to warrant the additional time required. Essentially, it is important to know that children who select a library book to read independently will probably select an easier book than the one used in their reading group. This is the way it should be. The teacher is providing extra scaffolding and support to children during the lessons that is not available during independent reading. Children with strong interests in a theme or topic might select books for independent reading at higher levels, but the extra motivation of a child reading about the butterflies he or she collects will compensate for the added difficulty.

This is also good information to convey to parents: When they help their children select books at the library or the bookstore, they should not steer the children to books at the same level as the textbooks they are using in the classroom. Children's independent reading should be done at a level at which they are very comfortable, reading for enjoyment and not struggling with decoding tasks or difficult vocabulary and concepts. Your own recreational reading as an adult is probably similar: You are likely to read more John Grisham than Marcel Proust.

myeducationlab
The Power of Classroom Practice
www.myeducationlab.com

Learn how to gather information about individual students by completing the activity "Administering Informal Reading Inventories." (To find this activity, go to the topic *Assessment* in MyEducationLab and click on Building Teaching Skills and Dispositions.)

Other Measures of Comprehension

IRIs afford a great deal of insight into a reader's comprehension, but they do so at a high cost of time required. Also, they must be administered to one child at a time, and completing an IRI with a child in third or fourth grade can take an hour. They are most useful for diagnostic testing, to identify strengths and weaknesses of a child's reading ability in order to guide instruction. Even when a full IRI is not administered, questions of the type just described can be made up by the teacher and used with any text passage, of course. Many teachers include a variety of questions like these during informal observations. For the more frequent testing that is used to monitor children's progress in learning to read, teachers rely on other, quicker means of assessing comprehension. These include oral retellings and fluency measures.

After a child has read a passage, the teacher asks the child to give an *oral retelling*— that is, to retell the passage in his own words. The teacher then makes a mental calculation of how much of the information from the text the child retold. For a slightly more exact way of evaluating the retellings, teachers may use a retelling checklist, which is a list of pieces of information contained in the text, prepared in advance. The teacher checks off the pieces of information that the child retold, and then computes the score as a percentage of the whole list of items.

Another way of assessing reading comprehension is to use a structured observation procedure. The teacher sits alone with a child and has the child read a passage aloud. The teacher may ask the student questions before, during, and after the student reads. A checklist for guiding observations may then be used, such as Figure 7.10 in Chapter 7.

Fluency measures are sometimes used as a "proxy check" of comprehension. Fluency measures can be administered more quickly than actual comprehension measures because they involve no follow-up questions and answers. Also, because fluency measures have been shown to predict growth in reading ability, including reading comprehension (Pinnell, et al., 1995), they are often used as monitoring assessments throughout the year.

Reading: Measuring Attitudes and Interest

It has long been noted, and was recently very eloquently affirmed (Allington, 2005), that children learn to read by reading. As we noted in Chapter 6, children differ enormously in the amount of reading they do, and as Stanovich (1992) has pointed out, those who read more benefit enormously in increased vocabulary, increased world knowledge, better spelling, and even greater measured intelligence. Somewhere between reading ability and the amount of reading that actually gets done is the will to read, a positive attitude toward reading, and a deep interest in books and reading. Where that motivation and interest is lacking, we have a problem. Teachers would do well to assess students' attitudes toward reading.

Surveys can look into children's general attitude toward reading. *The Elementary Reading Attitude Survey* (McKenna & Kear, 1990) is one widely used instrument that reveals how students are feeling about reading and reading instruction in general. This instrument can tell if a school or a classroom is succeeding in promoting an interest in reading among groups of children, as well as an individual child's attitude. It has also been used in research to track large groups of students' attitudes toward reading.

Reading interest inventories are intended to find out individual students' interests and preferences, to help teachers and librarians match them up with books and learning experiences they will enjoy. A reading interest inventory from a librarian in Michigan is found in Figure 11.5.

Assessing Spelling Knowledge

Children's knowledge of spelling develops in two ways. One is the level of words they can spell. For instance, we would expect a second-grade child to be able to spell *train, queer,* and *float,* but not *conceive* or *profitable,* while a sixth grader should be able to spell the harder words. Another is that they work their way through stages of spelling or phases of knowledge, and each stage brings new thinking about how written words are structured.

USING WORDS FROM SPELLING TEXTBOOKS. Commercial spelling and language arts programs normally provide lists of words children are expected to learn every week. Those lists are arranged at difficulty levels according to their grades. Publishers use various means to level words, including surveys of children's writing and studies of the vocabularies of textbooks and trade books.

If you are using a spelling series, or if you are teaching grade-level-based spelling lists every week, it is important to find children's instructional level in spelling. The range of spelling abilities of a typical classroom of children is very wide. If students in a typical classroom were asked to spell words they had not yet been taught, their scores might range from less than 10 percent to more than 90 percent (Morris, Nelson, & Perney, 1986). But if the lowest scoring spellers were taught words at their instructional level of spelling instead of words at their grade-placement level, they might fill in the foundational spelling concepts that are taught at the lower grades and that they need for further learning—and in the long run actually make more progress learning to spell the harder words. This was exactly what Darrell Morris and his colleagues (Morris et al., 1995) found in an experimental study.

The instructional level of spelling is found by testing children on spelling words they have not been taught and finding the grade level of words where the children score from 50 percent to 75 percent (Henderson, 1990). To assess children's spelling ability for grade-level placement, construct a *spelling inventory*, consisting of twenty randomly chosen words from each grade level in grades 1 through 6 of the spelling program. (These lists are usually found as an appendix in the teacher's guide.) You can test a whole class by beginning

Figure 11.5

Reading Interest Inventory.

1. Do you like to read?

2. How much time do you spend reading?

3. What are some of the books you have read lately?

4. Do you have a library card? How often do you use it?

5. Do you ever get books from the school library?

6. About how many books do you own?

7. What are some books you would like to own?

8. Put a check mark next to the kind of reading you like best. (topics you might like to read about)

____history	____travel	____plays
____sports	____science fiction	____adventure
____romance	____detective stories	____war stories
____poetry	____car stories	____novels
____biography	____supernatural stories	____astrology
____humor	____folktales	____how-to-do-it books
____mysteries	____art	____westerns

9. Do you like to read the newspaper?

10. If 'yes', place a check next to the part of the newspaper listed below you like to read.

____Advertisements	____Entertainment	____Columnists
____Headlines	____Comic Strips	____Political Stories
____Current Events	____Sports	____Editorials
____Others: (please list)		

11. What are your favorite television programs?

12. How much time do you spend watching television?

13. What is your favorite magazine?

14. Do you have a hobby? If so, what is it?

15. What are the two best movies you have ever seen?

16. Who are your favorite entertainers and/or movie stars?

17. When you were little, did you enjoy having someone read aloud to you?

18. List topics, subjects, etc. which you might like to read about.

19. What does the word 'reading' mean to you?

20. Say anything else that you would like to say about reading.

Source: D. Hildebrant (2001), pp. 34–37.

Writing and Reading Connections

Why is children's spelling and word knowledge so important to their reading and writing development?

with the words one year below grade level and calling out the words as the children spell them. Then call out the correct spellings, or display them on an overhead transparency, and have the children mark their own errors. Call out words from higher-level lists and have the children continue to spell words until they misspell 50 percent of the words. Children who score 50 percent spelling errors can stop. After you look over their papers, you can go back and privately ask some children to spell words from easier lists if they did not reach the instructional level on the first list you called.

ASSESSING SPELLING QUALITATIVELY. Students work their way through stages of spelling development that reflect how they think about the structure of words. Those stages are described in Table 11.6. The student's spelling level suggests ways that she or he can be taught to spell.

Table 11.6　Stages of Invented Spelling

STAGE	ALSO KNOWN AS	EXAMPLES	TYPICAL AGE
Prephonetic	Preliterate	*bumpy* = R4TSX	Preschool and kindergarten
Early phonemic	Early phonetic	*bumpy* = BP	Kindergarten and early first grade
Letter-name	Phonetic	*bumpy* = BOPE	Early to mid-first grade
Common patterns	Transitional, within-word pattern	*bumpy* = BUPPY	Late first to mid-second grade
Syllable juncture		*batted* = BATID	Mid-second grade through third grade
Derivational constancy	Conventional	*photograph* = FOTOGRAF	Fourth grade and above

Source: Bear, Invernizzi, Templeton, and Johnston (2000), Gentry (1981); Henderson (1990); Schlagal (1989); Temple, Nathan, Burris, and Temple (1993).

To assess a child's level of developmental spelling, you can administer a list of words that are arranged to elicit invented spellings at different levels. A typical list of such words is found in Figure 11.6. See also Richard Gentry's *Monster Test* on pages 137–141 of this book.

Developmental spelling inventories with full explanations are available in *Words Their Way* (Bear et al., 2007) and *Word Journeys* (Ganske, 2003). As all of these publications make clear, improving children's spelling knowledge improves their word knowledge, especially if they are taught to use what they learn in the context of writing and reading.

Differentiated Instruction

Differentiated instruction begins with good assessment. *Screening assessment* indicates which students are where they are expected to be, which are above grade level, and which need additional support. *Diagnostic assessment* indicates how strong each student is in different aspects of reading and writing development. Based on diagnostic assessment, students will have different kinds of instruction designed for them. They will be assigned different levels of books for guided reading. They will be given different groups of words for word study and possibly will be placed in different points in the sequence of phonics instruction. The teacher will construct focused lessons on aspects of comprehension—on setting purposes for reading, summarizing, visualizing, making inferences, understanding vocabulary from context, learning new information, and interpreting the text. The students will be placed in groups that read different levels of text for fluency practice. They will be placed at their instructional level of spelling words to learn, even if that falls a year above or below their grade-placement level. The assessment picture will be rounded out by other information gained from interviews with the students

Analytic Phonics Lesson

Fluency Oriented Oral Reading

1. lit	6. peeked	11. spacious	16. physician
2. chap	7. sailed	12. design	17. biographical
3. rock	8. shove	13. brilliance	18. sympathetic
4. truck	9. sitter	14. traction	19. adjournment
5. lend	10. batted	15. doubting	20. collegial

Source: Temple, Crawford, and Gillet, *Developmental Literacy Inventory: Reading and Spelling from Emergent to Mature Levels.* © 2009. Reprinted by Permission of Pearson Education, Inc.

Figure 11.6
Words to Elicit Different Levels of Invented Spelling.

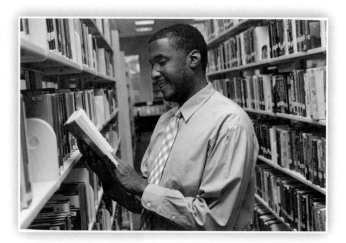

Both beginning and experienced teachers have the professional obligation of keeping abreast of developments in fields that impact their classrooms. (Corbis RF)

to determine the topics they are interested in, the kind of reading they most prefer, and the conditions they need to help them learn.

Once courses of instruction have been established for all students, they are given periodic *monitoring assessments*. Unlike the daily observations, these are more formalized and done on a schedule. The results may be shared with other teachers or with the reading specialist, and provide guidance for determining whether the present plan of instruction should be followed or if different strategies should be tried to improve a student's learning. In addition, the teacher should practice kidwatching by making a habit of selecting a small number of children every day and observing how they are working, what exactly they are doing when they read and write, what they appear to be interested in, what kinds of tasks they are succeeding in, when they work best, and when they get off task, and in sum, how the teacher can help each one be successful in this class.

Late in the year, children take outcomes-based assessments, which are based on the state learning standards for each grade level. This is a serious accountability event. While the daily informal assessments and the periodic monitoring assessments focus on children's development as readers, writers, and learners in general, these assessments also have one eye on the outcomes of instruction.

Teacher Self-Assessment

As new entrants to a profession, beginning teachers must have the professional knowledge they will need to be successful in the classroom. Experienced teachers, too, have the obligation as professionals to keep abreast of developments in the field of literacy and other domains of knowledge that impact their classroom and to continually perform **teacher self-assessment** activities.

Some years ago, Donald Schön (1983) developed the influential model of the *reflective practitioner*, a professional who is able to learn from experience and create his or her own practical knowledge and skill. This model is still useful today. Professors in your teacher education classes undoubtedly encourage you to observe as closely as you can individual children and whole classrooms, to sense patterns and find possibilities for action.

Becoming a reflective practitioner is not a solitary activity, however. As Taylor and Pearson (2005) noted, in "schools that beat the odds," where students outperform what is predicted for them, teachers come together to share information about their students, about teaching, and about what works in their schools.

Following is an example of a second-grade teacher's observation/assessment discussion with her team teachers:

> I worked with Michele today. She is putting extra vowels in some words and leaving needed vowels out in others. Today, she spelled chin as CHIAN and cream as CREM; this is a pattern for her. I looked it up in a textbook, and this means that she is using but confusing vowel- and consonant-patterned words. Easy to see, but now what? She is on the verge of getting it but needs help. Here is what I am thinking. First of all, I don't think she can read the words she is trying to spell—chin and cream are not known words for her. I need to step back to a point at which she can succeed. What do you think? Give me some feedback.

This teacher received suggestions from the team on increasing assessments of Michele's understanding of the words she attempts to spell. They also suggested she give

Michele more opportunities to write. Someone suggested word sorting by patterns—*chin, pin, tin, in*. They made a date for her to try some of these suggestions and report back to the group.

Teachers benefit from comparing and contrasting their ideas with those of others and from using multiple assessment measures. If the opportunity for collaboration does not exist in your building, you should create it with at least one other teacher. With teachers in your building, create regular meetings to talk shop before or after school, at planning times, or during working lunches.

Because of their many variables, teaching and learning are always in flux. Assessment helps to make order and sense of teaching and learning. For direction and planning, you will learn on a daily basis what children know and can do. Professional organizations as well as state governments have something to say about the assessment of teachers, too. The International Reading Association (IRA) and the National Council for the Accreditation of Teacher Education (NCATE) jointly publish a set of *Standards for Reading Professionals* (2006) that outlines what a committee of reading educators believes teachers of reading should know. The standards are available online at http://www.reading.org/resources/community/ncate_standards.html. The IRA/NCATE standards have been incorporated by many schools of education to guide their curricula, and they were also consulted in preparing this textbook. James Zarrillo has written a self-administered guide based on the standards entitled *Are You Prepared to Teach Reading?* (2010). It includes a sample written test at the end of the book.

Word Sorting

For Review

Assessment is used in this chapter as a term to cover deciding what we need to know about children's learning, considering what means we will need to use to get the information and possibly designing our own, collecting the information, and interpreting the information to help us make instructional decisions to help the students.

With the federal No Child Left Behind Act there has been an intensified interest in assessment. Reading First requires that teachers assess children at four moments: for *screening*, for *diagnosis*, for *progress monitoring*, and to assess *outcomes*.

Several different kinds of assessment instruments are available to teachers. Standardized or norm-based tests compare children to other children; and standards-based tests look at their accomplishment of curricular standards. Curriculum-based measurement takes brief snapshots of learning, usually for monitoring purposes, and these are closely tied to the outcomes that are desired at the end of the year. Informal assessments such as the Informal Read-

ing Inventory, the Reading Miscue Inventory, and running records reveal a rich array of information about children's reading. However, teachers need to pay attention to the validity (the extent to which the test measures what it claims to) and reliability (the extent to which the findings of the tests are stable) of tests they use.

Assessments are done of various aspects of emergent literacy, including print concepts, language awareness, and letter knowledge. Once children can begin to read, we can assess reading levels (independent, instructional, and frustration) as well as their word recognition, fluency, vocabulary, and comprehension. The readability of the texts they read can be assessed by means of a readability formula or the cloze procedure. Their spelling and writing should be assessed, too. Finally, teachers and teachers-to-be should practice self-assessment, both to make sure they are acquiring professional knowledge and skills, and to keep advancing along with the growth of knowledge in the field of literacy.

For Your Journal

1. Now that you have read the chapter, return to the anticipation guide at the beginning. What differences are there in how you would answer those questions now?

2. Choose a grade that you would like to teach, or that you do teach. First describe what aspects of reading and writing you would want to test for in your screening and diagnostic assessments. Second, explain what instruments you would use and why.

3. Go online and find your state's standards for literacy at your chosen grade level. Read the information about the outcomes-based assessments given. Then, for each set of abilities and concepts that they list, describe the way you would monitor students' progress toward achieving those outcomes.

Taking It to the World

Now that you have read about the emphasis on accountability and the regimen of assessments that have been ushered in by the No Child Left Behind Act, go online with a search engine and look up "standards-based assessment" and "high-stakes testing." Be ready to see sparks fly! Who are the different groups posting things on the topic? What are they saying? Why are they saying it? Be sure to check at least one opinion poll, too, such as Public Agenda.

New Literacies Connections

Go online and look up the services that are offered by DIBELS (http://dibels.uoregon.edu/) and Developmental Reading Assessment (http://www.pearsonlearning.com/dra/). What exactly do they do for teachers and for schools? How do those services meet the mandates of the No Child Left Behind Act? Which services are required to meet the requirements of Reading First? How much do the services cost?

PEARSON myeducationlab

Now go to MyEducationLab (www.myeducationlab.com), where you can:

- Find learning outcomes for the topics covered in this chapter, along with the national standards that connect to these outcomes.

- Complete Assignments and Activities that can help you more deeply understand the chapter content.

- Engage in Building Teaching Skills and Dispositions exercises, in which you can apply and practice core teaching skills identified in the chapter.

12

Putting Effective Literacy Instruction into Practice: Grades K to 2

Anticipation Guide

The following statements will help you begin thinking about the topics covered in this chapter. Answer *true* or *false* in response to each statement. As you read and learn more about the topics mentioned in the statements, think back on your answers. See what interests you and prompts your curiosity toward more understanding.

_____ 1. Establishing a friendly and supportive psychological/social climate in the classroom should be a teacher's first concern in teaching early literacy.

_____ 2. It is more important for children to learn to follow the teacher's rules than to manage their own behavior.

_____ 3. In classroom management, it is useful to make a distinction between teaching children procedures and enforcing discipline.

_____ 4. When children practice learning procedures, they eventually become routines.

_____ 5. Reading to children is valuable in kindergarten when most children cannot read for themselves, but it has little value after that.

_____ 6. The "five-finger test" is a way of telling if a book is too difficult for primary grade children to read: If children miss five words on a page, the book is probably too hard.

_____ 7. Children can learn about phonics from writing and using invented or temporary spelling.

_____ 8. Children who are English language learners will not profit from formal instruction in English reading until they reach an intermediate level of proficiency in English.

_____ 9. Elkonin boxes are useful devices for teaching children phonemic segmentation.

_____ 10. Learning centers should be carefully designed to teach only reading or writing skills. It is not advisable to mix content from other subjects such as social studies or science into them.

Putting Effective Literacy Instruction into Practice: Grades K to 2

Creating the Learning Place p. 366

Developing Knowledge and Skills p. 374

Organizing for Instruction p. 379

Reaching All Children p. 391

Assessment p. 397

Literacy Activities in a First-Grade Classroom

It's October. Nineteen children are looking at books while Ana Lopes sets the big book, *Bread, Bread, Bread* (Morris, 1989) on the easel. Her students come from many international backgrounds, and they all appear to enjoy this informational book with photos of people making and eating bread—including Mexican tortillas, Indian nan, French baguettes, and others.

Ms. Lopes speaks to a small group of children who are not scheduled to participate in this lesson. She offers them a choice of two literacy activities: They can work on a poster in progress for a science project or in the classroom interest center. Once they are settled, Ms. Lopes motions to the other children to join her on the reading rug. She asks them to look at the pictures first, and then whisper their ideas about the book to one another. Now actively involved, children in the larger group whisper and then talk with Ms. Lopes about many kinds of bread. As she reads the book, she uses a long pointer to indicate each complete word (emphasizing that the groups of letters separated by a space are words) while she encourages the children to read with her.

Ms. Lopes stops reading to spark discus-

sions—sometimes about the story and other times about the writing. She says, " I really like the way this author talks about making bread. Do any of you know something about making bread?"

One child says, "I like the way it smells!"

"Oh yes, does anyone else have something to say?" says Ms. Lopes. Several children raise their hands and engage in a short conversation with her. Next, the children who didn't get a turn at speaking are invited to whisper what they know about bread-making comments in one another's ears. Everyone gets a turn!

By drawing the children into talking about the meaning of the text and the nature of the written presentation, Ms. Lopes is teaching good reader behaviors and encouraging the children to think and relate personally to books. She also shows the children that she is interested in what they know or are thinking.

After the reading, children are encouraged to identify words they know. Ms. Lopes points out that some words begin with two letters, such as /br/ in bread: Those words begin with consonant blends. As the lesson continues, Ms. Lopes points out that some

words with consonant blends are repeated in the text, such as "bread, bread, bread." She asks the students to find other words that are repeated. A child responds, "I see the word *eat*. And we saw it before, too."

"Excellent word watching!" Ms. Lopes responds. "Now let's see if we can spot the word *eat* repeated yet again."

This teacher draws the children into more focused reading by asking them to think about the book's words as she points to words on the word wall (see page 381) that share features with the words in the book: They end with the same phonogram pattern, or they begin with consonant blends.

As Ms. Lopes brings the lesson to a conclusion, the children move into a session of play as they pretend to make and eat bread. While they are engaged in this play, Ms. Lopes returns to her desk to make quick notes on her observations of children who actively participated and those who needed nudging into the lesson. She also makes notes on the sense children seemed to make about letter-to-sound relationships. Then she motions for all the children to return to their seats.

Creating the Learning Place

School beginnings are important. Teachers focus first of all on setting up a learning place: a classroom environment and instructional procedures that support learning. In the complex act of teaching, we strive for children to become *readers* who not only "know the words" but also engage their whole minds. The goals of early-grade literacy instruction are to nurture children intellectually, emotionally, and socially as we immerse them in spoken and written language, instill concepts about print, and develop their joy in reading and writing (IRA & NAEYC, 1998). Effective teachers create a *learning place* as they carefully craft their lessons so that children experience success and come to believe in themselves as competent learners on the path to literacy. Because nothing succeeds like success, your students' success ensures your success.

A learning place is created in a classroom that is steeped in mutual respect and responsibility. Young children come to school believing that they will learn to read and write. The effective and caring teacher in the early grades can go a long way toward fulfilling that expectation. Teaching requires sustained energy and dedication, which becomes self-sustaining in the teacher when it is supported by certain attributes:

- Strong principles
- A strong sense of responsibility for student learning and motivation
- A desire to search for personal strengths
- An enjoyment of interactions with students and an abiding compassion for them (Ayers, 1993).

Classroom Management

As they set about creating a productive classroom, many teachers, especially beginning teachers, think first about classroom management. Even the most creative teaching can achieve little unless it takes place in a well-ordered environment in which children can focus on learning and discovering.

In order to achieve a well-ordered classroom, it is useful to distinguish between establishing *routines* and maintaining *discipline* (Wong & Wong, 2009). Having **routines** ensures that children know what to do at all times during the school day so that many young people occupying the same space at the same time can work productively and enjoyably. Routines apply to such things as coming into the classroom in the morning and getting to work, working in learning centers, feeding the fish, watering the plants, walking to and from the classroom library, hosting visitors to the classroom, rotating assignments and carrying out classroom tasks, reading with a partner, settling disagreements, borrowing books and returning them, distributing hand-outs, reading with a partner, participating in a guided reading group, cleaning up after art work, and getting ready to leave at the end of the school day. Having well-understood routines helps ensure that children are able to control themselves peacefully. Behavioral routines also deal with the limits of what is acceptable and what happens when behavior is unacceptable.

ESTABLISHING ROUTINES.   It takes the first few weeks of school to establish procedures that will become routines. There are many procedures that students must learn to carry out; teachers must prioritize and select just a few to teach at first, and add more as the year goes on. Some of the procedures have to do with general classroom order, such as:

- Entering the classroom in the morning
- Going over the day's schedule
- Performing tasks assigned for the day and learning week-long tasks
- Taking turns speaking
- Moving about the classroom or asking to be excused
- Getting ready to leave for recess
- Moving as a group through the hallway
- Cleaning up after artwork and other tasks that involve materials
- Getting ready to go home

Other procedures are more specific to language and literacy instruction:

- Coming to the reading circle and participating in an interactive read-aloud
- Listening to the morning message

Morning Message

Figure 12.1
Procedure Poster.

> **When Mr. Acevedo Reads a Book Aloud**
>
> 1. Listen and watch
>
> 2. Keep your hands to yourself
>
> 3. Make pictures in your mind
>
> 4. Wonder what will happen next
>
> 5. Be ready to say what the book makes you think of

- Participating in a guided reading lesson
- Using the quiet reading area
- Choosing, using, and returning books from the classroom library
- Reading with a partner
- Learning what to do during independent reading time
- Learning what to do during independent writing time
- Sharing writing
- Working in a learning center
- Learning what to do when you come across an unknown word in reading
- Learning what to do when you need to spell an unknown word in writing
- Participating in group work
- Sharing and critiquing written work

Teach It! 52

Shared Writing

To teach a procedure, you should carefully explain and demonstrate it to the class. You may end the lesson by showing the students a poster with the procedure explained in bulleted steps (for younger children who cannot yet read many words, the steps may be identified by graphic symbols). The posters will be hung around the room. See Figure 12.1 for an example of a classroom procedure.

After you teach the procedure, be sure to practice it. Just as schools have many fire drills early in the year and a few periodically thereafter, many wise teachers provide guided practice in carrying out a procedure until every student knows how it is done. Remind the students from time to time how to do the procedure, especially if problems arise with children not performing it properly. But even if it goes well, make sure the procedure is well engrained in the students' behavior. Once the procedure is so well learned that it is second nature, it becomes a routine.

Teaching procedures is a good way to gradually place responsibility on the students to control their own behavior. As they learn, let them know that you have confidence in their ability to manage themselves. Guide children toward self-management. Take whatever time is needed.

ESTABLISHING AND MAINTAINING PRODUCTIVE BEHAVIOR. Before children arrive in your classroom, you should have in mind ways in which you will help them learn to manage their own behaviors. For example, generate a few simple classroom rules or guidelines for the first days of school and show great appreciation for the children's efforts to comply with them. Be generous with time and respect. Some kindergarteners may have been to preschool, and others have not; some have traveled and known various people and places, and others have had none of these experiences. Some have siblings in other grades, others have not.

A useful strategy in the first weeks of school is to use a form such as the Teacher Observation Form (Tattershaw & Penderville, 1995) for recording observations to identify where some trouble spots may arise (see Figure 12.2). Often children do not know what to do in school; in fact, learning to "do school" at first or in a new classroom is quite a challenge for many of them. Some children may need frequent redirecting to learn what is expected of them. After carrying out several structured observations, you can tell at a glance who needs more of your guidance.

BEHAVIOR CONTRACTS. If you repeatedly show the child, physically and verbally, what to do, but are still unsuccessful, you may try writing a contract. A simple written document nicely integrates literacy into a way for children to learn more about controlling their own behavior. One copy for the child and one for the teacher helps both to adhere to the contract. Here are some simple ideas you may want incorporated on a contract:

- List the child's name and yours, using one piece of paper or several pieces stapled together.
- Insert a line about the daily meeting that will be dated by both you and the child. Pick a moment right before school starts or ends and show the child your observation form, or simply discuss your notes on the target behavior(s); limit the focus to one or two behaviors.
- Insert a line for the child to check off or write in the good behaviors achieved that day. Make this part of your talk very upbeat and enjoyable, celebrating the smallest positive move. Also insert a space where you can list what the child and you want her to work on the next day and write that in. Then, read over the contract together.

Contract writing is particularly helpful with students who have difficulty adjusting or who have learning challenges. Keep your teacher observation forms and contracts as needed in children's files.

From the first day of school, talk with the children about what will happen during the day. It's a mystery to them! Post a daily schedule on a large chart; knowing what will happen next will create comfort in the classroom. Note that in doing this you are also inviting the children into literacy. Strive for all classroom routines to have some written language aspects. Repeating the day's routine again and again, providing special attention as needed, and drawing the children into play and song activities all help calm anxiety, particularly for the youngest children. By second grade or even perhaps in first grade, you might want to include students in your planning; this encourages them to take on more responsibility.

"I HAVE A PROBLEM." Regardless of your careful work, children will have problems that can interrupt the classroom. A literacy strategy that helps teachers and children deal with conflict and think critically through reasoning and evidence is an "I have a problem" writing place. Post a sign, and provide writing materials and a "problem basket." Assure children that the two of you will read their writing and solve the problem together. Figure 12.3 is an example of the kind of message that you might get.

Learning Centers

Learning centers are spaces set aside in the classroom where individuals, pairs, and small groups of students go to engage in activities that extend their learning. A learning center can be arranged on tables with space for children to work on both sides. It can also be an easel with a big book on it and space in front for students to work or a pocket chart hung in a place away from classroom traffic. Many teachers create learning centers in tubs of various sizes. It can be a space in the window where plants grow, with a desk for children

Writing and Reading Connections

How can the teacher motivate young children to begin to manage their own behavior?

Figure 12.2 Teacher Observation Form.

Teacher Observations

Student's name: _____ Date: _____

Teacher's name: _____

Please use the following statements to guide your observations of the child on a typical school day. Write your comments after each statement.

1. The child seems to know the order of events in a typical class day.

   Yes No Comments: _____
   ☐   ☐   _____

2. The child looks in your direction when you are standing in your usual teaching spot.

   Yes No Comments: _____
   ☐   ☐   _____

3. The child responds appropriately and in a timely manner to your signals for attention.

   Yes No Comments: _____
   ☐   ☐   _____

4. The child can usually restate directions that you have given in his or her own words when asked to do so.

   Yes No Comments: _____
   ☐   ☐   _____

5. The child restates only the first part of directions.

   Yes No Comments: _____
   ☐   ☐   _____

6. The child restates only the last part of directions.

   Yes No Comments: _____
   ☐   ☐   _____

7. The child responds appropriately to your signals for transitions. (For example, the child puts away materials used for prior tasks, gets out materials for the new activity, or looks at you with apparent readiness for the new information or activity.)

   Yes No Comments: _____
   ☐   ☐   _____

8. The child seems to have difficulty leaving a project or task when you signal a transition.

   Yes No Comments: _____
   ☐   ☐   _____

9. The child seems to look at and follow peers' actions rather than respond independently to your signal for transitions.

   Yes No Comments: _____
   ☐   ☐   _____

10. The child's comments are appropriate for the topic under discussion.

    Yes No Comments: _____
    ☐   ☐   _____

11. The child seems able to understand and follow the rules and procedures of a game or classroom activity.

    Yes No Comments: _____
    ☐   ☐   _____

12. The child follows the class rules for behavior without reminders.

    Yes No Comments: _____
    ☐   ☐   _____

Source: From *Using Familiar Routines in Language Assessment and Intervention* by S. Tattershaw and J. Prendeville. Copyright © 1995. Permission granted by Sandra Tattershaw.

Figure 12.3
"I Have a Problem"
Note.

> simon   5/12/02
> I have a problem.
>
> Today Bob pushed me into
> the lunch line and sed bad
> words. I told him to stop he din't
> stop

to read and write about seed pods and take measurements, and then read their writing back to themselves and others. It can be a puppet theater, or a dramatic play area decorated according to the theme of a book the class is reading.

Most center materials can be purchased, but many teachers enjoy the creative act of making their own—going to garage sales to search for books on weekends and collecting articles from retiring teachers or friends. Building a collection of books for your centers will be easier if you share books with other teachers. This may come about as you engage in mapping curriculum (Jacobs, 1997, 2006).

There are several criteria to keep in mind as you prepare learning centers:

1. They should address learning objectives from at least one content area, and perhaps more than one.

2. Learning center activities should be planned so that they can synchronize with other activities being conducted at the same time—not too short, but not too long.

3. The procedures should be straightforward and require neither elaborate explanation nor direct supervision.

4. There should be some end product or other indication that the student has completed the center. Most of these should be suitable for evaluating, albeit informally.

5. Learning centers should be long on use and short on preparation! Learning centers should be engaging enough and variable enough for children to rotate through the same one several times over several weeks. Alternatively, durable frameworks (the same design, the same instructions, the same space) can be set up for learning centers in which different content can be substituted each week.

To create a literacy-rich classroom, it's important to include an array of books that appeal to all children's needs and interests. (Lindfors Photography)

Scheduling and monitoring students' progress through learning centers requires that a system be devised and carefully followed.

- A wall chart can specify which students will be assigned to which center weekly.

- Each child can have a pocket folder with a "center schedule" anchored in the middle with brads. For younger children, an icon representing each center can be printed on the schedule, with instructions for the child to color the icon as soon as she has completed the center. Worksheets or other written products can be kept in the folder all week, and handed in at the end of the week to be graded (http://www. mrsmcdowell.com/centers.htm).

- Each child can have a "center lariat" to hang around his or her neck, with icons printed on it that correspond to the centers. The students check off or color each icon once the center has been completed.

Time for students to work in learning centers is scheduled in rotation with small group instruction with the teacher, independent reading time, and perhaps independent writing time. Begin small group reading and writing instruction and start using learning centers as soon as you have the whole class well organized and the day running smoothly.

Learning centers should begin in kindergarten, even before children are reading and writing well. These centers usually focus on such topics as alphabet learning (opportunities for children to copy and write letters, write, experiment with writing names, create labels for areas of the classroom, and so on), blocks (a great old stand-by that interests boys and girls in building and learning spatial concepts), math (primarily counting and sorting), dress up (dramatic play), art (clay/play dough), and home living. Special centers such as a store or post office are also popular kindergarten learning centers. In today's world, learning centers should be aligned with your state standards; they help provide an effective way to meet benchmarks. As you implement learning centers to help meet standards/benchmarks, remember that kindergarten children are still very young, and they need the old, stand-by centers too. These centers are very valuable in the healthy development of young children, as research in early childhood has established (Christie, 1991; Morrow, 2003; Christie & Roskos, 2001). These centers provide important "no stress periods" from the children's regular work in literacy and in integrated curriculum. Much learning will occur in these centers. Make no mistake: Young children learn a great deal in productive play. Activity and interest centers should be part of the schedule each day or week, depending on the maturity and needs of the children you teach.

Integrated Curriculum

In other chapters we have stressed the importance of multiple and repeated opportunities for children to read and write in all their lessons, whether they are learning science, social studies, or math. Everything children are learning in the literacy-rich twenty-first century classroom—from recognizing the English alphabet to the new literacies they now must learn—documents that the "benchmarks" for adequate literacy learning happen right before our eyes. It is incredibly critical for all students to have as much reading and writing practice as possible in school, in the home, and in the community! See Chapters 2 and 4 for more on these topics. From kindergarten through middle and high school, students should be reading and writing in every class or lesson they experience.

Just think about what your primary classroom centers, over and above your integrated curriculum in formal lessons, will offer when each and every center integrates all language arts modalities, including:

- Oral language (remember, a silent primary classroom is a boring, frustrating, and stifling place)
- Writing and drawing, using stamps, markers, crayons, stickers, and other kinds of tools to create images and make meaning
- Writing and reading as tools for "behavior contracts," to label and mark all sorts of classroom places and objects
- Reading for pleasure, for research (by second grade!), for self-selected projects, and more

See the feature "Integrating Across the Curriculum: Teaching Reading and Writing through Science in a Learning Center" for an example.

Working with Names to Teach the Alphabet

Reflect on a primary grade teacher's use of learning centers by completing the activity "Managing Learning Centers." Answer the questions that follow. (To find this activity, go to the topic *Organization and Management* in MyEducationLab and click on Assignments and Activities.)

"Word Conversations" for Primary Grades

The theme of this science learning center is What Do Plants Need to Grow. We need the following materials for the center: a table large enough for children to work; radish seeds; soil; paper cups; rulers; markers; paper for children to record their findings, including a large piece of graph paper on the wall with 1" squares (each pair or small group of students working together needs its own column on the graph paper). We need a chart or chalkboard space on the wall above the center upon which we write:

Science Center: What Do Plants Need to Grow?

In addition, we will provide the following books from the school and classroom libraries:

The Magic School Bus Plants Seeds: A Book about How Living Things Grow by J. Cole; *How Plants Grow* by R. A. Martin; *Eddie's Kitchen and How to Make Good Things to Eat* by S. Garland, and other books and articles that the teacher adds. Because of the range of reading levels in a second grade classroom, all of these materials are pictured or written at levels appropriate for children from grades K–3.

We will also provide task cards with instructions that range from those that are illustrated for struggling readers to cards written at levels appropriate for most second graders. Many learning center activities are cooperative in nature, so children will be working together to solve problems that arise, such as a child who is unable to read a difficult word. The teacher needs to introduce the new science center activity to the class before they begin to use it independently. Completing some of the task cards will require adult supervision—a paraprofessional or a parent volunteer can help the children with some of the more complex tasks the first day or two they work, for example, the graphing task card. After that, the children should be able to continue gathering and recording information on their own.

Below are examples of instructions from some of the task cards:

- Make a list of things plants need to grow. Read one of the books in the center with a buddy. Look for things in the book that plants need to grow. Write those down, too. Are the two lists the same? Are they different? Now circle each thing that your radish seeds need in order to grow. Draw a picture of each thing circled on your list.

- After you plant your radish seed in the cup, be sure it has everything it needs to grow. Draw a picture of the seed. Draw a new picture of your plant every two or three days as it grows. Be sure to write the date under each picture.

- With a friend, plant a new radish seed, but leave out one thing from your list of things that plants need to grow. Make a prediction about what will happen. Draw a picture of what happens each day. Be sure to write the date under each picture. See if your prediction comes true. Why?

- When your first radish plant is one inch high, start measuring it every day with a ruler. Fill in one square on your graph each day your plant reaches another inch. Write the date inside the square. Ask for help the first time you do this.

As we have seen above, a learning center provides an excellent opportunity to teach across the curriculum in a primary classroom. This second grade learning center incorporates content and activities in science, reading, writing, and mathematics. It addresses the following benchmarks (standards) from the Florida Department of Education (2007):

Reading and language arts:

LA.2.1.6.5: The student will relate new vocabulary to familiar words.

LA.2.1.7.4: The student will identify cause-and-effect relationships in text.

Science:

SC.K.N.1.2: Make observations of the natural world and know that they are descriptors collected using the five senses.

SC.K.N.1.3: Keep records as appropriate—such as pictorial records—of investigations conducted.

Mathematics:

MA.2.G.3.1: Estimate and use standard units, including inches and centimeters, to partition and measure lengths of objects.

MA.2.A.2.4: Solve addition and subtraction problems that involve measurement and geometry.

Developing Knowledge and Skills

★ ★ **A**s a primary teacher, you might ask, "What are the most important learning opportunities teachers should provide for children in the earliest years of reading instruction?" First, children must learn to love school and certain books or online readings, and they must learn basic skills of literacy. Second, the teacher must know the reading process and understand well the developmental changes that new readers experience. You have read a good deal about literacy development in previous chapters. If you become a K–2 teacher, the previous chapters and this one will serve you well. Use this book for teaching support, for classroom design, and for your own family's enrichment!

Instruction in grades K–2 focuses not only on the five elements of reading that the U.S. Department of Education emphasizes—awareness of sounds in words, awareness of letter-to-sound relationships, fluency, vocabulary, and comprehension—but also on developing children's oral language (Ogle & Beers 2009) and helping them think of themselves as readers. Written language is grounded in oral language, and its development is supported by teachers' reading aloud, social interactions, and children's talk (lots of talk about work and classroom life!). A silent classroom is a barrier to learning. As children move through the stages of reading development, the goal is that they all arrive at fluent oral reading and silent reading by the beginning of third grade. Some will gain these abilities by the end of first grade and many by the end of second grade. Children become better readers as a result of:

- High-quality guided reading instruction
- Reading some more challenging books as time goes on and reading many, many easy books at their developmental level
- Becoming more aware of reading strategies and then using them
- Taking more independent action based on their learning

See The World of Reading box for an example of teachers' quality questioning and see Figure 12.4 for an example of children's self-directed practice in word strategies.

Helping children learn good strategies builds metacognition and extends skills to all areas of their education and even their personal lives. These skills open up the world to children. Kathleen and Katie explain just what those strategies are in Figures 12.5A and 12.5B.

Figure 12.4
Word Strategies.

Name Will   Date May 14, 2001
What you read today The town mouse and county mouse

Word Strategies

1. List the strategies you used to figure out words when you were reading today.
   CHunK, skip, sound,

2. Write down a sentence that had a word you had trouble with and underline the word.
   She had never seen such delicacies

3. Tell what you did to figure out what this word meant.
   I chunked The wiled out

The World of Reading

Quality Questioning

Good questioning on the part of a teacher promotes critical thinking in children and provides high-quality oral language teaching and practice. Open-ended questions require children to infer, reason, use language to express thought, and think deeply. Open-ended questions call forth more thinking and expressive oral language. Open-ended questions might include: Why do you think that? Why did the author of our story write about _____? What do you think will happen? What would you do? Can you tell me more about that? What is your prediction? Show how you can confirm that. Show us why you make that prediction. How do you think this problem can be resolved? Consider the following examples of open-ended questions and the child's answers:

Teacher	Child
What did the princess do to help?	She went off on her own to take care of the dragon.
Why did she do that?	She just did. Cause the prince wouldn't.
How could she do that?	She was brave, and she wasn't afraid.
How did the princess and prince dress?	Well, the prince was in nice prince clothes, but all the princess had was a dirty paper bag.
Why?	Because of the dragon. He burned up everything even her clothes.

What did the prince do?	He just stayed in the cave and said her clothes were a mess. And her hair too. That wasn't very nice.

Notice the vocabulary and textlike phrasing use: *brave, nice, prince, clothes*. Notice the length of the sentences and the clarity of thought, and consider the critical analysis that occurs in the child's last sentence. "That wasn't very nice." This child's responses demonstrate the use of inference.

Now consider this same discussion but with the teacher employing constrained, or closed, questions:

Teacher	Child
What happened to the princess?	She ran away.
The prince was no _____?	Help
Who was the prince afraid of?	The dragon.
What did the princess do to the dragon?	Made him tired.

Children can respond "correctly" to constrained/closed questions, yet totally miss the real meaning in the book. With practice, teachers learn open questioning. Some examples of open questions should be kept by your side as you teach. It is important to preread and know the children's literature you will use.

Figure 12.5A

I Am a Good Reader—Kathleen.

Figure 12.5B

I Am a Good Reader—Katie.

Teach It! 1

Reading Aloud

Teacher read-alouds in grades K–2 may well be the most common teaching practice in the United States and perhaps throughout the world. At least we hope so! This essential practice at school and at home should continue throughout children's education from preschool through the elementary grades and into middle and high school (Trelease, 2006). In elementary school, being read to stimulates children's literacy growth (Adams, 1990). Reading aloud to children supports those who have factors associated with risk, such as living in poverty, having less involved parents, being English language learners, and having limited language development (Temple & Makinster, 2005). Good primary grade teachers read to children three to five times daily in literacy lessons and for sheer pleasure and instructional conversations. Through an analysis of the oral and written language of well-read-to young children, Victoria Purcell-Gates (1991) found that those children understood the vocabulary and structures of written language even before they learned to read. Thus, children who have had extensive read-aloud experiences before starting school have an important advantage. In another study with low-income children who had not been well read to before starting school, and who then received extensive teacher read-alouds in kindergarten and first grade, Purcell-Gates, McIntyre, and Freppon (1995) found that by the end of first grade, these children's knowledge of written language was comparable to that of upper- and high-middle income, well-read-to children. It is reasonable to infer that teachers' read-alouds compensated for the children's limited reading experiences prior to school.

Competent middle school teachers value and practice reading aloud (Alley, 2008; McEwan-Adkins, 2001), and many effective high school teachers are finding reading aloud a successful instructional strategy. McEwan-Adkins (2006) reports raising middle and high school reading achievement by reading aloud.

Interactive reading aloud demonstrates to children that reading is thinking, and that thinking should be critical. It prompts children to use oral language; it also engages them in comprehending more deeply, and in hearing and using sophisticated vocabulary. All this and more happens when teachers regularly read aloud and ask open-ended and high-quality questions. Naturally, reading aloud comes alive with meaning for students and teachers when it's interactive. These examples show the "value added" teaching that is done explicitly and implicitly in reading aloud. Reading aloud is also useful in organizing and managing classrooms in the following ways:

- Getting the day or period off to a good start
- Changing classroom activities in an orderly way such as getting ready for the next class, next lesson, recess, or lunch (just start reading the current read-aloud and see what happens during such changes)
- Building a love of books
- Promoting motivation to read
- Appreciating and knowing books in various genres and authors
- Ending the day on a positive note

Phonics Knowledge and Skills

Phonics and Phonological Awareness

Why is it important to teach phonics in context of children's needs?

As you know, phonics knowledge is a necessary condition for learning to read, but not a sufficient one. In literacy lessons, phonics shares attention with oral language development, concepts about print, vocabulary, fluency, comprehension, instantaneous word recognition, and developing the habit of reading.

Phonics is certainly an important part of balanced literacy instruction. As much as a total of thirty minutes a day in the early grades may be spent on various kinds of phonics instruction.

Teach It!

Refer to the Teach It! appendix at the end of the book for further activities you can use to reinforce concepts discussed in this chapter.

Reading Aloud

You certainly do not need advanced training to read a book aloud successfully with children! Nonetheless, good preparation is rewarded by a more satisfying experience all around. We suggest following these steps when reading aloud to children:

1. Prepare to Read the Book. Read the book through yourself before you read it to children. Decide whether it is suitable for your group. Does it have enough excitement or depth to hold the interest of a whole group? If it is suitable, decide how you want to read it — with humor, with drama, with questions to whet curiosity? If there are voices to bring to life, decide how you want to make each one sound. If you decide to stop reading to ask for predictions or discussion, decide where the stopping places should be. If there are any words or ideas that will be unfamiliar to the children, make a note to pronounce them carefully and explain them to the children.

If the book has illustrations large enough for the children to see, practice reading the book through while you hold it facing away from you, where the children will be able to see it.

2. Prepare the Children. Make sure the children are seated comfortably where they can see and hear you. Most teachers prefer to have the children sit on a carpet or cushions in front of them. Remind the children, if you need to, of the behavior you expect of good listeners: hands to themselves, eyes on the teacher, and ears for the story.

3. Begin to Read. Show the children the cover of the book. Ask them what they know about the topic. If you want to arouse more curiosity, quickly show them some other pictures in the interior of the book (but not the last pages — keep the children in suspense about those). Ask the children to make predictions about what will happen or what they expect to find out in the book.

Turn to the title page. Read the author's and the illustrator's names. Talk about what each person contributed to the book. It might help to point out that if only one name is given, then the illustrator and author are the same person. Otherwise, the children should know that the author and the illustrator both have important things to do to bring the book into being. (Publishers usually pay authors and illustrators equally and frequently encourage them to work independently of each other.) Remind the children of any other books they know by this author or this illustrator.

4. While Reading. As you read the book through the first time, ask for comments about what is going on. How is the character feeling? What is the character's problem? What do they think the character can do to solve the problem? Ask the students to predict what will happen. Read a few pages; then stop again. Ask how things look for the character now. What is the character doing to solve the problem? How is it working? What do the children think will happen now? Why do they think so? Stop right before the end and ask for last predictions. You can add to the suspense if you take an obvious quick look at the last page, but don't let the children see it. Then ask the children to predict what will be on the last page.

5. Follow up the Reading. Ask the children whether the book turned out the way they thought it would. What made them think it would turn out that way, or why were they surprised? What did they like about the book? How did it make them feel? Why?

6. Reread the Book. Read the book through a second time. This time, you might want to take more time to look at the ways the illustrator pictured the action. If there are any chants given in the book, ask children to repeat them. Ask questions about characters, motives, and other things you and the students find interesting about the book.

7. Leave the Book Available to the Children. Put the book on display in the library corner, and encourage children to read it later during scheduled time in the reading center or between other activities. The children might especially enjoy taking turns reading it to each other.

Phonics instruction should be **systematic**; that is, the teacher should have in mind a set of concepts about the English spelling system and she or he should make sure that they are being taught and learned.

Phonics instruction should be **developmental**; that is, the teacher should recognize that at an early level, phonics instruction makes children aware of words themselves, and the sounds within them. Then, it focuses on the matches between letters and sounds. At a later level, it focuses on relations between larger chunks of sound and clusters of letters. Beyond that, it emphasizes what happens when vowels in words are "marked" long or short, or when morphological endings are added to words. And still later it explores etymologies of words. (All of these matters were discussed in Chapters 4 and 5.)

Phonics instruction should also be done in the context of reading or writing. Dahl and colleagues (2001, p. ix) write, "Phonics in context means: in the context of children's needs, in the context of children's developing language knowledge, [and] in the context

Teach It! 5

Language Experience with Authentic Children's Literature

Teach It!

Refer to the Teach It! appendix at the end of the book for further activities you can use to reinforce concepts discussed in this chapter.

Phonics in the Context of Children's Needs

Daniel Woo is teaching a group of eighteen children in a transitional first grade. They have completed kindergarten, but are not yet ready for first grade. Most of the children struggled in kindergarten, and some are English language learners. Mr. Woo's school and its teachers recognize the need for an additional year of expert teaching before first grade to prevent later failure.

In the following lesson, Mr. Woo engages the children in explicit word study that is highly interactive and appealing to them. He has arranged for half of his class to go to music in the morning and half in the afternoon. In this way, Mr. Woo can provide more focused attention to specific children with similar needs in a smaller group. His needs-based lesson follows:

Mr. Woo asks the children to raise their left thumb if they are ready for word play. The children love word play and eagerly help one another find their left thumb.

He then asks the children to give him their "important" word, cautioning them that it must be a real word. This activity is similar to key vocabulary teaching. Mr. Woo says, "Tell us your word and new letters you want to try."

Taking turns, the children say their words and letters they want to substitute as the beginning letter. A child volunteers the word Lex (his dog's name) and the letters D and B.

Mr. Woo writes the word Lex on the board; then the children spell Dex and Bex. Mr. Woo then writes these words on the board. Next, he asks the children to work with the two words bat and big, and he writes the words on the board. He and the class change the beginning letters to make new real words, with the children leading the conversation.

Mr. Woo guides the instructional conversation, but makes every effort to "lead from behind." He employs scaffolding actions—warmth and responsiveness, coming to shared understandings with children, staying in their zone of proximal development—as he teaches.

For consolidation, he guides the children's participation in word learning practice. He chants, "If I know pig, I know jig." The children read this refrain with him from chart paper. The teacher and the children continue: "If I know day, I know play. If I know . . . ."

As an application and extension of the lesson, Mr. Woo distributes word cards that have the letter/sound patterns just taught and has the children engage in exclusive word learning practice in partner groups and individually.

As part of his ongoing assessment, Mr. Woo takes notes on several children after he has observed and interacted with them as they sort through the word cards. He makes a note to do a formal phonemic awareness test with three children he is worried about.

Contributed by Linda Headings, M.Ed.

Guiding Student Self-Assessment

Picture the teacher—he has observed his students during a rhyming word lesson and has decided to work with a few children who avoided participating or seemed lost during the activity. For a ten-to-fifteen-minute informal assessment, he gathers a selection of rhyming word cards (single syllable and consonant blend) including words from a lesson just taught: table, able, chair, Blair, rag, bag, tag, goat, boat, float. The children sort the words into rhyming matches independently—they are seated spaced apart at a table.

Having told the children he would make some notes, he watches for accurate matches, mistakes, self-corrections (a sign of confidence), and signs of uncertainty. With a small group of four or five children, the teacher is able to make notes on each child. After this brief word sort, he asks the children to move together. Of course, the cards are slightly mixed up as they are slid across the desks, but this gives the children another opportunity to quickly arrange their rhyming matches.

Beginning with accurate matches, the teacher asks why they are matches. He aims to guide children to identify rhyming patterns ("It's the ending letters!") and to encourage self-assessment. Through dialogue, the teacher and children discuss "good matches" and engage in "good fixes." This brings the assessment to a dynamic level; learners self-correct and feel accomplished. During this conversation the teacher affirms, repeats children's accurate reasoning, and corrects as needed. Some direct correcting is needed, but not very much because having begun with talk about accurate matches and why they are accurate, incorrect ones are more readily identified and fixed by the children.

Assessment notes are filed in children's folders as they return to their seats. Which is more informative, an assessment such as this or corrected worksheets? Which is a better use of the teacher's and the students' time? Which is more interesting to you as a professional reading teacher?

of classroom reading and writing activities." Encouraging young children to write and to use invented or temporary spelling calls their attention to the alphabetic nature of English spelling and leads them to explore letter-to-sound relations (Templeton & Morris, 1999).

Organizing for Instruction

Nearly all young children benefit from and enjoy learning literacy with their peers. Young children approximate literate reading and writing behaviors through pretend-reading and pretend-writing for some time before the behaviors become part of their repertoire. But not all children enter school with the same abilities. Some children have been in preschool for three or four years, while others are having their first school experience (Riley, 2007). Some might have disabilities, some might read independently, others might have literacy skills typical of a three-year-old, and for some, English might be a second language. Therefore, instruction must have breadth and great flexibility. In the early years, teachers need to know what to expect in children's development and be able to recognize differences, manage a broad range of development, and use research-based strategies that are designed for a range of development. (See the Differentiated Instruction box.)

Differentiate Instruction through Grouping and Planning

Grouping children and planning for instruction are major teaching strategies designed to address differences in children's learning. Traditional grouping, which identified students as having high, medium, or low ability, nearly guaranteed underachievement for many children and teachers. How could teachers be effective and still have the same children in the same low-ability group for nine months? For years? This concept is based on an invalid deficit learning model, and it invites a "blame the kid" attitude (Pressley et al., 2001, p. 233).

Research shows that once a child has been assigned to the low reading group, it is highly unlikely he or she will ever be moved to a higher group (Good & Marshall, 1984; Hiebert, 1983). Children in low groups often have low self-esteem and receive instruction with fewer opportunities to think and work with meaning (Allington, 1983; Allington & McGill-Franzen, 1989; Eder, 1983).

Two well-known approaches offer grouping ideas that are designed to help avoid the pitfalls of traditional grouping. Each approach makes a distinction between the organizational structures and the kind of instruction that goes on in them. Grouping strategies and other organizations for literacy instruction (e.g., writing time, word time, reading group time) are not prescriptions for effective teaching. Rather, what teachers *do* with children in these blocks of time is what matters. However, a well-designed lesson structure is essential to managing the classroom, which, of course, frees you to teach your personal best!

DYNAMIC GROUPING.   Fountas and Pinnell (2001, 2007) developed the concept of dynamic grouping as a way to target guided reading opportunities. Dynamic grouping involves the creation of several kinds of reading and writing groups that work together and receive instruction over the course of a school day. For example, dynamic groups allow for non–ability-based interest groups, peer tutoring and cooperative learning pairs, cross-grade buddies, and needs-based small groups (flexible and ability-based). In needs-based groups, children are moved regularly so that no child is stuck in any one group all year.

A Rural Primary Classroom

Plans for a week of reading lessons in a Readers' Workshop. One lesson set supports children at several developmental levels, another provides for two interest groups, and another gives children opportunities to read their weekly "challenge" books. In teaching, focus on reading comprehension, fluency, and word recognition skills (vocabulary and phonics), as well as children's enjoyment.

For the guided reading groups, get multiple copies of the following books leveled by Reading Recovery:

- Books for more emergent readers:

  Wake up Dad (Randell, 1996c)

  At the Zoo (Peters, 1995)

  The Animals Went to Bed (Theodorou, 1996)

- Books for the solid beginning readers:

  Mrs. Wishy-Washy (Cowley, 1990)

  Baby Bear Goes Fishing (Randell, 1996a)

- Books for those farther along:

  Happy Birthday Sam (Hutchins, 1978)

  Henny Penny (Galdone, 1968)

  Leo the Late Bloomer (Krauss, 1987).

For interest groups, have several new books. For primary fiction include *Ace Lacewing: Bug Detective, Mr. Tuggle's Troubles,* and *Russell the Sheep.* For nonfiction include *Jose! Born to Dance, Brave Dogs, Gentle Dogs: How They Guard Sheep,* and *Recess at 20 Below.* During the week, children will have several opportunities to take turns reading these books alone and in pairs. As with all reading groups, attend to comprehension strategies and word recognition skills.

Have the children select challenge books from the classroom or school library. While you teach the guided reading group, instruct the students not in the group to read their self-selected books at their tables (or desks pushed together). Later in the day, meet and observe several readers. Something is always gained with the self-selected books, including new vocabulary and boosted motivation for the students to read. You gain too by learning what your students can do given varied and flexible opportunities to read with your guidance.

Teach It! 10

Guided Reading and the Four Blocks Approach

GUIDED READING AND FOUR BLOCKS.   As described in Chapter 1, guided reading often takes place within a **four-blocks** language arts period. However, **guided reading** could take place in other approaches. For example, a wise and creative teacher can effectively guide children's reading using basal texts. This is because by definition guided reading creates "a context in which the teacher supports each reader's development of effective strategies for reading texts at increasingly challenging levels of difficulty" (Fountas & Pinnell, 2001). Children in first and second grade can often select their own challenge books.

Four blocks is a well-balanced structure for reading instruction. It describes four specialized reading periods that address some of teachers' most challenging issues. No matter what reading program is used, all teachers are faced with the responsibility of teaching a class of twenty to thirty students in ways that meet their needs, without having some children labeled and taught as "low-ability" all year. Additionally, the question of how to grade young children looms large. Cunningham, Hall, and Sigmon (2007) and Cunningham, Hall, and Defree (1991) created a framework to address these questions and issues and to provide guidelines for organization, planning, teaching, and grading. (Grading is discussed later in this chapter.) The four blocks provide varied and ample opportunities for primary grade children to learn and for teachers to teach reading and writing.

The framework of four reading periods occurs during the school day and includes (1) guided reading, (2) self-selected reading, (3) working with words, and (4) writing. Within each block, specific structured activities take place. A major goal of four blocks is to give children a balance of reading, writing, and word instruction. Four-blocks structure provides what it takes for teachers to make each block as multileveled as possible. **Multileveled groups** include children with different needs and strengths (Cunningham & Allington,

1999, Cunningham, Hall, & Defree, 1991). These four blocks contain key elements of instruction for all classrooms with dynamic or multileveled groups:

- **Guided Reading.** For thirty to forty minutes, the teacher helps children learn children's literature (fiction and non-fiction) and reading comprehension. The lesson focuses on developing prior knowledge, oral language, meaningful vocabulary, self-confidence, and motivation. In guided reading the teacher works with small groups, teaches reading concepts and strategies (such as guessing an unknown word with what is known about how the word is spelled and if it makes sense in the sentence). There is no doubt that small group reading instruction is superior to whole class instruction. This is one reason it is critical for your students to be able to manage their behavior well in centers! Within guided reading periods, children often engage in shared reading—the teacher reads to the children, the children read with the teacher in unison, or the children take turns reading, etc. They read a big book or sets of the same little books. Following instruction, children read with their partners (often two children who read at somewhat different levels, but who are compatible enough to read together) and the teacher watches partners closely and intervenes to stress use of strategies and provide encouragement. Next, the group comes together again to discuss the book. The children or both the teacher and the children usually write something about their reading.

- **Self-Selected Reading.** The goal of self-selected reading is to share different kinds of books, or various genres, and build motivation. The teacher encourages reading interests, provides developmental-level books, and gently "coaches" some children's reading. Children read their selected books with help as needed and confer with the teacher individually. They may also draw and write about their books. This block lasts about thirty minutes.

- **Working with Words.** For about thirty minutes, the teacher and the children engage in various word-related activities, such as reading both familiar words on the word walls and the new ones that are added weekly (approximately five). The teacher asks the children to review the wall words and talks with them about the importance of these words (sight words, high-frequency words, and words in units of study such as science and social studies). Children write the words, say the words, look for patterns in words, and discuss and practice the words' spelling patterns. The teacher writes the words, showing how the letters and words are formed and pointing out word patterns (rhyming, blends, diagraphs, short or long vowel words, and so on, according to children's literacy development). The children practice making words and sorting them with games and word cards.

- **Writing.** A minilesson also occurs in writing workshop. It begins each writing period, which lasts forty-five to sixty minutes, depending on how young children get along in an extended time period. Goals vary from kindergarten to second grade; for example, first graders may focus on having every sentence make sense and using capital letters and punctuation to end a sentence. In addition, the writing block focuses on spelling. Children write during the minilesson, on their own and with partners. This is an easy block to teach on multiple levels. Children write books, stories, and information pieces; illustrate their writing; and have conferences with the teacher for individual instruction. The word wall helps children to find words they need and to work on spelling. Writing time concludes with sharing writing in the author's chair. Be aware that different teachers use different formats and structures for writing workshops. What is important is that all writing workshops include the basic essentials, such as time to write, writing and spelling instruction, strong support, and a warm and inviting work environment. Cunningham and Allington (1999) provide some basic guidelines to consider in using four-blocks teaching:

- Long-term planning for four-blocks teaching is organized around units of study such as inquiry units in science, math, and social studies; four-blocks teaching also contributes greatly to integrated curriculum. Short-term planning is laid out in both daily and weekly descriptions. This is the time when some of the arts can be integrated into the already integrated curriculum.

- Oral language is not a specific part of the four blocks, but many conversations take place in all four blocks.

- Four-blocks teaching does not eliminate the need for interventions such as Reading Recovery; it is not an add-on and can be used with other approaches such as response to intervention (RTI) (see Chapter 2).

- Volunteers and paraprofessionals can help support four-blocks teaching.

- The four blocks can be arranged in any order that works in your classroom.

- Finally, it is fine to do whole class instruction at other times during the day; for example, reading big books with the teacher is a popular way to include all the children in one lesson. As you know by now, children learn from one another as well as from their teacher.

Lesson Structures

Because children need many and varied learning opportunities, teachers use different types of lessons to accomplish the desired outcomes. In all lessons, the teacher uses a before, during, and after structure. For example, there is an introduction to the lesson, a period in which the heart of the lesson is conducted, and a conclusion, which is usually followed by an extension and application of what has been taught. Each type of lesson has structural aspects that help teachers meet their goals. That is, some lessons are more comprehensive and include a strong focus on word study, while reading or writing is also taught. Other types of lessons include mini-lessons, teachable moments, and think-alouds.

MINI-LESSONS.   Mini-lessons require fewer materials and are planned and taught fairly quickly. A mini-lesson is often taught at the beginning and focuses on one or two teaching points, such as self-monitoring one's comprehension and metacognition, providing the anticipation and focus of the lesson. The following is an example of a writing mini-lesson conducted by teacher Dr. Jill Dillard:

> Recess is over and the second graders are either reading or sitting at tables playing word games. Dr. Dillard asks the children to get ready for writing workshop. They gather around her and she talks with the children about yesterday's topic lesson, "I'm an expert." Several children generated new topics after that mini-lesson: Jarad selected a pet story; Sammie Ann selected a soccer story; and Kyle selected a story about his baseball team (see Figure 12.6A and Figure 12.6B). Dr. Dillard invites the children to talk to a neighbor about their writing topic. During this time, she circulates among the children prompting and encouraging. Dr. Dillard confirms the children's good ideas for stories and information writing and then asks the class whether they are ready to begin. With the children's consensus, she calls Monday's small writing group to meet with her to talk about their writing before Annie, the high school volunteer, arrives.

TEACHABLE MOMENTS.   Teachable moments are lessons in which the teacher seizes on an incident or observation to reinforce a concept. For busy teachers, teachable moments are superior opportunities for providing individual instruction in the context of a child's need. The next example demonstrates how much a good teacher can do in a very short time:

> First-grader Ransika is working in the writing center. As Mr. López walks by to check on him, he notices that Ransika is putting capital letters in the middle of some of his words.

Figure 12.6A

I Am an Expert—Kyle.

I'm a EXpert at bassball.
I'm a Pitcher.
I threw three peeoel out.
I'm all so gode at batting.
I hit two homeruns in eve
ry game.
I'm a EXpert at foot ball to.
I scored ten tuch downs
in a year. I'm a quar
ter back. I through fiv
e touch downs. We won a
lot of games.

Figure 12.6B

I Am an Expert—Sammie Ann.

Socer
when I play Socer I am
usholly defens or the side
plays kecase I am good
at the side and defens
be case when I am on the
side I nick the
ball of that side
and when I am defens
I block the gole line
the goley and I
can stand on a
Socer ball

Mr. López intervenes immediately, asking Ransika if he is using capital letters. Ransika nods yes, and Mr. López reviews the morning talk about when to use capital letters. With a sheepish grin, Ransika realizes his errors and begins to erase. Mr. López nods approval and turns to help another child.

With that interaction, Mr. López was able to reinforce the morning's lesson quickly and positively. And, importantly, his speaking to Ransika reminded him, and he self-corrected! Self-correcting is powerful stuff for all of us—and especially young learners.

THINK-ALOUDS. Think-alouds are lessons that demonstrate and model. They often show children how to think like a reader, writer, or speller. The following is an example of a reading comprehension think-aloud:

Ms. Novacek rereads Sheila Rae, the Brave (Henkes, 1987) to her first and second graders in a multiage classroom. This book is a favorite, as is Lilly's Purple Plastic Purse, also by Henkes (1996). The children and Ms. Novacek discuss the topic of bravery, which the children think is the book's theme. For discussion among the children, Ms. Novacek has paired a slightly less experienced reader with a somewhat more experienced reader. Ms. Novacek's goal is to help the children work toward understanding a deeper meaning, one that has to be inferred.

Henkes's books provide opportunities to teach children to infer meaning, and the implied meaning in *Sheila Rae, the Brave* is about sibling relationships. Ms. Novacek engages in the following think-aloud: "Class I've been thinking about this book and what Sheila Rae is like. I'm going to read a bit and keep thinking." Ms. Novacek reads and says, "I make a connection with Sheila Rae. When I was a child, I had a little brother, and I wasn't always nice to him. Sometimes I'd say mean things. What do you think about this?" The children discuss the idea, and Ms. Novacek picks up on their levels of understanding and carefully guides them to make inferences.

The use of wall charts for things such as lunch schedules and attendance helps students learn classroom routines. How does this carry over to benefit children's learning and your classroom management?

Daily Routines in K–2 Classrooms

As mentioned earlier, well-balanced daily schedules help young children to adapt more quickly and happily to the school day. Teachers incorporate a variety of strategies for implementing classroom routines. The following routines and lessons serve as examples of systematic routines that provide opportunities to work on important skills, such as word recognition and reading comprehension, in highly authentic situations.

KINDERGARTEN ROUTINES.   A typical day in a kindergarten class would include many, if not all, of the following routines (Vukelich, Christie, & Enz, 2002, pages 45, 54–57):

- *Morning Greeting.* Engage in one-on-one conversations with the children, and use this time to observe how children talk with each other and which centers they self-select (e.g., reading center, writing center). This allows you to check for interest and avoidance.

- *Taking Attendance.* Use a creative technique to take attendance, such as singing a song that includes the children's names. Children sing along and learn one another's names. Use large name tags that children read and hang on the attendance chart during the singing. Point to the words as they are sung.

- *Shared Reading.* Read aloud predictable books with repeated phrases. As the children become familiar with the words and phrases, have them join in. Figure 12.7 provides a typical read-aloud lesson plan.

- *Shared Writing.* Model aspects of writing, such as letter formation, thinking about what to say, or using conventions such as periods and capital letters. Then have the children take turns writing letters and words. This provides high-level scaffolding.

- *Writing Center.* Encourage use of the writing center where children can self-select and write on their own and experiment with invented spelling and letter formation (See Figure 12.8).

- *Group Time.* Use group time to emphasize oral language. Demonstrate purposeful speaking, good listening, taking turns, and idea sharing. Use group time to discuss the daily schedule and some center assignments. After center assignments have been made, assign a group of approximately six children to sharing time.

Shared Reading

Shared Writing

Figure 12.7

Reading Aloud Lesson Plan.

Objectives: Engage children (through a shared reading).

Goals: Provide rich oral and written language experiences. Demonstrate the joy of reading.

Increase intrinsic motivation. (Guthrie & Wigfield, 2000)

Materials: Big book copy of The Wheels on the Bus (Kovalski, 1987), drawing paper, and crayons.

Demonstrate what is going to happen.

Immerse children in the literacy event by discussing illustrations.

Provide Word Study, and Guided Practice by reading the book, rereading children's favorite parts, building knowledge by singing and rereading.

Apply and Extend by having children draw their favorite part of the story.

Share several new little Wheels on the Bus books; invite children to read them as much as they wish.

Ongoing assessments: Write and file notes on level of participation, enjoyment, skills, and interest on the three to five children you select as focal for the week.

- *Sharing Time.* In smaller groups, children can be more at ease and engaged than they are in larger groups. You also have opportunities to ask natural questions, such as "What happened next, Mark?" or "Does anyone have a question for Michael?" (Moffett & Wagner, 1991).

Beginnings are important, and good teachers teach children many things on the first day of school. The Teach It! box on page 386 provides a model of how one teacher organizes her first day of kindergarten.

FIRST-GRADE ROUTINES.   Routines that incorporated authentic reading and writing in kindergarten also work well with first and second graders. For example, taking attendance, lunch count, and accounting for jobs for the day require children to read and think. Wall charts that are used as tools in everyday teaching also serve children well. In early first grade, children need the support of illustrations and pictures to comprehend the reading they need to do. Later, these supports are removed as children become better able to read without them.

Each day, at some point during the day, all children engage in the following: guided reading, being read to, self-selected reading, peer or buddy reading, and writing. Read-alouds might begin to introduce some reading from information books on science or social

Figure 12.8

Topics of Interest. Invitation to Fisher David Cook's Pirate Party!

Teach It!

Refer to the Teach It! appendix at the end of the book for further activities you can use to reinforce concepts discussed in this chapter.

First Day of Kindergarten

The following schedule was contributed by Linda Headings, M.Ed., a highly effective kindergarten and first-grade teacher.

Half-Day Kindergarten Schedule

Before the first day of school with all the children together, the children come to school in groups of about seven for one or two days until all have been transitioned into classroom life. Teacher Linda Headings welcomes the children and teaches them about centers and the number of children allowed in a center, how to work with the materials, and so on. She introduces a teacher-made attendance chart with all the children's names. Pictures of children taken on the transition days are mounted on the "Our Class" poster. Ms. Headings has used the first partial days to gather some personal information about each child from parents or from children's conversations in class.

Goals: Begin (a) relationship building with children, (b) establishing daily routines, and (c) gathering data by observing children's interactions with environmental and class-created print and with read-alouds.

First Day of Kindergarten with All the Children

Greeting: Greet children by name at eye level with a smile as they come in.

Remind children to put their belongings away in their cubby, to hang up their name on the attendance chart, and to sit on the group rug (use warmth, caring, and support).

Demonstrate and Immerse

Review the Daily Schedule: Tell children what is going to happen; be descriptive and lively while discussing group time, story time, taking a school tour, recess, center time, and time to go home. [*Use a schedule chart at children's eye level, and point to the words as you talk.*]

After reviewing the schedule, put it at the children's eye level for review. [*Going over the schedule often comforts an anxious child. The chart demonstrates that print carries meaning and that it carries important information.*]

Working with Words

Attendance and Reading: Hold up each child's name written on a large sentence strip. Have the child wave when his or her name is read so that the children can start to put the name with the face. As their name is called, children wave, and you make a personal connection—for example "Hi, Billy Jack. I hear you like animals."

Apply and Extend

- Do sorting activities with children's names. Use a magnetic board on an easel. Sort name strips by boys and girls. Note beginning letters in names.

- Read *Dogger* by Shirley Hughes (1977). Introduce the main character, Alfie, and share that, "We will be reading other stories about Alfie the rest of the week." [*Teaches about authors.*]

- In small groups, invite sharing from the children of their favorite "lovey" brought from home. [*Show warmth and caring.*]

School tour: Review the locations of restrooms and the principal's office; talk about walking in line and using appropriate voices. Take children out to play on the playground for about fifteen minutes. If someone is having separation problems, delay playing outside. Work in a little recess when all the children are calm.

Center time: After returning to the classroom, review the names of the centers and their rules: (1) Only five children can be in a center at one time, and (2) children put their names on a waiting list so that everyone can have a turn. Demonstrate using waiting lists with role-play. [*Shows children the function and power of print.*] Review options if the waiting list is long. Role-play frequently. Dismiss the children from the group rug to the centers.

Centers and Materials:

- Writing center: Pencils, markers, note cards, name word cards, a variety of papers, etc.

- Reading center: Big books, manipulative charts, books on tape, bookshelf, magnetic letters, flannel board story

- Dramatic play center: Shoe store (correlation with buying new shoes for school), shoes, rulers, boxes, calculators, chairs, storage shelf, paper and pencil, receipts, a mirror (for looking at shoes)

- Math center: Blocks, Unifix cubes™, puzzles, sorting items, counting games

- Science center: Magnets, materials to experiment with, a scale, paper and pencils

As children use centers, monitor and observe who works well together, who engages, who likes to work by themselves, group dynamics, problem solving, who uses the waiting lists, and so on. Intervene as needed.

Transitions:

- Signify a transition by a bell or singing softly; ring the bell twice to signify clean-up.

End of day: In the whole-group meeting area, review the day, and explain something interesting that will be happening tomorrow. Close with the song *The More We Get Together* (Raffi, 1996), which has been written on a chart in advance. Point to the words as you sing. [*Demonstrate meaning and enjoyment of print.*]

Dismiss:

- Tell children to gather their gear and line up at the door when you call their names.

- Make a quick trip to the teachers' lounge, coffee break, and prepare for the afternoon group.

Table 12.1 Daily Schedule

OCTOBER	WEEK 1	GUIDED READING	BUDDY READING	INQUIRY CENTER
	Monday			
Daily read-alouds		Ben, Shealee, Sam, Tessa, Mark, Jenny	Books of choice (oral language practice)	Book research: work with frog facts (write findings)
	Tuesday			
Reading and writing		Joe, Michael, Dan, Angela	Listening center and read together	Report writing: science
Literature study		Jerriann, Nicki, Don		
		Helen, Jane, Chris, Mickey	Oral language practice	Author study (write and share)

Source: Adapted from Fountas and Pinnell (1996).

studies topics. Far too often, the primary grade curriculum is strongly based on storybooks (fiction). Providing plenty of reading from information books in the early school years helps prepare children for the heavy reading of these books in later grades. Children really enjoy information books and often these books pave the way to reading for boys (Duke, 2000; Duke & Bennett-Armistead, 2003).

Establish learning centers where children can focus on particular reading and writing skills. Centers might include a writing area, an inquiry study area, a listening area with audio books, a computer area with options for self-selecting from two or three activities posted on the computers, a word work center, and, perhaps, an interest center. These centers, along with the teacher's guidance, provide vital reading experiences. Children should be rotated through the learning centers, and these assignments should be charted for the children to see. They can check the chart for center assignments and go to work in them while you teach small groups blocks of reading and writing.

SECOND-GRADE ROUTINES.   On the first day of second grade, you and the children might follow a schedule that is highly similar to the one used in first grade, but with more advanced materials and activities. Just as in first grade, each day should include guided reading, being read to, self-selected reading, peer or buddy reading, writing, and word study and spelling. Table 12.1 models part of a weekly schedule for second grade. Creating such schedules helps to ensure that many varied learning opportunities are included daily.

Second-grade planning proceeds until all children are scheduled for a week of varied learning opportunities. The teacher's long-range plans need to be open to change and should include daily read-alouds, small-group reading, children's self-selected reading, spelling and word work, and at least twice-weekly comprehensive writing workshops with daily writing activities. You might also want to incorporate a block of pleasure reading, perhaps every Monday, Wednesday, and Friday for twenty minutes right before the end of the day.

Teach It! 55

The Writing Workshop

Providing Appropriate Materials

Before the children come through the door on the first day of school, teachers have prepared the classroom for learning. They have also thought about the materials they will need to assist them.

Teach It!

Refer to the Teach It! appendix at the end of the book for further activities you can use to reinforce concepts discussed in this chapter.

First Day of First Grade

Goals: Begin relationship building with children. Begin establishing daily routines. Begin gathering data by observing children's interaction with environmental and class-created print and with read-alouds.

Greeting: Greet children at the door at eye level; invite them to put their personal items on any table and come to sit on the gathering rug. Take attendance and lunch count. Children stand and point to their names on attendance chart and point to wording on lunch chart.

Opening: Introduce yourself by sharing objects that tell the children about you. Pull individual items out of a pillowcase, and share what they mean to you. Draw a web or graphic organizer of the pillowcase contents. [*This provides a visual introduction to webbing, organizing ideas, and storytelling and building relationships.*]

Graphic Organizer: Pillowcase

Tell the children that one of your favorite things to do on Saturday mornings, for example, is to go out to garage sales to find books for the classroom and to hunt for other treasures the class can use at bargain prices.

Welcome: Welcome children as a group by doing some sorting activities and writing them down on large pieces of white construction paper in front of the children. [*Introduce making a class big book.*] Use one page for each pair of children. [*Collaboration begins.*]

Sorting examples that create the first class-made book are:

- Number of children in classroom enrolled along with number of boys and girls
- Number of children who walk, who ride the bus, who are dropped off
- Types and number of pets children own
- Favorite foods
- Favorite holiday

After selection of the sorting topics, the pairs of children dictate pages. After each page is written, read it together, pointing at each word. Observe who is attending and participating.

School tour of locations: Show children the bathrooms, lunchroom, office, nurse, music, gym, and art room.

Read aloud: Read *A Porcupine Named Fluffy* (Lester, 1986). [*The focus is on adjusting to a different place and making friends.*]

Work on book illustrations: Hand out to the class book pages from earlier in the morning for each pair of children to illustrate. [*This is collaboration in action.*] Talk about the size of illustrations and filling up the page so that the pictures can be seen from far away. Demonstrate by comparing the size of illustrations in a standard text to a big book's illustrations.

Classroom explorations: Following the book illustrations, allow children free exploration of the classroom. Items in the room for their explorations include puzzles, a variety of books, books on tape, Unifix cubes, magnets, pattern blocks, magnetic letters, checkers, art supplies, flannel board with story props, and some simple games.

After children's exploration, clean up and line up for lunch by holding up the last name of each child. Observe and record impressions. Read as needed.

Lunch time.

CLASSROOM LIBRARIES. Classroom libraries are essential in a literacy-rich classroom. Teachers and children use book collections for lessons, pleasure reading, and inquiry lessons. This supports an **integrated curriculum** that includes reading and writing in science, math, and social studies. Work with your school librarian to build your collection. In addition, join book clubs that offer good children's literature at reduced prices; leave no garage sale, yard sale, or library sale unexamined; find used bookstores; and contact the local public library to see if they have a program for obtaining children's books on a regular basis. Involve parents in helping to find ways to obtain books. A good source for identifying great books is *The Reading Teacher*, which can be accessed at http://www.reading.org/choices/. Provide a wide variety of reading materials, including informational materials such as brochures from stores, automobile sales offices, community information centers, and the local police and fire departments. As you know from Chapter 4, children's own writing and published books and whole-class created books make excellent reading materials!

After lunch read aloud *Tacky the Penguin* (Lester, 1993). [*Expand on the theme in* A Porcupine Named Fluffy.]

Journals: Introduce journal writing using the overhead projector. Illustrate a think-aloud writing of an idea. Write a bit on the topic idea. Tell the children that they will write in their journals. Encourage inventive spelling: "Spell words the way they sound to you. Don't worry about spelling, this is just practice." Ask all children to add an illustration to their writing until you are familiar with their spelling proficiency. (Collect written artifacts to check for writing, sketching, and illustration.)

Before children begin journal writing, divide them into two groups. Group 1 works on journals, and group 2 engages in buddy reading in the rug area. Use leveled books, kindergarten to late first grade, from the Wright Group or Rigby Books. Circulate among the two groups, observe, and talk with children about their work.

There are always lots of hesitations and questions when children start journals. Working with half the class helps keep order. Work in blocks of about twenty minutes and then have the children switch. Observe and record students who worked quickly, but shabbily, who procrastinated, who struggled, who went to the bathroom, and who seemed to love the writing process. As children finish their journals, they must check in with you to read their writing aloud. Observe and teach voice/print matching. Keep journal writing and reading to a time limit to regulate and work on pacing.

Science: The sink and float experiment.

Students sit in a circle on the group rug with a large shallow tub of water. Ask the children what types of objects sink or float in water? [*Taps prior experiences and supports oral language.*] Pull out objects individually from a container.

Help the children hypothesize by predicting with thumbs up or down on what will happen when an object is placed in water. Assess. [*Watch for interactions. Who is in the lesson and who is out?*] Have small groups of children search the classroom to find one item they would like to test. Engage in the hypothesize/test cycle. Write group conclusions on chart paper. [*This is the first inquiry study.*]

Closing: Review the teacher-made attendance and lunch charts. Request that they hang up their names on the attendance chart and make their lunch request on the lunch chart before coming to the rug area the next morning.

Homework: Instructions to the children: To share their interests, bring some personal items to school tomorrow in a labeled bag. Six children will share each day. Two children share in the morning, two after lunch, and two at the end of the school day. [*This introduces sharing to the classroom community.*] Put the homework paper describing the project in the home/school correspondence folders.

Introduce correspondence folders: Discuss the folders with the children, and show them the basket where the folders are kept. The children are to bring their folders to school every day and place them in the basket first thing in the morning. Ask the children where they will put their folders at home. [*Use role-play.*]

Dismiss: Children line up to go home by responding to a riddle: "I'm holding the folder of a boy whose name begins with the sound of /ch/." Observe and record their responses.

The ideas and procedures presented on the first day of first grade are easily modified for second or third graders. Revise this first-grade summary after reviewing the developmental levels at which you find your students. For example, older children can collaborate on making the class-made book by doing some or most of the writing and illustrating. Children might also write and illustrate their own little books.

LEVELED BOOKS. Review the leveled books your school has to offer. These books provide excellent materials for reading lessons, children's self-selected reading, and books you ask children to read repeatedly. Once they are at the mid to late point of first grade (finger pointing), children need large amounts of easy reading at their level in order to gain fluency and confidence. A good way to encourage repeated readings includes:

- Write up a simple contract with a situation in which the child will read to others, such as the principal, cafeteria staff, custodian, or children in other classrooms (clear this with the teachers first).
- Decide on a reasonable date for the child to leave your classroom for her or his "performance reading."
- Encourage children to practice reading until they are ready to read with confidence.

Teacher Linda Headings conducts a journal writing exercise with her students.

- Provide a time for a rehearsal with you or with other children in your own classroom.
- Arrange for the child to leave the classroom (or read to buddies in the classroom) on the appointed day.

Children will practice long and hard for the privilege of doing performance reading. Excellent websites for leveled books and many other excellent materials are www.readinga-z.com and www.starfall.com. These sites require membership, but they are well worth it (specific grade levels could share a membership).

It is also important for teachers to be aware of each child's independent reading level, and to furnish books at one or more higher levels to nudge young readers forward. Having high-interest, higher-level books to choose from provides essential support for moving all children along in reading. This can take time, but nearly always, patience, excellent reading instruction, and much encouragement will work wonders. Finding a book that is of particular interest to the child facilitates this process.

Leveled books are rated by a child's reading development stage, not by age or grade. Basal readers and other texts are often leveled only by grade. Often grade-level ratings are not sufficiently helpful. If a basal series is required, you can also use Reading Recovery (or Fountas & Pinnell, 1996) books for more precise leveling. Features that distinguish leveled books include the following: level of syntactical complexity, number of words in sentences or on a page, accumulating vocabulary (number of high-frequency words and new words introduced), and level of support from illustrations. Fountas and Pinnell (2001, 2007) provide criteria for book selection:

- Sentence complexity (length of sentence)
- Vocabulary (number of high-frequency words)
- Print features (length of book, illustrations, format of the book)
- Language features (similar to oral language, high-level written language)
- Content (children's special interest, universal themes)

Reading recovery leveled books are rated from A to Z, with levels A–C for kindergarten, D–E and F–H for first grade, and F–H and I–K for grade 2. These books use much the same criteria as Fountas and Pinnell. Many children will be able to read above these levels, but the system provides a place to begin in selecting books.

Assessing Book Levels.   Some children need guidance when self-selecting books. The teacher might offer an array of books and ask the children to look them over and select from this array. The "five-finger test" offers one simple method: The child holds up fingers and thumb, reads the book, and turns down one finger for each word missed on a page. If the child gets to the thumb, the book is probably too difficult. However, children should be permitted to read books they self-select regardless of level of difficulty—this builds interest! Children should not continue to read a book they do not like. There are far too many wonderful books available for that to happen. Be aware of easy books that might hold high appeal for struggling readers and diverse language learners so that they can experience success. Nothing succeeds like success! All readers can make some progress; some just need more time and support than others.

NEW LITERACIES.   Computers are an important component of today's classroom materials. It is necessary that every primary classroom has them. Computer grants are still fairly easy to get, and even the youngest school child should have computer access. The importance of new literacy skills is evident even in the first few years of school as the following situation illustrates.

Picture a second grader stopping a visiting teacher in her classroom. The child is poised to sit down at a computer to take her turn, and she asks for help. She has to do research on animals and doesn't know where to look. The visitor says, "Well try www.animals.org," the child types in this address and says, "Great, I've got what I need now, thanks." (Personal communication Dr. Jill Dillard, May 14, 2009)

New Literacies

Why should we begin to help children be comfortable and learn how to navigate on the computer screen in the primary grades?

We will never know how this research project turned out, but we do know the challenge it can be to search for information. The fact is that by second grade, children need a number of computer skills. Be very explicit in your teaching. Know that it requires much patience, and that early on, children's "playing around" on the keyboard or screen is a good way to learn. We have all learned some things this way.

A brief list of computer skills, dispositions, and goals that need to be integrated into your practice starting in kindergarten and through the primary grades follows:

- Small muscle motor coordination for (1) booting up or turning on, and logging off, (2) navigating with the mouse, and (3) beginning keyboarding should be taught. Teachers should set aside time and use patience to teach these skills. Fortunately, children are usually very eager to have time on the computer, and those with some home technology experience will learn more quickly. Your classroom learning place's is open and democratic disposition will help children learn to take turns and share.

- Simple keyboarding and on-screen looking, not only left to right, but in various directions in order to point and click and solve search problems are essential activities as the child matures. Knowing where to look is not easy and not always obvious! Teachers should model and demonstrate skills, and allow time for children's sufficient low-key practice (being hurried will frustrate them). Work out a weekly schedule so all children have their time "on" all year.

- In first grade, facilitate children's learning to share playing a game or working on a reading activity on the same computer and finding the help they need from computer center charts of directions or from another child. Children can begin to buddy up on the computer and thus double their practice time.

- By the end of second grade, classroom technology instruction and practice should enable students to: (1) look, search, and click successfully without stress in appropriate software; (2) follow the text while they read it and click on unknown words; (3) think about and experiment with key word searches; and (4) navigate with the mouse in order to conduct specific searches and get support when they need it (again classroom charts, other children and sometimes the teacher).

Reaching All Children

There is little doubt that you will have English language learners and struggling readers in your classes during your teaching career. Teaching these children is one of your primary responsibilities. Previous chapters have provided information on these learners, and you will learn more in upcoming ones (especially Chapter 15). We focus here on the early grades.

English Language Learners

As with older students, young English language learners' English listening comprehension is more advanced than their ability to speak the new language, let alone read and write it. Much of the focus in the early years needs to be on oral language development. Helpful teaching includes the following, which reviews some of what you read in Chapter 4:

- Warm acceptance and valuing of differences
- Reading (or read-alouds of) the same book(s) in the English language learners' mother tongue and later in English

Language and Diversity

How can we address the needs of English language learners?

Language Experience with English-Language Learners

- Using parents and paraprofessionals, community volunteers, and anyone available in the school (all other support staff) to read and write with the children in their mother tongue
- Playing naming games of classroom objects in both languages, but in one language at a time
- Singing songs in two languages
- Providing many positive and comforting experiences with cultural differences

Use snacks, dramatic play with culturally appropriate clothing, holiday and birthday celebrations, and units of study with home and family, friends, and visitors to demonstrate culturally interesting facts about the children's homelands. Volunteers who include parents and business and community people can provide much-needed support if they speak an English language learner's mother tongue.

ENGLISH LANGUAGE LEARNERS IN KINDERGARTEN.   For children who come to school with some English proficiency, learning will move more rapidly than for those with little or no English proficiency. A few might be ready for phonemic awareness activities in English by late kindergarten but probably not before—and certainly not before they reach an intermediate level in spoken English. For a quick assessment of the intermediate level, try the following strategy:

- Read a predictable storybook in English to a small group of children.
- See if they can respond well to most comprehension questions.
- If so, try some simple phonemic awareness picture sorts (see Chapters 1 and 5).
- If children are successful, continue instruction.
- If children are not successful, step back and continue oral language development, and perhaps try the language experience approach (LEA) (see Chapter 13).
- Repeat the cycle of teach, assess, and teach accordingly.

Few English language learners will reach the intermediate level at a young age unless they speak English in addition to their mother tongue at home. As critical as explicit instruction is, other high-quality learning happens in the well-managed classroom, which is confirmed in a study by McCafferty and Iddings (2001). See how classroom organization provides for meaningful and frequent oral language practice in the example below:

Picture two Hispanic kindergarten children, one more advanced in English than the other, seated in the housekeeping center. Nicole (the more experienced English language learner) is reading a very well-known storybook in English to Jorge (as assigned by the teacher). Nicole knows the story by heart, and despite the fact that this lesson is appropriate for these children, they soon become less and less engaged and eventually toss the book aside. Nicole then stands up and begins to pretend that she is preparing food for Jorge. She speaks in English as she makes a sandwich, and Jorge responds. He immediately joins in the pretend play. The two children engage in an extended English conversation in which Jorge actually speaks more English than Nicole!

Productive play episodes such as this are exactly what Jorge needs to gain the oral proficiency necessary for moving into written language instruction. "Real-life" pretend-play situations provide rich opportunities, and sometimes being "off-task" provides valuable support. In play, young children learn to infer and will engage in useful language experiences (Christie & Roskos, 2009). Productive play is most likely to occur when the teacher has encouraged it in the primary classroom. Centers such as housekeeping, puppet theater, post office, restaurant, and others are present, and there is time for children to engage in them.

Moreover, children respond well to vocabulary words of personal significance to them, and book reading is a perfect place to teach vocabulary. Provide personal dictionaries (for home and school) in which children's favorite words may be kept. When your English language learners are ready for reading instruction, use **voice to print matching** (matching voice to print or word, focusing on word after word in order, and pointing to each word read), with small groups and frequent instructional conversations.

Children may be ready for phonemic awareness activities in their mother tongue, but not yet in English. (See Chapter 15 for discussion on sheltered English and sheltered instruction observation protocol [SIOP].) Here is an example of an ESL lesson for intermediate English language learners who speak Spanish.

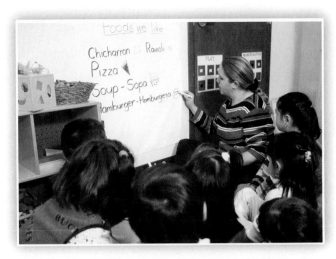

Using children's favorite foods in an LEA activity is a highly meaningful way to provide guided reading instruction for young children at the kindergarten or first grade levels. (Lindfors Photography)

- Read a storybook in English that the children already know in their mother tongue (someone else might have read the Spanish version to them). For example, *The Very Hungry Caterpillar* (Carle, 1987) is also available in a Spanish language version entitled *La Oruga Muy Hambrienta* (Carle, 1994).

- Engage the children in an enjoyable conversation, and then reread the book using children's suggestions for their favorite parts and using rich, scaffolded, or high-support discussion. With an English big book version or the same text on large chart paper, use voice to print matching and more discussion. Demonstrate how to identify a word, and help children identify words. To teach the concept of word, put your fingers and then their fingers at the beginning and end of a word. Make both book editions available for children's use in other explicit lessons and for self-selected use in pleasure reading and partner reading. The shared reading techniques described throughout this book help to extend this lesson. Use shared writing in similar ways with both languages as much as possible.

ENGLISH LANGUAGE LEARNERS IN FIRST AND SECOND GRADES.   Remember that some English language learners might enter your classroom having had no previous school experiences. As such, they are many months away from being ready for phonemic awareness activities in English. Their greatest need is for a strong emphasis on ESL lessons. Having developed English only at the level of basic interpersonal communication skills, a conversational level (Cummins, 2001), pronunciation difficulties often complicate letter-to-sound relationships and phonics learning.

As you will see in Chapters 13 and 15, many English language learners must learn to read first in English because of schools' limited resources to teach them more effectively in their mother tongue or because of state or district policies. Unfortunately, they have probably not mastered English at an oral level sufficient to support academic instruction in English. The primary focus of your reading instruction therefore needs to be on word recognition and comprehension.

Phonics will be the English language learners' weakest modality for learning to read, even after they have learned to communicate orally in English. A phonetic approach is based on knowledge of the sound system, and English language learners probably speak English with a heavy accent—a very strong indicator that they have not yet mastered the sound system of English.

Does this mean that you cannot teach these children to read until they master the phonetic approach? Not at all! Lessons discussed throughout this book provide varied and reliable instruction for teaching these children. Here are some helpful hints:

Teach It! 19

Word Wall Activities

- Focus on children's dictated texts (the language-experience approach [LEA]—revisit Chapter 4 and look ahead to Chapter 13 for details).

Making a book available in your students' mother tongue as well as in English can help them make the connection between the languages. (Lindfors Photography)

Using Questions to Teach English Language Learners

Struggling Reader

How can Elkonin boxes provide extra support to struggling readers?

- Work with teacher- and child-selected sight words for practice.
- Focus on *meaning*; use word walls, sorting cards, word hunts and games (all described in previous chapters).
- Work on *vocabulary* (and whole words). Your English language learners might know the word *big*, but not *huge*, *gigantic*, or *enormous*. (Use Chapter 6 to help you create sensible vocabulary instruction.)

Using children's "favorites" in an LEA activity is a meaningful way to provide guided reading instruction to young children at the emergent or beginning phase of reading.

Above all, involve the children, engage in conversations throughout the day—make it real for them! Often, children making the transition from their mother tongue to English have periods of stuttering or other issues, such as pronunciation and articulation difficulties. However, these periods do not usually signal a language disorder. Eventually, most of these children will improve. If they don't show improvement over time, seek help from school experts and work with parents who may not know where to turn. It is important to keep in mind that English language learners are no different than any other populations of children; and, just as with English speakers, a few may have problems with literacy learning (even in their mother tongue). However, the vast majority simply speak a language other than English and have many challenges to overcome as they develop English proficiency.

Struggling Readers

Young children who do not show steady reading, writing, and spelling growth close to that of their peers need careful evaluation and immediate intervention. The causes of delayed development may include a lack of early literacy experience or true lags in neurophysiological, psychological, and cognitive development.

Interventions such as Reading Recovery and the **Elkonin box** (Clay, 1985) provide support for struggling first graders. High-quality summer programs and tutoring are also recommended. The Elkonin box may well be an intervention used even in kindergarten with children who have been screened for possible problems in the Response to Intervention (RTI) program you read about in Chapter 2. Further discussion of RTI comes later in this chapter.

The Elkonin-box strategy focuses children's attention on letter-to-sound relationships. The routine goes as follows: The teacher might begin by asking a child to identify the problem word. When the child points to the word, the teacher writes the word.

Then, together, they segment the word in chunks of letters and draw boxes around each letter chunk

as they have a good deal of discussion about the letter-to-sound relationships. A variation on this would be for the teacher to draw the boxes first and then coach the child to write the letters in the boxes as he or she works through the letter-to-sound relationships.

If the child cannot pronounce the word, the teacher provides support by saying the word first. To consolidate the lesson, the student and teacher write the word in a sentence and use it orally in a sentence.

The Elkonin box strategy fills several needs. For older children who still need help, the strategy clarifies segmenting and manipulating letter-to-sound relationships. The Elkonin box can also be used as a visual aid in working with multiple-syllable words. For young children, the Elkonin box strategy is extremely helpful for those needing help with phonemic awareness and who struggle in perceiving and matching letter-to-sound relationships. Figure 12.9 provides an example of an accomplished teacher using this strategy with a struggling first grader.

Using sound reading instruction with young at-risk readers can result in tremendous benefits years later. (Ulrike Welsch/PhotoEdit)

Interventions

The earlier the intervention begins, the better the potential outcome. However, children in intervention programs are rarely able to function at grade level after the intervention stops (Bronfenbrenner, 1974; Spache, 1981). Gaskins (1998, p. 534) states that there is "more to [helping] delayed readers than good instruction." Here is a list of insights and recommendations provided by Gaskins and the teachers at Benchmark School in Media, Pennsylvania:

- Engage in extensive reading instruction.
- Show respect and teach the children self-monitoring and self-directing.
- Hold the idea that all teachers can change is their own approach to children and that children change as a result of teacher and teaching change.
- Focus on academic and nonacademic roadblocks (issues with engagement, having a disposition for learning, self-esteem).
- Work with other teachers, school experts, outside services, and parents to plan goals and plot the most efficient route to achieve the goals.
- Realize that long-term intervention is critical; most delayed readers need help from kindergarten through middle school and high school.

At Benchmark, the teachers work with children's dispositions or characteristics, such as attentiveness, organization, and conscientiousness. Research indicates that accelerating reading ability was not sufficient for at-risk learners. They must also acquire a disposition for learning and other affective or cognitive abilities. Among the many instructional foci used at Benchmark, one of the most important is teaching the *active search for meaning*. Graphic organizers, rich discussion, and other techniques need to be used intensively over time with struggling readers. If a child receives intervention, the specialist's instruction and the teacher's instruction must be in accord (Gaskins, 1998). Children are often put even more at risk when the specialist teaches in one way and the classroom teacher in another. In addition, teachers can learn a great deal by communicating with school specialists.

Cunningham and Allington (1999) suggest the following strategies for providing struggling readers with extra practice:

- Organize an after-lunch bunch in which you work with these children for ten or fifteen minutes reading easy books just for fun.
- Organize an easy reading time for ten or fifteen minutes after school using the same strategies as with the after-lunch bunch.
- Create a classroom learning center and have at least thirty minutes, perhaps two fifteen-minute periods of the day, set aside for struggling readers to work in this center.
- Include in the learning center materials such as Legos™, puzzles, computer games, word board games, math and science manipulatives, Play-Doh™, chalk (slates), markers, pencils, stickers and stamps, children's magazines, and a TV connection for watching Reading Rainbow or other educational videos.

Figure 12.9   Elkonin Box.

Elkonin Box Teacher and Child Conversation

Teacher: That was a wonderful job retelling that story. What would you like to write about that story?

Child: I want to say, "The crocodile got on."

T: That will be a fun sentence to write. [Here is where the teacher can encourage a more complex or a simpler sentence, depending on the needs of the child.] How would you begin the sentence, "The crocodile got on."?

C: With 'the.' I know 'the.'

T: I know you do! Write it on our book writing page. [The book writing page is the page where everything appears correct.]

Child writes the word 'The'.

T: I noticed you put a capital 'T'. Why did you do that?

C: 'Cause it starts the sentence.

T: You are just learning so much about writing! OK, say your sentence again.

C: The crocodile got on. I need crocodile.

T: Yes, let's see if we can work on that one together. What sounds do you hear in 'crocodile'?

C: Is it a 'c' or a 'k'?

T: What do you think?

C: 'c'

T: You got it! What else do you hear?

C: [*child stretches word*] 'r' and another 'c'

T: There is an 'r' and a 'c'; put the 'r' down and listen as I say the word. What do you hear before that other 'c'? [*Teacher stretches word*]

C: Oh! I hear an 'ah'. Ah, ah, octopus! 'O'!

T: You are really listening carefully for those sounds. OK, write o and the 'c' you heard. What does that much say?

C: The croc

T: Yes, let's finish this word together [Teacher and student sound word together and collaborate on writing letters—student supplies all but the silent e, which the teacher adds] So now we have The crocodile; we need to finish the sentence. What did you want to say?

C: The crocodile got on. I need got.

T: I want you to work out got by yourself. I know you can do it! I'll tell you that 'got' has 3 sounds. [Teacher draws 3 lines on the try page; some teachers use boxes]

C: I know it starts with 'g'

T: Yes, sir! What do you hear next?

C: [*Stretches word*] A 't'!

T: 'T' is in that word! But where do you hear it? Say it again and listen.

C: 'Got'—it's at the end. 'Got'. Oh, I know! It's 'o' again! G-o-t

T: Wonderful work! I could just see your brain in action! Now, what do we need to finish your sentence?

C: The crocodile got on. We need on, a –n, right?

T: Let's think about it. You just told me crocodile had an 'o' for the 'ah' sound; and got had an 'o' for the 'ah' sound. So what do you think makes the first sound in ah-ah on?

C: 'o'!

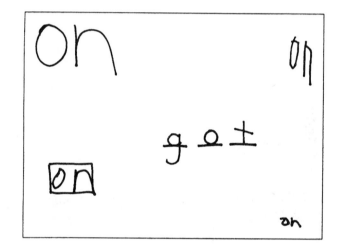

Source: Contributed by Karen Morrow Durica.

Remember that children who struggle can become defensive and lose interest in learning. This stance can be well established early. Sometimes fear of failure can be traced to instruction that focused on right answers at the expense of making sense, of focusing on meaning, and of using errors to increase learning.

Some children engage in negative behaviors, such as refusing to turn in their homework, because of a deep fear that it will be incorrect or because of a family problem. Children who are troubled often engage in behaviors that are self-destructive. These children need help, not blame. Children with struggles need the entire school system working for them. Beyond the risk of reading failure for students, their failures deeply hurt teachers, parents, and families (Dudley-Marling, 1990, 2000). Failure is suffering that no child, family, or teacher should have to experience.

Assessment

In Chapter 2, you read about Response to Intervention (RTI). Review this introduction and keep the following information in mind. Screening for possible learning difficulties will likely begin in kindergarten. RTI is adopted by an entire district; individual schools or classrooms cannot decide against implementing it. Screening may not occur until first or even second grade, and often, as you already know, these testing materials are usually from the Reading First program. However, some school districts decide

Standards and Literacy

Teaching in Accord with Standards

Despite the controversies surrounding standards-based education, **standards** can provide good guidance for schools and teachers. However, most standards call for an overwhelming number of student performance evaluations and can result in frustration. You might feel that you are expected to do everything and know you cannot. And you might feel as if you have no idea where to begin. Here are some recommendations for teaching in accord with standards (Caldwell, 2002):

- Don't agonize. Talk with colleagues, attend workshops and conferences, and take graduate classes that offer more knowledge. Let your administrator know that you want support. If you are interviewing for your first, or new position, ask about the support the school or district provides for teaching according to standards. Be proactive.

- Hold onto what you know is true and right. Keep your teaching in line with children's development. Find ways of consolidating standards and focusing on those that are most important for your students.

- Keep looking at the big picture and see what your standards really mean. Although stated in discrete pieces, standards cover overarching concepts that are critical to learning to read and learning from reading. Work with colleagues, and find ways to consolidate and group standards according to categories you relate to, add subcategories as you move along, and reread to consolidate.

- If the school or district mandates a basal or other reading program that you are expected to follow, work backward from the lesson you must teach to the skills and knowledge in the standards. This way you can match your lesson objectives with standards' benchmarks and grade-level indicators. It might work well to read a group of consolidated benchmarks and indicators you have categorized and plan accordingly.

Caldwell (2002) advises connecting instruction and assessment according to standards. Each state and each school district provides a list of standards and benchmarks that are required. Look at these benchmarks and indicators, and think about how you want to teach them. Because you know how to teach and assess, you can link your instruction with standards, benchmarks, and indicators, and the matches will make sense when you teach young children.

to elect their own, scientifically grounded screening tests. The following are some additional points that you will find useful in your teaching:

- A leadership team (LT) consists of about six to eight highly competent teachers and sometimes the principal or special education teacher.
- The LT is responsible for supporting the classroom teacher to ensure implementation of the reading program, such as four blocks with guided reading; it monitors the classroom teaching to ensure that there is fidelity to and consistency in this instruction. (Writing is also taught and monitored according to sound principles; see Chapter 9.)
- If, as a result of thorough screening and teacher input, a child is found to be struggling, an RTI "Tier One" phase is begun. Tier One means that specific high-quality, comprehensive instruction such as is described in this book is carried out for a specific time by the classroom teacher (progress is monitored and records are kept).
- If a child's progress is still not satisfactory according to RTI guidelines, "Tier Two" is begun. This is similar to Tier One, but it has a longer time line and more intensive classroom teacher instruction; more intensive support from the LT should also occur.
- If, with high fidelity to RTI guidelines and strong LT, well-documented support finds that the two previous Tiers are unsuccessful, Tier Three is begun and serious consideration among teachers, the LT, and parents takes place. It is possible that if Tier Three is unsuccessful, the child will be placed in special education classes.

Grading

Because grading is a challenge and a trial, Cunningham and her colleagues note that the concept of grading young children in the typical sense is simply not realistic. Putting a number or letter grade on young children is not informative or helpful because children vary so much. In traditional grading, the struggling reader or English language learner will almost always receive lower grades (marking them as "not as good as others"), and the more experienced and fortunate children will almost always receive higher grades (marking them as "better than others"). Teachers work hard to communicate to parents and school administrators that grades should reflect individual effort and growth. What matters most in teaching is that children are developing and making progress. Avoid marking any child as a learner with static ability. In *Classrooms That Work* (1999), Cunningham and Allington argue that we must change the way grades are determined. The typical grading system tells children who struggle: "You are a failure."

Many schools throughout the country do not assign letter grades to young primary children, focusing instead on their development. Even if you must work with a mandated traditional grading or report card system, you can maintain an encouraging attitude that is explicitly conveyed to children. Donald Graves (1983, p. 93) states, "Grading is a fact of life. It's the most difficult responsibility placed on teachers." He advises teachers to use grades to encourage children and to document well what children do in class.

Caldwell (2002) cites the limits of most report cards. She suggests adding to report cards in ways that show the children's growth and hard work. Here are some examples of this:

- Add a list of good comprehension strategies the child is working on and uses.
- Do something similar for word learning.

To keep grading records such as these, divide the grade book into sections labeled with your teaching emphasis—for example, *predicts in reading, connects self and the world to books, is learning sight words*. If you have a narrative report card, divide the report into categories, and keep information on all children in the same categories (reading comprehension, letter-to-sound relationships or phonics, spelling, etc.). In this way, you provide continuity in your report cards and even-handedness for all the children (Afflerbach, 1993).

Anecdotal Notes

Another tool that is vital for evaluating children's progress is the use of teachers' anecdotal notes. Anecdotal notes are narrative notes written while observing a child or children (E. McIntyre, personal communication, September 10, 2005). They are descriptive (avoid a rush to judgment). They may pose questions ("Why is he doing that?") and hunches ("I wonder if he understands the flexibility of writing?"). Anecdotal notes are based on what is actually seen and heard. They ask good questions, such as: Where is the child on meeting the first-grade standard benchmark indicator? Is he successful with help? What do I need to do?

Teachers take anecdotal notes to understand children's development and plan instruction, and to demonstrate accountability when called upon. Teachers write about what happens when they intervene, reteach, and provide high-level scaffolding, such as the Elkonin Box. It is hard to imagine effective instruction without data gathered and analyzed, and this data should be based on frequent notes and work samples.

A teacher who writes anecdotal notes on children's demonstrations of state benchmark knowledge and skill will have very important information at his fingertips for lesson planning, report cards, parent meetings, and meetings with other school experts. For example, a child might meet a benchmark regularly, sometimes, or rarely. This observation, with a line or two of description about what the child is doing, creates reliable data when carried out consistently.

In the beginning, it is often difficult to know when to write, so carry a clipboard or pack of sticky notes with you so that you can write anecdotal notes throughout the day. Use your notes to look for patterns. For example, identify a child who never seems to know short or long vowel words, who wanders around the room, or who is consistently left out of social activities. Recognizing patterns is the first step in intervention and knowing patterns provides critical information for assessment.

For Review

This chapter connects research-based information on children's learning with effective teaching from kindergarten through the second grade. It provides practical information for new and practicing teachers. Included are grading, four blocks (Cunningham & Alllington (1999), guided reading and dynamic grouping (Fountas & Pinnell, 1996), Reading First, assessment, and information on standards. English language learners and struggling readers are comprehensive topics.

A significant portion of this chapter is devoted to practice that develops both the knowledge and skills of young children and your own! Discussion of routines that teach and "first day of school" illustrations provide concrete guidance. Organization and management of the classroom learning community include helping children learn to manage their own behavior. Included also are discussions of family, community, materials, leveled books, Response to Intervention (RTI) and New Literacies connections.

For Your Journal

Write the notes below in your journal. Then analyze each for its value as anecdotal notes made when observing children.

1. Victoria is driving me crazy. I think her mother is at the root of this. Mom works and is never home!

2. Cody pretend-read *Frog and Toad* to me today; he uses a lot of text like phrases and his own mix of oral language. This little guy maintains a story formation with a beginning, middle, and end. He even connected the real frog he had with Frog in the story!

Taking It to the World

Develop a home literacy project that will help make school life more authentic and draw families into the school community. For such a project, it is wise to connect homework activities with inquiry projects and to have culminating activities in the classroom to which parents and caregivers are invited. Identify an inquiry project that would provide an excellent forum for family member or caregiver involvement. Create questions the children could use for interviews, and plan for how they might be able to supplement the information with photos, toys, or perhaps articles of clothing. How would the children be able to tell their stories?

New Literacies Connections

1. Children in grades K–2 nearly always go through a period of intense interest in dinosaurs. Build on children's natural interest in dinosaurs and increase your teaching opportunities by using the following websites and books to enhance pleasure reading:
   - www.enchantedlearning.com/subjects/dinosaurs (an interactive child-friendly site with basic information about dinosaurs and extinction)
   - www.fieldmuseum.org/sue (a site dedicated to Sue, the largest tyrannosaurus rex yet discovered)

2. Nearly all teachers are concerned with motivation, and many experts believe that technology has motivational advantages over conventional teaching methods. Explore the following websites, and identify one that might work well with younger children (K–2). Add your views on why you think they would be useful.
   - www.youthtrust.org—then click on "e-mentoring"
   - www.itown.com/athens/mentor

3. Try these websites for teaching practices:
   - Teaching Reading K–2 Workshop at www .learner.org/resources/series175.html
   - Teaching Reading K–2: A Library of Classroom Practices at www.learner.org/resources/series162 .html

---

PEARSON myeducationlab

Now go to MyEducationLab (**www.myeducationlab.com**), where you can:

- Find learning outcomes for the topics covered in this chapter, along with the national standards that connect to these outcomes.

- Complete Assignments and Activities that can help you more deeply understand the chapter content.

- Engage in Building Teaching Skills and Dispositions exercises, in which you can apply and practice core teaching skills identified in the chapter.

Putting Effective Literacy Instruction into Practice: Grades 3 to 5

Anticipation Guide

The following statements will help you begin thinking about the topics of this chapter. Answer *true* or *false* in response to each statement. As you read and learn more about the topics mentioned in these statements, think back on your answers. See what interests you and prompts your curiosity toward more understanding.

_____ 1. When children enter the third grade, there is little change from the first grade in the use of literature, in word recognition instruction, in reading in the content areas, and in writing.

_____ 2. Teachers in grades 3 to 5 devote much less attention to phonemic awareness and phonics than teachers in grades K to 2.

_____ 3. When children move from grades K to 2 to grades 3 to 5, the balance between oral reading and silent reading is about the same.

_____ 4. As children reach higher grades, there is a greater range between their achievement levels, resulting in the need for careful grouping for instruction.

_____ 5. The child's home can be the source of many family literacy activities.

_____ 6. When children are reading orally for fluency, it is not possible to judge their comprehension.

_____ 7. Formal assessment processes such as standardized testing do not provide information that is valuable in diagnosing the needs of individual students.

_____ 8. Teaching English phonics to English language learners is the same as teaching it to native English speakers.

_____ 9. Most children go through similar stages of spelling development.

_____ 10. Computer technology is more useful in writing instruction than in reading instruction.

Putting Effective Literacy Instruction into Practice: Grades 3 to 5

Literacy Activities in a Third-Grade Classroom

Chantell DeLaney is a third-grade teacher in a suburban classroom. Her 27 students represent many different cultures and ethnic groups, but all are proficient in English. Today she has organized her students into three groups according to their levels of reading comprehension. One group reads slightly below grade level, another group reads at grade level, and some children read at fourth- and fifth-grade levels. Ms. DeLaney's children come together in these groups from time to time, but her overall approach to grouping for instruction is flexible, according to the children's needs and to the goals and standards she is addressing.

In today's lesson with a group of 12 children who are reading at grade level, Ms. DeLaney's plan reflects a three-stage structure: anticipation activities, building knowledge, and consolidation. She begins with two anticipation strategies. She first conducts a read-aloud of the story title and the first page of the story, asking the students questions about the illustration on the page, which she shows them from her copy of the book. She asks, "Based on the title and the illustration on this page, what prediction can you make about the story?"

Vinh says, "It's about a big animal. What is it?"

"Who knows?" asks Ms. DeLaney.

Theodore responds, "A hippopotamus!"

"How large is a hippopotamus?" asks Ms. DeLaney.

"Really big!" they shout.

She then introduces two new vocabulary words from the story, "huge" and "gigantic," with a t-graph, a graphic organizer.

For the part of the lesson in which the children build knowledge through reading, Ms. DeLaney uses two strategies that are often used in tandem: guided reading and chunking. She focuses the children's reading by asking a higher-order (comprehension-level) question before they read and by chunking the amount of reading they do after she asks the question, usually a single page, occasionally more than one page, or sometimes only a paragraph or two in difficult material. After she poses the purpose-setting question, the children read silently to find the answer and then discuss what they have found out. Ms. DeLaney then proceeds to the next question and the next chunk. She uses the questions as a scaffolding strategy in a Directed Reading Activity (DRA). Placing the focus on the children's reading comprehension of what they read silently instead of only on accurate pronunciation and speed strengthens the children's abilities to understand what they are reading.

Ms. DeLaney's procedure is as follows: "Boys and girls, we are going to read a story about a girl who tries to hide from her mother the pet hippopotamus she found. Look in the table of contents for the story, turn to the first page, and close your book with your finger in the place. I am going to ask you a question before you read, and I want you to read to find the answer. How does Kamesha solve the problem of feeding her new pet so that her mother doesn't find out about it? Please read silently to find the answer." The children read silently and, one by one, they raise their hands as they find the answer. Ms. DeLaney repeats the question

and calls on Theodore, who responds correctly. She says, "That's correct, Theodore. Now, please read us the sentence that proves your answer." Other children offer their own opinions. She asks another question about the same page or chunk that they have just read. Then they move on to the next page, repeating this procedure for several pages.

In a consolidation activity after the children have read about half of the story, Ms. DeLaney asks them to retell the story so far in their own words, each child contributing part of the retelling. She asks, "How did our story begin?"

Tran contributes, "Kamesha found a huge hippopotamus at the park."

Nestor adds, "Her mother will be angry if she sees it."

"Why?" asks Ms. DeLaney.

"Because it will eat a lot of food," responds Nestor.

The children continue, negotiating with each other when there are disagreements or something is left out. Ms. DeLaney then asks the children to write two or three sentences predicting what Kamesha's mother will do when she discovers the hippopotamus. They can choose to read a library book or play one of the many reading games available to them as independent activities after they finish their writing. They will finish the story the next day, but with only a brief review activity before the children continue reading.

As children move into grades 3 through 5, most have acquired a concept of print and can decode the majority of the words they encounter—especially when the words are contextualized in connected text—and the children are reading silently, are understanding what they read, and are expressing themselves in writing. The purpose of Chapter 13 is to weave together the major elements of a comprehensive and balanced reading program for implementation in self-contained classrooms in grades 3 through 5.

Developing Knowledge and Skills

As you saw in earlier chapters, there is much variation in beginning reading programs for kindergarten and first and second grades. The range extends from scripted, direct instruction, one-size-fits-all programs of explicit phonics to literature-based programs in which shared reading of authentic connected text is a major activity. Phonemic awareness and phonics are taught in the context of words the children have already learned to recognize. A basal reading program is also frequently employed. Such programs are less scripted than formal code-emphasis programs, but have more connected text for the children to read. Phonics elements and skills are systematically sequenced and presented explicitly. The text they read might be authentic in the case of anthologies of original versions of children's literature, but less so in the case of traditional basal readers. In these programs, text is often manipulated to conform to various criteria.

Consolidating Primary-Grade Gains in Grade 3

Teachers in grades 3 to 5 must organize reading instruction according to the experiences the children had in kindergarten and first and second grades and according to their degree of success there. Several very basic changes from children's initial reading experiences begin to appear in their reading instruction in the late second grade, continuing into the third grade. Individual differences among children not only continue to exist but also grow into even greater differences. Some children have not been successful in kindergarten through second grade, most have been moderately successful, and others are leaping ahead in their abilities to process and benefit from both narrative and expository text. The result is an increased need for flexible grouping according to different needs. There is also an increased need for a variety of instructional materials on several levels, and a need for more sensitive instructional strategies, especially for children who are not meeting standards for the grade level. Although this process might not always be under the control of the individual classroom teacher, he or she should have the knowledge and skill necessary to develop such a program where that opportunity does exist or to adapt and augment the adopted program where possible.

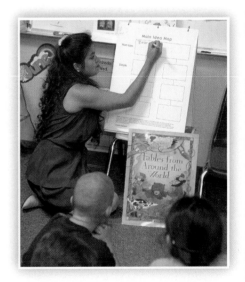

Whether you use a basal program or a literature-based program in your classroom, what is most important is making sure sound reading principles and instructional techniques are incorporated to meet the needs of your particular students. (David Young-Wolff/PhotoEdit)

USING CODE-EMPHASIS PRIMARY-GRADE PROGRAMS. A trend in some school districts is a reading program through which all children proceed at the same pace. Differences in home language, proficiency in English, previous experiences or lack of experiences with print, knowledge of the sound system of English, availability of print in the home and community, and parent roles in providing emergent literacy experiences are not considered. Typically, these programs focus on phonemic awareness and explicit decoding skills, with text reading occurring in decodable text or fragments of text that are written specifically to provide regular practice in decoding. The major goal of such programs is for the children to achieve **automaticity**, which involves rapid and accurate pronunciation of words that follow phonic generalizations.

Children may be discouraged from using cueing systems other than the graphophonic system. The obvious strength of such a program is seen in the formidable decoding skills of successful students when they attack regular words. But there are also problems with such a methodology:

Word Sorting

- The focus of instruction is on accurate and rapid pronunciation, not on comprehension.
- Motivation is a frequent problem in that decodable text tends to be less interesting than authentic literature.
- Because of the systematic and sequential nature of instruction, children who fail to master some skills and elements have difficulty learning subsequent skills and elements that are based on previous teaching. Similarly, some children are already able to decode virtually any unknown words through skilled use of all cueing systems, but they are required to follow the program nonetheless.
- Many children have difficulty in the application of phonics generalizations to words that are not regular, especially if they lack experience in using other cueing systems as tools in the decoding of unknown words.
- Many English language learners must try to learn to decode in a language they do not understand and in which they have not mastered the sound system.

These children will benefit from additional emphases in their later reading instructional experiences:

- Extensive reading of authentic children's literature and expository text
- Instruction in strategies from other cueing systems for use with new words that do not yield to analysis with regular phonics generalizations, such as using context clues, ignoring unknown words and reading on, using structural analysis skills, and questioning whether or not the word makes sense in the passage
- An increasing focus on silent reading as children gain proficiency in the middle grades, with questions to scaffold or guide that silent reading, followed by discussion

This situation was very much on Ms. DeLaney's mind when she planned her third-grade reading program. In grades 1 and 2, her children's teachers used a code-emphasis reading program that was characterized by explicit and systematic phonics in a highly scripted, direct instruction approach.

To meet their comprehension needs, Ms. DeLaney selected a basal program that has particularly attractive and interesting literature. She continued to build their phonics and related word recognition skills from the program, but she drew those brief lessons out of the literature that the children were reading in the program in a process called "breaking the lockstep." She taught the components in the program, but not always in the order in which they occurred in the teacher's manual.

USING BASAL PRIMARY-GRADE PROGRAMS. Basal reading programs tend to be broad and eclectic. Basal programs provide detailed teachers' manuals, often to the point of being scripted. Attention to phonemic awareness and phonics is usually ample. Instruction in the use of reading strategies, such as decoding, comprehension, and content reading skills, is provided in a sequence linked with the text to be read. Teachers often need to break the sequence by providing additional instruction related to a skill that is presented with a given story. This instruction might take several days. In the meantime, the children continue their reading of stories apart from this instruction, sometimes falling behind with respect to the skills presented with each story. A teacher might wisely decide to skip some direct skill development for children who have already demonstrated these abilities.

Making and Breaking Words

As children move into the middle grades from a basal reading program, you might choose the following options:

- Augment with multiple copies of trade books, apart from the basal reader or anthology.
- Provide scaffolding activities beyond those recommended in the basal reader when the children lack background knowledge about a story theme.
- Supplement skill development in decoding when gaps are encountered in the children's knowledge and skills, sometimes by reviewing word recognition lessons from previous levels of the program and sometimes by preparing new brief focused lessons.

Word Wall Activities

USING LITERATURE-BASED PRIMARY-GRADE PROGRAMS. Some children might have had a less structured experience in the primary grades, such as those who have been in a language-experience approach or a literature-based program. Children who were in a literature-based program have often had extensive experiences with shared reading in the primary grades. Their texts are often group sets of authentic literature, for example, multiple copies of *The Very Hungry Caterpillar* (Carle, 1983), that a group of children works with for a week or two before moving on to another piece of literature. These books are often leveled, with their difficulty having been assessed and taken into account before they are selected for use (Pinnell, Bridges, & Fountas, 1999).

Shared Reading

Decoding skills are sometimes taught opportunistically rather than systematically. For example, teachers using this approach might notice several words in a piece of text that begin with the same sound/letter correspondence. It might be an element that the children have not examined formally, such as the consonant blend *spl*. The teacher develops a lesson on this sound/letter correspondence that has emerged from words the children have encountered in the story.

When you teach a group of children who have such an experiential background, there might be a need for a more systematic approach to word recognition to augment their earlier instruction and for exposure to many types of comprehension scaffolding strategies.

Moving toward Independence in Grades 4 and 5

As children move further into the middle and upper grades, the same elements of the reading framework are in place, but the emphasis in each area and in the content changes. First, much more independent work takes place now that the children can read and write on their own. They still need support from the teacher, but they are much more self-sufficient.

Second, there is a diminished focus on skill development because the children have now mastered most of the word recognition skills they need to acquire. The focus on working with words in the four blocks is now more on vocabulary study than on letters and sounds, although occasional lessons are taught on letter/sound correspondences that are less regular or less frequently encountered, such as the silent consonants in *knee*, *write*, *pneumonia*, and *psychology* or prefixes of Greek origin, such as *poly-* and *biblio-*.

Word Origins and Derivations

A third major change is that more instruction emphasizes reading in the content areas of the curriculum, with some lessons focusing as much on science or social studies as on reading. Writing activities are also broadening out from early narrative efforts into various aspects of expository writing, including persuasion and argumentation.

Building Fluency in Reading

Although the reading **fluency** of many children is well established by the end of second grade, some children will benefit from continuing emphasis in this area. According to the report of the National Reading Panel (2000), children should read orally with appropriate timing, expressiveness, stress, and intonation (prosody). When necessary, fluency can be promoted through the following contextualized activities in grades 3 to 5:

- Providing daily self-selected reading of easy books at the children's independent levels
- Asking children to rehearse by reading to themselves before reading aloud
- Discouraging children from interrupting and correcting each other's oral reading
- Disregarding errors that do not change the meaning of the text and providing time for self-correction
- Focusing on comprehension by asking whether what was read incorrectly made sense when correction is needed
- Incorporating daily writing and encouraging invented spelling

Helping struggling readers to develop fluency in the middle grades is always a challenge because they already might be discouraged and they do not want to be perceived as needing to read easy books. Fielding and Roller (1992) suggest that the teacher can sometimes make more difficult books accessible to such children by doing the following:

- Having the children read to themselves first before reading aloud
- Providing paired reading opportunities in which a stronger reader supports a weaker reader (Caution: This can be overdone to the detriment of the more able reader.)
- Building background knowledge with easier books
- Having older troubled readers read easy books to younger children, which provides a good rationale for using less challenging materials at their independent reading levels
- Having children read the text in the mother tongue before reading orally in English (Crawford, 1993)

Finally, older children need extensive time for free-choice **sustained silent reading**, the self-selected reading aspect of the four blocks model. Worthy and Broaddus (2002) suggest beginning with about ten minutes each day, increasing to about thirty-five minutes each day as the children become capable of maintaining their attention and motivation for longer periods of time. Of course, the students need large numbers of high-interest books in a wide variety of genres.

Instructional Planning Structures

Throughout this book, you have seen and will continue to see numerous strategies that support various aspects of reading instruction. Teachers must make decisions daily, and sometimes by the hour and minute, as to which strategies to use, when to use them, how to sequence them, why to use them, and even how many to use.

A major factor in planning reading instruction relates to the type of program being implemented. A highly scripted program requires little planning in the sense of organizing instruction, but it might be necessary to prepare charts and other materials to be used with the lesson from the manual. Basal programs are also highly organized with many activities, usually more than can be accomplished during a typical lesson.

The task, then, is to plan the comprehensive reading program, assuming you have the latitude to combine elements and strategies from many sources to provide instruction that addresses the needs and interests of your students and the standards established for

Phonics and Phonological Awareness

How can we further develop children's reading fluency in grades 3 to 5?

myeducationlab
The Power of Classroom Practice
www.myeducationlab.com

Complete the activity "Developing Effective Fluency Interventions" to reflect on a third grade teacher's scaffolding of reading fluency in an individual conference. (To find this activity, go to the topic *Fluency* in MyEducationLab and click on Assignments and Activities.)

Teach It! 27

Paired Reading

the school. When that latitude is limited or does not exist at all, the opportunity to address children's individual needs precisely is diminished.

Planning at the Daily Level

When planning daily reading lessons, consider the elements recommended in the four blocks approach in Chapter 1:

Guided Reading and the Four Blocks Approach

1. Demonstration of authentic acts of reading and writing in meaningful literacy activities
2. Attention to working with words and developing students' knowledge of the structure of written language
3. Guided practice in meaningful reading and writing so that the children internalize effective strategies
4. Carrying out independent activities in which they apply and extend their reading and writing abilities and develop lifelong habits of literacy

State-adopted standards should also be reflected in lesson elements.

In grades 3 through 5, there will likely be more than one reading group in the classroom, sometimes three or four. Furthermore, one or more of those groups might be learning to read in Spanish or another language before moving into reading English later. The amount of planning that is necessary can be daunting for a beginning teacher, but just a year of teaching experience will lead to efficiencies that facilitate the planning process.

Most lesson plans contain several common elements:

- One or more student objectives that emerge from student needs and standards
- Necessary text and instructional materials
- An estimated amount of time planned for the lesson
- The body of the lesson:
  - Anticipation activities to motivate and to activate or introduce needed background knowledge and vocabulary
  - Reading activities to build knowledge for guiding and scaffolding the students' reading and comprehension of the text
  - Consolidation activities, in which students apply new knowledge, often by writing
- A brief focused word study lesson, usually an element that is related to or emerging from the text to be read
- Assessment, often incorporated into a consolidation activity after reading, and also part of an ongoing process of observation and record keeping described in Chapter 11

The Standards and Literacy box illustrates a lesson plan that might be designed to address some version of Little Red Riding Hood, a story that is familiar to most children. There are three objectives in the lesson, each emerging from one or more state standards—from the state of Massachusetts in this case. A description of materials that the teacher will need is provided, along with an estimated amount of time scheduled for the lesson.

The body of the lesson contains the three elements that make up most reading lessons. The prereading *anticipation activities* are brief and simple because the story is well known to most children. The *activities to build knowledge* during reading are focused on higher-order questions. The children read silently to find information needed to answer the teacher's questions, and they occasionally read evidence aloud to support their responses. The postreading *consolidation activities* allow them to negotiate the story during the oral retelling. They enjoy the authentic writing activity at the end. They are

Standards and Literacy

Sample Lesson Plan

Daily Lesson Plan: Third-Grade Level

Little Red Riding Hood

Prepared to align with standards from the Massachusetts Language Arts Curriculum Framework, 2000.

Reading and Literature Strand

Standard 12: Students will identify, analyze, and apply knowledge of the structure, elements, and theme of a work of fiction and provide evidence from the text to support their understanding.

Objective: Students read silently and respond to inferential questions about the text.

Reading and Literature Strand

Standard 7: Students will understand the conventions of print and the relationship of letters and spelling patterns to the sounds of speech.

Objective: Students correctly pronounce the unvoiced consonant digraph /th/ in final position in new words (brief focused lesson).

Composition Strands

Standard 19: Writing. Students will write compositions, such as narratives, summaries, essays, letters, or directions, with a clear focus supported by logically related ideas and sufficient detail.

Standard 20: Consideration of Audience and Purpose: Students will write for different audiences and purposes.

Objective: Students write letters that present a coherent argument and in which writing conventions of spelling, punctuation, and grammar are grade-level appropriate.

Materials: Twelve copies of the story text—Little Red Riding Hood; easel and chart paper, markers

Time: Forty minutes

Body of Lesson Plan *Anticipation reading activities:* The teacher shows the book cover, and the children immediately recognize a familiar story. The teacher asks one or two students to share the beginning of the story before they begin reading. The teacher introduces two vocabulary words using the context of the sentences in which they occur: *hood* and *forest*.

Building knowledge through reading activities: guided silent reading, chunking, and discussion

Read the first two pages to find out how the author told you that Little Red Riding Hood was a disobedient girl.

How did you know that the wolf was hungry? Please read the sentence that proves your answer. Let's read the next page to find out the effect on the wolf of his great hunger.

When Little Red Riding Hood returns home, what will her mother say to her? Why?

Read the next page to find out what kind of man the hunter was. How do you know that?

How do you know that this is a fantasy story?

Consolidation Reading Activities *Oral retelling of the story:* The children retell the story in their own words.

Writing activity: The teacher appoints each child to be an attorney for the wolf, who is in jail. Each child is to write a letter to the judge, asking for the release of the wolf. The teacher is the judge who will decide the wolf's fate in response to each letter. RAFT: Role is attorney; Audience is judge; Format is formal letter; Theme is getting the wolf out of jail (Buehl, 2001).

Read another fairy tale of your choice. Find two story elements that are similar to Little Red Riding Hood and two that are different and make notes about them. Be ready to talk about them tomorrow.

Brief Focused Lesson on Phonics Element *Step One:* Students listen to words that contain the final unvoiced consonant /th/, such as *teeth* (the wolf's teeth from the story), *both*, and *bath*. The teacher asks how the words sound alike, as well as other questions that focus the children on the target sound.

Step Two: The teacher shows known words that contain the sound, asking how the words look alike. The teacher asks the students to focus on the letters that make up the sound and where they are.

Step Three: The teacher shows new words that contain the same element in the final position and asks the children to pronounce them. The teacher then asks the children to make a rule about the letters and the sound they have pronounced.

Assessment *Reading comprehension during reading:* Success of the children in responding to inferential questions about the story and giving evidence for their answers.

Writing assignment: Coherence and persuasiveness of the argument to release the wolf; attention to the conventions of spelling, punctuation, and syntax.

Focused lesson on phonic element: Success of the children in decoding new words and correctly pronouncing the final sound of /th/ in them.

writing to a real audience—the judge (their teacher)—and they have an authentic purpose for writing. They will enjoy reading the teacher's judgments about the culpability of the wolf. The assessment of the children's achievement during the lesson is also authentic because the teacher is observing their actual listening, reading, thinking, and writing behaviors.

This teacher has incorporated a brief focused lesson on phonics that reflects a need of the children and uses vocabulary from the story as a base for the phonics mini-lesson. In this case, the unvoiced final sound of /th/ is the focus of the lesson, and the teacher will check phonemic awareness, even though the children will undoubtedly have no problem with this aspect in the third grade. Then the teacher moves from the sound to words the children already know that end in the element, some of which come from the story they have read. Finally, the children combine their background knowledge about the sound and the letters that make up the consonant digraph and draw a conclusion about the sound in that position in new and unknown words. The focused lesson on phonics is brief and explicit, only about five minutes, but it is related to and emerging from the literature they have read. It is in the analytic or whole-part-whole mode.

As this lesson plan is examined in terms of the four block multimethod, multilevel approach (Cunningham, Hall, & Sigmon, 2007), each of the four blocks—guided or directed reading, writing, self-selected reading, and working with words—is found. What is not readily seen in this example is the multilevel aspect of the four blocks approach. This could be accomplished by teaching the lesson to the entire class, making the text accessible to all students with multiple readings involving read-aloud, paired reading, and small flexible groups. There would be no problem in incorporating the writing and self-selected reading blocks of the approach, but the word study block might be less successfully applied in this example for grades 3 to 5. Some lower-achieving students might still not be comfortable with the unvoiced /th/ in the initial position, which they should probably know before moving on to that phoneme in the final position. And some children might have learned the sound/symbol correspondence of the final unvoiced /th/ years before.

Phonics and Phonological Awareness

How can phonics instruction emerge naturally from children's reading?

Strategies to Integrate into Daily Lessons

The rich variety of instructional strategies we introduced in earlier chapters can be used as scaffolding strategies to support children's reading comprehension for use in reading lessons (see Table 13.1). Scaffolding is the temporary support provided by teachers when children are engaged in a task within Vygotsky's "zone of proximal development." Bruner (1978) has described scaffolding as a temporary launching platform designed to support and encourage children's language development to higher levels of complexity. Pearson (1985) later described the temporary nature of scaffolding as the gradual release of responsibility. Good teachers intuitively use such scaffolding strategies to help children maintain their participation in learning activities (Crawford, 1994a).

Some strategies are appropriate as anticipation activities to prepare children for the reading they will do. Others might be helpful for building knowledge during their reading, supporting their comprehension, engaging them in the ideas they will encounter, and providing them with a structure to share their ideas with other students and the teacher. Others are most appropriate as consolidation activities to be completed at the conclusion of a lesson or even as homework. Some anticipation strategies, such as semantic mapping and semantic feature analysis, can be revisited as consolidation activities at the end of lessons for additions and revisions of initial predictions.

As you think about how these many strategies can be used in lessons, first consider that, as in choosing a meal in a cafeteria, you will take from each category the strategies that support your instruction, but not so many that the lesson becomes confused. Over the period of a year, you will likely use most or all of these strategies, but there is no need to use each one every week or even every month. As in all things, moderation is important. The most important activity in every lesson is the reading of connected text.

Teach It! 24

Semantic Analysis Feature

Table 13.1	Examples of Scaffolding Strategies to Support Reading Comprehension

ANTICIPATION ACTIVITIES BEFORE READING

Teacher read-aloud of beginning or selected parts of text

Discussion and predictions from book cover, title page, illustrations

Motivation by relating text to students' previous experiences

Think-pair-share

Quick-Write

Introduction of new vocabulary with semantic map, contextualized discussion

Activation or installation of background knowledge with semantic map, semantic feature analysis, advance organizer, shared discussion

ACTIVITIES TO BUILD KNOWLEDGE DURING READING

Guided or directed silent reading

Oral reading (generally limited to plays, dramatic activities, puppet shows, reading for expression, providing evidence)

Silent sustained reading

Think-aloud

Specific strategies, such as K-W-L, reader response, literature circles, the ReQuest procedure, reciprocal teaching, and questioning the author

CONSOLIDATION ACTIVITIES AFTER READING

Oral retelling

Written retelling

Review and elaboration of semantic map, semantic feature analysis from anticipation activities before reading

Writing workshop

Role-audience-format-theme (RAFT)

Reader's theater

Paired reading

Silent sustained reading

And more reading

And yet more reading

The recommended strategies that follow are those that will provide the underlying support, or scaffolding, needed for reading comprehension. It is the isolated skills development that you should consider carefully. Skill development should be viewed as an outcome of learning to read, not as its cause. When a child's needs suggest that a directed skill lesson is needed, you can seek out an appropriate one in the teacher's editions and workbooks of traditional reading and language arts programs.

Finally, the structure of the following strategies has been applied to the narrative text in the chapter-opening vignette, but it can also be applied to expository text in science and social studies textbooks and related readings. Reading can be taught in many other subject areas of the curriculum.

ANTICIPATION STRATEGIES BEFORE READING. An examination of Ms. De-Laney's lesson in the opening vignette makes it clear that she has given deep thought to organizing her instructional program in reading. She has identified the children's needs and has planned a program that addresses them carefully. She includes anticipation activities before the part of her lesson during which children read so they can activate background knowledge about the story and become familiar with the meanings of any new vocabulary words that might be needed. There are many strategies that she could use for these two purposes, but she uses only two to move the lesson along to the most important part: the reading.

Many strategies can be used to prepare children to read the text selected for a reading lesson. Two important factors affecting their readiness for reading are the background knowledge they bring to the task and vocabulary. Literature or expository text can be grouped into three levels of challenge with respect to these factors (see Table 13.2). The first category of text is not challenging because the background knowledge and vocabulary needed to understand it are present in the culture and language of the children who will read it. In addition, the story might be in their oral tradition, or they might have been exposed to the story in a read-aloud or storytelling activity before their reading. In this case, you might elect to skip unneeded preparation activities that are provided in the teacher's manual of the typical basal reading program. When English language learners have read a story in the mother tongue in a parallel version of their reading program, the story might fall into this category.

The second category of text requires some activation of background knowledge and introduction of new vocabulary, and those anticipatory activities are usually provided for in the teacher's manual. If not, you can develop the needed activities, as Ms. DeLaney did.

The third category of text is very difficult because the children have little background knowledge about it, and new vocabulary is extensive and challenging. Although anticipatory activities are provided in the teacher's manual, you might decide that they are insufficient or inadequate. One option is to skip the story or text and move on to the next one. Another is to augment the anticipatory activities before reading, especially in areas of need for the children. How do you know into which of the three categories the text falls? That decision requires a professional judgment based on your knowledge of the children's strengths and needs and on analysis of the text before they begin reading.

All children have acquired background knowledge, but there is often a discontinuity between the background knowledge a child has and that assumed by the authors of instructional materials or literature used in the classroom. Crawford (1994a) indicates that the discontinuity between the assumption and the reality is deeper when the child comes from a culture or speaks a language different from that of the children for whom the materials are designed or intended—usually middle-class native English speakers. A very effective anticipation strategy for activating and developing background knowledge is **semantic feature analysis** (Pittelman et al., 1991). This strategy involves helping students build

Teach It! 30

Terms in Advance

Table 13.2   Choosing Reading Texts Based on Readiness

TEXT LEVEL	READINESS CRITERIA		
	VOCABULARY	BACKGROUND KNOWLEDGE	TEACHER ACTION
easy	Part of oral traditions	Present in daily culture	Preparatory activities may not be necessary
1	Introduces some new vocabulary	Part of oral traditions	Some activities necessary to introduce new vocabulary
2		Some activation of background knowledge	
3	Extensive new vocabulary		Augment anticipation activities as necessary
difficult	Very difficult	Little activation of background knowledge	

Teach It!

Refer to the Teach It! appendix at the end of the book for further activities you can use to reinforce concepts discussed in this chapter.

Semantic Feature Analysis

Students in a suburban school may have limited background knowledge about the falcon, the topic of expository text from a science book. Related areas about which students in a suburban school would already likely have background knowledge might be *parrot, chicken,* and *crow.* These topics are listed on the *x*-axis of a chart (the top) and generic elements that relate to parrots, chickens, crows, and falcons are listed on the *y*-axis (the left) (see the chart on the right). The teacher prepares the chart before the lesson and presents it on the chalkboard, a transparency, or a large piece of paper. Information about the falcon should be available in the text to be read. In a prereading group activity led by the teacher, the students discuss, marking a plus (+) where they know that a relationship is true, a minus (–) where they know that it is not true, and a question mark (?) where they do not have information or do not agree.

On the sample chart, the prereading predictions of a student group are listed and marked accordingly. The students then read the text on falcons, looking for information about elements from the chart.

At the conclusion of the reading, the students discuss the text and return to the semantic feature analysis chart as a consolidation activity. They discuss again, change incorrect predictions, providing evidence they have found in the text, and fill in areas where question marks were indicated.

Unlike some other text-based strategies, semantic feature analysis lends itself well to reading expository text in mathematics and the sciences. For example, a mathematics teacher might list the following elements in the left column: triangle, isosceles triangle, parallelogram, trapezoid, square, rectangle, right triangle, equilateral triangle, and circle. Across the top, the teacher might list such elements as parallel lines, nonparallel lines, straight lines, no straight lines, equal lines, pairs of equal lines, angles, equal angles, pairs of equal angles, and right angles.

Semantic Feature Analysis Chart
The Falcon

	parrot	chicken	crow	falcon
What color are they?				
Brilliant colors	+	–	–	?
Brown	–	+	–	?
Blue	–	–	–	–
Black	–	–	+	?
What do they eat?				
Meat	–	–	+	?
Fruit	+	–	+	?
Seeds	–	+	–	+
Where do they live?				
In the jungle	+	–	–	?
In the mountains	–	–	–	?
On the farm	–	+	+	–
In the desert	–	–	–	?
In the city	–	–	+	?

knowledge about a new topic by comparing it to knowledge of related topics about which students do have background knowledge. The Teach It! box illustrates this effective anticipation strategy.

READING STRATEGIES FOR BUILDING KNOWLEDGE DURING READING. Children learn to read by reading. This fundamental idea should underlie your thinking about how children's time is best spent during reading instruction. Rather than having children study about reading by mastering skills, maximize the amount of reading they do. Some obvious counterproductive strategies are pencil-and-paper exercises. Another is the still-common practice of round-robin oral reading, in which each child takes a turn reading aloud to the group or class. This usually consists of having a child laboriously reading aloud a passage she or he has never before read, even silently, while the rest of the children in the group pretend to listen or read along. You might have memories of counting the children ahead of you in the first grade so that you could determine which paragraph you would read, although some wise teachers skipped around to thwart that strategy.

The child reading aloud usually focuses on pronunciation, not on understanding what is being read. The other children are either bored or preparing to read when their turn comes. This practice is especially deceiving in regard to children who learned to read first

Table 13.3	Reasons for Minimizing Round-Robin Oral Reading

- It diminishes the amount of actual reading that children do.
- The focus is on pronunciation, not comprehension.
- Strong readers love to perform by reading orally, but they could read more, and faster, by reading silently.
- Poor readers hate to read aloud, disclosing their reading problems for the whole class to hear.
- Both children and teachers dislike listening to the agonizing efforts of poor readers.
- Although teachers can informally assess student outcomes during oral reading, a more systematic approach is needed (see the informal reading inventory discussed in Chapter 11).
- Teachers sometimes convert an oral reading lesson into a phonics lesson that interferes with comprehension.

in Spanish, for example. They can read orally with confidence in English, albeit with a Spanish accent and no comprehension. They are, in fact, pronouncing and not reading. Table 13.3 identifies various reasons why round-robin reading should be kept to a minimum.

There are, however, some excellent uses for oral reading: reading a sentence aloud to provide evidence for a response to a question; reading poetry; reading roles in puppet shows and readers' theater; assessment; sharing writing; buddy reading or paired reading as a practice activity; read-aloud to parents, grandparents, or siblings; and improvement of fluency. Otherwise, valuable instructional time in grades 3 to 5 should be used for guided silent reading and comprehension development.

It is more difficult for teachers to provide extra support to English language learners because their need for it might be less obvious during the largely independent activity of reading silently. The need should be based on children's abilities to interact with the teacher and each other about what they have been reading—that is, their comprehension of what they have been reading.

Guiding children's reading with questions, a variation on DRA, provides valuable support in maintaining comprehension (Crawford, 1993). The teacher needs to precede the children's reading of a page or passage of a piece of literature by asking a higher-order question, that is, an open-ended question whose answer requires the child to use background knowledge and combine it with information from the selection to be read. An example of such a question is "Please read page 71 to find out why the main character is worried." Students will read page 71 to find the answer to the question. It focuses them on comprehension, not on production and accurate oral reading.

This questioning strategy brings key story concepts to children's attention as they read, and, perhaps more important, it provides moral support, interest, and motivation from someone who cares about them: the teacher. Children who cannot or will not read a lengthy selection alone might do so in chunks of a paragraph, or a page or two at a time within the security of a supportive teacher-directed group. These chunks are manageable and comprehensible sections, and questions can be used very effectively and naturally to accomplish this chunking. You can structure children's reading with questions that elicit predictions, with timely resolution of those predictions through discussion and any needed mediation.

Although there is considerable debate about the value of teaching reading comprehension skills through direct instruction, there are enough other reasons to guide silent reading with higher-order or comprehension-level questions. Table 13.4 provides some examples of poor low-level questions and strong higher-order questions. It takes no longer to formulate and ask a higher-order comprehension question than a low-level recall question before asking children to read to find the answer. Guided silent reading provides an

Teach It! 28

Readers' Theater

Teach It! 31

Directed Reading-Thinking Activity (DRTA)

Table 13.4	Examples of Different Levels of Questions from "Little Red Riding Hood"

LOW-LEVEL RECALL QUESTIONS

Tell what happened on the first page of the story.

Where did the wolf first see Little Red Riding Hood?

What color is Little Red Riding Hood's cape?

Where is Little Red Riding Hood taking the food basket?

HIGHER-ORDER COMPREHENSION QUESTIONS

How did the author tell you that Little Red Riding Hood was a disobedient girl?

How did you know that the wolf was hungry?

What was the effect on the wolf of his great hunger?

When Little Red Riding Hood returns home, what do you think her mother will say to her? Why?

Why did Little Red Riding Hood go to Grandmother's house by the forest road?

What kind of man was the hunter? How do you know that?

What advice would you give to Little Red Riding Hood for the future? Why?

opportunity for children to make inferences and predictions, identify cause-and-effect relationships, and apply other higher-order critical thinking skills when their comprehension is supported (Crawford, 1993). This is seen in Ms. DeLaney's lesson in the chapter-opening vignette. Her students are now in the third grade, and they need to read silently with a focus on comprehension. But their abilities in this area are still limited, and she therefore scaffolded their comprehension by guiding their silent reading with carefully formulated higher-order questions. She also limited how much they read after each question to an amount they could understand and remember for the discussion that followed each chunk. Ms. DeLaney provided occasional opportunities for oral reading, as described in her lesson. She often asked children to read aloud the sentence or sentences that provided evidence for their responses to her higher-order questions.

CONSOLIDATION STRATEGIES AFTER READING. Ms. DeLaney concluded her lesson with two consolidation activities. She integrated an **oral retelling** and a small authentic writing assignment into the closing part of the lesson—part to be done while she was with the group and the rest to be done after she left them. She collected the children's written predictions and later responded briefly in writing to the content of each one. If she noted a spelling error in a child's prediction, she used the word correctly in her response to that child. She also reviewed their papers for common problems, such as the correct use of the comma in a series. Instead of correcting that error, she would plan a minilesson on the element or detail for the next day. The children could then examine their own work and make needed changes or corrections.

Retelling is an excellent consolidation activity after reading. An oral retelling provides children with the opportunity to negotiate with each other about the meaning of the selection and requires them to listen very attentively to each other (Brown & Cambourne, 1990). Through this process, children can often incorporate new information gained through reading into existing background knowledge. They also observe that retelling promotes multiple readings of text as a part of the negotiation process. Koskinen et al. (1988) found that the verbal rehearsal that occurs in the retelling process also serves to improve the reading comprehension of less proficient readers. English language learners might elect to retell in their mother tongue what they read or heard in their second language (Crawford, 1993).

Retelling also provides a means for integrating writing into the program. Either through a cooperative learning process or through individual or paired writing, children can prepare a written retelling (Strickland & Feeley, 1985). As a result of their earlier discussion, the knowledge they gained through reading, and such prereading activities as semantic mapping and the examination of story grammar, children are better prepared to write a well-structured retelling. Like the demonstration that they provide during read-alouds, teachers should also model retelling with an actual example.

The most obvious consolidation activity after reading should not be overlooked: more reading. If you are successful in providing high-quality literature that children will choose to read and in supporting their comprehension, then you can expect gains in all areas of the language arts. Reading is more powerful than direct instruction in developing vocabulary, grammar, spelling, and reading comprehension, especially for English language learners. Provide extensive free voluntary reading with messages that are understood in low-anxiety situations. Good writing is promoted more by extensive reading than by writing (Krashen, 1985, 1993).

Writing and Reading Connections

How can writing be incorporated into the consolidation activity of retelling?

Teach It! 40

Story Maps

Long-Term Planning Using Thematic Units

The **thematic unit** is a very useful structure for organizing reading instruction across the curriculum around a topic that is of interest to children. It consists of a framework for organizing the work of several days or weeks (Zarrillo, 1994). Thematic units usually include goals and objectives, learning activities, instructional materials, and assessment, with connections to standards in several areas of the curriculum. The thematic unit provides an opportunity for the teacher to integrate reading and writing across the curriculum because a part of the unit can incorporate expository text from social science, science, and other subject areas. Narrative text on the theme from related literature, videos, images, and music found on the Internet can be included, as well. As we said in Chapter 1, reading instruction is often more productive when it is combined with content—when it is used to teach knowledge worth knowing.

The thematic unit included in the Integrating Across the Curriculum feature that follows also incorporated critical literacy strategies in several activities that addressed the cross-cutting issue of environmental education. These included reading news accounts of dolphin kills and checking tuna can labels to look for the dolphin-safe symbol, and culminated in social action: student posters urging shoppers to buy only dolphin-safe tuna. It is also an excellent place to incorporate the writing process, especially persuasive writing. Powell, Cantrell, and Adams (2001) provide several assumptions that underlie critical literacy and that apply in the thematic unit:

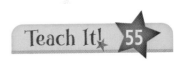

Teach It! 55

The Writing Workshop

- Literacy instruction can never be neutral because of the decisions teachers make in planning every lesson.
- Critical literacy is a major element of a strong democratic system, requiring shared decision making in society.
- Literacy instruction can lead to transformative action.

This thematic unit provides opportunities for teachers to address standards across the curriculum. Activities that lead children to meet science standards in this thematic unit will also involve reading both expository text and narrative text, performing an experiment that requires graphing outcomes, writing a report about those outcomes, or searching a website to learn what others have found out about the problem being explored.

Standards from the different subject areas of social studies, science, and other disciplines guide teachers as they choose content and skills from the content areas to combine into literacy-rich thematic units. There is much to teach, and teaching time is limited.

Integrating Across the Curriculum
A Thematic Unit on Endangered Dolphins

Goals/Objectives*	Activities	Assessment	Text Sources	Interval**
Formulate questions about dolphins and their endangered status	View video	Quality of student questions generated	Nat'l Geographic's Dolphins: The Wild Side (VHS); news videos; cans of tuna	One day
Read with fluency	Paired reading	Accuracy of oral reading in primary level book	In Dolphin Time by Kathleen Dudzinski	Periodic over four weeks
Read silently with comprehension	Guided reading in small groups; discuss findings in literature circles	Observation; quality of discussion	See and Explore Library: Whales, Dolphins, and Porpoises by Mark Carwardine; other sources	Four days
Read silently with comprehension	Guided reading during science lesson	Observation; quality of discussion	Science textbook	Two days
Locate information on the Internet or in newspapers; interest groups formed to work together	Select theme to research: Poem about dolphins; Miami Dolphins football team; Greek myth about dolphins; other themes of interest	Criteria: use of descriptors, refinement of descriptors, appropriateness of selected text	Google.com	Periodic over four weeks
Write informational and persuasive text about protecting endangered dolphins	RAFT (Role/Audience/Format/Theme) Word processing	Rubrics	Dolphins: What They Can Teach Us by Mary M. Cerullo	Three days following research activities
Illustrate informational writing accurately	Illustrate informational and persuasive writings	Relationship of illustrations to text written by students	Drawing Whales and Dolphins by Books Watermill	One day following writing activities
Read silently with comprehension	Silent sustained reading of self-selected narrative and expository books about dolphins and related ocean mammals	Motivation, conferences	Island of the Blue Dolphins by Scott O'Dell, Diving Dolphins by Laura Hamilton Waxman, and other leveled books	Periodic over four weeks

* Goals and objectives reflect Texas state standards (TEKS) below.
** Note: Days do not have to be consecutive.

The objectives of this thematic unit address many standards from English language and reading, science, and social studies from the Texas Essential Knowledge and Skills (TEKS) (Texas Education Agency, 2009).

English Language Arts and Reading, 2009–2010

- Distinguish fact from opinion in a text and explain how to verify what is a fact (Reading/Comprehension of informational text/Procedural texts)
- Explain the positive and negative impacts of advertisement techniques used in various genres of media to impact consumer behavior (Reading/Media literacy)
- Write responses to literary or expository texts and provide evidence from the text to demonstrate understanding (Writing/expository and procedural texts)

Science

- Make wise choices in the use and conservation of resources and the disposal or recycling of materials (Scientific processes)
- Analyze and interpret information to construct reasonable explanations from direct and indirect evidence (Scientific processes)

Social Studies

- Identify different points of view about an issue or topic (Social studies skills)

Addressing subject area contents and skills at the same time as teaching literacy is a welcome time-saver. But there are other considerations besides saving time. Contents from social studies, science, literature, and other subjects must be developed thoughtfully and well—requiring that concepts and skills be introduced in careful sequences and practiced, deepened, and extended in subsequent lessons. Thus the development of integrated thematic units and other integrated curricular frameworks across the school year, and from year to year, can lead to thoughtful discussions among teachers. Extensive planning sessions may be devoted to **curriculum mapping**. Curriculum mapping is the careful sequencing, articulation, and integration of contents and skills, usually across multiple years of instruction. Authors such as Heidi Hayes Jacobs (2004, 2006), James Beane (1997), Susan Drake (1998), and Anthony Fredericks (1998) have written valuable resources for teachers involved in this fascinating and challenging work.

Assessment: Revisiting the Informal Reading Inventory

Although there are already differences in achievement among children at each level from kindergarten to second grade, there is a much broader range of levels of proficiency in reading and writing in grades 3 through 5. Most states and school districts now conduct an annual or biannual assessment of children's reading achievement at several grade levels, but the data that those standardized tests yield are not designed for use in planning instruction for individual children. Teachers need to gather information about the individual strengths and needs of each child in order to plan instruction, select appropriate instructional materials, and group children.

In the chapter-opening vignette, Ms. DeLaney had divided her students into ability groups for that part of her instruction. According to results from the informal assessment she administered during the first week of school, the 27 students in her classroom were reading at grade levels from second to fifth, with one group reading slightly below grade level, one group reading at grade level, and some children reading at the fourth- and fifth-grade levels. See Chapter 11 for details on how she completed this task.

Language and Diversity

What is the effect of language and dialectical differences on the interpretation of oral reading errors in the informal reading inventory?

Interpreting IRI Results for Linguistically Diverse Students

Most assessment strategies used with English speakers function well in other languages and also in English with English language learners. Some adaptations are indicated, however. For example, one element of evaluating oral reading accuracy in the informal reading inventory is mispronunciation, each occurrence of which is counted as an oral reading error or miscue. When a mispronunciation error can be attributed to a conflict point with the mother tongue or dialect of English and when it does not interfere with comprehension, a short *i* pronounced as a long *e*, for example, then an error would not be counted.

Kenneth Johnson (personal communication, 1977) provides a test sentence to illustrate this principle for the African American child whose mother tongue is African American Vernacular English. The sentence often elicits a mispronunciation that has the potential to interfere with comprehension. The child is asked to read the following sentence aloud: "As I passed the sign, I read it." In conformance with African American Vernacular English, the African American child sometimes pronounces *passed* as *pass*, dropping the *-ed* suffix that is also a past tense marker. If the child comprehends the marker, that is, understands that *passed* is in the past tense even though he pronounced it as in the present tense, then the child will pronounce *read* in the past tense. If not, the child will pronounce *read* in the present tense. According to Johnson, these children invariably

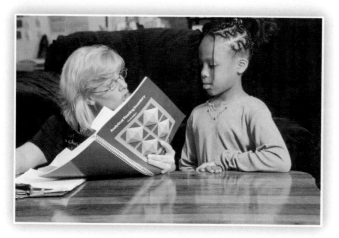

Reading assessments can help identify a child's reading level as well as comprehension. How can a teacher use this information to plan for instruction? (Lindfors Photography)

correctly pronounce *read* in the past tense. In a study of teachers who administered IRIs to Spanish-speaking children, Lamberg, Rodríguez, and Tomas (1978) concluded that to avoid such problems, teachers need special training to use them with English language learners.

Other Informal Measures of Reading and Writing

As you saw in Chapter 11, there are many informal measures that teachers can use to assess their students' progress through the developmental processes of learning to read and write. Chantell DeLaney, the teacher in the chapter-opening vignette, uses many of these measures daily. Although she makes effective use of the informal reading inventory periodically for all students, and when needed for individual students, she can observe the frustration level in her students' physical behaviors. She might note that some children rarely participate in discussion activities after silent reading, even with the support of the many scaffolding activities she provides. She takes careful notes about these observations and uses them in planning future instruction.

Each student in Ms. DeLaney's classroom has a portfolio of writing products. She urges them to add a sample of writing to their portfolios from their work each week. This can be used as a motivation tool when students are able to observe their progress as they page through the portfolio, week after week. It is also a valuable tool for use in parent conferences to document for parents their children's progress.

Transitioning English Language Learners

It is often during grade 3 that English language learners who have been in a mother tongue bilingual education reading program since first grade begin a process of transitioning to English language reading instruction. This may occur earlier or later for some children, depending on their age when they arrived. When children speak and understand English at an intermediate level, and when they are reading confidently in the mother tongue at least at a second- or third-grade level, they are ready to begin a formal transition to English, although they will have had many English language reading experiences before the formal transition. How can teachers help English language learners begin to make the transition into English language reading instruction?

What can you do to help your ESL students make the transition to English-language reading instruction?

Using the Language Experience Approach in English

In the past, it was commonly held that second-language learners should not begin learning to read and write at all in the second language until they had reached an intermediate level of fluency in speaking it. Teachers now recognize that informal processes of reading and writing in the second language can begin early in the English language acquisition process, especially for children who have developed literacy skills in the

The World of Reading

Using the IRI Capacity Level as a Measure of English Language Proficiency

Many commercial instruments are available for assessing English language proficiency. Most examine pronunciation, knowledge of syntax, vocabulary knowledge, and other discrete skills. Because state and federal funds are often involved for qualifying students, English language learners are usually assessed for redesignation as fluent English speakers in a very formalistic and legalistic process. The information gained from this type of assessment is less useful for instructional planning. To teach English language learners to read in English, teachers need to know how well they comprehend English.

According to A. Crawford (1982, 2000), teachers can use the reading capacity level, another level yielded by informal reading inventory, as a measure of listening comprehension that is a useful reflection of English language proficiency. They can use the IRI to make an informed decision about readiness for English language reading instruction in given materials by reading a selected passage aloud to the child. Crawford reported that children who read in the mother tongue and also respond correctly to 75 percent of comprehension-level questions about the material read to them in English usually have sufficient second-

language proficiency to begin learning to read at the highest level at which they successfully respond to those questions.

For example, a second-grade teacher who believes that an English language learner may be ready for formal English reading instruction would read a passage of 100 to 200 words aloud to the child from the second-grade text used for teaching English reading in the classroom. Children who can respond correctly to three of four comprehension-level (not recall) questions about the text in English when it is read to them are providing evidence that they are ready to begin formal reading instruction in English at the second-grade level. This level is described as one of cognitive academic-language proficiency (CALP), explained in detail in Chapter 15. For those children learning to read in their mother tongue in a bilingual program, this is often at or near the grade level at which they are reading in that mother tongue. They will need all of the scaffolding support described in this chapter. The levels of their English vocabulary and syntax will in no way correspond to those of children who have been communicating in English since birth.

mother tongue. This early reading instruction is informal and incidental; it is not a formal English reading program. In addition, this incidental instruction should not be substituted for mother tongue instruction when it is possible to provide it.

Bilingual teachers who teach reading in the mother tongue recognize that children's motivation to begin reading and writing in the English language is strong. It has already been noted that, where possible, it is most beneficial for children to learn to read and write first in the mother tongue, but teachers can begin a cautious, early introduction to literacy in a second language to take advantage of that motivation. Although it is employed mostly with young children, the language-experience approach (LEA) can also be used in grades beyond second grade when children are just beginning to learn to read in English or when older preliterate children need more time at the earliest stages of English reading, especially if they are unable to read in the mother tongue. Some migrant children or the children of refugees might never have been in school, even though they are ten or twelve years of age, or older.

There are many LEA activities that can be adapted for English language learners. For example, multiple readings of the text are helpful (Crawford, Allen, & Hall, 1995). Using a copy of the text with empty spaces where words have been left out, children can practice reading the text and try to predict what words should be in the spaces. This practice is known as an **oral cloze procedure**. When reading the text with the children, the teacher can pause briefly upon encountering each missing word, and then write in those words as the children identify them.

Children may accumulate new words they learn, with these collections serving as their personal word files. After they have fifteen or twenty words, they can do sorting activities with their word files (Bear et al., 2007). Finding words that start with the same letter and sound is a way in which some children learn to associate letters and sounds, allowing them

Language Experience with English-Language Learners

Making and Using Word Banks

to learn best about letters and sounds from words they already know. They can look for words that are names of people, places, animals, colors, foods, and clothing.

If children are collecting the words they can read, they can try to build sentences with them. You might need to demonstrate before asking them to try it. Read their sentences to them if they cannot read them independently. Children can also try to reconstruct the same sentences they have used in their dictated texts.

One nonthreatening way to elicit text that reflects more mature syntax and vocabulary is an adaptation called the *collaborative chart story*. When children are dictating and beginning to read with confidence later in the process, ask them to negotiate their suggested text with the group. You can invite questions from other children about a suggested sentence, for example, by asking how they feel about the way it is stated and how effectively the vocabulary provided expresses what the group wants to say. When children who have dictated sentences with grammatical errors hear suggestions from other children about how it might be said in another way, they invariably agree to the change. The children do not view this collaboration as correction, but rather as reflecting the contributions they all make together in communicating with the audience that will read their text later. It is probably better to accept exactly what is dictated at the beginning of the LEA process so that children can see the direct links among what they say, what you write down, and what the group reads back later.

The language-experience approach can be used with students who are learning to read in English as their second language as a way to initiate students into print of interest and relevance to them (Dixon & Nessel, 1983; Moustafa & Penrose, 1985; Nessel & Jones, 1981). According to Crawford (1993), the language-experience approach also provides a means through which students can experience authentic literature in English that is above their ability to read and comprehend for themselves. After you tell or read a story aloud, the students can then dictate the story back, that is, retell it for you to record, although probably in a less complicated version than the original.

Beginning a language-experience approach activity with a piece of authentic literature will often result in a better structured dictation than the random list of sentences that often results from LEA dictations stimulated by an illustration, a manipulative, or other prompts. Peck (1989) suggests that listening to read-aloud stories helps children to develop a sense of story structure, which should be reflected in their dictated version, and it enhances their abilities to predict in this and other stories. The dictated text allows children to think, talk, read, and write about the piece of literature and to be exposed to its valuable cultural content. At the same time, they are actively interacting with it at a level of comprehension and of second-language proficiency appropriate for their stage of development.

Vocabulary Development

Reading is also a major factor in the vocabulary development of English language learners. Second-language acquisition and literacy in English can contribute mutually to each other's development for intermediate English language learners. In keeping with a meaning-based approach to teaching English language learners, Harmon (1998) provides an excellent contextualized strategy for vocabulary development. She provides two examples of how a teacher uses a new term and then elaborates and expands its meaning immediately:

> *"Let's start recounting the events of the story. Let's tell about the beginning, middle, and end."*
> *"This is an excerpt—a small part."*

In another strategy described by Nagy and colleagues (1993) and by Cummins and Corson (1997), Spanish-speaking students can use cognates they recognize from Spanish and English to support their reading comprehension in English. Words such as *general* are the same in spelling and meaning in both languages, and many other cognates are the same in meaning and similar in spelling, such as an example provided by Nagy and colleagues: *transform* in English and *transformar* in Spanish. But looking beyond their study, children must also be taught to be wary of such false cognates as *actual*, which means *nowadays* in Spanish, and *dime*, which means *give me.*

When children read, their lack of vocabulary knowledge is often an obstacle to comprehension. Because they may have insufficient academically related background knowledge and vocabulary development in the mother tongue that would accompany it, this can be an even greater problem for children who must read in their second language. Although vocabulary is an aspect of background knowledge in prereading, it is treated separately here so we can examine several concepts that relate more specifically to this topic.

One aspect of vocabulary development relates to the richness of language that surrounds children. It is well recognized that children become familiar with the meanings of words when those meanings are highly contextualized, not when they are studied in isolation as new vocabulary words. It follows, then, that a richer language environment should result in increased exposure to contextualized vocabulary and therefore to greater understanding of meanings (Crawford, 1994b).

What can you do to help your ESL students make the transition to English-language reading instruction? (Michael Newman/PhotoEdit)

Schools often postpone or even eliminate instruction for at-risk children, however, in the very areas of the curriculum where new vocabulary words will be offered in the most highly contextualized ways—in science, social studies, art, music, health, and other areas of the curriculum. This is even more common for children who are learning in their second language. According to Crawford (1993), teachers must ensure that these areas of the curriculum are provided for all children, including English language learners, and that they are presented in such a way that contextualized exposure to a rich vocabulary is promoted.

Another aspect of vocabulary is the issue of direct instruction. Although many vocabulary words will be acquired incidentally, some literature or content selections will contain a few vocabulary words that must be clearly grasped if the text is to be understood. There will be other words not known to the children that need not be addressed through direct instruction because they are not critical to understanding the selection or because they can be quickly analyzed through the context in which they appear.

Many of the strategies recommended for the activation or development of background knowledge constitute direct approaches to vocabulary instruction. Semantic mapping is one of these strategies, but its application should be limited to those key and conceptually difficult vocabulary terms that are more in the realm of background knowledge. Otherwise, there will be little time left for reading following the completion of anticipation activities before reading.

"Word Conversations" for Primary Grades

Adapting Phonics and Decoding Strategies for English Language Learners

English language learners bring to the classroom phonemic awareness of sounds in the mother tongue. They should first learn phonics in the mother tongue out of the context of words they already recognize on sight, probably acquired from their print environment and from language experience charts and big books. English language learners who learn phonics in the mother tongue generally have a much easier time learning phonics in English than do children who must learn phonics first in English. Some languages, such as Spanish and Korean, are very regular in their sound/letter relationships. Not only is phonics easier to learn, but children have more confidence in the process than do children who are learning to read in a language in which sound/letter relationships are not regular, such as English.

The language-experience approach and shared reading are holistic strategies for teaching reading. In these strategies, teachers do not begin with phonics. But learning

Language and Diversity

What advantages may English language learners have in learning phonics in English if they first learn to read in the mother tongue?

about letters and sounds (phonics) is a part of learning to read in all methods, including these. In a developmental approach to teaching about letters and sounds, children should learn about reading first. They should dictate many LEA charts and read them, learning to read some 100 to 200 words on sight. They should have many shared book reading experiences, and then they are ready to learn about letters and sounds using words they already know in English.

The real dilemma for English language learners is when they must learn phonics in English first. Although they might have learned to speak and understand English, they still lack the phonemic awareness skills in English that a native speaker has. For example, a native Spanish-speaking child will speak the forty-three sounds of English using the twenty-five sounds of Spanish. There are only five vowel sounds in Spanish, but fifteen in English. This accounts for the difficulty that Spanish-speaking children have in pronouncing short vowels in English, especially the schwa; they have similar difficulty in "reading" (correctly pronouncing) these sounds in a phonetic approach to reading. Although there are variations in the differences between other languages and English, similar difficulties arise for children who speak those languages. However, for children who learn phonics in their mother tongue, the process of learning English phonics is much easier because they have already figured out how the process works. The process transfers from the mother tongue, even if many of the sounds do not.

Finally, Sleeter and Grant (1999) remind teachers that they need to distinguish between mechanics and meaning when teaching students whose mother tongue is not English or standard American English. They concluded that teachers should not be bogged down in remediation whenever they encounter gaps in student learning that relate more to mechanics than to understanding.

Writing and Spelling

A major principle of a developmental view of literacy is the interdependence of listening, speaking, reading, and writing. Hudelson (1984) observed that English language learners address the four language processes as a totality, not as separate entities. According to Fitzgerald (1993), writing begins when children can draw, and there is no need to wait for reading. These ideas can be extended to English language learners, who should be encouraged to write in the second language early, especially if they have writing skills in their mother tongue. The errors they make should be viewed in the same way that errors in oral production are viewed: as a part of the natural processes of approximation and acquisition (Crawford, 1994a).

Language and Diversity

How can we support the development of writing in English for English language learners?

For English language learners, writing can flow out of a variety of language acquisition activities, including the key vocabulary and language-experience approaches to reading and the consolidation strategy of written retellings after reading text. The structuring of their writing or their selection of vocabulary may be further supported through the use of semantic maps.

Spelling is another area in which instructional strategies must be adapted for English language learners. Consistent with the communicative approach principle of minimizing error correction and with the developmental nature of second-language acquisition and literacy, described in Chapter 15, teachers of English language learners, like teachers of English speakers, should accept the invented spellings of their students as a very natural aspect of their developmental growth in writing. There are differences, however, in how English language learners will progress through some of the developmental stages of invented spelling.

In the letter name–alphabetic spelling stage of Bear et al. (2007), English language learners begin to approximate an alphabetic orthography and to conceptualize the alphabetic principle (see Chapter 5). They begin to demonstrate the relationship between sound and letter, and they sometimes use letter names as words. They begin to understand the left-to-right convention, and they may begin to segment words. Differences in the nature of invented spelling between languages will appear. The use of consonants tends to predominate over the use of vowels when children write in English as a mother tongue, for example, but vowels predominate over consonants when children write in Spanish as a mother tongue (Ferreiro & Rodríguez, 1994).

In the within-word pattern spelling stage of Bear and colleagues (2007), children have learned most basic rules of the orthographic system. They are aware of such word structures as prefixes, suffixes, contractions, compound words, and homonyms, and they continue to learn some less common spelling patterns and rules. It is at this stage that they begin to recognize when a word looks correct, a phenomenon that corresponds to the natural approach characteristic in which second-language learners begin to recognize when something sounds right or feels right. They are able to spell a large number of words automatically.

English language learners who are literate in another language will tend to move much more rapidly through developmental stages of spelling in their new second language of English than they did in their primary language. Nathenson-Mejia (1989) found that Spanish-speaking children in the beginning stages of English spelling made extensive use of Spanish pronunciation in their invented spellings in English writing. Edelsky (1982) made the same observation in a more generic sense when she adopted the positive point of view that children are applying some mother tongue writing skills to the second language rather than the negative point of view that it reflected interference from the first language on the second.

Interactive Writing

Scaffolding Strategies for Improving Reading Comprehension

Your own experiences in learning another language might remind you of the importance of reading for comprehension as opposed to word calling. Remember that comprehension and communication are the focus of reading and writing. There are many reading strategies that will help to ensure that children focus on comprehension instead of only on correct pronunciation.

The use of scaffolding strategies to support the comprehension of children in general is of great importance; but for English language learners, it is the difference between success and failure (Crawford, 1994a). There has been a tendency to place some English language learners in perpetual compensatory or remedial programs. There, teachers expect them to learn to read and write by acquiring isolated skills through interaction with incomplete fragments of language. These children rarely move successfully into the mainstream curriculum; more frequently, they leave these programs only when they complete their schooling—all too often as dropouts. Scaffolding strategies sometimes resemble most closely the enrichment activities that teachers of English language learners never seem to have time for because they are busy teaching the isolated skills that the children appear to lack. Variations of two common comprehension strategies are especially effective in working with English language learners.

THE CUMULATIVE SEMANTIC MAP. Ordinarily, a semantic map is used for activating background knowledge or introducing vocabulary as an anticipation activity before reading. It is developed and completed for one or two related lessons and not referred to subsequently. Teachers often find, however, that they are dealing with some language topics on repeated occasions. Therefore, it can be useful to return to a semantic map on such a topic, to add to it, and to contrast new additions with earlier ones. Crawford has identified this semantic mapping strategy as the **cumulative semantic map** (Crawford, 1994a).

Figure 13.1 shows a cumulative semantic map on the theme of feelings and emotions that has been augmented periodically during the first few weeks of school (Crawford, 2000). A teacher might introduce the new word *furious* from a piece of literature they are about to read and ask children where it should be added to the existing cumulative semantic map for words about feelings and emotions. At that point, the children can discuss how much anger the word *furious* implies, as compared to *miffed*, *enraged*, and *upset*, which had been added to the semantic map on earlier occasions. They add the new word *furious* to their cumulative semantic map. Many weeks later, the map has been elaborated, as seen in Figure 13.2, and, of course, this process continues through the school year.

Figure 13.1

A Cumulative Semantic
Map.

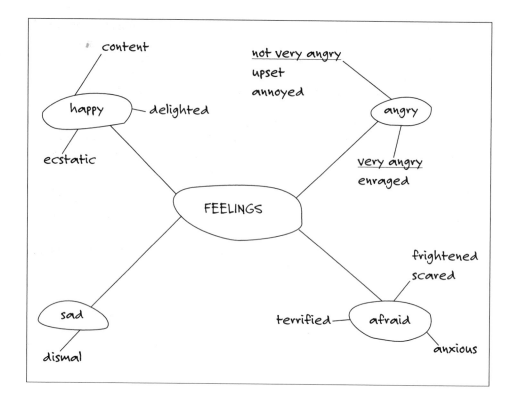

When written on sticky notes, the various words in a cumulative semantic map can be arranged and rearranged in ascending order of increasing anger as children negotiate the meanings with each other. Moustafa (1997) suggests placing words on cards for charts with cellophane tape across the top. The teacher can use the same piece of tape over and over by affixing the cards to a large wall chart made of plastic shower curtain material. This strategy can be adapted to the cumulative semantic map, which facilitates the mov-

Figure 13.2

An Elaborated
Cumulative Semantic
Map.

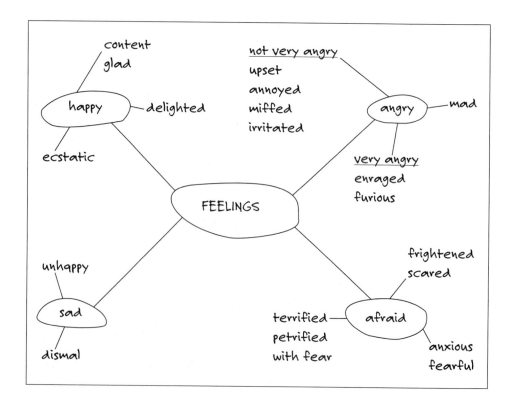

ing of words from one place to another on the chart or in making room for a new word to be added.

In a writing assignment perhaps several months later, English language learners might refer back to the cumulative semantic map on the wall when they want to select just the right word to convey the degree of anger they have in mind (Crawford, 1994a). Discussing the choice of word with the teacher or with other children will be particularly helpful. When children are ready to add yet another synonym for *angry* a week or a month later, they will have the opportunity to review other words or expressions for the same feeling, but within a context of known or somewhat familiar vocabulary. Teachers can view a well-developed cumulative semantic map as a "graphic thesaurus." Other suitable topics for cumulative semantic maps might include *see* (stare, peek, glare, etc.), *motion* (crawl, creep, dawdle, dash, poke along, lope, etc.), and *touch* (poke, tap, jab, stroke, etc.). Only the topics come from the teacher; the source of vocabulary is the literature the children are reading.

If your classroom has a word wall, this might be the place to attach several cumulative semantic maps that are used frequently. If there are so many that they do not all fit, several might be mounted on top of each other on the wall or an easel with a way of folding them up so the one in use during a lesson is visible. At the end of the school year, you might consider passing the cumulative semantic maps on to the children's teacher for the next grade, especially if most of the class will move to the new classroom intact as a group. Many teachers also save the children's portfolios for the children to pick up when they start the next school year. The children can take their portfolios to their new classroom and use them to introduce themselves to the new teacher.

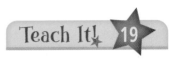

Word Wall Activities

READ-ALOUD ACTIVITIES.   English language learners often benefit from read-aloud activities by the teacher, followed by discussion. Vocabulary is presented in context, and someone in the group will likely have some knowledge of most words. Other words may be analyzed by reviewing the illustrations in a story or an appropriate illustration, manipulative, or visual aid provided by the teacher. Because illustrations provide important visual information, paging through a selection and discussing the illustrations before reading provides an opportunity for presenting new vocabulary and for making predictions about the text.

Occasionally, you might find that presenting the entire selection as a read-aloud is needed before English language learners read themselves, especially in a particularly challenging piece. When a parallel version of a text is available in the children's mother tongue, you might choose to read it aloud before the children read later in the second language. Children in school are not bored or disturbed by several exposures to the same literature selection. The familiarity of a story that is an old friend becomes a real comfort. Familiarity with the background knowledge and structure of a story permits children to read with better comprehension and with fewer time-consuming visual cues, especially for children's early literacy experiences in English. The read-aloud activity also provides the teacher with the opportunity to demonstrate and model predicting, thinking about context, and other metacognitive strategies in a think-aloud during the teacher's oral reading.

Differentiating Instruction in Grades 3 to 5

By now, you have doubtless concluded that a one-size-fits-all approach to teaching children to read is most inappropriate. Each child needs instruction at an appropriate level, but, fortunately, usually many children have needs in common. Grouping children for instruction is a tricky proposition, but it addresses the need for appropriate instruction for all children. Some advocate for teaching the entire class at one time, a strategy that can be very effective in some areas of the curriculum. For example, placing students in small groups according to individual needs is not a common practice in the areas of science, social science, art, and music.

Whole-Class Instruction

When instruction in reading is consistently conducted with the whole class, it is often characteristic of highly scripted and sequenced direct instruction reading programs. The use of this type of approach implies that all children are the same and that a one-size-fits-all program is adequate for all. In reality, this means that every time a lesson is taught, it is just right for some children, too difficult for children who were unsuccessful in earlier lessons and did not attain prerequisite skills, and repetitious and boring for children who mastered the material weeks, months, or years before. Instruction should be planned to meet individual needs. This does not imply a separate lesson for each individual child, but it does permit children with similar strengths or needs to be grouped together for appropriate instruction. There are some reading/language arts activities that can be conducted with the entire class, such as a review of how to avoid run-on sentences in writing when almost all children show the need, teacher read-aloud activities, library visits, using a video of a story, conducting a poetry hour, and readers' theater (Burns, Roe, & Ross, 1999).

Grouping: Why and Why Not?

Schools are sometimes tempted to group students homogeneously by reading ability on a classroom basis across an entire school. If there are five fourth-grade classes, why not place the students who are nonreaders in one classroom, those reading at grade level in another, those above grade level in yet another, and so on? The assumption is that each teacher will need to plan only a single reading lesson for the entire class. Teachers need to recognize that one result will often be racial, linguistic, and gender isolation. Another outcome is the classroom at each grade level with the lowest achieving children—twenty-five of thirty children are likely to be boys, and many of them will display behavior problems. English language learners often end up in the same class, despite their need to associate with native English speakers.

When all of these children with important needs are placed in the same classroom, the challenges for the teacher are extreme. The management of behavior in this classroom requires the most able and experienced teacher in the school, but all too often, this class is assigned to the newest teacher. The result can be negative attitudes, low self-esteem, and continuing low achievement. The classroom with the highest achievers will tend to have a preponderance of girls, along with much of the student leadership potential on the grade level. Although this classroom might seem to be an attractive assignment for most teachers, it is also a challenge.

There is really no such thing as a homogeneous group. Even children who have similar levels of achievement at the beginning of the school year will be very different from each other after a few months of instruction in which some gain more than others. In addition, teaching a reading lesson to a classroom-size group might not be the best way to provide effective instruction to them. If twenty children in a classroom are really reading at the same level and have similar strengths and needs, most experienced teachers would divide them into two groups and teach similar lessons to each smaller group to maximize individual attention.

In many countries, children are promoted from one grade to the next on the basis of their achievement, not their age. The tradition in the United States has been to promote on the basis of age because of research indicating that children do not benefit from being held back (Wheelock & Dorman, 1988). According to the Texas Education Agency (1996), being older than other students in your grade is a better predictor of future dropping out than underachievement is. In some states, attempts have been made to hold children back who do not reach a standard for their grade level, but most of these efforts are quickly abandoned when the numbers of children retained are much larger than was expected. The result is that children are usually grouped for instruction in reading to better address their different needs.

Grouping is most common in reading and mathematics. The higher the grade level, the greater is the need for grouping children as some fall behind and others forge ahead. In a first-grade classroom, as you have seen, most children are not reading, they are reading some, or they are reading well at a first-grade level. But in a fifth-grade classroom, the children might range from those not reading at all to some reading at a college level. Those who are not reading at all will tend to be children with severe reading disabilities or occasionally immigrant children with no school experience or very limited school experience.

Grouping children within the classroom can also have negative consequences. It does not matter what names the groups have; the children recognize that there are high groups and low groups, and they know which group they are in. This sends an unmistakable message to children in the "low" group. These expectations often become a self-fulfilling prophecy. Children in the "low" group in the first grade are all too often still there in the fifth grade.

What are the potential benefits of grouping students for instruction? (Mary Kate Denny/PhotoEdit)

Grouping Students without Tracking

The dilemma is how to meet individual cognitive and affective needs while avoiding the negative effects that can result from grouping by ability. Children need to receive reading instruction at their instructional levels, and so teachers must form groups that permit children to read at levels where they will be successful, interested, and engaged. Some fifth graders will be learning beginning reading concepts in the language-experience approach, and some in the same classroom will be reading and enjoying Shakespeare. It is difficult to put children from these two levels together when they are in guided reading lessons. There are two possible solutions to the dilemma, and they can be used at the same time: nonability-based groups and dynamic groups.

Guided Reading

GROUPS NOT BASED ON ABILITY AND ACHIEVEMENT. The interest group is a grouping structure that is not based on ability and achievement—perhaps a group of children who are interested in fairy tales. They can all read fairy tales, even the same fairy tale in the same lesson, but from books written at different levels or from the same book but with different levels of teacher support. This allows students who are working at a lower level to work with students reading at higher levels from time to time so that they are able to say, "Sometimes I am in the same reading group as Janie." Interest groups might meet one day a week instead of every day, and they might meet for a month before dissolving so that students can form new and different interest groups. Fountas and Pinnell (1996) add other structures to introduce flexibility, including peer tutoring, cooperative learning pairs, and cross-grade buddies. In literature circles, children who have decided to read the same book, poem, or other text compare and share ideas about what they have read (Daniels, 1994).

DYNAMIC GROUPING. Occasionally, the teacher should recognize that certain students need to work with a reading group other than their own for specific reasons. A bright but troubled and struggling reader might advance to a higher ability group to read a story for three days because the story will be of great interest to the student and because the student has much background knowledge about it. An otherwise high-achieving reader who has trouble decoding words with prefixes might join a lower-achieving group that happens to be working on that specific skill for a few days.

The ability grouping in Chantell DeLaney's third-grade classroom is what Fountas and Pinnell (1996, 2001) refer to as *dynamic grouping* (see Chapter 12), bringing students together for a period of time when, and for as long as, they have abilities and needs in common. The most capable students, reading at fourth- and fifth-grade levels in Ms. DeLaney's classroom, occasionally join the group working at the third-grade level, perhaps to learn or practice a needed word recognition skill or comprehension strategy. Often, however, they are working on individualized reading and on projects of interest, periodically meeting with Ms. DeLaney as a small group or conferencing with her.

Organizing and Managing a Learning Community

The lesson in the chapter-opening vignette seemed relatively simple and straightforward, but, of course, Ms. DeLaney doesn't just come in each morning and begin teaching. She has planned activities for students who are not working directly with her as she teaches small groups, she has arranged the furniture in the classroom, she has carefully selected instructional materials, she has scheduled precious instructional time, and she has made decisions about how to assess the outcomes of her teaching for the day.

Children's Identity and Motivation

In Ms. DeLaney's lesson on "Little Red Riding Hood," the focus was only on the group of children she was teaching. Over the period of a week, an observer in Ms. DeLaney's classroom sees a very complicated structure. She is usually working with one of several groups while the other two groups complete independent work, read trade books from the classroom library, write letters for the classroom postal system, work on projects in which reading and writing activities are integrated across the curriculum, use the classroom computers, and work in learning centers. There is much movement of students between groups, orchestrated by Ms. DeLaney as she assesses needs and asks students to join groups for a single lesson, a week, or even a month for activities to meet those needs.

A very important part of her planning involved the other two groups that were working independently while she was teaching the lesson to this group. The other large group that reads slightly below grade level needed much guidance and supervision. They had an independent assignment from the previous day's lesson to complete, but she also had learning centers that they could work in and a large variety of trade books at many levels for them to read. The group that was reading above the third-grade level required less direct supervision. Many of them were working on independent projects from social studies and science, and they were also deeply engrossed in library books that they were reading independently.

During Ms. DeLaney's guided reading lesson, there were intervals in which the children read silently for a few minutes. Ms. DeLaney took advantage of their focus and walked around the classroom to help children with questions. They knew that she would come around during the lesson and that they should not interrupt the group's work. In addition, she used her walks as a preventive classroom behavior management strategy, settling down children who were noisy or off task. But she always did this with a touch on the shoulder, a gentle tug on a pigtail, or a smile that said, "I caught you—back to work now." By the time the lesson group had finished the chunk they were reading, after just a minute or two, Ms. DeLaney was back with the group and seated, ready to continue with them until they read the next chunk of text.

On alternate Fridays, the children participate in an individualized reading program based on the many books Ms. DeLaney has accumulated for her extensive classroom library. They range from large-format picture books and simple stories to novels and nonfiction materials at upper grade and secondary levels. Self-selected silent sustained reading (SSR) characterizes the Friday program. As a good model for the children, Ms.

DIFFERENTIATED INSTRUCTION

SIOP®
Sheltered
Instruction
Observation
Protocol'

Providing Trade Books at the Independent Reading Level

Self-selected reading is an element of the four blocks approach to reading (Cunningham et al., 2007) that requires differentiated instruction, just as the more obvious teacher-directed aspects of reading programs do. Most self-selected reading activities are carried out by children individually, occasionally in paired reading. How then can teachers differentiate instruction in this part of the program?

One of the most important strategies is to provide text in the form of trade books or other reading matter that is at each child's independent level. For example, if a student has an instructional level at the third-grade level, but an independent level at the second-grade level, the teacher will provide formal and directed instruction at the instructional level, which is appropriate given the scaffolding support that the teacher will provide during the lessons: the introduction of new vocabulary, activating background knowledge, perhaps guiding reading with questions, and finally consolidation activities that allow the child to apply new knowledge.

But when the child selects a trade book to read for silent sustained reading (SSR) or self-selected reading, whether in the classroom or at home, that scaffolding support is often absent. The appropriate level of book then will usually be one or two grade levels lower for most children. By providing trade books for the classroom reading center at a variety of levels, a skilled teacher ensures that abundant books are available at the independent levels of all children.

But the teacher should also communicate the need for reading material at the independent level to parents. They will often provide books at home that are at the child's grade level, not the independent reading level. Librarians can help parents and children select books at an appropriate level for independent reading, and so can sales staff at specialized children's bookstores. At chain bookstores, however, parents may need guidance from the teacher about appropriate books. If motivation is high because a child has just received a computer and a book about how to use it, then a capable and highly motivated child might struggle and read successfully at the instructional level or even at the frustration level. But these are not the usual circumstances.

Teachers will find valuable information about the levels of hundreds, if not thousands, of trade books in Fountas and Pinnell's *Leveled Book List, K–8* (2005). Individual publishers of trade books also provide information about the levels of their books.

Echevarria, Vogt, and Short (2009) provide scaffolding suggestions to assist English language learners and other at-risk students in reading in the self-selected mode with books at the independent level. One recommendation is for the teacher to conduct a partial read-aloud of the piece of literature with the student or students who will read it. They can then pair up or work in small groups to continue through the material. Teachers can also scaffold by pointing out the text structure of what they are going to read—chronological in a biography or historical piece, for example.

DeLaney demonstrates how she reads for her own pleasure during part of the reading period, but she also spends much of her time conferencing with individual children about what they have been reading and encouraging them.

Managing Students and the Classroom for Learning

One important set of decisions for teachers in grades 3 through 5 concerns how to set up the classroom for instruction in reading and other subject areas. Some elements are inflexible, such as the positions of doors, windows, chalkboards, fixed cabinets, computer network connections, and the sink. But other elements indicate much about the philosophy of the program. Think about the difference between two university classrooms: one with chairs set up in straight rows facing the front, where a podium has been placed for the instructor, and another where there are round tables with chairs around them and no podium or front to the classroom.

One possible middle-grade classroom arrangement for reading/language arts instruction and also instruction in other areas of the curriculum would include the following:

- A U-shaped or kidney-shaped table for small-group lessons, with the teacher seated with back to the wall to be able to observe the entire classroom while teaching

- Movable individual children's desks that can be quickly and quietly rearranged when groups or activities change (two-student desks are only slightly less convenient)
- A library center with numerous trade books at many levels and places to sit, such as cushions on the floor, pillows in an old bathtub (for reading only), or a sofa (check the fire regulations)
- A computer center with at least two or three computers in the classroom
- The author's chair (Hanson & Graves, 1983), a very special chair in which children sit only when sharing their writing with others
- Other learning centers for individual or paired work, such as science, writing, or mathematics, with task cards that require children to read, write, and discuss
- A word wall above the writing center
- A listening center with earphones and a player for audiotapes, videotapes, and/or CD-ROMs
- Easels that can be moved from place to place, even for grades 3 to 5

Most teachers find it necessary to control or limit access to learning centers, which can often disrupt lessons. This can be done by doing the following:

- Limiting the number of students who can work in a center at the same time
- Limiting the amount of time each student can work in each center
- Assigning centers every day, with children rotating each day to a different one
- Occasionally informing children who misbehave when together that they cannot work in a center at the same time until they demonstrate more maturity

All of these controls have negative effects on children's spontaneity and their interests. Most teachers find that they can relax and even eliminate these controls over time, but they are very helpful early in the school year.

Selecting Appropriate Materials

There is a big difference between texts used to teach reading at the primary-grade levels and at the fifth-grade level. It is partly in the quantity; fifth-grade students will be able to read more text during a reading lesson than primary-grade students will, but the difficulty of the material is also a major factor. It is easy to observe that text in basal readers at the third-grade level has fewer difficult words and more complex sentences than text has at the fifth-grade level. There is a difference between text included in basal readers and that in authentic literature. The biggest difference between authentic literature and basal reader stories or so-called decodable text is the variety of vocabulary that skilled authors use when they select the precise word needed to best express an idea. This increases the difficulty of the text, but also the interest levels of the students (Crawford, 2000).

LEVELED BOOKS.   After the teacher determines student reading levels using an informal reading inventory, it is then helpful to be able to identify the levels of textbooks and especially of trade books so that they can be matched to the children's levels. Many thousands of children's trade books have been leveled for the text gradient, a measure of text difficulty developed as a part of the reading recovery program (Fountas & Pinnell, 2001).

According to Fountas and Pinnell (2001), text difficulty is a function of the following factors:

- Book and print features, such as length, print, layout, illustrations, graphic features, and organizational aids
- Themes and ideas, such as interest, sophistication, and maturity

- Language and literary features, such as literary and figurative language and dialogue
- Vocabulary, such as multisyllabic words and content-related words
- Sentence complexity, including length, embedded clauses, and punctuation
- Content, including topics, organization, and special graphic features
- Text structure, including fiction (narrative literary devices such as flashbacks) and nonfiction (compare and contrast, cause and effect, description, temporal sequence, and problem/solution)

As we saw in Chapter 12, the resulting text gradient ranges from A (kindergarten) through Z (grades 7 and 8). Grade-level ranges for typical children are assigned to each letter, which allows teachers to select books that are in the so-called Goldilocks range— not too difficult, not too easy, but just right. They are also within Vygotsky's zone of proximal development. Fountas and Pinnell provide lists of thousands of leveled books in their many publications (Fountas & Pinnell, 1996, 1999, 2001, 2009; Pinnell & Fountas, 2001).

USING TECHNOLOGY IN GRADES 3 TO 5.   Technology has the potential for creating many changes in the teaching of reading and language arts, some positive and some perhaps negative. Keep in mind, however, that the promise of instructional television and language laboratories to transform teaching never was realized (Griffith & Lynch-Brown, 2002). Possible roles for technology in grades 3 to 5 will be examined in two dimensions: reading and writing.

New Literacies

How can technology enrich reading and writing instruction in grades 3 to 5?

In Reading.   In the area of Web text reading, as contrasted to print text reading, Sutherland-Smith (2002) reported that students needed to use different reading strategies to acquire meaning from the two sources. She based this on student comments about the need to work fast on the Internet, in contrast to a more leisurely style of reading from books. She found that Web text reading was less linear, less hierarchical, and less sequential than print text reading. It was more interactive, allowing the reader to add, change, or move text, blurring the relationship between reader and writer. She described several strategies to help students in their Web text reading, all of which support the inquiry-based technology strategies already offered in Chapter 8:

Writing and Reading Connections

How can teachers incorporate a simplified approach to word processing into the writing program?

- Encourage "snatch-and-grab" reading, scanning or reading superficially to find pertinent information and returning to it later if it survived the culling needed when large quantities of information are found
- Help students to focus on finding keywords for searches as an important skill
- Encourage students to refine or delimit their problem or question so they are not overwhelmed with the amount of information they encounter
- Provide "sure-thing" links to students for their initial forays into the Internet
- Help students to differentiate between informative text and impressive visual images that might offer little information

In a related vein, Henry (2006) identifies new reading comprehension needs when reading on the Internet, in contrast to previous views of reading on the Internet as technological issues. For example, students need to read search engine results critically before clicking on them to read the actual website. Otherwise, they waste valuable time reading something in depth that will not be useful. Students need to recognize the need to evaluate entries quickly when they might turn up over a million somewhat relevant sites for each request. They also need to consider different kinds of results that particular search engines provide and select accordingly. When information is located, students need to consider whether the information is accurate, whether the author is an authority on the topic, possible biases of the author, whether the information is current, and how it compares with information found in other sources. These skills are clearly within the realm of critical thinking.

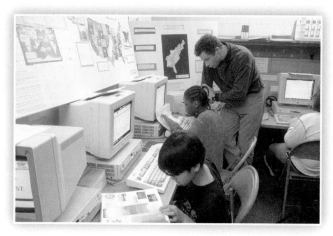

Computers can serve a number of purposes in the classroom. What do you think is the most common use of technology in the literacy classroom? (Brian Smith)

Baildon and Baildon (2008) recommended a set of resource questions for guiding the selection of a research source. First, the reader should consider the readability of the source, not in the sense of a Fry-type readability score, but rather whether the source is written at a level that is comprehensible to the student. Reading on the Internet is usually an independent activity, without the support systems that teachers provide during formal lessons. Second, the reader should ascertain if the source is trustworthy. Is the author known to be an expert on the subject? By checking the date, they can determine the currency of the source. They might also try to verify the accuracy of the information by locating another source that provides similar information or a similar point of view. Third, students should consider the usefulness of the information. Does it provide the information called for in the purpose of their project or paper? Does it meet their need?

In Writing. A very effective use of technology in teaching writing in grades 3 to 5 is in the area of word processing. Several word processors are designed for children, including *The Amazing Writing Machine* from Broderbund. Many teachers find that they can use Microsoft Word or the more simple word processing program included in Microsoft Works with children, teaching only the aspects of these complex programs that are needed for their writing. The appearance of the screen can be simplified by suppressing some of the toolbars and reducing the numbers of functions in those that remain to what is necessary for that grade level.

Finally, Wood (2000) has developed many interesting activities that incorporate the use of technology into the writing process:

- Use the Web to publish student work; it is very exciting for children to see the results of their writing published on the Internet, perhaps with digital photos they have taken.
- Initiate e-mail exchanges between children in which they write to each other about topics of common interest; Wood provides an example of two boys comparing Quidditch teams (from the Harry Potter books) they have organized (in their imaginations), whose members are well-known American professional basketball players.
- Help children to establish their writing portfolios on their personal or class Web page.
- Encourage children to develop their own writer's voice. They might even want to pretend to be someone else to write in a new voice.

Involving Family and Community

Adults other than teachers play major roles at home and at school in supporting literacy instruction, even in the middle grades.

Family Literacy

How can teachers take advantage of home literacy opportunities to enhance reading instruction in the classroom?

At Home

Authentic environmental print is a valuable resource that teachers can exploit in the home. Purcell-Gates, L'Allier, and Smith (1995) provide valuable print-embedded family literacy activities that are especially useful for children in grades 3 to 5 because they are authentic. Among them are the following:

- Daily living routines, such as shopping lists, reading recipes, and cooking together
- Entertainment, such as reading novels, storybooks, or television program descriptions
- School-related activity, such as homework or school assignments
- Interpersonal communication, such as notes on the refrigerator, e-mail
- Religion, including reading stories from the Bible, the Torah, the Koran, and other religious books treasured by the family
- Participating in information networks, such as sharing scores of sporting events, news of interest, and reactions to new films
- Work-related tasks, such as reading instructions, pay-stub information, and catalogs

Children enjoy reading in a comfortable, secure, and accepting place. (Paul Conklin/PhotoEdit)

Teachers often give students a consolidation or application activity to complete at home after their daily reading lesson. This activity may involve reading aloud to parents, siblings, or others who live in the home. When students are asked to read aloud, they should read something they have already read and practiced in the classroom. If they are to read something new, it should ordinarily be at their independent level, not at the instructional level (see the Differentiated Instruction box earlier in this chapter). When children struggle with reading aloud (which is potentially a very positive experience at school and one the teacher wants the child to have), it can turn into a negative experience with a well-meaning parent who tries to help by criticizing or by teaching a phonics lesson.

Similarly, the teacher might send the parents a note asking them to listen to the child read for ten minutes from an assigned book. The parent wants to do more and asks the child to read for thirty minutes from a more difficult book. Again, the well-meaning parent is trying to help the child, but fails to understand the importance of following the teacher's directions carefully.

Teach It! 2

Dialogic Reading

At School

The presence of other adults in the classroom can be an important asset. Teacher assistants or instructional aides are paid paraprofessionals who may work all day or part of a day to support the teacher. They might range from a minimally educated community resident to a university student who is ready for student teaching. Paraprofessionals are particularly important in working with English language learners.

Another source of adult support in the classroom is the parent volunteer, who might also be a grandparent or other extended family member or caregiver. Tinajero and Nagel (1975) suggest that you need only invite participation. They recommend that you ensure in advance that parents have the needed skills to accomplish assigned tasks and that the activities you request are culturally appropriate. You might find it helpful to demonstrate for adult volunteers so their roles are clear. Adult volunteers can make many important contributions, including sharing information in oral discussions; tutoring; participating in journal activities by responding to children's entries; reading aloud to students, including in the mother tongue other than English, where appropriate; helping with homework assignments in after-school study; storytelling; and sharing life events, personal oral histories, and job experiences.

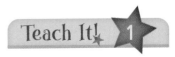

Teach It! 1

Reading Aloud

For Review

The reading program for most children changes as they proceed through the grades, with more emphasis on reading comprehension, silent reading, reading in the content areas of the curriculum, and writing in grades 3 through 5. There is still attention to phonics and other aspects of word recognition, but it occupies less time than it does in the primary grades. Developing fluency and automaticity may still receive some attention in the third grade.

The organizational structures for teaching reading are based on the four blocks framework that includes guided reading, working with words, self-selected reading, and writing. Teachers can use three typical stages of reading lessons for planning that reflects this framework: anticipation activities to build interest and connect students to background knowledge, guided reading activities to build knowledge through scaffolding students' reading and comprehension of text, and consolidation reading activities where students apply new knowledge and have opportunities for writing and self-selected reading. These stages are supplemented with mini-lessons focused on word study or another specific skill that usually have emerged from the text to be read in the lesson. Long-term planning can be systematized with thematic literature units that are often integrated with science and social studies instruction, even including critical literacy.

There is more variation in the reading levels of students in the middle grades than in the primary grades, and the need for grouping for instruction arises. Most useful is dynamic grouping that is flexible and includes multiple structures for instruction, including small ability groups, interest groups, buddy reading and cooperative learning pairs, peer tutoring, occasional whole-class instruction, and the frequent formation of temporary focused groups to address common weaknesses of students from all ability levels.

Most English language learners who have learned to read in the mother tongue are by now able to understand and speak English at an intermediate level. They are also often ready to begin a transition to English language reading in the third grade. Many scaffolding and support activities are particularly important for these students as they begin reading in their new second language, English.

You have now seen that students' abilities to understand text vary widely and students are grouped accordingly for some important comprehension instruction. Teachers must then be able to find textbooks, literature, and trade books that reflect those levels. Many thousands of books have been leveled on a gradient of difficulty, and teachers can quite accurately select books for students for whom they have assessment data. There is a growing role for the effective use of technology in the classroom in the middle grades. Children can do extensive reading on the Internet, but they must be prepared to deal with the immense amounts of information returned in the typical search. The introduction of new reading skills, such as identifying descriptors and criteria, scanning titles of returned references, and delimiting problems or assignments done on the Internet, will assist in their effectiveness. Children can make effective use of various types of word processors in the writing process at these grade levels.

Adults other than the teacher can make important contributions to students' progress in literacy. There are many activities that parents and caregivers can provide at home to complement efforts in the classroom. Teachers also need to take advantage of the services that other adults can provide in the classroom as paraprofessionals and volunteers.

For Your Journal

1. Using the lesson plan and the strategies illustrated in the chapter and the strategies you would like to incorporate from throughout this book, plan a similar lesson for the "Three Little Pigs," another story that most children know. Working with a partner should enrich your thinking as well as speed up completion of the task.

2. Identify a theme you could introduce to a class, such as "change." Visit the children's section of your local bookstore or public library, or look on a search engine for books, such as the one at amazon.com. Try to find three trade books at about the same grade level that fit into the theme of your unit. Develop activities and assessment tools for integrating these books into the unit.

Taking It to the World

1. Now that you have moved into grades 3 to 5, you have found that most children have acquired a concept of print; they are able to decode many words they encounter, especially when they are contextualized in connected text; they are beginning to read silently; they are understanding what they read; and they are beginning to express themselves in writing. What changes from a second-grade reading program do you now expect to find in the use of literature, in word recognition instruction, in reading in the content areas, and in writing as children enter the third grade?

2. Write down one or two thoughts with respect to each of these elements of literacy, and compare notes with another student. Try to agree on a single list of how the focus on these elements might be different from working with K–2 students.

New Literacies Connections

1. Using a search engine, such as Google (www.google.com), complete an Internet search for reviews on *Kid Pix*. What do the reviews say about this product for children? How could it be used in grades 3 to 5?

2. Visit Education World's "Technology in the Classroom Center" online at www.educationworld.com/a_tech. Identify at least three technology products recommended by Education World's tech experts as appropriate for students in grades 3 to 5. What do the experts say about these products?

PEARSON myeducationlab

Now go to MyEducationLab (**www.myeducationlab.com**), where you can:

- Find learning outcomes for the topics covered in this chapter, along with the national standards that connect to these outcomes.

- Complete Assignments and Activities that can help you more deeply understand the chapter content.
- Engage in Building Teaching Skills and Dispositions exercises, in which you can apply and practice core teaching skills identified in the chapter.

Putting Effective Literacy Instruction into Practice: Grades 6 to 8

Anticipation Guide

The following statements will help you begin thinking about the topics covered in this chapter. Answer *true* or *false* in response to each statement. As you read and learn more about the topics mentioned in these statements, think back on your answers. See what interests you and prompts your curiosity toward more understanding.

_____ 1. Schools can safely stop teaching reading by the time students reach the middle grades. Virtually all students will have learned to read adequately by then.

_____ 2. Middle grade students should be assured daily opportunities to read because reading ability grows with practice.

_____ 3. Having students post new words they have learned on a vocabulary bulletin board is effective because it helps for students to take ownership of their learning.

_____ 4. "Possible Sentences" is a method of fitting punishments to crimes, and "Personal Clues" is a means of locating criminals.

_____ 5. Reading aloud to students and encouraging them to listen to audiotapes and CDs is important because it provides an internal model of fluent reading.

_____ 6. Integrated instructional units help students build connections between literature and content learning in social studies and science.

_____ 7. An important form of assessment is for the teacher to learn to look and listen carefully as students read.

_____ 8. Part of a teacher's responsibility is to help students organize their time to afford more time for reading and studying.

_____ 9. It is pointless to ask students to reflect on their strategies when they read because fluent readers are simply unaware of what they are doing.

_____ 10. Teachers should be sure to give English language learners extra mini-lessons on reading materials before that material is discussed in class.

Putting Effective Literacy Instruction into Practice: Grades 6 to 8

- Reading in Adolescence p. 440
- Developing Knowledge and Skills p. 441
- Study Reading p. 457
- Assessment p. 453
- Metacognition p. 458
- Teaching All Students p. 461
- Organizing and Managing a Learning Community p. 472
- Organizing for Instruction p. 464

Integrated Reading Instruction in a Sixth-Grade Classroom

As part of an integrated unit on the Middle Ages, Rasheed Graham's sixth-grade students had the choice of reading one of Karen Cushman's books: *The Midwife's Apprentice* (1995) or *Catherine, Called Birdy* (1994). Mr. Graham was concerned that some of the students might encounter difficulty with the setting and he wanted to revisit a scene to emphasize its meaning and check for their understanding early on in the reading of one of the books. During Friday story share, Mr. Graham has students sit in a circle on the floor while he reads from what he considers a pivotal chapter in the *The Midwife's Apprentice*—where the main character is shopping at a medieval market. The students follow along with the text as he reads aloud. Mr. Graham's goal is to make sure the students reflect on the significance of this section. While reading aloud, he stops to comment and ask the students for their thoughts on the content, and then he asks them to make predictions: "I thought you'd like to revisit this chapter because it seems like such a big moment for the main character. Let's see how we all interpreted this section. What do you think about it? Let me

read this part again while you follow along. The setup, as you recall, is that Beetle, the main character, has been directed by the midwife to buy some items at the market. Beetle has never been there before, and she is overwhelmed by all the new sights, smells, and sounds."

Mr. Graham reads from Chapter 5, then stops after reading, "She sniffed all the spices for free before buying nutmeg and pepper. The hangman was doing a brisk trade in murderer's wash water." To help the students develop the skill of reading for understanding, Mr. Graham has the students think critically about a sentence that might otherwise be overlooked because of lack of understanding. He asks, "What do you think that means? It's not a beheading, but a hanging, so what do you think is going on?"

Jason speaks up, "'Murderer's wash water'? Isn't that just dirty bathing water? Why would anyone want that?"

"Does anyone have any ideas?"

"I guess it's like collecting things, you know, like stamps or rabbits' feet," offers Tran.

Next, Mr. Graham reads a section in which the main character sees an ivory comb at a

merchant's table. She loves the comb but has no money to buy it. Mr. Graham asks, "What do you think will happen? Will she use the money given her by the midwife to buy the comb or will something else transpire?"

Kayleigh states, "I hope she doesn't do that. If she does, the midwife will fire her, and she'll be worse off than she was before."

"I think she gonna steal it," calls out Deanna.

Mr. Graham continues to prod the students' thinking: "What makes you think that she would do that? Is there anything in her character that makes her out to be either a thief or irresponsible? Can you show that to me in the text?"

Here, Mr. Graham has asked students to match their predictions with the character's actual behavior so that they learn that predictions need to be linked to previous knowledge of events and actions. Then he continues reading and stops to help students focus on the key to this section: the development of the main character.

Reading in Adolescence

Reading instruction is needed just as much in the middle grades as it is in the first grade. This fact has been highlighted recently as state and national tests show that students are not reaching the levels of literacy needed for success in the twenty-first century. According to the 2007 National Assessment of Educational Progress (NAEP, 2007), 69 percent of eighth graders are not able to read grade-level materials proficiently. Several recent reports have championed the need for more attention to adolescent literacy. One of these, Reading Next (Biancarosa & Snow, 2006), makes fifteen recommendations for middle and high school literacy. These are included in Table 14.1. A recent U.S. Department of Education website, Doing what works (http://dww.ed.gov), has developed a whole section on Adolescent Literacy as part of its recognition of the need for more attention to upper level literacy. The Striving Readers Research studies and the professional

Table 14.1 Reading Next Recommendations

1. Direct, explicit comprehension instruction
2. Effective instructional principles embedded in content
3. Motivation and self-directed learning
4. Text-based collaborative learning
5. Strategic tutoring
6. Diverse texts
7. Intensive writing
8. A technology component
9. Ongoing formative assessment of students
10. Extended time for literacy
11. Professional development that is both long term and ongoing
12. Ongoing summative assessment of students and programs
13. Teacher teams
14. Leadership
15. A comprehensive and coordinated literacy program

development grants under the same name are also indications of the growing awareness of the need for a better understanding of how to increase students' literacy levels. Providing middle level students with expert reading instruction is essential also because reading is part of learning across the curriculum, and specific reading skills and strategies are needed in many different subject areas. Middle level readers have increasing demands placed on them to become flexible and competent in reading a much broader range of materials than was required in earlier grades.

As students mature, the range of reading strategies they need expands as well. Both national and state standards include a range of areas of reading expected during the middle school years. Most state standards specify levels of work that indicate students are able to read in these ways. Some show examples of the levels of response that can be expected from competent students. Some states also include lists of the books that students should know and be able to discuss for each grade level. State websites often have examples of proficient student work. If you are unsure of what middle grade students are capable of doing, these sources are good to use—and also to show students so that they can develop a realistic assessment of their own work in relation to what others are doing.

Adding to the complexity of reading instruction in the middle grades is the changing structure of this level of schooling. Many schools are organized into content departments, so students move from teacher to teacher, which creates challenges to educators' efforts to provide flexibility in time and integration of reading and writing with content-area learning. When students have multiple teachers and the curriculum becomes very content intense, aspects of good reading instruction often are overlooked. This chapter provides a framework for thinking about what needs to be taught and examines how different classrooms are organized so students have the opportunities to learn that they deserve. Recognizing the importance of reading for older students, the International Reading Association's Commission on Adolescent Reading (Moore et al., 1999) has published a document that lists seven reading rights of adolescents, as shown in Table 14.1.

Developing Knowledge and Skills

Given the wide range of reading development needed during the middle years, classroom instruction must be carefully structured so that all aspects of reading can be included. As a teacher, you need to ensure that you attend to each of these through the programs you develop. The following sections provide an overview of nine components to include in your reading program.

Daily Opportunities to Read

Reading is not a single activity, but one that is complex and that changes according to the situation, purpose, and type of text. For students to develop as flexible readers, they should be given a variety of purposeful reading opportunities each day. Each new type of text requires special attention, and the classroom teacher must supply assistance to students in approaching new materials. Teachers can remind students to adapt their reading strategies to their purposes and materials. Skimming headings and skipping from one chapter or section to another can be an appropriate strategy to use when reading for specific information. Reading and rereading may be the tactic to adopt when trying to understand and appreciate a poem. Some of the various purposes that students have for reading different texts include the following:

- Self-selected texts for personal enjoyment
- Texts for group discussions and sharing with others
- Content-area learning from textbook and resource materials, news magazines, newspapers, and electronic texts
- Experiences with poetry, humorous word plays, and cartoons
- Texts that enable students to perform tasks and follow directions
- Texts for specific problem-solving and learning activities

One of the most important kinds of reading is self-selected, independent reading. It is clear that students who read widely have a great advantage over students who do not read much or who never engage in self-selected reading. Cunningham and Stanovich's (1998) article, "What Reading Does for the Mind," makes a strong case for wide reading. The article summarizes data from various studies indicating that relying on oral input to learn is just not adequate. An analysis of the vocabulary load of various books and television programs demonstrates that even preschool children's books have a more sophisticated range of vocabulary than adult television shows. Students will never encounter the words and concepts they need to succeed in a professional world if they do not read. When middle level students read this information, many become convinced of the importance of their continued independent reading. It is through engagement in a great deal of reading that we encounter the concepts and forms of written discourse needed for life. We must keep reading!

Daily Reading at the Appropriate Instructional Level

Finding a balance between appropriately challenging reading materials and those that students can handle independently is part of each teacher's task. Students will improve in their reading when they have instructional-level materials that both challenge and reward them. If reading materials are too difficult, students cannot apply their skills to extend their proficiency. If materials are too easy, they do not need to apply their skills; thus, finding the instructional middle is essential. This is the zone in which students can develop as readers. Even so, situations in which students must deal with materials that are too easy or too hard will still occur. Students need some easy materials so that they can gain pleasure from reading and move comfortably through texts.

In whole-class instruction, many students also will be faced with materials that are above their instructional level. In spite of these situations, support mechanisms are available and should be used to assist students. Some of these support mechanisms include the following:

- Pre-reading activation of knowledge and vocabulary under teacher or adult guidance, which might involve viewing videos to set the context and build knowledge
- Audiotapes/CDs of texts
- Use of buddy or partner reading
- Assistance from older or adult readers
- Adapted, easier texts on the same topic

Integrating Reading and Writing

Both reading and writing develop better when they are taught as companion tools for learning about and expressing ideas. Integrating units of content instruction with language arts skill development provides a rich context in which to help students learn. With more extensive units, teachers have time to develop students' background knowledge and to help them formulate questions and expand their interests. Thus, the instruction can be personal and focused. Reading more deeply on a particular topic helps students to gain control of the ideas and learn the vocabulary and concepts more fully than a quick covering of curriculum often provides. As student knowledge of a topic increases, the student becomes more able to write about it with a sense of confidence and perspective. Examples of situations that encourage integration of curriculum and reading and writing are included in this chapter, both in the opening vignette and later as we explore organizational options for teachers. Additional options include the following:

- Science fairs, history fairs, family history projects, and other events put on by a class, school, or larger organization that encourage projects for which students, working as individuals, pairs, or small groups, choose topics, conduct research, and create exhibits. All language arts are integrated when students engage in these types of inquiry and sharing.
- Addressing broad questions, as in the Great Books Program (Plecha, 1992) and the Paidea program (Adler, 1982), with groups coming together after reading to discuss key issues and topics raised. After rich discussions, students can write their own points of view on one of the questions raised. They might begin by using a graphic organizer to help them compare and contrast ideas raised or to identify a theme statement and then list examples and details that support their perspective.
- Inquiry projects in which students frame their own areas of inquiry around current problems and questions in their world and then go about answering the questions they raised. Sharing the results of their inquiries becomes a community event, so students need to present their findings in visual, written, and oral formats.

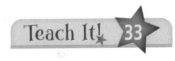

Instructional Conversations

Strategies for Independent Reading

Various types of texts and tasks can provide models for teaching specific strategic behaviors. To help students develop these strategies, you need to incorporate them in your planning for each part of the text lesson: before, during, and after the instruction as they *Anticipate, Build knowledge,* and *Consolidate* (ABC) what they learn. You need to explain how to use the strategies and the benefits that come from them. Then students can apply the specific strategies or make modifications that fit their own styles and preferences within the general ABC framework as they learn.

The World of Reading

The Nation's Report Card

Since 1969, the National Center for Education Statistics (NCES) has assessed the educational progress of our nation's children in a variety of subjects, including reading, mathematics, science, writing, history, civics, geography, and the arts. Known officially as the National Assessment of Educational Progress (NAEP), and unofficially called "the Nation's Report Card," these periodic assessments have two major goals: to measure student achievement in the context of instructional experiences and to track change in achievement of fourth-, eighth-, and twelfth-grade students over time in selected content domains.

The degree of interest in education today is unparalleled in American history. More than ever before, parents, educators, and policymakers are concerned with whether America's children will have the knowledge and skills necessary to be productive members of our global society. NCES points out, however, that we can only know if our schools are succeeding in this task if the nation has impartial information about what students know and can do, whether their performance has improved or declined, and the ways they study and learn. The Nation's Report Card is intended to provide a common yardstick across all states and districts for evaluating student performance objectively and to monitor whether that performance changes over time.

Although the NAEP has been conducted at some level since 1969, the fall of 2003 marked a significant step in the assessment. While participation in NAEP is voluntary, the No Child Left Behind Act provides strong incentives for school districts and states to participate. Beginning with the fall 2003 assessment, any state receiving Title 1 grants from the federal government must participate in national and state assessments at least once every two years in reading and mathematics in grades 4 and 8. Therefore, 2003 marked the first year all 50 states participated, which included approximately 187,000 fourth graders and 155,000 eighth graders. For the reading assessment, students answered a combination of multiple-choice and constructed-response questions after reading three types of texts from typical grade-appropriate sources, representing different contexts for reading:

- Reading for literary experience
- Reading for information
- Reading to perform a task (grade 8)

Achievement is reported in two ways—scale scores and achievement levels. Scale score results report the distribution of achievement for groups and subgroups. Achievement levels categorize student achievement as Basic, Proficient, and Advanced and are used to report results in terms of a set of standards for what students should know and be able to do. Under the No Child Left Behind Act, the goal is for all students to score as proficient in math and reading by 2014 or face sanctions.

Results from the 2003 NAEP for Reading indicate reading achievement remained relatively flat with little change from 1992 or 2002 in the average score for fourth graders, with the score for eighth graders decreasing one point from 2002. Eighth graders did show improvement over 1992 scores. However, although 63 percent of fourth graders and 74 percent of eighth graders read at or above basic level, 37 percent of fourth graders and 26 percent of eighth graders read at a below basic level.

Results from the 2007 NAEP test showed very modest improvements over previous years at both fourth and eighth grades. Now 67 percent of the fourth graders read at or above the basic level, a gain over 2003; but eighth graders stayed the same at 74 percent. The percentage of fourth graders reading below the basic level was down a few points to 34 percent, but eighth graders were up a point to 27 percent.

In addition to the national test, part of the NAEP testing in 2003 was the second step in the Trial Urban District Assessment (TUDA) of Educational Progress, funded as part of the No Child Left Behind Act. The first TUDA, conducted by NAEP in 2002, examined reading and writing in five urban districts. In 2003, nine public urban districts (including the original five) participated in the TUDA in reading and mathematics at grades 4 and 8. Scores showed continued differences between ethnic groups and males and females, although these gaps indicated some narrowing. Results of the TUDA portion of the NAEP indicate all but one of the participating urban districts scored lower than the national average at both grades 4 and 8, with more students reading at a level below the national average. In 2007, eleven school districts participated in TUDA: Atlanta, Austin, Boston, Charlotte, Chicago, Cleveland, District of Columbia, Houston, Los Angeles, New York City, and San Diego. The results showed modest gains over past years. Two cities had improved scores since the last testing. Gaps between racial groups remained considerable.

NAEP is not without its critics as some see what was once considered a relatively neutral assessment now being used to assess individual state testing as well. Critics worry that linking results to federal funds will ultimately lead to a national curriculum and remove individualism from states. Some educators also feel that such a national assessment could be an "indictment" in some cases and put added pressure on individuals and school systems. Regarding the test results, then–Secretary of Education Rod Paige remarked, "we are moving in the right direction; but we are nowhere near satisfied with what we are trying to accomplish. We will not be satisfied until the achievement gap is completely closed and all students are reading at very high levels, at proficient levels."

For a complete review of the findings and to examine sample questions and evaluations, visit the Nation's Report Card online at http://nces.ed.gov/nationsreportcard.

Source: National Center for Education Statistics, National Assessment of Educational Progress (NAEP), 2003 Reading Assessment.

ANTICIPATING. Students need to learn some simple strategies to use before reading that will assist their learning. First, they need to learn the importance of establishing purposes for reading. Remind students repeatedly that they can read texts in different ways and that the manner in which they read a text should grow out of their purpose for reading. Review several purposes for reading:

- Skimming a text or scanning some kind of reading material to see what it contains
- Reading for enjoyment
- Reading to learn how to do something
- Reading to remember facts and ideas

Second, show students how to survey or preview the materials to determine both the external and internal features of the text. Explain to students that visual clues and signal words are features provided as aids to make comprehension easier. External features include visual clues such as chapter and section headings, changes in typeface and font size, and illustrations and charts. Internal features include signal words that point to the text's structure. "Once upon a time," for example, signals the beginning of a fictional narrative. Words and phrases such as *consequently, therefore, because of,* and *as a result of* indicate the use of a cause-and-effect pattern.

Finally, students need to learn how to activate what is already known about the topic. Remind them that they will better understand what they read if they can connect it to what they already know both about the topic and about the way in which it is presented. Some ways to activate prior knowledge are the following:

- Brainstorming (Students can individually, in pairs, or in groups make lists of what they already know and then group these items into categories.)
- Writing out a list of questions they want answered
- Predicting what they expect will be in the text

BUILDING KNOWLEDGE. While reading, students add to what they know and deepen understanding as they construct meaning from the text ideas by doing the following:

- Making and confirming predictions
- Visualizing
- Summarizing and drawing inferences
- Generating questions
- Making connections
- Self-monitoring their progress
- Reflecting on an author's purposes and voice
- Checking accuracy of sources
- Comparing various texts on the same theme or topic

Ways of saving the ideas and images encountered in reading include using journals, bookmark notes, sticky notes, and graphic organizers. Writing and drawing require active thinking and processing and help to encode information in long-term memory as well as to create memory aids to help retrieve information later.

CONSOLIDATING NEW UNDERSTANDING. After students complete a text, they can review the whole and create a summary for themselves, generalize from the ideas,

Complete the activity "Teaching Text Structure to Aid Comprehension" and view a video of a teacher using a content area textbook to help her students identify text structures. Reflect on the video by answering the questions following. (To find this activity, go to the topic *Reading and Writing in the Content Areas* in MyEducationLab and click on Assignments and Activities.)

Paired Brainstorming

By the middle grades, instruction focuses on content area reading and helping students to develop a structured approach that will help them with formal school work. (Myrleen Ferguson Cate/PhotoEdit)

consider the text in relation to its purposes and content, make connections to other texts and their own experiences, participate in group sharing or writing experiences, identify themes and create interpretations of literary pieces (essential to the enjoyment and appreciation of literature), and reconstruct the major ideas of informational texts.

Engaging in Inquiry

Students also learn how to engage in inquiry projects and research. As they use their language skills in exploring new ideas, they have a real opportunity to make use of a wide variety of resources. Students engage their own thinking in both real and important pursuits. These applications of research and thinking abilities are not only made in language arts classes but across the curriculum. They need to develop their abilities to do the following:

- Ask good questions
- Seek appropriate sources of materials and evaluate their quality
- Synthesize ideas from multiple sources of information
- Use electronic media as a resource in learning—in seeking information, organizing it, and presenting ideas to others
- Create written, visual, or oral presentations to share findings

The Writing Workshop

At some point in the middle grades, schools introduce the more formal aspects of writing research papers and reports. This is where the teacher can provide a great deal of structure and guidance, because it is usually the first time such formal work has been required in which students need to show footnotes or references and develop a bibliography. Establish explicit guides for students and clear timetables for the work. You might have the students track their research and turn in weekly journal entries indicating what has been done during the time allocated so that you and the student ensure that things move forward at an appropriate pace. When there are questions or issues, conduct conferences with the students on their progress. This process of developing students' research skills is an example of where teachers can carefully scaffold the initial two components of good instruction: demonstration and immersion and attention to detail. Because the research takes so long to complete, you are preparing students for work they will be expected to do more independently in high school. Middle schools can help students to become more familiar with the research and writing process by giving added research opportunities with guided practice.

Strategies for Building Vocabulary

In the middle grades, students regularly encounter words in texts that they never hear in oral communication. Therefore, they must learn to attend to these new terms and have strategies to remember them. Vocabulary plays a crucial role in content learning because terms convey key concepts, and even familiar words often take on different and specific meanings. For example, consider the word *angle*: it means one thing in mathematics; in social studies, it has another meaning, as in "What was the government's angle on the incident?"; and in general use, it can be either a verb or a noun (e.g., "the stream angled through the woods" or "he loved angling in the stream").

There are many ways in which teachers help students develop their language facility. A key to students' continuing vocabulary development in the middle grades is increasing their understanding of the ways in which words are formed and also how words enter English. When students become sensitive to identifying new words that they perceive as important, the chances of their being interested in words and retaining the ones they select are higher (Blachowicz & Fisher, 1996). Encouraging students to look for words outside of the classroom also is an important component in their developing sensitivity to words. Beck and McKeown (1983) found that the most significant component of their rich vocab-

Table 14.2 Basic Elements of a Good Vocabulary Program

- The teacher models interest in language.
- Students engage in enjoyable word play.
- Students become attentive to new words and self-select words to learn.
- Students learn about the history and growth of English including the nature of words—affixes, combining forms, base words, and derivatives.
- Students develop basic strategies for learning and retaining new content-specific words.
- Students are involved in a great deal of reading that extends their knowledge.

ulary instruction program was the *word wall*. Almost incidentally at first, one of the teachers made bulletin board space and encouraged students to post examples of the new words they were learning in class. This factor alone significantly improved the students' learning. Making vocabulary learning interesting and giving students ownership are two key ingredients of successful activities. As you plan your approach to vocabulary development, keep in mind several important components. Just playing games with words, for instance, is not enough. Nor is doing spelling and vocabulary worksheets. Table 14.2 identifies six basic elements of a good vocabulary program.

TEACHER MODELING OF INTEREST IN LANGUAGE.   By keeping a small set of books about language growth and development on your desk and reading about words periodically, you help to build students' inquisitiveness about language. Books by Richard Lederer and Bill Bryson are great sources for read-aloud pieces on language. The *Readers Digest*'s regular vocabulary quiz is another easy resource that students (and teachers) enjoy taking and then exploring the definitions and uses of the terms. Jokes, too, often involve play with words and can be great starters for talk about language. Table 14.3 identifies some excellent books to keep as resources.

STUDENT ENGAGEMENT IN ENJOYABLE WORD PLAY.   Middle level students love to play with words and language. Music, clean rap word games, and jokes are wonderful ways they explore language. Even joke books should be considered for the classroom library. Comics are another favorite source of a very expansive vocabulary. The teacher can have great fun introducing strange and unusual forms of words and enjoying with students sesquipedalian words, portmanteau words, palindromes, and other strange

Table 14.3 Valuable Language Resources

Bryson, B. *The Mother Tongue: English and How It Got That Way.* New York: Avon Books, 1990.

Bryson, B. *Made in America: An Informal History of the English Language in the United States.* New York: Avon, 1994.

Lederer, R. *Crazy English: The Ultimate Joy Ride Through Our Language.* New York: Simon & Schuster, 1998.

Lederer, R. *The Miracle of Language.* New York: Pocket Books, 1999.

McNeil, R., & Cran, W. *Do You Speak American?* New York: Harvest Books, 2005.

Rheingold, H. *They Have a Word for It: A Lighthearted Lexicon of Untranslatable Words and Phrases.* Louisville, KY: Saraband Books, 2000.

Winchester, S. *The Professor and the Madman: A Tale of Murder, Insanity and the Making of the Oxford English Dictionary.* New York: Harper Collins, 2005.

word forms. Two great resources are *Superdupers: Really Funny Real Words* (Terban, 1989) and *A Cache of Jewels and Other Collective Nouns* (Heller, 1991).

SELF-SELECTION.   Students do better in learning language when they have some control over and choice about what they learn. Studies of students' ability to self-select words they want and need to learn have shown that students are quite good at determining key terms when they are given practice and opportunities to discuss their selections with others (Blachowicz & Fisher, 1996). By first modeling how to notice unfamiliar words, the teacher helps students to realize that this is part of what good readers do regularly. The teacher should then provide opportunities for students to build vocabulary by recording words they find interesting and new, trying to determine meaning from context and word parts, confirming hunches with dictionary or glossary checks, and then sharing their choices with others.

Word Origins and Derivations

UNDERSTANDING OF THE HISTORICAL DEVELOPMENT OF ENGLISH.   The way our language has grown and changed is fascinating. William and Mary Morris's (1962) *Dictionary of Word and Phrase Origins* still is a great source of information about our language, as is Bartlett's (2003) *Dictionary of Americanisms*. Having small sets of paperback books on language history available in the classroom gives students the opportunity to read and discuss the English language together. The talk about words and language also reinforces the use of new words and words used in new ways.

Students in the middle grades need to have some structured study of words and language, too. At this stage, they should be learning how affixes work, how to use Greek and Latin combining forms, and how to connect derivations with base words. Content-area learning involves a great many specialized terms, so knowing how to look for specialized meanings of common words is also valuable. Table 14.4 provides a list of affixes that students should learn. Two useful books are *Techniques of Teaching Vocabulary* (1971) by O'Rourke and Bamman and the more recent *Words Their Way* by Bear and colleagues (2007).

Figurative language is also important to highlight and teach, especially for English language learners in need of help in understanding the many expressions of English. The elementary *Amelia Bedelia* books (Parish, 1966) and *The King Who Rained* (Gwynne, 1989) offer good strategies for introducing figurative language and helping students become aware of the challenge of our language for English language learners.

LEARNING AND RETAINING OF CONTENT-SPECIFIC VOCABULARY.   Students' self-selection of words they want to learn is an important component of language growth. However, in content learning teachers don't want to leave to chance key terms that are necessary for students to make sense of the content. When content textbooks are used, a list of key terms can be developed from words suggested as important. Sometimes there is not a textbook program, and standards are used to develop curriculum. In these cases, a helpful guide to checking students' vocabulary knowledge and selecting words for particular attention is Marzano's (2004) book on academic vocabulary. He includes lists of key terms taken from standards in all the academic areas and chunks them by grade levels. He also suggests several activities to help students learn the terms, including keeping a vocabulary journal and playing games with the key words periodically. Good strategies are needed to draw students' attention to specific words and their meanings in the particular context being studied. A few of these are listed below:

- *Chunking and categorizing words.* The teacher provides a list of key terms and students are asked to chunk them together in groups that fit. Once the groups are made, students give each chunk a label or category. In preparing for the activity, the first step is to create a list of the most important terms that students will encounter in their reading. Next the teacher ensures that there are at least two or three words that can be chunked together. If there are not, the teacher adds some words from the content that will help students build categories of related words.

Table 14.4   Affixes

PREFIXES	MEANING	EXAMPLE
Un	not	*unhappy*
In	not	*incorrect*
Re	again	*repair, remove*
Dis	not or away	*disagree, dismiss*
Pre	before	*preschool, prepare*
Ex	out	*exhale, export*
Anti	against	*antifreeze, antiwar*
Sub	under, below	*subway, submarine*
Super	over, more than	*supersonic, superman*
Com	together, with	*complete, community*
Con		*connect*
Col		*collection*
Co		*cooperate*
Cor		*correspond*
Mid	in the middle	*midday, midsummer*
Mis	wrong	*misbehave, misunderstand*

NUMBER SUFFIXES	MEANING	EXAMPLE
Mono	one	*monotone*
Uni	one	*unicorn*
Bi	two	*bicycle*
Di	two	*dialogue*
Tri	three	*tricycle*
Deca	ten	*decade*
Centi	hundreth	*centipede*
Cent	hundreth	*century*

SUFFIXES	MEANING	EXAMPLE
s-es	plural	clo*cks*
s-ing-ed	verb, time	*sing, sin*
er, est	comparison	late, lat*er*, lat*est*
ly	how done	quick, quick*ly*
ful	full of	peace*ful*
ous	full of	fam*ous*
less	without	use*less*, sleep*less*
ist, ian	one skilled in	scient*ist*, physic*ian*
ness	state of being, having	sad*ness*, sick*ness*
ify, fy	to become, make	mag*nify*, de*ify*
en	make, cause, made of	soft*en*, wool*en*
able	can, able to, deserving	cap*able*, lov*able*
ible		poss*ible*, vis*ible*
tion	action, process	comple*tion*
ion		rebell*ion*
ish	have, quality of	fool*ish*, child*ish*
ment	state of, action	fulfill*ment*
ry, ery, ary	product or action of, place where	bake*ry*, potte*ry*
ize	make, made into	drama*tize*
ism	practice of, act of	hero*ism*, vandal*ism*, patriot*ism*

Sources: From *Vocabulary Building: A Process Approach* © Zaner-Bloser, Inc. Used with permission from Zaner-Bloser, Inc. All rights reserved.

- *Possible sentences.* The teacher gives students a list of the key terms that will be in the text and need to be learned. Working with a partner or individually, they try to connect two or three of the words into a sentence. They write these sentences and later share their possible sentences, even though they might be unsure of the real meanings of the words. The activity raises students' awareness of words they will need to attend to as they read.

- *Exclusion brainstorming.* The teacher gives students a list of words that includes both words they will need for the content being studied and some that do not relate to the topic. The teacher asks the students to predict which words do not fit the content. This activity is fun because it shifts the purpose of the task from what students normally get while highlighting new words.

- *Predict-o-gram.* The teacher presents students with a list of words that come from the story they will read. The teacher then asks the students to predict which words relate to the characters, setting, problem, or resolution. Students can use a graphic organizer with four blocks and space to write predictions they make about the story content after they complete the activity of categorizing the terms.

- *Vocabulary word cards.* Vocabulary word cards can be a fun and powerful way for students to build their vocabularies. They select the ten most important words from the unit of study and then create a 3 × 5 word card for each. On the front side of the card, they draw a picture to illustrate the meaning of the term. On the back side of the card, they write the word, the central definition, and added information to help them understand how to use the word. This might mean a sentence, some synonyms, or phrases in which the word might be found.

- *Personal clues.* The personal clue approach (Carr, 1985) is also an effective way to learn words in content areas. Words are grouped by the concept they are associated with or by the element or character in a piece of literature. Then students list attributes of the target words and think of one personal association that is the clue they will use to store the terms. For example, when learning *laconic*, one student wrote *terse* and *miserly* and associated them with Scrooge before Christmas. Then, on the second day, the student decided that from his study of American history, Calvin Coolidge was a better choice. On the third day, he added another clue: his New England uncle who hardly ever said more than three words. He had fun finding the right clue for *laconic*—but certainly wasn't laconic in his efforts (see the example in Figure 14.1).

- *Connect two.* Using the list of words being learned, students practice them by creating new and sometimes zany sentences containing either two or three of the new words. Doing this with a partner makes it more enjoyable for students because the sentences, which must respect the definitions of the words, can still be fun, and sharing makes it more enjoyable. Revisiting words is essential for retention.

Students also can use graphic organizers such as concept maps to help them learn new words. The organizer contains boxes or cells into which a question or concept is filled

Teach It! 22

Semantic or Concept Web for Upper Grades

Figure 14.1
Personal Clue.

Character
Laconic
- terse
- miserly
personal clue:
Calvin Coolidge was so laconic—
but Uncle Ben is more so!

in. For example, a concept of *definition map* could include questions such as "What is it?" "What is it like?" "What are some examples?" and "What are some attributes?" After creating the web, students can keep expanding their webs—some draw pictures of the concept, some add antonyms, and others collect sentences in which the term is used—to help deepen their understanding of the term. (See Chapter 7 for examples of various graphic organizers.)

WIDE READING.   Doing a great deal of reading is a critical way for students to build their recognition of vocabulary and to learn the specific contexts in which words are appropriate. There is no substitute for reading. Studies have shown that direct teaching of specific words can account for only part of the growth in word knowledge needed to develop an adequate vocabulary (Anderson & Nagy, 1991; Beck & McKeown, 1983). When students enjoy reading and are attentive to language and vocabulary, they continue to build their awareness and ability to use an increasingly wide range of vocabulary terms.

In summary, you can guide students in their development of vocabulary sensitivity and curiosity by having them do the following:

- Keep personal records of words new to them or new uses of known words.
- Develop strategies for building meanings for these words.
- Use appropriate visual or graphic organizers to build and retain meanings.
- Practice using new terms in speaking and writing.
- Use resources, especially dictionaries, thesauruses, and glossaries.
- Engage in word play by creating and enjoying jokes, word puzzles, poetry, and games such as *Scrabble*™ and *Pictionary*™.
- Understand how our language is evolving and how vocabulary grows and changes.
- Keep examples of new words and new usages. (Sports, pop music, and fashion are areas that keep inventing new words and usage that middle grade students are interested in following.)

Student Self-Reflection

In addition to self-monitoring, which refers to the active checking of one's own thinking while reading, students also become more confident readers when they learn to engage in reflection after completing the text. They learn to think about what they have just read and what is new or different. They also can reflect on their own active thinking processes and how well they have used their energies during reading. Questions such as "What did I learn?" "Was I using my energy wisely so I made best use of my time?" and "Did I use the best approach to the reading: visualizing, making a mental map of the text, outlining, or rephrasing as I read?" Adopting a reflective attitude encourages readers to take responsibility for their reading and to realize they can often do more to be effective readers. The teacher can encourage students to improve self-reflection by having them make marginal notes while reading and learning, discuss the process with peers, and keep a journal for self-reflections at the end of reading activities.

Another aspect of self-monitoring is learning to think about the process used in conducting research. Some teachers create guides for students to follow in forming and answering questions about their research: How did you begin your research process? How did you use your prior knowledge as a frame for deciding on what you would need to research? How did you compare and contrast different sources of information? Others have students keep journals of their research process and make notes of what they have done as they go. Another good way to increase students' self-reflection is to use the I-Search Paper model (Macrorie, 1988). In this model, students choose a topic and conduct research on it, but focus most directly on how they go about the process rather than just concentrating on the final paper. They reflect on how they went about their research, what caused

To learn more about how to effectively teach vocabulary, complete the activity "Teaching Academic Vocabulary" which outlines a sequence of instruction that will help students to not only learn the definitions of the target words, but also to be able to use and understand the new vocabulary in reading, writing, speaking, and listening. (To find this activity, go to the topic *Vocabulary* in MyEducationLab and click on Building Teaching Skills and Dispositions.)

Teach It! 61

Cumulative Semantic Map

problems for them, and what they would do the next time. The strategy creates a more reflective and powerful response to extended learning activities.

Opportunities to Model Fluent and Reflective Reading

The teacher can do a great deal to help students develop an internal model of what fluent reading is like by reading aloud to them on a regular basis. Selecting a variety of material to read helps students understand the beauty and depth of what can be communicated by writers. Contemporary students do not have many opportunities to engage in reflection about reading. Playing good audiotapes or CDs of texts being read can also help students begin to appreciate the sounds of written language read orally. For example, listening to books on tape such as James Joyce's *Dubliners* (1993) and Tony Hillerman reading his own mysteries helps students to gain an appreciation for the varieties of oral readers. This strategy can also help students to think of using their MP3 players and time spent in the car as potential time for listening to good books and poetry.

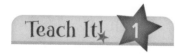

Reading Aloud

Reading aloud from interesting material also can be used to model critical thinking engaged in while reading. When reading to students, pay particular attention to reading with expression, asking questions as you read, and responding to the ideas in the text. Comments such as, "That was beautifully described—I can almost see it!" "Did I understand what the author just said?" "That doesn't sound possible to me" and "That reminds me of something else I just learned" are the kinds of reflections students need to use in their independent reading. Modeling such thinking encourages students to evaluate their own habits and can help them build new habits if they do not already have them. You can enhance the power of this thinking aloud by putting some of these "thinking asides" on the board or on strips hanging from the ceiling so that students are regularly reminded of them. Listening to you read aloud in this manner from a wide selection of texts provides students with many benefits, not the least of which are increased interest in print and sensitivity to vocabulary and language use. Think of the power of reading aloud in providing the following:

- A model of fluent reading
- A model of active and reflective reading
- A way to increase their store of knowledge about the world as well as their vocabulary

The amount of time you have with students will vary depending on how the school schedule is organized. Read the Being a Professional Reading Teacher box and think about your preferences.

Fluency through Repetition

Rereading texts improves students' word knowledge, reading speed, and accuracy while it deepens their understanding of that particular text. Effective methods for incorporating rereading and guided oral reading in the middle level classroom, and thus promoting fluency, include the following:

- Rereading poems and short passages using techniques such as choral reading, two-part reading, and echo reading
- Readers' theater, a technique that involves students in rehearsing and reading aloud their interpretation of a character's lines in passages from a short story
- Self-timing drills, a procedure in which students time themselves or partners in reading and rereading short passages to increase their speed

Readers' Theater

- An introduction to a variety of new books and genres, giving students short amounts of time to skim through several to see which they like best

Being a Professional Reading Teacher

Finding a Good Organization

Teaching reading in grades 6 to 8 is accomplished in varied ways depending on the school organizations. Some middle schools may have a separate reading teacher with major responsibility for teaching reading. However, some middle school organizations may have no designated reading period, with language arts and other content teachers assuming the responsibility of continuing the development of middle school students' reading abilities. In other communities these grades are part of elementary schools where teachers have self-contained classrooms, or they may be departmentalized for some subjects. Some have teams that teach together, with reading linked to social studies or science. Find out what instructional arrangements are used in your area schools. Think about how you would prefer teaching. If you are interested in these grades, investigate resources that are available for middle level teaching. Reflect on what is important at this level and how reading instruction changes for young people at these grade levels.

Your Portfolio

Teaching in grades 6 to 8 requires special classroom management skills. Teaching preadolescent and adolescent young people can be a challenge. Write some reflections about how you have identified potential behavior problems related to adolescence and how you have solved them in your volunteer and/or paraprofessional experiences. These could be excerpted from entries in your daily journal.

Teacher Resources

Related to student behavior issues, make a list of books you might refer to students experiencing problems such as isolation from peers, gender confusion, a divorce at home, or other critical social problems that adolescents often face. You can find many valuable sources by searching on the term "bibliotherapy" at www.google.com.

As you read more, think about the following questions:

- Why is knowledge of the English language such an important part of reading programs at this level?

- How can teachers teaming together in integrated content units (for example, reading biographies and historical fiction in literature while studying American history) be beneficial to students in the sixth- to eighth-grade classrooms?

- How can the teacher scaffold reading comprehension for English language learners in grades 6 to 8?

Assessment

Assessment is the starting point for good instruction. Students in the middle grades vary significantly in their reading abilities and interests, and, with the increasing range of reading genres and purposes that students this age must handle successfully, there is much teachers need to attend to. Throughout the year, the teacher's job is to monitor what all the students know and can do and to provide supportive instruction. Because this is a challenging task, it is also good to remember that the students themselves can be good assistants in the task of monitoring their knowledge and abilities. In fact, they should be made aware of their strengths and should participate in setting and monitoring their goals throughout the year.

Determining Reading Levels

As a result of the daily reading by students of materials in the classroom, the teacher should have a good idea of their development as readers and can guide them into reading appropriate materials. Determining students' instructional and independent reading levels can be done in a few ways.

INFORMAL READING INVENTORIES.   If a reading series is available, one of the easiest ways is to use an Informal Reading Inventory (IRI) provided for the reading program. As you read in Chapter 11, the IRI contains a series of increasingly difficult reading passages; students are asked to read the passages and then to demonstrate their comprehension by answering a series of questions. If the IRI asks for oral reading of the passages, the guideline is generally that oral reading with 99 percent accuracy and 90 percent comprehension indicates independence with the material. The range for instruction (where your guidance as a teacher supports the reading) is 95 percent word accuracy and 75 percent comprehension. Less success with passages indicates that the material is really too difficult for students to be asked to read. In the language of reading assessment, those texts are at a *frustration level* for students. If the IRI involves only silent reading, then the students' comprehension responses are the focus. Usually, the kinds of questions that are included on the inventory try to tap some basic recall of main ideas of the text, some inferences that can be drawn, and some vocabulary knowledge. Be sure to look at the questions in advance. If you are not satisfied that they give you the information you need about particular students, go back and talk over the answers students gave for them and find out why the students responded as they did. Asking students to write a summary of a text is another good way to get information on how well students can follow the main structure and ideas of a passage they read. Then, with students for whom there are questions, some individual discussion about their reading and thinking can be useful. You will not need to have an individual diagnostic discussion with each student, but instead can focus on those about whom you have some concerns.

ADVANCED INFORMAL INVENTORY.   As students mature, teachers also need to find out how well they can read information from more than one source, combine ideas, and learn to think critically about what they read. Teachers need to ask students to compare and contrast two different texts on some appropriate topic. A contemporary news story, two pieces of student writing with different perspectives, editorials in newspapers, and personal letters to the editor all make good content for student thinking. This will provide you with good data as you plan to have students do research (and use the Internet) and engage in extended projects. You can copy two short articles and create a few questions that require students to contrast the pieces, or ask students to write their opinion about the question addressed in the articles, citing references they find useful in the texts.

Another form of an advanced IRI is one that is specific for a content course. The teacher selects passages from the textbook or instructional materials that students read. Questions need to tap the range of reading comprehension tasks—from identifying key ideas, inferring relationships, and understanding specific vocabulary meanings to reading visual information contained in charts, maps, and graphs. This inventory can be completed in a group setting, so it saves much time for teachers.

LEVELED BOOKS.   Many districts now have leveled the books they have available according to difficulty, taking into account a variety of features, including vocabulary and concept load, complexity of sentences and redundancy, and layout of the materials. If you have this resource available, you can select a representative set of books at a range of levels and ask students to read short sections. Then summarize what they have read or have them answer a few of your questions and find their instructional levels this way.

Classroom Fluency Measure

One of the easiest ways to begin to get information on your students' reading is to use the **classroom fluency measure** (Blachowicz, Sullivan, & Cieply, 2001). For this quick assessment, select a passage from the reading anthology you will be using or from other material that you will be asking students to read. Type the passage for your use, and number each line in the margin. Set up a time when you can work with each student individually, either when the class is doing silent reading or before and after school. As you work with each student, ask the student to read orally for one minute while you follow the reading and then ask the student to recall what he or she can from the passage. While the student reads, record any deviations the student makes from the text and subtract the errors from the total number of words read during the minute. By marking the student's location at the end of one minute, you can do this calculation easily after the student tells what he or she recalls from the text. After you have completed the fluency check on all students, you can create a class grid, arranging the students' scores from lowest to highest. This gives you a clear sense of the range within your class and helps you to determine which students you need to do more assessment with immediately and which you can observe in other ways to plan for future instruction.

Strategy Knowledge

A third important component of students' reading that needs to be assessed early in the year is their awareness of the strategies they use to read successfully in different kinds of materials and for different purposes. One middle grade teacher begins her year by asking students to fill out a survey of what their strategies are for reading (see Figure 14.2). On it are examples of the kinds of reading tasks teachers in this departmentalized school expect of students. What the teacher and students learned by doing this survey one year was that the students were very "teacher and parent" dependent. Several students responded to the query about how to prepare for a social studies test that would be given on Friday by indicating that they would read over the chapter, maybe more than once, and then ask their mothers to quiz them using the end of chapter questions. When asked how to figure out a difficult mathematics problem, again the response was to ask Mom. Discussing responses to this kind of survey can be a starting place for developing students' awareness of what good readers do.

Another approach is to ask students to indicate what they are aware of doing as they read a challenging short article. Inform students that they can use sticky notes if they want to while reading so they do not forget their thinking or strategies. When finished reading, each student should write a reflection on what he or she did before starting to read, what he or she was conscious of doing while reading, and what he or she did afterward. If students are frustrated by this task, it means that they are not yet fully conscious of what reading is as a strategic behavior and there is much for the teacher to do with them during the year to develop a vocabulary for and awareness of reading strategies.

Content Reading

Another area that is important for students who are developing reading abilities is their flexibility in reading a variety of different informational texts and in developing strategies for using that information. The teacher needs to know whether students can use the features of informational textbooks as well as glossaries and thesauruses, and whether they can read and weave information from graphs, charts, tables, and pictures (with their captioned information) together with information in the narrative content. Do students use the physical layout of material they read to learn (see Chapter 8)? You may want to find an IRI that contains a good balance of fiction and informational text reading. Some of the newer tests have sections that ask students about their use of text features. Some even have actual articles and textbook formats, making the assessment quite similar to instructional tasks.

Vocabulary and Concept Learning

As you listen to students read and respond to what they read, attend to their use of the language of the text materials. Ask them to define some of the key terms. You might want to be more formal initially and prepare a short vocabulary assessment for one of the first articles or stories you have students read with you in a guided reading setting. Vocabulary knowledge is so important to reading comprehension that you do not want to leave it to chance. You want an idea of students' vocabulary knowledge, and then you want to know whether they have learned and use any self-conscious strategies for adding words to their use vocabularies.

Figure 14.2
Reading Strategies.

WHAT DO YOU KNOW ABOUT YOUR STRATEGIES FOR READING TO LEARN?

Your language arts teacher has set up a unit in which you will read novels in groups. Each night you will read one chapter. What strategies work best for you to help you enjoy and understand novels? What will you do?

_____

_____

_____

_____

Your social studies teacher has assigned you a 25-page chapter on Monday. On Friday you will have a test on the material. You are on your own to read and learn. There are lots of headings and boldfaced vocabulary in the text. At the end of the chapter, there are many questions and activities. What will you do this week with this chapter? What is your plan?

_____

_____

_____

_____

A quick way to find out how well students know the vocabulary of a particular novel, story, or informational text is to have them complete a Rate Your Knowledge chart (Blachowicz, 1986). Select eight to twelve key words that will be important for students to understand, and list them on a chart like the one shown in the Integrating Across the Curriculum feature that Rasheed Graham developed to check students' familiarity with terms in the novel _The Midwife's Apprentice_. Students do their own self-assessment by indicating their level of familiarity with the terms. They rate their own level of knowledge for each word. Including a column that asks students to define the words or create a drawing for words they mark as familiar can help keep students from overestimating their knowledge.

You also want to know whether students have any self-conscious strategies for learning new words and phrases and whether they are interested in vocabulary. Asking a few questions (orally or in written form) about how students note new terms that they think are important and how they then go about learning the terms can stimulate some new ideas and help make students more focused on this aspect of reading and learning. For others, you might find out a lot about how they learn language and what rehearsal tools they have found useful (making cards, drawing pictures of terms, writing and using the terms orally, etc.). Some English language learners can provide good ideas for all students, growing out of their high need for vocabulary. Highlight their experiences if they are willing to share how they learn language. This is a good place for you to be a model and share your own vocabulary-learning strategies as a way of stimulating students' reflection and realization of the importance of being self-conscious learners.

Understanding Students' Interests

If students are going to develop as readers, they need to be reading regularly both in school and beyond. Therefore, you will be able to encourage students most effectively if you are aware of what they are interested in reading and have an idea of their particular interests. This will allow you to help them combine these interests with new kinds of reading. For example, a student who is interested in snowboarding might find a magazine on the sport fascinating and develop an interest in deeper reading on this topic from articles in other magazines. You can find out about students' interests by observing them as they interact with others, by engaging them in conversations, and by doing some journal writing with them about their own lives and what they read and do. At the beginning of the school year, simply asking your students to write about their two favorite books can help you get a feel for them as readers. There are several commercially available Interest Inventories that can also help you and the students identify areas for more reading and for ways you can involve librarians in helping locate appropriate and new materials for the class.

Developing a Diagnostic Eye and Ear

One of the most important forms of assessment is what you observe students doing during your ongoing classroom reading activities. During these activities, you will see students engaged with texts and responding to them in a variety of ways. Use all of these typical situations to observe carefully and make notes of what students show about their developing reading abilities. Experiment with ways to record information from these classroom events and build profiles of your students as readers. Many teachers keep a clipboard nearby and focus on two or three students a day, making notes about their engagement in discussions, their responses to specific questions, or their thinking aloud as they read with a group. Other teachers prefer looking at the whole class and recording evidence of students' thinking, no matter who seems to be revealing their strategies and understanding. Writing short sticky notes of these occurrences and noting the students' names on the notes permits you to add these sticky notes to a student folder where a variety of performance indicators are collected along with samples of written work. Another approach is to shadow a particular student for a day, a form of observation that helps a teacher to create a more complete sense of how the student reads across a variety of situations.

Study Reading

As students enter the middle school years, many find the shift in expectations quite startling. Instead of having teachers guide them through their assigned work, students are expected to know how to read and learn from assigned materials; organize their own study time and come to class prepared; and be able to study and learn a vast amount of information. There are several areas in which teachers need to guide students so they can be successful.

Scheduling Time to Study

Allocating time for study is an important aspect of learning for middle school students. This is a good time to provide students with weekly schedules and talk through ways to find regular study periods on weeknights and weekends. However, students often are not inclined to listen well to a teacher's recommendations. You can stress the need to study by calling on older peer models. Invite former students from high schools and universities to talk with your students about their study habits. Some students in class might have older siblings who can speak with authority about their strategies for learning. When middle level students hear from older teens they respect, it becomes easier to guide them into more attentive reading and reflecting.

Students need to learn to keep a schedule for their study. You might ask visitors to bring their study plan books with them and show how important it is to develop a study schedule and keep records of assignments and time. Some of your own students might already have some form of study plan book or have parents who have given them planners. This can be a stimulus to help students review each week what they need to be working on and the time they will need to be prepared for all their assignments and projects.

Figure 14.3

Question-Answer
Relationships.

In the Book Questions	In My Head Questions
Right There The answer is in one place in the text.	**Author and Me** The reader needs to combine what he/she knows with what is in the text.
Think and Search The pieces of information are all in the text but the reader needs to put them together to answer the question.	**On My Own** The reader needs to use his/her own ideas to answer the question; it is not answered in the text.

Test Taking

Learning how to study for tests is important—and generally unknown to middle level students. Take time to make a grid for different kinds of study and discuss with students strategies that are effective, particularly the advantages of spaced study and repeated rehearsal of new concepts and terms. Practice tests are becoming very familiar—almost too familiar—in states with high-stakes testing. However, making students aware of the nature of those experiences is important. Talk through with the students how they went about answering questions. How did the format of the test influence their strategy for taking the test? When did they read the questions—before or after reading the story or passage? Did they skim through the text if it was fairly long? How did they finally make the decision to answer the question as they did?

Introducing the **Question Answer Relation (QAR) strategy** (Raphael, 1986) at this point is a good way to help students understand the difference between typical classroom questions that are often of a higher thinking nature and those asked on standardized tests. The QAR approach divides questions into four types: those that can be answered by finding one piece of information (right there), those that require searching the text (think and search), those that require drawing on background knowledge to add to the text (author and you), and those that go beyond information in the text itself (on your own). Standardized tests given to thousands of students must include answers that are available in the text passages themselves. Therefore, according to the QAR terminology, there are no "on your own" questions. All questions have answers that can be found either in a specific location in the text (right there) or by combining bits of information from sections of the text (think and search). See Figure 14.3 for a graphic representation of the QAR model.

Teacher Modeling

Another way to raise interest and awareness of the cognitive choices readers need to make as they read is to describe your own reading behaviors when you are learning. For example, you might describe how you study for a graduate course you are taking. Show students how you study, and get them to compare and contrast their own habits with yours. A key habit you can reinforce is the need to read the same text sections several times and make notes about what you consider to be important. Show students your own text markings or the sticky notes you insert at important points in a text.

Metacognition

Middle level students are very pragmatic and seem to always want to know "Why do we need to do this?" They often lack the knowledge of what reading really involves and are unable to describe what they do. Middle school students need to be better informed about what happens when they read and how they can become better readers. They need to develop **metacognition** about their learning, that is, an awareness of how they think. Metacognition involves three basic strategies: connecting new information to former knowledge; developing strategies for thinking; and planning, monitoring, and evaluating how they think (Dirkes, 1985). Activating metacognition can be done in a number of ways.

Active Reading

Students' metacognitive awareness of what good readers do while reading should be developed at this level. Teachers often begin this process by engaging in thinking aloud when they read orally. Using books that have margin notations on them is also a good way to stimulate students' attention to the thinking that goes on when good readers interact with pieces of text. You might create your own examples by having older students mark up a story or essay that your class is going to read. Go over the notations, and discuss them with the students by asking, "Why do you think this note was made? What would have stimulated this comment? How would you have responded?" Comparing two or three different people's responses to the same article gives students a clearer idea of the wide variety of ways in which people engage with text. Then you can build a list of the kinds of engagements that others have made and begin to use these as thinking strategies for your class; that is, visualizing, connecting to another text or author, marking it as providing an answer to a question, arguing with the text, and so on (see the Standards and Literacy box).

Many good teachers use sticky notes as a way of helping students monitor and develop their thinking as they read. They pose the question, "What kinds of thinking do we do as we read?" To explore their own minds during engaged reading, each student can be given several sticky notes and instructed to use them when ideas, images, and questions come to them while reading. When the group (either the whole class or a small group) is finished reading, the students can compare their notes and begin to understand how different students think about the same text. These different responses can then be categorized, and students can talk about how they think. Extending this activity to explore how the same students read a different kind of text also helps the students extend their understanding of the impact of the text on reading and thinking.

Self-Assessment

Once you have developed students' awareness of how to read and learn from text, they can then regularly include their own self-evaluations of the strategies they use in the work they do. You can do this by asking students at the end of class periods to fill out 3 × 5 cards on their class participation and work. You can alter the questions each day you hand out the cards with stems like these:

- What did you learn today?
- How did you learn best today?
- How was your class participation?
- What could you do better to help the class learn?
- What bothers you, or is still unclear?
- What was most interesting to you today?
- What would you like to learn more about?
- What questions do you have?

A teacher's feedback and guidance can help students learn to assess their own development. (Will Hart/PhotoEdit)

Standards and Literacy

Creating Visual Images While Reading

Having noticed that many of her students rushed through their reading of fiction, the teacher questioned three students about what images were being created in their heads when they read. She got blank stares in response. Knowing that this was one of the objectives of the state standards, she decided that it was time to provide a focus on visualizing and imaging while reading.

A State Standards Literacy Plan

From Texas state standards: Describe mental images that text descriptions evoke.

Teacher Decision Making About the Lesson

Focus of Instruction: Modeling imaging through a think-aloud process followed by students creating their own images as they read a short section of text.

Materials: The teacher creates an overhead transparency of a short paragraph that evokes images. The teacher makes copies of two paragraphs from a short story students can easily read that has good images.

Before the lesson: The teacher explains to the students that an important part of active reading is the creation of our own personal images—or seeing a movie in our mind. Some readers think of having a mind's eye that creates pictures from words on print.

Albert Einstein once said, "If I can't picture it, I can't understand it." A good way to ensure that you are comprehending when you read is to check to see whether you are creating mental pictures of what you read.

During the lesson: The teacher models the process by putting the paragraph on the transparency and uncovers the sentences one at a time. She thinks aloud about her own images as she reads each sentence. Then the teacher involves students in sharing any images they have. She writes down her own ideas on the transparency and does the same with the students' thoughts as they share.

> The woman slowly emerged from the hollow.
> In one hand she carried her good shoes.
> She carefully protected the large, bulging bag she carried over her shoulder.

After this introduction to imaging, the teacher asks students to take the copies of the two paragraphs she had copied for them and read them silently, drawing or writing about the images that were created as they read. She then asks them to share these images with their partner. When this is completed, the class comes back together to reflect on their imaging.

After the lesson: The teacher asks that as the students read their novels that evening, they make notes in their journals of images that came to them as they read. They will share their own images the next day in class. She suggests that if students prefer, they can find pictures in magazines that reflect their images and create a collage of ideas from the reading.

Begin the next class session by reviewing what the students wrote the day before. This simple process gives students a regular way to think about their learning and to know that the teacher is serious about taking advantage of class time to ensure learning. It also provides the teacher with important feedback on the success of the class sessions.

Learning Logs

Learning logs also give students a vehicle for ongoing self-reflection on their learning. At least weekly, students should be encouraged to review what they have learned that week, what questions they have, and how they have contributed to the class accomplishments. Key concepts and new vocabulary are also important to record in a learning log so that students stay focused on their primary purposes in school. This is serious business, yet it is very enjoyable when each student can keep a record of growth. Too often, students shift attention from learning to social acceptance at this age, and all the ways teachers can use to involve students in knowing and evaluating their own successes can help to balance the intense peer focus these students feel.

Extended Unit Assessment

Units of instruction are another place where student self-reflection is important. Right from the start, students should have a record of what they know and the questions they want to have answered from their study. Keeping this record in the form of a K-W-L chart in students' notebooks means that it will be available when students have completed their units. One teacher also asked students to generate a possible table of contents for the insect report they knew they would write as a culmination of their integrated language arts/science insect study and to make a semantic map of how those topics might be related. All of these pieces were kept in the students' notebooks throughout the unit. At the end of the unit, the teacher again asked students to look at their actual table of contents and compare it with the first one they had predicted would work. The teacher also had the students create a new semantic map and make a comparison with their first one. The teacher asked that the students respond in writing to some questions:

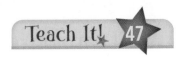

Know-Want to Know-Learn (K-W-L)

- What surprised you most about your learning?
- How did your first table of contents compare to your final one?
- What did you notice about your semantic maps?
- How do you feel about your learning?

Metacognitive Graphic Organizer

One student responded, *"I can't believe how much I learned! I even thought spiders were insects when we started. I learned what that crunchy sound is when you step on an insect—it is the exo-skeleton. I also learned how to create a semantic map and show the relation of body parts and what insects can do."* Students also can use personal notes like the sticky notes I-Chart (see Chapter 8) to evaluate their typical responses and thoughts while reading. When they compare their patterns with those of others in their class, they can begin to develop a broader sense of what reading can be and may consciously try to enhance their own thinking.

Portfolio Evaluation

Portfolios are great tools for student and teacher assessment at this level. These consist of personal collections of illustrative student work annotated to explain how they demonstrate learning or accomplishments. Students can collect examples of their own work that illustrate their best achievements and that also show the areas and goals they still need to work toward. When you have students annotate or add note cards to the pieces in the portfolios, the students' self-reflection is deepened. Be careful to give guidelines and set parameters for portfolios, however, because they can easily get out of hand. Students love to sort and annotate their work and can spend hours creating covers for the portfolios. Space to save the portfolios is also an ongoing concern. So, some clear guidelines about selecting a few pieces each quarter that illustrate both best work and work in progress can make the portfolio process integral to students' learning. Keeping a list of books and articles students have read with a short summary and evaluation can also become a lifetime habit. Students need visual records of what they are learning and reading, and the portfolio is a natural aid in helping them to celebrate the results of their efforts.

Teaching All Students

Each year that students grow and learn, their knowledge, skills, learning styles, and strengths and interests become more individualized. Good teaching encourages and nurtures the particular talents and differences in students' learning, so we all must celebrate these increasing variations! Research on multiple intelligences has helped us to understand that variations are natural and need to be considered in organizing for instruction.

Your students will bring with them a wide range of cultural and linguistic abilities. Many students know more than one language and have had experiences in diverse

Learning Journals

Finding out what students know about the content being studied at the beginning of a unit or lesson is important. This is particularly urgent when there are students from a variety of linguistic and cultural groups in the classroom. Yet these are the students who are most hesitant to speak in class and to write out their ideas. An easy way to elicit some of what they know is to have students keep modified Learning Journals in which they record what they are learning on a regular basis. For English language learners, these journals can be places where they can draw and create diagrams and graphic organizers of their knowledge. Rather than insisting that students write in traditional formats, these more visual forms of representing ideas can give English language learners more confidence in activating what they know. A part of their journals can be dual-language lists of key terms. When teachers provide a list of important terms at the beginning of the unit, students can write these in their own journals in both English and their first language. For new terms, teachers can encourage students to copy visual illustrations of the terms from their textbooks or dictionaries or find visual representations they can photocopy.

cultural settings. You can enrich your own learning and provide great resources to the whole class by using these opportunities sensitively and well. Therefore, as a teacher, you have real challenges in creating classroom experiences that meet students where they are and challenge them as literacy learners.

Identify Strengths

A key to reaching all of your students is being a careful observer, or, to use the term coined by Yetta Goodman (1978), becoming a good kidwatcher. Each day you can observe how your students come into your classroom; you can observe how they interact with their peers; you can listen to what they share; you can watch them as they read; and you can engage them in conversation. It takes just a few moments each day to become attuned to your students. The effort is most valuable. Keeping a notebook page with bits of information gained from informal observations can help you to build a profile of each student that can be useful over time. Then, at an opportune moment, the particular strengths of a student can be called forth. For example, who is good with music and can help to plan the background pieces to accompany the presentations by the novel groups? Who is good at drawing and can illustrate the class book or movie reviews? Who is great at organizing on the computer and can catalogue the independent reading records? Who is a good oral reader or actor and can help others visualize texts they are reading? Some of the less-adept readers and writers may have other strengths that will help them to learn more effectively and also contribute to the group in ways that can enhance their identity with literacy (see the Differentiated Instruction box).

Recognize Students' Cultures

Teachers can help to make all students feel a part of the classroom by ensuring that materials about their cultures and situations are available and by reading from some of these materials. Teachers can also sensitize students to the plights of immigrants and minority students by reading aloud from some stories that represent situations similar to those of students in the school. It is often from ignorance that young teens can seem callous and not caring. When they hear the stories of what others have had to experience, their sense of fairness and empathy can be expanded. Table 14.5 identifies some books that can be good for such read-alouds.

English language learners bring with them a wealth of knowledge about their own languages and often have the ability to contrast languages in ways that can be helpful to monolingual students in your classroom. Having bilingual or trilingual students in class can be a real asset. Help them to become comfortable talking about these differences in language and culture:

- When you are discussing characters in stories, ask students to reflect on how the same characters' actions would be perceived in their culture of origin. Discuss how the characters would have handled the same situations in their culture.

- Have students act out the behaviors of a character in a story as if the character were from their culture. Compare this with how the same character's actions are depicted by some other students.

- Analyze the language used. Would it be different if from another culture? For example, would characters express their emotions as they do in the story you are reading? How would they interact with strangers?

- When reading classic stories, ask whether students from other cultures have stories similar to those you are reading. Do they have the same story in translated form or is the story from their culture (e.g., *Arabian Nights*, *Aesop's Fables*, *Cinderella*, *The Nutcracker*)?

- Make lists of key vocabulary terms, and have students write the same words in their languages. These comparisons can often be the beginning point for discussion of where English has acquired its words.

- Graph the story structure of pieces you read with the class. Ask someone from another culture to show the structure of a typical tale from their culture. Are they the same? (For example, Athabaskan and Japanese tales often have a less-defined beginning and ending than Eurocentric tales do and can go on and on, leaving more to the reader to determine.)

- Read orally from news that reflects the world as represented by students in your school. Use maps so that the areas they come from become familiar to everyone. Use current events as the texts for some of the reading strategies you model. Often, students from abroad have a better sense of world events than do U.S. students, and their knowledge can be used to expand everyone's perspectives.

Story Maps

Adjusting Teaching for English Language Learners

When students are functioning in a second or third language, they need more time to process what they read and hear and more time to compose their own responses. Even when students have exited from bilingual programs, they have not had time to develop the depth of vocabulary and language usage required by middle school literature and content texts. The more the teacher can do to support their development of English, the better they will be able to engage fully in class activities and think deeply about content.

There are a few easy ways in which the teacher can support these students' learning within each area or theme. First, brainstorm the key terms you will be using, and check the students' familiarity with them. Create a glossary of the terms that are not known, and put these on a bookmark that students can keep with them while reading and studying. Second, as a way of introducing the writing of an author to students, have some parent volunteers record the first part of a text (a novel or story or a chapter of informational material) so that the students can hear the language and begin to recognize the connections between the oral and written forms.

A third way to help English language learners participate fully is to give them some pre-experiences before the class begins a new area of study. You might hear this referred to as "jump-starting" their thinking and learning. For example, if you are going to have a unit on survival tales and will read some of Gary Paulsen's books, check out a videotape showing the setting of Canada and the northlands so that students can more easily visualize as they read. You might also find some easier books or magazine stories that introduce the same concepts that you will deal with in a novel or informational unit and let students take these home and learn from them before delving into the more difficult class texts. You also might be able to find easier versions of some of the stories you will have students read, and these can be used as advance organizers to prepare your English language learners for the complete version. Many readers do better with texts when they have a good idea of what the content is about; this is particularly the case for English language learners. Help them to discover what works best for them, and then try to provide appropriate scaffolds for their learning.

Organizing for Instruction

Middle grades are just that—in the middle between self-contained elementary classrooms and high schools with their departmental structures. In some schools, grades 5 to 8 are treated much like the earlier elementary grades, in which one teacher has a single class with some special teachers perhaps providing elective courses in foreign language and music or computers for the students. Other schools create teams of students and teachers, so between 80 and 120 students are grouped together with four or five teachers, and the teams stay together for two or three years. Many middle school advocates have supported this model as a way to provide more guidance and create "home groups." Another variant is for students to have the same teacher for two or three subjects—usually language arts, reading, and social studies or a combined reading/language arts block. This core or combined teaching structure helps teachers to know their students more deeply, because they have fewer sections. Yet other schools are totally departmentalized with no groupings, so reading teachers teach four or five different groups of students each day. Any team teaching is done by individual teachers working together. Most new teachers have little say in how the school is organized. It is important that you know what kind of structure your school has in place because it provides the framework within which you have to teach.

There are several options for providing a range of reading opportunities that develop students' strategies and knowledge of reading, some of which are discussed in the following sections. The methods provided are certainly neither exhaustive of how good instruction can be organized nor are they comprehensive, but they provide a number of good options found in schools across this country. Recently, schools have also begun to use block scheduling to provide longer periods of time for students to work within a single content. Finding a balance among curriculum areas and language arts skills essential in learning content is challenging.

Integrating Content Areas

As one reads about the kinds of reading strategies and skills that middle grade students need to develop, the advantages of teachers either teaming or having students for two or three subjects are clear. Students need to learn to read many kinds of texts and for many purposes. They are more interested and engaged in developing these when they see the concrete and immediate use of them (Guthrie & Davis, 2003). For example, teaching students how to retain new and important vocabulary words is much easier if this instruction is provided when students need to master their history or science content. Helping them learn to read dense textbooks is easier when the teacher can use the students' own content textbooks. Middle graders are very pragmatic and concrete, and the more instruction is directly tied to needs, the more likely they are to attend and process the strategies.

There is so much that needs to be taught that teachers have come up with a variety of ways of organizing the curriculum to meet these wide-ranging aspects of reading. One of the basic issues to be faced is how to balance the reading of literature with reading in informational texts and helping students learn to use reading to learn. A good option is to divide the year into quarters and teach fictional literature and poetry for two quarters; use a thematic focus for one quarter, involving students in reading and evaluating multiple sources; and spend another quarter on inquiry and research, linking with either science or social studies teachers so that students have both the content and process as high priorities. Within this organization by quarters, there are many options for instruction.

In the example of integrated instruction described in the opening classroom story, Rasheed Graham, the language arts teacher, teamed with the social studies teacher, Elizabeth Raphael, so they could develop the deepest learning possible for their students. Mr. Graham had learned in previous years that his students couldn't read the novels he had selected with any depth of understanding unless they had a good foundation of knowledge about the Middle Ages and life in feudal Europe. This came from their work in social studies, where the whole structure of medieval life was explained and students had multiple experiences studying about medieval social structures and economics.

In developing this unit, the teachers began with the state standards and benchmarks in social studies and language arts (http://education.state.mn.us). In reading/language arts the key standards and benchmarks came from two areas: reading strategies and understanding the literature. Mr. Graham knew these standards and benchmarks were essential for his students.

For his part in this integrated unit Mr. Graham had selected a set of novels at different levels of difficulty so his students could engage in small groups and discuss the books together. He had used these literature circles for a few years and felt comfortable having students discuss ideas in small groups. He also knew that his students would be challenged by much of the vocabulary and so had developed some Rate Your Knowledge self-assessment guides for students to use. (The Integrating Across the Curriculum: An Integrated Unit on the Middle Ages and Life in Feudal Europe feature, shows an example.) Students complete their assessment of their knowledge of these terms at the beginning of each novel and then keep notes as they build understanding of the terms during the unit. At the end of the unit they return to the sheets to assess their growth.

As Ms. Raphael developed students' understanding of the medieval period in Europe, she used the textbook, videos, and other books and magazine articles so students could build a sense of the social order and life during that period and make comparisons with what they take for granted now. She was grateful that Mr. Graham provided opportunities for reflective analysis of the novels both in discussions and in student writing activities. Students kept vocabulary notebooks that were used across reading and social studies so they also understood the way their work in both classes overlapped and built a strong foundation for their understanding.

The final projects for this unit also were integrated with grades for both subjects. The students had choices for these: they could develop a character and write a diary or memoir of that person's life over a significant period; they could create a manor and the surrounding community (some did this on their computers and some built three-dimensional

Integrating Across the Curriculum
An Integrated Unit on the Middle Ages and Life in Feudal Europe

Put a check by the level of knowledge you have of each word. If you think you really know a term, then either write a few words to define it or draw what it means.

Key Words	Unfamiliar	Have seen	Know and Use	Definition/Drawing
Scavenge				
Scrawny				
Dung heap				
Midwife				
Apprentice				
Risk-taking				
Haggle				
Ointment				
Merchant				
Herbs				
Self-awareness				

The key social studies standards (MN standards) guiding this unit were:

	Standards	Benchmarks
World History, Substrand D. Early Medieval & Byzantium, 400 AD – 1000 AD	The student will demonstrate knowledge of Europe during the Middle Ages from about 500–1000 AD in terms of its impact on Western civilization.	1. Students will describe the spread and influence of Christianity throughout Europe and analyze its impact. 2. Students will explain the structure of feudal society and analyze how it impacted all aspects of feudal life.
E, Global Encounters, Exchanges, and Conflicts, 500 AD – 1500 AD	The student will demonstrate knowledge of social, economic, and political changes and cultural achievements in the late medieval period.	1. Students will describe the emergence of European states and analyze the impact. 3. Students will identify patterns of crisis and recovery related to the Black Death, and evaluate their impact.

Key Literature Standards & Benchmarks Guiding the Unit (MN Standards and benchmarks) Literary Standard: The student will actively engage in the reading process and read, understand, respond to, analyze, interpret, evaluate and appreciate a wide variety of fiction, poetic and nonfiction texts.

Literary benchmarks for sixth grade:
Identify and describe the relationships among elements of fiction including setting, character, plot, conflict/resolution, theme and tone.

4. Analyze characters through identifying thoughts, words, actions, and narrator's description.

5. Describe how figurative language (such as simile and metaphor) and literary devices contribute to the meaning of a text.

6. Relate a given literary work to historical events.

The reading standards and benchmarks (MN) that guided unit activities were:

C. Comprehension: The student will actively engage in the reading process and read, understand, respond to, analyze, interpret, evaluate and appreciate a wide variety of fiction, poetic and nonfiction texts.

Benchmarks:

3. Generate and answer literal, inferential, interpretive, and evaluative questions to demonstrate understanding about what is read.

4. Apply a range of monitoring strategies and self-correction methods.

5. Identify the main idea and supporting details.

6. Retell significant sequences of events or ideas.

displays); or they could research some aspect of medieval life and create a report that was presented to their classmates. In each of the project options, the students followed the guidelines and used the rubrics the teachers had prepared as they worked on the projects and later engaged in self-evaluation.

Teaching Literature

Most elementary students have been reading fiction and can anticipate the basic structures and techniques used in this kind of text. However, in the middle grades, several new genres are introduced, and they can pose problems for readers who are on automatic pilot much of the time in independent-level materials. Science fiction, fantasy, short stories, and stream-of-consciousness pieces are often new to these students. That said, with the current rage for *Harry Potter* and Tolkien's *Lord of the Rings* books, some fantasy texts are becoming better known even among younger students. Biography is another genre that is important to teach at this level because it provides a great link for students to the world at different periods of history and to people who have had important influences on the students' own development. Longer, narrative poetry is often given more attention in the middle grades, and students can be involved in dramatic play readings, choral reading, and readers' theater. Some teachers concentrate one unit on novel forms and a second on short stories, poetry, and drama. This is where the developmental continuum from fifth to eighth grades needs to be worked out among the reading and literature teachers so that students continue to learn more about literature each year. Teachers can develop their literature focus in at least three ways: using core novels and literature groups, literature circles, and guided reading and readers' workshops.

CORE NOVELS AND LITERATURE GROUPS. Use a core novel representing a genre you want to introduce with all students to begin the novel unit. Then have students select from four or five novels you have prearranged for their subsequent work in literature groups. By engaging all students in a single novel, you have a good context for introducing and

Literature Circles

modeling the concepts and strategies you think are important for students to be using independently later. With all students reading the same text, you can also help them develop good discussion skills and courteous behavior. Because a whole class is too large to hold engaging discussions most of the time, you can use a "fishbowl" technique and divide the class into two parts: Half the students sit in the center of the room and participate in oral discussion, and the other half sit around the outer part of the class and write their responses to the questions and flow of ideas and also monitor the participants' discussion behaviors. Use the same inner circle for the whole class period, or, if time permits, shift the roles halfway through the class period and give both groups the opportunity to participate both orally and in written form. By having the outer circle evaluate the participation of the inner circle, there is a good record of who has contributed and how the discussion proceeded. Students' written comments also serve as a good way to evaluate their own interpretation of the text and their response to the ideas discussed.

Supporting English Language Learners. Using a single novel also helps students who are English language learners participate more fully in the class. Before the unit begins, a few students or parents can tape-record the novel or the first half of it so that English language learners can hear the sounds of the language and become familiar with the text. The teacher can also prepare special guides for these students so that they can follow the plot, know the characters, and think of questions ahead of class discussion. Some teachers have found that giving English language learners mini-lessons before the general class sessions helps them to gain confidence in their understanding of the text; then they can relax and enjoy the discussion of the text during the class periods. Finally, students gain confidence in their ability to contribute to class discussions when the teacher provides time for them to talk with partners before responding in the whole class or fishbowl. Pose a question for the group, then let students turn to their partners to think aloud about their responses, find the words and ways of expressing ideas in English, and get feedback that either modifies their ideas or confirms what they have said. Then open the conversation to the larger group. With this slight modification, many English language learners feel much more confident and comfortable participating in larger class groups. It is also a good model for all students: Think before speaking!

Connecting Writing and Reading. While using a core novel with the whole class, you have the opportunity to model journal writing and use students' own responses to enhance the discussions. Students might need to learn how to respond to literature. Begin by showing your own journal entry for a part of the text the group is reading. Provide labels for the kinds of responses you make: connecting with the text (*this reminds me of . . .*), raising questions (*what does it matter if . . . ?*), visualizing (*I see . . . in my mind's eye*), responding emotionally (*I don't like ____ when . . .*), predicting (*I bet this problem will . . .*), and elaborating (*I know at this time in history there were often periods of . . .*). You might need to ask students to use two or three of the kinds of responses in their own journals so that they can develop the various ways of responding and then switch to other forms in the next entry. What you think is easy and automatic might be very uncomfortable for students. Rather than presuming a great deal, it is often better to start slowly and ensure that all students understand the tasks and intent of the journal experiences.

If students have a difficult time writing journal entries, they might do well to partner with another classmate and, between talk and writing, frame their joint responses to the text. You might find it useful to give students sticky notes to use while they are reading so that they don't lose the ideas that come to them while reading. Then they can return to those notes and elaborate on them as they write in their journals.

Journals can also serve as tools to help students focus on the features of the genre or other important elements of literature that you want to highlight. Students can keep a place in the journal where they record examples of specific literary elements, such as the setting in fantasy or futuristic elements in science fiction. They can also note special phrases or uses of language in the journal and share those later with other students. You can ask students to keep a section of their journals in which they can write new vocabulary items or new ways in which terms are used. If they record the pages on which the words occur,

Language and Diversity

English sounds different than the written words may suggest. How can students hear correct academic English?

Teach It! 32

Dual-Entry Diary

Writing and Reading Connections

Argue for the importance of writing across units of instruction.

they can begin to see how authors often repeat the same vocabulary in different contexts. Adding drawings of the terms helps many students to enjoy this activity and remember the new words more easily.

LITERATURE CIRCLES.   Students tend to discuss books better when teachers are not leading the groups (Almasi, 1995; Hynds, 1997; Raphael & McMahon, 1994; Short & Kauffman, 1995). Many teachers prefer conducting their literature units by having students self-select the books they read and work in small discussion groups rather than in teacher-led discussions of the same novel. They do their teaching in mini-lessons at the beginning of the class period so that all students can focus on the element the teacher highlights, but within their own texts, and then take on the role of active observers during book discussions led by the students. At times, teachers also serve as facilitators of the students' discussions, but they should not assume the role of "expert" at these times.

The nature of the mini-lessons that are used should derive from observations of the students as they are involved in reading and responding and by evaluating the written work of the students. The major framework that helps teachers to develop the foci for teaching comes also from the standards students should be able to meet.

In the standards in Minnesota and many other states, middle grade students are expected to learn to compare how authors and illustrators use text and art across materials to express ideas by employing foreshadowing, flashbacks, color, strong verbs, and language that inspires. Knowing that expectation, Mr. Graham developed the medieval unit using novels and art representing that time period. He selected a set of novels including *The Ramsey Scallop* (Temple, 1994), *Catherine, Called Birdy* (Cushman, 1994), and the *The Midwife's Apprentice* (Cushman, 1995). He added materials that exemplified life in medieval Europe in other artistic forms: books about life in medieval Europe, including *Anno's Journey* (Mitsumasa, 1997) and *Castle* (Macaulay, 1982); examples of tapestries from the collection at the Cloisters from the Metropolitan Museum of Art for students to observe; and tapes of Gregorian chants. On the day the unit was introduced, he had music playing in the background and showed slides of the art as he introduced each of the novels. Then he gave students time to look through each of the novels and make a decision about which books they wanted to read. Each student listed his or her first and second choices. From these lists, Mr. Graham could help guide students to appropriate texts; some were much harder than others, and he wanted all students to read somewhat challenging materials but not books they could not handle.

During the unit, Mr. Graham guided students to make comparisons about the techniques used by artists in different media. One of the journal guidelines for the students asked them to locate interesting examples of language used to create pictures of the times and to compare that with other works of art. At specific points in the unit, students compared the plots and literary devices used by the different authors. In these and many other ways the state standards and creative planning combined to develop a stimulating and enjoyable learning experience for the students.

Mr. Graham also created a variety of assignments to focus student learning. Most homework required students to read several pages of text and write two or three questions they wanted their literature circle group to discuss the next day. Because understanding point of view is another standard, some students were asked to keep a journal from the point of view of a character of their choice while doing their reading. Students reading the same novel selected different characters so the impact of the plot and events on them could be recognized. An assignment for another group of students was to take particular scenes and rewrite them from a point of view different from that of the author. This proved a very interesting and challenging task. As a culmination, one group created a short readers' theater production for their novel that required students to take on the personas of the characters in the novel. In all these ways, the focus was on creating engaging and challenging experiences so that the maximum was gained for the time spent reading and discussing the novels.

There are many advantages to having students in literature groups. First, the students' different reading abilities and interests can be accommodated much more easily this way, and all students can participate in the class activities. Assignments can be matched to the

How can students' assessments of each other's work help them to develop their comprehension and writing skills? (Will Hart/PhotoEdit)

Guided Reading

students' learning needs; not all able readers have developed the skills and strategies they need and can be focused through specific work. Using multiple texts permits teachers and students to make comparisons among authors and forms of art so authors' decisions and styles can be illustrated. Core vocabulary and concepts are generally repeated in various texts, so students gain a deeper understanding of the basic concepts and can develop better visual images of what they read. Students become resources for each other in very real ways when they are the authorities on particular texts. Speaking clearly, summarizing well, using good examples, and then listening to each other are very real communication skills that can be developed.

GUIDED READING AND READERS' WORKSHOPS. There is so much variety in the kinds of reading that students need to develop during the middle years that some group instruction by teachers is necessary. All students need to learn more about how textbooks are structured and the resources they contain. The differences in structures and discourse forms with which students must become familiar require teacher guidance. The various graphic aids and formats also need explanation and some direct attention. Then there is the issue of learning to do research and study independently. The middle years are when these become very important for students, and good schools provide a significant amount of time helping them learn to do research well and to construct reports and presentations. With computers now available in most classrooms, teachers need to provide instruction in the use of both the Web for collecting and evaluating information and the software for creating high-quality reports with digital pictures, imported pictures, and student-created diagrams and charts. For teachers who prefer doing most of their class work in fiction, this means that special segments of each week or a few weeks each quarter need to be devoted to informational reading and study.

Some teachers prefer to structure a portion of their reading program around student-selected individual reading. Atwell (1998) has developed the **reading workshop** model, during which students all read individually in books of their own choosing and keep logs of their reading to use when they conference with the teacher. When students come together to discuss their reading, Atwell characterizes the conversations as a "dining room table" conversation about what each person is reading. Although most of the time students read silently and write individual responses, the teacher brings students together periodically for mini-lessons in which aspects of literature or reading strategies can be explained. Later, students can apply these lesson foci when they engage in their own reading.

Depending on the amount of time the teacher has with students each day, the two components of a rich literacy program can be developed simultaneously or on alternating days and weeks. The two aspects can also be combined if teachers want to direct students' individual reading toward a particular theme or genre. For example, if the class is working on aspects of informational textbooks and scientific articles, then students could do their individual reading in books that include scientific essays, in magazines such as *Science* and *Scientific American* (or student magazines in the areas of science), and in biography. There are many great texts that students can read and use to enlarge their horizons in this more guided reading workshop.

Expository Texts: Thematic Units

Most middle level students enjoy exploring unanswered questions and making school relevant to their own lives. This is easier to do when a class is engaged in a focused group inquiry project or thematic unit of study. Because students are generally much less familiar with informational, expository texts than they are with fiction, providing a stimulating

Figure 14.4   Thematic Unit Overview.

THE AMERICAN DREAM UNIT OVERVIEW				
Thematic Statement: Personal goals and choices are influenced by our own values.				
Focus Question: Is it still possible to achieve the American Dream?				
Project: Persuasive Paper: Is the American dream still achievable for me?				
Selection	Genre	Perspective	Diversity	Period
The Grapes of Wrath	novel/realistic fiction	negative	Lower-class Anglo-American	1930s
The Great Gatsby	novel/realistic fiction	negative	Upper-class Anglo-American	1920s
"I Have A Dream"	speech	positive	African American	1960s
"Maya Angelou"	poem	positive	African American	1990s
"An American Dream"	magazine	positive	European	1990s
"Charlie Two Shoes & the American Dream"	magazine	positive	Asian	1950s
"Is the American Dream Still Alive?"	magazine	positive	Mexican-American	1990s
"False Gold"	magazine	negative	Lower-class America	1990s

context for the study of such materials is very advantageous. By having the students read several texts on the same topic, you can more easily illustrate the various text structures that are used and can help students to determine the advantages and disadvantages of each. You can also provide activities in which students write using those same structures. Attention to the varieties of forms of informational writing is important, as is the need to make it interesting. Therefore, many teachers have found that developing units around interesting content permits better teaching and learning than other skill-focused instruction. This can be achieved either by creating units with content teachers (in departmental structures) or by integrating reading and content when you teach content and reading to the same students.

One model for integrated units developed by Michigan educators uses a key question as the focus for each unit, such as "Can the American dream be achieved?" In collecting the resources students will read, they use a planning grid to ensure that multiple perspectives on the issues are presented and that a wide variety of literature, both fiction and nonfiction, is included. See the example in Figure 14.4 of the resources for one unit.

Essays and Biography

When teachers do not feel comfortable creating more extended units around themes or content topics, they can still provide guided instruction to help students handle informational reading. Contemporary magazines for middle school students contain much excellent writing and are good sources for reading development. *Cobblestones, Calliope, Faces, National Geographic World,* and *Boys' Life* magazines are great sources of articles. Collecting a variety of biographies, both long and short, is another way of

Readers' Theater exercises can be incorporated into all areas of the curriculum; this is a popular technique with young people. (Paul Conklin/PhotoEdit)

providing texts that permit the teacher to guide students toward reading more deeply in this genre. The different ways in which biographies are structured provide the opportunity to focus on organization and can be linked to students' writing of a biography later. Teachers can provide a good comparative study of how biographers represent the lives and accomplishments of well-known figures by structuring assignments so that students read and compare encyclopedia-type sketches and then read more in-depth book treatments of the same person. When more than one full-length biography is available, even more critical analysis is made possible, and students find it engaging. They easily become excited (and sometimes indignant) at how people are represented. Good questions analyzing the author's purpose, context, and perspective are natural outcomes of this investigation.

Drama and Choral Reading

One of the most interesting aspects of written language is hearing it read and performed orally. Middle level students also love these kinds of activities. Some teachers allocate two to three weeks during the year for production of a play or choral reading and having students perform before audiences. These dramatic events can comprise science and social studies content as well as literature units. There are websites specifically devoted to readers' theater scripts for teacher use. This makes including this oral form of reading (and rereading for fluency) much easier for busy teachers.

For English language learners, opportunities to participate in rehearsed oral language productions or even oral reading of poetry helps to instill a sense of the sounds of English language that can last a lifetime. Regular opportunities to memorize or at least reread and rehearse language provide valuable patterns that English language learners can rely on and build from later.

Organizing and Managing a Learning Community

As you plan instruction to include all that is important for middle grade students to learn, consider some of the options suggested in Figure 14.5 for weekly programs. These can shift over the course of the semester; however, you need to use your time wisely, and attention to planning will always pay off. Note the allotted time for whole-group activities, small groups, and individual work and reflection.

Adolescents' Identity and Motivation

Reaching and teaching young adolescents takes special consideration. Students at this period in their lives are going through enormous changes; one day they might seem like they are adults and very much in control, and the next day the same students behave as if they are children, definitely in need of adult structure and guidance. Younger adolescents

Figure 14.5 Weekly Schedule.

Monday	Tuesday	Wednesday	Thursday	Friday
Class focusing in whole group (10 min.) Share independent reading and viewing	Class focusing in whole group (5—10 min.) Teacher shares own reading	Class focusing in whole group (5—10 min.) Reflect on goals for week	Class focusing: teacher reads orally and thinks aloud—model use of target goal	Class focusing teacher/students share vocabulary
Teacher-guided lessons: reading and writing strategies attention to detail (30 min.+) & Small group and individual reading & writing activities: guided practice and independent work	Individual silent reading and writing (15—20 min.) & Partner/small group work (5—10 min.) Teacher conferences	Small group discussions (10—15 min.) and journal reflections Teacher observation of discussion—some participation Individual reading and writing (15 min.)	Teacher guided lessons: focus reading or vocabulary strategies (10—15 min.) Individual work reading, writing and research (10—15 min.)	Small group discussions (10—15 min.) journal reflections Individual work
Reflecting/ writing/planning ahead (5—10 min.)	Reflecting/ thinking ahead (5—10 min.)	Reflecting/ thinking ahead (5—10 min.)	Reflecting/ thinking ahead	Reflecting/ writing/ thinking ahead (1—10 min.)

also feel tremendous pressures from their peers. They want to be accepted and part of the peer group of those they admire. Often, this drives young teens away from adults and family, and teachers have to build their trust to create open, safe classrooms where students will engage fully.

Adding to the normal developmental changes that middle level students go through, our current culture inundates students with information and options—a sort of food court mentality. Everything students do involves choice, from what kind of milk to drink to which brand of French fries they want to eat. Even the cereals they eat in the morning might be their own selected favorites, chosen by no other family member. They become accustomed to having life tailored to their specific interests and preferences. This has real implications for their response to classroom activities. Choice needs to be a part of what is provided in terms of materials, groups, and learning activities. Children who are given choices outside of school expect them in school, too.

Young students live in a world that is ever changing and somewhat frightening to them. They look for classrooms that are safe and that respect their needs and interests. The teacher can do a great deal to make classrooms predictable and orderly simply by having clear routines and ways of engaging that students can anticipate. For instance, when students have several teachers each day, they often get confused about what kinds of participation each considers acceptable. Explaining how you want students to behave—when they have to raise their hands, when they can interrupt each other, when they can move around the room, and how they should interact in small group activities is helpful. Putting the rules on a chart that can be displayed regularly makes many others feel more comfortable. In addition, the clearer you make your expectations for the work students will do and how they will be evaluated, the more likely it is that students will relax and participate actively.

The humor, compassion, and idealism of young students are also wonderful attributes of this stage. They respond well to teachers who bring in humor, give them an opportunity to laugh, and encourage their fun sides. Many middle grade students find meaning by being able to work with younger students, and some classes make it a regular practice to build buddy programs with primary classrooms so that the middle level students serve as mentors and helpers for young children.

Finally, students at this stage need to see the relevance of the activities they are asked to do. The more learning can involve real inquiry about topics of concern to them, the more likely students are to become engaged. Beane (1991) advocates that middle school students themselves determine the units that they study. Being clear about the goals and purposes of class activities and how they relate to the students is important. Establishing a safe climate where students can ask questions, engage in extended inquiry, and express their own ideas and conclusions is a foundation to their learning.

Beamon (2001) suggests that adolescents learn best when activities are interactive and purposeful and include meaningful engagement. The five circumstances that make this most likely are as follows:

1. Adolescents do something that makes sense in a larger context, such as confronting real-life issues and problems.
2. Their personal initiative and energy are moved into action through meaningful involvement with relevant and current content.
3. Their cognitive and affective capabilities are challenged, such as when connections are made between difficult content and its application to personal experience.
4. They can draw on a variety of resources in the learning environment, including personal experience, the local community, and the Internet.
5. Their knowledge and understanding are substantively broadened or deepened.

Engage Students in Twenty-first Century Web-based Inquiry Projects

Children often come to middle grades with considerable skills in using electronic media. They are often motivated by opportunities to develop new media skills and share their learning using technology. One project that helps teachers engage students with new literacies focuses on student inquiry and development of their own websites. As they work with their own questions, students engage deeply in learning about both the content and then about the way websites are set up and how they can be used to communicate meaning. That is the purpose of the ThinkQuest Project sponsored by Oracle Education Foundation (ThinkQuest.org). The ThinkQuest Project is constructed so students choose an educational topic that captivates their interest—one that can be investigated from numerous viewpoints, is interdisciplinary, and creates interest by covering multiple academic disciplines—and then create a website that communicates what they learn.

The Foundation has created an online learning platform that facilitates students' ability to create their own websites to share the outcomes of their learning projects. The ThinkQuest project invites teams of students working with a teacher coach to participate in a global competition for the best websites. There are clear guidelines for the composition of the teams (3–6 students and a teacher/coach), the selection of the topic and investigation question (12 categories are given from which to select), the process of building a website to share student projects and the required components, and a set of criteria that are used for evaluating the projects. Winners receive prizes and some participate in the international competition. The student website are available at http://library.ThinkQuest .org.

As part of the Twenty-first Century Project in Orange, Massachusetts, one group of students decided to take on the challenge of creating their own website on global warming and ways to protect endangered species. Together with their teacher project advisors the three girls, Emily, Colleen, and Caroline, carefully read the guidelines for the projects and spent much of their after school hours engaging in research and in developing their website. During the winter, their area of Massachusetts was devastated by an ice storm that left them without electricity for most of a week. There was no heat, which led their teacher, Ms. Fredette, to challenge them with a practical problem: Could they create a portable, small heat source—Heat in a Box? They did, with the support of their parents, and added a most practical component to their project. Their website (http://library. ThinkQuest.org/08aug/0428) includes their Home Page, About Us, Global Warming, Climate Change, Environmental Effects, Spreading Disease, Threatened Species, and How to Help. The wealth of websites available on the Internet has become a valuable resource for students' learning. When students create their own websites, they become much more aware of the nature of these sites and how to use them effectively. They also become active contributors who share the outcomes of their own inquiries and research. See the results of this project and look at the winning websites for three divisions: 12 and under, 15 and under, and 19 and under. The winners for 2008-09 included teams from Romania and the United States. Read the reflections of both the students and their teacher coaches at http://library.ThinkQuest.org/.

Selecting Appropriate Materials

Most new teachers start out the year having to use materials that have already been selected—whether it is a reading anthology/basal series, a literature series, or a curriculum built around novels and thematic units of instruction. If there are classroom sets of novels, informational books, and magazines, these can be great resources for building a rich reading program. You want to make sure you can create a room that invites students into reading and writing. One element of immersion is creating the right environment; the visual statement of a classroom is a powerful one that all students notice. Having books and magazines is important, and ensuring that they are current and of interest is essential, as is displaying them attractively.

Assess what is available to you, and think of any holes that seem apparent. For example, check to see whether multiple levels of reading materials are available so that you can differentiate instruction for your students. Check to see whether fiction, poetry, plays, and readers' theater scripts are handy and that informational materials are in good supply. As you do your own inventory, also check with the school librarian and/or media specialist to see what resources they have for your use. And, of course, talk with the other teachers on your team or in your department so that you can be aware of all the collected materials that are available. Table 14.6 identifies some basic materials you will need to get started.

Given the current attention to state standards, a more focused curriculum is also quite likely. You will want to assess areas in which there are ample materials for your use when you want to go in depth and do some lessons that provide attention to detail in practice materials. Some of these might be available for use on computers; make an inventory of all the resources you can locate.

Because it is important that students learn to think critically about their reading, check for ways in which you can help students read from a variety of resources on the same topic or theme. If you have an anthology to use for literature selections, locate two or three pieces that complement or contrast with the core text so you can go beyond a single selection. If you are linking to content areas such as science and social studies, provide both fiction

Table 14.6　Materials Checklist

- Range of core text materials at varying reading levels
- Variety of types of materials (short stories, novels, informational texts, magazines, newspapers)
- Resource materials (how our language grows and changes, language usage and vocabulary, thesaurus, dictionaries)
- Practice materials (print and electronic) including vocabulary supports
- Materials that provide contrasting points of view
- Professional materials for your use and students' use, as appropriate

and nonfiction materials that will deepen the units of study and help you guide students into more sophisticated reading of these materials.

A wealth of resources is available for use with middle school learners. The following websites provide resources and links to literature discussions in which students can participate:

- The National Council for Social Studies provides a list of Notable Social Studies Books for Young People at www.socialstudies.org/resources/notable/.
- The National Science Teachers Association recommends a variety of resources, including books, at www.nsta.org/recommends/.
- The International Reading Association provides lists of choice books compiled by teachers, young adults, and children at www.reading.org/choices/.
- Many books also contain book lists. Junko Yokota's book *Kaleidoscope* (National Council of Teachers of English, 2001) includes a book list for grades K–8.
- Many local libraries have websites that provide links to online book clubs. Sometimes the libraries themselves sponsor book clubs. In many cases, libraries have partnered with the organization "Chapteraday," which has book clubs for teens as well as adults and covers a broad range of genres. Check out the following links to online book clubs: http://www.chapteraday.com, http://www.surfnetkids.com/bookclubs.htm, www.planetbookclub.com.

Assessing Reading Levels of Materials

Sometimes you may have a room full of materials, but you do not know whether they are appropriate for your students' reading development. You might want to do a quick fluency check to see how many of your students can handle the material easily. Sampling a few students who scored at the middle range, a few from the lower level, and a few from the upper level (as charted on your fluency scale) can give you a good idea of how you can use your material. One other easy way to check the match between any particular novel, text, or other material and your students is to develop a **cloze test** (Bormuth, 1968) and administer it to your students (see the Assessment box).

Involving Parents and the Community

Many parents of middle school students complain that their children no longer want to share with them what happens in school. One middle school decided to create a structure that would bring students and parents together. They initiated the Generations Literature Circle as a voluntary activity and then extended it to become a full part of school life. Parents and students agreed to read the same novel and come together for a book

Using Cloze Assessments

In the middle grades there is an increasingly wide variety of materials teachers can use to help students learn. One good tool to use to find out if the materials are within the reach of the students is the cloze procedure. It can be used with content textbooks, articles downloaded from the Internet, magazine articles, or any piece of text you consider using.

Cloze Assessment

To use the cloze test, take a passage of approximately 300 words from early in the text and retype it for your students, deleting every fifth word starting with the second sentence. Make sure that you have spaces of equal length for all the words that were left out and that the spaces are large enough that students can fill in what they think the author used. Then select one or two additional sections from later in the text if it is lengthy and do the same process.

Before giving the cloze test, model the procedure with your class because it might be unfamiliar to your students. Create a short sample from an article, leaving the first one or two sentences intact (see Figure 14.6). Then delete every fifth word until you have about five to ten spaces. Put the passage on the computer screen, on an overhead, or on the erasable board. Explain that you are going to try to fill in the exact words the author used, taking into account the style and total context of the piece. Let the students know that you are trying to determine whether the particular author has written in a way that matches their expectations and knowledge. Students might need another example that they can do independently or with a partner before completing the

full cloze passage you have developed (see Figure 14.7). If you use this second modeling, be sure that you take time to go over the answers and explain why particular choices are better than others.

Other Measures to Determine Levels

One of the most traditional ways to assess the difficulty level of materials is to use a formula that measures the difficulty of the words and the complexity of the sentences. Both the Dale-Chall (1948) Formula (for easy materials) and the Fry (1967) Readability Formula (appropriate through adult materials) use these indices of difficulty. Teachers can select a few passages from the text and determine their difficulty level; however, these formulas are general and provide only a rough estimate of difficulty for readers (see Chapter 10 for a review).

Use these tools just as rough starting places. Students' individual knowledge and interests influence how well they can understand texts they read. As students get older, the use of formulas becomes less predictive of the match between students and materials. Therefore, it is always good to check with students directly about their ability to understand materials. They can often provide clear feedback, and their ability to read and talk about what they read is the real measure we need. It is also true that the more students read on any topic, the more able they become to handle more difficult materials on the same topic. The same is true with authors; once students become familiar with an author's style, they can more easily independently handle more material by that particular author.

We have seen that the American colonists needed labor to build their fortunes and, in the process, build a nation. And we have seen their willingness to take that labor, by force, from Africans. But, African men and _____ did not willingly surrender _____ lives. The people who came _____ the boats were Africans, _____ by a strange tribe. _____ plantation owners did not _____ captives longing for freedom, _____ for ways to overthrow _____ who held them; they _____ slaves, people who would _____ without having to be _____ watched.

Taken from Now Is Your Time! by Walter Dean Myers (p. 36; HarperCollins, NY, 1991)

Exact words deleted: women, their, from, captured, The, want, looking, those, wanted, work, constantly

Figure 14.6
Cloze Passage.

When animal droppings and garbage and spoiled straw are piled up in a great heap, the rotting and moiling give forth heat. Usually no one gets close enough to notice because of the stench. But the girl noticed _____, on that frosty night, _____ deep into the warm, _____ muck, heedless of the _____. In any event, the _____ heap probably smelled little _____ than everything else in _____ life—the food scraps _____ from the kitchen yards, _____ stables and sties she _____ in when she could, _____ her own unwashed, unnourished, _____, and unlovely body.

Taken from The Midwife's Apprentice by Karen Cushman (p. 1; Clarion Books, NY, 1995)

Exact words deleted: and, burrowed, rotting, smell, dung, worse, her, scavenged, the, slept, and, unloved

Figure 14.7
Cloze Passage (Second Short Model).

discussion and share their responses to the book. Both groups read and made notes about favorite passages, and both groups developed questions they wanted to ask others about the book. Parents were not to ask those questions of their own children but could offer them to the whole group. The book discussion replaced part of the parent conference night. It provided a good way for parents to understand the new forms of book discussion being used by the reading and language arts department. As they experimented with the discussions, one class had fun using the inner/outer circle idea. First the students formed the inner circle and discussed some aspects of the book under teacher facilitation. Then the parents took their turn and discussed the same issues. Both groups had a great time understanding a little better the responses of the other generation.

Another exciting community reading event occurred when the mayor of Chicago declared that the whole city would read a book together. The first book that was chosen was *To Kill a Mockingbird*. This last year it was *House on Mango Street*. These books were already being used in many schools as part of the regular middle school literature/social studies curriculum. As a special focus, the middle school teachers in one K–8 building decided to involve the local school council members (the community school board) in a discussion of the book for the year. During the first part of the evening, the council members sat in the inner circle and discussed their responses to the book while the eighth graders listened. Then it was the eighth graders' turn while the adults listened. What a memorable night! And what different perspectives were enabled!

For Review

Middle level students are at a great stage of development—moving from childhood to maturity. They are eager and impatient to find themselves in the world, especially among their peers. Books and good instruction can provide great models and stimulate their best impulses. We as teachers have a great deal we can do to ensure that they develop into their best selves.

This chapter began by laying out the wide variety of literacy skills and strategies students need to develop in the middle grades. Particularly important changes occur at this point in schooling as teachers involve students more heavily in reading informational materials. Students need to become independent in their ability to apply appropriate strategies as they anticipate, build knowledge, and consolidate their learning. Vocabulary development is particularly important because students encounter so many words and concepts that are new to them. In the chapter, several activities that help students develop interest in and curiosity about words and strategies to retain new words for content learning and for their own personal vocabulary enhancement were described. Examples of good references to help teachers and students learn more about the rich nature of our language were also provided.

Because students in the middle grades possess a wide range of reading abilities, the section on assessment provided many avenues through which teachers can determine what students can do and what areas need more attention. These include using informal reading inventories, leveled books, fluency measures, and assessing awareness of text features, vocabulary, interests, and strategy knowledge.

Suggestions for how teachers can help students learn strategies for studying and retaining information from reading and develop their own self-monitoring of their learning were provided. A major component of middle level instruction is expanding the types of texts students read and developing their abilities to use reading and writing to learn new content. When teachers integrate their instruction in units that extend over time students have more substantial opportunities to think deeply and learn. The importance of students engaging in reading on a regular basis is a theme that continues throughout the chapter. Specific ways to reach all students, including English language learners, were introduced. The chapter suggested ways to organize for instruction with literature and informational texts. These include integrating content learning and reading instruction through thematic units and teaching literature by using core novels and literature groups, literature circles, and guided reading with readers' workshop.

The final section reminds teachers of the importance of organizing and managing a learning community by being sensitive to young adolescents and providing a rich array of materials that they can read with confidence and interest. Knowing students well is the beginning of good relationships and sets the foundation for meaningful instruction.

For Your Journal

1. What do you think is the optimal classroom environment in which to encourage and support middle level students?

2. After reading about different ways to organize classroom instruction, take some time to reflect on which ideas and structures you think you could use most productively. What are the reasons that you selected one over another? Have you seen other ways of organizing that you prefer?

3. Return to the questions in the Anticipation Guide and think about what you can add to your original thoughts. How have your ideas been expanded or altered?

Taking It to the World

1. A pair of eighth-grade teachers added a new dimension to the study of the Bill of Rights by having their students conduct a mock court trial. The issue: A student is accused of humming during the national anthem, a violation of a rule. The teacher faces a loss of job and pension. During a month-long study of the issues, students assembled arguments and witnesses and then argued the case. Because one teacher's spouse is a lawyer, the students did get some assistance in determining exactly how they should argue both sides of the case. Class members served as lawyers, jury, clerks, and witnesses. The students got so involved in their research and legal work that the local newspaper heard about the trial and photographed the final session.

2. Look carefully at the U.S. Constitution's Bill of Rights. Brainstorm with a friend ways you could make a thematic study of the rights practical for your students. What issues in the community could be highlighted?

New Literacies Connections

1. Middle-level students love to share their ideas and find out what their peers think. Now it is possible for students to extend these discussions worldwide with some of the good sites that have been established for international book discussions. Search for some of the sites that help students to connect with their peers in other countries.

2. Go to the U.S. Department of Education website, Doing what works (http://dww.ed.gov). The section on adolescent literacy has a whole set of resources for meeting the needs of readers needing intensive support. View some of the classroom clips and look at the ways teachers are reaching a wide range of students in middle schools across the country.

Chapter

15

Models and Strategies for Teaching ESL and for Teaching Reading in the Mother Tongue

Anticipation Guide

The following statements will help you begin thinking about the topics covered in this chapter. Answer *true* or *false* in response to each statement. As you read and learn more about the mentioned topics in these statements, think back on your answers. See what interests you and what prompts your curiosity toward more understanding.

_____ 1. English language learners can learn English in one year.

_____ 2. It is a waste of instructional time to teach a child to read in the child's mother tongue.

_____ 3. Phonics is the most important component of reading for an English language learner.

_____ 4. Children should always be grouped by level of English proficiency for English as a second language (ESL) lessons.

_____ 5. Children who learn to read in Spanish have to start over when they learn to read in English.

_____ 6. The teacher should always correct the grammatical errors of English language learners.

_____ 7. Children who have learned to read in their mother tongue have little difficulty learning to read in English.

_____ 8. English language learners should always respond in complete sentences.

_____ 9. Some adolescent English language learners are not able to read in any language.

Models and Strategies for Teaching ESL and for Teaching Reading in the Mother Tongue

Teaching the English Language Learner p. 485

Second Language Acquisition p. 491

Linking ESL Instruction and Literacy p. 500

Teaching Children to Read in Spanish p. 503

Assessing Oral Language and Reading Proficiency p. 510

Supervising Paraprofessionals p. 514

A Classroom Story

A Bilingual Teacher in a Bilingual Classroom

Ms. Ortega is a certified bilingual first-grade teacher. Her twenty-three students speak Spanish as their first language, and their English proficiency ranges from none to a few at a low-to-intermediate level. Her children are ready to learn to read in Spanish, and she is well prepared to teach them. The Spanish reading program she uses is parallel to the English language program used in other classrooms in her school, but it is not a direct translation. She also has a wealth of children's literature in Spanish.

Ms. Ortega begins her morning business in English. "Good morning, boys and girls." "Good morning, teacher," they respond, politely and respectfully addressing her by her title. After several weeks of school, the children can greet their teacher, respond to the roll and lunch count, and understand most classroom routines in English. Morning business is followed by a forty-minute ESL lesson that is characterized by simple dramatized commands, questions, many gestures and smiles, and much laughter.

After recess, the children have whole-class shared reading activities in Spanish with big books. In smaller groups, they dictate language-experience chart stories in Spanish, read them, put the sentences in order, illustrate, read to each other, and play word games with vocabulary they have used. Independently and in pairs, they will take turns "reading" big books to each other and reading language-experience stories to family members at home.

Some of the children are beginning to associate sounds with letters they recognize, and Ms. Ortega has begun to teach brief focused phonics lessons related to elements that have emerged from their language-experience charts and for which they have demonstrated phonemic awareness in language play activities. They also work in the more structured Spanish reading program with anthologies of stories and some expository text. The program includes more systematic and explicit activities designed to introduce the relationships between sounds and letters in Spanish several weeks into the school year and after they have developed a basic sight vocabulary.

The children in Ms. Ortega's classroom are indeed fortunate. They are in a full bilingual program with a highly qualified teacher and with appropriate instructional materials. She addresses them in English in the parts of her program where they are ready to understand. She consistently devotes thirty to forty minutes of instructional time each day to ESL, focusing on listening with nonverbal or simple responses at the beginning, with more emphasis on production later.

Her Spanish reading program is analytic or whole-part-whole, with children learning about letter/sound correspondences in the context of words they already recognize. The plentiful authentic literature in her classroom provides for a strong focus on comprehension and motivation.

The vignette also displays how Ms. Ortega presents the elements of the four blocks framework described in Chapter 1: guided reading and writing, self-selected reading, and working with words (Cunningham, Hall, & Sigmon, 2007). She demonstrates reading to her students in the shared reading activities with big books. She works with words in the brief focused phonics lessons that emerge from meaningful reading and writing activities. She provides guided practice both in the shared reading of big books and in the dictation and reading back of dictated language-experience charts. The children extend their reading practice in reading shared books to each other and language-experience charts to family members. They will soon begin to write in Spanish as an outgrowth of their LEA activities.

The purpose of this chapter is to examine the teaching of reading in the mother tongue and also the teaching of ESL as it relates to the teaching of reading and writing. The audience for the chapter is threefold: bilingual teachers who will teach reading and writing in a language other than English, teachers of English language learners whose mother tongue instruction will be conducted by a paraprofessional or other staff members under the teacher's supervision, and all teachers of English language learners who teach ESL.

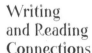

Writing and Reading Connections

How can teachers help English language learners develop vocabulary?

Options for Teaching the English Language Learner

There are two basic categories of instructional programs for teaching English language learners. These categories are presented in terms of the generic K–8 school program for them; the specific questions of second language and reading instruction are treated later in the chapter.

Teach Them in English

English-only options for teaching English language learners exist in several forms and for many reasons. In some cases, the numbers of children who have a non-English language in common at a grade level are small, and it is not feasible to offer a program of mother tongue instruction. A lack of trained teachers and mother tongue instructional materials may exacerbate this situation. Political considerations constitute another reason for providing only English language instruction, such as in California and Arizona, where statewide ballot propositions largely discourage or make difficult the use of mother tongue instruction and mandate the use of what is characterized as structured immersion in English. But there are many limitations in teaching English language learners only in English, as you will see.

IMMERSION INSTRUCTION.   One approach to second-language acquisition is *immersion*, sometimes called *structured immersion* (see Figure 15.1). Immersion instructional programs are focused on intensive English instruction during the first year, although it is well documented that children need more than one year to master enough English to learn academic subjects and reading in English (Thomas & Collier, 1997).

ESL instruction is the most important element in an immersion approach to teaching English language learners. Their academic instruction in reading, mathematics, science, and social science is also conducted in English, although English language learners gain little from this instruction. They do not understand or speak English, nor can they read in English at a sufficient level of comprehension. In some cases, support in the mother tongue is provided by a paraprofessional or parent volunteer. For example, that adult might sit down with the English language learners to assist them in understanding a lesson the teacher taught earlier in English and in completing independent work.

What is often called a *submersion* approach is a variation on structured immersion, and it is truly a sink-or-swim approach. Although most educators do not advocate its use, the submersion approach is often observed as the default methodology in working with English language learners. Non–English-speaking children are simply thrown to the mercies of a teacher, classmates, and instructional materials in English, with no concessions to their language or cultural needs. This sometimes occurs for political reasons. But many times it is simply a reflection of the school's inability to respond to the needs of a small number of non–English-speaking children who have a less common mother tongue.

Lambert (1975) contrasts additive and subtractive education programs for second-language learners. In an **additive program**, children add a new language and its accompanying culture to their mother tongue and culture, along with a positive self-image. In a **subtractive program**, English and its accompanying culture are substituted for the mother tongue and culture, often leading to low self-esteem, low academic achievement, increased dropout rates, and other negative consequences. Immersion programs are of the subtractive type.

Several major principles guide teachers' understanding of how to provide the best context for learning in general and for learning in a second language. Cummins (1986, 1989) describes two levels of language proficiency that demonstrate the need for high-level

Figure 15.1

Model Program
Structures for Meeting
the Needs of English
Language Learners.

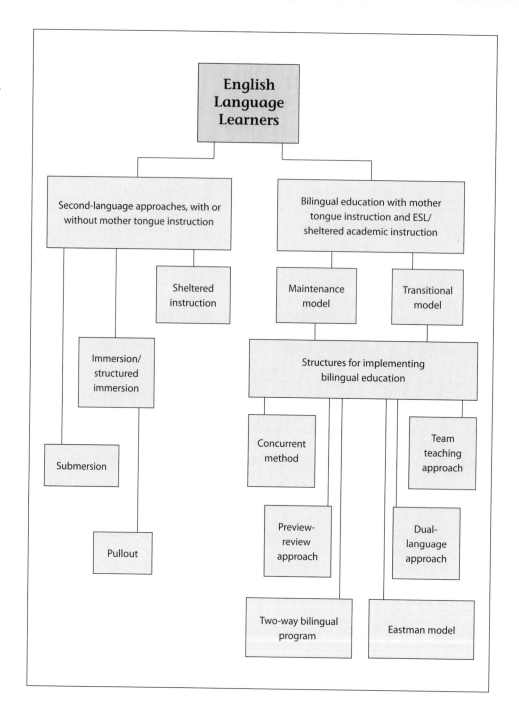

proficiency in the second language before academic instruction is provided in the second language. He describes **basic interpersonal communications skills (BICS)** as those that permit English language learners to carry on a simple conversation in the new second language, and they appear to be proficient. But a higher level of language proficiency, **cognitive academic language proficiency (CALP)**, is required for the student to learn to read in the second language or, for example, to learn the commutative principle of addition in mathematics. Cummins concludes that a threshold of language proficiency in the mother tongue must be reached for the student to attain academic proficiency in the mother tongue and later in a second language. This threshold is seldom met in programs of immersion in English.

STRUCTURES FOR PROVIDING ESL INSTRUCTION. The most common pattern for providing English language instruction is that in which the teacher in the self-contained classroom provides all instruction, including ESL. Another common pattern is the pull-out program, which is usually employed in elementary schools. ESL teachers have their own classrooms, and for periods of forty to sixty minutes, they pull children out of their self-contained classrooms for ESL instruction and then send them back. In semidepart-mentalized and departmentalized intermediate or junior high schools, usually at the fifth- or sixth-grade level and above, one teacher might have responsibility for teaching ESL to all English language learners.

Unfortunately, not every teacher is well prepared—or perhaps prepared at all—to teach ESL. An advantage of a pullout program is that a specialist can be very effective in providing this important instruction and will usually have high-quality materials for this purpose.

The pullout approach also has several disadvantages. Children miss instruction in the regular classroom, depending on the hour during which they are absent. English language learners are singled out as "special" or "different" when they leave for ESL instruction, which often has negative consequences. Pullout programs are usually organized according to homogeneous groups in that the ESL teacher will pull beginners from several class-rooms for a period of instruction, then intermediate learners from several classrooms, and so on. Even in the self-contained classroom, the teacher should consider teaching the Eng-lish language learners as a single group, regardless of their proficiency. As you will see later in this chapter, there are advantages to having children at several levels of English lan-guage proficiency during ESL/language development lessons, including the presence of capable English speakers.

SHELTERED ENGLISH INSTRUCTION, SDAIE, AND SIOP®. **Sheltered English instruction** is a very powerful approach for working with English language learners, but it is an intermediate approach. It is designed to follow an initial second-language acqui-sition program that takes students from non–English speaker status to that of intermedi-ate speaker of English.

In California, sheltered instruction is called Specially Designed Academic Instruc-tion in English (SDAIE) (CATESOL, 1992). A more recent model of sheltered instruc-tion is called the Sheltered Instruction Observation Protocol (SIOP®) (Echevarria, Vogt, & Short, 2009).

It is therefore an important second-language component of all education programs for English language learners, whether they have been in bilingual education or in an Eng-lish immersion program. It constitutes, however, a submersion approach when used, or misused, with beginning speakers of English. We examine sheltered English instruction later in this chapter.

Teach Them in the Language They Already Speak

The *Lau v. Nichols* decision (see Chapter 2) did not mandate bilingual education as a remedy, but school districts soon found that it was one of the few ways to ensure that Eng-lish language learners had equal access to education, that is, education in their mother tongue while they learned English. In most bilingual education programs, children learn to read and write and also to study the other subjects of the academic curriculum—math-ematics, social science, and science—in their mother tongue. Simultaneously, they learn English as a second language, a process that typically takes two to five years or more (Thomas & Collier, 1997). As the result of a transition process called **positive transfer of skills**, children can then do in English what they have learned to do in the mother tongue (Cummins, 1981). The knowledge that English language learners have in the mother tongue, they will also have in English. Furthermore, once a child is able to read in the mother tongue, learning to read in English as a second language is a relatively smooth and effortless process—the child learns to read only once. When children do not have the

Effective teachers recognize that English learners come to the classroom with a broad range of skills. Watch the video clip included in the activity "Creating a Supportive Environment for English Language Learners" to hear teachers stress the importance of responding to individual differences. (To find this activity, go to the topic *English Language Learners* in MyEducationLab and click on Assignments and Activities.)

opportunity to learn academic subjects in the mother tongue, they obviously fall behind in those subjects during the period of time they are learning English.

The underlying principles of bilingual education are as follows:

- Teach English language learners to understand and speak English as a second language.
- Teach the academic subjects, including reading and writing, in the mother tongue while the children are in the process of learning to understand and speak English.
- Transition the children from mother tongue academic instruction to English language instruction in a sheltered mode when they have an intermediate level of English.

Because of the lack of instructional materials and a shortage of trained bilingual teachers in many languages, non–Spanish-language bilingual education programs are less common and usually are limited in scope.

In *Preventing Reading Difficulties in Young Children*, Snow, Burns, and Griffin (1998) endorsed the efficacy of teaching children to read in the mother tongue wherever possible before teaching them to read in English. A major five-year developmental study conducted by Thomas and Collier (2002) provides additional evidence to support this point of view. Although many mother tongues were represented in their study of over 210,000 students in five school districts in Texas, Oregon, and Maine, most of the students were Spanish speaking. Thomas and Collier found that one-way or dual language bilingual enrichment programs that were 90:10 or 50:50 (the ratio of mother tongue instruction to English instruction) were the only programs in which students reached the fiftieth percentile in both languages and in which there were the fewest dropouts. Children whose parents refused bilingual education programs, insisting instead on English only, had much lower achievement. The strongest predictor of English language achievement in the study was the amount of formal mother tongue instruction. Thomas and Collier found that the highest achievement in bilingual education programs was associated with those that offered a natural learning environment in school, with rich oral and written language in both the mother tongue and English, problem solving, group student activities, media-rich learning, challenging thematic units, and use of the students' bilingual and bicultural knowledge to access new knowledge.

In a major meta-analysis of studies about the language and literacy development of language-minority students, The National Literacy Panel on Language-Minority Children and Youth published a report in 2006. Their conclusions paralleled those of the National Reading Panel (2000). First, they concluded that phonemic awareness, phonics, fluency, vocabulary, and text comprehension instruction were major factors in the development of literacy. They did, however, recommend that more focus be placed on working with particular phonemes that do not exist in their mother tongues.

Second, they found that although language-minority children were able to keep pace with their English-speaking classmates in the development of word recognition skills, they fell behind in comprehension and writing. They attributed this to the lower level of English language proficiency among these students.

Third, they concluded that children's oral proficiency and reading ability in the mother tongue can be used to facilitate the development of literacy in English as a result of the positive transfer of skills, a finding similar to that of Snow et al. in *Preventing Reading Difficulties* (1998) cited earlier.

Fourth, they concluded that there is a hierarchy of skills in English that must be attained before children can be successful in reading comprehension in English and that individual differences among children are a significant factor in this development. They further concluded that for language-minority children in special education programs, developing sight word reading and holistic learning strategies might be more effective in teaching them to read and write.

Fifth, they concluded that most assessment tools used with language-minority children are not effective in measuring their individual strengths and weaknesses. They also found little evidence of the effect of sociocultural variables on the development of literacy, except for the positive effect of home language experiences.

TRANSITIONAL VERSUS MAINTENANCE MODELS OF BILINGUAL EDUCATION. There are two underlying philosophies about how to conduct programs of bilingual education: transitional and maintenance. In the more common **transitional model**, children learn English as a second language. They learn their academic subjects, including reading and writing, in the mother tongue, and they make the transition to English language academic instruction in a sheltered mode when they have reached an intermediate level of English, usually between the late second grade and early fourth grade. The major goal of the transitional program is to produce a monolingual, monoliterate, and monocultural child who temporarily uses the mother tongue as a vehicle for learning. Children in transitional bilingual programs usually continue their academic studies only in English after the onset of transition to English, although they sometimes receive continuing support in the mother tongue from a paraprofessional, as needed.

In the **maintenance model**, the process is the same up to the point of transition. After the children begin academic instruction in English, they continue to receive periodic lessons in the mother tongue in all subject areas. The major outcome of the maintenance program is a bilingual, biliterate, and bicultural child who is able to function easily and comfortably in two languages and cultures.

STRUCTURES FOR ORGANIZING PROGRAMS OF BILINGUAL EDUCATION. Within the transitional and maintenance models are several structures for grouping children and for assigning teachers and paraprofessionals that can be used in either model.

Concurrent Method. One approach that is often used intuitively is called the *concurrent method*. The teacher says everything twice, once in the children's mother tongue, perhaps Hmong, and once in English, assuming there is only one non-English language in the classroom and the teacher is bilingual. When the teacher is not bilingual, a bilingual paraprofessional may fill that second role, basically serving as an interpreter. It is a time-efficient approach with an uncomplicated structure. It is also very ineffective. English language learners begin to tune out the English, which they cannot understand well or perhaps at all, and they listen only to their mother tongue. If they do learn some English as a part of the process, they learn it in terms of their mother tongue. The outcome is a compound bilingual child with two interdependent language systems. The result is a lifetime of unconscious translation from one language to another, a process that takes precious time, especially on examinations such as the SAT, the GRE, or the important high-stakes tests that are now required in many states. This approach also promotes code switching, the unconscious mixing of vocabulary and syntactical structures from two languages.

Team Teaching. The team-teaching approach is quite different. Two teachers, one bilingual, the other usually not, work together in the same classroom. They work independently, but when they teach, each teaches the entire class. The primary advantages of this approach are to provide outstanding language and cultural models to the children and to reduce the number of proficient bilingual teachers needed.

Dual Language. The dual-language model resembles the team-teaching model in that there are two teachers, one bilingual, the other usually not, but in separate classrooms. The monolingual English-speaking teacher teaches English as a second language and academic instruction in English for those in the two classrooms who are ready for it. The bilingual teacher teaches the academic subjects to the English language learners in the mother tongue and also teaches the other language as a second language.

The advantages of the dual-language model are that both teachers are working in a language of comfort to them and the children are learning English and their academic subjects from teachers who are good models. Unlike the concurrent method, they are not learning English in terms of the mother tongue but rather are developing as coordinate bilinguals with two independent language systems. The major disadvantage is that the English-speaking and non–English-speaking children are rarely working together because their needs are very different. It is important for English language learners to associate with English speakers because they learn English from those children as well as from their teacher. They can avoid the fossilization or stopping-in-place that can occur when children are separated from native and capable English-speaking peers. It is also important for groups of children from different languages and cultures to associate with each other to avoid ethnic, linguistic, and cultural isolation.

Preview-Review Model. The preview-review model is very complex, but it resolves some of the shortcomings of the other models. Two teachers work together as in the team-teaching and dual-language models: one bilingual, the other usually not. One teacher provides a preview of the lesson to the entire group in one language, and the other teacher then teaches the main body of the lesson to the entire group in the other language. Each teacher then reviews the main lesson with his or her language group after the main body of the lesson. The order of use of the languages is reversed in that subject area the next day. The children in whose language the main body of the lesson is not to be presented listen to a preview in their mother tongue. They also review the lesson in their mother tongue after the lesson is presented in their second language.

For example, two teachers, one bilingual and the other monolingual, teach a mathematics lesson. The bilingual teacher might conduct a ten-minute preview of the lesson in Korean for all children. The monolingual teacher would then teach the core of the lesson to all of the children in English, probably for thirty to forty minutes. Both teachers would then review the lesson in English and Korean, respectively, with children dominant in those languages for about ten to fifteen minutes. They would reverse the order the next day. The children always have the best possible model of both languages, and they are mixed for part of the lesson. The model also reduces the number of scarce bilingual teachers needed.

Eastman Model. The Eastman model (Krashen & Biber, 1988) of the Los Angeles Unified School District also effectively alleviates the problem of isolating students from each other at the elementary level. Spanish-speaking students are organized for mother tongue instruction in reading, the language arts, and academic areas of the curriculum during the morning, along with a program of ESL. English-speaking students are similarly organized for reading and academic instruction in English in the morning. In the afternoon, Spanish-speaking students are mainstreamed with English-speaking students in art, music, and physical education, which are conducted in English. As Spanish-speaking students gain English proficiency after two or three years, they begin to receive sheltered academic instruction in English in the more concrete areas of the curriculum, such as mathematics and science. Social studies in English is introduced later.

Two-Way Bilingual Education. The two-way bilingual education program has a different goal from mainstream bilingual education. It is used where two language groups of parents want their children to learn—and learn in—another language. Usually, one group of children will be native Spanish speakers learning English as a second language and academic subjects in Spanish. But another group of English-speaking students is in the classroom because their parents want them to learn Arabic and learn in Arabic. The program goal is additive in that each group learns the language and culture of the other group. The Eastman model is an effective organizational structure for conducting a two-way bilingual education program.

The English Language in the Bilingual Education Program

Teaching ESL is the underlying base of programs established to meet the academic needs of English language learners. It is the major element of the full bilingual education programs in which the mother tongue is used for academic instruction while children develop sufficient proficiency in English to benefit from academic instruction in English. And under No Child Left Behind requirements, it is the principal means of instruction.

Second-Language Acquisition

Regardless of whether children learn to read and write in their mother tongue, they clearly must learn to speak and understand English. In fact, it is not possible to address literacy for English language learners without considering the close links that must exist between the teaching of reading and writing and the teaching of ESL. Those links are rooted in the constructivist or whole-part-whole approaches that underlie effective practice in both.

At this point, we examine the contrast between constructivist and reductionist models of instruction. A constructivist view of instruction focuses on the construction of meaning, using what the child already knows and combining it with new knowledge, concepts, and skills to be integrated. It is learner centered and highly contextualized; these are important factors in working with students from diverse backgrounds, who are often at risk of failure. The factor of background knowledge is well recognized as being a key to success in reading and writing, especially in reading comprehension. English language learners have no lack of background knowledge, but there is often a discontinuity between the background knowledge they have and that assumed by the texts they will use in learning to read and reading to learn. Within the constructivist view, language acquisition is embedded in function. Skills are taught in a meaningful context, not in a rigid, artificial, isolated, and fragmented way. There are several approaches to second-language instruction that reflect the constructivist view; they are in the communicative category.

The foundation for communicative approaches to second-language acquisition is based on concepts, theories, and hypotheses that have converged around the interaction of constructivist notions about making meaning, including Vygotsky's (1978) zone of proximal development, as described in Chapter 2. Conversely, **reductionist models**, or skills-based models, focus on the disassembly or fragmentation of curricular elements so that isolated skills and concepts can be mastered within a linear paradigm. Traditionally, most students have studied a second language, whether English or a foreign language, using such grammar-based approaches as the grammar-translation and audiolingual methods. These are reductionist or skills-based approaches that move learners from part to whole.

COMMUNICATIVE-BASED APPROACHES.   The results of research have changed educators' conceptions of how a second language is acquired and how this acquisition is best promoted in the elementary and secondary classroom. There has been a major paradigm shift away from these grammar-based approaches to language learning and toward those called *communicative*, which are also consistent with meaning-based or constructivist approaches to literacy (Crawford, 1994a; Crawford, 2003).

Several important hypotheses underlie current practice in most communicative approaches to second-language acquisition (Krashen, 1982b). In his input hypothesis, Krashen concludes that growth in language occurs when learners receive comprehensible input, or input that contains vocabulary and structure at a slightly higher level than what they already understand. The input hypothesis reflects Vygotsky's zone of proximal development. The context of the input provides clues to maintain the integrity of the message. According to the input hypothesis, a grammatical sequence is not needed. The vocabulary and structures are provided and practiced as a natural part of the comprehensible input that the child receives, much as the process occurs with infants acquiring their mother tongue. Krashen (1981) relates the input hypothesis to the silent period, the interval before speech in either the mother tongue or second language in which the child listens to and develops an understanding of the language before beginning to produce language.

Krashen's (1991) updated input hypothesis includes what he calls "comprehensible input plus 1" or "i + 1." It is an "aspect of language the acquirer has not yet acquired but

To learn how to create learning environments that celebrate multiple languages and cultures, and provide all students opportunities to contribute to a community of learning complete the activity "Using Culturally Responsive Instruction to Meet the Needs of English Learners and Students from Diverse Cultures." (To find this activity, go to the topic *English Language Learners* in MyEducationLab and click on Building Teaching Skills and Dispositions.)

that he or she is ready to acquire" (p. 409). The i + 1 is a new element to be learned in what the teacher has already made comprehensible. It is contextualized, not isolated, and it may include academic language or other new elements, such as a new language structure.

In his acquisition-learning hypothesis, Krashen highlights the difference between the infant's subconscious acquisition of the mother tongue and the conscious learning of a second language of the secondary student of French. Students acquire language subconsciously, with a feel for correctness. Learning a language, by contrast, is a conscious process that involves knowing grammatical rules. The infant, of course, is almost always successful in acquiring communicative competence, whereas the secondary school foreign language learner is usually not (Crawford, 1994a; Crawford, 2003).

Gee (1992) elaborates Krashen's concept of acquisition to add a social factor reflecting Vygotsky's "zone of proximal development" and also the concept of approximation (1992).

> *Acquisition is a process of acquiring something subconsciously by exposure to models, a process of trial and error, and practice within social groups, without formal teaching. It happens in natural settings that are meaningful and functional in the sense that acquirers know that they need to acquire the thing they are exposed to in order to function and that they in fact want to so function.* (p. 113)

According to Krashen's (1982b) natural order hypothesis, grammatical structures are acquired in a predictable sequence, with certain elements usually acquired before others. He concludes that the orders for first- and second-language acquisition are similar but not identical. He does not, however, conclude that sequencing the teaching of language according to this natural order or any grammatical sequence is either necessary or desirable.

Krashen's (1982b) related *monitor hypothesis* describes how the child's conscious monitor or editor serves to make corrections as language is produced in speaking or writing. Several conditions are necessary for the application of the monitor:

- Time to apply it, a situation that is not present in most ordinary oral discourse, especially in classroom settings
- A focus on the form or correctness of what is said, rather than on the content of the message
- Knowledge of the grammatical rule to be applied

These conditions serve to illustrate why so few children or adults learn to understand and speak a foreign language in a grammar-translation or audiolingual foreign language course in the secondary school or university.

In his affective filter hypothesis, Krashen (1982b) concludes that several affective variables are associated with success in second-language acquisition. These include high motivation, self-confidence and a positive self-image and, most important, low anxiety in the learning environment. It is therefore important that teachers avoid high-pressure instruction and especially humiliation of students who are acquiring English.

OTHER BASIC PRINCIPLES.   Results from recent research have led to other major changes in educators' conceptions of how a second language is acquired and how this acquisition is best facilitated in the classroom, one of which is the obvious similarity between primary- and second-language acquisition. In both, primary- and second-language learners form an incomplete and incorrect interlanguage (Selinker, Swain, & Dumas, 1975), with most children moving through similar stages of development in this incomplete language.

The role of correction is also similar in both primary- and second-language acquisition. *Approximation* is a related process in which children imitate more proficient English speakers in all of the dimensions of language, oral and written, and test hypotheses about it. Approximation underlies oral and written language in that children are acquiring new understandings and skills within the context of authentic wholes. Children demonstrate behaviors in which they approximate the language behavior of their English models, growing closer and closer to their levels of proficiency. In his view of successive approximation, Holdaway (1979) describes the process as one in which Vygotsky's adults and more capable peers, that is, teachers and proficient English-speaking students, use information in the output from children's responses to construct, adjust, and finally eliminate the scaffolding that facilitates progress in learning.

Terrell (1982) and Krashen and Terrell (1983) conclude that correction should be viewed as a negative reinforcer that will raise the affective filter and the level of anxiety among English language learners. When errors do not interfere with comprehension, correcting them has no more place in the ESL program than it does when infants acquire their mother tongue. Caregivers might expand incorrect or incomplete forms, such as "me go" or "Kitty gots four feets," and say "Yes, you go" or "Yes, Kitty has four feet." There is little evidence, however, that this expansion has any positive effect. Errors are signs of immaturity, not incorrectness; they will disappear naturally as a part of approximation in the developmental process of language acquisition (Crawford, 1994a; Crawford, 2003).

These similarities between primary- and second-language acquisition are not consistent with either the grammar-translation or audiolingual approach. Children learning their first language do not rely on grammatical rules or on systematic acquisition of vocabulary. With its emphasis on early production instead of a silent period, on correct production instead of an acceptable though immature and incomplete interlanguage, and on grammatical sequence instead of function and communicative competence, the audiolingual approach bears little resemblance to the way primary or second languages are successfully acquired.

Finally, age is an important factor in second-language acquisition. Collier (1987) examined the relationship between the age of English language learners and their acquisition of a second language. She found that those who entered the second-language acquisition program at ages eight to eleven were the fastest achievers. Those who entered the program at ages five to seven were the lowest achievers, and they were one to three years behind children from eight to eleven years of age. Children who entered at twelve to fifteen years of age had the most difficulty acquiring the second language. She projected that they would need from six to eight years of classroom instruction to reach age-level norms in academic achievement.

Collier (1989) later analyzed other research on age and academic achievement in the second language and found that children who had academic instruction in the mother tongue generally required from four to seven years to reach national norms on standardized tests in reading, social studies, and science and as little as two years in mathematics and language arts, including spelling, punctuation, and grammar. She also found that children from ages eight to twelve who had at least two years of schooling in the mother tongue in their home country needed from five to seven years to reach the same levels of achievement in second-language reading, social studies, and science and two years in mathematics and language arts. Young children with no schooling in the mother tongue in either the home country or the new host country needed seven to ten years of instruction in reading, social studies, and science. Adolescent children with no ESL instruction and no opportunity for continued academic work in the mother tongue were projected, for the most part, to drop out of school before reaching national norms, regardless of whether they had a good academic background or interrupted schooling.

Instructional Strategies for Second-Language Acquisition

The implications of Krashen's hypotheses and of related similarities between first- and second-language acquisition are that approaches to second-language acquisition should do the following:

- Provide comprehensible input
- Focus on relevant and interesting topics instead of grammatical sequences
- Provide for a silent period without forcing early production

Using physical responses as a strategy of instruction in the bilingual classroom can help to reduce the anxiety ESL students might feel about the need to "perform." (Lindfors Photography)

- Avoid correction
- Maintain a low level of anxiety

There are approaches to second-language acquisition that meet these criteria. The communicative approaches most appropriate for elementary and secondary classrooms are the total physical response method and the natural approach.

THE TOTAL PHYSICAL RESPONSE METHOD.   Asher's (1982) total physical response (TPR) method is an important communicative approach in the initial stages of second-language acquisition. The TPR method provides for comprehensible input, a silent period, and a focus on relevant content rather than on grammatical form. The focus of TPR is on physical responses to verbal commands such as "Stand up" and "Put your book on the desk." Because little emphasis is put on production, the level of anxiety is low.

Lessons can be given to small groups or an entire class. In the beginning, the teacher models one-word commands. This is done first with a few children to introduce new vocabulary and structures, then with the entire group, then with small groups of children, and finally with individual children. For example, the teacher says, "Sit," and then models by sitting down. Later, the teacher issues the command without modeling. As the children's levels of language increase, the teacher begins to use two- and three-word commands, such as "Stand up" and "Bring the book."

The children demonstrate their understanding by physically carrying out the commands. The order of commands is varied so that the children cannot anticipate which is next. Old commands are combined with new ones to provide for review. Whenever the children do not appear to comprehend, the teacher returns to modeling. After a silent period of approximately ten hours of listening to commands and physically responding to them, a child then typically reverses roles with the teacher and begins to give those same commands to other children. It is important for the teacher to maintain a playful mood during classroom activities.

The TPR approach can be extended to higher levels of proficiency by using the technique of nesting commands. The teacher might say the following:

Jamal, take the book to Svetlana, or close the door.
Noriko, if Jamal took the book to Svetlana, raise your hand.
If he closed the door, stand up.

A high level of understanding is necessary to carry out such commands, but no oral production is needed. Parents of young children will recognize that their infants can understand and carry out such commands long before they begin to speak themselves.

THE NATURAL APPROACH.   Terrell's (1977) original concept of the natural approach provided for three major characteristics:

- Classroom activities were focused on acquisition, that is, communication with a content focus leading to an unconscious absorption of language and a feel for correctness, but not an explicit knowledge of grammar.
- Oral errors were not directly corrected.
- Learners could respond in the target language, their mother tongue, or a mixture of the two.

Krashen and Terrell (1983) later added four principles that underlie the natural approach to language acquisition:

1. Comprehension precedes production, which leads to several teacher behaviors: teacher use of the target language, a focus on a topic of interest to the children, and maintenance of the children's comprehension.

2. Production emerges in stages ranging from nonverbal responses to complex discourse, with children able to speak when they are ready and speech errors not corrected unless they interfere with communication.

3. The curriculum consists of communicative goals, with topics of interest comprising the syllabus, not a grammatical sequence.

4. Activities must result in a low level of anxiety, a lowering of the children's affective filter, which the teacher accomplishes by establishing and maintaining a good rapport.

Terrell's (1981) natural approach is based on three stages of language development: preproduction (comprehension), early production, and emergence of speech.

Ms. Ortega, the teacher in the bilingual classroom in the chapter-opening vignette, uses the natural approach. The curriculum of her ESL program is made up of themes that are supported by large-format posters and charts, big books, and concrete objects in the classroom. She also uses the four blocks approach to organizing her reading program that is described in Chapter 13 (Cunningham et al., 2007), but her program is a five blocks approach. She has added ESL as an important fifth reading/language arts area of the curriculum.

The Preproduction Stage.   In the preproduction stage, topical, interesting, and relevant comprehensible input is provided by the teacher in a close parallel with Asher's TPR approach. The teacher speaks slowly, maintaining comprehension with gestures. Children may respond with physical behaviors, shaking or nodding their heads, pointing at pictures or objects, and saying yes or no. It is important that input is dynamic, lively, fun, and comprehensible. Crawford (1994a) provides an example in which the teacher uses a pet turtle and says,

> *This is a turtle. It is four years old. Is it green? Who wants to hold it? [Hand to child.] Who has the turtle? Does Tran have the turtle? Yes, he does. Does Rosa have the turtle? No, she doesn't.*

This basic input can be repeated with other objects in the classroom, such as large-format posters and illustrations (Crawford, 1994a). Crawford suggests that each child in the group be given a different illustration, and the teacher provides input:

> *Who has a picture of an airplane? Yes, Olaf, you do. Is the airplane large? Olaf, give your picture to Zipour. Who has a picture of a boat? Yes, Nicole has a picture of a boat.*

These examples include three primary preproduction techniques of using TPR strategies, TPR strategies accompanied by naming objects, and pictures.

The required responses include movement, pointing, nodding or shaking the head, and using the names of other children in the group. Remember that nodding the head for an affirmative response and shaking it for a negative one are not appropriate in all cultures; it is the converse in Albania, for example. Children might also have to learn these nonverbal behaviors. Because the emphasis at this stage is on listening comprehension, verbal responses in the mother tongue are also acceptable. This might be a problem if the teacher cannot understand the children's mother tongue, but children usually find a way to help the teacher understand.

Classroom props allow for relevant expansion of this and subsequent stages of the natural approach (Crawford, 1994a; 2003). Any manipulative or concrete object is helpful, including flannel boards and puppets. Large colorful illustrations, such as those in big books, are also very helpful. Sources of free color illustrations include calendars (outdated or otherwise), travel posters, large posters available from textbook and trade book publishers, and colorful illustrations in the annual reports of many large corporations, which are often available on request through announcements in major business magazines.

The Early Production Stage. In the stage of early production, the child begins to produce one-word utterances, lists, and finally two-word answers, such as "big dog" and "in house." Some of the latter, such as "me want" and "no like," are grammatically incorrect or incomplete. According to Crawford (2003), teachers should view these responses as immature, not incorrect. In the presence of good models, these errors will disappear in time, just as they do among infants developing their mother tongue at home.

Several types of questions can be used to elicit one- and two-word responses that are within the reach of children as they move into the early production stage:

Question Format	Illustrative Question
Yes/no	Do you like hamburgers?
Here/there	Where is the picture of the cat?
Either/or	Is this a pen or a key?
One word	How many dogs are there?
Two word	What fruits are in the picture?

As in the preproduction stage, these strategies should be integrated into activities that permit a variety of responses, ranging from physical responses from those not ready for production, to brief oral responses from those who are. As the children begin production, conversations should increasingly require one-word responses. Within the same conversation, the teacher can address questions calling for longer responses to those children who are ready. Teacher questions and commands here are in italics, and student responses are in brackets []:

> *Kjell, show us your picture. What is in Kjell's picture?* [A sandwich.] *Yes, it is a sandwich. What is on the sandwich?* [Ketchup.] *Is there an apple on the sandwich?* [No. Laughter.] *What else is on the sandwich?* [Meat, mayonnaise.] *How does it taste?* [Good.] *What do you like with a sandwich?* [Cookies. Soda.] *I like chips with mine.*

The Emergence of Speech Stage. During the emergence of speech stage, children begin to produce structures that are richer in vocabulary, longer and more complex, and more correct. This production proceeds from three-word phrases to sentences, dialogue, extended discourse, and narrative, strategies that are also helpful in teaching standard American English to speakers of African American Vernacular English. At this stage, Terrell (1981) recommends such activities as games, group discussions, preference ranking, skits, art and music, radio, TV, pictures, filmstrips, readings, and filling out forms. An example of a chart that incorporates preference ranking is provided by Crawford (1994a) (see Figure 15.2). After surveying the children about their preferences for pizza toppings and recording them, the teacher uses the survey results in Figure 15.2 to ask questions at different levels, each directed at a particular student and designed to elicit a response that reflects that student's stage of English language development. Teacher questions are in italics, and student responses in brackets []:

Figure 15.2

Second-Language Preference Ranking Chart.

Name	Favorite Pizzas					
	Cheese	Sausage	Pepperoni	Tomato	Anchovy	Mushroom
Margarita	X			X		X
Sofik		X				
Abdul						
Nguyen	X		X	X		
Petra		X		X		X

Does Sofik like pizza? [Yes.] *What kind of meat does Sofik like?* [Sausage.] *How many like tomato on their pizza?* [Three, Margarita, Nguyen, and Petra.] *How much does Abdul like pizza?* [He doesn't like it.] *Which children like the same kind of pizza?* [Sofik and Petra.] *Is there a topping that no one likes?* [Yes.] *What is it?* [Anchovy.] *How do we know?* [Nobody wants anchovy.]

Not only is the chart a valuable source of comprehensible input, but the process of gathering the data for the chart is also. In addition, children begin to read each other's names and the words for popular foods in English.

Wordless picture books can also be used as a stimulus for the production of language at the emergence of speech stage. In an article that addresses struggling upper-grade readers, Ho (1999) describes strategies that will also be very effective for English language learners. After a brief book talk with the teacher, a small group of students creates a short text for a wordless book. One student member of the group records the text, although a paraprofessional or parent volunteer might fill this role when the students' writing abilities make this difficult. This is of even more value when two or three groups of students independently create their own text and then share it with the other groups.

BUILDING VOCABULARY WITH READ-ALOUDS.   The importance of read-alouds was demonstrated in Chapter 12. Collins (2005) found evidence that read-alouds were also a potent aid to the development of vocabulary among young English language learners, especially when rich explanations about new words were provided. In a related study of read-alouds done by parents at home and teachers at school, Roberts (2008) found that read-alouds in either the mother tongue or English produced vocabulary gains among preschool children. We can add that when these read-alouds are done with big books, then illustrations provide an important context to the process.

Reading Aloud

SHELTERED ENGLISH INSTRUCTION FOR INTERMEDIATE-LEVEL ENGLISH SPEAKERS.   When English language learners have reached an intermediate level of English proficiency, they are ready to move from academic instruction in the mother tongue to academic instruction in English by using sheltered English instruction, a mode that provides extensive support for comprehension. Sheltering strategies in the content areas of the curriculum add substantially to the knowledge and contextualized vocabulary that students need as a base for reading comprehension as they read and think in any language (Krashen, 1985). These strategies are consistent with the philosophy of communicative approaches to second-language acquisition, and they additionally provide access to academic areas of the curriculum in such a way that communication is maintained. Sheltered English strategies are also very appropriate in providing support for teaching standard American English to speakers of African American Vernacular dialect.

Cummins (1981) provides a set of intersecting continua that are very useful for conceptualizing the issue of balancing the complexity of curriculum content with demands on language proficiency (see Figure 15.3). The vertical continuum extends from cognitively undemanding to cognitively demanding—ranging, for example, from a conversation about what students ate for lunch on the cognitively undemanding side to a third-grade mathematics lesson about the distributive principle of multiplication on the cognitively demanding side.

Cummins's intersecting horizontal continuum extends from context embedded to context reduced, ranging, for example, from a science lesson on classification taught with concrete manipulatives on the context-embedded side to an abstract lecture/discussion about the principles of democracy on the context-reduced side. Sheltered instruction in English is most effective in subject areas of the curriculum that can be presented concretely, such as mathematics, science, art, music, and physical education. Although certain aspects of social studies can be taught concretely, such as geography and map skills, so many abstract concepts are taught that English language instruction in this area might well be delayed until students acquire additional English proficiency, especially if expository text in English is an important source of knowledge for the children.

Figure 15.3   Classifying Cognitive Level and Contextual Support of Language and Content Activities According to Cummins's Framework.

	Cognitively undemanding	Cognitively demanding
Context enhanced	Art lesson Playing kickball Conversation about lunch Playing a board game Singing a song	Mathematics lesson using manipulatives Conducting a science experiment about evaporation Making a map of the schoolyard Watching the news on television
Context reduced	Beginning reading skills Talking on the telephone Listening to the news on the radio Reading a set of instructions	Responding to higher-order reading comprehension questions Participating in a debate on capital punishment Taking the SAT or the GRE

Source: Based on Cummins (1981).

The purpose of a sheltered instruction approach to the core curriculum in English is to provide a focus on context-embedded activities, ensuring that comprehensible input is provided while treating increasingly cognitively demanding aspects of the core curriculum. The Los Angeles Unified School District (1985) prepared a set of English-language teaching strategies that provide the necessary scaffolding in content areas for intermediate English language learners. Recommended strategies for teachers include the following:

- Simplify input by speaking slowly and enunciating clearly.
- Use a controlled vocabulary within simple language structures.
- Where possible, use cognates and avoid the extensive use of idiomatic expressions.
- Use nonverbal language, including gestures, facial expressions, and dramatization.
- Use manipulatives and concrete materials, such as props, graphs, visuals, overhead transparencies, bulletin boards, maps, and realia.
- Maintain comprehension with gestures, dramatization, illustrations, and manipulatives.
- Check understanding by asking for confirmation of comprehension; by asking students to clarify, repeat, and expand; and by using a variety of questioning formats.

Teachers of English language learners can take two additional steps to ensure good communication with students as they teach: They should face the children, not the blackboard, when teaching; and male teachers should ensure that moustaches are trimmed so children can see the upper lip.

Schifini (1985) recommends a focus on student-centered activities, especially at the secondary level, where lecturing and textbook use predominate. Richard-Amato and Snow (1992) provide valuable strategies for content-area teachers of English language learners. For mainstream teachers, they recommend providing a warm learning environment, recording lectures and talks on tape for later review, rewriting some key parts of text material at lower levels, asking native-English-speaking students to share notes with English language learners, and avoiding competitive grading until students have achieved sufficient English proficiency to compete successfully with native speakers.

It is clear that many of these strategies are nothing more than effective teaching practices, but their absence is very damaging to English language learners who are struggling to learn mathematics, science, and social studies in English when they have reached an intermediate level of English proficiency.

Several other strategies provide scaffolding for English language learners in specially designed academic instruction activities in English. The highly contextualized interactions that take place in cooperative learning can make the difference between what Krashen (1985, 1991) describes as submersion, or sink or swim, and sheltered instruction, the type of scaffolded subject-matter instruction just described. Cooperative learning is most effective when, in the words of Vygotsky, more capable peers—that is, stronger speakers of English—are included in groups with English language learners at various levels.

SHELTERED INSTRUCTION OBSERVATION PROTOCOL.   The Sheltered Instruction Observation Protocol (SIOP®) (Echevarria et al., 2009) is a carefully organized professional development model that incorporates strategies you have seen in this chapter and previous chapters:

- *Preparation*: lesson planning, content objectives, instructional materials
- *Building background*: integrating student background knowledge and developing academic vocabulary
- *Comprehensible input*: teacher speech presentation strategies and multimodal techniques
- *Strategies*: scaffolding instruction and promoting higher-order thinking skills
- *Interaction*: encouraging elaborated student speech and grouping students appropriately
- *Practice/Application*: activities to extend student learning of language and content
- *Lesson delivery*: delivering lessons that meet teaching objectives
- *Review/Assessment*: teacher review of key language and content concepts, assessment of student learning, and feedback to students

A SIOP® lesson plan incorporates all of these elements. This model is designed for English language learners, but you can see how it would be very effective with speakers of African American Vernacular English and with any student struggling with language and literacy. As a framework for planning and teaching effective lessons, it highlights best teaching practice for all children.

All of these sheltered strategies build background knowledge that supports the reading comprehension of English language learners as they begin to read expository text in their new second language. When instruction in the mother tongue precedes the sheltered instruction in English, their background knowledge is much richer.

Grammar as Part of the Curriculum?

According to Crawford (1994a), teachers who would advocate teaching the first-person present indicative tense to a seven-year-old English-speaking child in a primary school classroom would be incredulous at the suggestion that a parent teach the same concept to a three-year-old at home. Of course, both children can use the tense correctly, neither as the result of instruction. It is clear that the content of second-language acquisition programs should be based primarily on content, not on grammatical sequence.

A communicative second-language curriculum is usually organized around a set of topics to ensure the introduction of new vocabulary and concepts of interest and utility to the children. Needed language structures emerge and are acquired naturally within the context of topical lessons. Some communicative curricula include grammatical sequences as a subcategory.

Terrell (1981) suggests that the initial content should be limited to ensuring that students understand the following:

- Commands for classroom management
- Names of objects in the classroom
- Colors and description words for those objects
- Words to describe people and family relationships
- Descriptions of children and their clothing; school areas and activities
- Names of objects in the school that are not in the classroom
- Foods, especially those eaten at school

Later in the acquisition process, topics of interest to children would include the children's families, their homes and neighborhoods, their favorite activities, and experiences they have had. They also enjoy discussing their preferences about food, colors, television programs and films, and other aspects of their lives.

Linking ESL Instruction and Literacy

There is a close link between literacy and the acquisition of a second language that becomes apparent when, as a part of the natural approach, Terrell (1981) recommends that key words be written on the chalkboard in the second language, especially for older children who are literate in their mother tongue. This corresponds to the key words to reading approach (Veatch, 1996; Veatch et al., 1979). In the early production stage of his natural approach, Terrell indicates that children may express themselves quite appropriately in one- or two-word utterances as they begin to acquire a second language. According to Crawford (1994a), it is altogether appropriate that they also begin to read key vocabulary that they have expressed for their teacher to write for them. They may later produce lists of related ideas, such as foods to eat at the school cafeteria, words that describe a favorite friend, or things to do after school. These topics and this output reflect the oral language common in the early production phase of Terrell's natural approach to language acquisition, output that is well suited for children to dictate for their teachers to record and for the children to read later.

Most bilingual teachers who teach reading in the mother tongue recognize that students' motivation to begin reading and writing in English early is strong. Although it is most beneficial for students to learn to read and write in the native language (Cummins, 1986, 1989; Krashen & Biber, 1988; Snow et al., 1998), where possible, teachers can begin an early introduction to literacy in English to take advantage of that motivation. The use of the key vocabulary and language-experience approaches should be done with caution to ensure that the second-language acquisition program does not evolve into an English literacy program presented before the student is ready. Being able to read and write in the mother tongue is always the most desirable base from which to establish literacy in English later because of the positive transfer of literacy skills to English.

As English proficiency increases, the key word approach to reading may give way to the language-experience approach described in Chapter 5. It is important that the teacher accept the language that the children use in their initial dictations. There will be incomplete sentences, missing words, and inappropriate vocabulary, but this represents the stage

Language Experience with
English Language Learners

at which they are working in their new second language, and correction will only serve to dampen enthusiasm and diminish active participation.

As mentioned earlier, big books are an excellent source of large-format illustrations for ESL lessons. Later in the process, teachers will find that many children benefit from read-alouds in their new second language, especially when these are based on the background knowledge that children have already acquired as a result of lessons using the illustrations in these big books. The big books that are of most value will be very predictable and have repetitive elements.

Other early second-language reading and writing activities that are useful in the emergence of speech stage of the natural approach include the creation of vocabulary cards, with a word in English and an accompanying illustration from a magazine or by the student. These can be used for word games, including some that begin to focus on beginning sounds; this is especially productive for students who are already learning to read in the mother tongue. Children can also use their vocabulary cards for building word banks, student dictionaries, and word walls. Many children will be anxious to begin writing in their new second language. Simple poetry forms, such as the cinquain (see Chapter 10) and diamante, are useful structures for their initial attempts.

In their efforts to use the mother tongue of children in their classes, teachers sometimes provide cards with a vocabulary word in the mother tongue on one side and in English on the other. They also often provide bulletin boards in the two languages, and they often search out children's books with text in English on one side of the page and in the mother tongue on the other side. Although these efforts are laudable, such practices lead children to approach their new language of English through their mother tongue instead of directly. Vocabulary cards in English are a good practice, but a picture on the other side is a better choice than the word in the mother tongue. Teachers can and should provide bulletin boards in both languages, but not with both languages represented on the same bulletin board. For example, a science bulletin board can be provided in English on one side of the classroom, and the same bulletin board in the mother tongue can be placed on the other side of the room. Providing the same literature in English and the mother tongue has many advantages, but it is better provided in two separate books. Children will learn their new second language of English better if they do not approach it through the mother tongue.

Shared Reading

Form Poems

Options for Teaching the English Language Learner to Read

There are two major options for teaching English language learners to read; these correspond to the two major categories of programs: English only and bilingual education.

In English

In an English-only instructional program, the children necessarily have to learn to read in English. This is not a positive approach, but it is often the only option when a mother tongue reading instruction program cannot be offered because of a very small number of children with a common non-English language, a lack of appropriate personnel and materials, or political considerations.

Assuming that an ESL program is offered beginning in kindergarten and extending into the primary grades, the English language learners should not be placed in a formal and systematic English reading program before they have any proficiency whatsoever in English. The reading program is not an appropriate place for beginning ESL instruction, which should instead focus on understanding and speaking. When reading in English is

How has our understanding of how English language learners learn changed in recent years? (Michael Newman/PhotoEdit)

included at the beginning stages of instruction in listening comprehension and speaking English, the ESL program all too often evolves into a phonics- and text-based reading program instead of an ESL program, with very negative results in terms of both language acquisition and reading.

As children gain vocabulary in English in their ESL program, they will be interested in writing the words they learn, and they will begin to learn to read them, too, especially if they are learning to read in the mother tongue at the same time. A complete treatment of teaching the English language learner to read in English is provided in Chapters 12 and 13 in two dimensions: (1) the very positive process of teaching the English language learner who has first learned to read in the mother tongue and who has also reached the intermediate level of proficiency in understanding and speaking English and (2) the less desirable, but sometimes necessary, process of teaching reading in English to an English language learner who has not learned to read in the mother tongue and/or who has not reached the intermediate level of English-language proficiency.

Finally, some families will insist that their children learn to read and write only in English, even though the children do not speak or understand that language. Often, the parents themselves can express that desire only in the mother tongue. A few parents might even believe that the purpose of using the minority language for literacy is to maintain speakers of that language in an inferior social position. In this case, teachers need to demonstrate respect for the mother tongue, and they need to assure the children and their families that they will also have the opportunity to learn to speak, read, and write English. In addition, they need to reinforce the idea that children learn to read and write only once and that learning to read and write in another language later, such as English, is a relatively simple transfer process that is well supported in research, as seen later. Finally, teachers need to reinforce the idea that reading is *comprehension*, not just pronouncing or "reading" sounds. Nonetheless, some parents still insist on English only, and most schools accept that parental decision.

In the Mother Tongue

A fundamental precept of literacy for children who are English language learners is that they learn to read and write more rapidly and more effectively in their mother tongue than in a second language that they learn later. The first important and authoritative position taken on this issue was that of a UNESCO conference (UNESCO, 1953), in which it was concluded that children learn better to read in a new second language if they first learn to read in the mother tongue. This conclusion has been corroborated by many investigators in subsequent years. Saville and Troike (1971) reported that once a child has learned to read, transferring that ability to another language is not a difficult matter. Modiano (1968) found that Maya children in Mexico learned to read more rapidly in their mother tongue of Quiché than did Maya children who learned to read in their second language of Spanish. Subsequently, the children who had initially learned to read in their mother tongue read better in Spanish than those who first learned to read in Spanish. Through succeeding years, the evidence consistently indicates that children learn to read most effectively in their second language by first learning to read in their primary language (Cummins, 1986, 1989; Krashen & Biber, 1988; National Reading Panel Report, 2006; Snow et al., 1998; UNESCO, 1953).

Cummins's (1986, 1989) linguistic interdependence hypothesis indicates that what students learn in two languages is interdependent. This common underlying proficiency (CUP) (Cummins, 1981) forms the basis for positive transfer of skills. Children have knowledge and skills that they have learned in the mother tongue, and they can use them in the second language. They do not have to learn this knowledge and these skills again. In fact, it is axiomatic that children learn to read only once. They can transfer reading and writing skills to their new second language, just as adults do when they study a foreign language. Cummins indicates that CUP explains why children who have attended school in their country (and language) of origin tend to demonstrate higher achievement in English later than do children who lack that experience. These principles lead to the counterintuitive, but inescapable, conclusion that success in English-language proficiency is closely related to students' learning of reading, writing, and academic concepts in the mother tongue (Collier, 1989; J. Crawford, 1989; Cummins, 1989; Hudelson, 1987; Krashen, 1985; Krashen & Biber, 1988; Ramírez, 1991).

Language policy is a factor of great importance in literacy for children. Clearly, children learn to read and write most quickly and most effectively in the mother tongue. Many factors must be taken into consideration, however, before that decision is made (Crawford, 1995). For example, if skilled bilingual teachers are available, if children speak a minority language for which there is a well-developed written form, and if there are instructional materials in that language, the children can be given instruction in the mother tongue. If this is not the case, then the teacher can consider using the language-experience approach in English, as described in Chapter 5 and also later in this chapter.

If children speak a language for which there is not a well-developed written form, such as Hmong, then the children must be taught to speak and understand English and later to read and write in English, probably using the language-experience approach and simple predictable literature in English. If bilingual teachers are not available, then even the presence of instructional materials will not be sufficient to permit mother tongue instruction. The school can also prepare a literate speaker of the minority language as a paraprofessional who works under the supervision of a fully trained teacher who is not proficient in the mother tongue of the children.

In the case of a program of bilingual education, the children will have the opportunity to learn to read in the mother tongue. If a bilingual program is provided for that population, children who speak another non-English language will likely be placed in an English-only approach instead.

In the case of Spanish and other languages that use the Latin or Roman alphabet, there is a close correspondence between literacy skills in English and these languages and therefore much transfer of skills from reading in the mother tongue to English:

- The letters of the alphabet in Spanish are almost without exception identical to those of English, except for a few diacritical markings, such as the tilde (~) in Spanish.
- The left-to-right and top-to-bottom directionalities of the languages are the same.
- The concept of print and the alphabetic principle operate in the same way.
- Most consonant sounds and some vowel sounds are the same.
- There are significant similarities in vocabulary because of the many cognates that exist between English and Spanish, although a few are false cognates, such as *actual*, which means *real* in English and *present* or *current* in Spanish.
- Reading comprehension and organization skills are the same. When a child has learned to read in Spanish, these skills do not need to be learned a second time.

You can think of your own experiences in studying a foreign language. There were many new vocabulary words and grammatical elements to learn, but you did not have to learn to read and write again.

Teaching Children to Read in Spanish

Most English language learners in American schools speak Spanish at home, and almost all formal programs of bilingual education are conducted in Spanish (Fradd & Tikunoff, 1987). In most areas, it is only in Spanish that a wide range of instructional materials are available and that sufficient certified bilingual teachers are available to conduct such a program. Therefore, this section of the chapter is devoted to the teaching of reading in Spanish to these children.

As you have seen, the reading and writing processes in English and Spanish have a common alphabet and similar writing conventions. A major difference between English and Spanish is in the regularity of phoneme/grapheme relationships. In English, they are very irregular and inconsistent, especially with respect to the vowels; but in Spanish, they are very regular and consistent, especially with respect to the vowels.

Given this difference, one might expect that reading methodologies in Spanish would focus on phonics to take advantage of that regularity, and many do. But Latin American educators have found that children who learn to read using decoding as their only word recognition skill fall short in comprehension, just as occurs in English reading. Their reading is characterized as *silabeando*, that is, reading syllable by syllable. Their focus is on oral reading accuracy and speed, with little or no attention to comprehension or enjoyment. This is often observed in children who have learned to read in Spanish in Latin America.

A great variety of approaches for teaching reading in Spanish is available, just as there is in English. Table 15.1 summarizes those approaches.

These approaches range from those that are highly synthetic to those that are whole-part-whole, even including what is characterized as constructivist or whole language in English. A balanced approach in the whole-part-whole tradition provides for a strong, well-rounded program that is characterized by the following:

- Extensive read-aloud activities to build background knowledge and vocabulary in the mother tongue
- Use of the key words to reading approach, the language-experience approach, and shared reading of authentic literature at the beginning stages to introduce the concept of print for children who do not have a rich print environment in the home
- Phonemic awareness activities emerging from vocabulary in children's background knowledge and from LEA charts and shared literature experiences
- An inductive whole-part-whole strategy for teaching phonics, with elements emerging from words the children have acquired in the activities just described
- Use of authentic literature in Spanish to serve as a basis for teaching reading comprehension
- Extensive and early opportunities for writing

Application of these strategies in Spanish is similar to that in English, with the exception of phonics, which is addressed later. These key instructional activities also represent the four blocks framework presented in Chapter 1 and, beyond the beginning stages of reading instruction, they should be augmented with the many highly effective strategies described throughout the book.

METHODOLOGIES FOR TEACHING READING IN SPANISH.   "He read slowly, spelling out each syllable and murmuring it quietly, as if with great relish, and when he'd mastered the whole word, he would repeat it in one breath." In *The Old Man Who Read Love Stories*, a prize-winning novel written by a Chilean author about an elderly man who lives in the rain forest of Ecuador, Luis Sepúlveda (1989) has described very accurately the way too many Latin American children read as the result of the syllabic approach to reading instruction used in almost every country in the region. It is not uncommon to find the use of similar methodologies in the United States, often in the hands of bilingual teachers who themselves were educated in Latin America, perhaps even trained as teachers there. These approaches have many limitations when used in isolation; their best use would be as an ancillary word attack skill program to use with high-quality children's literature. But as in reading English, children who read in Spanish need to employ all cueing systems in support of their word recognition efforts: the semantic, syntactic, and pragmatic systems, as well as the graphophonic.

Phonics and Phonological Awareness

Why is the sequence of teaching word recognition skills in Spanish different from English?

Table 15.1   Major Approaches for Teaching Reading in Spanish

CATEGORY OF APPROACH	METHODOLOGY	CHARACTERISTICS	CITATION
Part-whole	Alphabetic (alfabético)	Letter names taught first; sequence of vowels, consonants, syllables, words, phrases, and sentences	Barbosa Heldt (1971) de Braslavsky (2006)
	Phonetic (fonético)	Focus on sounds; sequence of vowels, consonants, syllables, words, phrases, and sentences	Barbosa Heldt (1971) de Braslavsky (2006)
	Syllabic (silábico)	Focus on syllables; sequence of vowels, consonants, syllables, words, phrases, and sentences	Barbosa Heldt (1971) de Braslavsky (2006)
	Onomatopoeic (onomatopéyico)	Focus on auditory associations between sounds of letters and natural sounds of the environment, such as the /s/ as the whistle of a fireworks rocket; sequence of vowels, consonants, syllables, words, phrases, and sentences	Barbosa Heldt (1971) Torres Quintero (1976)
Whole-part-whole	Everyday vocabulary (palabras normales)	An analytic approach in which words are broken into syllables, then into sounds, and then reassembled	Barbosa Heldt (1971) Rodríguez Fuenzalida (1982) Rébsamen (1949)
Global	Whole word (global)	Sequence of words and sentences, with little or no phonics	Barbosa Heldt (1971) de Braslavsky (2006)
	Generated words (palabras generadoras)	Sequence of sight words, syllables, and sounds; use of these elements to create new words, phrases, and sentences	Hendrix (1952) Barbosa Heldt (1971)
Eclectic	Eclectic (ecléctico)	Combination of sight word development and phonics; typical of basal reader programs in English and Spanish	Barbosa Heldt (1971)
Constructivist	Whole language (lenguaje integral)	Focus on literature and authentic text; similar to whole-language focus in English; phonics taught implicitly and when need demonstrated (not explicit and systematic)	Freinet (1974) Solé (1992) Goodman (1989) Arellano Osuna (1992) Salmon (1995)

ISSUES RELATED TO THE SOUND SYSTEMS OF SPANISH AND ENGLISH. The sequence in which Spanish phonics is introduced is different from that of English. It begins with vowel sounds because they are few in number and regular (see Table 15.2 on page 508). Consonants follow in an order that reflects their frequency and regularity. Few word recognition problems appear in reading in Spanish, but there are several difficult points in Spanish, as in English, in which one letter represents several sounds. These are often observed in the invented spelling of children, as seen in Figure 15.4 on page 506.

The invented spelling in the student's work presented in Figure 15.4 is very typical of children who write in Spanish, and it is also consistent with Gentry's phonetic stage (Gentry, 1981), where there is substitution of incorrect letters with similar or the same pronunciation. The word *castillo* is spelled *castio*, which yields the correct pronunciation of the word, but not the correct spelling. In the words *paresio* and *isieron*, the student substituted the letter *s* for *c*, again yielding the correct pronunciation of the word, but the wrong spelling. In addition, the silent *h* of *hicieron* was omitted. There is much confusion between the sounds of *b* and *v* in Spanish, both being pronounced similarly to the /b/ in English in the initial position and like /v/ in English when between vowels, resulting in the very typical substitution of *v* for *b* in *estava*.

Teach It!

Refer to the Teach It! appendix at the end of the book for further activities you can use to reinforce concepts discussed in this chapter.

Inductive Phonics Lesson

In a simple three-step inductive lesson structure, the first step of auditory discrimination serves to verify students' phonological awareness of the sound stated in the objective of the lesson (see the figure on the next page). If the students are not successful in this first step, substitute phonological awareness activities for the second and third steps of the lesson, such as those described in Chapters 5 and 11. If the students are successful, as they usually will be in the first grade, proceed to the second stage of the lesson, which is to verify that the students can already read the sight words used in the first stage of the lesson and also indicate that they recognize the letter and its position in the words.

The third stage, that of associating the sound with the letter, is the key step in the lesson. The students who can correctly pronounce the letter or syllable indicated in the objective in unknown words in the association stage should be able to use that skill to recognize and pronounce that sound in the same position in other unknown words.

Many of the children will be able to state a rule or generalization when asked how they know how to pronounce the target sound in the unknown word. A six-year-old's rule might be a statement that he or she remembered other known words with that letter in the same position, thought about how it sounded in those words, and pronounced it that way in the new word. The purpose of the extra stimulus question ("If that word is 'cola,' what is this word? 'Bala.' ") is for the teacher to provide the part of the word that is not the subject of the lesson objective—only the initial syllable /ba/ is of interest.

This model lesson is inductive in that you ask questions that lead children to think about what they already know about sounds, letters, and words. You do not tell or explain. Many children will not be able to state a rule or generalization at the beginning of this type of inductive lesson, although most will be able to correctly pronounce the target element in the words. But after a number of lessons, increasing numbers of children will be able to formulate a rule. These generalizations will be remembered and applied more easily if they are derived by the children. If you provide them in a direct instruction activity, then the child must rely on memory to recall the rule later. When children learn to derive their own rules, they can transfer this ability to new unknown words. They can also transfer this generalized ability to English.

The instructional time required for the model lesson presented in the figure should be about five minutes, certainly less than ten minutes. Most instructional activities in beginning reading in Spanish should focus on comprehension through shared reading and, later, in small-group lessons in which children are reading in a directed or guided reading mode.

Figure 15.4

Invented Spelling in Children's Writing in Spanish.

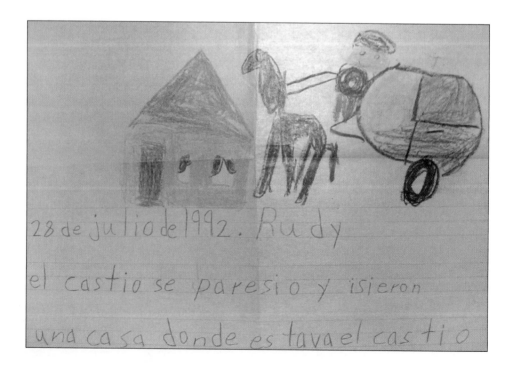

Inductive Phonics Lesson (Spanish/English)

Spanish lesson plan	English version of Spanish lesson plan
Objetivo: pronunciar el sonido inicial de palabras nuevas que empiecen con la sílaba /ba/	**Objective:** pronounce the initial sound of new words that begin with the syllable /ba/
Etapa de discriminacíon auditiva (verificar conciencia fonémica)	***Auditory discrimination stage (confirm phonemic awareness)***
Les voy a decir tres palabras. Escuchen bien.	I'm going to tell you three words. Listen to them carefully.
bajo baño bate	(short) (bath) (bat)
¿Cómo se parecen? ¿Qué tienen en común?	How are they alike? What do they have in common?
¿En qué parte de cada palabra se encuentra este sonido?	In what part of each word do you hear this sound?
Les voy a decir tres otras palabras. ¿Cuál no pertenece a este grupo?	I'm going to tell you three more words. Which one doesn't belong with the others?
ballena mesa barra	(whale) (table) (bar)
¿Cuál es diferente? ¿Por qué? ¿Cómo es diferente? ¿En qué parte?	Which is different? Why? How is it different? Which part is different?
¿Qué otras cosas pueden ver en el salón que empiecen con el mismo sonido?	What other things in the classroom can you see that begin with the same sound?
Etapa de discriminación visual	***Visual discrimination stage***
Vamos a leer tres palabras.	Let's read these three words.
Levanta la mano si quieres leer la primera palabra.	Raise your hand if you want to read the first word.
bajo, baño, bate Muy bien, etc.	(short) (bath) (bat [baseball])
¿Cómo se parecen estas tres palabras?	How do these three words look the same?
¿En qué parte de las palabras se encuentra la letra?	In what part of these words do you see that letter?
Etapa de asociación	***Association stage***
Ahora quiero que lean algunas palabras nuevas. ¿Quién quiere tratar de leer la primera palabra nueva? ¿Cómo sabias leeria?	Now we're going to read some new words. Who wants to read the first word? How did you know how to read it?
bala base barra ballena	bala base barra ballena
Si esa palabra dice "cola" ¿qué dice esta palabra? "Bala."	If that word is "cola," what is this word? "Bala."
cola	cola

Finally, there is a grammatical error that reflects a troublesome issue even for some adults. The conventions of Spanish require that the sequential repetition of a sound be avoided. Therefore, *y hicieron* should be written as *e hicieron* to avoid the repetition of the *y* (and) and the *hi* in *hicieron*, both of which carry the same sound (in Spanish, *y* followed by *hi* would sound like two English long *e* sounds in succession).

We have already discussed the issue of positive transfer of skills, that a reading skill or concept acquired in the mother tongue doesn't have to be taught again in the second language of English. Yopp and Stapleton (2008) provide evidence from a review of research and from their own work that phonemic awareness in Spanish transfers to English. They provide a variety of activities and book resources that support the kind of language play that leads to phonemic awareness in Spanish and that transfers to English.

Phonics lessons in Spanish should be drawn out of vocabulary from key words to reading lessons, language-experience approach lessons, and the shared reading experiences of children. The words used in the lessons should be within the children's sight vocabulary, moving from the whole (word) to the part (element to be taught) and back to whole (word)

Table 15.2 Sequence of Phonics Generalizations in Spanish

INITIAL SOUNDS	FINAL SOUNDS	WORD ENDINGS
a	a	os
e	e	as
i	o	diminutives
o	augmentatives	
u	d	verbs -ar
	l	verbs -er
m	n	verbs -ir
t	s	
l	r	Substitution of initial
p	z	consonants
n		
d	i	Substitution of final
s	u	elements
f		
r	**CONSONANT BLENDS**	Medial diphthongs
b		
g (soft)	br	Compound words
ll	cr	
c (hard)	dr	Verb endings
j	fr	
y	pr	Homonyms
h (mute)	tr	
ch	bl	Prefixes
z	cl	
qu	fl	Suffixes
g (hard)	gl	
c (soft)	pl	Homographs
gue, gui		
güe, güi		Grades of adjectives
x (medial)		
		Syllabication

again. Because of the nature of Spanish, elements are frequently syllables in the form of CV (consonant/vowel).

INSTRUCTIONAL MATERIALS IN SPANISH. The variety of instructional materials for reading in Spanish is almost as rich as that in English. These include formal reading programs, authentic children's literature, and electronic resources, including the Internet.

Print Resources. Most major publishers that provide an English reading program also offer a parallel program in Spanish. These programs would be fairly characterized as basal, although some have anthologies of original literature instead of contrived basal reader stories or decodable text. The best have children's literature from the Spanish-speaking world or children's stories written in Spanish by native Spanish-speaking authors. In both of these cases, the quality of Spanish language and the cultural appropriateness should be evaluated carefully.

Most Spanish programs also contain authentic children's literature translated from English. It is important to consider carefully the quality of translation and the cultural appropriateness. The best programs also offer selections of authentic Spanish-language lit-

New
Literacies

What technology resources are available for English language learners?

erature translated to English for their English versions, a demonstration of their respect for the literary traditions of both languages and cultures. A major strength of programs with parallel literature selections in two languages is that students who read a selection in the mother tongue as part of their mother tongue reading program have a powerful source of background knowledge when they later read an English version of the same story.

There is also a wealth of children's books and big books available in Spanish. The teacher who wishes to use authentic literature for a Spanish reading program instead of anthologies or basal readers will find the constantly expanding series of books on recommended children's literature in Spanish prepared by Schon (2000) to be an invaluable resource. In addition, she has published a compendium of children's books in Spanish with themes from around the world (Schon, 2001, 2002).

Electronic Resources for English Language Learners and Their Teachers. As we discussed in Chapter 2, access to technology is a major issue for English language learners and other children in urban and rural environments characterized by poverty. But what resources can English language learners and their teachers access when technology is available?

Many websites can provide support to English language learners and their teachers, both in the areas of English language development and in Spanish. For example, an international school website registry provides the home pages of schools around the world that are interested in establishing relationships such as pen pal arrangements with other schools (Greenlaw, 2001). These have the advantage of allowing English language learners to correspond in their developing second language of English with students in other countries who are also studying English, probably as a foreign language. In addition, they may have opportunities to correspond in their shared mother tongues. Two site registries are found at http://ppi.searchy.net/ and http://www.ks-connection.org/. Teachers should carefully supervise this activity.

The Bilingual Writing Center is a useful word processing program for children in English and Spanish that is distributed by The Learning Company (Wepner, Valmont, & Thurlow, 2000). A Google search on "student writing center" will reveal resources to meet this need.

In the area of ESL for teachers, the Internet TESLK website provides sample lessons and teaching ideas for teachers (Greenlaw, 2001). There are also articles and research papers, as well as other classroom activities. Click on http://h-net.msu.edu/cgi-bin/log-browse.pl?;trx=vx&list=EDTECH&month=9401&week=b&msg=RRyqEut43BLbd-SlqedxIrw&user=&pw= for a free subscription.

Another valuable website for the teacher who is searching for outstanding children's literature in Spanish is the Barahona Center for the Study of Books in Spanish for Children and Adolescents, directed by Isabel Schon, who was cited earlier for her books on this topic. The center's website can be found at http://www.csusm.edu/csb/.

Children Who Struggle Learning to Read in the Mother Tongue

Struggling Reader

Reading recovery has proven to be a very effective intervention strategy for children who experience reading difficulties in English (see Chapters 1 and 12). An authorized Spanish-language version of reading recovery, called *Descubriendo la Lectura*, has also been developed (Escamilla & Andrade, 1992). It follows the pattern of diagnosis and intervention of the original program, but in Spanish. Several adaptations to language and culture were necessary, including the need to locate children's literature in Spanish. The resulting program includes more than 300 books at twenty different levels of difficulty, with about twenty books per level.

How can English language learners be helped by programs such as Reading Recovery?

A Spanish diagnostic survey for the identification of students includes six observational tasks: (1) letter identification, (2) a word test, (3) concepts about print, (4) writing vocabulary, (5) dictation, and (6) running records of text reading. Procedures generally parallel those in the English language program, including the rereading of familiar books, a running record of the new book from the previous day, writing, rearranging a cutup story, and introducing a new book. The program is designed for first graders in the lowest 20 percent of the class after one year of reading instruction in the regular classroom.

In a national study of *Descubriendo la Lectura*, Escamilla et al. (1998) found that the program had a very positive outcome with Spanish-speaking second and third graders, with more than 90 percent of students at each grade level scoring above average on Spanish text reading. On the SABE, a standardized achievement test in Spanish, more than 75 percent of students at each grade level met or exceeded the average score.

Assessing the Oral Language Proficiency and Reading Proficiency of English Language Learners

Assessing the language and reading outcomes of English language learners is accomplished very much as is done for English speakers (Kame'enui et al., 2001). A number of measures of English language proficiency are used for placement of students in bilingual education programs or programs for English language learners, depending on their levels of achievement (see Table 15.3). In general, they measure the language production of children in English, including vocabulary, syntactical complexity, and auditory discrimination/pronunciation. State and local school district authorities typically establish criteria for the reclassification or identification of children whose English proficiency has advanced sufficiently for mainstream placement in regular classroom programs of instruction, although usually with extra support from a paraprofessional or other speaker of the mother tongue at the beginning of the transition process.

There are also several widely used standardized or normed tests of Spanish reading proficiency that usually parallel similar tests in English (see Table 15.3). The results of

The World of Reading

My 24 First Graders Speak 14 Different Mother Tongues: What Can I Do?

An increasingly common scenario in American classrooms is the presence of children who speak many different home languages. A bilingual education program usually cannot be provided for most of them for the following reasons:

- The teacher is not proficient in more than one of the languages, if that.

- Reading materials are not available in the languages.

- It would not be feasible to provide reading instruction in several languages, even with a proficient teacher and adequate materials.

- There might not be enough children with a common language at a grade level to support a full bilingual education program.

When many children at a grade level have a common language and are scattered among several classrooms, it might be possible to gather all of them into a single classroom. This is especially desirable if there is a teacher who can teach them in their mother tongue or if a paraprofessional or parent volunteer can provide mother tongue support to lessons taught in English. Usually, these children will be taught only in English in an immersion program. Because English is the only language common to most, they acquire basic interpersonal communication skills rather quickly. Formal reading instruction is usually delayed, although children can work with key words and the language-experience approach early in the process of acquiring English. Shared big books also provide excellent comprehensible input in English, as well as an early introduction to the concept of print and much valuable background knowledge.

these tests are often used to evaluate the progress of groups of children or the effectiveness of programs, but they are not very useful to teachers in identifying the levels of children for assignment to instructional groups or levels of textbooks.

In contrast, the informal reading inventory (IRI) serves the same function in Spanish as it does in English. It is an authentic measure of reading accuracy and comprehension, and the outcomes that it yields in Spanish, as in English, can be used to place children in reading groups and textbooks with some confidence (see Chapters 11 and 13 for discussions of using the IRI in English). Some major publishers with Spanish-language reading programs provide IRIs for them.

Teachers can also construct their own IRIs by selecting passages from basal readers or anthologies to represent each grade level, just as is done in English. Teachers should verify the levels of the passages by using a readability graph for Spanish (Crawford, 1995) (see the Assessment box). As in constructing an IRI in English, the teacher should ensure that the content of each passage in Spanish corresponds to background and cultural knowledge that the child has in Spanish. With a passage selected for each grade level and four comprehension-level questions developed for each passage, the teacher can employ the same process and accuracy and comprehension criteria for Spanish as for English, as described in Chapters 11 and 13. The IRI in Spanish yields frustration, instructional, independent, and capacity levels, just as it does in English and with the same criteria.

Readability measures are often misused, and the teacher should be aware of their limitations. These measures assess only surface structure features of language, and they ignore

DIFFERENTIATED INSTRUCTION

Teaching Older Children Who Are Preliterate

SIOP® Sheltered Instruction Observation Protocol

It is not uncommon for teachers of older English language learners from other countries to observe that a few lack literacy skills. Some have been in refugee camps without educational services, others have been working to contribute to family income, and still others have lived in very rural or isolated areas where attending school was not possible because of long distances and inadequate transportation. Many indigenous children from Latin America leave school because instruction is only provided in Spanish, which they might not speak or might not speak well. There are communities of speakers of Zapotec, Mixtec, Maya, Quechua, and many other indigenous languages living in the United States. Their Spanish might be very limited.

Other English language learners have had very limited school experience and left school, either for the reasons just cited, or occasionally because of the poor quality of education. According to Schifini (1996), many have large gaps in instruction in the primary grades, and they struggle as nonreaders in the higher grades. Schifini recommends several strategies for meeting the needs of these older preliterate English language learners:

- Develop a print-rich classroom environment that reflects student interests, including advertisements, brochures, bumper stickers, comics, drawings, magazines, murals, newspapers, photos, postcards, posters, recipes, and examples of their own work.

- Include native language print in the classroom environment.

- Use reading and writing workshop strategies and shared reading and literature studies.

- Use read-aloud activities for access to the core curriculum not available through reading.

- Use writing activities such as quick-writes to connect students to background knowledge.

- Provide shared book experiences with predictable and patterned books that are of standard textbook size and have mature story lines.

- Use collaborative chart stories, language-experience charts, and other forms of shared writing.

In their SIOP model, mentioned earlier in several chapters, Echevarria et al. (2004) recommend additional sheltered instruction strategies effective with preliterate older English language learners:

- Use graphic organizers, such as Venn diagrams, timelines, flow charts, and semantic maps, especially for reading in content areas of the curriculum.

- Use scaffolding techniques, such as paraphrasing or restating students' responses, and think-alouds.

Table 15.3　Assessment Measures for Spanish-Speaking English Learners

TYPE OF MEASURE	NAME OF MEASURE	SUBTESTS	ELEMENTS MEASURED	SOURCE OF MEASURE
English language Grades K–12	Basic Inventory of Natural Language (BINL)	N/A	Oral language production, language dominance, fluency, syntax, vocabulary, structural complexity	Checkpoint Systems
English-language development All LEP	California English Language Development Test (CELDT)	Listening and speaking Reading Writing	Oral language (one-on-one) Reading Writing	CTB/McGraw-Hill
English language Grades K–5	Language Assessment Scales (LAS)	N/A	Auditory discrimination, vocabulary, phoneme production, sentence comprehension, oral production of English and Spanish	CTB/McGraw-Hill
English language Grades K–12	Bilingual Syntax Measure (BSM)	N/A	Syntax, language dominance, second-language level, maintenance of first language	Psychological Corporation
English language (or other language) (observation rating scale) Grades 1–12	SOLOM	N/A	Comprehension, vocabulary, fluency, pronunciation, grammar	San Jose USD
Spanish reading (normed test) Grades 1–12	Aprenda: Prueba de Logros en Español, Second Edition	Sonidos y letras	Phoneme matching, letter identification, letter/sound correspondence	Psychological Corporation
		Lectura de palabras	Word matching with picture, word identification	
		Lectura de oraciones	Sentence match with picture	
		Vocabulario	Synonym matching, defining words in context	
		Comprensión de lectura	Reading comprehension of riddles, modified cloze tests, comprehension questions	
Spanish reading (normed test) Grades K–3+	La Prueba de Realización, Second Edition	Reading	Matching written words, matching spoken words with written words, picture–word matching	Riverside Publishing
Spanish reading (normed test) Grades K–8	Comprehensive Tests of Basic Skills	Reading	Word attack, vocabulary, reading comprehension	CTB/McGraw-Hill
Spanish reading (normed test) Grades 1–8	Spanish Assessment of Basic Education (SABE), Second Edition, Level 1	Reading	Basic skills of reading, spelling, language skills	Hampton-Brown

Spanish Readability Graph

Number of sentences

Number of syllables	1.0	1.5	2.0	2.5	3.0	3.5	4.0	4.5	5.0	5.5	6.0	6.5
220												4.3
218												3.8
216												3.3
214											5.3	2.8
212									9.7	7.2	4.8	2.3
210									9.2	6.7	4.3	1.9
208									8.7	6.3	3.8	1.4
206							13.1	10.7	8.2	5.8	3.4	1.0
204							12.6	10.2	7.8	5.3	2.9	
202							12.2	9.8	7.3	4.8	2.4	
200					16.6	14.1	11.7	9.2	6.8	4.4	1.9	
198					16.1	13.6	11.2	8.8	6.3	3.9		
196					15.6	13.2	10.7	8.3	5.8	3.4		
194					15.1	12.7	10.2	7.8	5.4	2.9		
192					14.6	12.2	9.8	7.3	4.5	2.4		
190			19.0	16.6	14.2	11.7	9.3	6.8				
188			18.6	16.1	13.7	11.2	8.8	6.4				
186	23.0	20.5	18.1	15.6	13.2	10.8	8.3	5.9				
184	22.5	20.0	17.6	15.2	12.7	10.3	7.8	5.4				
182	22.0	19.6	17.1	14.7	12.2	9.8	7.4	4.9				
180	21.5	19.1	16.6	14.2	11.8	9.3	6.9	4.5				
178	21.0	18.6	16.2	13.7	11.3	8.9	6.4	4.0				
176	20.6	18.1	15.7	13.3	10.8	8.4	5.9	3.5				
174	20.1	17.7	15.2	12.8								
172	19.6	17.2	14.7	12.3								
170	19.1	16.7	14.3	11.8								
168	18.7	16.2										

Approximate level of readability

Instructions:

1. Count the first 100 words in the sample.

2. Count the number of sentences in the 100 words, rounding to the nearest tenth of a sentence.

3. Count the number of syllables in the 100 words.

4. Look for the number of syllables in the left column of the graph. Trace to the right to find the number of sentences. The number at the foot of that column is the approximate grade level of the passage.

5. If the text consists of more than a few pages, take samples from every three pages and compute the mean for each variable.

6. If the proportion of sentences to syllables for each 100 words does not appear on the graph, then the readability of the passage cannot be determined.

Source: Crawford, A.N. (1985) Formula y grafico para determinarla comprensabilidad de textos del nivel primario en castellano. *Lectura y Vida 6*(4), 18–24.

Permission to copy with credit to the author.

the level of content and the background knowledge required of children. Teachers should carefully judge the content of passages they select for inclusion in IRIs for the children they will assess. Finally, teachers are often tempted to rewrite text, changing sentence length or vocabulary to raise or lower readability levels. This is a dangerous practice that should be avoided. A readability graph should be used only as a rough measure and never as a tool for writing to a level.

Mother Tongue Support in the Bilingual Classroom

Monolingual classroom teachers who are unable to teach in their students' mother tongue might be able to use the services of a paraprofessional who can. Those paraprofessionals' services can extend from follow-up mother tongue support of lessons taught in English by the teacher to instruction provided in the mother tongue under the close and careful supervision of the teacher.

Vignette of a Nonbilingual Teacher and a Bilingual Paraprofessional in a Bilingual Classroom

There are twenty-six third-grade children in Room 14. Of the twenty-six native Spanish-speaking children, eleven have made the transition into English reading. Ten continue reading instruction in Spanish while receiving ESL instruction. They will make the transition to English reading within a few weeks or months as they become ready. Five new arrivals to the United States speak only Spanish.

Their teacher, Mr. Scott, is a certified elementary school teacher, but he does not speak Spanish. He is a very good teacher, and he provides all ESL and English reading instruction. But the Spanish reading program is conducted by Ms. Morales, a part-time paraprofessional and university student who plans to become a bilingual teacher. She is occasionally assisted by two Spanish-speaking parent volunteers who read to the children and tell stories from their childhood.

Today, Ms. Morales is teaching a reading lesson from an anthology of stories in Spanish, part of a reading program in English and Spanish that Mr. Scott is also using with the English-speaking students. Ms. Morales begins by introducing new vocabulary that students will encounter in the guided silent reading they will do in a few minutes. In addition, she helps them to construct a semantic map so that they can share background knowledge they have about the topic of the story: a young girl who lives in the Amazon forest of South America. She guides their silent reading with higher-order questions from the teacher manual and additional questions she has formulated herself. After today's lesson, during which they read the first half of the story, the children will write predictions about how the story might end when they complete it the next day. In the meantime, Mr. Scott is teaching a word analysis lesson to the English-speaking students on the other side of the room, which will be followed by a similar literature lesson from the English version of the same anthology that Ms. Morales uses in Spanish.

Mr. Scott meets daily with Ms. Morales to help her plan instruction, to answer questions about how to use the teacher's manual for the Spanish reading program, which is provided in both English and Spanish for his convenience, and to assess children's progress in Spanish reading. As they teach in parallel through the morning, he observes and monitors her activities. She also assists in parent conferences when needed.

Mr. Scott and Ms. Morales have molded themselves into a highly effective team, both making indispensable contributions to the language and reading development of the children in the classroom. She gains much from his long teaching experience as they plan instruction for the next day and, on a longer-term basis, for future days, weeks, and months.

At the same time, he gains insights from the valuable background she has in the children's mother tongue and their culture.

Although the two are usually teaching parallel to each other, Mr. Scott is able to supervise Ms. Morales's work from his teaching station in the classroom, and he periodically walks around the classroom to encourage and reinforce the work of the children in both groups. Although he does not speak Spanish, he finds that he is able to understand much of what is occurring in her lessons.

The parallel structure of the English and Spanish anthologies from the third-grade reading program they use has many advantages. The teacher's manual for the Spanish part of the program has English and Spanish instructions on opposite sides of the teaching manual, so Mr. Scott can quickly determine the students' progress in their lessons. In addition, they will eventually read in English the stories they are now reading in Spanish. Their prior experience with the stories and the background knowledge developed will constitute an important part of scaffolding their comprehension as they move into reading in their new second language.

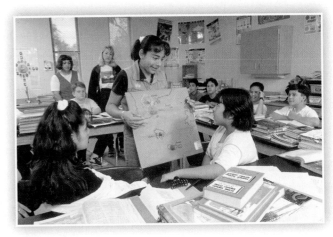

The help of bilingual classroom aides is extremely beneficial in the ESL/ELL classroom, but it is important that the teacher and the aides carefully coordinate their instruction so the messages to the students are consistent. (Will Hart)

Supervising the Paraprofessional Who Teaches in the Mother Tongue

It is a challenging task for monolingual teachers to supervise the instructional activities of bilingual paraprofessionals. Teachers should first model for their paraprofessionals in English the teaching manner, approaches, and strategies that are to be employed in Spanish or another language. Teachers should then observe their paraprofessionals, assessing the effectiveness of their modeling. Even though teachers might not understand the paraprofessionals' words, the teachers' knowledge of what is being taught should support good communication. A major emphasis of teachers should be to impress on paraprofessionals the importance of building up the children's self-concepts and of avoiding harsh words, which can undo the effects of even excellent teaching.

At an operational level, there should be outstanding communication between the teacher and the paraprofessional. They should meet in the morning to plan before school and again before the paraprofessional leaves at the end of the day, discussing the activities of the day and planning for lessons to follow. Because the teacher and paraprofessional complement each other so well, the development of mutual respect between them is important. The teacher has skills and knowledge about teaching, and the paraprofessional contributes vital communication skills and cultural knowledge.

Many bilingual paraprofessionals are university students who are in varying stages of the teacher preparation programs. They are highly motivated to become teachers, proud of their abilities to manage two languages and two cultures, and anxious to assume leadership in their own classrooms as soon as possible. As they approach and then enter their own student teaching experience, many are able to teach parallel to the regular teacher with careful supervision.

Some paraprofessionals exhibit those same language and cultural skills, but they view their paraprofessional role as their final career goal. They are often members of the local community who might have minimal academic preparation and training as instructional aides. It is perhaps among the members of this group that teachers who do not share the language and culture with the paraprofessional must exercise their most careful judgment. Because they are not trained teachers, their strategies in interacting positively and constructively with children must be carefully monitored. Because the supervising teacher often does not understand what the paraprofessional is saying to the children, it will be important to note the tone of the paraprofessional's voice and the children's reactions.

Parent Volunteers

Parent volunteers can be an important support to the nonbilingual teacher in the bilingual classroom. An important aspect of preparation for literacy in the mother tongue and English later is oral language development in the mother tongue. Family resources in the form of stories from parents, grandparents, and extended family can make a major contribution to this part of the program. Teachers can invite these adults into the classroom to tell stories to the children that can be used as a source of content for language-experience stories, for example.

McQuillan and Tse (1998) describe strategies for extending these storytelling experiences into the English language. The narratives that teachers, parents, grandparents, and other sources use constitute comprehensible input in the hands of an expert storyteller. The children are exposed to rich vocabulary and their background knowledge on a variety of valuable topics is enriched.

McQuillan and Tse indicate that students begin to write and tell their own stories as their own language production flourishes. When stories are related in English, the children's second language, students should be allowed to listen to stories in that target language without concerns about understanding everything. They should focus on the main ideas. Four steps then follow: (1) telling a short and simple version of the story; (2) revising the story by retelling it with different characters or settings, extending the story beyond its original ending, and narrating the story from the point of view of another character;

Family Literacy

What is the role of parent and family volunteers in working with English language learners?

Standards and Literacy

Standards for English Language Learners

Some states have developed English-language development standards for English language learners. These are helpful in planning curriculum, instruction, and assessment for the ESL programs that these students need. California has one of the most fully developed sets of standards for this purpose (California State Board of Education, 1999). The California standards are organized into the following categories:

- Listening and speaking
- Reading: Word analysis
  Fluency and systematic vocabulary development
  Reading comprehension
- Writing: Strategies and applications
  Conventions
- Reading: Literary response and analysis

Standards in these categories are provided at beginning, intermediate, and advanced levels. They are designed to be used at K–12 levels

but can be used as appropriate to the developmental level of the student. Some students may demonstrate that they have met advanced standards in the first grade, whereas a recent arrival may be just reaching beginning standards in the seventh grade. Here are examples of their standards:

Examples of English-Language Development Standards in Reading

Reading comprehension
Beginning level: Respond orally to stories read to the student, using physical actions and other means of nonverbal communication (e.g., matching objects, pointing to an answer, drawing pictures).
Intermediate level: Read and orally identify the main ideas and draw inferences about written text using detailed sentences.
Advanced level: Read and respond orally to familiar stories and other texts by answering factual comprehension questions about cause-and-effect relationships.

(3) the creation of a class story, which might involve considerable negotiation among the children; and (4) individual or small group creation of stories and books.

While McQuillan and Tse are most concerned about using the process to provide comprehensible input in English, the same strategies can be used to provide a stronger base of vocabulary and background knowledge in the mother tongue. In addition, this permits parents, grandparents, and other members of the extended family to play a valued role in the classroom. Finally, it validates and reinforces the value of the mother tongue and culture.

For Review

In this chapter, we examined the teaching of reading in languages other than English and also the teaching of English as a second language (ESL), as it relates to the teaching of reading. The chapter addressed three audiences: bilingual teachers who are capable of teaching reading and writing in a language other than English, teachers of English language learners whose mother tongue instruction will be conducted by a paraprofessional or other staff members under the teacher's supervision, and teachers who are responsible for teaching ESL.

There are various structures and models for teaching English language learners. One major direction is English only, that is, teaching ESL and also teaching all academic subjects, including reading, only in English. This is popularly known as immersion or structured immersion, and no evidence indicates it is an effective approach. The alternative is known as bilingual education. It consists of an ESL program as in the other approach, but academic instruction is provided in the children's mother tongue during the two to three years that are required for learning English sufficiently to support academic instruction (CALP), as opposed to a conversational level (BICS). There is substantial research support for this approach, although its application is highly political.

ESL is the major component of both immersion and bilingual education approaches. There are many approaches and methods for teaching ESL, but the natural approach is well supported in the literature. It resembles most closely the language environment of the child learning the mother tongue, a process almost always successful. It is based on themes rather than on grammar. Its major features are the provision of comprehensible input, the avoidance of correction, the acceptance of immature language structures at the beginning, a silent period during which children respond with gestures instead of producing language, and the maintenance of a low anxiety level in the classroom.

The natural approach consists of three stages: preproduction (comprehension), early production, and emergence of speech. During the intermediate stage that follows, children are ready to begin academic instruction in English, but in a sheltered or supported mode.

Strategies for teaching English language learners to read in English are given in Chapters 12, 13, and 14. In this chapter, the focus was on teaching reading in the mother tongue rather than English. Children learn to read only once. For children who learn to read in the mother tongue, there is a positive transfer of skills from mother tongue reading to the second language: English.

Learning to read in Spanish is not greatly different from learning to read in English. Teaching word recognition skills is easier in Spanish because of the regular correspondences between sounds and letters in Spanish, but it is slightly different because Spanish is a highly syllabic language. Children tend to learn syllables instead of the sounds of individual letters.

Teachers have no difficulty finding instructional materials in Spanish for all subject areas. Spanish reading is an especially rich area; most major publishers provide Spanish language reading programs that are parallel to their English language programs. In addition, there is ample children's literature in Spanish, some originating in Spanish and some in the form of translations from English. Because of a lack of materials in most other languages, it is uncommon to find reading programs except in Spanish, especially beyond the first or second grade.

Assessment in Spanish is similar to assessment in English, and many formal measures have Spanish language versions. Instructions were provided for locating or constructing an informal reading inventory (IRI) in Spanish. A Spanish language version of reading recovery, *Descubriendo la Lectura*, provides support to young children who are struggling.

Many teachers who do not speak their students' mother tongue find themselves in a bilingual classroom nonetheless. They are usually provided with a bilingual paraprofessional who conducts the mother tongue instruction under the teacher's supervision. It is important for each teacher to develop a strong spirit of teamwork in which the paraprofessional benefits from the professional training and experience of the classroom teacher, who in turn benefits from the language and cultural skills of the paraprofessional.

Many technological resources are also available that support the teacher who is working with ESL and mother tongue reading instruction. There are websites that provide background information about teaching ESL and computer-based resources that children can access.

For Your Journal

1. Find a classmate who did not speak English on arrival at the school or spoke English as a second language but who speaks English now. Interview this person about his or her experiences in learning English and learning to read. If you have ever traveled to a foreign country and did not speak or read the language, what did you do to adjust? Discuss the feelings you might have had if you had experienced this as a child.

Taking It to the World

1. You should now have a very clear idea of the challenges facing English language learners in their new classrooms. If you were the parent of a six-year-old child and you were to move to Croatia, describe the language and reading program you would want for your child. What additional information would you need before making a final decision?

New Literacies Connections

1. Yahoo.com provides a primitive translation website where children can cut and paste text to be translated to and from English and Spanish, as well as French, Portuguese, German, and Italian. The resulting translations are only fair in quality, but it is an interesting and revealing exercise for children. Visit the website at http://babelfish.yahoo.com/ and experiment with it for yourself. How might you be able to use this site when teaching?

2. Little Explorer is a multilingual website with a picture dictionary and graphics and multiple language translations provided. The site also includes links to other related sites. Visit Little Explorer (http://www.LittleExplorers.com) and explore for yourself. Why might this site be a valuable resource in the multilingual classroom?

PEARSON myeducationlab

Now go to MyEducationLab (www.myeducationlab.com), where you can:

- Find learning outcomes for the topics covered in this chapter, along with the national standards that connect to these outcomes.

- Complete Assignments and Activities that can help you more deeply understand the chapter content.

- Engage in Building Teaching Skills and Dispositions exercises, in which you can apply and practice core teaching skills identified in the chapter.

Appendix A

All Children Read and Professional Literacy Standards

Throughout this book, the impact of standards on the Literacy profession is discussed in various chapters and particularly in a special "Standards and Literacy" feature found in appropriate chapters. Discussions are intended to promote an understanding of how standards affect curriculum and instruction throughout the country. Two sets of standards of particular interest to reading professionals are the International Reading Association (IRA) *Standards for Reading Professionals* (2003) and the National Council of Teachers of English (NCTE) and IRA *Standards for the English Language Arts* (1996). In this appendix, we will provide you with a correlation of where the Standards are addressed within *All Children Read*.

How does *All Children Read* correlate to the International Reading Association *Standards for Reading Professionals?*

Standard	Chapter Coverage
1. Foundational Knowledge: Candidates have knowledge of the foundations of reading and writing processes and instruction.	
1.1 Demonstrate knowledge of psychological, sociological, and linguistic foundations of reading and writing processes and instruction	2–5, 6, 10
1.2 Demonstrate knowledge of reading research and histories of reading	1–15
1.3 Demonstrate knowledge of language development and reading acquisition and the variations related to cultural and linguistic diversity	1–5, 7, 10–12, 15
1.4 Demonstrate knowledge of the major components of reading (phonics, vocabulary and background knowledge, fluency, comprehension strategies, and motivation) and how they are integrated in fluent reading	1–13
2. Instructional Strategies and Curriculum Materials: Candidates use a wide range of instructional practices, approaches, methods, and curriculum materials to support reading and writing instruction and the variations related to cultural and linguistic diversity.	
2.1 Use instructional grouping options (individual, small-group, whole-class, and computer-based) as appropriate for accomplishing given purposes	2, 4–15
2.2 Use a wide range of instructional practices, approaches, and methods, including technology-based practices for learners at differing stages of development and from differing cultural and linguistic backgrounds	2, 4–15
2.3 Use a wide range of curriculum materials in effective reading instruction for learners at different stages of reading and writing development and from different cultural and linguistic backgrounds	2, 4–15
3. Assessment, Diagnosis, and Evaluation: Candidates use a variety of assessment tools and practices to plan and evaluate effective reading instruction.	

Standard	Chapter Coverage
3.1 Use a wide range of assessment tools and practices that range from individual and group standardized tests to individual and group informal classroom assessment strategies, including technology-based assessment tools	4–13
3.2 Place students along a developmental continuum and identify students' proficiencies and difficulties	2–13
3.3 Use assessment information to plan, evaluate, and revise effective instruction that meets the needs of all students, including those at different developmental stages and those from different cultural and linguistic backgrounds	2–15
3.4 Communicate results of assessments to specific individuals (students, parents, caregivers, colleagues, administrators, policymakers, policy officials, community, etc.)	1, 2, 4, 8–15
4. Creating a Literate Environment: Candidates create a literate environment that fosters reading and writing by integrating foundational knowledge, use of instructional practices, approaches and methods, curriculum materials, and the appropriate use of assessments.	
4.1 Use students' interests, reading abilities, and backgrounds as foundations for the reading and writing program	2–13
4.2 Use a large supply of books, technology-based information, and nonprint materials representing multiple levels, broad interests, and cultural and linguistic backgrounds	2, 4–15
4.3 Model reading and writing enthusiastically as valued lifelong activities	2, 4–15
4.4 Motivate learners to be lifelong readers	1, 2, 4–15
5. Professional Development: Candidates view professional development as a career-long effort and responsibility.	2
5.1 Display positive dispositions related to reading and the teaching of reading	1–2
5.2 Continue to pursue the development of professional knowledge and dispositions	2
5.3 Work with colleagues to observe, evaluate, and provide feedback on each other's practice	2, 10, 13
5.4 Participate in, initiate, implement, and evaluate professional development programs	2

Source: International Reading Association. (2003). Standards for Reading Professionals. Reprinted with permission of the International Reading Association. http://www.reading.org/downloads/resources/545standards2003/index.html

How Does *All Children Read* correlate to the National Council of Teachers of English & International Reading Association *Standards for the English Language Arts?*

Standard	Chapter(s)
1. Students read a wide range of print and non-print texts to build an understanding of texts, of themselves and the culture of the United States and the world; to acquire new information; to respond to the needs and demands of society and the workplace; and for personal fulfillment. Among these texts are fiction and nonfiction, classic and contemporary works.	2, 6, 7
2. Students read a wide range of literature from many periods in many genres to build an understanding of the many dimensions (e.g., philosophical, ethical, aesthetic) of human experience.	1, 2, 5, 6, 7
3. Students apply a wide range of strategies to comprehend, interpret, evaluate, and appreciate texts. They draw on their prior experience, their interactions with other readers and writers, their knowledge of word meaning and of other texts, their word identification strategies, and their understanding of textual features (e.g., sound-letter correspondence, sentence structure, context, graphics).	2–13
4. Students adjust their use of spoken, written, and visual language (e.g., conventions, style, vocabulary) to communicate effectively with a variety of audiences and for different purposes.	3–5, 8–12
5. Students employ a wide range of strategies as they write and use different writing process elements appropriately to communicate with different audiences for a variety of purposes.	3, 4, 8, 9, 12
6. Students apply knowledge of language structure, language conventions (e.g., spelling, punctuation), media techniques, figurative language, and genre, to create, critique, and discuss print and non-print texts.	3, 4, 9–12
7. Students conduct research on issues and interests by generating ideas and questions, and by posing problems. They gather, evaluate, and synthesize data from a variety of sources (e.g., print and non-print texts, artifacts, people) to communicate their discoveries in ways that suit their purpose and audience.	6, 7, 9, 11, 12
8. Students use a variety of technological and informational resources (e.g., libraries, databases, computer networks, video) to gather and synthesize information and to create and communicate knowledge.	1–15
9. Students develop an understanding of and respect for diversity in language use, patterns, and dialects across cultures, ethnic groups, geographic regions, and social roles.	2, 3, 5, 10, 11, 13, 15
10. Students whose first language is not English make use of their first language to develop competency in the English language arts and to develop understanding of content across the curriculum.	2, 4–15
11. Students participate as knowledgeable, reflective, creative, and critical members of a variety of literacy communities.	1–15
12. Students use spoken, written, and visual language to accomplish their own purposes (e.g., for learning, enjoyment, persuasion, and the exchange of information).	2–13

Source: *Standards for the English Language Arts*, by the International Reading Association and the National Council of Teachers of English, Copyright 1996 by the International Reading Association and the National Council of Teachers of English. Reprinted with permission. www.ncte.org/standards

Appendix B

Teach It! Instructional Activities

Codruţa Temple, *State University of New York at Cortland*
and
Jean Wallace Gillet

Contents

Overview

These lesson plans follow the order of their presentation in the text. They are designed for implementation by preservice teachers or by teacher education students in a practicum setting. They include a wide variety of activities featuring oral language development, emergent and beginning reading skills and concepts, reading comprehension, writing, and vocabulary development. Each of the activities is discussed in detail in the text.

Most of the featured lessons are intended for small group instruction within a regular classroom, and most can be readily adapted for individuals or larger groups, including whole classes. They provide opportunities for preservice teachers to practice instructional planning, lesson implementation, and classroom management while helping students develop critical language and literacy skills.

Each lesson plan includes a statement of objectives, stating what the activity is intended to teach or develop; a list of necessary materials, which should be gathered beforehand; and an estimated duration, or length of the lesson. Most lesson plans also include a list of suggested variations or extensions, which can be used to provide variety in subsequent lessons and to extend and enrich the learning experience. These can themselves become subsequent lessons, guided practice activities, or independent learning activities.

Each of these lessons can easily be modified to meet the individual needs of the preservice teacher, the supervising teacher, and the students in the classroom. Group size can be adapted and procedures and instructions can be modified to fit the needs and abilities of the students. Each activity is specific to one or more fundamental literacy skills, but each is also generic in that it can be productively retaught by changing the literature selection, writing stimulus, discussion props, and so forth. Each activity is one that preservice teachers should be familiar with and able to implement in the classroom.

Guidelines for Lesson Planning

- Plan every lesson ahead of time. Your mental preparation will enable you to present your lesson with skill and confidence. Planning ahead ensures that all necessary materials are at hand, allowing you to focus more on the students than on yourself.

- Select lessons to implement based on students' learning needs, not on your interests, strengths, or time constraints. Every lesson has an instructional purpose; knowing it will increase your confidence and enthusiasm.

- Collect and check all materials, supplies, and equipment beforehand. Missing markers, a mislaid book, or a burned-out overhead projector bulb can sabotage the best lesson.

- Be a positive language and literacy role model. Use precise, correct language, model enthusiasm for reading and literature, and show your enjoyment of learning.

- Reinforce positive behavior and effort by specifically drawing attention to what students did, rather than using empty praise. Point out when students use a strategy, attempt something difficult, or persist when having difficulty.

- Whenever possible, allow students choices, even if the range of choices is narrow. Having choices increases students' feeling of ownership and empowerment. Encourage diversity in answers to questions, ways to show comprehension, and choices of literature.

- Encourage and foster personalization and creativity. Show that you value students' attempts to relate what they are learning about to their own lives and experiences.

- Be prepared to handle interruptions, schedule changes, and the unforeseen with poise. No lesson ever unfolds exactly as planned, and an unexpected outcome can be even better than the planned outcome! Each lesson is a journey, and the "getting there" is as important as the destination.

- Evaluate each lesson you teach, even if your evaluation is only a brief self-reflection. If possible, jot down a few notes about what went well and what you'd do differently another time in a personal journal. Self-evaluation is one key to improving your teaching.

Reading Activities for Emergent and Beginning Readers

1. Reading Aloud

Objectives: To develop children's ability to comprehend written language; to raise children's awareness of the structure of different types of texts; to expand children's vocabulary; to encourage enthusiasm for literacy

Materials: An age-appropriate book

Duration: 10–15 minutes

1. Prepare to read the book.
   a. Read the book through yourself before you read it to the children to decide whether it is suitable for your class.
   b. Decide how you want to read it—with humor, with drama, with questions to whet curiosity.
   c. If there are voices to bring to life, decide how you want to make each one sound.
   d. If you decide to stop reading to ask for predictions or for discussion, decide where the stopping places should be.
   e. If there are any words or ideas that will be unfamiliar to the children, make a note to pronounce them carefully and explain them to the children.
   f. If the book has illustrations large enough for the children to see, practice reading the book through while you hold it in front of and facing away from you, where the children will be able to read it.
2. Prepare the children.
   a. Make sure the children are seated comfortably where they can see and hear you.
   b. Remind the children, if you need to, of the behavior you expect of good listeners: hands to themselves, eyes on the teacher, and ears for the story.
3. Read the title.
4. Show the children the cover of the book, ask them what they know about the topic, and ask them to make predictions about what will happen or what they expect to find out in the book.
5. Turn to the title page. Read the author's name and the illustrator's. Talk about what each contributed to the book. Remind the children of any other books they know by this author or this illustrator.
6. As you read the book through the first time, ask for comments about what is going on and for predictions about what will happen.
7. Follow up the reading with a whole-class discussion about the book.
8. Read the book a second time through, taking more time to look at the illustrations and to talk about characters, their motives, or other things you and the students find interesting about the book.
9. Leave the book available to the children in the library corner, and encourage them to read it later during scheduled time in the reading center or between other activi-

ties. The children might especially enjoy taking turns reading it to each other.

2. Dialogic Reading

Objectives: To develop children's oral language and concepts about print

Materials: An age-appropriate book

Duration: 10–15 minutes

A. Dialogic reading for younger children (PEER)
   1. Prompt the child to name objects in the book and talk about the story.
   2. Evaluate the child's responses and offer praise for adequate responses and alternatives for inadequate ones.
   3. Expand on the child's statements with additional words.
   4. Ask the child to repeat the adult's utterances.
B. Dialogic reading for older children (CROWD)
   While reading the book to the child, ask the following types of questions:
   1. Completion questions. Ask the child to supply a word or phrase that has been omitted. (For example, "I see a yellow duck looking at _____.")
   2. Recall questions. Ask the child about things that occurred earlier in the book. ("Do you remember some animals that Brown Bear saw?")
   3. Open-ended questions. Ask the child to respond to the story in his or her own words. ("Now it's your turn: You say what is happening on this page.")
   4. Wh- questions. Ask what, where, who, and why questions. ("What is that yellow creature called? Who do you think Brown Bear will see next?")
   5. Distancing questions. Ask the child to relate the content of the book to life experiences. ("Do you remember when we saw a yellow duck like that one swimming in the lake? Was it as big as this one?")

3. Morning Message

Objectives: To help emergent readers develop familiarity with written language; to focus attention on words

Materials: Chart paper

Duration: 15–20 minutes

1. Tell students that as a class you will write two or three things about your morning, such as the date, the weather, and anything that makes the morning special.
2. Invite students to suggest a sentence. Repeat the sentence.
3. Ask students what word you should write first. Ask what letter it should begin with and whether it should be an uppercase or a lowercase letter. Have a volunteer come forward

and write some of the letters of the first word for you. Continue until you have written the complete sentence.

4. Read the sentence, pointing to each word. Have students read the sentence as you point to each word.

5. Repeat steps 2–4 to write two or three additional sentences.

6. Write some of the words that are often repeated on separate pieces of thick paper and tape them to the bottom of the chart or on the chalkboard.

7. Invite a student to come forward, pick one of the pieces of paper, and read the word on it. Then have the student find the same word in a sentence. Have her read the sentence aloud, then place the word on top of the same word in the sentence. Finally, ask the student to read the sentence again with the word in place.

8. Repeat step 7 for all of the words written on pieces of paper.

9. Have all of the students read the lines of text with you as you point to each word.

10. Have students choral-read the whole text.

11. Have students echo-read the text.

12. Invite different groups of children to read the morning message.

13. Ask individual children to come forward and point to any words they can read in isolation. Bracket each word with your hands as the child reads it, so the surrounding words cannot be seen. If the child is successful, write the word on a piece of thick paper and have the student add it to her word bank for later practice.

4. Language Experience or Group Dictated Story

Objectives: To help emergent readers develop oral language fluency, print directionality, concept of word, sight word recognition, and phonemic awareness

Materials: An object, shared experience, favorite song or book, or other stimulus for the dictation; large chart tablet or 24 × 36-inch paper on easel or chalkboard; large marker

Duration: 10–30 minutes; additional time for follow-up activities listed below

1. Select a group of 4–10 children to participate.

2. Select and prepare a stimulus for dictation: for example, an interesting concrete object, classroom pet, familiar story for retelling, or recent classroom event.

3. Invite participants to gather close to the chart paper. Introduce the activity by explaining that they will talk together about the stimulus and create statements about it that you will write for them on the chart paper. They will learn to read the sentences for themselves by rereading them together and pointing to the words.

4. Invite discussion of the stimulus, encouraging students to describe, narrate, and add verbal details. If necessary, ask open-ended questions like "What else do you notice?" "What else do you remember?" or "What happened after that?"

5. Ask for volunteers to contribute sentences for the dictation.

6. Write students' sentences verbatim, allowing changes or additions. Print neatly and clearly in large letters, with clear spaces between each word. Limit the account to 5–7 sentences.

7. Read the completed story expressively and at a natural pace, pointing to each word as you read.

8. Reread the story chorally several times until students have memorized it. Continue pointing to each word. (Keep up the pace so the reading sounds natural, not word by word.) If students have trouble memorizing the whole text, divide it into sections of two or three sentences each.

9. Invite volunteers to come to the chart and recite a part or the whole story while pointing to each word. Continue until each student who volunteers has read the story individually.

10. Point to individual words and invite students to identify the words, reading from the beginning to the target word if necessary.

5. Language Experience with Authentic Children's Literature

Objectives: To help emergent readers develop oral language fluency, print directionality, concept of word, sight word recognition, and phonemic awareness; to stimulate interest in and engagement with children's literature

Materials: A culturally appropriate piece of children's literature; chart paper or chalkboard; large marker or chalk

Duration: 15–30 minutes

1. As a stimulus for a language-experience dictation, conduct a read-aloud of a piece of children's literature that is culturally appropriate for your class.

2. During the read-aloud, share the illustrations in the book and ask questions about the unfolding story.

3. Have the children dictate their brief version of the story.

4. Accept the dictations of the children as stated, regardless of any cultural affectations, as long as other children do not suggest changes. However, spell the words correctly irrespective of students' pronunciation.

5. Make sure the children have many opportunities to read the text in a shared reading mode as the dictation is recorded and after the children's rendition of the story is completed.

6. Optionally, follow up with some of the activities suggested for the Language Experience or Group Dictated Story.

Follow-Up Activities for Group Dictated Story

• Repeat choral and individual reading and pointing on subsequent days until all students can read the story fluently and point accurately.

• Create an exact copy of the story on another sheet of chart paper. Cut the sentences or lines apart. Place in a center for students to reorder the lines and compare to the original.

- Copy each sentence onto a sentence strip. Have volunteers hold up each strip in correct order. (These can also be used for independent practice with a hanging pocket chart.)

- Create exact copies of the story on copy paper. Duplicate several copies for each participant. In different lessons, students can paste copies on construction paper or in journals and illustrate them, cut lines and sentences apart and put them in correct order, cut sentences into phrases and put them in correct order, and use sentences for handwriting practice.

- Have students find individual words they recognize in isolation and begin building individual word banks with known words on cards. Students should sort and review word banks daily.

- Have students sort words in their word banks in a variety of ways: matching beginning sounds, number of syllables, alphabetical order, and so forth.

- Select one or several familiar words beginning with consonants. Using individual letter cards or magnetic letters, show students how to "make and break" the words by removing the initial letter or sound and substituting another, creating new words. (Change THAT to HAT, PAT, RAT, and CAT; MATCH to PATCH, BATCH, and SCRATCH; MAKE to TAKE, RAKE, FAKE, and LAKE.)

- Have students write known sight words using magnetic letters on cookie sheets, individual letters cut out of sandpaper, wallpaper scraps, or felt, glue and sand or glitter, pipe cleaners, heavy yarn, macaroni letters, mini-marshmallows, dried beans, and so forth. (The more ways they practice making the same words, the more automatic these words will become!)

- Begin personal dictionaries by folding eight to ten sheets of paper vertically and stapling in the fold to create individual books. Have students write a letter at the top of each page (group infrequent letters like q, u, x, y, and z with others) and begin collecting mastered sight words in their dictionaries.

6. Big Book Lesson

Objectives: To help emergent readers develop familiarity with book language patterns, print directionality, concept of word, sight word recognition, and phonemic awareness

Materials: A big book of your choice; for follow-up activities, a Word Hider (index card), sentence strips, pocket chart

Duration: 10–30 minutes; additional time for follow-up activities listed below

1. Display the big book, closed, on an easel or display stand (so your hands are free). Invite students to gather close enough to the book so everyone can clearly see the print.

2. Read the title, pointing to the words, and encourage students' observations about the cover art. Invite predictions of what the book might be about or what might happen based on the title and cover.

3. Open to the title page and read the author's and illustrator's names, pointing to the words. Be sure everyone knows what the author and the illustrator did. Make connections to other familiar books by the author or illustrator, if appropriate.

4. Read the first page fluently and expressively, pointing to the words. Comment, or invite student comments, on the illustrations. Review previous predictions and have students revise or confirm predictions based on what is now known.

5. Repeat this step with each page, or several pages at a time, depending on the length and complexity of the text and the illustrations. Continue pointing to the words as you read. Continue inviting new or revised predictions as the story unfolds.

6. As you near the story's conclusion, invite final predictions of how it will end. Read to the end of the story.

7. Invite students' comments about the story and illustrations. Encourage them to talk about characters or story parts they liked, appealing illustrations, and so forth. You may wish to go back to particular illustrations to reexamine them, looking for details, or just for enjoyment.

Five-Day Plan for Using a Big Book

Day 1: Follow the preceding plan for the first reading. Goals for this lesson include introduction to the story, forming and revising predictions based on illustrations and unfolding plot, perusal of illustrations, and general enjoyment of the book activity.

Day 2: Either reread the story in its entirety, pointing to the words, or echo-read the story with students. (You read a sentence or two, pointing to the words, then students repeat verbatim or "echo.") At relevant points, stop to discuss predictions made during previous reading, and help students verbalize how they arrived at those predictions. Reexamine illustrations, this time for features overlooked the first time, details of colors, borders, and so forth. If appropriate, compare this book to familiar others by the same author or illustrator.

Day 3: Reread the story, inviting students to "chime in" or read along with you (choral-read) as desired. Some may be more ready to do so than others. Predictable lines, repeating refrains, and rhyming elements will support choral reading. Continue pointing to the words as you read. Emphasize comprehension in this lesson; ask questions about the story events, characters, setting, and so forth, inviting students to use both the text and illustrations to find information and justify their answers.

Day 4: Reread chorally, encouraging all students to read with you as much as they can. Many will have memorized the story by now. (If many are still unable to choral-read it, break the story into sections to work on.) Emphasize "word work" in this lesson. Point to and have volunteers identify selected words. Use the Word Hider (index card) to cover selected words, have students read from the beginning of the sentence and identify the hidden word; uncover to confirm. See how many times students can find the same word on the same and subsequent pages, find other words with the same beginning sound, or match words to familiar words on the Word Wall.

Day 5: Reread chorally, letting your voice "fade" so students are reading more independently. Have volunteers come forward to read one or more sentences, pointing to the words as they read. Distribute sentences on sentence strips and have students put them in order in pocket chart. Have students act out the story and/or do related art, cooking, or other extension activities to enrich the literary experience.

7. Making Individual Small Books

Objectives: To provide students with small easily read books they can read independently at school and home

Materials: Two sheets of $8\frac{1}{2} \times 11$ plain paper for each student, supply of old magazines with colorful illustrations, scissors, glue, markers, stapler

Duration: 15–30 minutes, depending on number of students participating

1. Prepare a blank book for each student by placing two sheets of paper together, 11-inch side at top, folding vertically down the middle. Staple vertically in the fold, creating a book about $5\frac{1}{2} \times 8\frac{1}{2}$ with front and back covers and six inner pages.
2. Select a group of six to eight students. For larger groups, another adult is needed to assist students. Give each student a magazine, or magazine pages with colorful pictures, and scissors.
3. Select a group of eight or fewer students. If the group is larger, have another adult available to assist students. Gather around a work table where supplies have been placed.
4. Show students a premade model book: A magazine picture has been cut out and glued to each of the six pages of a book, and an adult has labeled the picture underneath with a simple phrase or sentence: "The dog is jumping," "A box is round," "A red apple," and so forth.
5. Assist students in choosing a picture and gluing it to the first page. Have them continue to complete the remaining pages. Using a marker, write the student's dictated sentence or phrase neatly and clearly under each picture. Have students copy a title onto the cover, print their names, and if desired write or draw on the back cover.
6. Assist each student in reading the entire book and practicing it so each can read his or her book fluently to the group or class during sharing time.

Variations: Give each book a theme and a title: Things That Are Round, What Is Square? (shapes); Red Is Everywhere, Things That Are Blue (colors); Animals All Around, Outdoors, We Can Play (various play activities); What Starts with B? (initial letters/sounds); It's Spring! (seasons or holidays), Foods We Love.

8. Modified Reading Recovery Lesson

Objectives: To help emergent readers develop oral language fluency, print directionality, concept of word, sight word recognition, and phonemic awareness

Materials: Individual copy of a short, predictable, clearly illustrated "little book" at Guided Reading levels A–D or Reading Recovery levels 1–8 for each participant

Duration: 10–15 minutes, depending on length and difficulty of text

1. Select one to three emergent readers to participate. (If more than one, have students take turns during the following steps.)
2. Preview the book by reading the title, encouraging student/s to examine the cover illustration and predict what might happen or what the book might be about.
3. Guide student/s in looking at the illustration on each page, naming objects and/or describing the picture, and if necessary modeling expanded oral language by repeating students' remarks in expanded form (S: "A dog." T: "Yes, there's a dog. It's a brown dog.")
4. Read and point to an important word or phrase, or repeated phrases, on each page as you examine the illustrations. (T: "Here's the word *dog*.") In this way you smooth the way for the reader/s to read each page independently.
5. Return to the first page and invite the student/s to read each page as independently as possible. Provide assistance on unfamiliar words, and encourage the student/s to use the picture, beginning sounds, and sentence context to attempt unknown words. Point out strategies you observe the student/s using: "You were smart to go back and read that sentence again when you got stuck," "I saw you get your mouth ready to say the beginning sound," or "You did what good readers do when you looked at the picture."
6. Choral-read the book with the student/s one or more times to gain familiarity with the sound of the sentences being read smoothly.
7. Invite student/s to read the whole book one more time with less teacher support. Encourage the student/s to reread the book several times independently at school and/or at home for fluency.

9. Guided Reading

Objectives: To develop effective strategies for processing novel text at increasingly challenging levels of difficulty; to develop students' ability to read silently

Materials: Multiple copies of leveled books

Duration: 5 minutes prior to reading; time necessary to complete reading and to respond to the story

1. Select a group of 4–6 children who are reading at about the same level.

2. Introduce a new text at students' instructional level. Encourage the students to converse about the text, to ask questions, and to build expectations.
3. Have the children read the entire text, or a unified part of it, to themselves silently (or softly in the case of younger readers). Allow them to ask for help when needed.
4. While the students are reading, observe their problem-solving strategies and provide assistance by suggesting other suitable strategies.
5. After the reading, involve the children in responding to the story through such activities as writing, discussion, paired reading, or sharing personal responses.
6. For subsequent guided reading sessions, regroup the children in accordance with outcomes that you have observed and assessed.

10. Guided Reading and the Four Blocks Approach

Objectives: To develop effective strategies for processing novel text at increasingly challenging levels of difficulty; to develop children's ability to read silently; to increase children's writing fluency; to teach word study skills in a meaningful context

Materials: Multiple copies of leveled books; optionally, a big book; chart paper for whole-class word study activities

Duration: 40–60 minutes

A. Working with small groups
   1. Follow steps 1–4 of the Guided Reading strategy as described earlier.
   2. Have the students respond to the story in writing. Suggest writing prompts that are appropriate to students' level of writing development.
   3. Follow the writing block with 10–15 minutes of self-selected reading time. Help students select texts at their independent reading level.
   4. Teach word study skills tailored to the needs of the children in the group.
B. Working with the whole class
   1. Make the text accessible to all students with multiple readings involving read-aloud, shared reading, and paired reading.
   2. Have the students respond to the story in writing.
   3. Follow the writing block with 10–15 minutes of self-selected reading time. Help students select texts at their independent reading level.
   4. In the last block, do word study with the whole class, with all students working on the same skills, or, if possible, teach appropriate skills in smaller groups.

11. Shared Reading

Objectives: To develop comprehension by modeling comprehension strategies; provide guided practice in using comprehension strategies

Materials: Fiction or nonfiction book students will read together

Duration: 10–30 minutes depending on length of book and size of group

1. Select a text for students to read. A big book can be used with younger readers.
2. Select two or more comprehension strategies to demonstrate; for example, organizing prior information before reading, predicting story outcomes, creating good questions, visualizing scenes, self-monitoring comprehension, making inferences about information not directly stated, using context to understand new words, identifying and clarifying difficult parts, or summarizing.
3. Preview the book with students; examine the title and cover illustration, predict what the topic of the book might be or what might happen in the story, and look at each page, examining illustrations and pointing out important words.
4. After previewing, read the text to or with students, depending on how well they can handle the text. Students can read predictable or repeated parts, echo-read or choral-read, or alternate reading with you.
5. While reading, "think aloud" to model effective reading: Pause to wonder or predict what might happen next, tell what a part reminds you of, wonder about word meanings, demonstrate how to use word parts or context to figure out new words, identify and reread difficult parts, and comment on illustrations. Emphasize the strategies you selected beforehand. For example, if you selected visualizing, think aloud about how you are imagining the setting, characters, and action; if you selected inferring, demonstrate making an inference from several related facts or ideas. Model what good readers do as they read.
6. Invite students' comments and predictions about the text. Ask and invite thoughtful questions.
7. Reread the text in its entirety to "put the pieces together" and experience the material as a whole. With greater familiarity, students may be able to read more of the text themselves.
8. Make the text available for students to reread independently.

Word Study Activities

12. Phonemic Segmentation with Elkonin Boxes

Objectives: To develop phonemic awareness and ability to segment phonemes in words

Materials: Elkonin boxes (series of connected squares) drawn on paper or sentence strips: two boxes for words with two phonemes, and so forth; "counters" such as poker chips or dried lima beans for the student to move; letter cards or magnetic letters

Duration: 5–10 minutes

1. Select a word with 2–4 phonemes (for example, *to*, *cat*, *trip*) to segment. Use the Elkonin box with the appropriate number of spaces. Say the word, then say the word phoneme by phoneme; as you say each phoneme, push or place a counter into a box. Have the student watch as you do this. If necessary, repeat.
2. Have the student copy what you did: Say the word, and then say each sound while pushing the counters into the boxes. If an error occurs, stop the student by placing your hand over his or hers and modeling again, saying, "Watch again. Now you try." Repeat until the student can segment the phonemes and place the counters correctly.
3. Repeat the process with another word. You may choose another word with the same number of phonemes (*to*, *in*, *at*) or proceed to a word with one more phoneme (*in*, *pin*, *spin*).
4. When the student has mastered segmenting the phonemes and moving the counters, begin using letter cards or magnetic letters instead of counters, placing the letters in the boxes. (Keep letters representing digraph sounds together; for example, *that* has three phonemes, and the letters *th* are placed together in the first box.)
5. When the student has mastered moving the letters into boxes, you can remove the boxes altogether and continue practicing using just the letters.

13. Working with Names to Teach the Alphabet

Objectives: To develop knowledge of the alphabet

Materials: Pieces of cardboard, a box

Duration: 5 minutes

1. Write each child's name on a piece of cardboard and put all the names in a box.
2. Each day draw out a name, call the child forward, and interview her (about favorite pastimes, pets, games, etc.).
3. Then put the child's name on the bulletin board and explain that this word is a name.
4. Point to the letters in the name, reading left to right.
5. Have the children count the letters.

6. Call attention to the first letter of the name. Have students notice that it is a big letter. Explain that all names begin with a big letter. Show them the lowercase letter as well. Ask if anyone else has that letter in their name. Write other names that contain the letter on the chalkboard.
7. Repeat the activity every day with another child's name.

14. Beginning Sounds Picture Sorting

Objectives: To develop phonemic awareness, ability to distinguish among several different beginning sounds, and ability to categorize pictures of objects with same beginning sound

Materials: Set of commercial beginning sounds sorting cards, or teacher-made cards with clear pictures of common objects, six to eight of each of two or more initial consonant sounds; pocket chart

Duration: 10–15 minutes

1. Preselect two or more beginning consonant sounds that are clearly different; begin with two contrasting sounds, and add more as students gain familiarity with the procedure. Select pictures of objects with these beginning sounds.
2. Gather a group of 4–10 students in front of the pocket chart.
3. Hold up each card and have students name each object. Be sure all students can name each object accurately.
4. Place one card for each sound at the top of the pocket chart. Tell students they will name the object on each card and place each card below the picture that begins with the same sound.
5. Mix up the remaining cards. Hold up each one and have students name the object chorally. Give each successive card to a different student. Have the student come to the chart, say a "sorting sentence" naming the two objects such as "Basket starts like baby," and place it in the correct column.
6. As each card is added to a column, have students name all the objects in that column chorally to check that they all have the same beginning sound.
7. When all pictures have been correctly sorted, have students name all the objects in each column one more time to reinforce the beginning sound. You may leave the cards near the pocket chart for students to sort independently as time allows.

Variations: Place one example of each sound at the top of the pocket chart. Distribute the remaining cards to students. Have students holding a card beginning with one sound come to the chart, say the sorting sentence, and place their cards in a column. Repeat with the other sound(s). Or dispense with the pocket chart: Have students line up next to each other, all the students with cards beginning with the same sound in one line. Have them name all the objects with the same beginning sound chorally.

15. Word Sorting

Objectives: To learn to discern patterns of similarity among words with similar sound, spelling, grammatical, or meaning patterns

Materials: Word cards with printed words that share a particular feature; pocket chart

Duration: 5–15 minutes, depending on number of words to sort and size of group

1. From a word wall, sight word banks, spelling list, or other source of words recognized at sight, select 2–4 features to contrast (for example, different beginning consonants, beginning blends, short or long vowel patterns, or parts of speech) and 4–6 words that share the same feature for each category. When introducing a new feature, or with struggling readers, contrast only two features at one time.
2. Review all the word cards with students; hold each up and have them identify the word chorally. Discard any words not recognized quickly.
3. Select one word from each group to represent the feature; read it and place it at the top of the pocket chart. Words sharing that feature will be placed below it in vertical columns. Point out the critical feature: "Let's find all the words that begin with the same sound as ball," "... have the same vowel sound as run," "... mean more than one," or "... are adjectives, words that describe things."
4. Mix up the remaining cards and hold each one up, having students read it aloud. Have volunteers come forward to place the word in the correct column and say the "sorting sentence"; for example, "Men means more than one man" or "Pretty is an adjective."
5. When all words have been correctly sorted, have students read each column chorally beginning with the example word.
6. Leave the example words displayed, remove and mix up the cards, and leave them near the pocket chart for independent sorting.

Variations: Have students sort their word banks and create their own individual sorts on the floor or table in front of them, using the example words you give them. Have students create their own individual sorts using word bank or word wall words, and let others guess the common feature. Have students sort their spelling words and write the words in categories as a practice exercise.

16. Word Hunts

Objectives: To develop children's ability to make connections between the spelling and the pronunciation of words

Materials: Chart paper

Duration: 10–15 minutes

1. Select a short rhymed poem and write it in large print on a piece of chart paper.
2. Read the poem to the children.
3. Read it a second time with the children reading along.
4. Have the children reread the poem in partner groups.
5. Ask the children what they notice about the words at the end of each line. Elicit examples of rhyming words.
6. Tell the children you want to go on a word hunt for two words that don't rhyme. Thinking aloud, select two words that don't rhyme and, on another piece of chart paper, write them as the headings of two columns.
7. Tell the students to copy the columns and the headings into their notebooks.
8. Organize the class in pairs.
9. Tell the children that each pair has to find as many rhyming words as they can that match the top word in each column. The words can be new ones that they think of, words from the word walls, and words in the poem.
10. Have the pairs share the words they have found.
11. Talk about what makes words rhyme.

17. Making and Breaking Words

Objectives: To develop phonemic awareness and ability to segment onset (beginning sound) and rime (the rest of the word without the beginning sound)

Materials: Magnetic letters or letter cards for students (metal cookie sheets for magnetic letters, and "letter holders" [sheet of paper folded 2 inches up from bottom and stapled vertically to create three or four pockets for letter cards] are helpful but optional); a large set of letter cards for demonstration

Duration: 10–15 minutes

1. Preselect two to four common phonograms that can become several different words by changing the initial consonant; these are often called "word families." Examples are -an, -am, -to, -ock, -in, -ake, -ike, and -ill. Preselect letters for these phonograms and the beginning sounds.
2. Select a group of students. Each student needs a set of letters or cards to make the phonograms and the necessary beginning letters. Gather around a table so students can manipulate letters.
3. Use large letter cards on the table or in a pocket chart to demonstrate. Put up the letters necessary to make a word such as *man*. Then remove the *m* and substitute another letter, such as *p*. Ask students to read the new word, *pan*.
4. Have students repeat the procedure themselves, using the magnetic letters or letter cards. Have them say the initial word, then say the new word as the initial letter is substituted. On the display set, again remove the initial letter and substitute another such as *r*, this time asking, "What word did I make this time? That's right, *ran*. Use your letters to make *ran*."
5. Continue until all real words have been made. (Avoid creating nonsense words like *zan*.)

6. Using the demonstration letters, quickly "make and break" all the words in one word family and have students read each word. Then have students use their letters to quickly make the words as you call them out. Repeat with the other word families used.

18. Making and Using Word Banks

Objectives: To develop sight word recognition

Materials: Index cards cut in half or pieces of thick paper or cardboard; a box or a zip-lock plastic bag

Duration: 5 minutes

1. Once a student has demonstrated that she can read a word out of context, write that word on a piece of thick paper and have the student put it in her word bank (a box or plastic bag that contains all the sight words a student has learned).
2. Have students practice reading the words in their word banks every day in one of the following ways:
   - By reading them to a partner or a parent volunteer;
   - By grouping the words into categories (e.g., animals, things, actions);
   - By grouping all the words that begin with the same letter;
   - By doing "word hunts," that is, looking for the same words in a children's book.
3. Have each student read the words in his or her word bank to you every week or every ten days. If a child cannot read a word correctly, put it in a special envelope inside the word bank. Have students practice reading the words in the special envelope. When a word is read correctly, add it to the word bank.

19. Word Wall Activities

Objectives: To develop automatic (sight) recognition of words

Materials: Large bulletin board or wall space for display of word collections, with room to add 5–10 new words per week; blank word cards or sentence strips; heavy black and/or colored markers

Duration: 2–3 minutes to introduce each new word; 10+ minutes for a daily review of all words

1. To create a word wall of high-utility sight words, select 5–10 high-utility or frequently occurring words per week that students can recognize; begin with the simplest, like *I, a, the, is, am,* and so forth, and continue adding words weekly as students encounter them over and over in reading and writing. Divide the word wall space alphabetically; use letter cards to create spaces so words can be added with others beginning with the same letter.
2. To add a new word, print the word in large neat letters on a letter card. Hold up the card and "say-and-spell" the word aloud: "Good. G-O-O-D. Good."
3. Have students say-and-spell chorally, clapping as they say each letter. Repeat if students had difficulty.

4. Print the word on the board, or trace each letter with your finger, spelling aloud as you go. Say the word again.
5. Have students print the word or trace the letters with their fingers on desktops, the floor, or the back of their other hand, spelling the word aloud as they write/trace and repeating the whole word.
6. Have students "help you" find the letter category the new word goes in, and attach it to the word wall. Say-and-spell it again in unison. Quickly review all the words in that letter category.
7. Review at least some of the word wall words daily; point to the word and say-and-spell chorally. Have students practice "reading the wall" independently throughout the day.

Variations: Instead of, or in addition to, sight words, word walls can be made of word families (-*ike*, -*op*, etc.); beginning consonants, blends, and digraphs; vowel patterns; plurals; synonyms and antonyms; parts of speech (adjectives, prepositions, etc.); unusual words; subject-area words (math, science, health, history, etc.); holidays; sports; music; homophones; contractions; base words with their derivational forms; prefixes and suffixes; words with related Latin and Greek bases (*bio-*, *tele-*, *graph*, etc.); and words from a particular work of literature.

20. Analytic Phonics Lesson

Objectives: To help students learn to recognize new words by analogy to similar known words; to help develop phonemic awareness

Materials: Chalkboard, chart paper, or transparency, or letter cards and pocket chart, or magnetic letters and cookie sheet

Duration: 5–10 minutes

1. Select a word students know that can become several different words by changing the initial consonant, or have a student suggest a word they know to make new words from.
2. Write and say the word. Then say, "If I know _____, I know _____" while you remove or cover the initial consonant or cluster and replace it with another. (For example, "If I know ship, I know slip.") Repeat the process while the students say, "If I know ___, I know ___."
3. Repeat with the other initial letters to continue making new words. Invite volunteers to come forward to move the letters and make new words while saying the sentence as above.
4. Have students practice with a partner making and reading new words using letter cards or magnetic letters.

Variations: Have students write all the new words they can make from one known word. Add words to the Word Wall as needed. As students are able to recognize the new words at sight, have them add them to their individual word banks. Have students use the new words in oral and written sentences. Add new words to personal dictionaries.

21. "Word Conversation" for Primary Grades

Objectives: Introduce students to new vocabulary; help students learn the pronunciation, meaning, and use of new words

Materials: A fiction or nonfiction book to read aloud to students; chalkboard or chart paper

Duration: 5–10 minutes for each new word taught; sufficient time to read the book aloud

1. Select a book featuring rich use of language to read to the class or group. Select one to three unfamiliar words to teach. Read the book to the group or class.
2. After the reading, print the new word on the board. Point to it as you put the new word into the context of the book by using the word in a sentence about the book; for example, "In this story (*Best Friends* by Steven Kellogg), Kathy wishes Louise would get a contagious disease so Louise could come home. Say that word with me: *contagious*." Point to the word as children repeat it.
3. Give a one-sentence definition of the word in terms the students can understand: "*Contagious* means that an illness is catching; you can catch it from someone else."
4. Give an example or two that children will be able to understand: "Colds are contagious; you can get a cold from someone else if that person sneezes or coughs near you and you breathe in the germs. Chicken pox is very contagious; if one child in a family gets it, usually the other children get it soon afterward."
5. Ask children to provide their own examples of the word: "I got chicken pox from my best friend in kindergarten." "When I got pinkeye I had to stay home because I was contagious for one day."
6. Have students echo as you say the word and its meaning again: "Contagious means that an illness is catching."

Extensions: Add the new word to a poster, bulletin board, "new word" Word Wall, or other display of interesting vocabulary words. Have students make up and act out brief skits to demonstrate the word's meaning. Have students write the new word and illustrate it. Have them add their illustration to individual vocabulary books they create and add to systematically. Designate it the "Word of the Day," and see how many ways students can use the word in meaningful sentences. Add the new word as a bonus word to the weekly spelling list.

22. Semantic or Concept Web for Upper Grades

Objectives: To learn specific meanings of synonyms and to categorize synonymous words by connotative meanings or shades of meaning

Materials: List of synonyms or words related by meaning; chalkboard, overhead transparency, or chart paper

Duration: 10–20 minutes, depending on number of synonyms and size of group

1. From a Word Wall, thesaurus, student writing, reading material, or other source, select a group of words sharing a common meaning; for example, these words relate to the concept of "more than enough": *plenty, excess, ample, lavish, copious, plethora, surfeit, myriad, superfluous, profuse*.
2. Write each word, pronounce it, and brainstorm with students what each one means. Provide several good context sentences to help them determine specific meanings.
3. Help students generate several categories into which the words can be sorted; for example, these words may suggest *many, enough,* and *too much*. Create a web on the board, transparency, or chart paper with circles or boxes that are large enough to write all the words in that category inside it. (Students often make their circles too small.) Or have students fold a sheet of paper to create the required number of boxes: in half for two, thirds for three, or quarters for four. They label each folded section and list the words in it that fit that category.
4. Have students sort the words into their appropriate categories; for example, "many" may include *lavish, ample, myriad, profuse, copious,* and *plethora*; "enough" may include *plenty* and *surfeit*; and "too much" may include *excess* and *superfluous*.
5. Have students come up with their own context sentences that illustrate the meanings of each word.

23. Connect Two

Objectives: Help students learn new vocabulary by predicting meanings of and relationships among key terms from a selection prior to reading

Materials: List of key terms from a selection to be read by students

Duration: 5–15 minutes depending on number and familiarity of terms selected

1. Preview a selection students will read. Collect five or more key terms from the selection, including technical vocabulary and unusual or unfamiliar uses of known words. List them on the board, a transparency, or duplicated worksheets.
2. Explain that all of the terms are used in the selection, and thinking about them before reading will help students recognize and understand them when they encounter them in the text. Pronounce each word.
3. Pair students and have each pair select two terms and use them together in a meaningful sentence. Sentences

should, if possible, reflect what students think the words mean or how they are related.

4. Have students write their sentence for each pair of words and, if desired, draw a sketch to accompany it. Then have each pair share the sentences and comments about them with the larger group.

Variation: Instead of creating sentences, have students categorize terms they think go together, give each category a title or heading, and explain why they grouped them together when they share.

24. Semantic Feature Analysis

Objectives: To enrich vocabulary; help students relate a new concept to familiar concepts

Materials: Nonfiction text; chalkboard, chart paper, or transparency; marker

Duration: 10–15 minutes

1. Select a concept from a nonfiction text about which students may have limited prior knowledge or experience.

Think of several related concepts about which students may know a little more to compare to it.

2. Create a chart on the board, chart paper, or transparency with a vertical (y) and a horizontal (x) axis. On the x-axis, list the new concept and the related concepts; on the y-axis, list several features of the concepts they may share.

3. Prior to reading, engage students in using what they may already know and their predictions to complete the chart. Start with the concepts they may be more familiar with, and ask if each feature is true; if the concept has that feature, mark it with a plus (+), and if the concept does not have that feature, with a minus (–). End with the new concept; students may not know if it has a particular feature but are to predict based on what they already know.

4. Have students complete the reading of the selection. Have them watch for information about the concept that they predicted about.

5. After reading, reexamine the chart. Have them compare their predictions about the new concept to what they learned from the reading, and change the chart as needed. Review what is now known about the new concept.

Fluency Activities

25. Repeated Reading

Objectives: To develop children's reading fluency

Materials: A reading passage of 50–500 words, depending on the child's reading rate

Duration: 10 minutes

1. Find a text (informational or fictional but not poetry or lists) written at the student's instructional level.
2. Sit next to the student in a quiet place, and listen as the student practices reading the text repeatedly.
3. Keep a copy of the text yourself on which you can mark the student's reading errors. (Errors are words that are omitted, or for which other words are substituted, or which are mispronounced. If the student does not say a word, wait 2 seconds and say the word yourself, and count that as an error.)
4. Time the student's reading for exactly 60 seconds; then stop the student, count the total number of words read, and subtract the errors from the total.
5. Have the student practice reading the text several times— preferably until the child reaches the criterion score for his or her grade level. Remember to offer adequate praise each time.

26. Fluency Oriented Oral Reading (FOOR)

Objectives: To develop reading fluency

Materials: Copies of text at students' instructional level

Duration: Three days (10 minutes each day)

1. Assemble a group of students who are at roughly the same instructional level. Provide copies of the text to all the students.

2. *Day 1:*
   - Read the text fluently while the students are following along.
   - Think aloud: call attention to the way you read words in groups and to how you emphasize important words.
   - Briefly discuss the meaning of the text with the students.
   - Echo read the text (you read one sentence fluently and the students read it at the same pace and with the same intonation).

3. *Day 2:*
   - Pair up the students and have them take turns reading the text, each one reading a sentence or a paragraph.
   - Circulate among the pairs and provide help as needed.

4. *Day 3:*
   - Have students come back together in the original group and choral read the text with you.

Extension: Step 4 may be followed by a Readers' Theater activity.

27. Paired Reading

Objectives: To develop reading fluency

Material: Text at the less fluent reader's instructional level

Duration: 5–10 minutes

1. Match up a fluent reader (a parent volunteer, a tutor, or an older student) with a less fluent reader. Instruct the more fluent reader to carry out steps 3–6.
2. Choose a text at the instructional level of the less fluent reader.
3. The more fluent reader reads the text to the less fluent reader.
4. The two readers read the passage several times in unison.
5. The less fluent reader reads the text, while the more fluent reader monitors her reading (corrects the errors by saying the words correctly, has the partner reread a sentence in which a word was misread, models the adequate intonation for a sentence and has the partner try to mimic it).
6. Repeat step 5 once or twice.

28. Readers' Theater

Objectives: To develop students' reading fluency and comprehension

Materials: A fictional text that contains dialogue, preferably among several characters

Duration: 15–25 minutes

1. Make a photocopy of the text you plan to use for readers' theater.
2. Read through the text and mark the parts that should be read by different readers. Create a code for different readers, such as a capital letter to represent the name of each different character, and a capital N followed by a number for narrator number 1, 2, 3, and so on.
3. Put brackets [ ] around the parts that will be read by each reader, and write in a letter over each section to indicate who should read it.
4. Strike through any parts that do not need to be read. Often "He said," "she replied," and the like, can be eliminated without affecting the meaning.

5. As they prepare to read a fictional text with readers' theater, have the students discuss the setting of the text, who the characters are, and what they are like.
6. Have the students read portions of the text several times in order to read the lines fluently and with the expression called for.
7. Offer coaching, asking the students questions such as,
   - "What is your character feeling right now? How do you sound when you feel that way? Should your voice be loud or soft? Fast or slow?"
   - "What might your character think about what the other character is saying? How will your character sound then?"
   - "What is going on at this point in the story? How is your character reacting to it?"
   - "How is your character changing as the story proceeds?"
8. Offer comments and suggestions after each practice reading and invite the students to do the same.

29. Choral Reading

Objectives: To develop reading fluency in a meaningful context

Materials: Poems with a strong rhythmic pattern

Duration: 10–15 minutes

1. Prepare the children to choral-read a text by discussing the circumstances or the context in which it might be said. Ask the children to imagine the situation and to describe the sounds they associate with it. Offer suggestions as necessary.
2. Decide how the poem should be read, for example, by the whole chorus, by individuals, by pairs, or by two alternating sections; in loud or soft voices; rapidly or slowly; melodiously, angrily, giggling, or seriously.
3. Have each student or group of students practice reading their part until they can keep the rhythm perfectly.
4. Have the whole class practice reading the poem in the manner previously agreed on until they sound like a good chorus. Invite and give feedback after each performance.

Comprehension Activities with Fictional Texts

30. Terms in Advance

Objectives: To develop comprehension by recalling and organizing prior information before reading; enable students to predict what a reading passage might be about; familiarize students with key vocabulary and concepts prior to reading

Materials: List of key terms or phrases from the text to be read, chart paper or transparency, marker

Duration: 5–15 minutes, depending on size of group, number of terms, familiarity of terms

1. From a reading passage students are going to read, collect a group of key words and/or phrases that bear importantly on the content of the passage. Try to include both familiar and unfamiliar terms; don't just collect all the hardest or least familiar vocabulary.

2. Display the words on a chart or transparency with space around each one for recording students' ideas of what each term means and/or how it might bear on the passage they will read.

3. If your main goal for the activity is to encourage predictions about what the text to be read will be about, have students hypothesize about ways in which the terms might be related in the story. Optionally, you may allow them to write down their predictions before sharing them with the class. Accept all hypotheses or predictions encouragingly.

4. If your main goal is to introduce new vocabulary, have students dictate or write sentences explaining the meaning of one or more of the terms, or make up sentences that combine two or more of the terms in one sentence.

5. As students read the text and the meaning of various terms becomes clear, modify the chart or transparency to show what each term means in the passage and to reflect new information gained during reading. Alternatively, ask students to compare the story they read to their initial predictions.

31. Directed Reading-Thinking Activity (DRTA)

Objectives: To develop comprehension by recalling and organizing prior information before reading

Materials: Fiction selection; chalkboard, chart paper, or transparency; marker

Duration: 10–30 minutes or longer, depending on length of selection

1. Select a story with a well-structured plot that revolves around a character's attempts to solve a problem or achieve a goal, with a clear resolution of the conflict at the end.

2. Plan from two to five stopping points in the story, where students will stop reading to discuss what they have read and make predictions about forthcoming parts of the story. Plan the stops just before some major event or piece of information.

3. Explain to students that they will be making predictions, or educated guesses, about what might happen in the story, and they will base their predictions on the title, illustrations, and what they read in preceding sections. They will read up to, but not beyond, the stopping points and will not read ahead. They will justify their predictions based on what they learn as the story unfolds. All predictions will be accepted respectfully by everyone. The process of predicting, not whether their predictions are proved or disproved, is what is important.

4. Have students read the title, examine cover art and initial illustrations, and perhaps the first section of the story. Elicit predictions by asking, "What might happen in this story?" or "What might this story be about?" and "Why do you think so?" Jot down key phrases from different predictions. Have students read the next section to find out and stop at the next stopping point.

5. After each section, have students briefly review what they know so far and new information revealed in the prior section. Review and check predictions that still seem likely or possible. Elicit further predictions about the next section.

6. Repeat this cycle of "review-predict-read to prove" to the end. At the conclusion of the story, briefly discuss with students how they used clues and events to predict the outcome.

Variation: Read the story aloud to the group as a Directed Listening-Thinking Activity, following the same procedures.

32. Dual-Entry Diary

Objectives: To encourage personal responses to literature; to develop writing fluency

Materials: Response journals

Duration: 10–15 minutes

1. Model the technique on the overhead projector or on the chalkboard. Draw a vertical line in the middle of a blank sheet of paper:
   - On the left-hand side, write a passage from the text that students are reading. Explain that you chose to write it down because you found it particularly striking (because it reminded you of your own experience, or because you disagree with it, or because it is unexpected, etc.).
   - On the right-hand side, write a comment about the passage. (Why did you write it down? What did it make you think of? What question do you have about it?)

2. Instruct students to use their response journals as dual-entry diaries and, as they read the text, to pause and make entries. You may choose to assign a minimal number of entries per text.

Extension: If students are reading a longer text, you may collect the dual-entry diaries periodically and write comments in them. You may also ask students to share some of their entries in a discussion group or use them to structure a whole-class discussion.

33. Instructional Conversations

Objectives: To develop comprehension; to develop critical thinking; to develop conversational skills

Materials: Story or passages from a book

Duration: 30–60 minutes

1. Decide on what the theme or issue for the conversation should be (a real issue that real people might wonder about, one that invites different responses, one to which students can relate and that is likely to engage them).

2. Select a story or passages from a book and have the students (re)read it/them.
3. Explain that you will have a conversation about the text and that everyone is invited to think hard about it and share ideas.
4. Clarify the rules for participation: Students do not need to raise hands; however, they need to listen to each other carefully, be respectful, and wait for others to finish before contributing.
5. Begin the conversation with an open-ended question. Make sure that the students can resort to their background knowledge, interests, and experience to answer it.
6. Keep the conversation loosely focused on the main theme. Do take the time to explore collateral issues raised by students, but tactfully steer the conversation back to the main topic.
7. As the conversation proceeds, explain points that are not clear, provide background information that you notice students do not have, provide new vocabulary that students may need to express their emerging insights in a more sophisticated manner.
8. Ask students to support their ideas with evidence from the text throughout the conversation.

34. Save the Last Word for Me

Objectives: To develop comprehension; encourage thoughtful discussion of a shared text

Materials: 3 × 5 file cards or sheets of paper cut in quarters; 1–4 cards per student

Duration: 10–20 minutes depending on size of group

1. Distribute blank file cards or papers to students.
2. After they have finished reading a selection, have them find a sentence or short section (no longer than a few sentences, or as short as one sentence) in the text that they find particularly interesting, surprising, evocative, or otherwise noteworthy and write the quotation on one side of a card. On the reverse side they write a comment or response: why they found it interesting, what it made them think about, something it reminded them of, and so forth. Older students and those reading longer or more complex texts can complete several cards in the same way; younger readers or those reading shorter texts can complete one.
3. When completed, ask a volunteer to read his or her selected quotation aloud and call on several other students to comment on or respond to the quotation. Discussion of each other's comments is allowed. After several others have commented, the first student shares his or her written comment on the quotation. No discussion follows; the original writer has "the last word."
4. Another student is selected by the first student or the teacher to repeat the procedure; read the quotation, invite others to comment, then share his or her written comment. In small discussion groups or literature circles, all students may be able to participate; in larger groups or with the whole class, only some will be able to share each time.

35. Literature Circles

Objectives: To develop comprehension; promote thoughtful discussion and interpretation of shared literature

Materials: A shared work of literature (all students in the group read the same text)

Duration: 20 minutes or longer, depending on the group size, degree of experience with the procedure, and students' interest in discussion

1. Assign students participating to read the same text; they may read a short text in one sitting or read a section such as a chapter of a longer work.
2. Convene a group of all the students reading the shared work; for best interaction, group size should not exceed 5 or 6. If more students are reading the same text, create two groups.
3. Assign each student a role for that meeting; see textbook, Table 7.2, for a list of possible roles. The roles most often used include the Questioner, sometimes called the Discussion Director, who creates three or four thoughtful questions about the main events of the selection for the group to discuss; the Quotation Finder, sometimes called the Passage Master, who selects one or more excerpts to practice and read aloud; the Artist, or Illustrator, who illustrates the selection with written captions; and the Word Finder, or Word Wizard, who locates and explains interesting or important words, figurative language, expressions or idioms, and the like, to the group.
4. Monitor the execution of the various roles in the group discussion; model reflective questioning and responding to the text without lecturing or dominating; move the discussion forward when necessary by drawing all students into the discussion, and use literary terms such as *episode*, *climax*, *resolution*, and so forth, as appropriate.
5. If students are reading a longer work in sections, assist them in deciding how far they will read before the next meeting and when they will next meet.
6. Have all students regardless of their role write a summary, response, or other piece in their literature or reading journals about the section just discussed.
7. Rotate the roles so all students participate and have different responsibilities.

36. Shared Inquiry

Objectives: To develop comprehension and critical thinking

Materials: A shared work of literature (all students have read the same text)

Duration: 20–40 minutes

1. Choose a text or part of a text that encourages discussion (that is, one that lends itself to multiple interpretations or raises interesting or even controversial issues) and which students have read carefully.
2. Prepare four or five discussion questions that meet the following three criteria: (1) they are questions that real

people would ask in real life; (2) they have more than one possible answer; and (3) they lead the discussion into the text, that is, they invite revisiting the text as a source of evidence in support of possible answers.

3. Write the first question on the chalkboard and invite the students to think about it and briefly write down their answers.

4. Invite students (including reluctant speakers) to share what they wrote. Point out differences between responses and invite their authors and the rest of the class to expand on those differences. Press them to support their views with references to the text and to restate their ideas more clearly if necessary. Do not correct any answer and do not suggest that it is right or wrong. Do not offer your own answer to the question.

5. Use a seating chart to record what each student has contributed.

6. When the discussion of a question has run its course, summarize it based on your notes and ask if anyone has anything to add.

7. Repeat steps 3–6 with each of the discussion questions you have prepared.

Extension: Have students respond to one of the discussion questions in writing.

37. Discussion Web

Objectives: To develop comprehension; promote thoughtful discussion and interpretation of shared literature; help students perceive and understand both sides of a position or argument

Materials: A shared work of literature (all students in the group read the same text)

Duration: 15–30 minutes

1. Assign students participating to read the same text; they may read a short text in one sitting or read a section such as a chapter of a longer work. Text may be fiction or nonfiction.

2. Generate a discussion question that can reasonably be argued from both sides, sometimes called a binary question; for example, "Was it wrong for _____ (story character) to _____ (act in a way that some might consider wrong, but for which he or she had a reason or rationale)?" "Was _____ (story character) _____ or _____ (two opposite or opposing characteristics, like brave/reckless, caring/selfish, or wise/foolish)?" or "Is (or was) it right or wrong to _____ (nonfiction text or subject area issue: secede from the Union, hunt whales, log the rain forest, send Japanese Americans to internment camps, etc.)?" Write the question so students can refer to it as they reflect.

3. Assign students to pairs. Have each pair answer the question from both sides of the argument, listing three reasons, examples, and so forth, to support each side.

4. Combine two pairs to create groups of four. Have students combine their lists so all positions are included.

Then have each foursome reach agreement on one side of the argument and prepare to defend it.

5. Have each foursome summarize and defend its work to the larger group.

Extension: When two or more groups take opposing positions, a formal debate can follow. Groups taking the same position can join forces to share arguments and prepare to present them as forcefully and logically as possible, prepare notes, select spokespersons, and if desired conduct research on their position. Establish strict ground rules (no personal attacks, no raised voices, etc.) and time limits for arguments and rebuttal. Have each side briefly summarize its arguments in closing.

38. Debate

Objectives: To develop critical thinking skills; to give students practice in making claims and defending them with reasons

Materials: Chalkboard

Duration: 20–30 minutes

1. Find a binary question (one that has a yes/no answer) that you think will divide students' opinions roughly equally and write it on the chalkboard.

2. Give students five minutes to discuss it freely in pairs or groups of four.

3. Ask the students who believe one answer to the question is right to go stand along the wall on one side of the room, and those who think the other answer is right to stand along the wall on the other side. If there are undecided students, instruct them to stand along the wall in the middle.

4. Explain the ground rules:
   a. Argue politely!
   b. If you hear an argument that makes you want to change your mind, walk to the other side or to the middle.

5. Ask the students on each side to spend 2–3 minutes in their groups to come up with a sentence that states their position and to appoint someone to say that sentence.

6. Begin the debate by asking each team, including the undecided group, to state their position.

7. Invite students on both teams to respond—either with a counterargument/rebuttal or with more reasons in support of one of the positions expressed.

8. Ask for clarifications as needed. Offer an idea or two from the devil's advocate position to liven up the debate. Change sides when you hear a compelling argument. Encourage students to change sides if they are persuaded to.

9. When the debate has proceeded for 10–15 minutes, ask each side to summarize what they have said.

Extension: Ask the students to write down what they think about the issue and why.

39. Value Line

Objectives: To develop critical thinking; to give students practice in making arguments

Materials: A shared text (one that all the students have read)

Duration: 15–20 minutes

1. After the students have read a text carefully, ask a question about it to which the answers may vary along a continuum.
2. Give the students three minutes to write down their individual answers.
3. Stand at one end of the room and announce that you represent one pole, or extreme position, of the argument. State your position.
4. Invite a student to stand at the other end of the room to represent the other pole of the argument. Help her state that position.
5. Invite the students to line up between the two of you. Instruct them to choose a point on the imaginary line between the two poles of the argument that reflects their position on the question.
6. Tell the students to compare their views with those of the students around them to make sure they are standing in the right spots. Encourage them to move one way or another on the value line after hearing others' ideas and to continue discussing their answers until they find a group that shares the same position on the question.
7. Identify three or four clusters of students who seem to represent different views. Invite them to prepare a statement of their position and to share it with the class.

Variation: After step 6, you may want to fold the value line in the middle so that students with divergent views may debate their answers, while students with similar views may be helped to think of additional reasons in support of their position.

Extension: Have students write an argumentative or persuasive essay in response to the question.

40. Story Maps

Objectives: To develop comprehension; help students identify and sequence key story elements and events

Materials: Shared fiction text; story map graphic organizer, with key story elements for students to label

Duration: 10–20 minutes

1. Have students read, or read to them, a well-structured story that has a clear plot line including a well-defined main character; a problem, goal, challenge, or defining event faced by the main character; a series of attempts by the character to solve the problem or achieve the goal, the first several of which are unsuccessful, often referred to as the *rising action*; a final attempt that is successful, although not always as the character expected, forming the climax; and a resolution of the story, in which the character is often changed in some way.
2. Create a simple graphic organizer that labels the major parts of the story and allows students to fill in spaces on a chart, timeline, or flowchart. (There are many different kinds of premade story map graphic organizers available in teacher resource books, textbooks, basal manuals, comprehension kits, and so forth, or you can make your own.) For emergent and beginning readers, divide a sheet of paper into thirds vertically and label the sections *Beginning*, *Middle*, and *End*; students retell the story, then draw a picture to represent each part and write or dictate one or two sentences telling what happened in that part.
3. Have students include important details supporting the plot, including the setting and supporting characters.
4. Allow students to share their story maps by using them to retell the story.

Extensions: Provide students free access to a variety of types of story maps they can complete as they finish a work of fiction. Carefully completed story maps can be substituted for book reports or reviews when students must demonstrate their comprehension of a completed story. They can be shared during oral book reports. When students are writing fiction, completing a story map during the planning stage of the writing cycle helps students plan a complete story before they start and helps them structure their stories. (See "Story Maps for Writing" activity.)

41. Character Clusters and Character Maps

Objectives: To develop comprehension; help students understand characteristics or traits of story characters and relationships among characters

Materials: Shared work of fiction; chalkboard, transparency, or chart paper

Duration: 10–15 minutes

A. Character Cluster
   1. Have students identify the main character in a shared work of fiction. (If a work has more than one central character, create a separate cluster for each main character.)
   2. Create a web graphic organizer by placing the main character's name in a circle in the center of the web. Have students brainstorm characteristics or traits of that character (e.g., brave, funny, a loyal friend, loves wildlife, shy, etc.). Have students select three to five that are most descriptive of that character and write those traits in circles around the center circle, connected to it by lines.
   3. For each characteristic, have students generate examples of the character's words, actions, and attitudes from the story that illustrate that trait. Write these examples in circles that are connected by lines to the trait circles; for example, *brave*: chased away the mean dog, told the truth about breaking the lamp.

B. Character Map

1. List with students the main and supporting characters in a work of fiction they have read or are reading. Have students identify the main character/s.
2. Write the names of the main character in a central circle and the supporting characters in circles arranged around the central one. (Leave plenty of writing space between the circles.) Have students briefly describe how the main character feels about the supporting character. Draw an arrow from the main character to a supporting character; along the line, write a sentence that describes those feelings. Repeat for the other supporting characters.
3. With student help as above, draw arrows from the supporting characters to the main character and to other supporting characters. Along the arrows, write these characters' feelings about each other.

Comprehension Activities with Nonfictional Texts

42. Think–Pair–Share

Objectives: To reflect on and thoughtfully respond to a question and share responses with a peer; encourage reflective thinking and respectful listening; develop comprehension by recalling and organizing prior information before reading

Materials: Students may write their initial responses in journals or learning logs or on scrap paper; otherwise, no materials are needed

Duration: 5 minutes or less

1. Ask an open-ended question—that is, a question that can be answered many ways depending on the opinions, experiences, predictions, or preferences of the individuals answering it. For example; "What could we do as a class to show our concern for the environment?" "How could this story character have behaved differently so the story had a different outcome?" or "What traits or characteristics make a person a good leader?" Write the question so students can reread it as they think.
2. Have students think, then write in brief form their thoughts in their journals, learning logs, or on scrap paper.
3. After a short interval for writing, have each student turn to a partner and share his or her answers to the questions, taking turns. Remind students to talk to their partners, not read their papers to them, and to listen respectfully and attentively to each other.
4. Have a few volunteers share their thoughts with the larger group or restate their partner's response instead of their own.

Variation: Paired Brainstorming In a situation where students will share factual information, for example before reading expository text when students are recalling and organizing their prior information about the topic, have individuals briefly list the information they already know during the "Think" phase. After a minute or two, each student joins a partner and the two lists are quickly combined during the "Pair" stage. Finally, a few key facts from each pair are listed on the board, chart paper, or a transparency during the "Share" stage. Students can compare what they knew before reading to information they acquire during and after reading.

43. Paired Brainstorming

Objectives: To activate prior knowledge of a topic

Materials: Journals or scrap paper

Duration: 6–10 minutes

1. Announce the topic of the lesson and ask the students to brainstorm (that is, to think of everything that comes to mind) about it and list the facts or ideas on a sheet of paper in 2–3 minutes. Tell them that they may also list questions they have about the topic.
2. When time is up, instruct the students to turn to a classmate and combine their lists.
3. Have volunteers share their ideas and make a master list on the chalkboard, arranging the ideas in categories if possible.
4. Leave the master list on the board and have students compare it to the ideas they have after they have read a text or at the end of the lesson.

44. Anticipation Guide

Objectives: To develop comprehension by recalling and organizing prior information before reading

Materials: Teacher-made anticipation guides, duplicated for each student

Duration: 5–10 minutes to complete the guide prior to reading and again after reading the material

1. Read through the material your students are going to read. Select a number of important facts, terms, and so forth, you want students to remember and understand from the reading.
2. Create a set of statements to which students will respond by agreeing or disagreeing, marking them True or False, or checking the statements they think are true; for example, "There were thirteen southern colonies," "Maple syrup is made by crushing the leaves of the maple tree," or "Only native-born U.S. citizens can become president."

3. Type each statement, preceding each one with a blank on the left side of the paper and following each one with a blank on the right side of the paper. Head the left-side column of blanks "BEFORE" and the right-hand column "AFTER."

4. Distribute the anticipation guides *before* reading or discussing the text material, and have students read and mark each statement true/false, agree/disagree, and so forth, in the BEFORE (before reading) column. (Be sure they understand they are not expected to know all the right answers, just to make an attempt at each item based on what, if anything, they might already know about the topic, and their answers will not be corrected, graded, etc.) Collect the guides and keep them for later. Briefly discuss students' responses to each statement, but do not tell them the correct answer.

5. Read and discuss the text material as you would normally do. After students have thoroughly read and discussed the material, participated in comprehension activities, and so forth, redistribute the original anticipation guides and have students respond to each item, this time marking in the AFTER (after reading) column. These responses should now represent the correct information; therefore, answers in the AFTER column may be checked for correctness or graded. Be sure students understand that their initial attempts were "best guesses," and only their responses after the reading will be checked.

6. Students can fold the BEFORE column under and keep their anticipation guides as a form of class notes or study guides on the topic.

45. Graphic Organizers

Objectives: To help students organize information in text

Materials: Blank graphic organizers for students to fill in before, during, and after reading

Duration: 5–30 minutes depending on length and complexity of text and the graphic organizer used

1. Select or create a graphic organizer that fits the organization of the text: for example, a timeline or sequential flow-chart for sequences of events, Venn diagram for comparison/contrast, or web for main and subordinate categories.

2. Have students preview or skim the material to find some of the main topics or categories of information and enter them on the graphic organizer. With textbook material, chapter headings and subheadings often contain this information.

3. Have students attempt to recall and organize their prior information about these topics before reading, and note what they already know in pencil on the organizer. (If they are later disproved, these entries can easily be changed.)

4. As students read, they continue to enter new information they encounter on the organizer: for example, dates and places of historical events, short- and long-term effects of events, biographical information, and other important supporting details.

5. After the reading, have students compare their organizers in pairs or small groups, adding or moving information as needed to make their organizers clear and accurate. They can then be used as outlines for writing or for study guides.

46. Metacognitive Graphic Organizer

Objectives: To develop awareness of text organization; to assist students in self-monitoring their comprehension of nonfiction texts; to help students create a personal guide for reading and study

Materials: Article or textbook chapter

Duration: Varies with the length of the text

1. Have students place the title of the article or chapter in the center of a sheet of paper and then add the major headings as they survey the material.

2. Instruct students to look at the visual information in charts, diagrams, etc. and add key ideas from these to the graphic organizer, under the appropriate headings.

3. Have students read the text and make notes on the graphic organizer or on sticky notes as they read.

4. When they finish reading, instruct students to review the graphic and the notes made and decide whether to (a) revise the graphic (if the actual organization of the text is different from what students initially drew), (b) add sub-headings (if several ideas can be grouped under one sub-heading), or (c) write extended notes to clarify the important ideas (if there are many new ideas). Students may choose to do any or all of these depending on their own learning needs.

Extension: Have students use their graphic organizers to write a summary of the article or chapter.

47. Know–Want to Know–Learn (K–W–L)

Objectives: To develop comprehension by recalling and organizing prior information before reading; organize new information gained by reading and relate it to prior information

Materials: Nonfiction material; chalkboard, chart paper, or transparency; duplicated K-W-L charts

Duration: 10–30 minutes or longer, depending on length of selection and students' prior information

1. Create a K-W-L chart on the board, chart paper, or transparency consisting of three vertical columns; label the left-side column K: What We Know; the center column W: What We Want to Find Out; and the right-side column L: What We Learned. Write the topic at the top. Duplicate and distribute blank charts.

2. Prior to reading, have students write some things they already know about the topic in the K column on their charts. Have volunteers share some of their ideas; record

them in the K column on the group chart. Ask direct questions about important information in the passage that no one mentioned.

3. When disagreements occur or when questions arise that can't be answered prior to reading, note these in the W column. Have students generate and write on their charts one question they can't answer; write some of these on the group chart and have students include them on their charts as well.

4. Briefly review with students what they already know and are uncertain about. Read the passage.

5. After reading, review the K column with students; check those ideas that were borne out by the passage; and cross off those that were disproved, writing the correct information in the L column. Review the W column; check those questions that were answered by the passage, writing the corresponding information in the L column. Mark those questions still unanswered with a question mark for further research. Add to the L column any other new information gathered from the passage.

6. Have students reorganize and add to their own charts as you do so with the group chart.

48. What? So What? Now What?

Objectives: To help students organize facts and arguments to prepare to do persuasive writing or speaking

Materials: Blank organizer on board, chart paper, or transparency; duplicated copies of blank organizer for students to complete

Duration: 10–15 minutes

1. Prepare a model organizer for the group to complete on the board, chart paper, or a transparency. Create three columns across the top: label the left-side column WHAT?, the center column SO WHAT?, and the right-side column NOW WHAT? Explain that this chart will help them organize their facts and opinions to write or speak persuasively on an issue they have read about (e.g., environmental pollution, species endangerment, cafeteria recycling, logging of national forest lands, etc.).

2. On the left side of the chart, list factual information students have learned about the topic: for example, "Since 1950, _____ species have become endangered and _____ have become extinct," or "Species are now becoming endangered at an average rate of _____." In the central column, list students' reasons why these facts are important or why others should care about them. In the right-side column, write students' suggestions of actions that could affect or improve the situation.

3. Using the completed group chart, have students compose persuasive essays or speeches presenting the relevant facts, explaining their importance, and urging their audience to pursue a course of action.

Variations: When an issue arises that students care about, complete this chart with them to help them sort out facts from opinions, create persuasive arguments, and determine how they can act on their beliefs. Then follow

through as a group on one or more actions to address the situation.

Extensions: Have students organize the information in the L column in categories and construct a web or other graphic organizer of the information. Have students use their K-W-L charts as study guides or as resources for writing summaries and reports. Gather related reading materials and have students research answers to questions still listed in the W column. Follow up with a "What? So What? Now What?" activity to help students determine actions that can be taken based on what they learned.

49. Reciprocal Teaching

Objectives: To model and practice comprehension strategies of summarizing, questioning, clarifying, and predicting

Materials: Nonfiction text; chalkboard, chart paper or transparency

Duration: 15–30 minutes or longer, depending on length and difficulty of text

1. Survey and break the text into segments for students to read; depending on the length and difficulty of the entire selection, segments may be as short as one or two paragraphs or as long as a chapter section. Students can use sticky notes to mark the end of a segment. Create groups of four students each.

2. Read the first segment with students. Then model how to use the four strategies: First, summarize the section in one or two sentences, writing them on the board, chart paper, or transparency; second, ask one or two good questions to be answered by students; third, clarify by identifying the most difficult part of the section (may be a word or phrase, sentence, example, or concept) and explain it or tell how you could figure it out (look it up, check an encyclopedia, use surrounding context, etc.); fourth, predict what the next section might contain based on what you've already read.

3. Assign each student in a group a task for the next section: summarizer, questioner, clarifier, or predictor. (Job cards help students remember what they are to do.) Read the next section with students.

4. After reading, each student is to complete his or her task following your model. Allow time for task completion. Each student then shares his or her work with the group, starting with the summary statement and ending with the prediction. The group should discuss and amend the summary as needed, use the text to answer the questions, examine the difficult part and add to the explanation, and discuss the prediction.

5. Repeat the teacher modeling of the strategies after reading the next section. Depending on time available and students' success with the procedure, you can continue to alternate teacher modeling and student practice through the remaining sections or have students work through subsequent sections as above, rotating tasks within the group so each student completes a different task each time.

50. Jigsaw

Objectives: To develop comprehension; to provide practice in using comprehension strategies in cooperative learning groups

Materials: Nonfiction text; expert sheets

Duration: 40–60 minutes

1. Before the lesson select a text, divide it into four sections, and prepare four different expert sheets numbered 1–4. The expert sheets are sets of 4–6 questions that will focus students' attention on the most important points in each section. Make sure you include not only recall questions, but also questions that invite higher order thinking.
2. Begin the activity by explaining that everybody will be reading a text and be responsible for learning all the material. Add that each person will become an expert in one part of the text and will teach others about it.
3. Assign students to home groups of four or five members.
4. Distribute copies of the text to all students. Also distribute a different expert sheet to each student in a group. If there are more than four members in a home group, make sure that no more than two students receive the same expert sheet.
5. Have the class read the entire text. Instruct students that finish early to take notes on the section of the text that pertains to their expert sheet.
6. Reassign the students to one of four expert groups based on the number of their expert sheet.
7. Instruct the expert groups to discuss the questions on their expert sheets and take notes on the answers that the group offers to the questions. Encourage the students to clarify the material as best they can. Explain that each person in the group will be responsible for helping the others in their home group understand the material in the section to which the questions on the expert sheet pertain.
8. Circulate among the expert groups to make sure they stay on task and to provide help as needed.
9. When all the expert groups have answered their questions, have students return to their home groups. Each student should take about five minutes to present in the home group what she learned in the expert group. In addition to explaining the material in her section of the text, the expert should also ask and entertain questions from the group, to make sure everyone learned her piece of the text.

51. ReQuest Procedure

Objectives: To develop comprehension; to provide practice in asking higher order thinking questions as a way of developing principled knowledge of the topic

Materials: Nonfiction text

Duration: 10–20 minutes

1. Select a text you want your students to read using this technique. To model the kinds of questions you want them to ask, read the first paragraph aloud and ask students to read along. Ask 3–4 questions about the paragraph (e.g., "What is the main idea of the paragraph?" "Why might this piece of information be important?" "How does this new information relate to…?" "How does this compare to…?") and have students answer them.
2. Have one student read the second paragraph aloud while the class and you read along. Have the student who has read aloud ask you questions about the paragraph. Answer those questions by referring to the text as much as possible.
3. Instruct the class to continue to read the text in pairs, paragraph by paragraph, taking turns at reading aloud and reading along. Tell them to stop after each paragraph, ask each other questions about it, and try to answer them as best they can. Encourage them to refer to the text to support their answers.

Variations: (1) When the students are familiar with the ReQuest procedure, assign them to groups of three and have them take turns reading aloud and asking and answering questions. (2) Use the Paired Reading/Paired Summarizing technique, in which the student who reads a paragraph aloud also summarizes it, while the other student asks questions that probe the meaning of the passage and that both students attempt to answer.

Writing Activities

52. Shared Writing

Objectives: To engage students in composing a written text; to raise students' awareness of letter-sound relationships

Materials: Chart paper

Duration: 10–15 minutes

1. Choose a topic that the students are excited about (e.g., a field trip) and discuss it with the class.
2. Gather the students around an easel and ask them to help you write a few sentences about the topic.
3. Have students suggest the first sentence they want to write and have them say it several times so everyone is aware of the words.
4. Ask students to help you write the first word. Ask what the first sound in the word is, what letter needs to be written, etc.
5. Before you repeat step 4 for the second word, explain that you need to leave a blank space between the two words.

Demonstrate the blank space by putting a finger after the first word.

6. Continue writing the sentence in this manner, inviting the students to come forward and supply the letters they can. Pronounce the sounds the children may skip and provide letters for them. If a child makes an error in writing, put a piece of correction tape over the error and help the children write the correct letter.

53. Interactive Writing

Objectives: To help emergent and beginning readers and writers explore the writing system in its details

Materials: Chart paper

Duration: 15–20 minutes

1. Working with a medium-size group of students, begin by agreeing on a topic to write about. The topic might be a retelling of a story or a poem or a song, the daily news, or an idea that the class is studying.
2. Ask the children to offer a sentence about the topic.
3. Have them repeat the sentence many times and even count the words to fix them firmly in their minds.
4. Ask the children for the first word; then pronounce that word slowly, writing its letters.
5. Ask for the next word and invite a child up to write the whole word, a few letters, or a single letter. Fill in letters the children miss.
6. Point to the words and have the children read back the text. Repeat this step each time a word is added.
7. To help the children orient themselves to the text and add letters, you may write blanks where the letters should go.
8. Use correction tape to paste over letters that are poorly formed, and write them correctly.
9. As the lesson progresses, teach about words and print (remind children of words they know or almost know, remind them of spelling patterns they have seen before, remind them to leave spaces between words, and to add punctuation).

54. Pillowcase, or Me in a Box

Objectives: To introduce yourself to students by displaying objects representing aspects of your life; encourage discussion; provide springboard for personal writing

Materials: Pillowcase, bag, box, or similar container; objects representing your interests, family, pets, hobbies, and so forth, in a container

Duration: 5–10 minutes to share and discuss objects; extended time for discussion and/or writing

1. Collect a number of objects that represent things about you to share with students: for example, photos, sports trophy, dog toy, college banner, map, vacation postcards, and so forth. Put them in the container.
2. Explain that the objects you collected tell about you as a person. As you show each object, explain what it represents.

3. Have students write or dictate a few sentences about you based on what they learned.
4. Invite students to collect objects in the same way and tell the group about themselves. Schedule a few talks per day so students know when to bring in their things. (Remind them to get parents' permission before bringing anything valuable or personal to school.)
5. Have students use their collections to help them write about themselves.

Variations: Invite other teachers, the principal, or other school personnel to share in the same way. Have students draw self-portraits, or use a digital camera or school pictures from cumulative files to illustrate their writing. Collect the compositions in a class book. Display them in or outside the classroom. Make a "Students of the Week" bulletin board to display several students' writings at a time until all have been displayed. Create a web graphic organizer as you model this activity; write your name in the center, the objects in circles around it, and words or phrases explaining the objects projecting from the circles. Show how the web can help you organize your writing.

55. The Writing Workshop

Objectives: To familiarize students with the writing process

Materials: Notebooks

Duration: Sessions of 30–60 minutes scheduled at regular intervals over a longer period of time, with time set aside for five distinct activities in each session

1. *Rehearsing.* Have students think of what they might like to write about. You can do this in one of the ways listed below. For a–c, demonstrate how you yourself would settle on a topic.
   a. Have the students brainstorm possible topics. Optionally, have them create a graphic organizer, such as a cluster or semantic web, with the topic listed in the center connected to "satellites" around it.
   b. Have the students interview each other to find a story.
   c. Have the students research a topic before they write about it (by reading about it, by interviewing experts, or by doing an Internet search).
   d. Ask the students to compose one work together as a class before writing their own. This will allow you to help them if they have difficulty beginning.
2. *Drafting.* Have the students set out their ideas on paper, so they can see more of what they want to say about a topic. Tell them not to worry about spelling, punctuation, and handwriting at this stage. Remember to tell the students to write on every other line, so they can make subsequent changes to the draft.
3. *Revising.* Have students consider how their ideas can be stated more clearly. Teach revising skills through the following:
   a. Focused lessons on different aspects of writing, from word-choice issues such as showing, not telling, to composition-related issues such as ways to write strong

introductions and closings. In one of the early focused lessons, show students how to use arrows, carets (^), and stapled-on sections to indicate on a draft how it should be rewritten. Remember to demonstrate how you would revise your own draft each time.

    b. Teacher-led conferences with groups or individual students. Ask students questions to help them focus on areas to improve their writing, and provide checklists of things to watch out for.

    c. Peer-led conferences. Put together a checklist of good questions to ask as students conference with each other, such as the following:

- Did my opening lines interest you? How might I improve it?
- Do I need more information anywhere? That is, where could I be more specific?
- Do you ever get lost while reading my draft?
- Do I stay on topic?
- Do I come to a good conclusion?

4. *Editing.* Have the students check their revised drafts for spelling, punctuation, run-on sentences, and so forth.

5. *Publishing/Sharing of work in progress.* Choose two or three students to share who are far along in a draft or whose work displays an interesting issue. Different students should share each time. Model giving feedback to the writers and elicit comments from the class.

56. Descriptive Writing

Objectives: To familiarize students with genre of descriptive writing; provide practice in descriptive writing

Materials: Excerpt from text that is vividly descriptive; paper bag containing a concrete object; journals or writing folders

Duration: 15–30 minutes depending on length of text excerpt and size of group

1. Select a descriptive passage, fiction or nonfiction, to read aloud. The passage should exemplify good descriptive writing.

2. Place an object in a paper bag for students to feel without looking at it. It should be small and light enough to be held in one hand, unusual enough so students may not recognize it instantly, and safe to feel without looking (no sharp edges, points, etc.).

3. Read the excerpt to the group. Invite students' comments about how the author used vivid descriptive language. Discuss the author's use of sensory words and images to create description.

4. Have students take turns silently feeling the object in the bag without looking at it. Caution them not to say what they think it is or what it feels like. After feeling the object, each one is to brainstorm and write in journals descriptive words or phrases to describe the object without naming it. Then they are to use their list of words to write descriptive sentences or a paragraph about the object, again without saying what it is.

5. Have students share their descriptive writing before naming the object.

Variations: Use senses other than touch to explore an object; with eyes closed, have students sniff objects like a sliced orange, blooming flower, cinnamon stick or other edible spice, school paste, ground coffee, pine or eucalyptus branch; listen to environmental or recorded sounds like wind, flowing water, heavy machinery, rain, surf, traffic; or taste safe and edible substances like toothpaste, coarse sugar, dry gelatin powder, baking chocolate, or pickles. Collect, or have students collect, small objects like keys, erasers, shells, bottle caps, or toys, and place one on each desk; give students a few minutes to write a complete description of the object, and then switch objects with someone else and repeat. Have students write what an object reminds them of rather than describing its physical features alone.

57. RAFT (Role, Audience, Format, Topic)

Objectives: To develop students' awareness of genres

Materials: Blank sheets of paper; newsprint

Duration: 40–60 minutes

1. After the students have studied a topic thoroughly, have them brainstorm 4–5 roles of people or characters that have a stake in the issue. Write down the roles on the chalkboard and have each student choose one role.

2. Assign students to groups based on their roles.

3. Explain that each group will write a message expressing their position on the issue.

4. Ask each group to choose an audience for their message out of the roles listed on the chalkboard.

5. Once all the groups have selected their audience, have them decide what format their message will take (a letter, a newspaper editorial, an advertisement, etc.).

6. Allow the groups about 15 minutes to write their message.

7. Have each group share their message with the class.

8. Engage the students in critiquing the messages. (Is the format appropriate for the targeted audience? Is the register appropriate for the audience? Is the message consistent with the characteristics of the role?)

Extension: Distribute the messages to students in the class. Instruct them to adopt the role of the audience and respond to the messages.

58. Story Maps for Writing

Objectives: To assist writers in planning a cohesive story

Materials: Blank story map on board, chart paper, or transparency; duplicated copies of the blank map for students to complete as they plan their stories

Duration: 5–15 minutes

1. On the board, chart paper, or a transparency, construct a story map containing elements similar to the following: Once there was a _____ named _____ who lived _____. He/she wanted _____. So he/she _____, but _____ (so he/she _____, but _____). Then, he/she _____. Finally, _____. So, _____. Leave plenty of space after each sentence starter.

2. Invite students to help you plan to write a story by suggesting elements to go in each blank space; for example, a boy named Sam who lived in a small apartment in the city, who wanted a dog, so he asked his parents ... and so forth. Remind students that the story elements they suggest need to fit together to make sense. Select suggestions to write in the blanks that will make a meaningful story. To set off the sentence starters from the rest of the text, use a different color to complete the sentences.

3. Read through the completed story map, showing students where details could be added that would help readers visualize the story. Focus attention on the character's problem or goal, attempts to solve the problem or achieve the goal, and the final resolution of the conflict. Display the group story for students to refer to as they write.

4. Distribute blank story maps and have students generate their own stories, filling in the blanks to create a skeletal story. Allow time to share ideas and completed plans with partners or small groups.

5. Have students write their stories following their story maps. Encourage them to write several sentences or a paragraph after each sentence starter, to discourage them from recopying their maps as completed stories. Allow time for sharing of completed stories.

Variations: Before attempting to write a story solo, allow pairs to create a shared story after participating in the group

story. Encourage students to revise, edit, and illustrate their stories, then display or publish them. Collect illustrated stories in a binder and place in the classroom library.

59. Form Poems

Objectives: To familiarize students with structured poems; increase students' awareness of how form and meaning can shape each other in poetry

Materials: Examples of form poems

Duration: 10–20 minutes

1. Show the students an example of a well-written poem that follows the form. (You might need to write this yourself or save it from a previous class.)

2. Discuss the formal characteristics of the poem with the class.

3. Have the students help you create a poem as a group. Discuss each choice they make so they understand the process well.

4. Have individuals or pairs write their own poems.

5. Share several of the poems, and discuss their qualities. Also call attention to the ways in which the poems followed the structure.

6. Talk about why a writer might choose to write a poem structured that way.

7. Make a wall chart in which you feature several of the students' poems; also outline the procedures for writing a poem with the structure in question.

Activities for English Language Learners

60. Language Experience with English Language Learners

Objectives: To help English language learners develop English fluency, print concepts, sight word recognition, and phonemic awareness

Materials: An object, photograph, shared experience, shared literature, or other stimulus; chalkboard, chart tablet, or transparency; marker

Duration: 10–30 minutes; additional time for follow-up activities

1. Select an individual student or a group of English language learners.

2. Select a topic for dictation: an interesting concrete object, classroom pet, familiar story for retelling, recent classroom event, and so forth. Younger students benefit from a concrete or immediate stimulus, whereas older students can talk about past events, friends, families, and

other more abstract topics. Encourage students to select topics.

3. Explain that you can write what students say, that they can learn to read what was written, and that learning words in these sentences will help them learn to read and write many other words.

4. Invite discussion of the stimulus, encouraging students to use as elaborated language as they can. Ask open-ended questions that encourage extended answers. If students give brief or incomplete sentences, model elaborated language using their words: S: "Green. Fuzzy." T: "It's green and fuzzy."

5. Ask for volunteers to contribute sentences for the dictation.

6. Write students' sentences, allowing changes or additions. If you want students to learn to read each other's names, include their names in the text. Print neatly with clear spaces between each word.

7. Read the completed story expressively and at a natural pace, pointing to each word as you read.

8. Reread the story chorally several times until students have memorized it. Continue pointing to each word. (Keep up the pace so the reading sounds natural, not word by word.) If students have trouble memorizing the whole text, divide it into sections of two or three sentences each.

9. Invite volunteers to come to the chart and recite a part or the whole story while pointing to each word. Continue until each student who volunteers has read the story individually.

10. Point to individual words and invite students to identify the words, reading from the beginning to the target word if necessary.

Follow-Up Activities for English Language Learners

1. Repeat choral and individual reading and pointing on subsequent days until students can read the story fluently and point accurately. (Older students can reread and point using duplicated copies of the story rather than at a chart.)

2. Copy each sentence onto a sentence strip. Have volunteers hold up each strip in correct order. (These can also be used for independent practice with a hanging pocket chart.)

3. Create exact copies of the story on copy paper. Duplicate several copies for each student. Students can paste copies on construction paper or in journals and illustrate them, cut lines and sentences apart and put them in correct order, cut sentences into phrases and put them in correct order, and use sentences for handwriting practice.

4. Have students find individual words they recognize in isolation and begin building individual word banks with known words on cards. Students should sort and review word banks daily.

5. Have students sort words in their word banks in a variety of ways: matching beginning sounds, number of syllables, alphabetical order, words that are related by meaning, and so forth.

6. Select one or several familiar words beginning with consonants. Using individual letter cards or magnetic letters, show students how to "make and break" the words by removing the initial letter or sound and substituting another, creating new words.

7. Students can write known sight words using magnetic letters on cookie sheets, individual letters cut out of sandpaper, wallpaper scraps, felt, glue and sand or glitter, pipe cleaners, gel pens, macaroni letters, letters cut from magazines, and so forth. They can also search for known words in newspaper and magazine ads and headlines, and cut them out.

8. Begin personal dictionaries by folding eight to ten sheets of paper vertically and stapling in the fold to create individual books. Have students write a letter at the top of each page (group infrequent letters like *q, u, x, y,* and *z* with others) and begin collecting mastered sight words in their dictionaries.

9. As students' word banks grow, have them construct sentences with word cards.

61. Cumulative Semantic Map

Objectives: To foster vocabulary growth; help students learn meanings of related words

Materials: Large paper chart that can be displayed and added to periodically

Duration: 5–15 minutes each time new words are added

1. Have students begin collecting words that are related by meaning: for example, synonyms, color words, action words, and so forth.

2. Construct a web graphic organizer on the chart, with one or more general categories in the center and related words radiating from them. For example, a cumulative semantic web on temperature words might show HOT and COLD in central circles, with various temperature words attached to them: *burning, boiling, sizzling, blistering, icy, freezing, frigid, polar,* and so forth.

3. As students encounter related words in their reading, or as you encounter such words in literature you read to them, return to the web and have students suggest where such words might be added or where new categories might be entered. For example, a new category of WARM words could be added, to include *comfortable, mild, tepid,* and *lukewarm.*

4. Encourage students to use words from the charts in their writing and to continue to watch for words that could be added to the collection.

62. Word Origins and Derivations

Objectives: To develop vocabulary; teach meanings of bases and affixes to help students figure out meanings of unfamiliar words; engage students in language learning

Materials: Space for Word Walls, charts, and bulletin board words; paper and markers; resource materials (dictionaries that include word histories, thesauruses, books on idioms, etc.)

Duration: 10–15 minutes several times weekly

1. Encourage students to begin collecting words they need to learn for subject areas and interesting or unfamiliar words they encounter during reading. Have them copy the sentence in which the word occurs, or share the text, so they can practice using context as a meaning clue. Make a Word Wall or chart of student-selected words, their context sentences, and meanings.

2. Teach vocabulary words in groups that have a shared base or affix; for example, *ex* (out): *exhale, exclaim, expand, exorcise, expectorate, exfoliate, explode, expire; in-/im-/il-* (not): *illiterate, illogical, illegal, illegible, immature, imbalance, impassable, immortal, incapable, inappropriate, inaudible, inconvenient.* Create word families and add new words as students encounter them.

3. Teach the meanings of the Latin and Greek bases or stems that have consistent meanings: for example, *photo* (light), *graph* (write), *mega* (large), *cap* (head), *corp*

(body), *ped* (foot), *manu* (hand), *scrib* (write), *retro* (backward), *poly* (many), *phone* (sound), *mono* (single), *bi* (two), *tri* (three), *cent* (hundred). Draw attention to these word parts and their meanings whenever they occur.

4. Avoid having students copy dictionary definitions, which they rarely understand. Instead, have them predict a word's meaning from word parts they know and context sentences before looking it up. Have them write meanings in their own words rather than a dictionary definition.

5. Have students divide word cards into three sections to include (a) the word, (b) its meaning in their own words, and (c) synonyms and opposites. On the back have them draw a sketch that illustrates the meaning, and write a caption for the drawing.

6. Limit the number of new words students have to learn each week; teach a group of related words and have students really learn fewer words rather than superficially memorize a long list.

63. Visualization

Objectives: To develop comprehension; model and practice visualizing or mentally seeing images a writer creates with words

Materials: Shared text; reading journals or literature logs; duplicated copies of the text that students can draw on; sticky notes; pencils

Duration: 5 minutes or less at various points in a text

1. Copy a short (1–2 paragraphs) excerpt of vivid or descriptive text onto the board, chart paper, or a transparency. Explain that you will model what good readers do as they visualize text.

2. Read the passage expressively; as you read it, pause and think aloud by telling students what you are mentally seeing or imagining. Mark the words, phrases, or sentences that are particularly vivid to you. Make a quick sketch in the margin that represents what you are visualizing, and explain what it means to you.

3. Distribute duplicated copies of similar text or portions of a text students are reading together. Read aloud a short section while students follow along. Have volunteers say what they visualized as you read, following your model. Have all students sketch in the margin as above, or distribute sticky notes and have students sketch on them and place them over or near the appropriate sections. Ask each student to tell briefly what they drew; they do not need to display the drawings because they are a sort of personal code.

4. In later lessons, students can write ("jot") what they are visualizing, using brief phrases, in addition to or instead of sketching. Students may prefer one method over the other; neither one is "better."

Variations: As students read longer or more difficult passages, encourage them to use the "jot" or "sketch" methods independently to help them visualize by making sticky notes available during reading, by having them jot or

sketch in their reading journals at the end of each day's reading, and by periodically repeating the activity with different kinds of text. Use visualization in combination with the Think-Pair-Share activity; after visualizing and drawing, each student shares with a single partner and then each pair with another pair. Encourage students to use sketches, drawings, or cutout magazine pictures to illustrate their writing about what they are reading.

64. Using Questions to Teach English Language Learners

Objectives: Vocabulary development; to help students learning English to acquire words, follow directions, and converse with others

Materials: Props to talk about: magazine pictures, picture cards, small objects like keys, toy cars, plastic fruit and other foods from children's kitchen toys, puppets, stuffed animals, and so forth

Duration: 5–15 minutes or longer, depending on students' age, English fluency, and size of group

1. Select a group of students who are similar in English fluency. Gather pictures or props to use.

2. Determine the general fluency level of students and plan the activity to meet their English abilities: preproduction, where students understand a few words but speak little; early production, where students understand simple sentences and produce very short utterances; or speech emergence, where students understand many words and sentences and produce longer, more varied sentences.

3. For preproduction students, use very simple, repetitive sentences accompanied by gesture and sound effects: "This is an apple. Is it red? Yes, it's red. Is it green? No, not green." "Can Maria hold the apple? Yes, she can. Can Nguyen hold the apple? Yes, he can. Can I hold the apple? Yes, I can." "Who has a frog? Juan has a frog. Who has a bird? Irma has a bird."

4. For early production students, use questions that require short answers, including yes/no, here/there, either/or, how many ..., what color ..., and common prepositions like in/out/under: "Is this a dog or a bird? What color is the bird? Do you like birds?" "Is this the mother or the father? Where is the baby? How many children are there?"

5. For speech emergence students, ask questions requiring longer answers, description, and simple sentences. Use wordless picture books, tell what is happening on each page, and ask students to retell. Read simple versions of stories several times, and have students retell or act out the stories using puppets or a flannel board. Play direction-following games like Simon Says, and have students give each other directions to follow: Stand behind your chair; open and close the door; raise your left hand. Practice naming objects: foods, clothing, tools, vehicles, classroom objects, colors, temperature words, animals, family members, areas of the school and home, and people (teacher, principal, nurse, bus driver).

References

Achilles, C. M. (1999). *Let's put kids first, finally: Getting class size right*. Thousand Oaks, CA: Corwin Press.

Ada, A. F., & Campoy, I. (1998). *Authors in the classroom*. Washington, DC: Del Sol Press.

Adams, M. J. (1990). *Beginning to read: Thinking and learning about print*. Cambridge, MA: MIT Press.

Adams, M. J. (1998). The three cuing system. In J. Osborne & F. Lehr (Eds.), *Literacy for all: Issues in teaching and learning*. New York, NY: Guilford Press.

Adler, M. (1982). The Paideia proposal: Rediscovering the essence of education. *American School Board Journal, 169*(7), 17–20.

Afflerbach, P. (1993). Report cards and reading. *The Reading Teacher, 46,* 458–465.

Alexander, P. (1998). The nature of disciplinary and domain learning: The knowledge, interest and strategic dimensions of learning from subject matter text. In C. Hynd (Ed.), *Learning from text across conceptual domains*. Mahwah, NJ: Erlbaum.

Alexander, P. A. (2000). Learning from text: A multidimensional and developmental perspective. In M. Kamil, P. B. Mosenthal, P. D. Pearson, & R. Barr (Eds.), *Handbook of reading research, volume III*. Hillsdale, NJ: Erlbaum.

Alexander, P., Jetton, T. L., Kulikowich, J. M., & Woehler, C. (1994). Contrasting instructional and structural importance: The seductive effect of teacher questions. *Journal of Reading Behavior, 26,* 19–45.

Allard, H. (1977). *Miss Nelson is missing!* Illustrated by J. Marshall. Boston, MA: Houghton Mifflin.

Alley, K. M. (2008). *Teaching integrated reading strategies in the middle school library media center*. Westport, CT: Libraries Unlimited, a member of Greenwood Publishing Group.

Allington, R. L. (1983). Fluency: The neglected reading goal. *The Reading Teacher, 36*(6), 556–561.

Allington, R. L. (1983). The reading instruction provided to readers of differing reading ability. *Elementary School Journal, 83,* 549–558.

Allington, R. L. (1997). Overselling phonics. *Reading Today, 14,* 15.

Allington, R. L. (2001). *What really matters for struggling readers: Designing research-based programs*. New York, NY: Longman.

Allington, R. L. (2005). *What really matters for struggling readers*. Boston, MA: Allyn & Bacon.

Allington, R. L. (2008). *What really matters in response to intervention*. Boston, MA: Allyn & Bacon.

Allington, R. L., & Johnson, P. H. (2002). *Reading to learn: Lessons from exemplary fourth-grade classrooms*. New York, NY: Guilford Press.

Allington, R. L., & McGill-Franzen, A. (1989). School response to reading failure: Instruction for chapter one and special educa-tion students in grades two, four, and eight. *Elementary School Journal, 89*(5), 529–542.

Allington, R. L., & Walmsley, S. A. *No quick fix: Rethinking pro-grams in America's elementary schools* (1995, 2007 [preface]). Newark, DE: International Reading Association.

Almasi, J. F. (1995). The nature of fourth graders' socio-cognitive conflicts in peer-led and teacher-led discussions of literature. *Reading Research Quarterly, 30*(3), 314–351.

Anderson, R. C., & Nagy, W. E. (1991). Word meanings. In R. Barr, M. L. Kamil, P. B. Mosenthal, & P. D. Pearson (Eds.), *Handbook of reading research* (Vol. 2). New York, NY: Longman.

Anderson, R. C., & Nagy, W. E. (1992). The vocabulary conun-drum. *American Educator, 16,* 14–18, 44–47.

Anderson, R. C., & Pearson, P. D. (1984). A schema-theoretic view of basic processes in reading. In P. D. Pearson (Ed.), *Handbook of reading research*. New York, NY: Longman.

Anderson, R. C., Wilson, P. T., & Fielding, L. (1988). Growth in reading and how children spend their time outside of school. *Reading Research Quarterly, 23,* 285–303.

Andrade, H. G. (2002). *Understanding rubrics*. http://learnweb .harvard.edu/ALPS/ thinking/docs/rubricar.htm

Archambault, J., & Martin, B. Jr. (1989). *White dynamite and the curly kid*. Illustrated by Ted Rand. New York, NY: Henry Holt.

Arellano Osuna, A. (1992). *El lenguaje integral: Una alternativa para la educación*. Mérida, Venezuela: Editorial Venezolana.

Armbruster, B. B., Lehr, F., & Osborn, J. (2001). *Put reading first: The research building blocks for teaching children to read. Kindergarten through grade 3*. Washington, DC: National Insti-tute for Literacy.

Asher, J. J. (1982). The total physical response approach. In R. W. Blair (Ed.), *Innovative approaches to language teaching* (pp. 54–66). Rowley, MA: Newbury House.

Ashton-Warner, S. (1963). *Teacher*. New York, NY: Simon & Schus-ter.

Atwell, N. (1985). *In the middle*. Portsmouth, NH: Heinemann.

Atwell, N. (1998). *In the middle: New understandings about writing, reading, and learning*. Portsmouth, NH: Heinemann.

Atwell, N. (1998). *In the middle: Writing, reading and learning with adolescents* (2nd ed.). Portsmouth, NH: Boynton/ Cook.

Ayers, W. (1993). *To teach*. New York, NY: Teachers College Press.

Baildon, R., & Baildon, M. (2008). Guiding independence: Devel-oping a research tool to support student decision making in selecting online information sources. *The Reading Teacher, 61*(8), 636–647.

Baker, L., Serpell, R., & Sonnenschein, S. (1995). Opportunities for literacy learning in the homes of urban preschoolers. In

L. M. Morrow (Ed.), *Family literacy: Connections in schools and communities* (pp. 236–252). Newark, DE: International Reading Association.

Banks, J. A. (2003). *Teaching strategies for ethnic studies*. Boston, MA: Allyn & Bacon.

Barbosa Heldt, A. (1971). *Cómo han aprendido a leer y a escribir los mexicanos*. Mexico City, Mexico: Editorial Pax México, Librería Carlos Cesarmán.

Barger, J. (2003). *Comparing the DIBELS Oral Reading Fluency indicator and the North Carolina end of grade reading assessment* (Tech. Rep.). Asheville: North Carolina Teacher Academy.

Barker, C. (2006). How many syllables does English have? Retrieved from http://ling.ucsd.edu/ %7Ebarker/Syllables/index.txt

Barone, D. (1992). That reminds me of . . .: Using dialogue journals with young readers. In C. Temple & P. Collins (Eds.), *Stories and readers: New perspectives on literature in the elementary classroom*. Norwood, MA: Christopher-Gordon.

Barone, D., Hardman, D., & Taylor, J. (2006). *Reading first in the classroom*. New York, NY: Pearson.

Barthes, R. (1974). *S/Z*. New York, NY: Hill and Wang.

Bartlett, J. R. (2003). *Dictionary of Americanisms*. Hoboken, NJ: John Wiley & Sons.

Baumann, J., Kameenui, E., & Ash, G. (2003). Research on vocabulary instruction: Voltaire redux. In J. Flood, D. Lapp, J. Squire, & J. Jensen (Eds.), *Handbook of research on teaching the English language arts* (2nd ed.). Mahwah, NJ: Erlbaum.

Beamon, G. W. (2001). *Teaching with adolescent learning in mind*. Arlington Heights, IL: Skylight Professional Development.

Beane, J. (1991, October). The middle school: The natural home of integrated curriculum. *Educational Leadership, 49*(2), 9–13.

Beane, J. A. (1997). *Curriculum integration: Designing the core of a democratic education*. New York, NY: Teachers College Press.

Beane, J. (2002). Beyond self-interest: A democratic core curriculum. *Educational Leadership, 59*, 25–28.

Bear, D. R., Invernizzi, M., Templeton, S., & Johnston, F. (2007). *Words their way: Word study for phonics, vocabulary, and spelling instruction* (4th ed.). Englewood Cliffs, NJ: Prentice Hall.

Beck, I. L., & McKeown, M. G. (1983). Learning words well—a program to enhance vocabulary and comprehension. *The Reading Teacher, 36*, 622–625.

Beck, I. L., McKeown, M. G., & Kucan, L. (2002). *Bringing words to life: Robust vocabulary instruction*. New York, NY: Guilford Press.

Beck, I. L., McKeown, M. G., Hamilton, R. L., & Kucan, L. (1997). *Questioning the author: An approach for enhancing student engagement with text*. Newark, DE: International Reading Association.

Becker, H. J. (2000). Who's wired and who's not: Children's access to and use of computer technology. *Children and Computer Technology, 10*, 44–75.

Bettelheim, B. (1975). *The uses of enchantment*. New York, NY: Vintage.

Betts, A. E. (1946). *Foundations of reading instruction, with emphasis on differentiated guidance*. Chicago, IL: American Book Company.

Biancarosa, G., & Snow, C. E. (2004). *Reading next—A vision for action and research in middle and high school literacy: A report to Carnegie Corporation of New York*. Washington, DC: Alliance for Excellent Education.

Biancarosa, C., & Snow, C. E. (2006). *Reading Next: A vision for action and research in middle and high school literacy. A report to Carnegie Corporation of New York* (2nd ed.). Washington, DC: Alliance for Excellent Education.

Blachman, B. (2008). *Road to reading: A program for preventing and remediating reading difficulties*. Baltimore, MD: Paul Brookes.

Blachowicz, C. L. Z. (1986). Making connections: Alternatives to the vocabulary notebook. *Journal of Reading, 29*, 643–649.

Blachowicz, C. L. Z., & Fisher, P. (1996). *Teaching vocabulary in all classrooms*. Englewood Cliffs, NJ: Prentice Hall.

Blachowicz, C. L. Z., & Fisher, P. (2000). Vocabulary instruction. In M. L. Kamil., P. Mosenthal, P. D. Pearson, & R. Barr (Eds.), *Handbook of reading research* (Vol. 3). New York, NY: Longman.

Blachowicz, C. L. Z., & Fisher, P. (2006). *Teaching vocabulary in all classrooms* (4th ed.). New York, NY: Pearson-Prentice Hall.

Blachowicz, C. L. Z., Fisher, P., Ogle, D., & Watts-Taff, S. (2006). Vocabulary: Questions from the classroom. *Reading Research Quarterly, 41*(4), 524–539.

Blachowicz, C. L. Z., Sullivan, D., & Cieply, C. (2001). Fluency snapshots: A quick screening tool for your classroom. *Reading Psychology, 22*(2), 95–109.

Bleich, D. (1970). *Subjective criticism*. Baltimore, MD: Johns Hopkins University Press.

Bleich, D. (1978). *Subjective criticism*. Baltimore, MD: Johns Hopkins University.

Block, C. C., & Pressley, M. (Eds.). (2001). *Comprehension instruction: Research-based best practices*. New York, NY: Guilford.

Booth, D. (2006). *Reading doesn't matter any more: Shattering the myths of literacy*. Portland, ME: Stenhouse.

Booth, D., & Schwartz, L. (2004). *Literacy strategies*. Portland, ME: Stenhouse Publishers.

Bormuth, J. R. (1968, Autumn). Cloze test readability: Criterion reference scores. *Journal of Educational Measurement, 5*(3), 189–196.

Bos, C. S., & Anders, P. L. (1989). Developing higher level thinking skills through interactive teaching. *Journal of Reading, Writing, and Learning Disabilities International, 4*(4), 259–274.

Bos, C., & Anders, P. (1990, Winter). Effects of interactive vocabulary instruction on the vocabulary learning and reading comprehension of junior-high learning disabled students. *Learning Disability Quarterly, 13*(1), 31–42.

Bradley, L., & Bryant, P. (1985). *Rhyme and reason in reading and spelling*. Ann Arbor: University of Michigan Press.

Bradbury, B., & Jäntti, M. (1999). *Child poverty across industrialized nations*. Florence: UNICEF International Child Development Center.

Bransford, J. D., Brown, A. L., & Cocking, R. (Eds.). (1999). *How people learn: Brain, mind, experience, and school*. New York, NY: National Research Council.

Brenner, B. (1992). *Group soup*. New York, NY: Viking.

Britton, J. (1970). *Language and learning*. Harmondsworth, England: Penguin Books.

Bromley, K. (1999). Key components of sound writing instruction. In L. Gambrell, L. Mandell Morrow, S. B. Neuman, & M. Pressley (Eds.), *Best practices in literacy instruction* (pp. 152–174). New York, NY: Guilford Press.

Bronfenbrenner, U. (1979). *The ecology of human development*. Cambridge, MA: Harvard University Press.

Brooks, W. (2006). Reading representations of themselves: Urban youth use culture and African American textual features to develop literary understandings. *Reading Research Quarterly*, 41(3), 372–392.

Brooks, W. M. (2005). Reading linguistic features: Middle school students' response to the African American literary tradition. In B. Hammond, M. E. Rhodes Hoover, & McPhail, I. P. (Eds.), *Teaching African American learners to read* (pp. 253–263). Newark, DE: International Reading Association.

Brown, H., & Cambourne, B. (1990). *Read and retell: A strategy for the whole-language/natural learning classroom.* Portsmouth, NH: Heinemann.

Brown, M. (1947). *Stone soup.* New York, NY: Aladdin Paperback.

Brown, M. (1949). *The important book.* New York, NY: Harper.

Brown, R. (1955). *Words and things.* Garden City, NY: Basic Books.

Bruner, J. (1978). The role of dialogue in language acquisition. In A. Sinclair, R. J. Jarvella, & W. M. Levelt (Eds.), *The child's conception of language* (pp. 241–256). New York, NY: Springer-Verlag.

Buck, J., & Torgesen, J. (2003). *The relationship between performance on a measure of oral reading fluency and performance on the Florida Comprehensive Assessment Test* (FCRR Tech. Rep. #1). Tallahassee, FL: Florida Center for Reading Research.

Buehl, D. (2001). *Classroom strategies for interactive learning* (2nd ed.). Newark, DE: International Reading Association.

Burniske, R. W. (2008). *Literacy in the digital age.* Thousand Oaks, CA: Corwin Press.

Burns, P. C., Roe, B. D., & Ross, E. P. (1999). *Teaching reading in today's elementary schools.* Boston, MA: Houghton Mifflin.

Butler, A., & Turbill, J. (1985). *Towards a reading-writing classroom.* Portsmouth, NH: Heinemann.

Caldwell, J. S. (2002). *Reading assessment: A primer for teachers and tutors.* New York, NY: Guilford Press.

California State Board of Education. (1999). *English language development standards.* Sacramento, CA: Author.

California State Department of Education. (2009). Response to instruction and intervention (RTI²). http://pubs.cde.ca.gov/tcsii/ch2/responsetointerven.aspx

Calkins, L. (1994). *The art of teaching writing.* Portsmouth, NH: Heinemann.

Calkins, L. (1996). *The art of teaching writing.* Portsmouth, NH: Heinemann.

Campbell, J. (2008). *The hero with a thousand faces.* Princeton, NJ: Bolingen Press.

Campo-Flores, A. (2001, June 4). A town's two faces. *Newsweek*, 34–35.

Carle, E. (1987). *The very hungry caterpillar.* New York, NY: Philomel Books.

Carle, E. (1994). *La oruga muy hambrienta.* New York, NY: Philomel Books.

Carlisle, J. F. (2000). Awareness of the structure and meaning of morphologically complex words: Impact on reading. *Reading and writing: An interdisciplinary journal*, 12, 169–190.

Carlisle, J. F., & Stone, C. A. (2005). Exploring the role of morphemes in word reading. *Reading Research Quarterly*, 40, 428–449.

Carr, E. M. (1985). The vocabulary overview guide: A metacognitive strategy to improve vocabulary, comprehension and retention. *Journal of Reading*, 28, 684–689.

Carr, E. M., & Ogle, D. (1987). K-W-L Plus: A strategy for comprehension and summarization. *Journal of Reading*, 30, 626–631.

Castañeda v. *Pickard*, 648 F.2d 989, 5th Circuit (1981).

CATESOL. (1992). *Position statement on specially-designed academic instruction in English (sheltered instruction).* Orinda: California Teachers of English to Speakers of Other Languages.

Cervetti, G.N., Pearson, P. D., Barber, J., Hiebert, E. H., & Bravo, M. A. (2007). Integrating literacy and science: The research we have, the research we need. In M. Pressley, A. K. Billman, K. Perry, K. Refitt, & J. Reynolds (Eds.), *Shaping literacy achievement* (pp. 157–174). New York, NY: Guilford.

Chall, J. (1967). *Learning to read: The great debate* (Rev. ed.). New York, NY: McGraw-Hill.

Chomsky, C. (1971). Write first, read later. *Childhood Education*, 47(6), 296–299.

Christie, J. (1991). *Play and early literacy development.* Albany, NY: State University of New York Press.

Christie, J., & Roskos, K. (2001). Examining the play-literacy interface. *Journal of Early Childhood Literacy*, 1(1), 59–89.

Christie, J., & Roskos, K. (2009). Play's potential in early literacy development. *Encyclopedia on Early Childhood Development.* Montreal, Quebec: Center for Excellence in Early Childhood Development.

Clay, M. M. (1975). *What did I write?* Portsmouth, NH: Heinemann.

Clay, M. M. (1985). *The early detection of reading difficulties: A diagnostic survey with recovery procedures.* Portsmouth, NH: Heinemann.

Clay, M. M. (1987). *Writing begins at home: Preparing children for writing before they go to school.* Portsmouth, NH: Heinemann.

Clay, M. M. (1993). *An observational survey of early literacy achievement.* Portsmouth, NH: Heinemann.

Clay, M. M. (1993). *Reading recovery: A guidebook for teachers in training.* Portsmouth, NH: Heinemann.

Clay, M. M. (2000). *Concepts about print: What have children learned about the way we print language?* Portsmouth, NH: Heinemann.

Cleary, B. (1997). *Ramona and her father.* New York, NY: Harper Trophy.

Clymer, T. (1996, November). The utility of phonic generalizations in the primary grades. *The Reading Teacher*, 50, 3, pp. 182–187.

Coiro, J. (2009). Rethinking assessment in a digital age. *Educational Leadership*, 66, 59–63.

Coiro, J., & Dobler, E. (2007). Exploring the online reading comprehension strategies used by sixth-grade skilled readers to search for and locate information on the Internet. *Reading Research Quarterly*, 42, 214–257.

Coleman, J. S., Campbell, E. Q., Hobson, C. J., McPartland, J., Mood, A. M., Weinfeld, F. D., & York, R. L. (1966). *Equality of educational opportunity.* Washington, DC: U.S. Government Printing Office.

Collier, V. P. (1987). Age and rate of acquisition of second language for academic purposes. *TESOL Quarterly*, 21, 617–641.

Collier, V. P. (1989). How long? A synthesis of research on academic achievement in a second language. *TESOL Quarterly*, 23, 509–539.

Collins, J. L. (1998). *Strategies for struggling writers.* New York, NY: Guilford Press.

Collins, M. F. (2005). ESL preschoolers' English vocabulary acquisition from storybook reading. *Reading Research Quarterly*, 40(4), 406–408.

Conrad, P. (1992). *Pedro's journal.* New York, NY: Scholastic.

Cowhey, M. (2006). *Black ants and Buddhists.* Portland, ME: Stenhouse.

Crawford, A., Saul, E., & Mathews, S. (2005). *Teaching and learning lessons for the thinking classroom*. New York, NY: Central European University Press.

Crawford, A. N. (1982). From Spanish reading to English reading: The transition process. In M. P. Douglass (Ed.), *Claremont reading conference yearbook* (pp. 159–165). Claremont, CA: Claremont Reading Conference.

Crawford, A. N. (1993). Literature, integrated language arts, and the language minority child: A focus on meaning. In A. Carrasquillo & C. Hedley (Eds.), *Whole language and the bilingual learner* (pp. 61–75). Norwood, NJ: Ablex.

Crawford, A. N. (1994a). Communicative approaches to second language acquisition: From oral language development into the core curriculum and L₂ literacy. In C. F. Leyba (Ed.), *Schooling and language minority students: A theoretical framework* (2nd ed., pp. 79–121). Los Angeles, CA: California State University, Los Angeles, Evaluation, Dissemination and Assessment Center.

Crawford, A. N. (1994b). Estrategias para promover la comprensión lectora en estudiantes de alto riesgo. *Lectura y Vida, 15*(1), 21–27.

Crawford, A. N. (1995). Language policy, second language learning, and literacy. In A. N. Crawford (Ed.), *A practical guidebook for adult literacy programmes in developing nations* (pp. 9–16). Paris: UNESCO.

Crawford, A. N. (2000). Strategies for teaching reading and writing to English language learners. In J. W. Gillet, C. Temple, A. N. Crawford, S. R. Mathews, & J. P. Young (Eds.), *Understanding reading problems: Assessment and instruction* (pp. 416–453). New York, NY: Longman.

Crawford, A. N. (2003). Communicative approaches to second language acquisition: The bridge to second language literacy. In G. García (Ed.), *English learners: Reaching the highest level of English literacy* (pp. 152–181). Newark, DE: International Reading Association.

Crawford, A. N., Allen, R. V., & Hall, M. (1995). The language experience approach. In A. N. Crawford (Ed.), *A practical guidebook for adult literacy programs in developing nations* (pp. 17–46). Paris: UNESCO.

Crawford, A., Saul, W., Mathews, S., & MaKinster, J. (2005). *Lessons from the thinking classroom*. New York, NY: IDEA.

Crawford, J. (1989). *Bilingual education: History, politics, theory and practice*. Trenton, NJ: Crane.

Cuban, L. (2001). *Oversold and underused: Computers in classrooms*. Cambridge, MA: Harvard University Press.

Cummins, J. (1980). The construct of language proficiency in bilingual education. In J. E. Alatis (Ed.), *Georgetown University roundtable on languages and linguistics* (pp. 76–93). Washington, DC: Georgetown University Press.

Cummins, J. (1981). The role of primary language development in promoting educational success for language minority students. In California State Department of Education (Ed.), *Schooling and language minority students: A theoretical framework* (pp. 3–49). Los Angeles, CA: California State University, Los Angeles, Evaluation, Dissemination and Assessment Center.

Cummins, J. (1986). Empowering minority students: A framework for intervention. *Harvard Educational Review, 56*, 18–36.

Cummins, J. (1989). *Empowering minority students*. Sacramento: California Association for Bilingual Education.

Cummins, J. (2001). *Language, power, pedagogy: Bilingual children in the crossfire*. Bristol, UK: Multilingual Matters Limited.

Cummins, J., & Corson, D. (1997). *Bilingual education*. Amsterdam: Kluwer.

Cunningham, A. E., & Stanovich, K. E. (1997). Early reading acquisition and its relation to reading experience and ability 10 years later. *Developmental Psychology, 33*(6), 934–945.

Cunningham, A. E., & Stanovich, K. E. (1998, Spring-Summer). What reading does for the mind. *The American Educator*, pp. 8–17.

Cunningham, P. M. (1995). *Phonics they use: Words for reading and writing* (2nd ed.). New York, NY: HarperCollins.

Cunningham, P. M., & Allington, R. L. (1999). *Classrooms that work: They can all read and write* (2nd ed.). Reading, MA: Addison-Wesley.

Cunningham, P. M., & Allington, R. L. (2003). *Classrooms that work: They can ALL read and write* (3rd ed.). Boston, MA: Allyn & Bacon.

Cunningham, P. M., Hall, D. P., & Defree, M. (1991). Non-ability grouped, multileveled instruction: A year in a first-grade classroom. *The Reading Teacher, 44*, 566–571.

Cunningham, P. M., Hall, D. P., & Sigmon, C. M. (1998). *The teacher's guide to the four blocks*. Greensboro, NC: Carson-Dellosa Publishing.

Cunningham, P. M., Hall, D. P., & Sigmon, C. M. (2007). *The teacher's guide to the four blocks*. Greensboro, NC: Carson-Dellosa.

Curtis, C. P. (2000). *Bud, not buddy*. New York, NY: Yearling.

Dahl, K. L., Scharer, P. L., Lawson, L. L., & Grogan, P. R. (2001). *Rethinking phonics: Making the best teaching decisions*. Portsmouth, NH: Heinemann.

Dahl, R. (1998). *Danny, the champion of the world*. Illustrated by Quentin Blake. New York, NY: Puffin.

Damico, J. S. (1991). Descriptive assessment of communicative ability in limited English proficient students. In E. Hamayan & J. S. Damico (Eds.), *Limiting bias in the assessment of bilingual students* (pp. 157–218). Austin, TX: PRO-ED.

Daniels, H. (1994). *Literature circles: Voice and choice in one student-centered classroom*. York, ME: Stenhouse.

Daniels, H. (2001). *Literature circles: Voice and choice in book clubs and reading groups*. Augusta, ME: Stenhouse.

Daniels, H. (2002). *Literature circles: Voice and choice in book clubs & reading groups* (2nd ed.). Markham, Ontario: Pembroke.

Darling-Hammond, L., Pearson, P. D., Schoenfeld, A. H., Barron, B., & Stage, E. K. (2008). *Powerful learning: What we know about teaching for understanding*. San Francisco, CA: Jossey-Bass.

Davis, F. B. (1944). Fundamental factors of comprehension in reading. *Psychometrica, 9*, 195–197.

Davis, F. B. (1968). Research in comprehension in reading. *Reading Research Quarterly, 3*, 499–454.

de Braslavsky, B. P. (2006). *Adquisición inicial de la lectura y escritura en escuelas para la diversidad*, Tomo 1. Buenos Aires: Fundación Perez Companc.

Delpit, L. (1990). Language diversity and learning. In S. Hynds & D. Rubin (Eds.), *Perspectives on talk and learning* (pp. 247–266). Urbana, IL: NCTE.

Delpit, L. (1995). *Other people's children: Cultural conflict in the classroom*. New York, NY: The New Press.

Delpit, L. (1996). Skills and other dilemmas of a progressive black educator. In L. Delpit (Ed.), *Other people's children*. New York, NY: The New Press.

Delpit, L. (2008). Introduction. In L. Delpit (Ed.), *The skin that we speak: Thoughts on language and culture in the classroom* (pp. xxii–xxvi). New York, NY: The New Press.

Dewey, J. (1913). *Interest and effort in education*. Boston, MA: Riverside.

Diana v. State Board of Education of California, Action No. C-7037RFP (N. D. Cal. Jan. 7, 1970 & June 18, 1973).

Dirkes, M. A. (1985). Metacognition: Students in charge of their thinking. *Roeper Review*, 8(2), 96–100.

Dixon, C. N., & Nessel, D. (1983). *Language experience approach to reading and writing: LEA for ESL*. Hayward, CA: Alemany Press.

Donahue, P. L., Finnegan, R. J., Lutkus, A. D., Allen, N. L., & Campbell, J. R. (2001). *The nation's report card: Fourth-grade reading 2000.* (NCES 2001-499). Washington, DC: U.S. Department of Education, National Center for Education Statistics.

Drake, S. M. (1998). *Creating integrated curriculum: Proven ways to increase student learning*. Thousand Oaks, CA: Corwyn.

Droop, M., & Verhoeven, L. (2003). Language proficiency and reading ability in first and second language learners. *Reading Research Quarterly*, 38, 78–103.

Dudley-Marling, C. (1990). *When school is a struggle*. Richmond Hill, Ontario: Scholastic.

Dudley-Marling, C. (2000). *A family affair: When school troubles come home*. Portsmouth, NH: Heinemann.

Dudley-Marling, C. (2009). *A classroom teacher's guide to struggling writers: How to provide differentiated support and ongoing assessment*. Portsmouth, NH: Heinemann.

Duffy, G. G., & Roehler, L. R. (1989). Why strategy instruction is so difficult and what we need to do about it. In C. B. McCormick, G. Miller, & M. Pressley (Eds.), *Cognitive strategy research: From basic research to educational applications*. New York, NY: Springer-Verlag.

Duffy-Hester, A. (1999). Teaching struggling readers in elementary school classrooms: A review of classroom reading programs and principles for instruction. *The Reading Teacher*, 52, 480–495.

Duke, N. K. (2000). 3–6 minutes per day: The scarcity of informational texts in first grade. *Reading Research Quarterly*, 35(2), 202–224.

Duke, N. K., & Bennett-Armistead, V. S. (2003). *Reading and writing informational text in the primary grades*. New York, NY: Scholastic.

Duke, N. K., Purcell-Gates, V., Hall, L., & Tower, C. (2006). Authentic literacy activities for developing comprehension and writing. *Reading Teacher*, 60, 344–355.

Durkin, D. (1978–1979). What classroom observations reveal about reading comprehension instruction. *Reading Research Quarterly*, 15, 481–433.

Dyson, A. H. (1989). *Multiple worlds of child writers: Friends learning to write*. New York, NY: Teachers College Press.

Echevarria, J., Vogt, M. E., & Short, D. J. (2009). *Making content comprehensible for elementary English learners: The SIOP® model*. Boston, MA: Allyn & Bacon.

Edelsky, C. (1982). Writing in a bilingual program: The relation of L_1 and L_2 texts. *TESOL Quarterly*, 16, 211–228.

Eder, D. (1983). Ability grouping and students' academic self-concepts: A case study. *Elementary School Journal*, 84(2), 149–161.

Edwards, S.A., Malloy, R. W., & Verock-O'Laughlin, R. (2003). *Ways of writing with young kids*. Boston, MA: Allyn & Bacon.

Eeds, M., & Wells, D. (1989). Grand conversations: An exploration of meaning construction in literature discussion groups. *Research in the Teaching of English*, 23, 4–29.

Ehrenreich, B. (2001). *Nickled and dimed: On (not) getting by in America*. New York, NY: Owl Books.

Ehri, L. C. (1991). Development of the ability to read words. In R. Barr, M. Kamil, P. B. Mosenthal, & P. D. Pearson (Eds.), *Handbook of reading research* (Vol. 2). New York, NY: Longman.

Ehri, L. C. (1995). Phases of development in learning to read by sight. *Journal of Research in Reading*, 18, 116–125.

Ehri, L. C. (1997a). Learning to read and learning to spell are one and the same, almost. In C. Perfetti, L. Rieben, & M. Fayol (Eds.), *Learning to spell* (pp. 237–269). Hillsdale, NJ: Erlbaum.

Ehri, L. C. (1997b). *The development of children's ability to read words*. Paper presented at the convention of the International Reading Association, Atlanta, GA.

Elkonin, D. B. (1973). USSR. In J. Downing (Ed.), *Comparative reading*. New York, NY: Macmillan.

Elley, W. (1992). *How in the world do students read?* The Hague: The International Association for the Evaluation of Educational Achievement.

Elley, W. (1996). *The IEA study of reading literacy*. Oxford, England: Pergamon.

Escamilla, K., & Andrade, A. (1992). Descubriendo la lectura: An application of *Reading Recovery* in Spanish. *Education and Urban Society*, 24, 212–226.

Escamilla, K., Loera, M., Ruiz, O., & Rodriguez, Y. (1998). An examination of sustaining effects in *Descubriendo la Lectura* programs. *Literacy Teaching and Learning*, 3, 59–81.

Federal Register. (2006). Title I—Improving the Academic Achievement of the Disadvantaged; Final Rule. 34 CFR Part 200, September 13, 2006. Washington, DC: Department of Education.

Ferreiro, E., & Rodríguez, B. (1994). *Las condiciones de alfabetización en medio rural*. México: CINVESTAV.

Ferreiro, E., & Tebersoky, A. (1982). *Literacy before schooling*. Portsmouth, NH: Heinemann.

Fielding, L., & Roller, C. (1992). Making difficult books accessible and easy books acceptable. *The Reading Teacher*, 45, 678–685.

Fisher, A. (2001). *Critical thinking*. New York, NY: Cambridge University Press.

Fisher, P., Blachowicz, C., & Smith, J. (1991). Vocabulary learning in literature discussion groups. In J. Zutell & S. McCormick (Eds.), *Learner factors/ Teacher factors: Issues in literacy research and instruction* (pp. 201–209). Fortieth yearbook of the National Reading Conference. Chicago, IL: National Reading Conference.

Fitzgerald, J. (1993). Literacy and students who are learning English as a second language. *The Reading Teacher*, 46, 638–647.

Fitzgerald, J. (1995). English-as-a-second-language reading instruction in the United States: A research review. *Journal of Reading Behavior*, 27, 115–152.

Flesch, R. (1956). *Why Johnny can't read*. New York, NY: Popular Library.

Florida Department of Education (2007). Retrieved from http://www.floridastandards.org/Standards/FLStandardSearch.aspx

Fogelberg, E., Skalinder, C., Satz, P., Hiller, B., Bernstein, L., & Vitantonio, S. (2008). *Integrating literacy and math: Strategies for K–6 teachers*. New York, NY: Guilford.

Foorman, B. R., & Mehta, P. (2002, November). *Definitions of fluency: Conceptual and methodological challenges*. PowerPoint presentation at A Focus on Fluency Forum, San Francisco, CA. Retrieved from www.prel.org/programs/rel/fluency/Foorman. ppt

Fountas, I. C., & Pinnell, G. S. (1996). *Guided reading: Good first teaching for all children.* Portsmouth, NH: Heinemann.

Fountas, I. C., & Pinnell, G. S. (1999). *Matching books to readers: Using leveled books in guided reading, K–3.* Portsmouth, NH: Heinemann.

Fountas, I. C., & Pinnell, G. S. (2001). *Guiding readers and writers: Grades 3–6.* Portsmouth, NH: Heinemann.

Fountas, I. C., & Pinnell, G. S. (2001). *Guiding readers and writers: Teaching comprehension, genre, and content literacy.* Portsmouth, NH: Heinemann.

Fountas, I. C., & Pinnell, G. S. (2001). *Leveled books, K–8: Matching texts to readers for effective teaching.* Portsmouth, NH: Heinemann.

Fountas, I. C., & Pinnell, G. S. (2007). *The continuum of literacy learning grades K–2.* Portsmouth, NH: Heinemann.

Fountas, I. C., & Pinnell, G. S. (2009). *The Fountas & Pinnell leveled book list, K–8+: 2010–2012.* Portsmouth, NH: Heinemann.

Fradd, S. H., & Tikunoff, W. J. (Eds.). (1987). *Bilingual and bilingual special education: An administrator's guide.* Boston, MA: Little, Brown.

Frazier, D. (2000). *Miss Alaineus: A vocabulary disaster.* San Diego, CA: Harcourt.

Fredericks, A. D. (1998). *The integrated curriculum: Books for reluctant readers, Grades 2–5.* Englewood, CO: Teacher Ideas Press.

Freebody, P., & Luke, A. (1990). Literacies programs: Debates and demands in cultural context. *Prospect: Australian Journal of TESOL, 5*(7), 7–16.

Freeman, D. (1978). *Corduroy.* New York, NY: Viking Junior.

Freinet, C. (1974). *El método natural de lectura.* Barcelona, Spain: Editorial Laia.

Freppon, P. A. (1987). Radices docere: Teaching roots. *Ohio Reading Teacher, 21,* 20–25.

Frith, U. (1985). Beneath the surface of developmental dyslexia. In K. E. Patterson, J. C. Marshall, & M. Coltheart (Eds.), *Surface dyslexia* (pp. 310–330). London: Erlbaum.

Fry, E. (1967). Fry's readability graph: Clarifications, validity, and extension to level 17. *Journal of Reading, 21,* 242–252.

Frye, Northrop. (1951). The archetypes of literature. In C. Kaplan & W. Anderson, *Criticism: the Major Statements* (3rd ed., pp. 500–514). New York, NY: St. Martin's, 1991.

Fuchs, L. S., Deno, S. L., & Mirkin, P. K. (1984, Summer). The effects of frequent curriculum-based measurement and evaluation on pedagogy, student achievement, and student awareness of learning. *American Educational Research Journal, 21*(2), pp. 449–460.

Ganske, K. (2000). *Word journeys.* New York, NY: Guilford Press.

Ganske, K. (2003). *Word journeys.* New York, NY: Guilford Press.

Ganske, K. (2006). *Word sorts and more: Sound pattern and meaning exploration K–3.* New York, NY: Guilford Press.

Garbarino, J. (2000). *The lost boys: Why our sons turn violent and how we can save them.* New York, NY: Anchor Books.

García, E. E. (2005). *Teaching and learning in two languages: Bilingualism and schooling in the United States.* New York, NY: Teachers College Press.

Garcia, E. (1991, Autumn). Factors influencing the English reading test performance of Spanish-speaking Hispanic children. *Reading Research Quarterly, 26*(4), 371–392.

Gaskins, I. W. (1998). There's more to teaching at-risk and delayed readers than good reading instruction. *The Reading Teacher, 51,* 534–547.

Gee, J. P. (1992). *The social mind: Ideology and social practice.* New York, NY: Bergin & Garvey.

Gelman, R., & Greeno, J. G. (1989). On the nature of competence: Principles for understanding in a domain. In L. Resnick (Ed.), *Knowing, learning, and instruction: Essays in honor of Robert Glaser.* Hillsdale, NJ: Erlbaum.

Gentry, J. R. (1981). Learning to spell developmentally. *The Reading Teacher, 34,* 378–381.

Gentry, J. R. (1989). *Spel . . . is a four-letter word.* Portsmouth, NH: Heinemann.

Gentry, J. R. (2007). *Breakthrough in beginning reading and writing.* New York, NY: Scholastic.

Gentry, J. R. (2008). *Step-by-step assessment guide to code breaking.* New York, NY: Scholastic.

Gersten, R. (1998). Recent advances in instructional research for students with learning disabilities: An overview. *Learning Disabilities Research and Practice, 13*(3), 162–170.

Gersten, R., & Baker, S. (2000). What we know about effective instructional practices for English-language learners. *Exceptional Children, 66,* 454–470.

Gibson, E., & Levin, H. (1975). *The psychology of reading.* Cambridge, MA: MIT Press.

Gillet, J. W., & Temple, C. (1978, December). Developing word knowledge: A cognitive view. *Reading World, 18*(2), 132–140.

Gillet, J. W., Temple, C., & Crawford, A. (2004). *Understanding reading problems* (6th ed.). Boston, MA: Allyn & Bacon.

Gillet, J. W., Temple, C., & Crawford, A. (2007). *Understanding reading problems* (7th ed.). Boston, MA: Allyn & Bacon.

Gleitman, L. R., & Rozin, P. (1973). Teaching reading by use of a syllabary. *Reading Research Quarterly, 8,* 4 (Summer, 1973), 447–483.

Goatley, V. J., Brock, C. H., & Raphael, T. E. (1995). Diverse learners participating in regular education "book clubs." *Reading Research Quarterly, 30*(3), 352–380.

Goldman, S. R., & Rakestraw, Jr., J. A. (2000). Structural aspects of constructing meaning from text. In M. L. Kamil, P. Mosenthal, P. D. Pearson, & R. Barr (Eds.), *Handbook of reading research* (Vol. 3, pp. 311–335). Mahwah, NJ: Erlbaum.

Gollnick, D. M., & Chinn, P. C. (2008). *Multicultural education in a pluralistic society.* Boston, MA: Allyn & Bacon.

Gomes de Matos, F. (2002). Teaching peace- promoting vocabulary: A new frontier. *Glosas Didacticas,* Spring.

Goodman, K. S. (1967). Reading: A psycholinguistic guessing game. *Journal of the Reading Specialist, 6,* 126–135.

Goodman, K. S. (1986). *What's whole in whole language?* Portsmouth, NH: Heinemann.

Goodman, K. S. (1989). *Lenguaje integral.* Mérida, Venezuela: Editorial Venezolana.

Goodman, Y. M. (1978). Kid watching: An alternative to testing. *National Elementary Principal, 57,* 4, 41–45.

Goodman, Y. M. (1985). Kid watching: Observing children in the classroom. In A. Jaggar & M. T. Smith-Burke (Eds.), *Observing the language learner* (pp. 9–18). New York, NY: New York University. Co-published by the International Reading Association and the National Council of Teachers of English, 1985.

Goodman, Y. M. (2006). *Kidwatching.* Retrieved July 22, 2006, from www.reading.org/downloads/publications/books/bk558-27-Goodman_Kidwatching.pdf

Goodman, Y. M., & Burke, C. L. (1972). *Reading miscue inventory: Procedure for diagnosis and evaluation.* New York, NY: Macmillan.

Goodman, Y. M., Watson, D. J., & Burke, C. L. (2005). *Reading miscue inventory: From evaluation to instruction.* Katonah, NY: Richard C. Owen.

Goswami, U. (2000). Phonological and lexical processes. In M. Kamil, P. Mosenthal, P. D. Pearson, & R. Barr (Eds.), *Handbook of reading research* (Vol. 3). New York, NY: Longman.

Graves, D. H. (1982). *Writing: Students and teachers at work.* Portsmouth, NH: Heinemann.

Graves, D. H. (1983). *Writing: Teachers and children at work.* Exeter, NH: Heinemann Educational Books.

Graves, M. (2006). *The vocabulary book: Learning and instruction.* Champaign, IL: NCTE.

Greenlaw, W. (2001). *English language arts and reading on the Internet.* Columbus, OH: Merrill Prentice Hall.

Griffith, P. L., & Lynch-Brown, C. (2002). Owning technology. *The Reading Teacher, 55,* 614–615.

Gronlund, N. E., Linn, R. L., & Davis, K. (2000). *Measurement and assessment in teaching.* Englewood Cliffs, NJ: Prentice Hall.

Guthrie, J. T., & Davis, M. H. (2003). Motivating struggling readers in middle school through an engagement model of classroom practice. *Reading & Writing Quarterly, 19,* 59–185.

Guthrie, J. T., & Wigfield, A. (2000). Engagement and motivation in reading. In M. L. Mamil, P. B. Mosenthal, P. D. Pearson, & R. Barr (Eds.), *The handbook of reading research.* Mahwah, NJ: Erlbaum.

Gwynne, F. (1988). *A chocolate moose for dinner.* New York, NY: Aladdin.

Gwynne, F. (2006). *The king who rained.* New York, NY: Aladdin Paperbacks.

Hall, E. T. (1966). *The hidden dimension.* New York, NY: Doubleday.

Hall, E. T. (1983). *The dance of life.* New York, NY: Doubleday.

Hall, S. L., & Moats, L. C. (1999). *Straight talk about reading.* Lincolnwood, IL: Contemporary Books.

Halle, T., Kurtz-Costes, B., & Mahoney, J. (1997). Family influences on school achievement in low-income African American children. *Journal of Educational Psychology, 89,* 527–537.

Hanson, J., & Graves, D. (1983). The author's chair. *Language Arts, 60,* 176–183.

Harmon, J. M. (1998). Vocabulary teaching and learning in a seventh-grade literature-based classroom. *Journal of Adolescent & Adult Literacy, 41,* 518–529.

Harris, K., & Graham, S. (1996). *Making the writing process work: Strategies for composition and self-regulation.* Cambridge, MA: Brookline Books.

Harste, J., Woodward, J., & Burke, C. (1984). *Language stories and literacy lessons.* Portsmouth, NH: Heinemann.

Hart, B., & Risley, T. R. (1995). *Meaningful differences in the everyday experiences of young American children.* Baltimore, MD: Brookes.

Harter, M. (2000). *A framework for reading for information.* Workshop presented at Reading Leadership Institute, National-Louis University, June 2000.

Harvey, S., & Goudvis, A. (2000). *Strategies that work: Teaching comprehension to enhance understanding.* Portland, ME: Stenhouse.

Hauerwas, L. B., & Walker, J. (2004). What can children's spelling of *running* and *jumped* tell us about their need for spelling instruction? *The Reading Teacher, 58*(2), 168–176.

Heath, S. B. (1983). *Ways with words: Language, life, and work in communities and classrooms.* Cambridge, England: Cambridge University Press.

Heath, S. B. (1986). Sociocultural contexts of language development. In *Beyond language: Social and cultural factors in schooling language minority students* (pp. 143–182). Sacramento, CA: Bilingual Education Office, California State Department of Education.

Heller, R. (1991). *A cache of jewels and other collective nouns.* New York, NY: Putnam Juvenile.

Henderson, E. H. (1982). *Learning to read and spell: A child's knowledge of words.* Carbondale, IL: University of Southern Illinois.

Henderson, E. H. (1990). *Teaching spelling.* Boston, MA: Houghton Mifflin.

Henderson, E. H. (1995). *Teaching spelling.* Boston, MA: Houghton Mifflin.

Hendrix, C. (1952). *Cómo enseñar a leer por el método global.* Buenos Aires, Argentina: Editorial Kapelusz.

Henkes, K. (1987). *Sheila Rae the brave.* New York, NY: Greenwillow.

Henkes, K. (1996). *Lilly's purple plastic purse.* New York, NY: Greenwillow.

Henkes, K. (2006). *Lilly's big day.* New York, NY: HarperCollins Children's Books.

Henry, L. A. (2006). SEARCHing for an answer: The critical role of new literacies while reading on the Internet. *The Reading Teacher, 59*(7), 614–627.

Hickman, J. (1979). *Response to literature in a school environment.* Unpublished doctoral dissertation, Ohio State University, Columbus.

Hickman, J. (1981). A new perspective on response to literature. *Research in the Teaching of English, 15,* 343–354.

Hickman, J. (1992). What comes naturally. In C. Temple & P. Collins (Eds.), *Stories and readers.* Norwood, MA: Christopher-Gordon.

Hildebrandt, D. (2000, Fall). "But there's nothing good to read" (In the library media center). *Media Spectrum: The Journal for Library Media Specialists in Michigan,* 34–37.

Hill, R., Carjuzaa, J., Aramburo, D., & Baca, L. (1993). Culturally and linguistically diverse teachers in special education: Repairing or redesigning the leaky pipeline. *Teacher Education and Special Education, 16,* 258–269.

Ho, D. B. (1999). Using wordless picture books to support struggling sixth grade readers and writers. *The California Reader, 32,* 9–11.

Hoban, R. (1995). *Bedtime for Frances.* Illustrated by Garth Williams. New York, NY: HarperTrophy.

Hoberman, M. A. (2000). *The eeensy weensy spider.* Boston, MA: Little, Brown.

Hoff-Ginsburg, E. (1998). *What explains the SES-related difference in children's vocabularies and what does that reveal about the process of word learning?* Paper presented at the Boston University Conference on Language Development, Boston, November 6–8.

Hoffman, J. V. (1992). Critical reading/thinking across the curriculum: Using I-Charts to support learning. *Language Arts, 69,* 121–127.

Hohmann, M. (2002). *Fee, fie, phonemic awareness.* Ypsilanti, MI: Highscope Press.

Holdaway, D. (1979). *Foundations of literacy.* Portsmouth, NH: Heinemann.

Hudelson, S. (1984). Kan yu ret an rayt en Ingles: Children become literate in English as a second language. *TESOL Quarterly, 18,* 221–238.

Hudelson, S. (1987). The role of native language literacy in the education of language minority children. *Language Arts, 64,* 827–840.

Huey, E. B. (1908). *The psychology and pedagogy of reading.* Cambridge, MA: MIT Press.

Hynds, S. (1997). *On the brink: Negotiating literature and life with adolescents.* New York, NY: Teachers College Press.

Individuals with Disabilities Education Act 1997 (Reauthorization). (1997). 20 U.S.C. 1400 et seq.

Individuals with Disabilities Education Improvement Act of 2004. (IDEA).

International Association for the Evaluation of Educational Achievement (IEA). (2006). *Progress in International Reading Literacy Study, 2006.* Boston, MA: Lynch School of Education, Boston College.

International Reading Association & National Association for the Education of Young Children. (1998, July). Learning to read and write: Developmentally appropriate practices for young children: A joint position statement of the International Reading Association (IRA) and National Association for the Education of Young Children (NAEYC). Newark, DE and Washington, DC: Authors.

International Reading Association and the National Council for the Accreditation of Teacher Education. (2006). *Standards for reading professionals.* Newark, DE: Author.

International Reading Association. (2001). *Second-language literacy instruction: A position statement of the International Reading Association.* Newark, DE: Author.

Iser, W. (1978). *The act of reading.* Baltimore, MD: Johns Hopkins University Press.

Ivey, G., & Broaddus, K. (2001). "Just plain reading": A survey of what makes students want to read in middle school classrooms. *Reading Research Quarterly, 36,* 350–371.

Jacobs, H. H. (1997). *Mapping the big picture: Integrating curriculum and assessment.* Alexandria, VA: Association for Supervision and Curriculum Development.

Jacobs, H. H. (2004). *Getting results with curriculum mapping.* Alexandria, VA: ASCD.

Jacobs, H. H. (2006). *Active literacy across the curriculum.* Larchmont, NY: Eye on Education.

Johnson, K. R., & Simons, H. D. (1974). Teaching reading to children who speak Black English. In *MetroVoices (Teacher's edition).* Beverly Hills, CA: Benziger.

Johnson-Coleman, L. (2001, May). *Keep on keepin' on: Motivation for the young and young at heart.* Keynote address presented at the annual conference of the International Reading Association, New Orleans, LA.

Juel, C. (1988). Learning to read and write: A longitudinal study of 54 children from first through fourth grades. *Journal of Educational Psychology, 80,* 415–447.

Kagan, S. (1997). *Cooperative learning.* San Clemente, CA: Kagan.

Kame'enui, E. J. (1998). The rhetoric of all, the reality of some, and the unmistakable smell of mortality. In J. Osborn & F. Lehr (Eds.), *Literacy for all: Issues in teaching and learning.* New York, NY: Guilford Press.

Kame'enui, E., Simmons, D., Cornachione, C., Thompson-Hoffman, S., Ginsburg, A., Marcy, E., Mittleman, J., Irwin, J., & Baker, M. (2001). *A practical guide to reading assessments.* Washington, DC: U.S. Department of Education.

Katz, L., & Feldman, L. B. (1981). Linguistic coding in word recognition: Comparisons between a deep and a shallow orthography. In A. M. Lesgold & C. A. Perfetti (Eds.), *Interactive processes in reading.* Mahwah, NJ: Erlbaum.

Katzir, T., & Pare-Blagoev, J. (2006). Applying cognitive neuroscience research to education: The case of literacy. *Educational Psychologist 41*(1), 53–74.

Kawakami-Arakaki, A. J., Oshiro, M. E., & Farran, D. C. (1988). *Research to practice: Integrating reading and writing in a kindergarten curriculum.* Champaign, IL: University of Illinois at Urbana-Champaign—Center for the Study of Reading.

Keene, E., & Zimmerman, S. (1997). *Mosaic of thought.* Portsmouth, NH: Heinemann.

Kelly, M. (2000). *Of dreams and new realities: Mexican immigrant women in transition.* Unpublished doctoral dissertation. National-Louis University.

Kieff, J. (2003). Revising the read aloud. *Childhood Education, 80*(1): 28.

Kirsch, I. S., Jungeblatt, A., Jenkins, L., & Coldstat, A. (2002). *Adult literacy in America: A first look at the results of the National Adult Literacy Survey* (3rd ed.). Washington, DC: National Center for Educational Statistics.

Kissner, E. (2008). *The forest and the trees.* Portsmouth, NH: Heinemann.

Klenk, L., & Kibby, M. W. (2000). Re-mediating reading difficulties: Appraising the past, reconciling the present, constructing the future. In M. L. Kamil, P. B. Mosenthal, P. D. Pearson, & R. Barr (Eds.), *Handbook of reading research* (Vol. 3, pp. 545–562). Mahwah, NJ: Erlbaum.

Koskinen, P. S., & Blum, I. H. (1986). Paired repeated reading: A classroom strategy for developing fluent reading. *The Reading Teacher, 40,* 70–75.

Koskinen, P. S., Gambrell, L. B., Kapinus, B. A., & Heathington, B. S. (1988). Retelling: A strategy for enhancing students' reading comprehension. *The Reading Teacher, 41,* 892–896.

Kovalski, M. (1987). *The wheels on the bus.* Boston, MA: Joy Street Books.

Krashen, S. D. (1981). Bilingual education and second language acquisition theory. In California State Department of Education (Ed.), *Schooling and language minority students: A theoretical framework* (pp. 51–79). Sacramento: California State Department of Education, Office of Bilingual Bicultural Education.

Krashen, S. D. (1982). *Principles and practice in second language acquisition.* New York, NY: Pergamon Press.

Krashen, S. D. (1985). *Inquiries and insights: Second language teaching, immersion and bilingual education, literacy.* Hayward, CA: Alemany Press.

Krashen, S. D. (1991). *Bilingual education: A focus on current research.* Washington, DC: National Clearinghouse for Bilingual Education.

Krashen, S. D. (1991). The input hypothesis: An update. In J. E. Alatis (Ed.), *Georgetown University Round Table on Languages and Linguistics 1991, Linguistics and language pedagogy: The state of the art.* Washington, DC: Georgetown University Press.

Krashen, S. D. (1993). *The power of reading: Insights from the research.* Greenwood Village, CO: Libraries Unlimited.

Krashen, S. D. (1997). Conflicting claims concerning computers: A comment on Hinkson (1996). *The California Reader, 30,* 16–17.

Krashen, S. D., & Biber, D. (1988). *On course: Bilingual education's success in California.* Sacramento: California Association for Bilingual Education.

Krashen, S. D., & Terrell, T. D. (1983). *The natural approach: Language acquisition in the classroom.* New York, NY: Pergamon/Alemany.

Kuhn, M. R., & Stahl, S. A. (2003). Fluency: A review of developmental and remedial practices. *Journal of Educational Psychology, 95,* 3–21.

Labbo, L. D., & Teale, W. H. (1990). Cross age reading: A strategy for helping poor readers. *The Reading Teacher, 43,* 363–369.

LaBerge, D., & Samuels, S. J. (1974). Toward a theory of automatic information processing in reading. *Cognitive Psychology, 6,* 293–323.

Labov, W. (1970). *The study of non-standard English.* Champaign, IL: NCTE.

Labov, W. (1972). *Language in the inner city: Studies in Black English vernacular.* Philadelphia, PA: University of Pennsylvania Press.

Ladson-Billings, G. (1994). *The dreamkeepers: Successful teachers of African American children.* San Francisco, CA: Jossey-Bass.

Ladson-Billings, G. (2009). The dream-keepers: Successful teachers of African American children. San Francisco, CA: Jossey-Bass.

Lamberg, W. J., Rodríguez, L., & Tomas, D. A. (1978). Training in identifying oral reading departures from text which can be explained as Spanish-English phonological differences. *The Bilingual Review/ La Revista Bilingue, 5,* 65–75.

Lambert, W. E. (1975). Culture and language as factors in learning and education. In A. Wolfgang (Ed.), *Education of immigrant students.* Toronto: O.I.S.E.

Landrum, J. (2001). Selecting intermediate novels that feature characters with disabilities. *The Reading Teacher, 55,* 252–258.

Lau v. Nichols, 414 US 563 (1974).

Lee, J., Grigg, W. S., & Donahue, P. L. (2007). *The nation's report card: Reading 2007.* Washington, DC: National Center for Educational Statistics. http://nces.ed.gov/nationsreportcard/pubs/main2007/2007496.asp. Accessed May 20, 2009.

Lehr, F., Osborn, J., & Hiebert, E. (2006). *A focus on vocabulary.* Honolulu, HI: Pacific Resources for Education and Learning.

Lehr, S. (1988). Children's developing sense of theme as a response to literature. *Reading Research Quarterly, 23,* 337–357.

Lennon, C., & Burdick, H. (2004). *The Lexile Framework as an approach for reading measurement and success.* Durham, NC: MetaMetrics.

Leslie, L., & Caldwell, J. (2005). *Qualitative reading inventory* (4th ed.). Boston, MA: Allyn & Bacon.

Lester, H. (1986). *A porcupine named fluffy.* Boston, MA: Houghton Mifflin.

Lester, H. (1993). *Tacky the penguin.* Boston, MA: Houghton Mifflin.

Leu, D. J., Coiro, J., Castek, J., Hartman, D. K., Henry, L. A., & Reinking, D. (2010). Research on instruction and assessment in the new literacies of online reading comprehension. In C. C. Block & S. Parris (Eds.), *Comprehension instruction: Research-based best practices.* New York, NY: Guilford Press.

Leu, D. J., Zawilinski, L., Castek, J., Banerjee, M., Housand, B., Liu, Y., & O'Neil, M. (2007). What is new about the new literacies of online reading comprehension? In L. Rush, A. Berger, & J. Eakle (Eds.), *Secondary school reading and writing: What research reveals for classroom practices* (pp. 37–68). Chicago, IL: NCTE/NCRL.

Levi-Strauss. C. (1970). *Structural anthropology.* Garden City, NY: Basic Books.

Loban, W. (1976). *Language development: Kindergarten through twelfth grade.* Urbana, IL: National Council of Teachers of English.

Los Angeles Unified School District. (1985). *Strategies for sheltered English instruction.* Los Angeles, CA: Author.

Luke, A. (2000). Critical literacy in Australia: A matter of context and standpoint. *Journal of Adolescent and Adult Literacy 43*(5), 448–461.

Luke, A., & Freebody, P. (1999). A map of possible practices: Further notes on the four resources model. *Practically Primary, 4,* 2.

Luria, A. R. (1976). *Cognitive development: Its cultural and social foundations.* Cambridge, MA: Harvard University Press.

Mandler, M. J., & Johnson, N. S. (1977). The remembrance of things parsed: Story structure and recall. *Cognitive Psychology, 9,* 51–91.

Manzo, A. V. (1969). The ReQuest procedure. *Journal of Reading, 13,* 123–126.

Marsh, G., Friedman, M., Welch, V., & Desberg, P. (1981). A cognitive-developmental theory of reading acquisition. In G. MacKinnon & T. Waller (Eds.), *Reading research advances in theory and practice,* volume 3. New York, NY: Academic Press.

Marshall, E. (1994). *Fox and his friends.* Illustrated by James Marshall. New York, NY: Puffin.

Martinez, M., Roser, N., & Strecker, S. (1999). "I never thought I could be a star": A readers theatre ticket to reading fluency. *The Reading Teacher, 52,* 326–334.

Marzano, R. J. (2004). *Building background knowledge for academic achievement: Research on what works in schools.* Alexandria, VA: ASCD.

Maya Simon, M., Graziano, M., & Lenhart, M. A. (2001). *The Internet and education.* Washington, DC: Pew Research Center.

Mayer, M. (2002). *Beauty and the beast.* Illustrated by Mercer Mayer. New York, NY: Macmillan.

McCafferty, S. G., & Iddings, C. (2001). *Carnival: Putting a round peg in a square hole.* Paper presented at the meeting of the National Reading Conference, San Antonio, TX.

McEwan-Adkins, K. (2006). *Raising reading achievement in middle and high school: Five simple-to-follow strategies.* Thousand Oaks, CA: Corwin Press.

McGee, L., & Morrow, L. (2005). *Teaching literacy in kindergarten.* New York, NY: Guilford.

McGee, L. M., & Richgels, D. J. (2003). *Literacy's beginnings: Supporting young readers and writers* (3rd ed.). Boston, MA: Allyn & Bacon.

McKee, J., & Ogle, D. (2005). *Integrating instruction: Literacy and science.* New York, NY: Guilford.

McKenna, M. C., & Kear, D. J. (1990, May). Measuring attitudes toward reading: A new tool for teachers. *The Reading Teacher, 43*(9), 626–639.

McKissack, P. C. (1997). *Ma Dear's aprons.* New York, NY: Alladin.

McLaughlin, M., & Vogt, M. (1996). *Portfolios in teacher education.* Newark, DE: International Reading Association.

McMahon, S., & Wells, J. (2006). *Teaching literacy in fifth grade.* New York, NY: Guilford.

McPhail, E. P. (2005). On literacy and liberation: The African American experience. In B. Hammond, M. E. Rhodes Hoover, & I. P. McPhail (Eds.), *Teaching African American learners to read* (pp. 9–23). Newark, DE: International Reading Association.

McQuillan, J., & Tse, L. (1998). What's the story? Using the narrative approach in beginning language classrooms. *TESOL Journal, 7*, 18–23.

McTighe, J., & Lyman, F. T. (1988). Cueing thinking in the classroom: The promise of theory-embedded tools. *Educational Leadership, 45*, 18–24.

Mehan, J. (1979). *Learning lessons.* Cambridge, MA: Harvard University Press.

Meier, D. (2004). *Many children left behind: How the No Child Left Behind Act is damaging our children and our schools.* New York, NY: Beacon Press.

Mesmer, E. M., & Mesmer, H. A. E. (2008/2009). Response to intervention (RTI): What teachers of reading need to know. *The Reading Teacher, 62*(4), 280–290.

Miller, J., & Schwanenflugel, P. J. (2008). A longitudinal study of the development of reading prosody as a dimension of oral reading fluency in early elementary school children. *Reading Research Quarterly, 43*(4), 336–354.

Modiano, N. (1968). Bilingual education for children of linguistic minorities. *American Indígena, 28*, 405–414.

Moffett, J. (1976). *Teaching the universe of discourse.* New York, NY: Holt, Rinehart & Winston.

Moffett, J., & Wagner B. J. (1991). *Student centered language arts K–12.* Portsmouth NH: Boynton/Cook.

Moore, D. W., Bean, T., Berdyshaw, D., & Lycis, J. (1999). *Adolescent literacy: A position statement for the commission on adolescent literacy of the International Reading Association.* Newark, DE: International Reading Association.

Morris, A. & Hevman, K. (1989). *Bread, bread, bread.* New York, NY: HarperCollins.

Morris, R. D. (2005). *Case studies in beginning reading.* New York, NY: Guilford.

Morris, R. D. (2005). *The Howard Street tutoring manual* (2nd ed.). New York, NY: Guilford.

Morris, R. D., Blanton, L., Blanton, W. E., Nowacek, J., & Perney, J. (1995, November). Teaching low-achieving spellers at their "instructional level." *Elementary School Journal, 96*(2), 163–177.

Morris, R. D., Nelson, L., & Perney, J. (1986). Exploring the concept of "spelling instructional level" through the analysis of error types. *Elementary School Journal, 87*, 181–200.

Morris, W., & Morris, M. (1962). *Dictionary of word and phrase origins.* New York, NY: Harper & Row.

Morrow, L. M. (1990). Preparing the classroom environment to promote literacy during play. *Early Childhood Research Quarterly, 27*, 203–225.

Morrow, L. M. (2003). Organizing and managing the language arts block. New York, NY: Guilford Press.

Morrow, L. M., & Gambrell, L. (2004). *Using children's literature in preschool: Comprehending and enjoying books.* Newark, DE: International Reading Association.

Moskal, M. K., & Blachowicz, C. (2006). *Partnering for fluency.* New York, NY: Guilford Press.

Moustafa, M. (1997). *Beyond traditional phonics.* Portsmouth, NH: Heinemann.

Moustafa, M., & Penrose, J. (1985). Comprehensible input PLUS the language experience approach: Reading instruction for limited English speaking students. *The Reading Teacher, 38*, 640–647.

Murray, D. (1985). *A writer teaches writing.* Boston, MA: Houghton Mifflin.

Muth, J. (2003). *Stone soup.* New York, NY: Scholastic.

Nagy, W. E., Anderson, R. C., & Herman, P. A. (1987). Learning word meanings from context during normal reading. *American Educational Research Journal, 24*, 237–270.

Nagy, W. E., Anderson, R., Schommer, M., Scott, J., & Stallman, A. (1989). Morphological families and word recognition. *Reading Research Quarterly, 24*, 262–282.

Nagy, W. E., García, G. E., Durgunoglu, A. Y., & Hancin-Bhatt, B. (1993). Spanish-English bilingual students' use of cognates in English reading. *Journal of Reading Behavior, 25*, 241–259.

Nagy, W., & Anderson, R. C. (1984). How many words are there in printed school English? *Reading Research Quarterly, 19*, 304–330.

Nagy, W. E., & Scott, J. A. (2000). Vocabulary processes. In M. L. Kamil., P. Mosenthal, P. D. Pearson, & R. Barr (Eds.), *Handbook of reading research* (Vol. 3). New York, NY: Longman.

Nathan, R., Temple, F., Juntunen, K., & Temple, C. (1988). *Classroom strategies that work: An elementary teacher's guide to process writing.* Portsmouth, NH: Heinemann.

Nathenson-Mejia, S. (1989). Writing in a second language: Negotiating meaning through invented spelling. *Language Arts, 66*, 516–526.

Nation, I. S. P. (2001). *Learning vocabulary in another language.* New York, NY: Cambridge University Press.

National Assessment Governing Board. (2008). *Reading framework for the 2009 National Assessment of Educational Progress.* Washington, DC: U.S. Government Printing Office.

National Center for Education Statistics. (1999). *Digest of education statistics, 1998.* Washington, DC: U.S. Department of Education.

National Center for Education Statistics. (1999). *The condition of education.* Washington, DC: U.S. Government Printing Office. Available at http://nces.ed.gov/programs/coe/

National Center for Education Statistics. (2000). *Elementary and secondary education: An international perspective.* Washington, DC: U.S. Department of Education. Retrieved from http://nces.ed.gov/ pubs2000/ 2000033.pdf

National Center for Educational Statistics. (2006). *National assessment of educational progress: The nation's report card.* Washington, DC: U.S. Department of Education.

National Center for Educational Statistics (NCES). (2006). Parental involvement in preschoolers' educational activities at home. Retrieved from http://nces.ed.gov/pubs2006/earlychild/06.asp

National Center for Educational Statistics (NCES). (2009). Parent and family involvement in education. Retrieved from http://nces.ed.gov/programs/coe/2009/section4/indicator30.asp

National Early Literacy Panel. (2008). *Developing early literacy: Report of the National Early Literacy Panel.* Washington, DC: National Institute for Literacy.

National Institute for Literacy. (2008). Retrieved from http://www.nifl.gov/nifl/facts/facts.html.

National Literacy Panel on Language–Minority Children and Youth. (2006). *Developing literacy in second–language learners: Report of the National Literacy Panel on Language–Minority Children and Youth* (D. August and T. Shanahan, Eds.). Mahwah, NJ: Erlbaum.

National Reading Panel Web site. (2003). *Reports.* Retrieved from http://www.nationalreadingpanel.org

National Reading Panel. (2000, December). *Teaching children to read: An evidence-based assessment of the scientific research literature on reading and its implications for reading instruction.* (Reports of the Subgroups). Washington, DC: National Institute of Child Health and Human Development, National Institutes of Health.

NCELA (National Clearinghouse for English Language Acquisition and Language Instruction Educational Programs). (2006). U.S. Department of Education. Introduction to Language Instruction Educational Programs. Retrieved July 19, 2006, from http://www.ncela.gwu.edu/about/lieps/

NEA [National Education Association]. (2004). *NCLB: The intersection of access and outcomes.* Washington, DC: National Education Association.

Nessel, D. D., & Jones, M. B. (1981). *The language-experience approach to reading.* New York, NY: Teachers College Press.

Neuman, S. B., & Celano, D. (2001). Access to print in low-income and middle-income communities: An ecological study of four neighborhoods. *Reading Research Quarterly, 56,* 8–28.

Neuman, S., & Roskos, K. (1991). The influence of literacy-enriched play centers on preschoolers' conceptions of the functions of print. In J. Christie (Ed.), *Play and early literacy development* (pp. 167–187). Albany, NY: State University of New York Press.

O'Leary, D. (2002). *2002 widening achievement gap.* Tucson, AZ: League of Latin American Citizens (LULAC).

O'Rourke, J., & Bamman, H. A. (1971). *Techniques of teaching vocabulary.* Menlo Park, CA: Benjamin/ Cummings Publishing Company

Office of English Language Acquisition (OELA). (2004). Retrieved July 19, 2006, from http://www.ed.gov/print/programs/sfgp/index.html

Ogle, D. (1986). K-W-L: A teaching model that develops active reading of expository text. *Reading Teacher, 40,* 564–570.

Ogle, D. (1991). The know, want to know, learn strategy. In N. Muth (Ed.), *Children's comprehension of text: Research and practice* (pp. 22–23). Newark, DE: International Reading Association.

Ogle, D. (2000). Make it visual: A picture is worth a thousand words. In M. McLaughlin & M. Vogt (Eds.), *Creativity and innovation in content area teaching.* Norwood, MA: Christopher-Gordon.

Ogle, D., & Beers, J. W. (2009). *Engaging in the language arts: Exploring the power of language.* New York, NY: Pearson.

Ogle, D., & Blachowicz, C. (2001). Beyond literature circles: Helping students comprehend informational texts. In C. C. Block & M. Pressley (Eds.), *Comprehension instruction: Research-based best practices.* New York, NY: Guilford Press.

Olson, M. W., & Gee, T. C. (1988). A review of story grammar research. *Childhood Education, 64*(4), 302–306.

Organization for Economic Cooperation and Development. (1995). *Employment outlook.* Paris: Author.

Organization for Economic Cooperation and Development. (2000). *Program for international student assessment.* New York, NY: The United Nations. Retrieved from http://www.pisa.oecd.org/

Organization for Economic Cooperation and Development. (2001). *Knowledge and skills for life: First results from PISA 2000.* Paris: OECD.

Organization for Economic Cooperation and Development. (2009). *Program of international reading and literacy survey: 2009.* Retrieved from http://timss.bc.edu/PDF/P06_IR_Ch1.pdf.

Osborn, J., Lehr, F., & Hiebert, E. H. (2003). *A focus on fluency.* Honolulu, HI: Pacific Resources for Education and Learning. Retrieved from http://www.prel.org

Owocki, G., & Goodman, Y. (2002). *Kidwatching: Documenting children's literacy development.* Portsmouth, NH: Heinemann.

Palincsar, A. S., & Brown, A. L. (1986). Interactive teaching to promote independent learning from text. *The Reading Teacher, 39,* 771–777.

Parish, P. (1992). *Amelia Bedelia.* Illustrated by Fritz Siebel. New York, NY: HarperCollins.

Patterson, E. (1984). *Language, letters, and learning.* Lecture at Hobart and William Smith Colleges, Geneva, NY.

Pearson, P. D. (1985). Changing the face of reading comprehension instruction. *The Reading Teacher, 38,* 724–738.

Pearson, P. D., & Anderson, R. C. (1985). A schema theoretic view of the learning to read process. In P. D. Pearson, R. Barr, & P. Mosenthal (Eds.), *Handbook of reading research: Volume 1.* New York, NY: MacMillan.

Pearson, P. D., Cervetti, G. N., & Tilson, J. L. (2008). Reading for understanding. In L. Darling-Hammond et al., *Powerful learning: What we know about teaching for understanding* (pp. 71–111). San Francisco, CA: Jossey-Bass.

Peck, J. (1989). Using storytelling to promote language and literacy development. *The Reading Teacher, 43,* 138–141.

Pennycook, A. (1985). Actions speak louder than words: Paralanguage, communication, and education. *TESOL Quarterly, 19,* 259–282.

Perfetti, C. A. (1985). *Reading ability.* New York, NY: Oxford University Press.

Perfetti, C. A. (1986). Cognitive and linguistic components of reading ability. In B. Foorman & A. Siegel (Eds.), *Acquisition of reading skills, cultural constraints and cognitive universals* (pp. 11–40). Hillsdale, NJ: Erlbaum.

Perfetti, C. A. (1992). *Reading ability.* New York, NY: Oxford University Press.

Peterson, P. E., & West, M. R. (Eds.). (2003). *No child left behind?: The politics and practice of school accountability.* New York, NY: Brookings Institution Press.

Pilkey, D. (2000). *Captain Underpants boxed set.* New York, NY: Scholastic.

Pinnell, G. S., & Fountas, I. (1998). *Word matters.* Portsmouth, NH: Heinemann.

Pinnell, G. S., & Fountas, I. C. (2001). *Leveled books for readers, grades 3–6.* Portsmouth, NH: Heinemann.

Pinnell, G. S., Bridges, L. B., & Fountas, I. C. (1999). *Matching books to readers: Using leveled books in guided reading.* Portsmouth, NH: Heinemann.

Pinnell, G. S., Pikulski, J. J., Wixson, K. K., Campbell, J. R., Gough, P. B., & Beatty, A. S. (1995). *Listening to children read aloud: Oral fluency.* Washington, DC: National Center for Education Statistics, U.S. Department of Education.

Pittelman, S. D., Heimlich, J. E., Berglund, R. L., & French M. P. (1991). *Semantic feature analysis: Classroom applications.* Newark, DE: International Reading Association.

Plecha, J. (1992). Shared inquiry: The Great Books method of interpretive reading and discussion. In D. Temple & P. Collins (Eds.), *Stories and readers: New perspectives on literature, the elementary classroom* (pp. 103–114). Norwood, MA: Christopher-Gordon.

Powell, R., Cantrell, S. C., & Adams, S. (2001). Saving Black Mountain: The promise of critical literacy in a multicultural democracy. *The Reading Teacher, 54,* 772–781.

Preece, A. (1998, July 1). Personal Communication. Sinaia, Romania.

Pressley, M. (1999). Self-regulated comprehension processing and its development through instruction. In L. B. Gambrell, L. M. Morrow, S. B. Neuman, & M. Pressley (Eds.), *Best practices in literacy instruction*. New York, NY: Guilford Press.

Pressley, M. (2000). "What should comprehension instruction be the instruction of?" In M. L. Kamil, P. B. Mosenthal, P. D. Pearson, & R. Barr (Eds.), *Handbook of reading research* (Vol. 3, pp. 545–562). Mahwah, NJ: Erlbaum.

Pressley, M. (2002). Metacognition and self-regulated comprehension. In A. E. Farstrup & S. J. Samuels (Eds.), *What research has to say about reading instruction* (pp. 291–309). Newark, DE: International Reading Association.

Pressley, M., & Afflerbach, P. (1995). *Verbal protocols of reading: The nature of constructively responsive reading*. Hillsdale, NJ: Erlbaum.

Pressley, M., Allington, R. L., Wharton-McDonald, R., Block, C. C., & Morrow, L. M. (Eds.). (2001). *Learning to read: Lessons from exemplary first-grade classrooms*. New York, NY: Guilford Press.

Pressley, M., Rankin, J., & Yokoi, L. (1996). A survey of instructional practices of primary teachers nominated as effective in promoting literacy. *Elementary School Journal*, 96, 363–384.

Pressley, M., Wharton-McDonald, R., Mistretta, J., & Echevarria, M. (1998). The nature of literacy instruction in ten grade 4/5 classrooms in upstate New York. *Scientific Studies of Reading*, 2, 159–191.

Purcell-Gates, V. (1991). Ability of well-read-to kindergartners to decontextualise/recontextualise experience into a written-narrative register. *Language and Education: An International Journal*, 5(3), 177–188.

Purcell-Gates, V. (1995). *Other people's words: The cycle of low literacy*. Cambridge, MA: Harvard University Press.

Purcell-Gates, V., L'Allier, S., & Smith, D. (1995). Literacy at the Harts' and the Larsons': Diversity among poor inner city families. *The Reading Teacher*, 48, 572–578.

Purcell-Gates, V., McIntyre, E., & Freppon, P. A. (1995). Learning written storybook language in school: A comparison of low-SES children in skills-based and whole language classrooms. *American Educational Research Journal*, 32(3), 659–685.

Radcliffe, R., Caverly, D., Hand, J., & Franke, D. (2008, February). Improving reading in a middle school science classroom. *Journal of Adolescent and Adult Literacy*, 51(5), 398–408.

Raffi. (1996). The more we get together. *Raffi Sampler*. [CD]. Cambridge, MA: Rounder Records.

Ramírez, J. D. (1991). *Final report: Longitudinal study of structured English immersion strategy, early-exit and late-exit bilingual education programs*. NTIS, 300-87-0156. Washington, DC: U.S. Department of Education.

Raphael, T. E. (1986). Teaching question answer relationships, revisited. *The Reading Teacher*, 39(6), 516–522.

Raphael, T. E. (1998). Balanced instruction and the role of classroom discourse. In J. Osborn & F. Lehr (Eds.), *Literacy for all: Issues in teaching and learning*. New York, NY: Guilford Press.

Raphael, T. E., & McMahon, S. I. (1994). Book club: An alternative framework for reading instruction. *The Reading Teacher*, 48, 102–117.

Raphael, T. E., Goatley, V., McMahon, S., & Woodman, D. (1995). Teaching literacy through student book clubs. In N. Roser & M. Martinez (Eds.), *Book talk and beyond: Children and teachers respond to literature* (pp. 66–79). Newark, DE: International Reading Association.

Rasinski, T. V. (2003). *The fluent reader: Oral strategies for building word recognition, fluency, and comprehension*. New York, NY: Scholastic.

Rasinski, T., & Padak, N. (2005). *Three-minute reading assessments: Word recognition, fluency, and comprehension*. New York, NY: Scholastic.

Rasinski, T., Blachowicz, C., & Lems, K. (Eds.). (2005). *Fluency instruction: Research-based best practices*. New York, NY: Guilford Press.

Read, C. (1975). *Children's categorization of speech sounds in English* (Research Report No. 17). Urbana, IL: National Council of Teachers of English.

Rébsamen, E. C. (1949). *La enseñanza de la escritura y lectura en el primer año escolar: Guía metodológica*. Paris: Librería de la Vda de Ch. Bouret.

Recht, D. R., & Leslie, L. (1988). Effect of prior knowledge on good and poor readers' memory of text. *Journal of Educational Psychology*, 80(1), 16–20.

Reichle, E. D., & Perfetti, C. A. (2003). Morphology in word identification: A word experience model that accounts for morpheme frequency effects. *Scientific Studies of Reading*, 7, 219–237.

Richard-Amato, P., & Snow, M. A. (1992). *The multicultural classroom: Readings for content content area teachers*. New York, NY: Longman.

Rickford, J. R. (1999). *African American Vernacular English*. Malden, MA: Blackwell Publishers.

Rickford, R. R., & Rickford, A. E. (1995). Dialect readers revisited. *Linguistics and Education*, 7, 107–128.

Rideout, V., Roberts, D. F., & Foerh, U. G. (2005). *Generation M: Media in the lives of 8–18 year-olds*. Kaiser Family Foundation http://www.kff.org/entmedia/upload/Executive-Summary-Generation-M-Media-in-the-Lives-of-8-18-Year-olds.pdf

Riley, J. (2007). *Learning in the early years*. London, UK: Sage Publications.

Roberts, T. A. (2008). Home storybook reading in primary or second language with preschool children: Evidence of equal effectiveness for second-language vocabulary acquisition. *Reading Research Quarterly*, 43(2), 103–130.

Rodríguez Fuenzalida, E. (1982). *Metodologías de alfabetización en América Latina*. Pátzcuaro, Michoacán, México: UNESCO/CREFAL.

Rosen, M. (2003). *We're going on a bear hunt*. Illustrated by H. Oxenbury. New York, NY: Alladin.

Rosenblatt, L. (1978). *The reader, the text, and the poem*. Carbondale, IL: Southern Illinois University Press.

Roser, N. L., Hoffman, J. V., & Farest, C. (1992, January). Language charts: A record of story talk. *Language Arts*, 69(1), 44–52.

Ross, T. (1992). *Stone soup*. New York, NY: Dial Books.

Routman, R. (1996). *Literacy at the crossroads: Crucial talk about reading, writing, and other teaching dilemmas*. Portsmouth, NH: Heinemann.

Rowe, M. B. (1974). Wait-time and rewards as instructional variables: Their influence on language, logic and fate control: Part one—Wait time. *Journal of Research in Science Teaching*, 11(2), 81–94.

Sainsbury, M. (2001). *The 2001 IEA progress in international reading literacy study*. Paper presented at the 12th European Conference on Reading. Dublin, July.

Salmon, K. (1995). *Lenguaje integral: Una alternativa para la enseñanza-aprendizaje de la lecto-escritura.* Quito, Ecuador: Abrapalabra Editores.

Samuels, S. J., & Farstrup, A. E. (Eds.). (2006). *What research has to say about fluency instruction.* Newark, DE: International Reading Association.

Sanacore, J. (2004). Genuine caring and literacy learning for African American children. *The Reading Teacher, 57*(8), 744–753.

Santa, C. M. (1988). *Content reading including study systems: Reading, writing and studying across the curriculum.* Dubuque, IA: Kendall Hunt.

Saville, M. R., & Troike, R. C. (1971). *A handbook of bilingual education.* Washington, DC: Teachers of English to Speakers of Other Languages.

Scarcella, R. (1990). *Teaching language minority students in multicultural classrooms.* New York, NY: Longman.

Schifini, A. (1985). *Sheltered English: Content area instruction for limited English proficient students.* Los Angeles, CA: Los Angeles County Office of Education.

Schifini, A. (1996). Reading instruction for the pre-literate and struggling older student. *NABE News, 20,* 5–6, 20, 30.

Schlagal, R. C. (1989). Constancy and change in spelling development. *Reading Psychology, 10*(3), 207–232.

Schön, D. (1983). *The reflective practitioner: How professionals think in action.* New York, NY: Basic Books.

Schon, I. (2000). *Recommended books in Spanish for children and young adults, 1996–1999.* Lanham, MD: Scarecrow Press.

Schon, I. (2001). Los niños y el mundo: Children's books in Spanish from around the world. *The Reading Teacher, 54,* 692–698.

Schon, I. (2002). From Pulgarcito to Shakespeare. *Language, 2,* 28–30.

Schon, I. (2004). *Recommended books in Spanish for children and young adults, 2000 through 2004.* Lanham, MD: Scarecrow Press.

Schon, I., & Corona Berkin, S. (1996). *Introducción a la literatura infantil y juvenil.* Newark, DE: International Reading Association.

Scieszka, J. (2001). *Baloney (Henry P.).* Illustrated by Lane Smith. New York, NY: Viking Junior.

Scragg, D. G. (1974). *A history of English spelling.* New York, NY: Barnes & Noble.

Selinker, L., Swain, M., & Dumas, G. (1975). The interlanguage hypothesis extended to children. *Language Learning, 25,* 129–152.

Sepúlveda, L. (1989). *The old man who read love stories.* New York, NY: Harcourt Brace.

Shanahan, T. (2002). *A sin of the second kind: The neglect of fluency instruction and what we can do about it.* PowerPoint presentation at A Focus on Fluency Forum, San Francisco, CA. Available at www.prel.org/programs/rel/fluency/Shanahan.ppt

Shaw, R., & Shaw, D. (2002). *DIBELS Oral Reading Fluency-based indicators of third grade reading skills for Colorado State Assessment Program (CSAP)* (Tech. Rep.) Eugene, OR: University of Oregon.

Shaywitz, S. E., Escobar, M. D., Shaywitz, B. A., Fletcher, J. M., & Makuch, J. R. (1992). Evidence that dyslexia may represent the lower tail of a normal distribution of reading ability. *New England Journal of Medicine, 326,* 145–150.

Shinn, M. R. (Ed.). (1989). *Curriculum-based measurement: Assessing special children.* New York, NY: Guilford.

Short, K., & Kauffman, G. (1995). So what do I do? The role of the teacher in literature circles. In N. Roser & M. Martinez (Eds.), *Book talk and beyond: Children and teachers respond to literature* (pp. 140–149). Newark, DE: International Reading Association.

Short, K., Harste, J., & Burke, C. (1996). *Creating classrooms for authors and inquirers.* Portsmouth, NH: Heinemann.

Simpkins, G., Holt, G., & Simpkins, C. (1974). *Bridge: A cross-culture reading program.* Boston, MA: Houghton Mifflin.

Sleeter, C. E., & Grant, C. A. (1999). *Making choices for multicultural education.* Upper Saddle River, NJ: Merrill.

Smith, C. B. (1997). Vocabulary instruction and reading comprehension. *ERIC Digest.* ERIC Clearinghouse on Reading English and Communication #126.

Smith, F. (1973). *Psycholinguistics and reading.* New York, NY: Holt, Rinehart & Winston.

Smith, F. (1986). *Keynote address: How education backed the wrong horse.* Presented at the meeting of the California Reading Association, Fresno.

Snow, C. E., Burns, M. S., & Griffin, P. (Eds.). (1998). *Preventing reading difficulties in young children.* Committee on the Prevention of Reading Difficulties in Young Children. Commission on Behavioral and Social Sciences and Education, National Research Council. Washington, DC: National Academy Press.

Snow, C. E., Tabors, P. O., & Dickenson, D. K. (2001). Language development in the preschool years. In D. K. Dickinson & P. O. Tabors (Eds.), *Beginning literacy with language.* Baltimore, MD: Brookes.

Snowling, M. J. (2000). *Dyslexia.* London, England: Blackwell.

Solé, I. (1994). *Estrategias de lectura.* Barcelona, Spain: Graó Editorial.

Souriau, E. (1955). *Les deux cent milles situations dramatiques.* Paris, France: Flamarion.

Spache, G. (1981). *Diagnosing and correcting reading disabilities* (2nd ed.). Boston, MA: Allyn & Bacon.

Spandel, V. (1996). *Seeing with new eyes.* Portland, OR: Northwest Regional Educational Laboratory.

Spandel, V. (2000). *Creating writers through 6-trait writing assessment and instruction* (3rd ed.). Boston, MA: Allyn & Bacon.

Spandel, V. (2008). *Creating writers through 6-trait writing assessment and instruction* (5th ed.). Boston, MA: Allyn & Bacon.

Spinelli, J. (1990a). *Maniac Magee.* Boston, MA: Little, Brown.

Spinelli, J. (1990b). *Maniac Magee.* New York, NY: Scholastic. Large-print version from Library Reproduction Service, ISBN 0-590-45203-7.

Spolin, V. (1986). *Theater games for the classroom.* Evanston, IL: Northwestern University Press.

Stahl, S. A., & Fairbanks, M. (1986). The effects of vocabulary instruction: A model-based meta-analysis. *Review of Educational Research, 56,* 76–110.

Stanovich, K. E. (1986). Matthew effects in reading: Some consequences of individual differences in the acquisition of literacy. *Reading Research Quarterly, 21,* 360–407.

Stanovich, K. E. (1992). Are we overselling literacy? In C. Temple & P. Collins (Eds.), *Stories and readers.* Norwood, MA: Christopher Gordon.

Stanovich, K. E., & Siegel, L. S. (1994). Phenotypic performance profiles of children with reading disabilities: A regression-based test of the phonological core variable-difference model. *Journal of Educational Psychology, 86,* 24–53.

Stauffer, R. (1975). *The language experience approach to the teaching of reading.* New York, NY: Harper.

Steele, J. L., & Meredith, K. E. (1997). *Critical thinking.* New York, NY: Open Society Institute.

Stein, N. L., & Glenn, C. F. (1979). An analysis of story comprehension in elementary school children. In R. O. Freedle (Ed.), *New directions in discourse processing: Vol. 2. Advances in discourse processes* (pp. 53–120). Norwood, NJ: Ablex.

Sternberg, R., & Powell, J. (1983). Comprehending verbal comprehension. *American Psychologist, 38,* 878–893.

Stoll, D. R. (Ed.). (1977). *Magazines for kids and teens.* Newark, DE: International Reading Association.

Strickland, D. S. (1991). Cooperative, collaborative learning for children and teachers (emerging readers and writers). *Reading Teacher, 44,* 600–602.

Strickland, D. S. (2006). Balanced literacy: Teaching the skills AND thrills of reading. Available from *Scholastic on-line:* http://www2.scholastic.com/browse/article.jsp?id=4315

Strickland, D. S., & Schickedanz, J. (2004). *Learning about print in preschool.* Newark, DE: International Reading Association.

Strickland, D. S., & Feeley, J. T. (1985). Using children's concept of story to improve reading and writing. In T. Harris & E. Cooper (Eds.), *Reading, thinking, and concept development* (pp. 163–175). New York, NY: The College Board.

Suárez-Orozco, C., Suárez-Orozco, M. M., & Todovora, I. (2008). *Learning in a new land: Immigrant students in American society.* Cambridge, MA: The Belknap Press of Harvard University Press.

Sulzby, E. (1985). Kindergarteners as writers and readers. In M. Farr (Ed.), *Advances in writing research: Vol. 1. Children's early writing development* (pp. 127–199). Norwood, NJ: Ablex.

Suro, R., & Singer, A. (2002). *Latino growth in metropolitan America: Changing patterns, new locations.* Washington, DC: Brookings.

Sutherland-Smith, W. (2002). Weaving the literacy web: Changes in reading from page to screen. *The Reading Teacher, 55,* 662–669.

Sutton-Smith, B. (1981). *The folk stories of children.* New York Olympic Marketing.

Tattershaw, S., & Prendeville, J. (1995). *Using familiar routines in language assessment and intervention.* San Antonio, TX: Communication Skill Builders.

Taylor, B., Pearson, P. D., Clark, K., & Walpole, S. (1999). *Beating the odds in teaching all children to read.* Ann Arbor, MI: CIERA. http://www.ciera.org/library/reports/inquiry-1/1-010/1-010.pdf

Taylor, B. M., & Pearson, P. D. (2005). Using study groups and reading assessment data to improve reading instruction within a school. In S. Paris & S. A. Stahl (Eds.), *Children's reading comprehension and assessment* (pp. 237–255). Mahwah, NJ: Erlbaum.

Taylor, W. L. (1953). Cloze procedure: A new device for measuring readability. *Journalism Quarterly, 45,* 415–433.

Teale, W. H., & Sulzby, E. (1986). *Emergent literacy.* Portsmouth, NH: Heinemann.

Teale, W. H., & Sulzby, E. (1987). Literacy acquisition in early childhood: The roles of access and mediation in storybook reading. In D. Wagner (Ed.), *The future of literacy in a changing world* (pp. 111–130). New York, NY: Pergamon Press.

Temple, C. (1994). The "global method" of Celestin Freinet: Whole language in a European setting? *The Reading Teacher 48,* 1 (September, 1994) pp. 86–89.

Temple, C. (2000). What can we learn from 15,000 teachers in Central Europe and Central Asia? *Reading Teacher, 54*(3), 312–315.

Temple, C., Crawford, A., & Gillet, J. W. (2009). *Developmental literacy inventory.* Boston, MA: Pearson.

Temple C., & MaKinster, J. (2005). *Intervening for literacy.* Boston, MA: Allyn & Bacon.

Temple, C., Martinez, M., & Yokota, J. (2010). *Children's books in children's hands* (4th ed.). Boston, MA: Allyn & Bacon.

Temple, C., Nathan, R., & Burris, N. (1982). *The beginnings of writing.* Boston, MA: Allyn & Bacon.

Temple, C., Nathan, R., Burris, N., & Temple, F. (1993). *The beginnings of writing* (3rd ed.). Boston, MA: Allyn & Bacon.

Temple, F. (1992). *Tiger soup.* New York, NY: Orchard.

Temple, F. (1994). *The Ramsay scallop.* New York, NY: Orchard.

Temple, F. (1995). *Tonight, by sea.* New York, NY: Harper Trophy.

Temple, F. (1996). *The Beduin's gazelle.* New York, NY: Orchard.

Templeton, S. (1991). Teaching and learning the English spelling system: Reconceptualizing method and purpose. *Elementary School Journal, 92,* 183–199.

Templeton, S., & Morris, D. (1999). Questions teachers ask about spelling. *Reading Research Quarterly, 34*(1), 102–112.

Templeton, S., & Morris, D. (2000). Spelling: Reconceptualizing spelling development and instruction. In M. Kamil, P. B. Mosenthal, P. D. Pearson, & R. Barr (Eds.), *Handbook of reading research* (Vol. 3, pp. 525–539). Mahwah, NJ: Erlbaum.

Terban, M. (1989). *Superdupers: Really funny real words.* New York, NY: Clarion.

Terman, L. (1916). *The measurement of intelligence.* Stanford, CA: Stanford University Press.

Terrell, T. D. (1977). A natural approach to second language acquisition and learning. *Modern Language Journal, 6,* 325–337.

Terrell, T. D. (1981). The natural approach in bilingual education. In California State Department of Education (Ed.), *School and language minority students: A theoretical framework* (pp. 117–146). California State University, Los Angeles, Los Angeles: Evaluation, Dissemination and Assessment Center.

Terrell, T. D. (1982). The natural approach to language teaching: An update. *Modern Language Journal, 66,* 121–122.

TESOL. (1997). *Policy statement of the TESOL board on African American vernacular English.* Arlington, VA: Center for Applied Linguistics.

Texas Education Agency. (1996). *Comprehensive biennial report on Texas public schools: A report to the 75th Texas legislature.* Austin: Author.

Texas Education Agency. (2009). Retrieved from http://ritter.tea.state.tx.us/teks/

Tharp, R., & Gallimore, R. (1991). *The instructional conversation: Teaching and learning in social activity* (Research Report 2). Santa Cruz, CA: The National Center for Research on Cultural Diversity and Second Language Learning, University of California, Santa Cruz.

Thomas, W. P., & Collier, V. (1997). *School effectiveness for language minority students.* Washington, DC: National Clearinghouse for Bilingual Education.

Thomas, W. P., & Collier, V. P. (2002). *A national study of school effectiveness for language minority students' long-term academic achievement final report: Project 1.1.* Santa Cruz, CA: Center for Research on Education, Diversity and Excellence.

Tinajero, J. V., & Nagel, G. (1995). "I never know I was needed until you called!": Promoting parent involvement in schools. *The Reading Teacher, 48,* 614–617.

Tomlinson, C. A. (2000). Differentiation of instruction in the elementary grades. Champaign, IL: ERIC Clearinghouse on Elementary and Early Childhood Education. http://ceep.crc.uiuc .edu/eecearchive/digests/2000/tomlin00.pdf

Tompkins, G. (2000). *Teaching writing: Balancing process and product*. Columbus, OH: Merrill.

Topping, K. J. (1987). Paired reading: A powerful technique for parent use. *The Reading Teacher, 40*, 608–614.

Torres Quintero, G. (1976). *Método onomatopéyico*. Mexico City: Editorial Patria.

Trelease, J. (2006). *The read-aloud handbook* (6th ed.). New York, NY: Penguin Books.

Trieman, R. (1985). Onsets and rimes as units of spoken syllables: Evidence from children. *Journal of Experimental Child Psychology, 39*, 161–181.

Trout, B. (1993, November). Little dogies, lay down. *Highlights for Children*.

U.S. Census Bureau. (2000). *U.S. Census 2000*. Washington, DC: U.S. Department of Commerce.

U.S. Census Bureau. (2007). *Income, poverty, and health insurance coverage in the United States: 2007*, Report P60, n. 235, Table B-2, pp. 60–65.

U.S. Department of Education. (2000). *Report of the National Reading Panel: Teaching children to read, an evidence-based assessment of the scientific research literature on reading and its implications for reading instruction*. Washington, DC: U.S. Government Printing Office.

U.S. Department of Education. (2001). *No child left behind*. Retrieved from http://www.ed.gov/offices/OESE/esea/

UNESCO. (1953). *The use of vernacular languages in education*. Paris: UNESCO.

University of Wisconsin–Eau Claire. (2000). *Hmong population research project*. Retrieved August 3, 2001, from www.uwec. edu/Academic/Econ/HmongResearch/HPopulation.htm

Urrea, L. A. (1996). *By the lake of sleeping children: The secret life of the Mexican border*. New York, NY: Anchor Books.

Vacca, R., & Vacca, J. (1986). *Content area reading*. Boston, MA: Allyn & Bacon.

Vacca, R., & Vacca, J. (1996). *Content area reading* (5th ed.). New York, NY: HarperCollins.

Valencia, S., Hiebert, E. & Afflerbach, P. (1993). *Authentic reading assessment: Practices and possibilities*. Newark, DE: International Reading Association.

Vasquez, V. (2004). *Negotiating critical literacies with young children*. Mahwah, NJ: Erlbaum.

Vaughn, J., & Estes, T. (1986). *Reading and reasoning beyond the primary grades*. Boston, MA: Allyn & Bacon.

Veatch, J. (1996). From the vantage of retirement. *The Reading Teacher, 49*, 510–516.

Veatch, J., Sawicki, F., Elliott, G., Flake, E., & Blakey, J. (1979). *Key words to reading: The language experience approach begins*. Columbus, OH: Merrill.

Vellutino, F. R., & Scanlon, D. M. (2001). Emergent literacy skills, early instruction, and individual differences as determinants of difficulties in learning to read: The case for early intervention. In S. B. Newman & D. K. Dickinson (Eds.), *Handbook of early literacy research*. New York, NY: Guilford Press.

Vellutino, F. R., Scanlon, D. M., Sipay, E. R., Small, S. G., Pratt, A., Chen, R., & Denckla, M. B. (1996). Cognitive profiles of difficult-to-remediate and readily remediated poor readers: Early intervention as a vehicle for distinguishing between cognitive and experiential deficits as a basic cause of specific reading disability. *Journal of Educational Psychology, 88*, 601–638.

Verhoeven, L. (1990, Spring). Acquisition of reading in a second language. *Reading Research Quarterly, 25*(2), 90–114.

Vernon-Feagans, L., Hammer, C. S., Miccio, A., & Manlove, E. (2001). Early language and literacy skills in low-income African American and Hispanic children. In D. K. Dickenson & S. B. Newman (Eds.), *Handbook of early literacy research*. New York, NY: Guilford.

Vogt, M. E. (2000). Content learning for students needing modifications: An issue of access. In M. McLaughlin & M. E. Vogt (Eds.), *Creativity and innovation in content area teaching* (pp. 329–351). Norwood, MA: Christopher-Gordon.

Von Franz, M. L. (1996). *The interpretation of fairy tales*. Boston, MA: Shamhala.

Vukelich, C., Christie, J., & Enz, B. (2002). *Helping young children learn language and literacy*. Boston, MA: Allyn & Bacon.

Vygotsky, L. (1976). *Thought and language*. Cambridge, MA: MIT Press.

Vygotsky, L. S. (1978). *Mind in society: The development of higher psychological processes*. Cambridge, MA: Harvard University Press.

Wagner, B. J. (1999). *Dorothy Heathcote: Drama as a learning medium*. Portsmouth, NH: Heinemann.

Walsh, D.J., Price, G. G., & Gillingham, M. G. (1988). The critical but transitory importance of letter naming. *Reading Research Quarterly, 23*, 108–122.

Webb, S. (2000). *My season with penguins*. Boston, MA: Houghton Mifflin.

Wepner, W. B., Valmont, W. J., & Thurlow, R. (Eds.). (2000). *Linking literacy and technology: A guide for K–8 classrooms*. Newark, DE: International Reading Association.

Wheelock, A., & Dorman, G. (1988). *Before it's too late: Dropout prevention in the middle grades*. Boston, MA: Massachusetts Advocacy Center and Chapel Hill Center for Early Adolescence.

Whipple, G. (Ed.). (1925). *The twenty-fourth yearbook of the National Society for the Study of Education: Report of the National Committee on Reading*. Bloomington, IN: Public School Publishing.

White, E. B. (1980). *Charlotte's web*. New York, NY: Harper Trophy. (Original work published 1952)

Whitehurst, G. J. (1994). *Dialogic reading for parents: Headstart, K, and pre-K* (available from G. J. Whitehurst, State University of New York at Stony Brook, Stony Brook, NY 11794–2500).

Whitehurst, G., & Lonigan, C. (2001). Child development and emergent literacy. *Child Development, 69*, 848–872.

Whitehurst, G. J., & Lonigan, C. J. (2001). Emergent literacy: From pre-readers to readers. In S. B. Neuman & D. K. Dickinson (Eds.), *Handbook of early literacy research*. New York, NY: Guilford Press.

Whorf, B. L. (1964). *Language, thought, and reality* (J. B. Carroll, Ed.). Cambridge, MA: MIT Press.

Wiggins, G., & McTighe, J. (2005). *Thinking by design, expanded edition*. Washington, DC: Association for Supervision and Curriculum Development.

Williams, S. (1991). Classroom use of African American Language: Educational tool or social weapon? In C. Sleeter (Ed.), *Empowering through multicultural education* (pp. 199–215). New York, NY: State University of New York.

Willms, J. D. (1999). *International adult literacy survey: Inequalities in literacy skills among youth in Canada and the United States*. Ottawa, Ontario: Ministry of Industry.

Wilson, J. (2005). *The relationship of Dynamic Indicators of Basic Early Literacy Skills (DIBELS) Oral Reading Fluency to performance on Arizona Instrument to Measure Standards (AIMS)*. Tempe, AZ: Tempe School District No. 3.

Wilson, P. (1992). Among non-readers. In C. Temple & P. Collins (Eds.), *Stories and readers*. Norwood, MA: Christopher-Gordon.

Wong, H. K., & Wong, R. T. (2009). *First days of school: How to be an effective teacher* (4th ed.). Mountain View, CA: Harry K. Wong Publications, Inc.

Wong-Fillmore, L., & Snow, C. (2000). *What teachers need to know about language*. Washington, DC: U.S. Department of Education, OERI.

Wood, J. M. (2000). *A marriage waiting to happen: Computers and process writing*. Newton, MA: Education Development Center.

Worthy, J., & Broaddus, K. (2002). Fluency beyond the primary grades: From group performance to silent, independent reading. *The Reading Teacher, 55*, 334–343.

Wylie, R. E., & Durrell, D. D. (1970). Teaching vowels through phonograms. *Elementary English Journal, 47*, 787–791.

Yopp, H. K., & Stapleton, L. (2008). Conciencia fonémica en español (Phonemic awareness in Spanish). *The Reading Teacher, 61*(5), 374–382.

Young, J. P., & Brozo, W. G. (2001). Boys will be boys, or will they? Literacy and masculinities. *Reading Research Quarterly, 36*(3), 316–325.

Zambo, D. (2007). Using picture books to provide archetypes for young boys: Extending the ideas of William Brozo. *The Reading Teacher, 61*(2), 124–131.

Zarrillo, J. (1994). *Multicultural literature, multicultural teaching: Units for the elementary grades*. Fort Worth, TX: Harcourt Brace.

Zarrillo, J. (2010). *Are you prepared to teach reading?* (2nd ed.). Englewood Cliffs, NJ: Prentice Hall.

Zemach, H. (1964). *Nail soup*. Chicago, IL: Follett.

Zutell, J. (1999). Sorting it out through word sorts. In I. C. Fountas & G. S. Pinnell (Eds.), *Voices on word matters* (pp. 103–113). Portsmouth, NH: Heinemann.

Zutell, J., & Rasinski, T. (1991). Training teachers to attend to their students' oral reading fluency. *Theory into Practice, 30*, 212–217.

Name Index

Durica, K. M., 396
Durkin, D., 192
Durrell, D. D., 75

E

Echevarria, J., 56, 431, 487, 499, 511
Edelsky, C., 425
Eder, D., 379
Edwards, S., 310
Eeds, M., 3, 207
Ehrenreich, B., 5
Ehri, L. C., 81, 134, 138, 139, 149
Einstein, A., 459
Elkonin, D. B., 117
Elley, W., 60
Enz, B., 384
Escamilla, K., 509, 510
Escobar, M. D., 4
Estes, T., 198, 199

F

Farah Al Jabar, 43–44
Farley, J., 171
Farran, D. C., 142
Farstrup, A. E., 112, 161
Federal Register, 49
Feeley, J. T., 417
Feldman, L. B., 76
Ferreiro, E., 81, 425
Fielding, L., 5, 408
Fielding, L. G., 162
Fisher, A., 265
Fisher, P., 174, 176, 179, 446, 448
Fitzgerald, J., 45, 424
Flesch, R., 342
Fletcher, J. M., 4
Florida Department of Education, 373
Fogelberg, E., 24
Folse, K. S., 175
Foorman, B. R., 161
Fountas, I. C., 18, 38, 113, 120, 144, 146, 199, 303, 305,
    345, 379, 380, 386, 390, 400, 407, 429, 431, 432–433
Fradd, S. H., 503
Franke, D., 250
Frasier, D., 177
Fredericks, A., 419
Freebody, P., 9, 266, 272, 288
Freeman, D., 183
Freinet, C., 320, 505
Freire, P., 278
Freppon, P. A., 375
Frith, U., 133, 134, 135
Fry, E., 342
Frye, N., 281
Fuchs, L. S., 331
Fuhrmann, J., 145

G

Galdone, P., 380
Gallimore, R., 203
Gambrell, L., 103
Ganske, K., 80, 138, 139, 347, 359
Garbarino, J., 320
García, E. E., 49, 175
Garland, S., 373
Gaskins, I. W., 395
Gee, J. P., 492
Gee, T. C., 93
Gelman, R., 229
Gentry, J. R., 80, 136, 137, 138, 139, 140, 141, 359, 505
Gersten, R., 57, 93
Gillet, J. W., 7, 102, 103, 185, 216, 332, 349, 351, 354,
    359
Gillingham, M., 103
Glassock, S., 171
Gleitman, L. R., 71
Glenn, C. F., 92, 93, 213, 268
Goatley, V. J., 3
Goldman, S. R., 228
Gollnick, D. M., 44
Good, T., 379
Goodman, K. S., 15, 50, 505
Goodman, Y. M., 332, 335, 336, 462
Goswami, U., 74, 133, 134, 135
Goudvis, A., 197
Graham, C., 116
Graham, S., 306
Grant, C. A., 424
Graves, D. H., 15, 176, 297, 398, 432
Greenlaw, W., 509
Greeno, J. G., 229
Griffin, P., 5, 338, 488
Griffith, P. L., 433
Grigg, W. S., 16
Gronlund, N. E., 337
Gurvitz, D., 234
Guthrie, J. T., 230, 384, 465
Gwynne, F., 79, 177, 448

H

Haggard, M. R., 179
Hall, D. P., 18, 144, 145, 380, 381, 411, 484
Hall, E. T., 47
Hall, M., 421
Hall, S. L., 74, 75
Halle, T., 60
Halliday, M. A. K., 74
Hamilton, R. L., 284
Hammer, C. S., 5
Hand, J., 250
Hanson, J., 432
Hardman, D., 348
Harmon, J. M., 422

P

Padak, N., 331
Palincsar, A. S., 249
Pare-Blagoev, J., 339
Parish, P., 79, 308, 448
Patterson, E., 176
Paulsen, G., 464
Pearson, P. D., 2, 15, 22, 193, 227, 342, 361, 411
Peck, J., 422
Pennycook, A., 47
Penrose, J., 422
Perfetti, C. A., 9, 87, 161, 335
Perney, J., 357
Peters, C., 380
Peterson, P. E., 330
Pew Internet and American Life Project, 3, 13
Piaget, J., 15
Pilkey, D., 59, 61
Pinnell, G. S., 18, 38, 113, 120, 144, 146, 161, 199, 303,
        305, 345, 356, 379, 380, 386, 390, 400, 407, 429,
        431, 432–433
PIRLS, 3
Pittelman, S. D., 414
Plecha, J., 35, 209, 443
Powell, J., 175
Powell, R., 417
Preece, A., 165
Prendeville, J., 369, 370
Pressley, M., 8, 9, 192, 194, 197, 198, 221, 230, 233, 379
Price, G., 103
Public Agenda On-Line, 330
Pugliano-Martin, C., 171
Purcell-Gates, V., 6, 375, 434

Q

Quinn, K. B., 216

R

Radcliffe, R., 250
Raffi, 387
Rakestraw, J. A., Jr., 228
Ramírez, J. D., 503
Randell, B., 380
Raphael, T. E., 3, 18, 35, 180, 184, 207, 254, 458, 469
Raschka, C., 115, 171
Rasinski, T., 162, 167, 331, 347, 358
Read, C., 74, 83, 134
Reardon, J., 72
Rébsamen, E. C., 505
Recht, D. R., 2
Reichle, E. D., 87
Rheingold, H., 447
Rice, D., 463
Richard-Amato, P., 499

Richgels, D. J., 144
Rickford, A. E., 52
Rickford, J. R., 50
Rickford, R. R., 52
Riley, J., 379
Risley, T. R., 6, 89, 90, 175
Roberts, T. A., 497
Rodríguez Fuenzalida, E., 505
Rodríguez, L., 420, 425
Roe, B. D., 216, 428
Roehler, L., 197, 231
Roller, C., 408
Rosen, M., 107
Rosenblatt, L., 193
Roser, N., 161, 215
Roser, N. L., 281
Roskos, K., 372, 392
Ross, E. P., 428
Routman, R., 302
Rowe, M. B., 46
Rozin, P., 71
Rylant, C., 120

S

Sachar, L., 269, 275
Sainsbury, M., 226
Salmon, K., 505
Samuels, J., 161
Samuels, S. J., 112, 161
Sanacore, J., 52, 53
Sanders, N. I., 171
Santa, C., 314
Satz, P., 24
Saville, M. R., 502
Scanlon, D., 5
Scarcella, R., 46
Schifini, A., 499, 511
Schiller, P., 116
Schlagel, R. C., 80, 138, 139, 359
Schön, D., 360
Schon, I., 60, 509
Schreiber, A., 196
Schwanenflugel, P. J., 347
Schwartz, L., 109
Schwartz, R. M., 180, 184
Scieszka, J., 177
Scragg, D. G., 78
Selinker, L., 492
Sepúlveda, L., 504
Serpell, R., 6
Seuss, Dr., 36, 120
Shanahan, T., 166
Shaw, D., 331
Shaw, N., 115
Shaw, R., 331

Subject Index

A

ABC model
   anticipation in. *See* Anticipation phase
   consolidation in. *See* Consolidation phase
   for informational texts, 232–233
   knowledge building in. *See* Building knowledge phase
   middle grade students and, 443, 445–446
   for narrative texts, 198–219
Academic Vocabulary List, 179
Acquisition-learning hypothesis, 492
Acrostics, 187, 309–310
Active reading, 243–255, 459
Additive ESL program, 485
Adjectives, 91
Adolescence. *See* Middle grades
Adverbs, 91
Affective factors, effect on reading, 54–55
Affective filter hypothesis, 492
Affixes. *See* Prefixes; Suffixes
Affricate consonants, 73
African American Vernacular English, 50–51, 419–420,
     496, 497, 499
   literacy issues and, 52–53
   Standard American English and, differences between, 51
African Americans, 32
   literacy issues for, 52–53
Age, in second-language acquisition, 493, 511
Alphabet, emergent literacy and, 118–120
Alphabet bingo game, 118
Alphabet books, 122
Alphabet knowledge, emergent literacy and, 103–105
Alphabetic language, components of, 72–74
Alphabetic reading phase, 134–135
   error type in, 137
   teaching reader in, 143–146
Alphabetic writing, 71
Amazing Fact Sheet, 225
American Library Association, 173
Américas Award, 164
Anecdotal notes, 399
Anglo-Saxon, English origins and, 88
Answering
   comprehending text and, 196

culturally-responsive, 46
Anticipation guides, 199, 200
Anticipation phase, in ABC model
   grades 3–5, 409, 412, 413–414
   for informational texts, 232
   middle grades, 445
   for narrative texts, 198–200
   teaching approaches in, 199–200
   teaching goals for, 199
Approximation, 492–493
Argumentative essay, structuring in, 287
Arguments
   analyzing in text, 287–288
   examining, 269–272
   producing, 286
   reading to follow, 284–288
   unclearly stated, 272–273, 288
   unfair, 271–272
Art, as response to story, 107
Articles (parts of speech), 91
Asian Americans, 48
Assessment, 327. *See also* Informal Reading Inventories
     (IRIs); Self-assessment
   accuracy of measures in, 340
   approaches to, 329–337
   authentic, 333, 335
   of beginning readers, 340–359
   of comprehension, 216, 217–219
   current practices, implications of, 63
   differentiated instruction and, 359–360
   for ELLs, 510–513
   of emergent readers, 338–340
   extended unit, 460–461
   forms of, 24
   in grades K–2, 397–398
   in grades 3–5, 419–420
   high-stakes, 226–227, 458
   in middle grades, 453–457
   monitoring, 360
   outcomes-based, 360
   purpose of, 24, 327–329
   Spanish Readability Graph, 513
   of spelling development, 85

Assessment *(Cont.)*
   student self-assessment. *See* Self-assessment, student
   teacher self-assessment, 360
   terms used in, 337–338
   of word knowledge, 136, 137, 140–141
   of word learning, 182
   of writing, 314–317
Assessment-criterion relationship validity, 337–338
Association for Library Services to Children, 173
At-risk students. *See also* Struggling readers
   contextualized exposure to vocabulary and, 64
   differentiated instruction for, 53–59
   racial/ethnic groups overrepresented in, 57
Attitudes, measuring, 357–358, 456–457. *See also* Motivation
Authentic assessment, 333–334
Authentic children's literature, 54
Author, imitating writing of, 307–308
Automaticity, 405

B

Background knowledge, 45
   informational texts and, 228–229
   narrative text and, 194–195
   reading readiness and, 413–414
Balanced literacy, approaches to, 19–22, 24
Balanced reading instruction, 18
   four blocks approach in, 380–382
Barahona Center for the Study of Books in Spanish for
      Children and Adolescents, 509
Barbara Bush Literacy Foundation, 126
Basal reading levels, publisher systems, 112–113
Basal reading programs, 20–21, 406–407
Basic interpersonal communication skills (BICS), 175, 486
Beginning readers, assessment of, 340–359
Behavior contracts, 369
Benchmark School (Media, PA), 395
BICS (basic interpersonal communication skills), 175, 486
Biculturalism. *See* Cultural diversity
Big books
   for ELLs, 501
   shared reading with, 109–110
Bilingual education, 48–49, 487–490. *See also* ELLs
      (English language learners); ESL (English as a
      second language) instruction
   classroom support structures for, 515–517
Bilingual paraprofessionals, 514, 515
Bilingual Writing Center, 509
Biographies, 471–472
Black dialect, 50–51
Board game, for word sorts, 147, 148
Book baggies, 123–124
Book clubs, 35, 207
Book It! program, 173
Books
   assessing level of, 390
   big books, 109, 501

   classroom-produced, 121–122
   leveled, 388–390, 432–434, 454–455
   little books, 112–113
   for reading aloud, 163–164, 239
   wordless, 496–497
Books program, 35
Bound morphemes, 84
Boys, as struggling readers, 59
   irreverent books for, 62–63
   print materials for, 61
Brainstorming
   exclusion, 450
   paired, 199
   in writing process, 297
Buddy reading, 35, 168, 202
Building knowledge phase, in ABC model
   grades 3–5, 412, 414–415
   for informational texts, 232
   middle grades, 445
   for narrative texts, 200–205

C

California Achievement Test, 329
California Young Reader Medal, 36
CALP (cognitive academic-language proficiency), 175,
      421, 486
Casteñeda v. Pickard, 49
Casual register, 95
Cause-and-effect charts, 312
Cause/effect idea organization, 238–239, 240
Caxton, William, 88
CBM (curriculum-based measurement), 331
Ceremonial register, 95
Certification, training requirements for, 18
Chants
   as response to story, 107
   teaching phonological awareness with, 116–118
   word wall, 145
Chapter graphic organizers, 235, 236
Chapteraday, 476
Character clusters, 200, 213–214
Character maps, 214
Characters
   behavior and rewards of, 281–283
   portraying during read-alouds, 163
   relationships between, 269, 282–284
   as stand-ins for other people, 268–269
Charts, in classroom, 120
Chat rooms, 319, 320
Child development
   emergent literacy, 124–125
   word knowledge, 138–139
Children's literature
   authentic, 54
   special needs portrayed in, evaluation criteria for, 57
Choral reading, 172–173, 472

SIOP®, 499
in Spanish and English, 507
Lessons. *See also* Mini-lessons (focused lessons)
daily, planning, 409, 411
emergent literacy strategies in, 109–120
sample plan, 410
teachable moments in, 382–383
think-alouds as, 205, 383–384
Letter name spelling phase, 80, 81–84, 134
Letter-to-sound relationships. *See* Phonics
Leveled books, 388–390, 432–434, 454–455
Lexile Framework, 344
Libraries/Librarians
access to, reading achievement and, 60
read-aloud recommendations by, 163
reading encouragement and, 173
Limited English Proficient (LEP) students, language
backgrounds of, 49
Linguistic diversity, 48–50, 54–55. *See also* ELLs (English
language learners)
IRI results and, 419–420
Linguistics, 70
sounds of language, 71–76
spelling development, 79–85
spelling-to-sound relationships, 76–79
syntax, 90–95
vocabulary, 88–90
word morphology, 86–88
Linguists, 74
List poems, 310–311
Listening games, for language awareness, 115–116
Literacy. *See also* Critical literacy; Emergent literacy
adults, programs for, 126
celebrating, school participation in, 36
and content instruction integration, 22, 24
critical, 9–10
diversity and. *See* Diversity
ESL instruction and, 500–501
of family, child's reading success and, 4–5
importance of, 2–3
in middle grades, 440–441
needs of culturally-diverse students, 45
new vs. traditional literacies, 13–14
social contexts of, 31–32
state standards and, 460
teaching grades K–2 and, 397
Literacy development
milestones in, 124–125
phonological awareness and, 75
Literacy history
of community, 31–32
of students, 30–31
Literacy play, 120
Literacy rich classroom, grades K–2, 371
Literacy Volunteers of America, 126
Literary performance, 170–172
Literature, teaching, 467–470

Literature circles, 207–209, 469–470
Literature-based primary-grade programs, 407
Little books, guided reading with, 112–113
Loan words, 79
Logographic reading, 133–134
error type in, 137
teaching, 141–143
Logographic writing, 71
logos, 268
Los Angeles Unified School District, 498
LULAC (League of United Latin American Citizens), 50

M

Main ideas
describing, 238–239, 240
recognizing, 196–197
summarizing and rehearsing, 197
Mainstreaming, 56–57
Maintenance model, of bilingual education, 489
Materials and resources
access to, 59–63
for ELLs, 508–509
for grades K–2, 387, 388–391
for language instruction, 447
for middle grades, 475–476
for teaching the alphabet, 121–122
for teaching writing, 314
Matthew effect, 62, 64, 230–232
Mature reading, 12–13
Meaning-based miscues, 333
Meaningful word parts, 135. *See also* Morphological
reading
Memory games, 147, 148
Messages, looking critically at, 288–289. *See also*
Arguments
Metacognition
informational texts and, 250–251, 458–461
middle grade students and, 458–461
strategies for building, 374
Mexican Americans, 32
Middle English, 88
Middle grades
ABC model use with, 443, 445–446
assessment in, 453–457
daily opportunities to read, 442
diversity and, 462–464
ELLs in, 463–464
fluency in, 452
identity and motivation in, 473–474
instructional level materials for, 442–443
integrating reading and writing, 443
involving parents and the community, 478
knowledge development in, 441–452
materials for, 475–476
metacognition in, 458–461
organizing for instruction in, 464–472

reading in, 440–441
reading rights and, 441
skills development in, 441–452
student self-reflection in, 451–452
studying in, 457–458
teacher modeling in, 458
vocabulary-building strategies, 446–451
Web-based inquiry projects and, 474–475
Mini-lessons (focused lessons), 382
in four block approach, 381
on phonics, 411
in writing workshop, 302–303
Misbehavior, 397
Miscues, types of, 333
Misunderstandings, cross-cultural examples, 46–47
Modal verbs, 91
Modeled writing, 304
Modeling, 458
arguments in texts, 287
critical thinking, 452
fluent and reflective reading, 452
interest in language, 447
reading fluency, 162
reading for learning, 458
teachers and, 36–37, 154–155
Monitor hypothesis, 492
Monitoring assessments, 360
Monochronism, 47
Monophthongs, 72–73
Monster Test, 137, 140–141
Morning message, 142–143
Morphemes, 78
bound, 84
and reading, 87
Morphologic spelling phase, 84
word recognition and, 135
Morphological reading, 151–152
error type in, 137
Morphology, of words, 86–88
Morphophonemics, 78
Motivation, 230
in adolescents, 473–474
in grades 3–5, 430–431
Multidimensional Fluency Scale, 337, 351
Multiple texts, comparing same theme between, 288–291
Multiple-meaning words, 177–178
mythos, 268

N

NAEP (National Assessment of Educational Progress),
reading level definitions, 3–4
Narrative, web of, 267–268
Narrative texts
with common themes, comparison of, 291
comprehension of. *See* Comprehension, narrative texts
elements of, 205

hero cycle in, 270
informational texts and, balanced reading of, 258
interpretation of. *See* Comprehension, narrative texts
structure of, thinking critically about, 267–269
strategies for, 279–286
Nasal consonants, 73
National Association for Bilingual Education (NABE), 41
National Center for Family Literacy, 123, 126
National Council for the Accreditation of Teacher
Education (NCATE), 361
National Council for the Social Studies (NCSS), 476
read-aloud book recommendations, 164
National Council of Teachers of English (NCTE), 41, 476
National Geographic Society, 321
National Institutes of Child Health and Human
Development (NICHD), 17
National Literacy Panel on Language-Minority Children
and Youth, 488
National Reading Panel, 17, 335, 488
ready fluency definition, 161
National Science Teachers Association, 476
read-aloud book recommendations, 164
Nation's Report Card, 444
Natural approach, to second-language acquisition,
494–497
NCATE (National Council for the Accreditation of
Teacher Education), 361
NCSS. *See* National Council for the Social Studies
(NCSS)
Negative behavior, 397
New literacies, 266–267
critical thinking and, 266
for grades K–2, 390–391
in teaching writing, 318–320
No Child Left Behind (NCLB) Act
assessment and, 24, 329, 338, 350
balanced literacy and, 19
bilingual education and, 49
reading fluency and, 162
standards development and, 17
students with disabilities and, 57
Nonfiction books. *See* Informational texts
Nonverbal communication, culturally responsive, 46–47
Norm-referenced tests, 329
Notes
anecdotal, 399
"I Have a Problem," 369, 371
Nouns, 91

O

Observational assessments, 216, 217–218
Observations, informal and structured, 335–336, 369, 370,
457
Old English (OE), 87
Omission error, 342, 355
One-on-one tutoring, 55

Preproduction phase, in second-language acquisition, 495

Prereading preparation, for informational texts, 242–248

Pretend-read strategy, 104

Preview-review model, of bilingual education, 490

Primary-grade programs
   basal, 406–407
   code-emphasis, 405–406
   literature-based, 407

Principled content knowledge, 229–230

Print awareness, 102–105

Print Concepts Assessment, 339

Print materials
   displaying, 121
   in home environment, 59–60
   in school environment, 60–62
   sources for, 61–62
   in Spanish, 508–509
   spoken language represented by, 101

Problem/solution idea organization, 238–239, 240

Procedure poster, 368

Productive behavior, establishing and maintaining, 368–369

Productive play, 392

Productive vocabulary, 174

Professional community, schools and, 40–42

Professional organizations, 41. *See also* specific organizations

Professional portfolios
   elements of, 42, 336, 453
   for evaluation, 461
   format for, 19
   student writing examples in, 314

Professional register, 95

Pronunciation, changes in, 72

Proofreading, in writing process, 299–300

Proper names, misreading, 342

Proposition 227 (California), 50

Propriety, 174–175

Props
   for literacy play, 120
   in second-language acquisition, 495

Prosody, 347

Proxemics, 47

Psycholinguistics, 15

Psychomotor factors, effect on reading, 54–55

Public Broadcasting Service, 321

Publishing, in writing process, 300–301

Pull-out programs, 55, 487

Q

Quantitative assessments, 216

Question Answer Relation (QAR) strategy, 458

Questionable texts, reading, 273–274

Questioning/Questions
   in anticipation phase, 199

   in comparative analysis of multiple texts with common themes, 288–290
   for Creative Dialogue activity, 280
   culturally-responsive, 46
   in Directed Reading Activity, 205
   in Directed Reading-Thinking Activity, 203
   guiding children's reading with, 415–416
   Informal Reading Inventories and, 352
   informational text comprehension and, 252–255
   interpretive, 210
   in principled knowledge development, 229
   quality of, 375
   in Socratic Seminar, 286
   taxonomies in, 254
   text comprehension and, 196
   Text-to-self, 210
   Text-to-text, 211
   Text-to-world, 211
   webbed, 184, 185

Questioning-the-author technique, 250, 284, 286

R

"Race Track" game, 147, 148

Radio reading, 168

RAFT (role, audience, format, topic) procedure, 314

Rainbow Reading, 38

Rate Your Knowledge chart, 178, 179, 182

Raw scores, 337

Readability
   assessment of, 341–345
   ELLs and, 511, 523
   measuring, 342–345
   reading levels and, 342
   Spanish language, 513

Read-alouds. *See* Reading aloud

Reader response
   in action, 194
   theory of, 193

Reader's theater, 170–172

Reader's workshops, 21, 470

Reading
   in adolescence, 440–441
   anticipation strategies before, 413–414
   attitudes toward and interest in, 357–358
   building knowledge during, 414–415
   consolidation strategies after, 416–417
   developmental stages in, 11–13
   fluency in. *See* Fluency
   grades 3–5 technology use and, 433–434
   habit of, developing, 6–7
   instruction in. *See* Teaching reading
   knowledge and skills development for, 374–379
   to learn. *See* Informational texts
   maturity in, 12–13
   morphemes and, 87

proficiency in ELLs, assessing, 510–513
readiness for, book choices and, 413
refusal, 104
for structured opposites, 282–284
teaching. *See* Teaching reading
wide, 451
for word histories/families, 136
Reading ability
components, 6–10
grouping and, 429
Reading achievement
factors contributing to, 101
grouping and, 429
home literacy environment and, 60
Reading aloud
activities augmenting, 107, 164–165
benefits of, 105
choosing/collecting texts for, 163–164, 239
for ELLs, 427
engaging students while, 164
with expression, 162–163
in grades K–2, 376, 377
in lesson plan, 384
modeling critical thinking and, 452
second-language acquisition and, 497
strategies for, 107
Reading corners, 34
Reading disabilities, 4–5
Reading errors, 136, 137, 342
scoring criteria, 342
Reading First, 53, 350
Reading interest inventory, 356, 358
Reading Is Fundamental (RIF), 62, 173
Reading levels, 3–4, 38
assessing, 341–345, 353
determining in middle grades, 453–454
measures compared, 345
NAEP definitions, 3–4
publisher systems, 112–113
teacher awareness and, 115
U.S. ranking, 3–4
Reading Miscue Inventory (RMI), 332, 335
Reading Next, recommendations from, 440, 441
Reading programs, 20–21. *See also individually named programs*
Reading rates, average by grade, 167
Reading Recovery Program, 12, 332–333, 344, 345, 380, 382, 394
Spanish version, 509, 510
Reading strategies, 230
assessing knowledge of, 455, 456
for comprehension, 243–255
for informational texts, 243–255, 459
for phonics and decoding, 423–424
for second-language acquisition, 493–499
for vocabulary building, 446–451

Reading to learn. *See* Comprehension, informational texts
Rebecca Caudill Awards Program, 36
Receptive vocabulary, 174
Reciprocal RAFT procedure, 314
Reciprocal teaching, 249–250, 251
Recorded reading, 168
Reduced vowels, 78
Reductionist view, of second-language acquisition, 491
Reflective practitioners, 360–361
Registers, language, 94–95
Rehearsing, in writing process model, 297–298
Relationships, characters and, 269, 282–284
Reliability, 338
Remedial programs, for at-risk students, 55
Repeated reading, 165–167
embedding in performance, 170–173
encouraging, 388–390
Repetition, reading fluency through, 452
Report writing, computers for, 320–321
ReQuest procedure, 255
Research
informational texts and, 255–257
on vocabulary, 175–176
in writing process, 298
Research-based instructional practice, 16–17
Resources. *See* Materials and resources
Response to Intervention (RTI), 58–59, 331, 382
grades K–2 and, 397–398
Retelling. *See* Oral retelling
Reversal error, 342
Revising, in writing process, 299
Rhyming games, 144. *See also* Chants
Riddle books, 122
RIF (Reading Is Fundamental), 62, 173
Rimes, 75, 76, 102, 117
RMI (Reading Miscue Inventory), 332, 335
"Roaming around the Known," 340
Role models. *See* Modeling
Roman alphabet, 73
Root words, 86
of Latin origin, 153, 154
Round-robin oral reading, 250, 415
Routines, grades K–2, 367–368, 384–386
RTI. *See* Response to Intervention (RTI)
RTI^2 (Response to Instruction and Intervention Squared), 58–59
Rubrics, 315–316, 336–337
Running records, 332–333, 334, 346

S

SABE achievement test, 510
Save the Last Word for Me, 206–207
SBRR (scientifically based reading research), 17
Scaffolding, 45
comprehension and, 197–198